PERGAMON MANAGEMENT AND BUSINESS SERIES

Fundamentals of Organizational Behavior

An Applied Perspective

(PMBS-5)

Fundamentals of Organizational Behavior

An Applied Perspective

Andrew J. DuBrin
College of Business,
Rochester Institute of Technology

PERGAMON PRESS INC.

New York · Toronto · Oxford · Sydney

PERGAMON PRESS INC.
Maxwell House, Fairview Park, Elmsford, N.Y. 10523

PERGAMON OF CANADA LTD.
207 Queen's Quay West, Toronto 117, Ontario

PERGAMON PRESS LTD.
Headington Hill Hall, Oxford

PERGAMON PRESS (AUST.) PTY. LTD.
Rushcutters Bay, Sydney, N.S.W.

Copyright © 1974, Pergamon Press Inc.
Library of Congress Cataloging in Publication Data

DuBrin, Andrew J
    Fundamentals of organizational behavior.

    (Pergamon management and business series, 5)
    Includes bibliographical references.
    1. Organization.   2. Decision-making.   3. Leader-
ship.   I.   Title.
HM131.D82   1974   301.18'32   73-12998
ISBN   0-08-017110-9
ISBN   0-08-017111-7   (pbk.)

Printed in the United States of America

To Douglas and Drew

Contents

List of Figures   xi

Preface   xiii

Acknowledgments   xv

PART I   Introduction   1

CHAPTER 1   Introduction to Organizational Behavior   3
The Knowledge Worker and Organizational Behavior. What Organizational Behavior Is Not. Conceptual Framework for Organizational Behavior. Plan of the Book. Guidelines for Action. Questions. Notes.

PART II   Individuals   31
Preview   32

CHAPTER 2   The Motivation to Work   33
Work, Leisure, and Motivation. Motivation and Satisfaction Are Different. Maslow's Hierarchy of Needs. Herzberg's Motivation–Hygiene Theory. Need Gratification Theory. Achievement Motivation. Equity Theory. Expectancy Theory. Work Motivation Schema. Role of Penalties and Threats. How Do You Motivate This Man? Motivational Consequences of Managerial Behavior. Relationship to Core Propositions. Guidelines for Action. Questions. Notes.

CHAPTER 3   Behavioral Aspects to Decision Making   71
The Decision-Making Schema. Problem Finding. Clarification of the Problem. Finding Creative Alternatives. Weighing Alternatives. Making the Choice. Evaluation of Outcomes. Repetitive Decision Making. Quantitative Decision Making. Decision Making and the Organizational System.

Relationship to Core Propositions.   Guidelines for Action.
Questions.   Notes.

CHAPTER 4   **Stresses in Managerial and Professional Life**   103
Relationship of Individual and Organizational Stress.   Reactions
to Stress.   Organizational Pressures.   Individual Conflicts.
Prevention of Dysfunctional Stress. Executive Health in
Perspective.   Relationship to Core Propositions.   Guidelines for
Action.   Questions.   Notes.

CHAPTER 5   **Political Maneuvering in Organizations**   137
What Causes Political Maneuvering?   Career-Advancement
Strategies.   Power-Acquisition Strategies.   Can Politics Be
Ignored?   Antidotes to Political Maneuvering.   Relationship to
Core Propositions.   Guidelines for Action.   Questions.   Notes.

PART III   **Small Groups**   177

Preview   178

CHAPTER 6   **Small Group Behavior**   179
What Is a Group?   A Framework for Understanding Small
Groups.   A Practical Theory of Small Group Behavior.   What
Functions Does a Group Perform?   Group Pressures Toward
Conformity.   Effective Work Groups.   Committees.   Office of
the President: Running a Company by Committee.   Temporary
Task Forces.   Relationship to Core Propositions.   Guidelines for
Action.   Questions.   Notes.

CHAPTER 7   **Leadership Styles**   211
Leader Traits and Leadership Situations.   Contingency Theory
of Leadership Effectiveness.   Managerial Grid Styles.   3-D
Theory of Leadership.   Path–Goal Theory of Leadership.   Dual
Leadership Theory.   Leadership Style and Productivity.
Determinants of Leadership Style.   Improving Your Leadership
Style.   Relationship to Core Propositions.   Guidelines for Action.
Questions.   Notes.

CHAPTER 8   Improving Subordinate Performance   **241**
Establishing Improvement Goals.   Framework for Coaching and
Counseling.   Counseling in Practice.   Identification with a
Superior.   Performance Appraisals and Improvement.
Punishing People to Improve Performance.   Group
√ Cohesiveness and Improved Performance.   Structural and
Technological Factors.   Relationship to Core Propositions.
Guidelines for Action.   Questions.   Notes.

CHAPTER 9   Interpersonal Communications   **269**
The Universal Communications Problem.   Communication is
Transactional.   An Interpersonal Communication Process
Model.   Interpersonal Communication Structures.   Technology
and Interpersonal Communication.   Barriers to Communication.
Coping with Barriers to Communication.   Transactional Analysis.
Communication, Productivity, and Satisfaction.   Relationship
to Core Propositions.   Guidelines for Action.   Questions.
Notes.

CHAPTER 10   Intergroup Conflict   **301**
A Systems Model of Intergroup Conflict.   Sources of
Conflict.   Consequences of Intergroup Conflict.   Reducing
Intergroup Conflict.   Behavioral Science Intervention in
Conflict.   Capitalizing on Conflict.   Relationship to Core
Propositions.   Guidelines for Action.   Questions.   Notes.

PART IV   Organizations   **329**

Preview   **330**

CHAPTER 11   Organizational Climate   **331**
A Framework for Viewing Organizational Climate.
Determinants of Climate.   Diagnosis of Organizational Climate.
Organizational Climate and Motivation.   Organizational
Climate and Behavior.   Organizational Climate and
Productivity.   Successful Versus Unsuccessful Organizations.
Relationship to Core Propositions.   Guidelines for Action.
Questions.   Notes.

Contents

CHAPTER 12   Management of Individual and Group Change   **363**
A Taxonomy of Change.   A Systems Model of Change.
Effects of Change on People.   Attitudes and Attitude Change.
Why People Resist Change.   Reducing Resistance to Change.
Managing Technological Innovation.   Managerial and
Professional Obsolescence.   Relationship to Core Propositions.
Guidelines for Action.   Questions.   Notes.

CHAPTER 13   Organizational Change   **397**
Organizational Change Strategies.   A Model for the
Management of Organizational Change.   Executive
Realignment.   Changing the Organizational Structure.
Changing the Technology.   Organization Development.
Relationship to Core Propositions.   Guidelines for Action.
Questions.   Notes.

PART V   The Future   **441**

CHAPTER 14   Managers and Organizations of the Future   **443**
Top Management Elite.   Flexible Organizational Structures.
More Power to the People.   Managers of Tomorrow.
Explorations in New Values.   Scientific Control of Behavior.
Guidelines for Action.   Questions.   Notes.

Index   **465**

List of Figures

1.1   Relationship of Organizational Behavior to Other Interdisciplinary Fields   4
1.2   Proportion of Three Different Occupational Groups in the
United States Labor Force, 1950–1975   9
1.3   Continuum of Knowledge Work   10
1.4   Organizational Behavior Follows the Principles of Human
Behavior   14
1.5   Determinants of Organizational Behavior   17
1.6   Organizational Behavior Is Systemic   20
1.7   Technical Changes at Biotronics Precipitate Other Changes in
the Organizational System   22
2.1   Path–Goals Analysis Version of Expectancy Theory   50
2.2   Work Motivation Schema   51
3.1   Three Conceptions of the Decision-Making Process   73
3.2   The Decision-Making Schema   74
3.3   Rational Analysis of Decision-Making Alternatives   91
4.1   A Model of Organizational and Individual Adaptation to Stress   105
5.1   Political Versus Social Approaches in Resolving Conflicts of
Interest   139
5.2   Percentage of White and Black Knowledge Workers in the
United States   146
6.1   A Framework for Understanding Small Groups   182
7.1   Illustrative Relationships Between Leadership Situations and
Leader Traits   215
7.2   Favorability of Eight Different Leadership Situations   217
7.3   The 3-D Theory of Leadership   220
7.4   Dual Leadership in Complex Organizations   226
8.1   Factors Potentially Influencing the Individual in the Organization Toward Improved Performance   241
8.2   Conditions Under Which Superior–Subordinate Coaching
Can Have Positive, Neutral, or Negative Consequences   246
9.1   One Experimental Task Used in a Comparative Study of
Unilateral and Bilateral Communication   273
9.2   An Elementary Model of the Interpersonal Communication
Process   274

9.3 Two Communications Networks: Wheel and All-Channel   277
9.4 Barriers to the Communications Process   281
10.1 A Systems Model of Intergroup Conflict   303
10.2 A Typology of Intergroup Conflict   313
11.1 A Framework for Viewing Organizational Climate   333
11.2 Questionnaire Items Used to Measure Organizational Climate   341
11.3 Organizational Climate of Two Hypothetical Resort Hotels   349
11.4 Schematic Model of the Organizational–Societal Interactions   355
11.5 Intercorrelations of Satisfactions of Seven Parties-at-Interest with 97 Business Firms   357
12.1 A Taxonomy of Some Changes Taking Place Within an Organizational Unit   364
12.2 A Systems Model of Change at the Individual, Group, and Organizational Level   368
13.1 A Model for the Management of Organizational Change   400
13.2 The Managerial Grid   428

Preface

Why would anyone attempt to write another book about the behavior of people at work? Behavioral scientists, management theorists, novelists, and a host of nonfiction writers have written about this topic in the past. Many new books covering the same topic are undoubtedly forthcoming. Immodestly, it is stated that this book has been written because the author feels he has a perspective that can contribute some new insights into the behavior of people in organizations. Next, I would like to share with its intended readers—mostly undergraduate and MBA students taking courses in organizational behavior, behavioral science, or human relations—the four-part rationale underlying the writing of this book.

First, colleagues of mine in the field of behavioral science and many students have complained that many books about organizational behavior are of relatively low reader interest. A strong attempt has been made in preparing this book to include topics and case illustrations of intrinsic interest to students, professionals, and managers. For example, the text contains separate chapters about political maneuvering in organizations ("politics") and the stresses and strains experienced by middle managers and professionals. Reference material for these topics, aside from professional journals and texts, includes sources such as *Playboy, Fortune, Dun's Review,* and first-hand case histories observed by the author.

Second, before embarking upon this project, the author had noted the need for a textbook about organizational behavior that was based more on recent research with professionals and managers than on older research with supervisors, production workers, and clerical workers. Readers of this book, in vast majority, are knowledge workers (managerial, technical, and professional personnel). Case illustrations and research findings presented in this text reflect this emphasis on the knowledge worker, although the careful observer will find some exceptions that have found their way into the manuscript. It was not our intent never to mention the terms production worker or clerk. Knowledge workers have some interactions with people at all levels in the organization.

Third, many books about people in organizations are over-inclusive in their attempt to cover the entire spectrum of personnel administration, organizational psychology, human relations, and the practice of management. An unfortunate negative side effect of this melange has been an overlapping of material among several courses in most business school programs. The present book is an attempt to focus attention on human behavior in organizations. Information about the practice of management, except for those processes directly involving superior–subordinate interaction, is omitted from consideration. Excluded are standard management topics such as planning, controlling, and organizing. Also excluded are discussions of personnel techniques such as selection testing, employment interviewing, and wage and salary administration. Only passing mention is made of older research such as the Hawthorne studies, which have already been the subject of lengthy discussion in almost every book written about human behavior in organizations.

Fourth, organizational behavior is a difficult problem to study and teach, in part because many of the concepts appear as abstractions to the student. Convenient frames of reference are missing for such abstract concepts as organizational climate or functional analysis (often due to lack of experience in organizations). This book attempts to present concepts about organizational behavior at an appropriate level of abstraction. This approach is implemented by presenting a conceptual framework for organizational behavior combined with numerous case illustrations and examples from live organizational settings. Abstract concepts and concrete examples are further blended by providing suggestions at the end of each chapter for the application of key ideas contained in the text. In short, the intent of this book has been to present material that is useful from the viewpoints of the intellectually rigorous academician and the pragmatically minded practitioner.

Feminist thinking has created a few minor editorial problems in the writing of this book. An attempt has been made not to infer by the use of personal pronouns such as "he" that all managers or professionals are male. However, unswerving attention to the avoidance of all sexist terms can create complicated and awkward sentences. In general, when the author is not quoting the statements of someone else, he has used such terms as chairperson, salesperson, or the double personal pronoun "he or she." Several times, nevertheless, case illustrations do refer to a male. For instance, when the author refers to an industrial engineer as "he," that person was probably a male, even though some industrial engineers are female.

Acknowledgments

An author of a book of this nature acts as a synthesizer, collector, and integrator of the published and unpublished ideas of many people. Footnotes included in the text, however scrupulously inserted, indicate the source of only some of the ideas. Many students in the MBA program at the Rochester Institute of Technology uncovered case illustrations that have worked their way into my writings. My peers have furnished me with valuable insights about organizational behavior and so have people I have worked with in a consultant–client relationship. The scope of organizational behavior is such that even people and situations I have observed in the process of my being a customer, visitor, student, client, traveler, or vacationer have been useful to me in the preparation of this book.

Drew and Douglas DuBrin, my beloved sons, receive my gratitude for their continued interest in my writing. Marcia Miller DuBrin, my wife, receives my deep-felt appreciation for the emotional support she provided me during the final stages of this project. Barbara M. Shapiro performed effectively as my typist for the first two drafts of the manuscript. K. Lois Smith typed the balance. Vicki F. Gary and Barbara S. Wagner performed a variety of necessary secretarial tasks for this project.

I thank Lester M. Cone, Jr., my consulting editor, for his hundreds of major and minor suggestions, the majority of which I followed. My indebtedness also extends to many members of the management and editorial staff at Pergamon Press for their technical and administrative support.

Rochester, New York   ANDREW J. DUBRIN

THE AUTHOR

Andrew J. DuBrin (Ph.D., Michigan State University) is Professor of Behavioral Science at the College of Business, Rochester Institute of Technology. Formerly a fulltime management consultant, his professional activities include management selection and development, and organizational development. His public appearances have included television and radio talk shows, and presentations to both management and women's groups. He is a certified psychologist in New York State and a Diplomate in Industrial and Organizational Psychology. In addition to having published a large number of scientific, trade, and popular articles, Dr. DuBrin is also the author of *The Practice of Managerial Psychology, Women in Transition,* and *The Singles Game.*

PART I

Introduction

Introduction to Organizational Behavior

"This is the most screwed up place I've ever worked. Nobody seems to know what the hell they are doing," lament countless people in both profit and nonprofit organizations. Complete answers to why organizations and people do not always function smoothly have yet to be found, but a field of inquiry has emerged to help unravel the complexities of organizations and the people in them. The study of *organizational behavior*, in its most basic conception, is a systematic attempt to understand the behavior of people in organizations of which these people are an integral part. Individuals, small groups, and total organizations comprise the units of observation for organizational behavior. Joe Kelly, an organizational psychologist from Sir George Williams University in Montreal, provides the following elegant definition of organizational behavior:[1]

> Organizational behaviour is concerned with the study of the behaviours and attitudes of man in an organizational setting; the organization's effect on his perceptions, feelings, and actions; and his effect on the organization, particularly how his behaviour affects the achievement of the organization's purposes.

Organizational behavior as a field of inquiry is broadly interdisciplinary in scope. Several other fields, all of which are interdisciplinary themselves, provide the knowledge base for organizational behavior. Adding to the difficulty in delimiting this field is the popularity of the term *behavioral science*. Essentially, behavioral science is the systematic study of behavior. It encompasses all aspects of scientific inquiry that relate to the understanding of human behavior. Psychology, sociology, anthropology, political science, and sometimes even economics are considered part of behavioral science. Escaping from this myriad of overlapping definitions, organizational behavior can be viewed as the application of behavioral science knowledge to organizational settings. The terms "organizational behavior" and "behavioral science" have come to be used interchangeably in colleges

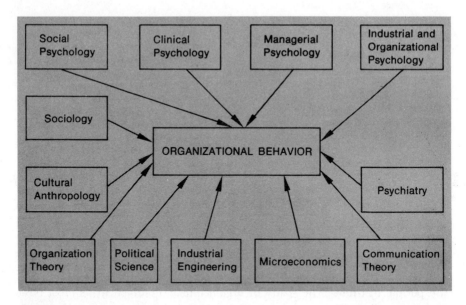

Figure 1.1 Relationship of organizational behavior to other interdisciplinary fields.

of business and schools of management in many American institutions of higher learning.

Figure 1.1 provides an approximate guideline to understanding the relationships among organizational behavior and twelve fields of inquiry that are themselves interdisciplinary in nature. Organizational behavior borrows information from each of these fields; and each of these fields overlaps with at least one other of the twelve fields. For instance, the conditions under which a group develops teamwork may represent a problem in social psychology, but sociology and communication theory would also have much to contribute about this topic. In short, organizational behavior is far from a field of independent inquiry. Scant knowledge exists that is *purely* or *uniquely* organizational behavior. This situation, however, does not diminish the relevance of arriving at a more in-depth understanding of organizations and the people in them. Contemporary life for most people is in large measure organizational life. Virtually everybody works, plays, or is educated in an organization.

Two of the twelve fields just mentioned overlap heavily with the conception of organizational behavior presented here. The relationship of these two interdisciplinary fields—organizational theory and industrial and organizational psychology—to organizational behavior is examined next. By emphasizing these two fields it is not implied that the other ten fields are irrelevant to the study of organizational behavior.

Organization theory attempts to provide an explanatory set of concepts to understand the phenomena of organizations. Included under organizational theory are the so-called "schools of management thought," discussed in almost any textbook about management. *The Process of Management,* a major work in the field of management, divides management thought into three subareas.[2] First is the classical or productivity approach, developed originally by production engineers. Frederick W. Taylor provided the intellectual and almost spiritual leadership to this approach, which is called *Scientific Management.* Beginning in the early 1900s in the United States, this movement provided the origins of a systematic and well-planned approach to production problems that has led to a range of managerial tools including production and inventory control, financial budgeting, and cost analysis.

Second came the behavioral approach to management thought, which in some ways was a reaction against the "efficiency expert" orientation of Taylor and his disciples. (The reader is cautioned not to share the misconception that Taylor ignored human factors. His approach was basically a method of coping with individual differences in productivity. Taylor's methods made it possible for unskilled workers to be highly productive.) The studies of informal organization and morale conducted by Elton Mayo and Fritz J. Roethlisberger at Western Electric have been quoted in virtually every book about management, organizational behavior, or industrial psychology. Their findings were the forerunners of the human relations movement of the late 1940s and 1950s. Human relations in industry was thus founded upon a dramatic example of serendipity. The *Hawthorne effect*—an increase in productivity stemming from the mere fact that people felt management cared about them—came about because of experiments to investigate the efficacy of modifying physical working conditions.

Later concepts and techniques of the behavioral approach to management include sensitivity training, organization development (OD), and role playing. The human relations movement in industry thus moved up the scale in sophistication from human relations training to attempts at increasing the ability of managers to understand people at a deeper level.

Third is the rationalistic–model approach, sometimes called the quantitative or management science approach. William H. Newman, Charles E. Summer, and E. Kirby Warren contend that operations research is the most promising of the rationalistic–model approach. Operations research

(OR) stems from attempts to solve a variety of complex logistical problems that the military faced during the Second World War.[3] For example, project teams were formed to investigate problems of shipping, scheduling, and submarine search. New tools were needed to solve such problems, and OR was the result.

Quantitative answers are provided by operations research methods to a variety of decision-making questions. Model building can be considered an operations research technique. For example, sometimes management relies upon models to help predict demand for a product. Few students graduate from business schools today without becoming broadly exposed to the rationalistic–model approach to management. Predictions have been made that this school of management thought will lead to the creation of a small group of specialists in large organizations who will do much of the planning.[4]

Industrial and organizational psychology provides much of the knowledge base for organizational behavior. It represents the joining together of personnel and organizational (industrial–social) psychology. Many of the "buzz words" of behavioral science are concepts and techniques developed by industrial and organizational psychologists. Job enrichment, job enlargement, the motivation–hygiene theory, and the Managerial Grid, to cite several examples, are all products of psychology.

Personnel psychology has provided the methodological underpinnings for many aspects of personnel work such as attitude surveys and employee selection methods. Underlying this field is the belief that individual differences exist among people and that these differences can be measured. Early-day industrial psychology, with its study of production workers and its close liaison with industrial engineering, complemented Scientific Management. In recent years personnel psychologists have shifted their emphasis from line workers and supervision to the study of management. Problems of sales selection have been an external concern of personnel psychologists.

Organizational psychology is almost indistinguishable from organizational behavior except that the latter has become broader in scope. Defined by Bernard M. Bass as the study of the interplay of men and organizations, organizational psychology places heavy emphasis on the study of groups.[5] The historic roots of the human relations movement and organizational psychology are almost identical. Modern organizational psychology stems from the early social psychology of Kurt Lewin.[6] Focus in organizational psychology is placed upon understanding universal principles of human behavior rather than individual differences. Organizational psychology represents a major component of the behavioral approach to management.

The scope of organizational behavior can be further understood by highlighting the contribution of a third interdisciplinary field of knowledge. *Industrial engineering* has provided organizational behavior with formal techniques to describe and analyze jobs and systems of work. Industrial engineers and a group of scholars identified as *technologists* have developed insights and understandings about the relationship between organizational structure and human behavior. The recent practice of *office landscaping* implies that structural elements—including actual physical layout—can influence employee morale and productivity. Office landscaping is a convenient device for esthetically partitioning off large work areas into smaller, more intimate groupings. The partitions used are "S"-shaped and attractively carpeted. Research on the utility of office landscaping is yet unavailable, but its proponents contend that people work more efficiently and experience higher job satisfaction when surrounded by office landscaping, in contrast to working in large undivided areas.

Studies conducted with 100 British firms, reported by Joan Woodward, illustrate at a broader level how organizational structure is related to organizational behavior.[7] One aspect of these studies concerned the interrelationships among levels of technical sophistication, organizational structure, and business success. An important finding was that successful low and high technology organizations tended toward the following structural characteristics: (a) less emphasis on precise written definitions of job duties—people were less constrained by rules and regulations, (b) a higher degree of delegation of authority—subordinates were given more decision-making responsibility, (c) a more permissive management style—less emphasis was placed upon authoritative management, and (d) less tightly organized work forces.

Successful firms in the middle ranges of technological sophistication exercised more supervision of production workers. Written communications were more frequent, control procedures were more elaborate, and deviation from company policy was more likely to be reprimanded in high or low technology organizations.[8]

Another important technological influence on organizational behavior is the computer. For instance, Jay W. Forrester has analyzed how computerized processing of information allows for a new information flow or system within organizations.[9] Modern electronic equipment, according to Forrester, permits a rearrangement of the information system into a radial or star shape with all storage files at the center. With a restructured system of this nature, information is directly accessible to people who previously operated with too little information to permit effective management or to establish a feeling of confidence. Technology is thus responsible for changes in behavior.

THE KNOWLEDGE WORKER AND ORGANIZATIONAL BEHAVIOR

Why is it necessary to have a new book about the behavior of people in organizations? Has the nature of people changed that much since the outpouring of books about human relations and personnel management that took place in the 1950s? New insights and understandings about organizational behavior are necessary not because the basic psychological makeup of people in organizations has changed. New insights and understandings are necessary because the *mix* of people in organizations has changed. Most readers of this book will never encounter the problems of the "man on the assembly line" or those of his supervisor. Many readers will be productively employed yet will never observe first-hand the production of things. They will deal with the production of ideas.

The knowledge worker in the knowledge society is becoming the dominant figure in organizational life. He has replaced in importance the production worker in a manufacturing-oriented (industrial) society. Peter F. Drucker describes this phenomenon of contemporary society with the following carefully reasoned conclusion:[10]

> The figures are impressive enough. Ninety percent of all scientists and technologists who ever lived are alive and at work today. In the first five hundred years since Gutenberg, from 1450 to 1950, some thirty million printed books were published in the world. In the last twenty-five years alone an equal number has appeared. Thirty years ago, on the eve of World War II, semi-skilled machine operators, the men on the assembly line, were the center of the American work force. Today the center is the knowledge worker, the man or woman who applies to productive work ideas, concepts, and information rather than manual skill or brawn. Our largest single occupation is teaching, that is, the systematic supply of knowledge and systematic training applying it.

Census data about the distribution of occupations in the United States are useful in quantifying the phenomenon of the rise of the knowledge worker. Drucker includes professional, managerial, and technical people in the knowledge worker classification. The ascendance of the knowledge worker, however, is more vivid in the professional and technical than in managerial groups. Major structural changes in the work force have been in the proportion of professionals and technicians, not the proportion of managers.

	1950	1960	1970	1975
Total Work Force	59,648	66,681	78,627	88,700
Professional and Technical Workers	4,490	7,475	11,140	13,200
Percentage of Labor Force	7.53	11.21	14.17	14.88
Managers, Officials, and Proprietors	6,429	7,067	8,289	9,200
Percentage of Labor Force	10.78	10.60	10.54	10.37
Sales Workers	3,822	4,401	4,854	5,800
Percentage of Labor Force	6.41	6.60	6.17	6.54

Figure 1.2 Proportion of three different occupational groups in the United States Labor Force, 1950–1975 (figures in thousands). SOURCE: U.S. Bureau of the Census, *Statistical Abstract of the United States: 1971*, 92nd edition (Washington, D.C., 1971), p. 222.

Figure 1.2 reflects these changes. Over the 25-year period summarized, approximately ten percent of the work force has been engaged in managerial work. Note, however, that the percentage of professional and technical workers has approximately doubled. In 1950 professional and technical workers comprised 7.53 percent of the work force; in 1970 they comprised 14.17 percent. Projections for 1975 are that professional and technical workers will comprise 14.88 percent of the work force.[11]

Who Is a Knowledge Worker?

Occupations are difficult to classify as purely "knowledge work" versus "nonknowledge work." The concepts of knowledge work and knowledge worker can best be understood as points on a continuum. Figure 1.3 expresses this idea schematically. At the extreme left-hand side are occupations requiring very little conceptual work and very much manual or physical work. (No job requires zero conceptual skill. Even the venerable floor cleaner must make a "sweep or mop" decision in order to remove a foreign element from the floor.)

At the extreme right-hand end of the continuum are jobs requiring considerable conceptual skill and almost no physical skill. (No job requires zero physical skill. Even the most theoretical physicist must be able to manipulate pencils, desk drawers, and elevator buttons.) At the middle of the

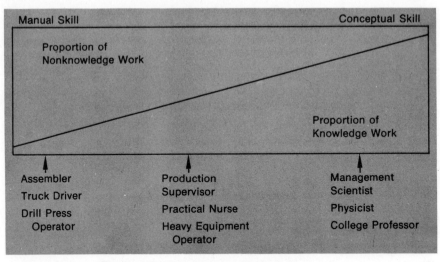

Figure 1.3 Continuum of knowledge work.

continuum are jobs requiring approximately equal proportions of conceptual and manual skill.

Implications for Organizational Behavior

A knowledge society densely populated by knowledge workers has far-reaching implications for organizational life. Knowledge industries will be subject to a different set of pressures than their manufacturing company counterparts of the past. Joseph W. McGuire has formulated a list of the possible consequences of the development of a knowledge organization.[12] His conclusions are corroborated by similar ideas presented by Fremont E. Kast and James E. Rosenzweig,[13] Dale E. Zand,[14] and Peter Drucker.[15]

1. *The ratio of salaried to wage employees in an industrialized society may be expected to increase steadily.* It will be more difficult to pay people directly for production of knowledge. Salaries may have to be adjusted to reward the acquisition of knowledge.

2. *Personnel, educational, and developmental departments within the enterprise are going to expand and play a more important and somewhat different role.* Personnel departments, for example, will be called upon to play an even more active role in the recruiting and upgrading of knowledge workers.

3. *The tendency toward professionalism in business will become more important.* A more professionalized work force will adhere to higher ethical standards of business conduct and will also place more demands upon management for challenging work. Robert F. Pearse observed in 1972 that the era of professional management is almost present. One unique barometer of

the trend is the Certified Administrative Manager (CAM) designation, reflecting a program launched in 1970. More about this new development is found in Chapter 14.[16]

4. *Increased demands for independence and competence will be associated with professionalism.* Professional workers are more cosmopolitan than local in their orientation. They tend to be more mobile and identify more with their occupation than with any single organization.

5. *In order to attract and hold educated workers, it will be necessary for companies to create task forces to work on interesting and stimulating projects that tend to optimize specific subgoals.* Project organization has become a widely used form of organizational structure. Despite their popularity, project organizations solve some problems and create others. For example, project managers who find themselves between assignments tend to become quite anxious.[17]

6. *Old concepts of line organization will be increasingly revised to take advantage of knowledge most efficiently.* One important implication of this development is that staff personnel (prime examples of the knowledge worker concept) become an integral part of the team.

7. *Organization communications will become a problem of growing significance.* Experts tend to discuss problems in their own unique jargon and symbols. Often they are unable to translate their ideas to management in a workable form. "A knowledge firm, therefore, runs the real risk of becoming a Tower of Babel, unable to move forward because of semantic and conceptual difficulties."[18]

8. *Adaptability lags within the business organization will have to be shortened.* An orientation toward knowledge implies an orientation toward change and unlimited growth; organizations that remain static rather than dynamic will not survive.

9. *The tasks of top management will be substantially altered.* Knowledge workers will react better to coordination than to control and direction, thus calling for more adaptive leadership styles. Decision making will become more complex and sophisticated.

10. *Finally, as a corollary to the preceding points, the work environment will have to be more conducive to innovation.* Business organizations, in order to survive, will have to encourage and reward innovative behavior.

Implications for this Book

The rise of the knowledge worker in organizational life implies that a formal study of organizational behavior should be oriented toward topics of vital concern to the knowledge worker. Less emphasis need be placed upon information relating to clerical or production workers. Toward this end, topics have been selected for this text on the basis of their relevance for managerial, professional, and technical personnel. For example, discussions about motivation, decision making, political maneuvering, and stress generated by jobs and organizations are largely based upon research or observations about knowledge workers. Creativity and innovation in the decision-making process will be highlighted.

A conception of leadership will be presented that has particular appeal to the motivational makeup of the knowledge worker. Discussion about organizational structure will also emphasize those types of organizational design in which the knowledge worker is most likely to find himself. Finally, the glimpse into the future presented in the conclusion to this book will reemphasize several of the ten forecasts made by McGuire.

WHAT ORGANIZATIONAL BEHAVIOR IS NOT

Some attempt must be made to delimit the field if organizational behavior is to become a recognized discipline. Toward this end, personnel techniques and principles of management are arbitrarily excluded from direct consideration in this book. The omnipresent discussion of planning, organizing, controlling, and directing will therefore not be repeated here. Similarly, many other books adequately treat personnel techniques and procedures such as selection, testing, manpower planning, performance appraisal, accident prevention, and management development.[19]

Quantitative approaches to management decision making such as PERT, decision trees, and management information systems are also considered to lie outside the direct purview of organizational behavior.

Organizational behavior, according to the present conception, does not include a direct study of basic human processes such as intelligence, perception, emotions, motivation, and learning. No study of people in organizations would be complete without such information, but these knowledge areas can best be acquired in any introductory course in psychology. Readers in search of an up-to-date, nontechnical presentation of basic human processes are referred to *Living Psychology* by Gerald L. Hershey and James C. Lugo.[20] A general schema of how basic human processes are related to organizational behavior is presented in the next section of this chapter.

Another body of knowledge to be excluded here is research methodology underlying organizational behavior. The philosophy and methods of science make a vital contribution to one's formal education, but they need not be considered part of the fundamentals of organizational behavior. Similarly, methods of data collection and analysis can be found in broad-scoped books such as Blair J. Kolasa's *Introduction to Behavioral Science for Business.*[21] Focus returns next to what this book *is* about—achieving insight into and understanding of the basic processes that take place among people in organizations.

CONCEPTUAL FRAMEWORK FOR ORGANIZATIONAL BEHAVIOR

Organizational behavior, as the reader may have surmised so far, is a far-reaching body of knowledge with permeable boundaries. A central purpose of this book is to simplify and unify much of the available knowledge about the behavior of people in organizations. Toward this end, a conceptual framework is presented consisting of four core propositions. Ideally, these propositions represent the bedrock upon which new insights about organizational behavior will emerge. At a minimum, they may be considered a "game plan" to which the reader should frequently return. Frequent mention will be made of these propositions throughout the book; they provide a theoretical base for interpreting human behavior in organizations. They will soon be examined in depth. In summary they are:

1. Organizational behavior follows the principles of human behavior.
2. Organizational behavior is situational.
3. Organizational behavior is systemic.
4. Organizational behavior represents a constant interaction between structure and process variables.

1. *Organizational behavior follows the principles of human behavior.* However elementary this statement, the importance of its implications cannot be overlooked. Human beings in organizations are governed by the same physiological mechanisms both on and off the job. Internal mechanisms provide people an extra spurt of the appropriate hormone under times of stress, whether this stress is job or nonjob related. Similarly, people at work are governed by the same psychological principles both inside and outside organizational life. Organizational behavior *is* human behavior in a particular setting.

Figure 1.4 presents a basic schema to explain how psychological and sociological principles intervene in or *mediate* organizational behavior. The behavior of a given individual in an organization is determined to some extent by basic psychological and sociological factors or internal and external factors. Intervening variables placed in the center of the schema are but

INTERVENING VARIABLES		

Figure 1.4 Organizational behavior follows the principles of human behavior.

a sampling of the multitude of forces that shape behavior. An undetermined number of interactions also take place between internal and external factors. For example, a person frustrated about losing a bowling tournament may be more sensitive to noise levels in the environment. The schema presented in Figure 1.4 will be explained further by three illustrations of how psychological and sociological factors influence (function as intervening variables in) human behavior in organizations.

Gloria Hayes, an administrative assistant in a large company, is very bright (*high learning ability*), ambitious (*motivation*), emotionally expressive (*emotions*), and has a high frustration tolerance (*frustration*). She learns one morning that in 30 days her position will be discontinued. Three weeks ago her performance was rated excellent. Gloria perceives the *reward system* as being unjust and her degree of *trust* in management is lowered. Gloria reacts to the *stress* of potential unemployment in a manner mediated by her personal characteristics. She is disappointed about losing her position, but her judgment combined with her high frustration tolerance shapes her behavior. She quietly inquires around the organization and learns of a new opening in another department without going through formal personnel channels.

Austin Bellows, a statistician in an insurance company, harbors negative *attitudes* toward authority figures. These attitudes shape his *perception* of management. He perceives most changes initiated by management as being more beneficial to the company than to employees. Austin is temporarily assigned to a profit-improvement task force, a newly formed but already *cohesive group*. Suspecting that management is really using this group as a "witch hunt" to eliminate unproductive employees, Austin is slow to assimilate himself into the group. Feeling somewhat alienated from the group, he is disappointed with the *social factors* surrounding the job. Alienation from the group soon becomes a source of *stress* to Austin and he becomes *frustrated* with his job situation. These events combine to reinforce his negative attitudes toward management.

Michael Levin, a physicist, is young, capable, and creative. Mike's *values* include desires for freedom and independence of action. Working after hours, Mike develops some ideas for a new product that he feels his company should manufacture and sell. His management brings some related company policy to his attention. First, new product ideas have to be submitted through channels to a new product committee. Once a new product idea is approved by the committee, a feasibility study is conducted. Mike is also informed that funds for new product development have already been spent this year. Michael Levin experiences feelings of frustration. Company *policy* (gradualness in exploring new products) has interacted with personal values (eagerness to try new things) to precipitate an internal state (frustration).

Many external factors in addition to those listed in Figure 1.4 can influence or mediate human behavior in organizations. Primarily external sociological factors are shown in Figure 1.4. This analysis can be extended to an array of factors that are structural or technological in nature. For instance, many people react emotionally to some aspects of automation. This emotional response may cloud their judgment about the contribution automation can make to their welfare.

To illustrate further, learning ability can be influenced by technological factors. A study conducted at International Business Machines Corporation demonstrated a ten percent savings in learning time attributable to computer-assisted instruction.[22] Seventy-nine electronic technicians received their required training in data-processing principles through programmed texts, the standard method used by the company. A contrast group of 25 equivalent students received the same training through a keyboard-operated device linked remotely to an IBM 1440 computer system. Although both groups showed an equivalent amount of learning, the group assisted by a computer device learned the same amount in ten percent less time.

2. *Organizational behavior is situational.* Psychologists and other behavioral scientists have emphasized for years that individual behavior is a function of the interaction between personal characteristics of the individual and environmental variables. In order to understand a person's behavior, the pressures placed upon him in a given situation must be understood. Aggressive behavior, for example, surfaces when a normally calm individual is forced into constant and close physical proximity with other

people. Ghetto dwellers and subway riders behave aggressively in large measure because of the pressures exerted upon them. Situational approaches to understanding leadership also emphasize the importance of understanding each situation in order to determine what constitutes effective leadership in that situation. By way of illustration, the director of research and development in a technologically sophisticated company should possess a different constellation of personal characteristics than the supervisor of a key-punch operation. He should also handle different situations that arise according to the dictates of each situation. Robert J. Mockler has developed a new formulation of the situational perspective in his *Situational Theory of Management.* His theory is flavored by the following kind of thinking:[23]

> A new wind is stirring through management theory, however—the *situational approach*—and it is affecting all major areas of management theory, including organization, leadership, staffing, control and planning. In doing any job, the manager's first step is to identify the major characteristics of the situation confronting him, either from his experience or his reading, and he will have guidelines at hand for dealing with it. If he is not lucky, he must develop his own solutions!

Mary Parker Follett, in the 1920s, provided some insights about the importance of studying the situation in carrying out the management process.[24] Her *law of the situation* provides guidelines for order giving. In order to avoid the extremes of "bossism" or a *laissez-faire* attitude, order giving must be depersonalized. The situation must be analyzed to discover the law of the situation. Orders then stem logically from this law. The question of giving and receiving orders disappears when orders are part of the situation. Following these dictates, authority is always the authority of the situation. Follett also cautions that, because the situation is always evolving, orders should never be stationary.

Paul Pigors and Charles A. Myers have developed the concept of situational thinking through six editions of *Personnel Administration.*[25] Their analysis suggests that four situational variables are basic for anyone responsible for getting results accomplished through people.

(a) *The human element.* In addition to individual differences this category includes interpersonal relationships and other social aspects of the situation.
(b) *The technical factor.* Included here are items such as production methods and equipment, management procedures, and specialized skills in any job function.

(c) *Space-time dimensions and relationships.* "Examples of spatial variables would be the size and location of a plant, office or work situation."[26] An example of a temporal factor would be the stage of personal development a manager has currently achieved.

(d) *Organization-wide policies designed to achieve major organizational objectives.* Policies affect behavior and their possible effect in each situation must be understood.

Situational thinking also underlies the contingency theory of leadership effectiveness developed by Fred E. Fiedler on the basis of elaborate experimentation and statistical analysis. Fiedler's situational approach to leadership is highlighted in Chapter 6. For now, a basic statement of his theory is sufficient to illustrate how situational thinking enhances an understanding of organizational behavior.[27]

> This theory suggests that leadership is an influence process where the ease or difficulty of exerting influence is a function of the favorableness of the group task situation for the leader. Although it has been recognized that the favorableness of each group task situation may depend on different variables, the three most commonly acknowledged determinants stated in their order of importance are leader–member relations, task structure, and position power.

Specifying all the factors that compose the environment is a complex and perhaps unmanageable task. Tentatively, the total environment can be subdivided into organizational structure, technological or product influences, peer group pressures, leadership style of one's superiors, organizational climate, and cultural influences. Organizational behavior—or the behavior of an individual in an organization—is thus a function of the interaction between his characteristics and all these environmental variables. These relationships are summarized in Figure 1.5 and can be represented by the equation **OB = f(IC, OS, TI, PGP, SLS, OC, CI)**. Verbally, this equation is illustrated with a hypothetical life situation.

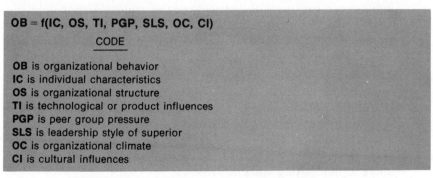

OB = f(IC, OS, TI, PGP, SLS, OC, CI)

CODE

OB is organizational behavior
IC is individual characteristics
OS is organizational structure
TI is technological or product influences
PGP is peer group pressure
SLS is leadership style of superior
OC is organizational climate
CI is cultural influences

Figure 1.5 Determinants of organizational behavior.

Barry Kindig is an English professor at Raymond College, a small liberal arts institution in New England. The behavior in question was Professor Kindig's condoning (or at least not stopping) college students from smoking marijuana while taking a final examination in a course entitled "The Contemporary Novel." Word of this situation came back to the administration and Professor Kindig's situation is being reviewed for possible disciplinary action, including a request for his resignation. In order to understand why Kindig behaved as he did (without attempting to defend or criticize his behavior) each term in the organizational behavior equation will be examined.

IC: Kindig's individual characteristics are such that he is a mild-mannered, tolerant, and permissive person. He enjoys his work and family life and has almost no need to condemn or criticize people for actions that do not adversely affect him. Additionally, he dislikes confrontation. Barry Kindig says that he is not a marijuana user himself and his attitudes about the subject of drugs are neutral to liberal. He also points out that since he does not use marijuana himself, he was not able to detect others using marijuana.

OS: Organizational structure contributed in no small way to Kindig's decision to adopt a *laissez-faire* policy about his students smoking "grass" during the contemporary novel final. Traditionally, the professor operates with almost complete autonomy while functioning in the classroom. Almost never is his decision subject to review from the administration. This organizational tradition predisposed Kindig toward thinking that his behavior in the classroom would not be subject to review.

TI: The product or technology in this situation is knowledge in general and the contemporary novel in particular. Marijuana smoking, it might be reasoned, is more appropriate while taking an examination in the contemporary novel than during an accounting or statistics exam. Extending this line of reasoning to fanciful extremes, if Kindig were a professor of surgery (and the students were conducting surgery), the technology—medicine—would have been entirely incompatible with marijuana smoking. Additionally, it would be highly illegal to conduct surgery under the influence of intoxicants or drugs.

PGP: Peer group pressures were almost nonexistent for Kindig in this particular situation. His colleagues looked upon marijuana in much the same light as cigarettes or whiskey. Barry Kindig and his colleagues had never even discussed what should be done if students used marijuana in the classroom. Any peer group pressure that existed at all would be nearer the lenient than the punitive end with respect to monitoring student behavior.

SLS: Superior leadership style probably contributed to Kindig's decision not to discourage students from smoking grass during his final. Dr. Beam, the Chairman of the English Department, saw his role as providing administrative support to the professors in his department. Beam disliked committee meetings and only held staff meetings about urgent matters. Kindig had seen Beam only twice in the last semester. The subject of imposing controls on student behavior while on campus had never once been a topic for departmental discussion. Under the influence of a more directive leader, Professor Kindig might have developed a policy beforehand about students using marijuana while taking a final exam.

OC: Organizational climate at Raymond College could be described as mildly, but not militantly, conservative. In earlier years, "panty raids" were tolerated, student demonstrations about the war in Viet Nam were treated sympathetically, and minor concessions were made about changes in the curriculum. Recently, demands for black studies, women's studies, and recognition of the Gay Liberation Front on campus were sympathetically reviewed but denied. Overall, Kindig did not think that the administration would take such extreme action about his students using marijuana on campus. First, he did not *push* marijuana; second, a more permissive atmosphere tends to exist during finals. In earlier years, even when cigarette smoking was not allowed in the classroom, exceptions were made for examination periods.

CI: Cultural or broader environmental influences undoubtedly had some preconscious effect upon Kindig. Pressures toward conformity in behavior have decreased since Barry Kindig's childhood. Although possession of marijuana is illegal in the United States, cultural mores suggested that "only pushers get busted." Furthermore, in recent years colleges have moved gradually away from playing the role of parents or policemen to college students. In short, to understand Barry Kindig's behavior, it is necessary to understand his personal characteristics and the total range of environmental influences to which he is subjected.

3. *Organizational behavior is systemic.* Systems thinking has become an integral part of modern organizational theory. Organizations are viewed as complex systems consisting of interrelated and interlocking subsystems. Changes or alterations in any one part of the system has both known and unknown consequences in other parts of the system. When modifications in the system lead to desired, positive consequences, they are called *functions.* Negative consequences in response to modifications in the system are called *dysfunctions.*[28] According to the system's point of view, every act or interven-

tion has both functions and dysfunctions. Astuteness is required to observe all these consequences taking place within the system.

Systemic properties of organizational behavior can be illustrated by the functions and dysfunctions that occur when several aggressive, young, and effective salesmen are introduced into a sales force of older and less effective salesmen. Among the positive consequences are increased sales and a feeling of competitiveness that spurs some of the more senior salesmen on toward higher levels of performance. Among the possible negative consequences are decreased morale and productivity on the part of some senior salesmen because they begin to feel less important to management. Junior members of the sales force tend to place disproportionate demands upon sales service and clerical support areas because they (the salesmen) lack familiarity with office procedures. Stress is often created for the credit department because younger and more aggressive salesmen take a less conservative view of what type of customer represents a sound credit risk.

General systems theory has been utilized in recent years to help understand the complex workings of organizations. The grand hope of general systems theory is the "... creation of a science of organizational universals—or if you will, a universal science—using the elements and processes common to all systems as a starting point."[29] William G. Scott and Terence R. Mitchell caution, however, that human organizations may not be directly comparable to computer or biological systems, and analogies have to be drawn·with

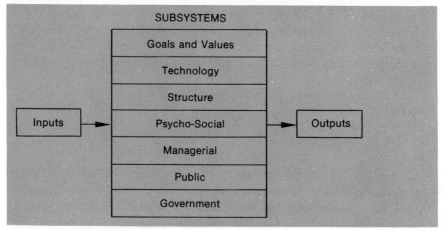

Flow of Material/Energy/Information

Figure 1.6 Organizational behavior is systemic. (Adapted from Fremont E. Kast and James E. Rosenzweig, *Organization and Management: A Systems Approach*. New York: McGraw-Hill, 1970, p. 121. Used with permission of McGraw-Hill Book Company).

caution. Nevertheless, systems theory does provide a useful framework for understanding the complex interrelationships that constitute organizational behavior. Recently, systems theory has been used to diagnose the organizational effectiveness of companies such as ITT and Penn Central.[30]

Human organizations, to carry systems thinking one step further, are in fact a complex of interdependent subsystems. A general systems model of an organization is presented in Figure 1.6. "Public" and "Government" have been added to this systems diagram developed by Kast and Rosenzweig because of today's emphasis on the relationship between organizations and their external environment. Ralph Nader and his followers have provided a renewed impetus in this on organizations receiving feedback from the external environment. Kast and Rosenzweig provide a rationale for Figure 1.6 that illustrates how systems thinking helps interpret organizational behavior.[31]

> The goals and values, as well as the technical, structural, and psycho-social, and managerial subsystems are shown as integral parts of the overall organization. This figure is an aid to understanding the evolution in organization theory. Traditional management theory emphasized the structural and managerial subsystems and was concerned with developing principles. The human relationists and behavioral scientists emphasized the psycho-social subsystem and focused their attention on motivation, group dynamics, and other related factors. The management science school emphasized the economic-technical subsystem and techniques for quantifying decision making and control processes. Thus each approach to organization and management has emphasized particular primary subsystems, with little recognition of the importance of the others. The modern approach views the organization as a structured, sociotechnical system and considers *each* of the primary subsystems *and* their interactions.

Organizational behavior and its systemic properties may also be illustrated with the variables discussed in core proposition 2. Figure 1.7 represents but one example of the complex network of interrelationships that exist in the organization system. Assume that one variable in the environment is substantially changed: Biotronics Engineering phases out of the manufacture of microscopes and phases into the manufacture of medical–electronic devices such as pacemakers to stimulate the heart. Following is but a sampling of the systemic changes that could conceivably take place. Theoretically, in a real system, every variable has an influence on every other variable. (Figure 1.7, if completed, would be a dense lattice of overlapping arrows!)

Changes in technology (technological influence) bring about changes in individual characteristics. For example, many of the engineers will automatically become obsolete from a technological standpoint. This obsoles-

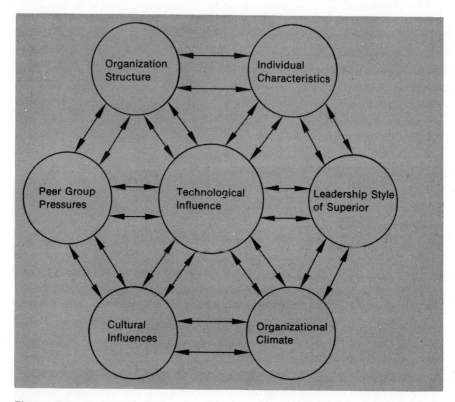

Figure 1.7 Technical changes at Biotronics precipitate other changes in the organizational system.

cence may change the feelings and attitudes of some engineers; they may suffer a loss of self-confidence and feel the threats of job insecurity. These feelings in turn will call for a more supportive leadership style on the part of their immediate superior.

Changes in technology generally bring about some changes in organizational structure. An electronics department may be created while the optical department (that dealt with microscopes) may be phased out. Peer group pressures may in turn change for many individuals because new organizational subunits will be formed as a result of organizational changes. Shifts in the organizational climate may also become observable. Companies specializing in the manufacture of microscopes tend to be "stodgy" and conservative because of the relative stability of their market, while companies engaged in the newer electronic technologies tend to be more dynamic, *avant-garde*, and "swinging."

Finally, changes in technology may ultimately carry with them changes in the cultural influences impinging upon the organization. Infusion of a new technology into an organization gradually brings about a change in the complexion of the work force. Younger, better educated, and more mobile people enter the organization in greater numbers than in the past. This changeover of personnel carries with it a new set of personal values, attitudes, and concerns. Part of a new cultural influence has been brought into the organization, carrying with it a heightened contrast between the "old guard" and the "new guard."

4. *Organizational behavior represents a constant interaction between structure and process variables.* Kelly has insightfully commented in the preface to his compendious book, *Organizational Behaviour,* "As I got nearer to the end of the book, it became clearer that the great division in this field, as in many others, is between structure and process."[32]

Structure refers to organizational shapes, definitions, and roles. The arrangement of boxes on an organization chart is an example of organizational *shape.* A statement in a personnel manual that a suggestion system "allows for upward communication of ideas for improvement and rewards employees for creativity" is an organizational *definition.* An organizational *role* is illustrated by the statement, "A company president is expected to interface with the community about problems of mutual concern to the company and the community."

Process refers to what happens, with or without the structure. A retail store may use both formal advertising and public relations functions (structure) to help build its image in the community. However, most of the store's image is formed by word-of-mouth from satisfied and dissatisfied customers and employees (the actual process of image building).

Processes emerging within a group or organization are often evident only after they are heading toward completion. Kelly notes that the student revolution "with its emphasis on confrontation, conflict, escalation and crisis" is an example of an organizational process breaking through the conventional structure of bureaucracy.[33] It is an almost structural requirement in any organization that managers deal with the discontents of their people, yet employees sometimes find other processes for handling them. The management of one casualty insurance company was shocked to learn that its claims representatives were ready to unionize. Management did not carefully observe the processes of reacting to discontent that were taking place within the organization.

The difference between structure and process represents a vital concept for understanding organizational behavior. Classical approaches to management theory appear sterile to many students because they neglect the interpersonal processes—the human side—of organizational life. Erring in the opposite direction (neglecting the influence of structural and technological factors) is a tendency on the part of some social psychologists. Deeper understandings of organizational behavior require an ability to follow the complex shifting in relative importance between structure and process variables.

The familiar dichotomy drawn between the formal and informal organization parallels the distinction between structure and process. The formal organization refers, in general, to written statements about how things should work. Edgar H. Schein describes the formal organization as fundamentally a "pattern of roles and a blueprint for their coordination" that "exists independently of particular people and can survive in spite of 100 percent turnover of membership." Informal organization, in contrast, refers to ". . . those patterns of coordination that arise among the members of a formal organization which are not called for by the blueprint."[34] *Custom* represents a useful synonym for informal organization. For example, in a research laboratory many good ideas are generated because scientists and engineers ask each other provocative, work-related questions. Stimulating each other intellectually is a custom, not a formal organizational requirement. The formal versus informal distinction is not absolute. In practice, the formal and informal organizations interact rather than exist independently of one another.

Structure versus process *interactions* can be illuminated here by way of two brief examples. Committees have some degree of formal structures. Assigning a committee chairman and forming the committee both represent an element of structure. Examining the structure, however, provides only the barest understanding of what the committee will actually accomplish during its tenure. Studying the interactions that take place among the people—process variables—will lead to more fruitful predictions about a particular committee's productivity. Structural considerations, however, cannot be ignored. The organization level to which the committee reports is one structural consideration of significance. Presidential committees, for example, obviously have more power and a greater sense of urgency pushing them toward accomplishment than committees appointed by a lower level manager.

Medical residents, according to their job descriptions and state law, have ultimate authority for patient welfare. The most inexperienced and incompetent resident thus has more formal authority than the most experienced and competent nurse. Fortunately, for the welfare of patients, most residents recognize that they are dependent upon experienced nurses for practical knowledge about day-to-day patient care. From a process standpoint, the experienced nurse has power equal to or exceeding that of the resident. Interpersonal conflicts between nurses and residents reach their peak when a resident who legalistically interprets his role (structure) interacts with a nurse with strong needs for dominance (process).

How might the reader make optimum use of these four core propositions? Ideally, one should simultaneously keep in mind all four concepts or perspectives during the reading of the entire text. Ideally, every behavioral phenomenon should be examined from all four perspectives: individual behavior, situational, systemic, and the interaction between structure and process. For instance, in the chapter about leadership style a case history is presented of a dynamic executive. The reader might ask the following kinds of questions about the case illustration: (1) What impact does his style have on the behavior of individuals? (2) How well does his leadership style fit the situation? (3) What impact does his style of leadership have on the organizational system? (4) How would his leadership style influence the ways in which executives under him implement company policy?

Admittedly, precise answers to questions such as these will be difficult to achieve. Behavioral incidents will be described in this book that cannot be conveniently analyzed by more than one or two of the core propositions. An element of speculation exists in even advancing these core concepts. The field of organizational behavior has not yet developed a set of tools that invariably provides useful insights to all situations taking place in organizations.

PLAN OF THE BOOK

Discussion so far has laid the conceptual groundwork for the balance of the book and indicated its knowledge worker flavor. Readers are urged to review the core propositions before and after reading Parts II, III, and IV. Part I has been both a brief introduction to organizational behavior and a framework for interpreting the balance of this text.

Readers of this book in large proportion either aspire toward managerial or professional roles in organizations or have already achieved such status. Emphasis throughout this book is therefore upon the concerns of managerial and professional personnel rather than upon supervisory, clerical, or production workers.

Information dealing more nearly with individuals than with small groups or total organizations is presented in Part II. Chapter 2 intends to provide some fresh insights in addition to reviewing some basic material on the ubiquitous topic of work motivation and satisfaction. Chapter 3 focuses upon psychological factors underlying how managerial and professional people go about making decisions and finding problems. Chapter 4 presents a lengthy analysis of the problems, frustrations, and "hang-ups" of managers and professionals in organizations. Chapter 5 provides some new knowledge about how individuals in organizations maneuver their way toward bigger jobs and more power.

Information dealing more nearly with groups than with individuals or organizations is the subject matter of Part III. Chapter 6 provides some general background information about how groups function. Special attention is also given to task forces and committees. Chapter 7 discusses leadership from both the trait and situational points of view. An overview of the different approaches to, or "styles" of, leadership also constitutes part of the subject matter. Chapter 8 discusses approaches that managers can use to improve subordinate performance, particularly with regard to the interpersonal processes involved. Chapter 9 provides some understandings of the intricate processes of interpersonal communication (both verbal and nonverbal) in organizational life. Intergroup conflict and its resolution is the subject matter of Chapter 10.

Information dealing more nearly with total organizations than with small groups or individuals constitutes the subject matter of Part IV. Chapter 11 examines organizational climate of the "personality" of organizations. The influence of organization policies and values on behavior is also studied in this chapter. Chapter 12 looks at the psychological and sociological aspects of coping with change, particularly at the individual and small group level—one of the key responsibilities of managers in contemporary society. The subject of management of change, however, could fit logically into any of the three major sections of the book. Chapter 13 then explores change from the standpoint of how organizations are changed and improved.

Part V concludes this analysis of organizational behavior with a chapter about the future of both organizations and the managers and professionals working in them.

Toward the end of each chapter a brief section labeled "Relationship to Core Propositions" appears. Its purpose is to assist the reader in relating chapter material to the framework for organizational behavior which undergirds this book. Relating such information to the core propositions should in turn help the reader integrate the body of knowledge called *organizational behavior* into a meaningful whole.

"Guidelines for Action" are presented toward the end of each chapter to offer suggestions on how to apply some of the insights provided in the text. Although the study of organizational behavior may not yet have reached the stage of being a prescriptive art, the author is fully aware of the typical reader's impatience for practical advice that can be used in live organizational settings. Hopefully, these guidelines for action will provide appeal to the reader's need for practicality and relevance.

Questions at the end of each chapter are designed to test insight and understanding, not content, about material in the text. Some of the questions simulate the activities of an applied behavioral scientist.

GUIDELINES FOR ACTION

1. In attempting to interpret and understand the behavior of people in organizations you must look at both their individual characteristics and the environmental situation in which they are working.
2. Every action taken in an organization has intended and unintended consequences on some other part of the organization. Your job as a staff person or manager is to predict and/or manage these consequences.
3. Job descriptions, organization charts, and the like represent only a starting point in predicting how people will behave in a given situation. You also have to examine the interactions among people that actually take place in order to understand organizational behavior.

QUESTIONS

1. What fields of knowledge outside of the physical and biological sciences do you feel are *not* part of organizational behavior?
2. Most business organizations have departments or divisions called marketing, accounting, manufacturing, and so forth. Should they also have departments of organizational behavior? Why or why not?
3. If Frederick W. Taylor (the father of Scientific Management) were alive today, what would his feelings be about the field of organizational behavior?
4. Robert J. Mockler has stated that "management is situational." What would the opposite or more traditional view of management contend?
5. If you were the president of Raymond College, how would you have handled the case of Professor Kindig? Why?
6. A basketball team can be considered a microcosm of a larger, more complex organization. What structural elements and processes can you identify that would be encountered during a game?
7. Assume that the change entered into the system at Biotronics Engineering was a shift from a permissive to an autocratic president. Describe the systemic consequences that might take place, using the variables included in the organizational behavior equation presented in this chapter.

NOTES

1. Joe Kelly, *Organizational Behaviour.* Homewood, Ill.: Richard D. Irwin and Dorsey Press, 1969, p. 1.
2. William H. Newman, Charles E. Summer, and E. Kirby Warren, *The Process of Management: Concepts, Behavior, and Practice,* third edition. Englewood Cliffs, N.J.: Prentice-Hall, 1972, pp. 6–10.
3. Martin K. Starr, *Management: A Modern Approach.* New York: Harcourt Brace Jovanovich, 1971, p. 33.
4. Andrew J. DuBrin, *The Practice of Managerial Psychology.* Elmsford, N.Y.: Pergamon Press, 1972, p. 285.
5. Bernard M. Bass, *Organizational Psychology.* Boston: Allyn & Bacon, 1965, p. 1.
6. *Ibid.,* p. 6.
7. Joan Woodward, *Industrial Organization: Theory and Practice.* London: Oxford University Press, 1965, pp. 68–80.
8. *Ibid.,* p. 80.
9. Jay W. Forrester, "A New Corporate Design," in Donald E. Porter, Philip B. Appelwhite, and Michael J. Misshauk, *Studies in Organizational Behavior and Management,* second edition. Scranton, Pa.: Intext Educational Publishers, 1971, pp. 830–831.
10. Peter F. Drucker, *The Age of Discontinuity: Guidelines to Our Changing Society.* New York: Harper & Row, 1969, p. 264.
11. Fremont E. Kast and James E. Rosenzweig, *Organization and Management: A Systems Approach.* New York: McGraw-Hill, 1970, p. 503.
12. Joseph W. McGuire, "Knowledge: The Basic Business Commodity," *Business Horizons,* Vol. 12, No. 6, June 1969, pp. 36–38. The ten italicized statements are quoted directly from McGuire.
13. Kast and Rosenzweig, *op. cit.,* pp. 505–508.
14. Dale E. Zand, "Managing the Knowledge Organization," in Peter F. Drucker (editor), *Preparing Tomorrow's Business Leaders Today.* Englewood Cliffs, N.J.: Prentice-Hall, 1969, pp. 112–136.
15. Drucker, *The Age of Discontinuity, op. cit.,* pp. 287–310.
16. Robert F. Pearse, "Certified Professional Managers: Concept into Reality?" *Personnel,* Vol. 49, No. 2, March–April 1972, pp. 26–35.
17. Clayton Reeser, "Some Potential Human Problems of the Project Form of Organization," *Academy of Management Journal,* Vol. 12, No. 4, December 1969, p. 467.
18. McGuire, *op. cit.,* p. 37.
19. One convenient source is John B. Miner, *Personnel Psychology.* New York: Macmillan, 1969.
20. Gerald L. Hershey and James C. Lugo, *Living Psychology.* Riverside, N.J.: Macmillan, 1970.
21. Blair J. Kolasa, *Introduction to Behavioral Science for Business.* New York: Wiley, 1969.
22. H. A. Schwartz and R. J. Haskell, Jr., "A Study of Computer-Assisted Instruction in Industrial Training" in Porter, Appelwhite, and Misshauk, *op. cit.,* p. 803, footnote 9.
23. Robert J. Mockler, "Situational Theory of Management," *Harvard Business Review,* Vol. 49, No. 3, May–June 1971, p. 146.
24. H. C. Metcalf and Lyndall Urwick (editors), *Dynamic Administration: The Collected Papers of Mary Parker Follett.* New York: Harper & Row, 1941.
25. Paul Pigors and Charles A. Myers, *Personnel Administration: A Point of View and a Method,* sixth edition. New York: McGraw-Hill, 1969, p. 238.
26. *Ibid.*
27. Walter Hill, "A Situational Approach to Leadership Effectiveness," *Journal of Applied Psychology,* Vol. 53, No. 6, December 1969, p. 513.

28. David R. Hampton, Charles E. Summer, and Ross A. Webber, *Organizational Behavior and the Practice of Management.* Glenview, Ill.: Scott, Foresman, 1968, pp. 20–21.

29. William G. Scott and Terence R. Mitchell, *Organization Theory: A Structural and Behavioral Analysis,* revised edition. Homewood, Ill.: Richard D. Irwin and Dorsey Press, 1972, p. 53.

30. Don Hellriegel and John W. Slocum, Jr., "Integrating Systems Concepts and Organizational Strategy," *Business Horizons,* Vol. 16, No. 4, April 1972, pp. 71–78.

31. Kast and Rosenzweig, *op. cit.,* pp. 121–122.

32. Kelly, *op. cit.,* p. vi.

33. *Ibid.*

34. Edgar H. Schein, *Organizational Psychology,* second edition. Englewood Cliffs, N.J.: Prentice-Hall, 1970, p. 10.

PART II

Individuals

Preview

Individuals rather than small groups or organizations are emphasized in this section of the book. The topics selected for inclusion are of vital concern to the knowledge worker in the knowledge organization. Some arbitrary decisions must be made by the author in excluding many topics that would also be of interest and concern to the knowledge worker. It is assumed, however, that basic topics such as perception and learning have already been studied by the student in psychology or social science courses.

Work motivation is the subject matter of Chapter 2. An attempt will be made to provide tentative answers for such basic issues as why people work (or choose not to work), why some people work harder than others, and also how one goes about motivating others to work harder. Chapter 3 deals with the issue of how managerial, professional, and technical people find problems and make decisions—the essence of the knowledge worker's contribution to an organization.

The last two chapters in Part II deal with topics that have as yet been given only scant attention in textbooks and scholarly journals. Middle managers and professional people encounter many frustrations, "hang-ups," disappointments, and dissatisfactions in organizational life. Readers will be given an inside look at the nature of these problems and, equally important, ideas about circumventing them. Chapter 5 provides an in-depth analysis of an almost taboo topic—the political maneuvering that takes place in most organizations. Pragmatically minded readers might interpret some of this information as a somewhat scholarly "survival kit" for career advancement.

2

The Motivation to Work

"Thank God it's Friday," exclaim most people, while some feel, "Oh, God it's Friday." Neither sentiment is correct nor incorrect, moral nor immoral; both are simply expressions of polar attitudes toward the meaning of work. Devotees of the "TGIF" philosophy perceive work as basically painful—an activity to be tolerated in order to pay for the luxuries of family life, community life, and recreational activities. In contrast, work zealots perceive their occupational role as a primary vehicle for recognition and self-fulfillment.

This capsule introduction to the meaning of work is one small step in unraveling the complexities of work-related motivation. Very few incontestable facts are found in the field of human motivation.

An attempt will be made in this chapter to achieve a balance between presenting widely known theories of motivation such as those of Maslow, Herzberg, and McClelland and newer conceptions such as equity theory, expectancy theory, and need gratification theory. The Work Motivation Schema, developed by this author, builds upon the work of other authors cited in this chapter. Prior to discussing motivation theories, an exploration will be made into the meaning of such vital concepts as work, leisure, motivation, and satisfaction.

WORK, LEISURE, AND MOTIVATION

The meaning of work and work motivation are inextricably bound. Why some people work harder than others is in some measure a function of their orientation toward work.

The Meaning of Work

What work means to people influences the amount of energy they are willing to expend at work. Readers seeking an extensive discussion of the meaning of work might consult *The Social Dimensions of Work* by Clifton D. Bryant.[1]

Work is a punishment, hardship, or an unpleasant obligation. Careful students of the Old Testament will note a familiar ring to this statement about the meaning of work. Adam and Eve were sentenced to work because they disobeyed certain divine laws. Later in history, the Athenian Greeks downgraded the value of work. Mundane chores, whenever possible, were delegated to a group of slaves. Arts, athletics, academics, and philosophical speculation were assigned higher value than traditional work. It should be carefully noted that these Biblical and Athenian interpretations of work focused upon the satisfaction of the necessities of life.[2] In present society, work performed strictly to satisfy such basic needs as food or shelter receives little prestige or status. Work conducted to satisfy higher level needs such as power or prestige (e.g., an independently wealthy individual running for political office) tends to be more highly valued.

Many people in contemporary society also attach negative connotations to work. Joseph W. McGuire notes that for most production and white-collar workers, work has an unpleasant connotation.[3] In contrast, most professional people and executives enjoy their occupations. Despite these group differences, individual differences must be recognized. Some people at the lowest end of the occupational hierarchy view work as a dominant form of satisfaction in their lives, while some people in the high status occupations find work basically distasteful. For instance, physicians exist who regard patient care as a necessary hardship they have to endure in order to purchase leisure activities for themselves and their families.

Closely related to the belief that work is punishment is the feeling of alienation many people—knowledge, production, and clerical workers included—develop toward their jobs and organizations. Concerns about the alienation of blue-collar workers were reawakened in recent years by problems encountered at the General Motors highly automated plant at Lordstown, Ohio.[4] Workers at this Vega assembly plant were predominantly in the 25-and-under age category. Underlying their alienation from work was the feeling that increased automation of the plant made work less creative yet equally arduous. A *Business Week* reporter observed that younger and better educated production workers complained the most about increased automation.[5] Increased absenteeism, high turnover, poorer quality work, and even sabotage have been attributed to feelings of alienation. Feelings of alienation experienced by managerial and professional personnel will be discussed in Chapter 4.

Douglas S. Sherwin, a business executive, observes that lack of commitment (alienation) underlies much of the behavior blamed for high costs and poor service.[6] He argues that organizational members lose or fail to gain commitment because organizations frustrate the psychological needs of people. Management, cautions Sherwin, must change some long-standing policies to "reverse a decline in production, employee morale, and concern for the company."[7] Several of the types of antidotes to worker alienation offered by Sherwin are discussed in Chapter 4. One novel suggestion that writer makes to management for gaining employee commitment will be mentioned now.

Sherwin contends that the "one-man, one-boss" concept prevalent in organizations adversely affects employee commitment by exerting a direct negative effect on communications. Communications, he reasons, is the lifeline for the survival of employee commitment.[8]

> When employees cannot communicate upward, they conclude that the organization does not care what they think and they turn themselves off.

Work is a duty to fulfill one's predestined "calling." During the Protestant Reformation, work took on many religious connotations.[9] Failure to work, or even failure to want to work, had an immoral connotation. Today, it appears that only a decreasing number of clergymen perceive their occupational role as a *calling.* One possible exception is the handful of zealots in any field who pursue their work with missionary fervor. Leaders of various movements and some franchise distributors display an almost driven quality to their promotional activities. Illustrative of the inspired franchise distributor was the "mink-oil king" who successfully promoted a pyramid-type distributorship before it was declared illegal in most states. Under the pyramid type of distributorship, each level of distributor is responsible for recruiting other distributors.

Work is central to life. Many individuals regard work as their dominant source of recognition, power, and status in life. Work gives them meaning and purpose. People at parties and other social gatherings are often asked their occupation before they are asked about their families, hobbies, or political attitudes. Many people spend more time with their work than with their families, hobbies and interests, or friends, combined. (Sleeping time is not included.) An important contributor to the *housewife syndrome* that affects approximately one-third of middle-class housewives is that homemaking as an occupational role has low prestige and status.[10] If the nature of work an individual performed was a less significant source of prestige in society, people would not feel uncomfortable about performing lower status work.

Primary focus in this chapter (and throughout the book) is upon people for whom work is a central force in their lives. Knowledge workers rarely perceive work as a punishment, a divine calling, or as a vehicle basically designed to provide the necessities of life.

The Meaning of Leisure

Work does not have a clear opposite. Tentatively, the concept of *leisure* or *play* can be accepted as the converse of work, but this is not an absolute distinction. McGuire, among others, has noted that for many workers—particularly professionals and executives—the boundary between work and leisure is obscure.[11] The photographer on assignment for *Life* shooting photographs for a story about African wildlife is probably engaging in one of his most preferred activities. This fortunate photographer derives more enjoyment from his work than most people do from their play.

One workable distinction that can be drawn between work and leisure is that leisure involves more discretion in choosing an activity. The management scientist whose daily work is mostly conceptual may choose to build a patio as a leisure activity. The construction worker whose work is mostly physical may choose to collect stamps for leisure. Next, three different orientations toward leisure will be presented. They are mentioned here because the importance people attach to leisure can readily influence their level of work motivation. For example, if the prospects of taking an annual European skiing trip turned you on, would you expend more effort on the job to attain that goal?

Leisure is an escape from work.   Many individuals, for a variety of reasons, feel they need to escape from their jobs. Some people feel that their jobs place too many physical and mental demands upon them. Others may find their jobs intrinsically boring and uninteresting. Leisure to these people is basically a way to relieve pent-up tensions stemming from work. Large numbers of managers, professionals, blue-collar workers, and clerical personnel on a given fall Sunday afternoon may dissociate themselves from their work (and family) by watching other people (football players) work.

Fishing trips, western movies, Civil War novels, and hikes in the woods (provided that no work-related thinking is allowed) are other popular forms of escape. The further removed the leisure activity is from the reality of work, the more effective it is as an escape mechanism.

Leisure is a source of prestige, accomplishment, and recognition. Many individuals use leisure to bring them a variety of satisfactions in life. *Conspicuous leisure* is the label McGuire gives to the prestige use of leisure resources.[12] Leisure becomes a vehicle for something other than recreation. People who purchase boats more for display purposes than because of an interest in boating are conspicuous users of leisure. "Snowbunnies"—those people who habituate ski resorts to be seen in fashionable ski attire—also fall into this category.

Leisure activities often provide people with more prestige and genuine accomplishment than they are able to derive from their jobs. Many tournament-level tennis, golf, and bridge players have less romantic and rewarding full-time occupations than their hobbies. Similarly, many painters and poets derive more prestige and feelings of accomplishment and recognition from their leisure than work activities. Significantly, the types of hobbies and leisure activities mentioned may require more hard work and concentration than their vocational activities. (Readers who have observed bridge tournaments will agree that most jobs would represent an escape from the demands of serious bridge.)

Leisure is a reward for hard work. A logical corollary of the belief that work is punishment is the viewpoint that people *deserve* leisure because they have worked hard. One manager of custodial services in the New York City school system noted that watching television and drinking beer was "the only reward I get for having knocked my head against the wall all day." Leisure is most likely to represent a reward for work to the extent that a person's work is lacking in intrinsic appeal.

The concept of leisure achieves new importance in society as an increased emphasis is placed upon retirement planning. A well-developed philosophy of leisure—including the corresponding development of skills and interests—makes retirement from work a less ominous prospect. For instance, those people who perceive leisure as a source of prestige, accomplishment, and recognition will look forward with anticipation to this *new* period in their lives called retirement.

MOTIVATION AND SATISFACTION ARE DIFFERENT

Motivation refers to expenditure of *effort* toward a goal. The congressman who works long and hard to meet the demands of his constituents shows high job motivation. The district sales manager who expends just enough effort to meet the minimum requirements of his position shows low job motivation. John P. Campbell, Marvin D. Dunnette, Edward E. Lawler, III, and Karl E. Weick, Jr. present a helpful description of what the concept of motivation includes:[13]

> .... an individual's motivation has to do with:
> 1. The *direction* of his behavior, or what he chooses to do when presented with a number of possible alternatives.
> 2. The *amplitude*, or strength, of the response (i.e. effort) once the choice is made.
> 3. The persistence of the behavior, or how long he sticks with it.

Satisfaction, in general, refers to the feelings of contentment related to work. Similar to motivation, satisfaction is a complex concept. Recent research has identified nine different operational meanings of job satisfaction.[14] One useful distinction made by John P. Wanous and Edward E. Lawler, III, is that between job satisfaction and attraction. Satisfaction, technically speaking, only applies to outcomes already possessed or experienced by an individual. Attraction, in contrast, refers to anticipated satisfaction of an outcome. Job satisfaction is primarily a "hedonism of the past," whereas job attraction is primarily a "hedonism of the future."[15]

Whether job satisfaction has nine meanings or one, these feelings range from extremely negative through neutral to extremely positive. The well-motivated congressman mentioned above might conceivably have low job satisfaction because of the long hours he works and also because he would prefer to be a senator. Nevertheless, he is well motivated. The poorly motivated sales manager mentioned above might have high job satisfaction. He prefers not to work hard and appreciates the opportunity to coast along in his career. His *motivation* is low but his job *satisfaction* is high.

Making this differentiation between satisfaction and motivation helps explain why high job satisfaction does not necessarily lead to high productivity. Poorly motivated individuals are content with jobs that do not require high productivity. Highly motivated workers persist in their efforts even when their job satisfaction is low. (This latter observation in turn explains why well-motivated people often represent high turnover risks. They work hard in spite of low job satisfaction, but leave organizations to find higher job satisfaction elsewhere.) Bernard M. Bass suggests that a productive worker may manifest more dissatisfaction with certain conflicting aspects of his work as a consequence of his involvement and interest in the work.[16]

Paul F. Wernimount, Paul Toren, and Henry Kapell[17] conducted an extensive empirical investigation about the relationship between motivation and satisfaction. They made statistical comparisons between the sources of personal satisfaction and of work motivation (job effort) among 775 scientists and technicians. Their results indicated that it is incorrect to use the terms *motivator* and *satisfier* interchangeably. For example, "personal accomplishment" was ranked as having a greater impact on satisfaction than on motivation. Thus, if work motivation and satisfaction have different sources, it can be inferred that they are basically different concepts.

MASLOW'S HIERARCHY OF NEEDS

The widespread acceptance of Abraham H. Maslow's *hierarchy of needs* conception of human motivation may be attributed to its apparent simplicity and utility. Similar to Douglas McGregor's Theory Y, this theory represents an optimistic and positive viewpoint about the motives of people.[18] According to the late Maslow, people have an internal motive (need) directing or pushing them toward self-fulfillment and personal superiority.[19] Higher order needs of this kind, however, become prepotent only after several more basic needs have been satisfied. In short, man strives to reach specific goals because he has an internally generated need to reach them.

Maslow's hierarchy of needs, beginning with lowest and ascending to the highest, is as follows:

Physiological Needs

These refer to bodily needs such as food, water, shelter, elimination, sleep, and sexual satisfaction. It would be difficult to identify jobs in business, industry, education or government which block the satisfaction of basic physiological needs. However, adverse working conditions such as poor ventilation and excessive noise might serve to frustrate some physiological desires for avoidance of irritation.

Safety Needs

These include actual physical safety as well as a feeling of being safe from both physical and emotional injury. You might argue that some people engage in occupations or recreational activities (such as stock-car racing or ski

39

jumping) that lead to frustration of safety needs. The stock-car racer, however, may use his occupation primarily to satisfy higher order needs such as esteem.

Love Needs

Physiological and safety needs center around the person himself. Belongingness or love needs involve interaction with other people for purposes of giving and receiving love, or simply to feel part of a group. Organizations usually provide opportunities to satisfy such social needs. Two exceptions might be when an individual dislikes his coworkers or is placed in an isolated position (e.g., the field claims examiner who works out of his home).

Esteem Needs

These needs are based on the belief that people want esteem in terms of both their own standards and the standards of others. There is a reciprocal relationship here. Respect from others usually leads to self-respect. In general, people must have positive attitudes toward the nature of their work (consider their occupation worthwhile) in order to satisfy esteem needs through their jobs.

Self-Actualization

This represents the highest level need: man's striving to become what he is capable of becoming. Extraordinary examples of self-actualized people such as Albert Einstein are often cited in popular discussions of this topic. The individual of average intelligence and scholastic aptitude who receives an Associates degree and eventually achieves his goal of becoming an effective general foreman is also self-actualized. Self-actualization takes into account an individual's own goals and potentials. Jobs which provide people opportunities to work toward self-actualization are infrequent. Higher level managerial and some professional jobs are among the kinds of occupational activities that can contribute to self-actualization.

Individual differences are taken into account in Maslow's theory. Some individuals never develop active needs for esteem and self-actualization. They are perpetually concerned with taking care of *deficits*: e.g., lack of love, lack of esteem. Reasons for this include neurosis, immaturity, or cultural values. A given individual may be motivated only to provide for the physiological and safety needs of his family. Attempting to motivate him by using "opportunity for creativity and decision making" as a reward is ineffectual. Conversely, self-actualizing people are not motivated to work harder because of increased medical insurance. Frederick Herzberg's theory, to be discussed next, builds upon this concept.

Different individuals have different need hierarchies, and the same individual may have a different need hierarchy at different stages in his or her life. A need hierarchy is a dynamic—not static—concept. One female executive began her business career at age 31—precisely the time when her youngest child began attending school. During the next decade this woman concentrated on career development in order to satisfy her highest level needs. While her children were of preschool age she was content to achieve satisfaction of only lesser needs such as love, affection, and nurturance.

HERZBERG'S MOTIVATION–HYGIENE THEORY

Underlying the motivation–hygiene theory of work motivation is the familiar dichotomy between job satisfiers and dissatisfiers. Elements within the *content* of the job are called satisfiers because positive feelings toward them provide personal satisfaction. For example, challenging work provides individuals with job satisfaction. Job *context* factors are called dissatisfiers because negative feelings toward them contribute to job dissatisfaction. For example, uncomfortable working conditions might make people dissatisfied, but comfortable working conditions do not make people satisfied. Satisfaction and dissatisfaction are thus separate factors, not end points on a continuum. Satisfiers are also called *motivators* because these factors were shown by Herzberg to be effective in motivating the employee to greater productivity.[20] Dissatisfiers are called *hygiene* factors because they prevent dissatisfaction from occurring but do not induce people toward extra effort.

Herzberg's theory of motivation follows the growth and deficit conceptual scheme of Maslow, discussed in the previous section. Factors that have a motivational thrust upon individuals are *growth* factors—those that provide the worker with a sense of accomplishment through the work itself and thus satisfy higher level needs. For example, providing a systems analyst with objective data about the efficacy of his system would be motivational. Herzberg criticizes attempts to motivate workers by reliance upon hygiene factors. For example, people may be dissatisfied if fringe benefits are missing or inadequate, but their existence does not elicit real motivation from people. Fringe benefits and other dissatisfiers appeal to deficit not growth needs.

Following is a classification of job factors into the traditional satisfier–dissatisfier dichotomy. The various terms used to describe essentially the same concepts as satisfier or dissatisfier are presented in parentheses.

Satisfiers (motivators, job content factors, intrinsic factors)

> Achievement
> Recognition
> Work itself
> Responsibility
> Advancement
> Growth

Dissatisfiers (hygiene, job context, maintenance, extrinsic factors)

> Company policy and administration
> Supervision
> Working conditions
> Interpersonal relations (with superiors,
>   subordinates, and peers)
> Salary
> Status
> Job security
> Personal life

The *motivation–hygiene* theory has received positive, neutral, and negative support from other researchers.[21,22] Criticisms include the observation that Herzberg's theory is an oversimplification of (a) the relationships between motivation and satisfaction and (b) the sources of job satisfaction and dissatisfaction. Herzberg's results are also criticized as being *method-bound.* Paper and pencil questionnaires might provide different results than the interview method used by Herzberg. One psychologically oriented criticism levied against the two-factor theory is offered by Victor H. Vroom:[23]

> Persons may be more likely to attribute the causes of satisfaction to their own achievements and accomplishments on the job. On the other hand, they may be more likely to attribute their dissatisfaction not to personal inadequacies or deficiencies, but to factors in the work environment, i.e., obstacles presented by company policies or supervision.

Recently, two behavioral scientists—H. Randolph Bobbitt, Jr., and Orlando Behling—conducted research suggesting that Vroom's alternate explanation of the two-factor theory is incorrect. Instead they posit that the motivator–hygiene dichotomy is related to an individual's attempt to protect a favorable self-concept.[24]

Martin G. Wolf's *need gratification theory* to be presented next claims to account for all the discrepant research results about job satisfaction and its relationship to motivation.

NEED GRATIFICATION THEORY

Wolf's need gratification theory of job motivation and its relationship to satisfaction builds upon the need hierarchy and motivation–hygiene theories. Its basic statements are based upon the writings of Maslow and the substantial research about Herzberg's two-factor theory of job satisfaction. Need gratification appears to have relevance for managers who wish to increase the job motivation (effort) of people. The reader is cautioned, however, that need gratification theory awaits empirical verification. Those aspects of this theory directly related to job motivation are discussed next.

Statement of the Theory and Interpretation

1. Job motivation can be considered as a sub-classification of general motivation; as such, it follows the principles of the need hierarchy (Maslow, 1954).[25] The individual will actively seek to gratify his active need or needs, essentially ignoring both lower level needs that are already gratified and higher level needs that have not yet emerged.[26]

For example, an engineer may receive a promotion to project leader. Before this promotion his most active needs centered around earning sufficient income to own a home. This might be considered as a manifestation of *esteem needs*. His promotion provided him with a high enough salary to finance a suitable home. The prospects of normal increments in income no longer *motivate* him (he will not expend extra job effort just for money). Another esteem need now becomes active. He looks toward opportunities for personal accomplishment as motivational. This need might be met by successfully completing his first several projects. Eventually he may be motivated by the opportunity to become nationally known as an engineer. This latter need approaches the self-actualization class of needs. For now national recognition is an inactive need, but it may become active after more ordinary forms of personal accomplishment have been achieved.[27]

2. Job motivation occurs when an individual perceives an opportunity to gratify an active need through job-related behaviors. The strength of the job motivation is a function of the individual's subjective probability estimate of the likelihood that the desired consequences will follow given job-related behaviors.

43

For example, a hotel manager has an active need for accomplishment or self-fulfillment. In terms of his frame of reference, accomplishment means managing the largest hotel in his company's chain of hotels. He is told by his superior that he will be promoted to that position with the following provision: he must first manage his present hotel (which is losing money) for two consecutive years without showing a loss; additionally, he must achieve these results without injurious effects upon employee morale or customer relations.

The hotel manager sees a direct positive relationship between his job performance and gratification of his need for accomplishment (managing the largest hotel in the chain). He is willing to expend considerable effort to turn the hotel into a financially profitable business situation. Promotion to his job ideal (as he perceives it) is almost guaranteed provided that specific objectives are realized. In short, a classic situation exists whereby there is a high probability of a need being gratified through job-related behaviors. Such behaviors might include establishing an incentive compensation for kitchen help or making the hotel more attractive for local business meetings.

Theoretical Relationship of Content and Context Elements to Job Motivation

Wolf contends that job *context* factors are essentially unrelated to job motivation—expenditure of effort. This is true because an individual cannot increase the level of gratification of his related needs through job-related behaviors. Context factors, as mentioned earlier, include company policy and administration, working conditions, job security, technical supervision, status, and interpersonal relations.

For example, unless an employee occupies a high-level management position, there is little he can do to change the company policy regarding his job security. Thus, there is generally no way for him to increase the level of gratification of related needs (such as security) through actions that will be as indicative of job motivation.

Wolf gives special consideration to the role of salary as a motivator. Salary is generally classified as a context job factor because its action is more like that of other context elements. According to the need gratification theory, salary (or financial compensation in general) acts as a motivator only when the employee sees a direct relationship between pay and job performance. (This, of course, is the implicit assumption underlying most forms of commission or incentive forms of compensation. Campbell and his associates express doubt, based upon their survey of 33 firms, that most

forms of managerial pay show a direct relationship to performance.[28])
When he does not perceive a direct relationship between pay and performance, "salary will act to lower satisfaction to the extent that the individual
perceives his salary as reducing or preventing the gratification of his active
needs."[29]

Content elements, in contrast to context elements, according to the need
gratification theory, are closely related to job motivation. The individual
can increase the gratification of his related needs through job-related behaviors. Achievement, recognition, work itself, responsibility, advancement, and growth are all job elements somewhat within the control of the
individual. Wolf provides the following example to illustrate his
reasoning:[30]

> If an individual has interesting work that allows him to exercise responsibility
> and obtain a sense of achievement while leading to personal growth and de-
> velopment, he can increase his level of gratification of the related higher level
> needs through the simple expedient of doing more of this job.

At this point in the need gratification theory, the tenets of Maslow, Herzberg, and Wolf are mutually supportive and congruent. For jobs to have
positive motivational impacts upon people they must provide opportunities
for satisfaction of higher level needs. This generality will, of course, surprise few managers or students of management.

ACHIEVEMENT MOTIVATION

High levels of accomplishment at work, according to the widely quoted
research and theory of David C. McClelland and his associates, are under-
girded by high achievement needs (n Ach).[31,32] People imbued with a high
achievement level are turned on by accomplishment for its own sake;
money, status, and power are secondary considerations. Accomplishment
to the person with a high need for achievement usually means improving
something that already exists or creating something entirely new. Extensive
research in many different countries and subcultures indicates that the
high achiever (a) takes personal responsibility to solve problems, (b) attempts to achieve moderate goals at calculated risks, and (c) prefers situations that provide frequent feedback on results.[33]

People High in *n* Ach

Innovative businessmen usually score high in achievement motivation
as measured by psychological tests. Founders of businesses—entrepreneurs—score quite high on achievement. McClelland notes that

45

patterns of achievement motivation are clearest in small companies. Presidents of smaller companies generally score higher than their associates. In larger companies, lower management personnel score the lowest; middle managers, just below the top, score highest. Big company executives tend to be somewhat average in achievement concern. McClelland notes that ". . . this seems strange, but possibly they have done well enough to relax a little."[34] Tentative evidence suggests that entrepreneurs are imbued with the idea of accomplishing things, while managers have stronger needs for power. Bureaucrats are probably only average in achievement motivation.

T. George Harris, editor of *Psychology Today*, observes that people high in *n* Ach exhibit many antiestablishment tendencies. They are concerned about solving new problems and do not over-rely on tradition. As suggested by Harris, "that may explain the high *n* Ach found among student radicals—they tend to be entrepreneurial, too, in the sense that they build new organizations."[35]

Contrary to widely held opinions, achievement motivation is not entirely a middle-class American phenomenon. Cross cultural research by McClelland and the many other psychologists who have investigated his theories provides some intriguing results. McClelland summarizes cross cultural observations about achievement motivation:[36]

> No, this thing is neither capitalist nor white, neither Western nor middle class. The Ethiopian people of the Gurage are fabulously high in *n* Ach. So are some tribes of American Indians, we've found, and the Biafran, or Ibo people. The Biafrans got into the usual trouble of achievement people, who are always getting beat on by power oriented people because the Biafrans are so pushy . . .
>
> Communist states like Poland and Russia now score very high in achievement motive, and they seem to have passed it on to China. Why not? In Poland, for instance, plant managers work under a quota system for output that demands solutions to problems and provides very clear feedback. It takes high *n* Ach people to meet that challenge, and the whole culture applauds the hero or heroine who gets things done. So the Communists have become entrepreneurial.

High achievement motivation, similar to any other phenomenon studied in organizational behavior, has some dysfunctional consequences. McClelland made the following comment about high achievers:[37]

> Some psychologists think that because I've done so much on *n* Ach I must like the kind of people who have strong need for achievement. I don't. I find them bores. They are not artistically sensitive. They're entrepreneurs, kind of driven—always trying to improve themselves and find a shorter route to the office or a faster way of reading their mail. . . .

Achievement Motivation Can Be Taught

Evidence has been gathered that entrepreneurial behavior—one vital manifestation of achievement motivation—can be developed even in people from cultures where desire for economic motivation is minimal. *Motivating Economic Achievement* by David C. McClelland and David G. Winter is a lengthy report of an attempt to test whether a training course designed to develop the ambition needed to succeed in business produced actual changes in entrepreneurial attitudes and behavior.[38]

Indian managers in small industry and commerce who participated in the training program later increased their entrepreneurial activity and accelerated increases in the economic growth rate of their communities. According to McClelland, the course doubled the natural rate of entrepreneurial activity in the experimental group. Specific examples cited included a banker who became less conservative in his money-lending practices and the owner of a small radio store who opened a paint and varnish factory after completion of the training program.[39]

Prior results with a small group of American businessmen also gave support to the notion that *n* Ach can be taught, and that, once learned, increases in entrepreneurial activity are forthcoming. The 11 participants studied were promoted faster than a comparable group of managers who attended a more standard program of management development. It is presumed that promotions were based upon entrepreneurial performance.

McClelland's approach to bringing about changes in entrepreneurial behavior centers around the belief that people can be taught how to "think, talk, act and perceive the world like a person with a high need for achievement."[40] *Prestige suggestion* is an important element of the training program. Managers come to believe that they have the power to change. Specific goals for change are established by managers, and progress toward these goals is measured every six months. The language of achievement is taught essentially by giving the managers insight into the specific thought content of individuals with demonstrated high *n* Ach. Participants even learned how to obtain high scores on a projective test used for the measurement of *n* Ach. Content of the training program also includes extensive cognitive information about research evidence on achievement motivation. Another important aspect of the program is the emotional support received from other group members. The sharing of experiences with other individuals who have similar concerns has a facilitating effect upon individual learning.

EQUITY THEORY

Popular conceptions of man such as the economic man or the achieving (self-actualizing) man do not satisfactorily explain many aspects of man's behavior. Equity theory, in attempting to fill this gap, posits that man acts to alleviate tensions by decreasing the inequity he feels exists in a given situation.[41] Stated differently, people strive to be treated fairly—a well-accepted principle of human relations. John B. Miner notes that the primary concern is with the "... relation between an individual's own input/outcome ratio and that of a person with whom he compares himself."[42] These ratios are shown as follows:

$$\frac{\text{Inputs}}{\text{Outcomes}} \text{ of mine in comparison to } \frac{\text{Inputs}}{\text{Outcomes}} \text{ of other people.}$$

Inputs are investments or contributions the employee feels that he is making to the job. Among these are education, intelligence, skill, age, sex, health, and effort expended on the job. For example, a male with a Ph.D. in physics from the California Institute of Technology and an MBA from Stanford, in good physical health, and working as an R&D manager would expect high compensation in comparison to many other people.

Equity theory has achieved good empirical support in research conducted with lower level jobs, particularly with regard to financial compensation.[43,44] As would be expected, no one theory of motivation can account for all the complexities involved in work motivation. Equity theory, so far, is limited in its ability to specify underlying motivational processes or to predict how a given individual will reduce tension.[45]

EXPECTANCY THEORY

Motivation theory has a new look that holds promise of someday assigning mathematical probabilities to predictions about work behavior. For example, it may become possible to state that the probability a given systems analyst will be motivated to produce an improved workflow design for a hospital operating room is 0.88 provided that (a) he feels 0.67 certain that he can do the job, (b) there is a 0.92 guarantee he will be given a salary increase if the new systems design works, and (c) he feels 0.89 certain that designing the system and receiving the salary increase will satisfy his need for recognition.

Expectancy theories of motivation have been developed by several behavioral scientists. Victor H. Vroom has formulated the most comprehensive expectancy theory relating to work behavior.[46] John P. Campbell and his associates later developed a *hybrid expectancy model* which both amplifies and simplifies the models developed by Vroom.[47] A recent synthesis of expectancy theory geared toward the serious scholar of organizational behavior has been prepared by Vance F. Mitchell.[48]

Expectancy theories have been given several intriguing labels, including preference–expectation theory, instrumentality theory, and path–goals analysis. The basic contents of all these theoretical explanations of work motivation are consistent with the Work Motivation Schema, presented later. Expectancy theory models, however, usually include several equations which have strengthened their credibility in the scientific community. Presented next is a general explanation and interpretation of expectancy theory.

Human behavior in a given situation is a joint function of the degree to which that behavior is *instrumental* (effective) in attaining an outcome and the *subjective probability* (hunch) that the outcome will be forthcoming.[49] Individuals choose that behavior which they perceive as most directly leading to the things they want. To illustrate, a serious tennis player will practice serves one hour per day if he believes such effort will enable him to survive one more round in most tournaments he enters. How badly somebody wants something—its valence for that person—is crucial in predicting the force he or she will exert to achieve that outcome. Vroom elegantly states the valence model in this fashion:[50]

> ... the valence of an outcome to a person is a monotonically increasing function of the algebraic sum of the products of the valences of all other outcomes and his conceptions of its instrumentality for the attainment of these other outcomes.

Adding the contribution of George Strauss and Leonard R. Sayles to those authors already cited, a simplified path–goals analysis schema can be constructed to illustrate how expectancy theory might work in an individual situation.[51] In general, this model suggests that a person will expend effort (show high work motivation) to produce (complete work) if that completed work leads to an incentive (reward) that will satisfy an important need. Furthermore, the need satisfaction must be intense enough to make the effort *feel* worthwhile, and the person must learn if effort leads to a reward (feedback). These relationships are shown in Figure 2.1. A verbal illustration can be added to demonstrate how expectancy theory aids in understanding individual situations.

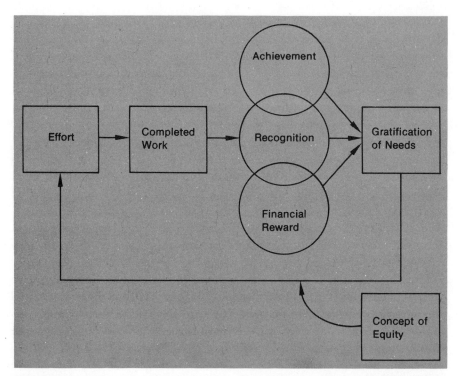

Figure 2.1 Path–goals analysis version of expectancy theory. (Adapted from George Strauss and Leonard R. Sayles, *Personnel: The Human Problems of Management,* third edition. Englewood Cliffs, N.J.: Prentice-Hall, 1972 , p. 135. By permission of Prentice-Hall, Inc., Englewood Cliffs, N.J.).

An assistant to the vice president of administration is asked by his boss, "Dave, why don't you come up with a tentative plan for reorganizing the company. I'll be in Europe during August. Let's get together when I return and discuss what ideas you have developed."

Dave is thus placed in a complex motivational situation. He will need to expend considerable effort to accomplish this task. It might even be necessary for him to conduct an informal survey or a formal study. From the perspective of expectancy theory, he must automatically or analytically arrive at answers to these questions:

1. Am I skilled enough now, or able to acquire the knowledge necessary to conduct organizational planning?
2. If I put time and effort into this assignment, what is the probability that my results will be used?
3. If the results are used, how much will my salary be increased? How much more recognition will I receive?

4. Will the amount of money, recognition, and status I receive be commensurate with the effort I have to put out?

In short, expectancy theory offers the following suggestion to those attempting to motivate others: people tend to expend more effort toward reaching goals when both the probability of receiving a reward and the magnitude of that reward are known in advance.

WORK MOTIVATION SCHEMA

This schema is a graphic representation of many of the basic concepts contained in the preceding theories of job motivation with particular emphasis upon gratification theory. Its purpose is to provide a framework for understanding the complexities involved (the many possible variables impinging on the situation) in attempting to elicit motivated behavior from another individual. The Work Motivation Schema depicted in Figure 2.2 will first be described by way of a specific illustration.

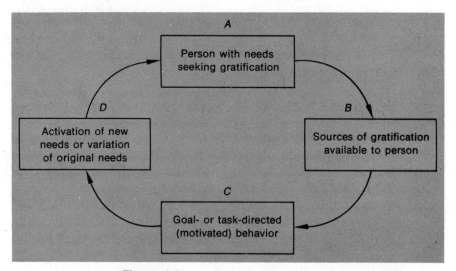

Figure 2.2 Work Motivation Schema.

1. Point A on the schema represents a normal (nonpathological) person with needs seeking gratification. His current active need is a variation of the self-fulfillment need. Specifically, the person is an accountant who decides that he must find new intellectual stimulation in his work. His subjective feelings are those of an individual "bored" with his job. If his need for new challenges are not soon met, a diminution in effort directed toward the job may occur.

51

2. Point *B* represents potential sources of need gratification available to a person. One potential need gratifier is presented to the individual. His manager discusses with the accountant the latter's possibilities of receiving a new position. An opening has occurred within the personnel department for a wage and salary analyst. The primary technical knowledge specified for the job (by this company) is that the incumbent have skill in preparing budgets. The accountant intuitively feels that this is an excellent personal opportunity. The accountant anticipates receiving new sources of intellectual challenge, and feels he will be able to transfer old skills to a new situation.

3. Point *C* represents goal- or task-directed behavior on the accountant's part. He accepts the new position with enthusiasm. He works hard to meet the demands of the position. For example, he studies reference material about wage and salary administration and carefully reviews the company's policies and procedures about this aspect of the business. Within one week he begins to make some preliminary contribution to the job. The effort he expends in this job is directed toward company goals. Management rightfully interprets his actions as indicative of his being a *motivated employee*. (As pointed out by Wolf, motivation from management's standpoint implies that the employee's efforts are directed toward goals and objectives the company thinks are worthwhile.)

4. Point *D* represents the temporary aspect to the gratification of human needs. This accountant has gratified one aspect of his need for self-fulfillment. He accepted a position as a wage and salary analyst in the pursuit of new intellectual challenges (or the avoidance of job challenge loss). His need for self-fulfillment now takes on a new manifestation. He establishes a modicum of self-confidence in his new job function, and he now aspires toward mastery over what he is presently doing. He perceives promotion to a corporate wage and salary analyst as one source of gratification of this need. Another potential vehicle for gratification is to become the manager of wage and salary administration in his present location. (It must be emphasized here that few needs come in pure or unidimensional form. Promotion may simultaneously satisfy needs for status, income, self-fulfillment, recognition, and perhaps others.)

5. The motivational cycle repeats itself. We return to Point *A* on the schema. The hypothetical accountant now has another set of needs seeking gratification. Continued expenditure of effort directed toward company goals may be contingent upon whether or not new sources of need gratification are available. Needs already gratified are no longer sources of motivation.

Next the four points in the motivational schema will be discussed in more detail to further illustrate the complex, multidetermined nature of work motivation.

Persons with Needs Seeking Gratification

The several theories of motivation discussed earlier should not be interpreted to mean that all people have the same needs or motives. These theories provide useful generalities about motivation that apply to most individuals, but they are not intended to describe the motivational pattern of a given individual. The uniqueness of each individual and the situation in which he is placed must be taken into consideration in understanding individual motivation. An essay entitled "Motives are Personal" in a book edited by Charles D. Flory emphasizes the *idiographic* nature of work-related motivation.[52]

> Human purposes and goals are personal. They influence behavior to the extent that they have vital significance and meaning for the individual. This fact suggests that the manager should recognize that people at one point in time or under one set of conditions are likely to respond positively to a certain kind of "reward." But this fact does not mean that they will respond in the same way to additional amounts of the same reward. Neither does it mean that they will respond to this reward under different circumstances.

Specific needs or motives show variation both between groups of individuals (e.g., managers versus nonmanagers) and between individuals belonging to the same group (e.g., all managers do not share the same level of ambition). Substantial empirical evidence has been accumulated that managers have stronger drives for accomplishment and achievement than do nonmanagers. Effective managers in turn have stronger needs for achievement, power, and economic rewards than less effective managers.[53]

Edwin E. Ghiselli conducted a large-scale investigation of motivational factors in the success of managers.[54] His results further illustrate the differences in needs or motives that exist among managers:

1. Middle managers (in comparison to workers in general) have a lower desire for security and for financial reward, and a higher desire for self-actualization.
2. Successful middle managers have less desire for security and financial reward than those who are unsuccessful. They also place more value on self-actualization than their less successful counterparts.

Observers of managerial behavior also recognize that even successful managers show marked individual differences in motives or needs. For example, some people simply enjoy working harder (show more goal-directed behavior) than do others. Some company presidents work 70 hours per week, others 45. Some professors publish 400 scholarly articles within their career, others just publish enough to establish tenure. Research may eventually substantiate the concept that there is an almost genetic, inherited difference in the temperament of people that underlies differences in drive level. Individuals with stronger drives for accomplishment may in fact be individuals with a greater reservoir of psychological energy.

Sources of Gratification

Needs of individuals are varied and, correspondingly, so are potential rewards available to gratify these needs. Wolf's need gratification theory is an excellent starting point for understanding what specific kinds of rewards are potent incentives for most people in a work situation. Briefly stated, job content elements are useful in motivating people. Again, however carefully derived, a theory of motivation cannot be used in lieu of understanding the individual or even a class of individuals. For example, a given manager may have strong active needs for status. He will expend more job effort if placed in an office with a large desk and private secretary. Job elements providing status are *motivators* for this unique ego-centered manager despite the wealth of evidence cited by Herzberg that status elements are *hygiene* factors for most people.

John G. Darley and T. Hagenah's *occupational level theory* is germane here with respect to classes of individuals. They contend that a person's occupational level determines whether context or content elements are involved in job satisfaction or dissatisfaction. Extending their theory to motivation, we can infer that a person's occupational level influences his outlook on whether or not a potential source of need gratification is rewarding. For example, offering a financially poor individual money incentives for good performance may stimulate him toward extra effort on the job. Financial incentives may not have the same potency for a wealthy individual. Darley and Hagenah contend:[55]

> Below some cut-off point in the occupational hierarchy, work is primarily a means to the end of survival and minimal subsistence; the tasks of the job are not in themselves (intrinsically) interesting, challenging, or satisfying. Above this cut-off point, survival and subsistence needs are met, and the tasks of the job may appear useful to intrinsic satisfactions, interacts and needs.

The *organizational climate* provides opportunities for need gratification. Some characteristics of an environment exert a positive motivating influence upon most people. One positive characteristic would be a reward system related to performance. An inference to be drawn from McGregor's Theory X/Theory Y is that bureaucratic organizations exert a demotivating influence on people because they centralize decision making and control people from above. Bureaucratic organizational climates, however, may not have the same demotivating effect on everybody. One executive in a bureaucratic style organization described what positive motivational influence he perceived to exist in his company:[56]

> I enjoy the fun and games around here. People complain about the red tape, but it's really a lot more challenging than the technical portions of my job. I work like the devil to figure out strategies to get around these layers of approvals you need to go ahead on a project.

The situation a manager is in should affect his behavior by arousing various motives. People show broad variation in their desire (and capacity) for displaying innovative behavior in relation to their work assignments.[57] Those individuals with strong needs and the capacity for creative expression will be motivated by an organizational climate or a superior that encourages creativity. In contrast, an individual with limited need or desire to make creative responses to his environment might display defensive or avoidant behavior in such an environment. This same individual would probably show high job satisfaction and high motivation in an environment that encouraged adherence to older modes of doing things.

Organizational climates can frustrate the need for creative expression, according to a theory of creativity developed by Jack R. Gibb.[58] He notes that defensive management mobilizes the defenses in the social system and may impede creative behavior or displace it in a direction that does not help the organization (e.g., creatively cheating on an expense account). Gibb's theory contends that "low-creativity management tends to be fearful, persuasive and controlling."[59] For instance, management behavior and attitudes might include a heavy component of fear and distrust. An emotional climate of this nature precipitates certain effects that constrain creative behavior. These effects include (a) fear of criticism, derision, and disapproval, (b) censoring others' ideas, (c) response inhibition, and (d) behavior that "goes underground."

The *leader himself* as a source of need gratification for subordinates requires further research and understanding. A leader acts as a *facilitator*; he or she helps establish conditions or a climate that elicits motivated behavior. For instance, if a leader encourages top management to pay people in his department an equitable wage, he contributes to employee motivation (particularly in accordance with equity theory). Even the leader's role in assigning work facilitates work motivation. Enriched, interesting jobs given to employees are more motivational than less enriched (impoverished) jobs.

Wolf's need gratification theory, and the studies by Herzberg, suggest that the role of the leader is a *context* element and thus not directly related to motivation.[60] However, the leader can in many instances gratify needs that are related to *content* elements of the job. Managers of people occupy a role that can directly contribute gratification of higher order needs. Assume that a middle manager has needs to grow as a person both in terms of the acquisition of job-related knowledge and responsibility. His manager, through coaching the man and recommending him for promotion, can help the subordinate gratify these needs. The analysis of the leader as a source of need gratification supports the commonly held contention that good leaders *motivate* people. Managers are also a potential source of need frustration and thus *demotivation.*

> Paul Dennis is an industrial engineering manager with at least average needs for recognition. He and his group helped design a plastic machine component that led to yearly cost savings of approximately $150,000. During a performance review Paul asked his manager what he thought of this project. His manager replied: "That's routine. Why do you think we bother hiring industrial engineers?"
>
> Paul's needs for recognition by others were sufficiently frustrated that he left his company at the next available opportunity. Some research evidence about the manager's influence on subordinate motivation will be discussed in the last section of this chapter.

Task or goal difficulty also influences the potential for need gratification. Having the opportunity to complete interesting and challenging work has a positive motivational impact on most people. Assignments that are perceived as too difficult may lead to need frustration and decreased job effort. Most of the research about this topic has been conducted in laboratory rather than field settings, but the results are reasonably congruent.[61] For tasks or goals to exert a positive, motivating influence upon people they should be specific rather than general and within the individual's capability. Assume a distributor of Japanese-made automobiles wanted to motivate the general manager of his Detroit dealership. A modest quota of units to be sold during the coming year might motivate the dealership head. (Particularly if these quotas were jointly established between the dealer and his superior.) Suggesting to him that "he make a terrific showing" next year might be demotivating for two reasons: (1) the task is difficult—American-made automobiles have a competitive advantage in Detroit, (2) the term "terrific year" is a vague goal.

Goal- or Task-Oriented Behavior

The third component of the Work Motivation Schema refers to the type of behavior manifested by the individual that indicates he is motivated. Again, from management's standpoint, goal-oriented behavior is that which leads to the attainment of organizational objectives. An advertising executive who daily takes two-hour lunches to write a novel is well motivated. He is expending extra effort directed toward recognition and perhaps self-fulfillment. His management, however, perceives his efforts as being unrelated to goals of the agency.

The expenditure of effort toward a goal does not inevitably lead to successful outcomes. High motivation must be accompanied by appropriate intelligence, knowledge, and external resources to insure successful completion of the task. The author recalls a well-motivated life insurance salesman who worked 50 hours a week, yet produced 50 percent less business than the average agent produced for the company. He was a compulsive talker who was unable to listen to prospects long enough to learn their needs. Much more than high motivation is required to meet organizational goals.

Activities people engage in to meet organizational objectives can have an inherent motivational value. The process of working hard can be both a source of satisfaction and motivation to an individual. This observation is indirectly supported by research that describes job enrichment as contributing to satisfaction and motivation.[62] The city planner exhibits goal-directed behavior when he starts to plan an improved neighborhood as part of his job requirement. He may expend additional effort when he perceives the planning activity itself as a worthwhile intellectual exercise. Some work is intrinsically motivating.

Activation of New Needs

Point D on the Work Motivation Schema characterizes both the insatiable and dynamic quality of human needs and motives. As mentioned earlier, an individual may express new variations of the same class of need once the original form of the need is gratified. The company president who successfully improves ("turns around") the performance of one company has an active need to improve the performance of another company. He perceives maintaining an ongoing, successful company operation as less psychologically rewarding than managing a company in difficulty. This phenomenon is sometimes described as the *insatiable* quality to human motivation. Needs for accomplishment characteristically have this insatiable quality. The inventor or entrepreneur is rarely satisfied with accomplishing something important *once* in his lifetime. He looks toward new sources of need gratification after each accomplishment.

Needs and motives are *dynamic* in the sense that they are subject to change within the same individual as a function of environmental circumstances. Changes in economic conditions, for example, may tend to activate the financial and security needs of people and temporarily lessen the desire to satisfy certain higher order needs. During a downturn in business, professional and technical personnel may put less pressure on management for ideal working conditions (such as more time for professional development). Presumably, decreased opportunities for movement to another company decreases their willingness to express dissatisfaction about present working conditions.

Degree of success in attaining goals can also influence what level of needs are dominant at a given time. The branch manager who fails in his first assignment as a manager might be less motivated by the prospects of additional responsibility than his counterpart who succeeded in his first assignment. An underlying factor here might be level of self-confidence. Successful task completion leads to feelings of self-confidence. Increases in self-confidence lead to a higher risk-taking attitude. Failure experiences, conversely, lead to a lowering of self-confidence and risk-taking attitude.

Both lower and higher level needs require continuous gratification for most people. The schema described here can also be interpreted as a need cycle. This makes need gratification a temporary phenomenon. Once one manifestation of a need is gratified it loses its motivational power. Financial bonuses could motivate some people toward a spurt in job performance before or after the bonus is distributed. Job motivation of this kind is short lived. Once the money is spent the motivational impact of the bonus is dissipated. This is perhaps the reason that research results have rarely classified money as an effective motivator.

Higher level managers show higher levels of motivation than individuals placed at lower positions in the organizational hierarchy.[63] They also manifest higher level needs.[64] Despite (or perhaps because of) this high level of motivation, executives seek constant gratification of needs such as accomplishment, power, and recognition. Illustrative here is the company president who looks to community or public service as a vehicle for accomplishment beyond his business success. You might want to furnish several examples of your own here of successful business executives who later in their careers expressed their needs for accomplishment, recognition, or power in community and government service. This statement does not exclude the possibility that community and public service does not also appeal to service or helping needs.

ROLE OF PENALTIES AND THREATS

The motivation schema presented has not discussed threats, punishment, withholding of rewards, and other forms of "negative motivation." This does not infer that the schema (or the formal theories of motivation reviewed in this chapter) ignores the role of punishment as a motivator. Most individuals, somewhere in their motivational pattern, have needs to avoid pain or to achieve financial or job security. The prepotency of such needs depends upon individual and situational differences, but they are usually lower order needs.

"Threatening" a corporate planner that he will lose his job if the next company acquisition he suggests loses money could conceivably motivate him to work harder. For this threat to elicit additional effort from the planner, he would need to be under the following conditions: (a) be a fairly self-confident individual who remained effective under threat, (b) feel that no other good alternatives to working for his company were available at this time, (c) have a motivational pattern of a psychologically primitive individual who required external threats to pursue high-level accomplishment.

Penalties and threats, in short, are poor motivators because their action is geared more toward lower than higher level needs. Note that positive motivational practices, according to Wolf and Herzberg, involved gratification of the higher level needs. Additionally, threats and punishments may precipitate retaliatory or defensive behavior, which is directed away from achieving organizational objectives. For example, the corporate planner mentioned above might react to his threat by preparing a lengthy report explaining how someone else was responsible for the last acquisition failure. The time and energy invested in preparing this report might have been more profitably directed toward meeting corporate objectives.

HOW DO YOU MOTIVATE THIS MAN?

Terry Paquette, age 32, joined the law firm of Malcolm, Thomas, Greely, and Barton four years ago. Up to this point his performance as a corporate attorney had been regarded as satisfactory. Most clients of the firm are business organizations requesting help in matters such as contracts and taxes. Complaints about Terry Paquette's handling of client problems had never previously been brought to the attention of senior members of the firm. He was respected by clients for his competence about legal matters, but his method of relating to them was somewhat abrupt and cold. Few clients mentioned that they enjoyed working with Terry. Recently, Terry's performance in legal areas was sufficiently below par to come to the attention of principals of the firm. Terry, for example, had made errors in interpreting tax regulations and failed to notice a serious loophole in a labor–management contract. He had also been absent from the last two luncheon meetings of the firm. Principals in the firm have tentatively concluded that Terry has "lost interest" in his work and is "poorly motivated."

Background information about Terry Paquette is helpful in understanding his present situation. Terry grew up in a poor section of Pittsburgh, as one of five children. His father, a drill press operator, decided early that Terry, the oldest son, deserved a better life than he (the father) had lived. Terry's father believed that by becoming a professional person, a young man could almost be guaranteed a satisfactory life. His father worked in a service station on weekends to save money for Terry's college and law school. Terry obligingly capitalized on the opportunity to become an attorney, but he never felt comfortable with his college classmates; he felt more uncomfortable with his law school classmates. His attitude was expressed in this manner: "I had nothing against them, but they were not my kind of people. I didn't belong." After graduating from law school, Terry worked as one member of a large legal department in a steel company located in Pittsburgh. He found his work interesting from a technical point of view, but questioned the relevance for him of protecting the interests of a substantial-sized steel company. Terry particularly disliked eating in the executive dining room. Finally he resigned, offering the reason, "I'm just not cut out to be an organization man."

Paquette looked forward with excitement to the prospects of working for a law firm. He reasoned that working with a small group of professionals would be more consistent with his interests than working for a large steel company. Terry began his work with some enthusiasm, but within two years he suffered the same motivational drag as he did with the steel company. At the beginning of the third year, Terry had one altercation with the principals of the firm. His employers suggested that he and his wife and children move to a "more fashionable" section of Boston. Terry had been living in a working-class section of Boston where he and his wife had formed some close personal friendships. After protesting, he begrudgingly rationalized that his family had outgrown the apartment and that schools might be better in the suburbs. Terry and his wife did buy a home in the suburbs in a neighborhood consisting mostly of young, middle managers, salesmen, and professional people.

Two principals of the firm met with Terry over a protracted lunch to delve into the reasons underlying his substandard job performance. Toward the end of a tense half hour, Terry was asked in several different ways whether or not he enjoyed working for the prestigious firm of Malcolm, Thomas, Greely, and Barton. It was further suggested that unless Terry could elevate his job performance, he perhaps should seek a position similar to his old job as a corporate attorney. Terry became visibly upset and retorted: "That's absolutely the last damn thing in this world I would ever do. I hate all the phoniness in big companies. I hate working for this stuffed shirt, old-fashioned, creepy law firm. All we do around here is lick the boots of clients. Even this stupid luncheon meeting is a waste of time. I'm not lazy, I just hate what I'm doing. I'm leaving the firm."

Terry Paquette and the principals of his firm must share the blame for this incident. Several hypotheses can be drawn to explain Terry's behavior other than assuming he was lazy: (1) Personal problems such as family illness or marital difficulties were adversely affecting his concentration. (2) Terry was involved in a personal disagreement with members of one of his client firms and could not work effectively with them. (3) Terry was poorly placed in his present occupation; limited opportunities to satisfy his interests in his present occupational role had become severe enough to lower his productivity.

Had the firm searched for an explanation of Terry's lowered job performance instead of accusing him of being lazy, the situation could have been handled in a more constructive manner. Terry is at fault for not having confronted himself with his real values earlier in his career. His core attitudes include a basic dislike for corporate affairs. Switching to a law firm from a steel company was only a minor change. He would still be serving the interests of management or the "establishment." Three months after resigning from his law firm, Terry Paquette found employment on the legal staff of the regional headquarters of a labor union. He was now working for a cause he could identify with, thus providing him more opportunity to satisfy higher level needs. For example, Terry may now experience more feelings of accomplishment because he believes that serving the interests of a labor union is intrinsically worthwhile. Seven years of his professional life were characterized by less than peak performance because he was not in a job situation that could appeal to his more potent *motivators.*

MOTIVATIONAL CONSEQUENCES OF MANAGERIAL BEHAVIOR

Managerial behavior can have a profound influence on the motivation of organizational members. For now, the motivational consequences of three aspects of managerial behavior will be examined: (a) compensation policies, (b) development of subordinates, and (c) "creative management." Each of these topics will be interwoven into other sections of the book because of their central importance in organizational life.

Optimizing the Role of Money

People are emotional about the topic of money. Findings of industrial psychologists that money is neither the most important source of job satisfaction nor work motivation thus frequently meets with skepticism, denial, or disbelief. I recall expressing to an accounting professor my desire for my first book to be a financial success. His retort was, "You behavioral scientists give me a chuckle. According to your theories money isn't important. But when it comes down to practice, you're just like anybody else."

Interrelationships between money and motivation are complex and subtle. Research-minded readers wishing to explore the depths of this topic should consult *Pay and Organizational Effectiveness*, by Edward E. Lawler, III.[65] For purposes of this chapter, five conditions will be mentioned that tend to optimize the role of money in eliciting motivated behavior from people.

First, money has more potency as a motivator when people have not yet reached their *relief of discomfort zone*. According to this concept, when income reaches a certain level it is possible to provide for the necessities of life and make such discretionary expenditures as buying a second car, taking two vacations, or sending children to college. Having the flexibility to make such purchases provides a relief of discomfort. Once a person's income takes him beyond this zone, money loses much of its influence as a motivator. According to one estimate, for most middle-class Americans living in the 1970s, $25,000 per annum is required to experience this relief of discomfort.

Obviously this figure of $25,000 is affected by inflation, cost of living differentials between one part of the country and another, and certain fringe benefits. In 1980, $30,000 may be required to take a middle-class family beyond the relief of discomfort zone. A family in a small town in Vermont requires less money than a family in metropolitan New York to achieve a comparable standard of living. Fringe benefits that substantially reduce out-of-pocket costs also affect the motivational value of money. Owning a company car, as one case in point, can increase a person's effective income by about $1500 to $3000 per year.

Second, according to the observations of Saul Gellerman, substantial amounts of money are required if money is to be an effective motivator. In practice this would imply that a salary increase should have the power of changing a person's lifestyle in order to exert a substantial motivational impact.[66] By implication, the traditional six percent salary increase exerts at best a minor motivational impact.

Third, amounts of money received by an individual should be directly related to performance, as suggested by need gratification theory. In practice, as cautioned earlier, this motivationally sound relationship between compensation and effort rarely exists. Not surprisingly, pay is directly related to results obtained in some occupations where the task at hand is notably difficult to achieve. For example, life insurance and door-to-door salesmen rely almost exclusively on commissions for compensation. Almost nobody would persist in cold canvassing life insurance prospects if pay were not directly related to results obtained.

In management's defense, lack of sophistication about human motivation does not explain entirely why pay is rarely tied directly to performance. Results obtained in many management positions, as a case in point, are both difficult to measure and often reflect group rather than individual output. Another complexity is that most people are willing to accept bonus pay for performance, but few will accept a decrease in pay for below-average results.

Fourth, the motivational impact of money is related more to relative than absolute wage levels. According to *equity theory*, people compare their income level to others they feel are making the same kind of contribution or performing similar kinds of work. Dissatisfaction and sometimes demotivation ensues when an individual feels underpaid in comparison to others performing comparable work in the same type of organization. Managers will often rationalize low absolute income by stating that in comparison to other managers within the same field or industry they are satisfactorily compensated.

Fifth, different occupational groups place different values on the meaning of money, thus influencing its incentive value. Paul F. Wernimount and Susan Fitzpatrick conducted research suggesting that money is a good incentive for upward-oriented persons including sales groups, technical supervisors, and managers.[67] Money appeared to have less incentive value for secretaries, scientists, and engineers. Hard-core trainees attached the least importance to money of the groups studied. Complicating the findings further, it was noted that hospital sisters and college students view money as less important than do hard-core trainees. One remote explanation here is that if you are deprived of money long enough, it begins to decrease in importance!

Development of Subordinates

Managers are in a strategic position to assist subordinates in their quest for personal growth and development. (In the context used here, development is related to growth or higher order needs.) To the extent that the manager helps his subordinates grow, advance, or develop, he (the manager) will elicit motivated behavior from subordinates. Research conducted by M. Scott Myers at Texas Instruments provides strong support for this statement.[68] In brief, managers with demonstrated effectiveness in developing their men were classified as *developmental*. A developmental manager, for example, recognizes performance, listens to new ideas and practices, and has sensitivity to the feelings of others. In contrast, those managers who were poor at developing subordinates were called *reductive*. A reductive manager, for example, reduces or inhibits expressions of creativity and induces withdrawal into positive patterns of conformity. Approximately one-half of the highly motivated managers had *developmental* bosses, but only eight percent had *reductive* bosses. Almost two-thirds of the poorly motivated managers had *reductive* bosses, but only eight percent had *developmental* bosses.

Creative Management

Shigeru Kobayashi, the Managing Director of Sony Corporation in Tokyo, uses the term "creative management" to describe a variety of behavioral science-oriented management practices employed by his firm. A review of Kobayashi's book, *Creative Management*, by Irving Paster highlights the types of managerial behaviors that contribute to the typical Sony employee's high level of motivation to work.[69]

Kobayashi places heavy reliance on the findings of behavioral scientists in his management of the Sony Corporation. He believes that wide-scale application of behavioral science-based management is the key to improved employer–employee relationships. The organizational climate at Sony is characterized by informality and mutual trust and respect between superiors and subordinates. Three specific examples of how creative management works in practice are presented next.

Honor system in the cafeteria.   Sony employees are provided with a book of meal coupons. They select whatever meals they would like on a self-service basis, add up their own checks, and deposit the appropriate number of coupons in a receiving box. Management feels that this system works because "everybody tries to live up to the trust placed in him."

No time clocks.   Sony has over 3000 employees, none of whom are required to punch time clocks. Instead, employees monitor their own attendance under a system that has worked satisfactorily, according to Kobayashi. The Sony Managing Director explains his policy about time clocks to employees in these words.[70]

> Obviously, we are here to make transistors. The only reason we joined this company is that we wanted this kind of job. I don't doubt at all that everybody is trying to do his job right. Therefore, let's decide that beginning tomorrow we will work according to the time schedule without any time clocks. Your own reporting of your absences will be sufficient. So will your own reporting of lateness or early leaving. The company will trust you. No one really wants to lose time; no one really wants to be absent when he ought to be working. What is important in this world is honesty. Let us try to be honest, then, from now on.

Formal communication channel.   Any employee wanting to receive or send information on certain topics may dial the number 2000. Types of information exchanged fall into the following three categories:

1. Latest information on company rumors.
2. Information on whom to call regarding job problems; information on any company related subject about which he is curious; information about receiving help with any of his ideas.
3. Information about possible job openings at Sony.

RELATIONSHIP TO CORE PROPOSITIONS

The following brief analyses are designed to help the reader integrate ideas about work motivation into the overall framework for organizational behavior presented in Chapter 1. Each of the four core propositions is mentioned separately.

Human Behavior

Work motivation follows quite closely principles of human behavior. As succinctly stated in the need gratification theory, job motivation can be considered as a subclassification of general motivation. Expectancy theory also is an extension of a general theory of human (and animal) motivation to a work environment.

Situational Nature

Work motivation is highly situational, as elaborated upon in the Work Motivation Schema. Individual differences among people, the leader himself or herself, and the organizational climate are among the many factors influencing the motivational level of workers. People who would exhibit high job motivation in some environments might also show low job motivation in others. Under extreme enough circumstances a climate can stifle job motivation.

Systemic Nature

Work motivation has several systemic properties. The Work Motivation Schema itself might be conceptualized as a minisystem. Changing any one of its components has ramifications for other components. For instance, if an individual finds a way to gratify his needs through job-related behavior (Component B on the Schema), he will work hard (Component C). Hard work leads to goal attainment, but it also leads to the activation of new needs (Component D).

Even the manipulation of financial incentives has systemic consequences. If a handful of individuals in an organization are given the opportunity to become wealthy through work, they will be turned on. Simultaneously, some other people in the same organization who are not given the same opportunity may become resentful, and may be turned off.

Structure and Process

Some elements of work motivation show the effects of interaction between structure and process. For example, every hierarchical organization has a formal system of incentives that purports to influence the work motivation of its members. Salary increases, fringe benefits, and formal titles all represent a structure for eliciting worker motivation. How these incentives interact with how they are administered (the process side of the equation) helps determine their effectiveness. One manager couples the formal structure of incentives (perhaps a change in title) with informal verbal recognition and good timing (processes). Another manager administers the change in title in a mechanistic, impersonal manner. The first manager is more likely to enhance employee motivation.

GUIDELINES FOR ACTION

1. Do not assume that employees with high levels of job satisfaction are necessarily well motivated or productive. Contrary to popular belief, dissatisfied workers are sometimes the most productive. (However, they also represent a high turnover risk.)
2. If money is to have a motivational impact on an employee, the amount of money he or she receives should be directly related to his or her effort. Also, the amount should "make a difference" to the person.
3. Job elements can be used to motivate people when the individual can gratify his or her needs by controlling that element. For example, the opportunity to attain recognition by receiving patents will motivate scientists because they control (within limits) the number of ideas or inventions they submit for patent application.
4. Penalties and other punishments have a low probability of effectively motivating ambitious, resourceful people. Conversely, these negative motivators may achieve at least short-range effectiveness with less ambitious, dependent individuals.
5. If you really want to elicit motivated behavior from another individual in a work situation, you would have to discover what needs he or she is attempting to satisfy through work. For example, at all levels in an organization some people are seeking more responsibility and accomplishment while others are in pursuit of a relaxed, comfortable work situation.

QUESTIONS

1. Can you think of any job element or factor that would increase your job satisfaction but would not influence your job motivation (the amount of effort you expend in reaching organizational objectives)?
2. What needs does occupying the role of a professional football quarterback satisfy? What needs are probably frustrated?
3. What sources of need gratification are available in a prison setting?
4. What is the difference between a "motive" in the Sherlock Holmes sense and a "need" in the motivation theory sense?
5. In one sentence, "How do you motivate people?"
6. Use the Work Motivation Schema presented in this chapter to explain why MBA students vary somewhat in the amount of effort they expend on course work.

NOTES

1. Clifton D. Bryant, *The Social Dimensions of Work.* Englewood Cliffs, N.J.: Prentice-Hall, 1972.
2. David R. Hampton, Charles E. Summer, and Ross A. Webber, *Organizational Behavior and the Practice of Management.* Glenview, Ill.: Scott, Foresman, 1968, pp. 4–5.
3. Joseph W. McGuire, *Business and Society.* New York: McGraw-Hill, 1963, p. 178.

4. "The Spreading Lordstown Syndrome," *Business Week*, March 4, 1972, pp. 69–70.
5. *Ibid.*, p. 69.
6. Douglas S. Sherwin, "Strategy for Winning Employee Commitment," *Harvard Business Review*, Vol. 50, No. 3, May–June 1972, pp. 37–47.
7. *Ibid.*, p. 37.
8. *Ibid.*, p. 42.
9. George Strauss and Leonard R. Sayles, *Personnel: The Human Problems of Management*, third edition. Englewood Cliffs, N.J.: Prentice-Hall, 1972, p. 23.
10. Andrew J. DuBrin, *Women in Transition*. Springfield, Ill.: Charles C. Thomas, 1972, pp. 3–23.
11. McGuire, *op. cit.*, p. 178.
12. *Ibid.*, p. 182.
13. John P. Campbell, Marvin D. Dunnette, Edward E. Lawler, III, and Karl E. Weick, Jr., *Managerial Behavior, Performance, and Effectiveness*. New York: McGraw-Hill, 1970, p. 340.
14. John P. Wanous and Edward E. Lawler, III, "Measurement and Meaning of Job Satisfaction," *Journal of Applied Psychology*, Vol. 56, No. 2, April 1972, pp. 95–105.
15. *Ibid.*, p. 104.
16. Bernard M. Bass, *Organizational Psychology*. Boston: Allyn & Bacon, 1965, p. 40.
17. Paul F. Wernimount, Paul Toren, and Henry Kapell, "Comparison of Personal Satisfaction and of Work Motivation," *Journal of Applied Psychology*, Vol. 54, No. 1, February 1970, pp. 95–102.
18. Douglas McGregor, *The Human Side of Enterprise*. New York: McGraw-Hill, 1960.
19. Abraham H. Maslow, "A Theory of Human Motivation: The Basic Needs," *Psychological Review*, Vol. 50, 1943, p. 395.
20. Frederick Herzberg, *Work and the Nature of Man*. Cleveland: World Book, 1966.
21. Robert J. House and Lawrence A. Wigdor, "Herzberg's Dual-Factor Theory of Job Satisfaction and Motivation," *Personnel Psychology*, Vol. 20, No. 4, Winter 1967, pp. 369–389.
22. Martin G. Wolf, "Need Gratification Theory: A Theoretical Reformulation of Job Satisfaction/Dissatisfaction and Job Motivation," *Journal of Applied Psychology*, Vol. 54, No. 1, February 1970, pp. 87–94.
23. Victor H. Vroom, *Work and Motivation*. New York: Wiley, 1964, p. 129.
24. H. Randolph Bobbitt, Jr. and Orlando Behling, "Defense Mechanisms as an Alternate Explanation of Herzberg's Motivator-Hygiene Results," *Journal of Applied Psychology*, Vol. 56, No. 1, February 1972, p. 27.
25. Abraham H. Maslow, *Motivation and Personality*. New York: Harper, 1954.
26. Wolf, *op. cit.*, p. 91.
27. *Ibid.*
28. Campbell *et al.*, *op. cit.*, p. 58.
29. Wolf, *op. cit.*, p. 92.
30. *Ibid.*
31. David C. McClelland, *The Achieving Society*. New York: Van-Nostrand, 1961.
32. Excerpted from "To Know Why Men Do What They Do: A Conversation with David C. McClelland and T. George Harris" in *Psychology Today Magazine*, January 1971, pp. 35–39, 70, 71, 74, 78, 79. Copyright © Communications/Research/Machines, Inc.
33. *Ibid.*, p. 36.
34. *Ibid.*, p. 70.
35. *Ibid.*
36. *Ibid.*
37. *Ibid.*, p. 36.
38. David C. McClelland and David G. Winter, *Motivating Economic Achievement*. New York: Free Press, 1969.
39. David C. McClelland, "Achievement Motivation Can Be Developed," *Harvard Business Review*, Vol. 43, No. 1, January–February 1965, pp. 6–24, 178.

40. *Ibid.*, p. 10.
41. Charles S. Telly, Wendell L. French, and William G. Scott, "The Relationship of Inequity to Turnover among Hourly Workers," *Administrative Science Quarterly*, Vol. 16, No. 1, March 1971, p. 164.
42. John B. Miner, *The Management Process: Theory, Research, and Practice.* New York: Macmillan, 1973, p. 312.
43. Paul S. Goodman and Abraham Friedman, "An Examination of Adam's Theory of Inequity," *Administrative Science Quarterly*, Vol. 16, No. 4, December 1971, pp. 271–288.
44. Telly *et al., op. cit.*
45. Miner, *op. cit.*, p. 313.
46. Vroom, *op. cit.*
47. Campbell *et al., op. cit.*, pp. 345–348.
48. Vance F. Mitchell, "Expectancy Theories of Managerial Motivation," *Proceedings of the 31st Annual Meeting of the Academy of Management*, pp. 210–220.
49. William G. Scott and Terence R. Mitchell, *Organization Theory: A Structural and Behavioral Analysis*, revised edition. Homewood, Ill.: Richard D. Irwin and Dorsey Press, 1972, p. 81.
50. Quoted in *ibid.*, p. 82.
51. Strauss and Sayles, *op. cit.*, pp. 135–137.
52. Charles D. Flory (editor), *Managing Through Insight.* New York: New American Library, 1968, p. 19.
53. Campbell *et al., op. cit.*, p. 361.
54. Edwin E. Ghiselli, "Some Motivational Factors in the Success of Managers," *Personnel Psychology*, Vol. 21, No. 4, Winter 1968, pp. 431–440.
55. John G. Darley and T. Hagenah, *Vocational Interest Measurement.* Minneapolis: University of Minnesota Press, 1955, p. 169.
56. From another point of view, this situation illustrates the potential dysfunctional consequences of a bureaucratic organization. This manager is diverted away from the constructive aspects of his job toward the way of "beating the system."
57. Premise number 5 of McGregor's Theory *Y* states that more people have the capacity to exercise imagination in the solution of organizational problems than is generally recognized. McGregor, *op. cit.*, p. 48.
58. Jack R. Gibb, "Managing for Creativity in the Organization," in Calvin W. Taylor (editor), *Climate for Creativity.* Elmsford, N.Y.: Pergamon Press, 1972, pp. 23–32.
59. *Ibid.*, p. 24.
60. Wolf, *op. cit.*, p. 91.
61. Campbell *et al., op. cit.*, pp. 374–377.
62. Frederick Herzberg, "One More Time: How Do You Motivate Employees?" *Harvard Business Review*, Vol. 46, No. 1, January–February 1968, pp. 53–62.
63. M. Scott Myers, "Conditions for Manager Motivation," *Harvard Business Review*, Vol. 44, No. 1, January–February 1966, pp. 58–71.
64. Ghiselli, *op. cit.*, p. 437.
65. Edward E. Lawler, III, *Pay and Organizational Effectiveness.* New York: McGraw-Hill, 1971.
66. Saul W. Gellerman, *Management by Motivation.* New York: American Management Association, 1968, pp. 203–218.
67. Paul F. Wernimount and Susan Fitzpatrick, "The Meaning of Money," *Journal of Applied Psychology*, Vol. 56, No. 3, June 1972, p. 226.
68. Myers, *op. cit.*
69. Shigeru Kobayashi, *Creative Management.* New York: American Management Association, 1971 (reviewed by Irving Paster, *Personnel Journal*, Vol. 50, No. 8, August 1971, pp. 649–650).
70. *Ibid.*, p. 650.

3

Behavioral Aspects to Decision Making

Rain is pouring down on Shea Stadium in New York City on a Sunday morning in May. The New York Mets are scheduled to play a double-header with the Cincinnati Reds. Within the next 50 minutes, the general manager must make a "play or postpone" decision. Potential side effects from making the wrong decision are far reaching. Among these are: (1) Should the general manager decide "the game is on" and conditions become unplayable, approximately 20,000 people will come to the stadium only to be frustrated, annoyed, and skeptical about the judgment of the front office. (2) Should the general manager decide to postpone the game and the weather suddenly improves, many fans will be frustrated, annoyed, and irritated because their plans for the day were needlessly canceled. Furthermore, changing the date of a doubleheader creates many scheduling complications later in the season.

Ben and John, two recent college graduates, have formed a manufacturer's representative company. Sales volume is on the increase and they have recently acquired two new lines of merchandise to sell. Currently they use a telephone answering service and part-time secretarial service. These two men face the decision of whether or not to rent an office and hire a full-time secretary. Deciding "yes" represents an annual investment of about $10,000. Both partners feel that having an office and a secretary would allow for better service to customers and simultaneously enhance the image of their firm. Nevertheless, $10,000 would represent a substantial investment that would drain away profits if it failed to stimulate sales.

The processes involved in making the kinds of decisions faced by the managements of the New York Mets and the small sales organization is the topic of this chapter. Decisions have to be made by managers at all levels in any organization. Some decisions may point an organization in an entirely new direction (e.g., should New York Life form a mutual fund of its own?), while others represent low risk, relatively minor considerations (e.g.,

71

should Cadet Dry Cleaners sell ties in its retail outlets?). Although decisions vary in the magnitude of their importance, the processes involved in reaching them are essentially the same.

Another way of conceptualizing the "big" versus "little" decision dichotomy is to think of some decisions as involving opportunities while others involve the maintenance of an ongoing system. Knowledge workers at different levels in the organization can find problems or make decisions that create new opportunities. One industrial engineering manager in a large organization decided that his department's efforts geared toward manufacturing efficiencies would have a greater payoff if attention were first directed toward resolving underlying interpersonal and intergroup problems. His unit of the organization thus acquired an organization development capability (*see* Chapter 13 for more about OD). The unit then dealt with the conflict underlying manufacturing problems before dealing with technological problems. Shifting the primary focus from manufacturing efficiency to interpersonal conflict *and* manufacturing efficiency created a new opportunity for his department and hopefully resulted in organizational improvement.

Focus in this chapter is upon managerial decision making, but the basic ideas presented here are also applicable to decisions faced by specialists. To illustrate, an investment analyst in advising about the purchase of IBM stock must go through the same processes as the warehouse manager who is contemplating the purchase of a forklift truck.

THE DECISION-MAKING SCHEMA

The Decision-Making Schema, shown in Figure 3.2, represents the core of the approach to understanding decision making taken here. Material presented at later points in the chapter is basically an elaboration of five key elements within the Schema: clarification of the problem, creative approaches, weighing alternatives, making the choice, and evaluating outcomes.

The Decision-Making Schema is based upon *process* or *flow* conception of decision making. Several other management theorists conceive of decision making in this manner, as summarized in Figure 3.1. For example, Donald W. Taylor conceptualizes decision making as a four-step process involving search, formulation of objectives, selection of alternatives, and lastly, evaluation of outcomes. William Emory and Powell Niland conceptualize three stages: purpose setting, task delineation, and solution finding. The basic

D. W. TAYLOR[1]	R. W. MORRELL[2]	W. EMORY and P. NILAND[3]
Search process to discover goals	Uncertainty	Purpose setting
↓	↓	↓
Formulation of objectives after search	Analysis and definition	Task delineation
↓	↓	↓
Selection of alternatives to accomplish objectives	Proposal of alternatives	Solution finding
↓	↓	
Evaluation of outcomes	Verification	

Figure 3.1 Three conceptions of the decision-making process.

core to the Schema follows the decision-making model presented by William H. Newman, Charles E. Summer, and E. Kirby Warren in *The Process of Management*.[4] Four pediatricians in group medical practice will serve as illustrative material for an excursion through the Decision-Making Schema.

Input

Dr. Swanson, the youngest member of the four man group practice, has *found* a *problem* (lower left-hand corner of the Schema). He informs Drs. McCausland, Green, and Carter that the group is taking too-conservative an approach to money management. "There must be a way for us to make money in addition to providing medical services." In many managerial decision-making situations, problems are *given*. This same medical group, to cite one illustration, might have been asked by the town council to relocate because their group practice violated zoning laws. Considerable activity would then be devoted to making a decision about where, when, and even how to relocate.

Intervening Variables

Note that under "Problem Found" is the notation, "Intervening variables *a* through *n*." An individual's capacity to find or discover a problem is related to a wide range of factors. These same factors are closely related to his capacity to make decisions. In combination, these factors or variables account for individual differences in decision-making ability. The total impact of these intervening variables defines the decision-making *situation*.

74

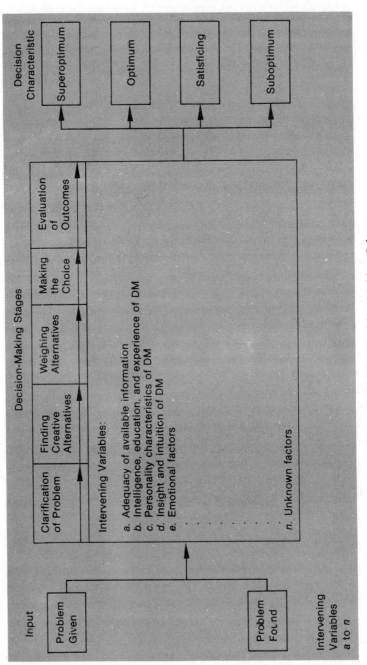

Figure 3.2 The Decision-Making Schema.

Adequacy of available information. People who have ready access to current, relevant, and vital information are in a good position to find problems and make decisions.[5] One merchandising manager carefully scanned census data for population trends that might affect the home furnishings industry. He noted that young women are staying single longer and, thus, are a better potential market for home furnishings. In the past, women took less pride in their premarital dwellings. This manager *found* a problem—conducting a marketing campaign directed toward single women. Similarly, the inventory control manager who has access to current computerized information about inventory throughout his company is in a better position to find problems than one who does not have or ignores this information.

Intelligence, education, and experience of decision maker. In general, intelligent, well-educated, and experienced managers are in a better position to find problems or make decisions than their counterparts of lesser intelligence, education, and experience. Common sense would suggest that this statement should go unchallenged because it is an obvious truism. Subtle exceptions, however, are known to exist. People without a well-developed facility for abstract reasoning (those of average intelligence) will sometimes see a problem or opportunity in its most rudimentary form. To cite one example, an industrial organization was embarking on a study to determine the root causes of low morale and high turnover in the organization. A worker at the very bottom level of the company made a spontaneous comment that proved to be the crux of the problem: "There's only one thing wrong with this place. The president is a cheap S.O.B." Lengthy experience in, or overexposure to a situation can also inhibit problem finding. One company came to a consulting firm, asking the question, "What other business should we get into? Our sales are slipping." The consultants found a different problem than the one presented to them: "Your problem is that you are in too many businesses. Pare down and concentrate on what you can do well."

Personality characteristics of decision maker. Traits and behavioral characteristics of a manager can also influence his or her ability to find problems and make decisions. People with a rigid mental set will have difficulty finding problems even when they are intelligent, well-educated, experienced, and have access to good information. Perfectionism can also inhibit problem finding. A scientist was hired because of his presumed inventive abilities. After one year had passed, this man had not only discovered nothing, he had failed to even completely define what kind of project he would like to pursue. His perfectionistic tendencies led him to rework one fundamental experiment until (in his words) its "scientific integrity is unquestionable." Similarly, cautious individuals have some difficulty in finding problems. Discovery of new opportunities requires an entrepreneurial, risk-taking flare.

Richard W. Pollay conducted a complicated set of laboratory experiments about the relationship between the difficulty of a decision problem and decision time.[6] Noteworthy here is that personality factors are somewhat related to decision behavior. For instance, people high in achievement potential (those who are described as persistent, industrious, forceful, dominant, independent, self-reliant, planful, and thorough) are able to make up their minds quickly about good and bad alternatives. They are also able to quickly reject poor alternatives to a decision.

Insight and intuition of decision maker. Another important intervening variable that influences whether or not problems will be found (or effective decisions made) is the basic insight and intuition of the manager. Finding problems or opportunities requires a person to make interpretations of trends that others have not already made. Documentation is difficult to find for something that does not already exist. Lyle Stuart, the owner of a publishing company, had the intuitive feel that the world was ready for a frivolous, shockingly candid portrayal of a woman's attitude toward sexual technique and behavior. He hired a public relations woman, "J", to write this book. *The Sensuous Woman* was the commercially successful monument to his business intuition. Shortly after this book came *The Sensuous Man* by "M", which was also a commercial success, lending more support to the publisher's intuition.

Rarely can a person make decisions solely on the basis of insight and intuition, however gifted he or she is in this area. Decision making is always a blend of relying upon both data and hunches. A purely intuitive approach to decision making is not being suggested here.

Emotional factors. These play a key role in problem finding and in all stages of decision making. Problem finding and decision making are not entirely rational processes. Intellect, reason, *and* emotion enter into most decisions. Even when decisions appear to be based almost entirely upon hard data, *which* data are selected for inclusion in the decision-making process is influenced to some degree by emotion and feeling. For instance, the marketing director of a company may attempt to convince his president that his company should launch a new product. Simultaneously, the controller may attempt to convince the president to pare down expenses in order to increase profits. Both the marketing and financial executives have "facts" to support their position. Which set of facts the president chooses to enter into his decision-making process is a function of his perceptual biases. Should he be feeling "bullish" these days, he will place more emphasis on the marketing facts; should he feel "bearish," he will give more weight to the controller's figures.

Decisions to retain unprofitable projects are often made on the basis of emotional (or subjective) rather than rational (objective) factors. One of the world's best-known optical companies sells a line of precision binoculars that, from a technical standpoint, are the envy of competitors. Financially, each sale results in a loss for the company, yet the company retains the line. A few company executives would argue that this "sacred cow" is a prestige item that serves as good publicity for the company's more profitable lines such as eye glasses. Most managers in the company contend that the binoculars are retained for sentimental and emotional reasons.

Problems and opportunities, even if rationally conceived, must be selected that will appeal to the emotions of other people. Illustrative here is the irrational (emotional) nature of charity drives. Diseases and disorders must be selected that have wide appeal. Without such an appeal, public support is difficult to garner. Emotional disorders, for example, have much less emotional appeal than most physical disorders, so it is presumably easier to collect money to combat leukemia than schizophrenia. The large majority of donors simply have more compassion for victims of leukemia than schizophrenia.

Unpredictable, uncontrollable factors. Problems are sometimes found (or correct decisions made) on the basis of luck or other unpredictable factors. Charles C. Thomas, a publishing company, is well respected for its medical, psychological, and police science books. Outsiders question how a firm originally specializing in medical books came to add a line of police science books. According to a company official, a principal of the firm originally published a police science book as a favor to a friend. Shortly, this book became one of the better selling books in the Thomas line. This served as a basis for publishing other books in the same general area. *Serendipity,* the gift of finding valuable things not sought for, is another unpredictable factor that enters the problem-finding or decision-making situation. It is rumored that New York State decided to charge an additional fee for special order license plates, such as those with an owner's initials. The purpose of the fee was to discourage state residents from making these special orders, Word spread that the New York State Motor Vehicle Department was now offering personalized plates for only a small fee beyond the regular plate. Demand for this new service was high and ultimately proved to be a worthwhile source of revenue. Minnesota Mining Company originally developed its Scotch Tape as an office product to mend torn documents. Scotch Tape shortly became a widely known household product. Current applications of cellophane tape include setting hair and holding bandages in place.

Decision-Making Stages

Proceeding to the middle component of the Decision-Making Schema, the first stage noted is *clarification of the problem.* The doctors mentioned earlier, who were deciding how to increase their income, might explore in greater depth the specific nature of their problem. Among the clarifications needed are: What proportion of the gross receipts does the medical practice want to invest? What kinds of things won't we do with our money? For example, the group agrees that investments in illegal or questionable activities are to be excluded as an alternative.

Finding creative alternatives, the next stage, involves intellectual free swinging. All kinds of possibilities are explored here, even if they appear too *avant garde* or unrealistic at the outset. Potential investments suggested at this time might include such diverse alternatives as: (a) purchase a cattle farm in Texas, (b) install coffee vending machines in the waiting room, (c) purchase shares in a mutual fund, (d) purchase a deferred compensation annuity, (e) establish a day-care center for children of working mothers, (f) buy an apartment building, (g) buy the building in which the medical offices are located, and (h) purchase a small, private hospital.

Weighing alternatives refers to comparing the relative value of all the alternatives just mentioned. Pros and cons of each possible decision should be carefully delineated. One decided advantage of the mutual fund alternative is that management of the doctors' excess money would be left to professional judgment. One disadvantage is that, for many people, investing in a mutual fund takes much of the fun and gamesmanship out of managing money. Also, the value of most funds is subject to wide fluctuation.

Weighing alternatives includes taking into consideration rudimentary financial considerations. On this basis, the coffee machine can be excluded from further consideration. All other alternatives involve a substantial outlay of capital. Another obvious consideration would be to classify those investment alternatives that require the doctors to invest only money versus those that require money plus time. Each alternative must also be considered in relation to the amount of capital each doctor decided to invest. Amount of capital invested remains a crucial variable in any financial decision.

Making the choice is next to the final stage in the decision-making process. In this situation, the group medical practice opted to purchase the building in which their practice was located and collect rent from other tenants. Another alternative open in any decision-making situation is to take no action. Deciding not to go ahead with a plan is psychologically different than ignoring the problem from the outset. As within any of the other three decision-making stages, the outcome in the final stage is somewhat dependent upon the intervening variables. Specifically, if the four pediatricians have neurotic attitudes about money, sound decision making will be difficult.

Evaluation of outcomes is the final stage of the decision-making process. Only by evaluating outcomes can the effectiveness of a decision be measured. William G. Scott and Terence R. Mitchell note that one method of evaluating outcomes is to compare them to the goals of the decision maker.[7] Thus, if the physicians wished to substantially increase their income, the coffee machine alternative would be a poor one.

Decision Characteristics

Every decision made in an organization has some kind of consequences. Subjective and objective measures are both required to determine the adequacy of each decision made. Several terms have developed in the behavioral science and management literature to describe the properties or characteristics of decisions; superoptimum, however, is a new term.

Superoptimum refers to those unique, breakthrough, entrepreneurial-type decisions that provide an organization with a new thrust. Decisions of this type are not called for in most organizational situations. The Ford Motor Company decision to manufacture and sell the Mustang illustrates a superoptimum decision in the history of American business. Conceivably, if the physicians in the hypothetical case presented in this chapter decided to invest in a small hospital, it would prove to be a superoptimum decision.

Optimum decisions are those that lead to most favorable outcomes. (Superoptimum decisions are in reality a special case of optimum decisions.) Alan C. Filley and Robert J. House note that a decision alternative is optimum only if "(1) there exists a set of criteria that permits all alternatives to be compared, and (2) the alternative in question is preferred, by these criteria, to all others.'"[8] Purchasing the building might have proven to be an optimum decision. Rentals from the building might generate enough revenue to satisfy all four partners. Also, this activity would not have interfered with the quality of medical service provided to patients.

Satisficing decisions are those that meet with a minimum standard of satisfaction; they are adequate, acceptable, passable, and "OK." Most decision makers continue their search until they find a satisficing alternative. Establishing a day-care center might have been satisficing; an acceptable level of profit might be possible, and the center would divert a moderate amount of the pediatricians' time away from medical practice.

Suboptimum decisions are those that lead to undesirable outcomes. Their consequences are dysfunctional to the system. Installing coffee vending machines in the waiting room might prove to be a suboptimum decision. The gross income would be meager, valuable space in the waiting room would be occupied by the machines, and such a maneuver might detract from the dignity of the medical practice. Decision characteristics, thus, may take into consideration both economic and noneconomic considerations.

PROBLEM FINDING

Before important decisions can be made in any organization, important problems or opportunities have to be found. Many managerial decisions are made about matters of relatively little consequence. A tobacco company, for example, might decide to change the package on a well-accepted brand of cigarettes. A decision of this magnitude will call for a flurry of activity from large numbers of people: package designers, printers, production people, paper manufacturers, and ink suppliers, among others. Concerns such as the dispensing of unsold cigarettes in the obsolete package even come to the fore. Unknown to the executives responsible for such a decision is whether or not this decision will have a meaningful impact on sales or corporate image. In short, it is not inconceivable that such a large decision was made about something that is *not even a problem*. Conversely, the individual who recognized that downhill skiing could never become a popular sport until mechanical methods of transporting people up the hill were developed had found both a problem and an opportunity. T-bars, rope tows, and chair lifts gave the skiing business its real impetus.

Rare is the individual who has the imagination, originality, and perception to find problems and opportunities. Opportunity finders are entrepreneurs and inventors. In ample supply, however, is the individual who can competently solve problems given to him or her by somebody else. Based upon extensive research, Norman H. Mackworth notes that problem finders are psychologically different than problem solvers. For one, "The most gifted problem finders rarely have outstanding scholastic records; those who do excel scholastically rarely are among the most effective problem finders."[9] Presented next are two examples of people who *found* problems.

> Robert Orlando was a lower middle manager in the organization. One of his responsibilities was to maintain liaison with local banks. After three months on the job, Bob concluded that his company was leaving an exorbitant amount of money on deposit in checking accounts. Among the analyses he conducted to find this problem was a calculation of the time taken by the average supplier to cash checks paid by his company. "I don't mind having friendly relations with the local banks, but why are we giving them such a large interest-free loan every month?" Finding this problem led to $20,000-a-year savings for the company (they put some of the excess funds in interest-bearing accounts) and a promotion for Bob Orlando.

> John Gillis, Tom Reebes, and Duane Cera (their real names) were three college students who had been "talking for some time about starting a business where we could make some money and have some fun, too."[10] First the group pursued the idea of starting a coffee shop in a downtown location to cater to young people. Among the unique features planned were (a) furniture made from telephone cable spools, (b) a closing time of 4:30 a.m., and (c) allowing amateur photographers to show their 16 mm movies on the premises. This plan failed because the site selected contained only one exit, which was in violation of local building codes. (John, Tom, and Duane lacked sufficient capital to have a second exit built.)

> Next, the group decided to make unusual hand-made things to supply to local head shops and boutiques. "... We went out and bought a potter's wheel and some molds, some plastic resin and dyes, and collected some driftwood from the beach and some leather from the garbage cans in the back of Hickok's belt factory. We made some pots and vases, ashtrays, translucent plastic plaques with the different astrological signs, and mounted them with driftwood and leather. We made a couple of lamps and some candles and then went around to the stores to get some orders."[11]

> Quickly it became apparent that the candles were the easiest to sell and manufacture. The group therefore made the decision to concen-

trate on these decorative candles. A store called the "Plum Tree" placed the first big order—50 candles on consignment. All were sold on the first day. The popularity of the candles spread rapidly. During the Christmas season, the candles were vended on pushcarts in a downtown location. John, Tom, and Duane, in an effort to match demand for their products, began to employ high school girls part time to make the candles. At this writing, the three principals are setting up a retail outlet in a choice location to sell these candles exclusively. Plans to distribute the candles regionally are also being formulated. After three months of operation, it can be safely concluded that a worthwhile opportunity had been found. Among the crucial characteristics of this product is that it is both decorative and consumable.

"Finding the right things to do" is the phrase Peter Drucker uses to describe opportunity finding.[12] Effective executives are characterized by this concentration on significant issues. Efficient executives, in contrast, expend mental effort and energy on much less significant matters. Here is how Drucker contrasts problem solving and opportunity finding:[13]

> All one can hope to get by solving a problem is to restore normality. All one can hope, at best, is to eliminate a restriction on the capacity of the business to obtain results. The results themselves must come from the exploitation of opportunities. . . .

Learning to become an opportunity or problem finder rather than a problem solver is difficult. In this author's experience, merely developing the mental set that problem finding is crucial can sometimes lead to improved results. Keeping the significance of problem finding in mind sensitizes a person to at least search for opportunities and problems. J. Sterling Livingston contends that guided practice in job environment is to date the best vehicle for acquiring skill in finding problems. Experience of this type, he contends, is of considerably more value than classroom education in learning how to find problems.[14]

CLARIFICATION OF THE PROBLEM

Once a person has discovered or been assigned a problem, that problem must be placed into clearer focus; a more definitive diagnosis is called for. Sound diagnosis of a problem, according to Newman, Summer, and Warren, should provide answers to the following three questions:[15]

1. Just what *gaps* exist between the results we desire and the existing or predicted state of affairs?
2. What are the direct, root *causes* and the intermediate causes of the gaps?
3. Does the broader *context* of the problem place limits within which we should find a satisfactory solution?

Gap Between Desired and Actual

Several years ago a pharmaceutical company discovered a gap between predicted and actual sales. Cough syrup sales had increased dramatically. In some retail outlets enough cough syrup was sold in three months to satisfy a normal five-year demand. Naively, one might assume that this is simply a manufacturing and distribution problem. The company's problem was simply to step up production to meet this sudden demand. Data about actual versus predicted sales were then collected at a regional and national level. Analysis of the data indicated that this "gap" appeared to be concentrated in two geographically adjacent regions. Before committing additional production resources to fill this gap, the company decided to discover *why* this gap existed.

Root and Intermediate Causes

Company representatives who visited field locations quickly identified an intermediate cause of the problem. Teenagers were responsible for the increased sales of cough medicine. Local druggists noted that young people were flocking to the store to purchase over-the-counter cough medicine, particularly this one brand. Notably, there was not a corresponding increase in the sale of cough drops, facial tissues, or aspirin. Few readers at this point will be surprised to learn the root cause. Teenagers were getting high on cough medicine, particularly with this brand because of its core ingredient. Questioning of police and sanitation department workers revealed that large numbers of cough syrup bottles were found each morning inside the town mall. Young people were congregating at night in the plaza to participate in "syrup parties."

Sociologically astute readers might argue that the pharmaceutical firm had failed to isolate the root cause. What must be answered is why do teenagers feel the need to get high? What is so bad about their lives that they seek to escape reality?

Broader Context of the Problem

Social ramifications of this problem are immense. Cough medicine, many would argue, serves constructive ends in society. At an absolute minimum, consumers of cough medicine feel better because they are doing something positive about their discomfort. Creating conditions that enable teenagers to get high, others would argue, is a destructive end. However, almost

83

every medicinal or health product can be and is put to some kind of destructive end. Large numbers of children take overdoses of aspirins, people attempt suicide with sleeping pills, and even "safe drugs" such as birth control pills have harmful side effects for a small proportion of women. The broader problem faced by the firm can be stated as follows: "How much responsibility does a pharmaceutical firm have for policing the end uses to which its products are put?" Automobile manufacturers are not asked to prevent people from speeding, and whiskey manufacturers are not asked to prevent people from becoming alcoholic.

FINDING CREATIVE ALTERNATIVES

Stage two in the Decision-Making Schema concerns finding creative alternatives to the problem at hand. Creativity, of course, is also welcomed at other stages in the decision-making process.[16] Creative behavior, for example, is required to find problems and opportunities; however, creativity is not called for in every organizational or business decision. Preestablished routines, systems, and procedures exist to solve many problems. Assume that a company finds itself in the enviable position of discovering that the demand for its products is in excess of its present capacity to produce. (The home safe business in the early 1970s is one prime example. Public concern about the high incidence of crime led to an unpredicted heavy demand for home safes.) Solutions to this problem, such as adding manufacturing capability and recruiting new personnel, have been worked out by many other companies in the past. Frequently other companies who have faced similar problems of expansion can be consulted about the problem.

Creativity is not a characteristic of artists and inventors exclusively. Creative responses to problems are possible in any field of endeavor including business, government, and education. Many readers associate names like Da Vinci, Edison, Einstein, Darwin, and Goethe with the concept of creativity. These individuals are indeed creative, but they represent extreme examples of creative genius. People of lesser renown are also creative. Consider the creative element involved in the following suggestion for dealing with a major social problem.[17]

> Helmut Schelsky, a German sociologist, advocates doing away with anonymity on the highway as a method of reducing the incidence of reckless driving. He notes that the automobile is depersonalizing. Aggressive behavior is encouraged because drivers "remain anonymous behind the mask of an apparatus called the automobile. People who would be very polite to each other meeting face to face in a doorway

will turn into aggressive idiots behind the wheel." The solution Schelsky recommends is *personalization* and *politicization.*

As a first step, names instead of numbers would be put on automobiles. At a minimum, he would let the police give out, on request, names corresponding to license numbers. Personalization would also be achieved by invoking peer group pressure. He would make good driving socially rewarding and dangerous driving socially unacceptable, perhaps by keeping peers posted on an individual's "driving morality."

Politicization would be achieved by demonstrations against unsafe driving like those against the Viet Nam War. "Why," Schelsky asks, "do the war dead arouse more protest in us than the victims of technology?"

What Kind of Person Is Creative?

Considerable opinion and some empirical evidence exist about the psychological makeup of the creative individual. According to popular stereotype, creative people are characterized by unusual dress and lack of inhibitions. Creative people are also thought to harbor deep-rooted personal conflicts. Support for these beliefs is usually found by newspaper accounts of writers and musicians who have undergone psychoanalysis or who lead chaotic personal lives. In reality, many creative people are conservative in appearance and behavior. Conversely, many noncreative people are unusual in appearance and behavior. Extensive studies about the nature of creative people have been conducted at the Institute for Personality Assessment Research located within the University of California, Berkeley campus.[18] Each person studied was rated on creativity by peers familiar with his or her work. Among the occupations studied were artists, writers, architects, mathematicians, and research scientists. Donald W. MacKinnon, one of the key researchers at the Institute, notes that architects represent what is most generally characteristic of creative persons. Because of this, many of the findings published by the Institute are based upon the psychological makeup of architects. MacKinnon reasons:[19]

> Architecture, as a field of creative endeavor, requires that the successful practitioner be both artist and scientist.... The successful and effective architect must, with the skill of a juggler, combine, reconcile, and exercise the diverse skills of businessman, lawyer, artist, engineer, and advertising man, as well as those of author and journalist, psychiatrist, educator, and psychologist. In what other professions can one expect better to observe the multifarious expressions of creativity?

Every participant in the research was involved in a weekend of intensive study at the Institute. Research methods included batteries of psychological tests, interviews, problem-solving experiments, and participation in simulated social situations. Statistical comparisons were made between individuals of varying amounts of creativity (as seen by peers). The dominant underlying theme revealed about the creative person is that he is more flexible than those who are less creative. Creative people, in short, are emotionally loose and open. Major findings revealed about the makeup of highly creative people reported by MacKinnon are summarized next:[20]

1. They tend to have a good opinion of themselves, yet they are able to talk quite frankly about their shortcomings.
2. They are not necessarily more intelligent than less creative individuals. (However, there is undoubtedly a critical minimum intelligence level required for creative output in any field. Can you imagine a feeble-minded person trying to write an advertising slogan?)
3. They are emotionally expressive and sensitive—character traits that are defined by contemporary society as being more *feminine* than *masculine.*
4. They have a preference for things that are complex and asymmetrical; they are open to new and unusual forms of experience.
5. They are more concerned with meanings and implications than with small details and facts for their own sake.
6. They have strong theoretical and esthetic values (in contrast, for example, to economic and political values).
7. They readily form unusual mental associations to words. For example, one creative person conjured up these associations to the stimulus word *wheel*: "round, motor, spin, axis, ovum, merry-go-round, reel, gear, big deal, heavy weight, cyclone, stock market, hurricane."

Improving Your Creativity

Considerable debate exists about the relative importance of heredity versus environment in contributing to an individual's creativity. Some people regard creativity as a mysterious, genetically determined talent possessed by a small minority of people. At the other extreme lies the viewpoint of those sponsors of creativity workshops who contend that "everybody can learn creativity." The position taken here is that most people can enhance their ability to provide creative responses to problems. Central to improv-

ing creativity is the development of more flexibility and emotional looseness. Methods to develop creativity are generally based upon this underlying principle. M. Gold, for example, recommends that the maintenance of
considerable spontaneity in the classroom is important in developing the
creativity of elementary school students. Children, according to his research, should choose some tasks for themselves rather than working exclusively upon assigned tasks.[21]

Overcoming perceptual blocks is one important key to the development of
creativity. Businessmen, similar to other people, frequently cannot find opportunities or solve problems in a creative manner because they are bound
by preconceived perceptions. The discovery of penicillin was contingent
upon overcoming the perception of mold as simply a substance that spoiled
pure cultures. Widely quoted is the anecdote about how Alexander Fleming one day realized that the same substance responsible for spoiling cultures could be used as a germ killer. Millions of lives have been saved because Fleming was able to overcome his perceptual blocks about mold. One
less dramatic illustration of overcoming perceptual blocks is found in the
field of fashion. Handbags ("purses" or "pocketbooks" depending upon
your region of the country) for many years were thought to be an exclusively female accessory. Men were expected to use pockets, attaché cases, or
sometimes fishing tackle boxes to carry small personal articles. Overcoming
the perceptual barrier that handbags are sex linked led to a small, but new
market—*manbags.*[22]

Brainstorming is still a widely used technique to enhance creative responses to problem solving and opportunity finding. Readers are probably
familiar with the basic elements of this technique, originally developed by a
prominent advertising executive, Alex F. Osborn.[23] A group of people
simultaneously call out solutions to a vexing problem. Any group member
is free to enhance, or "piggy back" upon, the contribution of any other
member of the group. Spontaneity and permissiveness are encouraged.
Ideas, however wild and undisciplined, are not censured nor criticized during the brainstorming sessions. Later, somebody may be assigned to sort out
and edit some of these undisciplined ideas. Newman, Summer, and Warren comment about the application of brainstorming to decision making in
organizations:[24]

> Executives have used this technique on a wide variety of problems including:
> how to find new uses for glass in autos, how to improve a company newspaper,
> how to design a new tire making machine, how to improve highway signs, and
> how to cut down absenteeism.

Placed in a group climate that is both permissive and cohesive, the individual is encouraged to be creative. Penalties are not levied, even for fanciful, half-processed, or trite ideas.

Brainstorming, similar to most well-publicized techniques for improving human potential, does not inevitably stand up well under the rigors of scientific scrutiny. Marvin D. Dunnette, John Campbell, and Kay Jaastad studied the relative effectiveness of group versus individual brainstorming sessions. The subjects in the study were research scientists and advertising personnel employed by a large corporation. One crucial aspect of the experimental design was that each person in the study participated in both individual and group brainstorming sessions. Here is one of the problems given to individuals and groups for potential solutions:[25]

> Suppose that discoveries in physiology and nutrition have so affected the diet of American children over a period of twenty years that the average height of Americans at age 20 has increased to 80 inches and the average weight has doubled. Comparative studies of the growth of children during the last five years indicate that the phenomenal change in stature is stabilized so that further increase is not expected. What would be the consequences? What adjustments would this situation require?

Results of this study were quite unfavorable to the group method of brainstorming, as shown in the table below. Numbers in the table refer to the mean total number of different solutions produced by the various groups. Individual brainstorming produced more different ideas and solutions than did group brainstorming. Furthermore, the quality of the solutions achieved by the individual brainstormers was judged to be equal to or greater than that of the group brainstormers.

	Research Personnel		Advertising Personnel	
	Individual	Group	Individual	Group
Total number of solutions for all four problems	140	110	141	97

Synectics is another training method for creative thinking that has achieved popularity in a wide number of organizations. The synectic methods, developed by William J. J. Gordon, are essentially mental devices for achieving new viewpoints and problem solutions. Similar to brainstorming, synectics is geared toward group problem solving but can be applied to individual problem solving. Gary A. Davis in his review of *Synectics* provides a colorful, capsule description of these methods:[26]

Gordon particularly emphasizes the use of analogies and meta-phors—especially those drawn from nature. For example, in attempting to devise a roof which is black in winter (to absorb heat), and white in summer (to reflect heat) the synectic group would speculate on how rabbits, chameleons, and some fish change colors. Gordon also describes a *personal analogy* method in which group members imagine themselves to be one of the problem objects. With his *fantasy analogy* method, members are encouraged to propose ideal but perhaps far-fetched solutions, such as having insects work on command to solve a transportation problem. Another metaphoric device is playing with word meanings. For example, group members free-associated to the stimulus word *opening* before being told that the specific problem was to devise a new can opener. Gordon also recommended "pushing laws out of phase" (e.g., repealing gravity) as a means of stimulating new viewpoints and ideas.

Self-discipline is an important aspect to any form of self-development and creativity is no exception. Developing the mental set or attitude that creativity is both desirable and necessary is an important starting point to-ward becoming more creative. Faced with a decision or problem calling for creativity, one effective starting point is to sit quietly with a pencil and pad and begin to generate possible solutions. Few people have developed the self-discipline to struggle with a problem in this manner for more than short periods of time.

Developing the self-discipline required to produce creative responses may begin with a paper clip! Simply sit alone in a room and write down 25 possible uses of an ordinary paper clip. During your next "creativity build-ing session" think of 25 uses for a rubber band. Next, think of five ways you might be able to raise money for yourself other than by performing your regular job. (Admittedly, such approaches may appear contrived and gim-micky, but in this author's experience they are a useful method of bringing forth part of the creative potential possessed by most individuals.) Creativ-ity, similar to other human characteristics, is a dimension of behavior that is normally distributed. Technically, people cannot be classified as creative versus noncreative but rather as having varying *amounts* of creativity.

Creativity Is Part of the Total Human System

Several days prior to his death, the famous psychologist Abraham H. Maslow completed an overview chapter entitled, "A Holistic Approach to Creativity."[27] Maslow conceives of creativity as inextricably bound up with other aspects of human functioning. He presents some data suggesting that the creative personality is remarkably similar to the self-actualized or self-fulfilled personality. Superior creativity is thus a by-product of being a superior person. Similarly, the way to improve the functioning of human kidneys is to improve the functioning of the total human system. Neither kidneys nor creativity exist in isolation: ". . . general creativeness, holistically conceived, emanates from the whole system, *generally* improved."[28]

Maslow's conclusions about the nature of creativity do not diminish the potential value of the creativity training techniques mentioned above. Although creativity is primarily part of the healthy person syndrome, it also has a specific factor. Given an already effective person, he or she can benefit from specific techniques designed to enhance creativity. Additionally, the total organizational environment can enhance or detract from the development of creativity as Jack R. Gibb has observed (*see* Chapter 2 on motivation and creativity).[29]

WEIGHING ALTERNATIVES

Once the managerial problem has been found (or given), clarified, and creative alternatives identified, the next stage is to make relative comparisons among these alternatives. Decision makers, it could be argued, automatically weigh each alternative; without such weighing a decision could never be reached. Despite the merit in this argument, decision making will probably be more effective when a rational analysis is made of the pros and cons of each alternative. Underlying the necessity for weighing each alternative is the basic proposition that *organizational behavior* is *systemic*. Every managerial action has more than one result. Any decision made in one part of the organization will have consequences, both intended and unintended, in other parts of the organization. One of the most difficult challenges facing any manager is to predict all the consequences of a given decision.

To illustrate the mental exercises required in the "weighing alternative" stage of the decision-making process, an actual decision faced by an advertising and sales promotion firm will be analyzed. Because of the embarrassing nature of this decision situation, the name of the firm and its client is disguised.

Allen Associates received a contract to supply Security Investment Corporation, a mutual fund, with 1000 vinyl carrying cases for its sales and managerial force. The words "Security Investment Corporation" were to be printed in gold on the front of each case. Shortly after the vinyl cases embossed in gold were delivered, a secretary in the client organization noted that the lettering read "Security Investor's Corporation." A representative from Security called Allen Associates, told

Decision Alternatives	Consequences	
	Positive	Negative
1. Allow mistake to stand.	(a) Profit margin will be retained. (b) Inconveniences of rework and frantic scheduling will be avoided.	(a) Client may refuse to pay or may sue for damages. (b) Client may accept decision but will be lost as potential future customer (c) Client may tell other potential customers that Allen is unreliable.
2. Print new set of cases.	(a) If completed on time client will be satisfied. (b) Quality reputation of Allen will be retained.	(a) Financial loss. (b) Rush scheduling may result in delays on other customers' jobs. (c) Company may appear too compliant to client. Could make future job negotiations difficult.
3. Grant client discount.	(a) Client will probably be placated. (b) Financial losses will be prevented. (c) Inconveniences of rework and frantic scheduling will be avoided.	(a) Profit from job will be eliminated. (b) Client will have use of cases, yet not pay fair price. (c) Company may appear too compliant to client. Could make future job negotiations difficult.

Figure 3.3 Rational analysis of decision-making alternatives.

them about the mistake, and said "Do you expect us to pay for this botch work? Our sales convention is ten days from now. What do you recommend?"

An analysis of the positive and negative consequences of three possible decisions by Allen Associates is summarized in Figure 3.3:

1. Allow the mistake to stand. Reason with the mutual fund company that it is too late to rectify the error.
2. Print a new set of vinyl cases and absorb the entire cost. (Cases embossed with another company's name have only salvage value.)

3. Ask the client to accept the shipment and offer them a discount price that will be high enough to cover costs of material, labor, and distribution.

Consequences presented in Figure 3.3 are illustrative, not exhaustive. Speculating on every potential consequence of this decision would encompass a wide range of rather trivial and minute considerations. For instance, rerunning the job would require additional output from the presses, thus shortening their useful life by the amount of time required to run the job.

MAKING THE CHOICE

Finally, someone has to gamble and make a decision. Assuming that the consequences of each alternative spelled out in Figure 3.3 are reasonably accurate, Allen Associates will have enough information to make a sound business decision. In this case illustration the firm chose alternative three—granting a discount as a penalty for the typographical error. Security Investment Corporation accepted this decision, and their sales representatives at this writing are still using the cases that read "Security Investor's Corporation." Allen Associates is now doing most of the printing and sales promotion work for Security. In this unique situation, the discount offered as a penalty payment proved to be a sound long-range business investment. Although less complex than many decisions faced in organizations, the Allen–Security incident illustrates two crucial behaviors that enter into making a final choice in a decision-making situation: establishing values and coping with ambiguity.

Ultimately, every important decision must be made on the basis of values, whether or not these values have been carefully thought through by the manager making the decision. Allen Associates placed a higher value on long-range customer good will than on short-range profit. Similarly, when an organization decides *not* to close a plant in a high unemployment town (although it would be more economical to relocate), it is placing more value on social concern than earnings per share.

Values do not inevitably connote social matters. Values play an important role in decision making, even when the issues are of a financial or business nature. Some multicompany organizations value return on invested capital more than product diversity. After having completed elaborate research into potential acquisitions, they will ultimately choose a company that holds promise of providing a predetermined rate of return on invested capital. All things being equal, another multicompany organization in the same situation might purchase a company that will put them in a new market. A well-known international company sought diversification into the education field. They were willing to pay a premium price for two educational companies, even though both companies had modest returns on investment; a higher value was placed on diversity and growth potential.

Coping with ambiguity is a vital aspect of managerial decision making. Even when decision alternatives are supported by charts, figures, and numbers, the decision maker is left with a feeling of ambiguity. Personnel decisions are the most ambiguous of all. Assume, for example, that an industrial psychologist told a company president that 70 percent of the time job enrichment increased the work motivation of production workers and that 80 percent of the time well-motivated workers were more productive. The president would have some probabilities as guidelines, but the decision "to enrich or not to enrich jobs" still has an element of uncertainty and ambiguity.

Decisions made by real estate developers, as another case in point, are fraught with ambiguity although quantitative data can be found upon which to base decisions. Urban planners provide real estate developers with impressive charts and graphs about population projections. Considerable information is also available about the present occupancy rate of local buildings, property taxes, and construction permits already applied for. Despite this abundance of information, the experienced real estate executive knows there is a high element of ambiguity in these figures. Often the really crucial information cannot be obtained. One such item of information is the frequency with which companies relocate administrative and manufacturing facilities. Such information is kept confidential until the last possible moment by companies contemplating relocation.

EVALUATION OF OUTCOMES

The final stage of the decision-making process can encompass a substantial portion of the knowledge worker's job. Answering the deceptively simple question, "How good (or bad) was the decision I made?" is a complex activity. Compounding the problem is the difficulty in establishing criteria by which the adequacy of managerial decisions can be judged. Evaluating outcomes of decisions is similar in scope to measuring managerial performance. Nevertheless, without some kind of accurate feedback, decision making can rarely be improved.

A major textile company in New York City made the decision to relocate its corporate offices to a small, nearby town in New Jersey. To evaluate the effectiveness of this decision, here are some of the outcomes that would have to be measured for both the short and long range:

1. What effects did relocation have on sales and costs?
2. How many key personnel were lost because of the move?
3. Is the effectiveness of the clerical labor pool better in that area of New Jersey than in New York City?
4. Has the corporate image improved because of relocation?
5. Are executives able to think more productively in their new environment?
6. Will the relocation assist in attracting new stockholders to the firm?

As described earlier, intervening variables influence every stage of the decision-making process. In the relocation of the textile firm, several intervening variables could have influenced the company president in question. *Emotional factors,* such as a distaste for New York City and positive attitudes toward New Jersey, might have been a major element in the decision to relocate. *Accurate information* about a more favorable tax structure in New Jersey than in New York may have influenced the decision. The dynamic, strong *personality* of the company president may have influenced subordinates to "tell him what he wanted to hear" about the advantages of relocation.

REPETITIVE DECISION MAKING

The decision-making process is not inevitably as complicated as that described by the Decision-Making Schema. Many routine, repetitive decisions are made by knowledge workers in every organization. As logic would suggest, the process of making a repetitive decision can be conceptualized in an easy to follow manner.

David L. Rados recently conducted research supporting the hypothesis that a two-step structure underlies the generation and selection of alternatives in repetitive decision making.[30] In step one, the decision maker generates and maintains a large, stable set of alternatives that are considered generally acceptable in the repetitive decision. In step two, a subset is chosen from the stable set, which narrows the number of alternatives. When the number of alternative solutions equals the number required by the decision, the decision maker accepts them (makes his or her decision). Creating the stable alternative list leads to economies in time. Without such a list (written or unwritten) considerable search would have to take place whenever the same decision situation reoccurred.[31]

G. P. E. Clarkson, in his book *Portfolio Selection*, explains how this two-step process works when investment offices face a stock purchase decision:[32]

> The basic list of stocks—the "B" List—that are considered to be suitable for trust investment by a particular bank will remain fairly stable over time, any changes being in the form of additions. Thus, for any given trust investor, the basic list of stocks from which he can choose is given to him by the historical record. At any particular point in time, an investor selects stocks from a subset of his basic list.

QUANTITATIVE DECISION MAKING

Comments made above about the ambiguity of managerial decision making even when quantitative data are employed do not discredit the contribution of management science. Most readers of this book undoubtedly have been (or shortly will be) broadly exposed to quantitative approaches to decision making. For this reason, and the fact that management science falls outside the scope of this book, quantitative approaches to decision making will only be briefly mentioned here. *Management: A Modern Approach*, by Martin K. Starr, is an exemplary treatment of this topic to which the interested reader might refer.[33] For now, the relationship of management science to the Decision-Making Schema will be explained.

First, it must be recognized that quantitative approaches to decision making are practiced more at lower than higher levels in the organization. Lower level decision making lends itself to quantitative analysis, while upper level decision making lends itself better to intuition and judgment.[34] To illustrate, quite specific information can be gathered to forecast how much computer time will be required to run a particular job on one computer versus another. Much less precise numerical data can be generated to forecast if one business machine will sell better than another one. Generalizing, it can be stated that management science-based input into the Decision-Making Schema is much more probable for lower level decisions. It has been predicted that, in the future, top management will make more extensive use of management science.[35]

Second, it can be argued that quantitative approaches to management are most applicable to the Decision-Making Schema at the "Intervening Variable *a*" and "Weighing Alternatives" stages. Thus, the impact of quantitative tools can be pervasive in the decision-making process. Assume that McDonald Hamburger was considering establishing three new locations in Toledo, Ohio. The contribution of operations research would be heroic in this instance if the following kinds of information could be accurately forecast:

1. Which are the three busiest streets in Toledo that are zoned for (but do not already have) a franchise, discount food chain?
2. At each of these three locations, what is the probability that a passerby will utilize a McDonald's restaurant?
3. Based upon experience in areas comparable to Toledo, to what extent would the opening of McDonald's create a demand for our food? How much of that demand will go to us versus competitors? (How many people seeing our sign will stop at a Carrol's?)
4. How much sales volume can we forecast for these three locations?

Answering these and similar questions accurately would improve the quality of decision making and lead to an *optimum* decision. Faced with decision-making stage four, "Making the Choice," the McDonald executive could reduce the ambiguity characteristic of most executive decisions.

Management science thus improves decision making by providing more accurate information upon which decisions can be based, and by analyzing information to make it more meaningful. Quantitative decision making, however, cannot (and does not intend to) overrule such factors as values in decision making. Assume that operations research suggested a location adjacent to a Howard Johnson's. The McDonald executive might "talk back to the computer" by making the value judgment that a McDonald's restaurant should not locate within a half mile of a Howard Johnson's.

Third, quantitative approaches to decision making have many subtle side effects in the total organizational system. In recent years attention has been devoted to the behavioral implications of management science and quantitative approaches to managerial decision making. L. S. Rosen and R. E. Schneck, for example, have summarized the behavioral dysfunctions of *information overload*. This term is defined as the amount of information input which exceeds the capacity of decision makers to adequately handle the information. Seven reactions to overload are quoted by Rosen and Schneck:[36]

(1) omission, failing to process some of the information;
(2) error, processing information incorrectly;
(3) queuing, delaying during periods of peak load in the hope of catching up during lulls;

(4) filtering, neglecting to process certain types of information, according to some scheme of priorities;

(5) approximation, or cutting categories of discrimination (a blanket and nonprecise way of responding);

(6) employing multiple channels, using parallel channels, as in decentralization; and

(7) escaping from the task.

DECISION MAKING AND THE ORGANIZATIONAL SYSTEM

Focus in this chapter has been on the decision-making processes of individuals. Decisions, however, are made within the context of the larger organizational system. Routine decision making may be carried out without approval from peers, superiors, or subordinates. Decisions that involve considerable innovation often meet resistance at all levels. (Chapter 11 examines this issue at length.) The organizational system has built-in subtle mechanisms that ward off some changes. For instance, an employee may be informed that although his or her suggested innovation appears to have merit, it will not be adopted because, "Although the present procedure isn't perfect, at least we are sure of its downside risks."

William G. Scott and Terence R. Mitchell have identified four systemic constraints on innovative changes recommended by individuals. Routine adjustments can be made by implementing existing programs. (A routine program is an established plan of action.) The quartet of constraints are presented next.[37]

First, the organization is unable to simultaneously adapt all aspects of its structure to change. Organizations, particularly when they are large, are cumbersome organisms. James G. March and Herbert A. Simon have noted that, for an organization to be adaptive, it requires some stable regulations and procedures that it can employ for carrying out its adaptive practices.[38] Innovation thus must proceed on a step-by-step basis throughout the organizational system. For instance, a New York textile company made the innovative decision to discourage accepting business from small clothing manufacturers. By the end of one year some salesmen were still selling to one or two small, long-term customers.

Second, innovation is limited by the range of information available in the system's memory. Organizations have vast storehouses of information accumulated that deal with problems solved in the past. Portions of this information are documented; other portions are found only in the memory banks of organizational members. Organizations may not implement innovative decisions or suggestions simply because their fund of knowledge for dealing with that idea is limited. For instance, an employee of a computer dating firm suggested to its owners that their best potential market was new arrivals in town who are divorced or separated. The proprietor agreed, but he did not have access to information about reaching these people.

Third, innovative suggestions ordinarily must fall within the scope of current policy. When an innovation suggested by an organizational member would violate existing policy if implemented, the organization will classify that innovative suggestion as "unusable." A behavioral scientist working for a large electronics firm provided management with a curious alternative to conducting another morale survey. His suggestion was to give every employee in the company ten dollars—the approximate per capita cost of conducting the survey. His hypothesis was that morale would more probably be increased this way than by conducting a survey and feeding back its results to employees. Management's principal objection was that his innovative suggestion was a "significant departure from company policy."

Fourth is the system's capacity to forget previously learned solutions to problems of change. According to Scott and Mitchell, this limitation implies that a system with too acute a memory might "narrow its behavioral choices to such an extent that innovation is stifled."[39] Old solutions to problems may be brought into play when the innovative solution offered by a given employee is optimum for the organization. "Here is how we used to handle that kind of problem" is an oft-repeated constraint on innovative decision making.

RELATIONSHIP TO CORE PROPOSITIONS

The process of decision making fits neatly into the framework for organizational behavior summarized by the four core propositions.

Human Behavior

Problem solving, problem finding, and decision making all closely follow the same psychological principles in and outside of organizational life. Ideas about the various stages in decision making apply to the solution of academic and business problems. For instance, the adverse influence of rigid mental set upon creativity applies equally well to business executives making product decisions and to college sophomores engaged in laboratory experiments.

To illustrate further, much of what is known about how people perceive according to need (selective perception) helps us to understand why so many decisions in organizational life disregard logical evidence. Executives, in general, may be more objective than most people, but they are not exempt from the influences of basic perceptual processes.

Situational Nature

Effective decision making is situational. Part of this core proposition was based on "the law of the situation," which implies that the exigencies of the situation should govern what type of orders are given. The Decision-Making Schema is highly situational. Most of the intervening variables in this model represent part of the decision-making situation. Characteristics of any decision (optimum, suboptimum, etc.) are influenced by such situational factors as the availability of accurate information and the personality characteristics of the decision maker. In short, it is difficult to imagine an effective decision that does not take situational variables into account.

Systemic Nature

The Decision-Making Schema, as alluded to earlier, is based on basic ideas borrowed from systems theory: inputs to the system are the problems to be solved; problems are processed through four stages (the fifth stage is a feedback mechanism); intervening variables influence the "processing of problems"; and outputs are the decisions reached.

Carrying this analogy further, any decision reached in an organization may have functional or dysfunctional consequences at other places in the organization. For example, a decision to tighten controls may breed newer, more innovative approaches to beating the system.

Structure and Process

To facilitate decision making (and to prevent chaos) most organizations establish standing plans and guidelines. To illustrate, a college might have the policy of lowering entrance qualifications once anticipated enrollment falls below a certain level. How quickly the college responds to this change will be a function of the interaction of the admissions office's ability to respond (are they intelligent, perceptive people, etc.) and the clarity of the policy statement. Decision making, in general, will be the most effective when flexible policies (structure) are implemented by capable people (process).

GUIDELINES FOR ACTION

1. Your chances of finding a problem or opportunity are enhanced when you immerse yourself in as much reliable information as you can find on that topic. This is true despite the valid counterargument that "sometimes you cannot see the forest for the trees." A subtle point is that you need all the data you can find (within time and budget constraints) but you have to be able to stand back and interpret its meaning.
2. Your decision-making ability will probably show improvement if you give careful attention to the five decision-making stages: clarification of the problem, finding creative alternatives, weighing alternatives, making the choice, and evaluating outcomes.
3. Emotional factors such as values, biases, and pet notions enter into almost any decision. You should search for and identify these when making any complex and important decision, to help discover *why* you chose the alternative you did.
4. One hopeful method of improving your creativity is to strive for more emotional looseness and flexibility in your approach to problems.
5. Self-discipline or "forcing yourself" to search for different alternatives to a problem is helpful in developing your creativity. Part of the benefits from creativity-inducing experiences such as brainstorming and synectics stem from forcing oneself to be creative.

QUESTIONS

1. You are awarded $50,000 in tax exempt money by SEE (The Society for the Encouragement of Entrepreneurs). Proceed with this hypothetical situation through the Decision-Making Schema. Be careful to include the influence of intervening variables.
2. How might being very intelligent and very well educated hamper decision making?
3. Name a satisficing decision that has been reached at your company or school. Why do you describe it as satisficing?
4. Does your present program of studies enhance or inhibit creativity? Discuss the evidence you have for your answer.
5. Problems of ecology, civil rights for blacks, and women's rights have received considerable attention in the past. What big problem do you think will be publicized next (Not including the energy crisis)?

NOTES

1. Donald W. Taylor, "Decision Making and Problem Solving," in James G. March (editor), *Handbook of Organizations.* Chicago: Rand McNally, 1965, pp. 48–86.
2. Robert W. Morrell, *Managerial Decision Making.* Milwaukee: Bruce, 1960, pp. 12–28.
3. William Emory and Powell Niland, *Making Management Decisions.* Boston: Houghton-Mifflin, 1968, pp. 12–15.
4. William H. Newman, Charles E. Summer, and E. Kirby Warren, *The Process of Management, Concepts, Behavior, and Practice,* third edition. Englewood Cliffs, N.J.: Prentice-Hall, 1972, Chapters 11, 12, 13, 14, 15.
5. Readers who wish to sample rigorous, algebraically-oriented approaches to the decision-making process might consult *Decision Sciences* (the journal for the American Institute for Decision Sciences).
6. Richard W. Pollay, "The Structure of Executive Decisions and Decision Times," *Administrative Science Quarterly,* Vol. 15, No. 4, December 1970, pp. 459–471.
7. William G. Scott and Terence R. Mitchell, *Organization Theory, A Structural and Behavioral Analysis,* revised edition. Homewood, Ill.: Richard D. Irwin and Dorsey Press, 1972, p. 171.
8. Alan C. Filley and Robert J. House, *Managerial Process and Organizational Behavior.* Glenview, Ill.: Scott, Foresman, 1969, p. 106.
9. Norman H. Mackworth, "Originality," in Dael Wolfle (editor), *The Discovery of Talent.* Cambridge, Mass.: Harvard University Press, 1969, p. 242 (reported in J. Sterling Livingston, "Myth of the Well-Educated Manager," *Harvard Business Review,* Vol. 49, No. 1, January–February 1971, p. 83).
10. Case report by John Gillis, Rochester Institute of Technology, March 1972.
11. *Ibid.*
12. Peter F. Drucker, *Managing for Results.* New York: Harper & Row, 1964, p. 5 [quoted in Livingston (note 9), *op. cit.,* p. 83].
13. *Ibid.*
14. *Ibid.*
15. Newman, Summer, and Warren, *op. cit.,* p. 250.
16. A good source of ideas about creative behavior is found in virtually any issue of the *Journal of Creative Behavior.*
17. "Behind the Auto Mask," *Time,* October 26, 1970, p. 63.
18. Donald W. MacKinnon, "The Nature and Nurture of Creative Talent," in *Readings in Managerial Psychology.* Chicago: University of Chicago Press, 1964, pp. 90–109.
19. *Ibid.,* p. 92.
20. *Ibid.,* pp. 95-102.
21. M. Gold, *Education of the Intellectually Gifted.* Columbus, Ohio: Merrill, 1965 (reported in James O. Whittaker, *Introduction to Psychology.* Philadelphia: Sanders, 1970, p. 397).
22. The influence of cultural relativity in regard to sex-linked fashion accessories is notable here. Lester M. Cone, Jr. notes that in Medellin, Colombia, South America, men have traditionally worn an over-the-shoulder bag.
23. Alex F. Osborn, *Applied Imagination,* revised edition. New York: Scribner, 1957.
24. Newman, Summer, and Warren, *op. cit.,* p. 276.
25. Marvin D. Dunnette, John Campbell, and Kay Jaastad, "The Effects of Group Participation on Brainstorming Effectiveness for Two Industrial Samples," *Journal of Applied Psychology,* Vol. 47, No. 1, February 1963, p. 31.
26. Gary A. Davis, "Review of William J. J. Gordon," *Synectics.* New York: Harper & Row, 1961, *Journal of Creative Behavior,* Vol. 1, No. 3, Summer 1961, p. 342.
27. Abraham H. Maslow, "A Holistic Approach to Creativity," in Calvin W. Taylor (editor), *Climate for Creativity.* Elmsford, N.Y.: Pergamon Press, 1972, pp. 287–293.

28. *Ibid.*, p. 290.
29. Jack R. Gibb, "Managing for Creativity in the Organization," in Taylor, *Climate for Creativity, op. cit.*, pp. 23–32.
30. David L. Rados, "Selection and Evaluation of Alternatives in Repetitive Decision Making," *Administrative Science Quarterly*, Vol. 17, No. 2, June 1972, pp. 196–204.
31. *Ibid.*, p. 196.
32. G. P. E. Clarkson, *Portfolio Selection: A Simulation of Trust Investment.* Englewood Cliffs, N.J.: Prentice-Hall, 1962, pp. 30–31.
33. Martin K. Starr, *Management: A Modern Approach.* New York: Harcourt Brace Jovanovich, 1971.
34. *Ibid.*, p. 121.
35. Andrew J. DuBrin, *The Practice of Managerial Psychology.* Elmsford, N.Y.: Pergamon Press, 1972, pp. 285–286.
36. L. S. Rosen and R. E. Schneck, "Some Behavioral Consequences of Accounting Measurement Systems," in William J. Bruns, Jr. and Don T. DeCoster (editors), *Accounting and Its Behavioral Implications.* New York: McGraw-Hill, 1969, p. 177.
37. Scott and Mitchell, *op. cit.*, pp. 177–178.
38. James G. March and Herbert A. Simon, *Organizations.* New York: Wiley, 1958, p. 53 (cited in Scott and Mitchell, *op. cit.*).
39. Scott and Mitchell, *op. cit.*, p. 178.

4

Stresses in Managerial and Professional Life

Feelings of conflict, frustration, disillusionment, apathy, indifference, dismay, and tension are familiar to large numbers of managers and professionals[1] in organizations. Underlying the mobility drives of many young people is the expectation that rewards will outweigh punishments once they achieve professional or managerial status. Anticipated is that the additional schooling and work effort required to achieve such levels of responsibility will yield higher levels of contentment with life. Unfortunately, the opposite is sometimes true. Managers and professionals find many stresses and strains in their lives. Jerome Steiner, a prominent New York City psychiatrist, recently made the following observation based upon his clinical experience with managers:[2]

> As today's business managers move into top executive positions, they become increasingly prone to interpersonal problems which are reflected in alcohol ingestion, marital instability, sexual maladjustment, and physical complaints that sometimes lead them fruitlessly from doctor to doctor.

This chapter focuses upon stresses experienced by individuals at the middle and upper levels of organizations. Problems to be described here go beyond minor job dissatisfactions and day-to-day inconveniences and disappointments. For instance, the business manager of a professional football team might complain that a sudden snowstorm has created problems for him in arranging transportation for the team. Job-related problems are present, but this is not a long-term stress situation. Similarly, the junior executive earning $17,000 per year in 1973 discovers that he and his wife are not saving money. They are concerned about this matter, but they do not perceive this lack of saving money as a stressful situation.

Business magazine coverage of this topic would suggest that managers and professionals experience more tension and anxiety now than they did in the past. "As a growing number of younger executives buckle under the pressures of job insecurity, personal problems, a rapidly changing society, stress appears to be the coming disease of civilization," proclaims a recent article in *Generation*.[3] George J. Berkwitt, observing the same phenomenon, notes that "The seeds of rebellion are spreading to the executive suite" in an article entitled "The Revolt of the Middle Managers."[4]

One major reason for devoting an entire chapter to the topic of managerial and professional stress (aside from its relevance to the knowledge worker) is the limited coverage this topic has received thus far in the scientific and professional literature. In contrast, the topic of discontentment, dissatisfaction, and pressures is widely discussed in the popular media and by knowledge workers and their spouses.

Stresses of managers and professionals will be examined from several dimensions. First, a model of organizational and individual adaptation to stress will be presented. Second, the symptoms and behaviors characteristic of managers and professionals under stress will be discussed. Third, forces that exert pressure or stress upon these people will be discussed. For clarity of presentation these forces are grouped broadly into organizational pressures and individual conflicts. Readers are cautioned that most stresses faced by managers and professionals are in reality a combination of individual conflicts and organizational pressures. Fourth, suggested remedial measures or antidotes to stress will be discussed.

RELATIONSHIP OF INDIVIDUAL AND ORGANIZATIONAL STRESS

Douglas T. Hall and Roger Mansfield have recently developed a systems model of the relationship between individual and organizational response to stress that integrates some of the ideas to be presented in this chapter.[5] This model is shown in Figure 4.1. *Stress*, in their conception, is an external force operating on a system, be that system an organization or a person. *Strain* is the change in the state of the internal system. (Stress and strain, thus, are not synonymous.) When individuals or organizations are subject to external stresses, it *may* lead to internal strains.

Organizational response to stress will change the organizational environment for the individual and may thus create strain for the individual. Stresses placed upon the organization thus may ultimately result in individual stress and strain. For example, a state-supported hospital may respond to budget cuts by not hiring replacements for many employees who leave through normal attrition. Employees will experience heavier workloads because a smaller number of people will be performing the same amount of work performed in the past by a larger number of people.

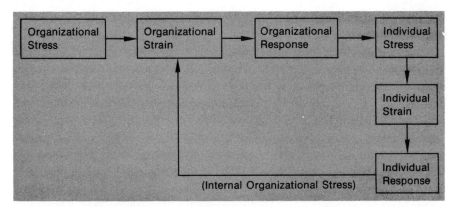

Figure 4.1 A model of organizational and individual adaptation to stress. (Reproduced with permission. Douglas T. Hall and Roger Mansfield, "Organizational and Individual Response to External Stress," *Administrative Science Quarterly*, Vol. 16, No. 4, December 1971, pp. 533–547.)

This increased workload may lead to strain for some people. Psychosomatic disorders (e.g., peptic ulcers) among some hospital employees can be traced to the intensification of anxiety created by budget cuts. Job insecurity is another potential response to the stress of budget cuts. A cautiousness about the consequences of making a mistake may lead to poorer organizational performance. Fewer people will be willing to risk implementing ideas that could prove costly to the organization if unsuccessful.

REACTIONS TO STRESS

Managers and professionals, similar to people in general, manifest a wide range of reactions to stress. The stress reaction of any single individual depends upon at least three sets of factors:

1. *His or her capacity to withstand stress.* For example, one marketing vice-president of a bank when told that he was fired stated simply, "Okay, I'll pick up my marbles and play this game someplace else." Within four weeks he secured a satisfactory position for himself. Another vice-president might react to the stress of being fired by excessive use of alcohol, marijuana, or other *chemical approaches* to problem solving.

2. *The magnitude of the stress exerted upon the individual.* Receiving a below-average performance appraisal would generally be considered a mild to average stress situation. Watching one's retail store burn down 20

days before Christmas, in contrast, might be classified as an above-average stress situation.

3. *Options available to the individual.* Sheri Montgomery is a fashion coordinator in a New York City store. Should job pressures mount, she has the option of leaving her job and finding employment elsewhere. Cindy Matthews is divorced, has three children, and works as a fashion coordinator in Grand Rapids, Michigan. Should job pressures mount, she will probably seek other approaches to dealing with stress than suddenly quitting her job. Fashion coordinator jobs are in short supply in Grand Rapids, and Cindy cannot risk unemployment. Instead, she might remain in her pressurized situation and project some of her anger onto children and friends.

Reactions to stress are usually complex and multiform. Under the stress of ambiguous job demands and a fatiguing work schedule, one executive might develop an ulcer, become defensive, and preoccupy himself with trivial job matters. Stress reactions are described one at a time here to provide the reader with a feel for the structural aspects of the subject and for ease of comprehension.

Normal Physiological Responses

Internal physiological changes are a universal reaction to stress. As stated by Hans Selye, the most widely quoted authority on stress reactions, "We can get high on our own stress hormones. Stress stimulates our glands to make hormones that can induce a kind of drunkenness."[6] More typically, the stress reaction takes place in three stages according to Selye's widely accepted *General Adaptation Syndrome*: (1) the alarm reaction, (2) the stage of resistance, and (3) the stage of exhaustion.

When the alarm is signaled, the body mobilizes its forces to combat the stress. Fatigue, for example, is a signal to the organism that stress is being exerted. If stress continues, the resistance stage comes to pass. An important part of the defense mechanism in the resistance stage is the pituitary gland, which produces ACTH, which in turn stimulates the adrenal cortex to produce adaptive hormones. Should these defenses overreact, bodily disturbances may occur. Hypertension and peptic ulcers are illustrative responses to such overreaction. When stress is prolonged and the body defenses are no longer adequate, the critical exhaustion stage is reached.

Psychosomatic Reactions

Frustration and anxiety resulting from stress are often taken out on the body in the form of psychosomatic reactions. Actual physical impairment results from emotional upset. Executives are subject to a wide range of psychosomatic reactions such as duodenal ulcer, hypertension, migraine, hay fever, colitis, dermatitis, and a host of allergies. Despite this awesome array of disorders, executives fare better than employees at the bottom of the organization with respect to mental health.[7]

Emotional Disorders

Anxiety in response to stress can be extreme enough to precipitate emotional disorder. Neurotic behavior patterns in response to pressure usually are found among individuals with a predisposition toward neurosis. For instance, a high strung, temperamental, and "nervous" individual might function quite adequately as a computer programmer until he or she is assigned a series of difficult programs to write under tight deadlines. Pressure of this type may precipitate the experiencing of severe anxiety attacks. The programmer and others might argue that job pressures "gave him a nervous breakdown," yet in reality his poorly developed ability to handle pressure is the root cause of his anxiety attack.

Psychotic reactions—bizarre behavior patterns characterized by a misinterpretation of reality—could conceivably be precipitated by job pressures, but only among the prepsychotic. One middle manager, later diagnosed as psychotic, exhibited the following behavior during a psychological examination. While he was taking self-administered tests, he wrote an "I love you" note to the female test administrator. After leaving the building, he was observed walking on a ledge with a 20-foot drop to the ground.

Alcoholism and Other Addictions

Alcoholism can be viewed as one more maladaptive response to stress; but again job pressures cannot be held responsible for the behavior of every alcoholic executive. Recent statistics suggest that about 2,000,000 workers in the United States are problem drinkers.[8] Managerial and professional personnel probably constitute about 100,000 of this figure. Aside from lost man-hours, poor health, and domestic problems, many faulty decisions are made under the influence of alcohol.

Dangerous drugs and marijuana are probably less frequently relied upon than alcohol as an escape from pressure by managers and professionals at this writing. It is conceivable that the next generation of managers and professionals will favor marijuana over whiskey as an escape mechanism. Robert D. Joyce describes an illustrative case where many technical errors in microfilming could be traced to drug usage by employees.[9]

Based on informal observations by the author, his students, and media coverage of the topic, drug usage is becoming more frequent among middle managers and white-collar personnel. One *Newsweek* article notes that on-the-job drug addiction among both blue- and white-collar workers has grown from a minor nuisance into a major dilemma. The reporter declares that "On Madison Avenue in New York, three advertising executives are caught shooting heroin in the men's room."[10]

Absenteeism

Stress is best escaped by absenting oneself from the source of the stressful situation. Absenteeism is thus another approach to coping with a stressful job. Part of the psychological dynamics underlying common colds, alcoholism, and minor psychosomatic disorders is the fact that these problems create conditions that legitimize being absent. Even the light headedness and dizzyness that characterize mild attacks of anxiety are sufficient to keep one home from a stressful job situation.

Defensive Behavior

Defense mechanisms are the universal response to anxiety and other uncomfortable feelings such as guilt and shame. Projection, rationalization, displacement, compensation, and the like are psychological terms that have become part of everyday language. Their purpose is to protect the ego. Robert H. Schaffer, a managerial psychologist, has developed an intriguing analysis of how defensive behavior relates specifically to executive life; illusion, denial, and xenophobia are the symptoms he cites.[11]

Illusion as a defense mechanism of managers is illustrated by the comment "I'm doing all I can in these circumstances," in response to criticism of his operation. Consultants frequently face this defensive maneuver when attempting to initiate changes. Managers are unconsciously saying, "Get away from me. Change is a painful, anxiety-provoking thing. If I tell the consultant that I'm already doing all I can, I won't be forced to make any more changes."

Denial of problems is sometimes used by managers to defend against the anxiety produced by a realistic assessment of the situation. Schaffer reports the following minicase to illustrate denial.[12]

> Even though a possibly competitive product was already being market tested, managers of one company convinced themselves that their key customers, many of years' standing, would never be so disloyal as to leave them.

Xenophobia (literally, hatred of foreigners) is another managerial defense mechanism. By the expedient of characterizing different business functions as "good guys" versus "bad guys" anxiety is reduced. Schaffer portrays executive xenophobia with the following statements made to a consultant:[13]

> "We're just not getting enough good products from R & D." The head of R & D told the consultant, "I can't set any directions for either our basic research or our product development because top management simply won't tell us where this company is supposed to be heading."

Preoccupation with Busywork

According to legend, Nero fiddled while Rome burned, and many managers expend time on unimportant matters while crucial problems go unresolved. Crucial problems are anxiety provoking and stressful; making decisions about office landscaping is less anxiety provoking than dealing with creditors. Managers looking for a behavioral escape from the stresses of dealing with important matters can find an ample number of trivial conferences to attend and unimportant memos to read and sort. In any large, complex organization, there are many lonely people eager to converse with managers about business-related, albeit unimportant, topics.

Schaffer describes *busyness* as the manager's "Linus Blanket." Busyness is an excellent defense against long-range planning. One of management's most frequent rationalizations is: "We've simply got to figure out how to get some time around here to do some more thinking and planning."[14]

Executive Flameout

Change is a source of stress for many people. "Flameout" is a term coined by Dr. Herbert Klemme, Director of Industrial Health at the Menninger Foundation, to describe the failure to adapt to change that sends many managers into active retirement at an early age.[15,16] Flameout is thus a behavioral escape from stress and another form of managerial obsolescence. The obsolete manager has withdrawn himself from the rigors of competition and adaptation to change. Managers become obsolete for a complex of reasons, some of which relate to factors not directly under their control. All situations of obsolescence are therefore not considered a behavioral escape from the rigors of change and competition.

Career Reorientation

Under ideal circumstances, a manager or professional person will react to the stress of his environment by finding a new career that he finds both less stressful and more rewarding. Few individuals in middle age have the courage or a life situation that enables them to make such a transition. Examples of second careers for managers and professional people of middle age are becoming more frequent. If the manager finding a new career is not merely bringing his personal problems to a new milieu, the *career reorientation* reaction to stress works effectively. Two representative vignettes of successful second careers are reported by Lewis E. Lachter in *Administrative Management.*[17]

> *Uses Experience to Help School.* Vice-President in charge of administration for a large southern textile manufacturer was a job that carried important responsibilities and a handsome paycheck. But this vp wasn't satisfied with his progress. He started a two year program to get his MBA at a local college. By the time he received his degree, he decided that his future was in education, not business. Today, this executive is dean of a business school at a small college in the south. "I believe the need for good administration is greater in educational institutions than in business," he says, "and I want to use my skills and 30 years of experience where they will count most. I've got a lot of ideas that will help this school, and the place is small enough for me to put my ideas into actual use."

> *Goes from 5 Day to 7 Day Week.* As controller for a large midwestern manufacturing firm, this executive was earning close to $30,000 a year. He worked hard, but at 5:30 p.m. he put on his hat and coat and went home. He rarely worked late, and Saturdays were out of the question. Today he owns a 30 unit motel near Chicago. His earnings were cut in half. He literally works seven days a week and sometimes close to 100 hours in those seven days. Why? "First of all I wanted to be my own boss. I'm paying for it, but I call all the shots around here. I don't commute into town anymore on an unreliable, uncomfortable train. My meals are home cooked, and I see my kids whenever I want to. I like to use my hands. There's plenty of opportunity for that. I also like to use my head, and taxes, payroll and purchasing keep my mind well-occupied. My schedule is getting better too, now that I can afford help."

ORGANIZATIONAL PRESSURES

Stress reactions, in the framework used in this book, result from the interaction between an individual's predisposition to stress and the force exerted by the environment. The term "environment" includes all factors and forces external to the individual. In this chapter, the organizational portion of the environment is emphasized. Other environmental forces contributing to stress of managerial and professional people include economic factors (e.g., recession and inflation), cultural values (e.g., success means movement up a hierarchy), and marital and family problems (e.g., my adolescent daughter is pregnant). Environmental factors such as general overcrowding and air, water, and sound pollution create stress for individuals. Stresses exerted by forces outside the job may have a spillover onto job behavior.

Neither organizational pressures nor individual conflicts exist in isolation. For example, *job insecurity,* one of the organizational pressures discussed in this section of the chapter, is much more of a threat to a psychologically insecure (or financially poor) individual than one who is self-confident (or financially rich). Eleven sources of managerial and professional stress are presented next; these are more nearly problems created by the organization than the product of individual conflicts or "hang-ups."

Underutilization of Abilities

Feelings of not being challenged, of one's intellectual abilities and formal education being wasted, and of being overqualified for present job responsibilities represent an omnipresent complaint of dissatisfied middle managers and professional people. The following statements made by a young research psychologist illustrate this type of organizational pressure.[18]

> I was hired here about one year ago for the purpose of conducting research on career adjustment problems of crippled people. The job sounded exciting. Not much solid research had been done in this area. One year later, I'm looking for a new job despite the fact that I've gotten a good salary increase and the director is satisfied. They won't let me do one worthwhile thing around here. In order to get a research project under way I have to write a 15-page proposal explaining what I will be doing and why I will be doing it. Then the proposal goes into committee and the administrators begin to argue about it. My second proposal was almost bought. But, finally, the agency head said my research implied that our agency was not already doing a competent job. He voted the proposal down. Now I'm back where I started looking for another research project that will be politically acceptable. Why was I hired in the first place?

Executives at high vantage point in an organization are also sometimes underutilized. Group vice-presidents, as a case in point, are executives in large multicompany organizations who supervise the activities of several company presidents. Some group vice-presidents and the company presidents who report to them, come to question the value of their function. Operations of the companies under their jurisdiction are directed by the company presidents, making the group vice-president a high-level staff advisor. Said one group executive to a former colleague, "I feel like a corporate *eunuch*. I no longer have as much power as I did when I was president of one of the divisions. Sometimes I wonder why the company created this position. You'll note that group vp's are the first to go in a recession."

Peter F. Drucker, perhaps the best publicized authority on management topics, feels that young people are critically underutilized in business, and that the picture for the forthcoming decade is even more pessimistic. He is quoted in an interview conducted for *Dun's Review* by Thomas J. Murray.[19]

And the young managers aren't really being given more authority, more complex jobs?

Don't believe anybody who tells you that jobs have become more complex. It just ain't true. Sure, the salaries have changed, and the titles, and the diploma one has to have. But the jobs have not been restructured. The trouble is that these young people—and many of my students among them—are hired with great expectations of challenging jobs, then dropped into training programs. They are given fancy titles and salaries and then given a file clerk's work. It serves no earthly purpose. It's work that doesn't have to be done.

Then the massive recruiting programs of the 1960's were really a big mistake?

The recruiting craze of the past ten years was insane. Nobody was asking, "How many do we need?" They were saying, "How many can we get?" Companies felt, rightly or wrongly, that they had to hire a good many of these well-trained young people, and raised their expectations with fairy tales about how every clerk is given a division to run. Now there are no jobs for them.

Job Insecurity

Traditionally, production workers were the first to be laid off during times of business downturn. More recently, top management has looked toward administrative and technical personnel as more dispensable than direct production workers, perhaps not without justification. As expressed by Drucker, "There is not one company I know of where a sharp cut in the number of executives wouldn't be a real improvement."[20] Fear of being fired thus poses another source of managerial stress to the manager and professional.

Conglomeration—jargon for the process of one company acquiring others—has created new job security threats for managerial personnel. Conglomerates, the companies that specialize in acquiring other companies, may not require the services of all the administrative staff working for the acquired company. An extra layer of management is often created by the acquisition process. Not atypical is the experience of Bill Bertrand, a labor relations executive.

> Bill Bertrand was the Corporate Vice-President of Labor Relations in Company A. His company was acquired by Company B. Unfortunately for Bill, Company B also had a Corporate Vice-President of Labor Relations. Both labor relations executives had ample size staffs reporting to them at division locations. Company A, prior to the acquisition, had received the usual reassurances that "The management teams of our acquired companies are left intact in order to ensure continuity in the management of the acquired companies. Deviations from this policy only take place under unusual circumstances." The circumstance of having two staff executives for industrial relations was considered unusual enough to deviate from policy. Bill Bertrand was fired, and explained to friends and prospective employers: "I've been a victim of *conglomeration.*"

Job insecurity has both psychological and financial roots. Loss of income, unpaid bills, and abandonment of luxury items constitute only part of the problem of a manager or professional being unemployed. Embarrassment, shame, and guilt are intertwined with the financial losses. Self-images in most cultures are in part dependent upon the type of work an individual performs. Unemployment thus weakens the self-image of those afflicted, according to a statement based on an interview with Harry Levinson:[21]

> And for the man who is fired, while the chances of him starving are nil, he is sure to lose face and confidence. He may feel compelled to switch careers, change his habits, reevaluate his own worth, strike a premature compromise with himself.

Uncertain Professional Status

Stresses created by underutilization of abilities and job insecurity contribute to feelings of uncertain professional status. An informal survey taken by this writer and his students enrolled in an MBA program suggests that many engineers, for example, question whether or not they should be classified as professionals. Bob Stedfield, the editor of *Machine Design,* has pointed out that, when unemployed, the engineer no longer feels like a professional; he is "just another guy out on the street hunting for a job."[22] One Hungarian engineer working in the United States commented, "In this country (United States) secretaries have more status than engineers. Nobody even talks to us."

Underlying the uncertain professional status of many professional-level workers, is the subtle fact that working for a nonprofessional automatically diminishes one's professional status. The employee who works for a large organization forfeits some of his identification with his primary professional group. For example, an attorney who works in the claims department of an insurance company will probably feel less professional status than his counterpart who works in a private law practice. Physicians, because they remain somewhat insulated from the rest of the organization even when employed full time by that organization, are better able to retain their professional status.

Insufficient Authority

Primers of management contend that authority should be commensurate with responsibility. Yet, this axiom is often violated in organization life. This discrepancy between power granted and power needed to accomplish a given task is a source of stress and frustration for many managers and professionals. Insufficient authority sometimes manifests itself in a manager not receiving the backing he needs from management to carry out its directives. Illustrative here is the experience of a production supervisor working for a commercial printer:

> Hank Parsons was responsible for one of the largest commercial printing operations in his city. Top management issued the directive that he cut operating costs by 25 percent in order to improve the firm's profit position. Parsons decided it was necessary to introduce two new pieces of labor-saving machinery to meet his cost-cutting objectives. The labor union objected to this machinery and expressed its dissatisfaction to top management. Hank Parsons was "called on the carpet" by his superiors, who wanted costs trimmed but were unwilling to accept strife from below. Parsons felt that management had placed him in the untenable position of not having sufficient power to carry out his responsibility.

Budget control is another key area in which the discrepancy between responsibility and authority creates stress—or at least aggravation—for many managers. Particularly vexing to some people is the lack of authority to expend funds that are already within their budgets. Reacting to the problem of budget control, one manager in a food products company made these comments:[23]

> If we're going to be given budget responsibility, we ought to be given the authority to exercise the judgments we've made on a present budget. If I've budgeted $500 for the quarterly period for travel, I ought to be able to use it.

Exorbitant Work Demands

Executives, many middle managers, and some professional employees often find themselves faced with a punishing workload. (This is not to deny that many such people use busy work schedules as a defense against having to deal with family problems.) Tightly scheduled work days, heavy travel, and simultaneous demands exert considerable stress. Work weeks of 60 hours or longer are not uncommon in management positions in business and some governmental and educational institutions. An article in *Time* suggests that it is not atypical for an executive to fly over 100,000 miles annually in conjunction with business.[24]

Fragmentation of a manager's time is an acute source of stress. George J. Berkwitt has observed that an executive in charge of a division may answer for the success or failure of 101 simultaneous projects, problems, and operations.[25] Constant interruptions characterize the executive's day. "I change hats every ten minutes," one financial vice-president reported to Berkwitt. "I act as a tax specialist for a while, a manager for the next few minutes, then a banker, a personnel specialist, and so on." Data such as these led Berkwitt to conclude:[26]

> ... What gives his job its nightmarish quality are the interruptions—the constant and seemingly endless telephone calls, sudden meetings and personnel problems that seem demonically designed to run his schedule off the track.

In an attempt to cope with the multiple demands and interruptions, many managers opt to perform their "paper work" at home. Familiar is the manager's lament that he devotes most weekday nights at home to cleaning out his in-basket. This approach to time management succeeds in freeing much of the workday for people-contact activities but creates stresses on most family situations. Stress sources are thus not eliminated but are displaced from the office to the home.[27]

Conflict Within Organizations

Intergroup and interpersonal conflict is an inevitable part of organizational life. Whenever individuals or groups of individuals compete for a limited supply of resources, some degree of conflict ensues. Conflict between groups is given separate attention in Chapter 10, and some aspects of conflicts between individuals competing for promotion is discussed in Chapter 5. The key point to be underscored in the present chapter is that prolonged and intense conflict has negative consequences for many individuals. Mental health can suffer when organizational conflict reaches a critical point. Each individual has his own level of frustration tolerance.

Prolonged conflict between production and engineering may precipitate ulcers in the production manager, while the engineering manager may look upon the same conflict as an intriguing game—a fringe benefit of belonging to a complex organization. A personnel manager describes the stress he was subjected to before he resigned to find a less conflictual environment:

> This was absolutely the worst place I have ever heard of. The working conditions were horrible. I pitied the lungs of the people we had working here. That black dust would kill anybody. One of my jobs was to recruit workers for the mill. We paid the bottom wages in the area, so we had to hire from the bottom of the labor pool. Many of the employees were old world people who could hardly speak English, but they were human beings and had common sense. After a while they would complain through their representative or quit outright. The plant superintendent would accuse me of not knowing my job because we couldn't keep a full labor force. Whenever I made suggestions about improving working conditions my boss would accuse me of being a union sympathizer or one of those soft-headed professor types. I just gave up. The job was ruining my mental health.

Conflict in any organizational environment can also be generated by *role ambiguity*. Studies by Robert L. Kahn have documented the discrepancy that exists between what people in organizations think they should be doing and what their subordinates think they should be doing.[28] As summarized by Levinson, "most of the people in that research project said they were not sure what they were supposed to do and what was expected of them."[29] Ambiguity, or lack of structure, makes most people anxious. Among the stress responses noted in this study were apathy, withdrawal, anger, and passing the buck.

Roles that demand creative problem solving according to Kahn also carry a high degree of role conflict and tension. Creative people are constantly battling more conventional thinkers who want to protect the status quo. Additionally, creative people find paper work and routine office-administrative tasks to be a source of conflict and tension. "Paper work, they say, is time-consuming, disrupts their creative work, and is generally unpalatable."[30] This type of conflict is also found in university settings. Professors with strong teaching, research, and writing interests who are promoted to administrative positions, often later ask to be reassigned to teaching. According to the value systems of these professors, research, writing, and teaching are more creative (and less anxiety provoking) than administrative work.

Large Organization Pettiness

Asked why he was so upset and tense, the management trainee told the industrial psychologist, "It's the chicken-shit around here that has driven me out of my tree." Expressed in the jargon of the management theorist, this young man is reacting to the stress created by a multitude of rules and regulations whose contribution to organizational goals is not apparent to organization members.

Berkwitt, in an insightful yet subjective analysis, contends that what most younger middle managers object to are the small, put-down type of practices indulged in by many corporations. Among the anecdotes provided by Berkwitt is the tale of a company executive who was transferred to headquarters from an out-of-state location:[31]

> First of all, the executive was given a small private office with a window—only to be told shortly after that it was a mistake: His rank did not entitle him to such a perquisite. So he was moved to a slightly larger office that he had to share with two other managers. Then when he moved to the new office, he took with him a metal-trimmed blotter. This was also taboo. A few days later, a senior executive visiting the office spotted the blotter and summarily ordered him to surrender it. It was, he was informed, an "executive blotter." The following morning he received an ordinary blotter. "Somehow," he related, "I kept thinking of Captain Queeg."

Younger people, many of whom are less impressed by considerations of status and rank, find such practices anxiety provoking and stressful. Older organization members, in contrast, are more culturally conditioned to accept rank and status. *Violation* of these customs creates tension and stress for them.

Information Stress

Computers and copying machines are not without dysfunctional consequences in terms of creating stress for managerial and professional personnel. In-baskets have reached an untenable size for many managers and professionals. More information is available to read than most managers have the time or desire to read. Added to this burden are business letters, intracompany memoranda, telephone calls, trade and technical journals, and normal newspaper reading. *Generation* magazine calls this form of overstimulation, decision stress: "The barrage of information and number of alternatives provided by computers alone can drive an executive into a corner."[32]

Large numbers of managers today either possess a technical background or supervise technical personnel, creating an obligation to maintain some degree of technical proficiency. (The term "technical" in this context relates to specific knowledge about any discipline, whether it relates to physical science, behavioral science, or business methods. Data processing and manager development, for example, are both fields with technologies of their own.) Movement from one position to another intensifies information stress. The mobile manager must quickly be conversant with the technology of a new or slightly different discipline.

"Instant experts"—those who have just read a general article about a technical field on how to maximize benefits from a technology—contribute to information stress. After the top management instant expert has read such an article, a middle manager is asked to explain why a competitive company has reduced costs or made profits implementing a particular modern development. Instant experts are armed with just enough jargon and generalizations to ask astute questions but not to comprehend an in-depth analysis of why a particular innovation won't fit the situation at hand.[33]

Information stress permeates all levels of management. Computer printouts and photocopied memoranda deluge all levels of management. Top management thus receives a smattering of knowledge about most company functions and can frustrate managers below them with embarrassing questions based upon their superficial knowledge. Middle managers and professional personnel are thus forced into playing the new organizational game "Guess what the boss will ask?" which creates another source of stress.

Pressures Toward Conformity

Individuals show wide variation in their willingness to conform to a norm established by the organization. For some individuals the pressure to conform represents a stress in their lives. Many managers and professional people, to cite one illustration, object to the pressures placed upon them to contribute to the Community Chest. Donations, under these circumstances, cease to be voluntary. An accountant relates how his organization pressures individuals into obeying parking regulations even when nonconformance to these rules would seem to be the solution of choice:

> When the accumulation of snow was heavy, a major part of the parking lot was used to stack the snow. This meant that the number of parking spaces was substantially reduced. To further aggravate the situation, people parked farther apart during periods of heavy snow-

fall. One day I arrived late and discovered that no parking space was left. I decided to park in the visitor's lot, even though this is illegal from the company standpoint. Here's how the company decided to punish me: A few days later a memo was circulated through my chain of command informing everybody that I had broken a rule. The whole thing embarrassed me and made me defend my actions to a whole bunch of people. I was quite ticked off about the whole incident.

Pressures also exist for organizational members to reshape or accommodate their ideas and suggestions to those of their superiors. This represents a more acute source of stress for some people than does conformity in behavior. Creative suggestions are frequently subjected to review by a wide range of people before they can be implemented. Several groups typically add their input to the original suggestion. Stress, or at least job dissatisfaction, can be the result when an original idea is watered down through the process of committee review. According to one young professional in an organization: "Each compromise, each appeasement, and each wording change to satisfy somebody (the infamous 'they') withdraws a little something from your bank of ambition."[34]

Job Design and Technical Problems

Pressures placed upon individuals discussed so far have dealt primarily with psychological and sociological factors and managerial practices. There also exists within any organization a vast source of stress centering around problems of organizational structure and technology. Automobile dealers, to cite one illustration, are subject to considerable stress when customers complain about the reliability of automobiles. These same automobile dealers have almost no control over the quality of automobiles purchased from the company. Similarly, there are several jobs in almost any organization that are inherently stressful—often with full awareness on the part of management and the employee. Collection agents for private finance companies rarely have a day that is not stressful. Reservation clerks in hotels or airlines must also learn to accept stress as part of their work routine.

Cataloguing the myriad ways in which job design, organizational structure, or technical errors can create stress for the individual goes beyond the scope and intent of this chapter. David R. Hampton, Charles E. Summer, and Ross A. Webber present an in-depth analysis of how faulty work design causes stress.[35] Among their key points is that stress created by an organization should be analyzed from the standpoint of the actual interaction patterns that take place between and among individuals. You will be under stress, for example, if your boss gives you orders and directions but you have no opportunity to initiate communication with him.

Inappropriate Leadership Style

Under extreme circumstances, the leadership style of a superior can create stress for a subordinate. An authoritarian and hostile leader might create more psychological pressure on a given individual than that person can comfortably handle. Moving to the other extreme, a superior who employs a *laissez-faire*, nondirective leadership style might create stress for an individual who is dependent upon structure. In general, autocratic managers create more stress upon subordinates than do permissive managers. Lester M. Cone, Jr. has summarized the potential adverse effects of an autocratic leadership style on individual development:[36]

> Much management literature indicates that any management style which does not aid in the process of self-actualization, and that creates submissiveness or dependency, is not as effective as one that focuses on utilizing the full capabilities of the individual, and promotes his growth through psychological success, achievement, and work commensurate with his capabilities.

INDIVIDUAL CONFLICTS

The seven stresses to be described next stem from conflicts that are *more nearly* a product of the individual's internal conflicts or perceptions than they are a product of organizational pressures. Assume that a young man conducts market research for an air conditioning company. Gradually he develops a mild stress reaction because his perception is that such activity lacks relevance. Defining relevance, of course, is a value judgment. Air conditioning, to many of its users, has considerable relevance because it satisfies their needs for comfort. For those unable to tolerate excessive heat and humidity, air conditioning might even prevent heart disorder. The organization has assigned the market research analyst work that lacks relevance for him but not necessarily for others. This issue will be examined further.

Lack of Relevance

Ideals have a strong enough impact upon the psyche to cause stress for some individuals when these ideals cannot be reached. Many managerial and professional people have developed a set of ideals which, as mentioned above, lead them to interpret their work in corporate life as lacking *relevance*. According to one General Electric psychologist, young managers are searching for "an opportunity for impact."[37] Today's young businessman, as interpreted by a variety of other observers, insists on meaning and a sense of social responsibility in his job and life in general. Judson Gooding, in a *Fortune* article, reports that younger managers want to improve the environment and society. Significantly, they insist that their companies work actively toward such goals.[38] Presumably, those more committed individuals suffer actual frustration and stress when their organizations do not comply. Corporations are expected by this new breed of managers to sanction socially relevant activities with financial support or through time off from the job.

Fortune contends that corporations face unprecedented demands from junior executives who want to "reform the world on company time."[39] Exemplary of this trend are the efforts of Michael Ghelardi, a 27-year-old assistant product manager at Lever Brothers. Ghelardi founded a Harlem limousine business in which drivers share the ownership. In addition, he helped organize a community action council in the Yorkville area of Manhattan to combat drug abuse and improve housing and local education.

Underlying the attempts of many executives, middle managers, and professional people to find teaching positions is a quest for work they perceive as relevant. Again, relevance is a value judgment. The individual manager who was managing a manufacturing department must decide for himself whether that work is less relevant than teaching manufacturing management to college students.

Frustrated Ambitions

Cultural pressures dictate—perhaps more so in the recent past than in the present—that members of hierarchical organizations must keep pushing toward a higher position on the corporate ladder. Maintaining yourself at a comfortable plateau, or being demoted, is thus interpreted as failure. Frustrated ambitions and goals are the cause of many psychosomatic reactions. Men and women suffer psychological stress from failure to be promoted even when their financial needs are satisfied at their present level of responsibility. Equally important, many managers experience feelings of failure about not being promoted even when they are poorly qualified for their present responsibilities.

Aspirants to greater responsibility far outnumber the positions of responsibility available; "the race to the top" is intensely competitive.

Levinson has analyzed some of the sources of tension that are created by this emphasis on vertical mobility.[40]

Change in social status creates an unusual type of stress for many individuals. Promotion that results in a new life style for a manager also carries with it an element of cultural shock. Blue-collar workers who work their way into managerial positions are particularly subject to this source of stress.[41]

> ... Put in simplest terms, a man who uses grammar incorrectly may fit well among blue-collar workers, but that deficiency may make him feel inadequate among his managerial colleagues. Not only are there different forms of speaking among various social classes within the same culture, but also what constitutes acceptable behavior varies widely. The glibness of a salesman, and his hail-fellow-well-met manner, so necessary to the selling task, may be viewed as lack of dignity in executive circles.

Blocked routes create another source of stress for the young manager. Factors that lie outside of a manager or professional person's competence may create roadblocks to his progress. Side roads may detour a man's progress and obstructions created by unpromotable superiors are two such examples. One detour cited by Levinson is to be assigned to a department or activity that is not in the main thrust of the organization, such as a warehouse or purchasing department. Politically astute managers, as described in Chapter 5, attempt to avoid such blocked routes.

Symbolic deprivation is a term Levinson uses to identify the unconscious source of tension that occurs when the organization disappoints a manager's expectations of being cared for by management. According to this concept, the organization is symbolically a "good father." Should the hard-working junior executive abide by the formal and informal organizational rules and then fail to be promoted, he feels unappreciated, unrecognized, and unrewarded for his efforts. Unconsciously, he may feel deprived by an untrustworthy father. Owing to its unconscious nature, this concept is difficult to verify empirically, but it remains an intriguing hypothesis.

Obsessive Concern for Work

Desires for vertical mobility sometimes reach obsessive proportions. Individuals obsessed with work operate under a high level of stress, pressure, and conflict. Time and effort expended by these people on their jobs far exceed the demands placed upon them by the organization. Obsessive devotion to work does not inevitably lead to the most productive output. Neurotic conflicts may interfere with, rather than enhance, some types of business decisions or creative effort. The tragic case of R.B., prepared by Albert Porter, Arthur F. Menton, and Seymour Halpern, illustrates the extremes that can be reached when sufficient pressure is applied on maladjusted men.[42]

> ... R.B. was a rising executive in his mid-thirties. Married, with three children, he lived in one of the wealthier New York suburbs and was active in civic and church groups. Already director of marketing in a large consumer products company, it appeared that R.B. was destined for a much higher position. At this stage, R.B. and his family appeared to be the epitome of the American dream. Closer scrutiny, unfortunately, would have revealed overextended financial commitments, inability to manage mundane daily affairs, and a lack of communication with the family. These conditions existed because R.B. had no time for his family except in those activities which complimented his drive towards the top of his organization.
>
> When a wrong decision by R.B. resulted in the loss of several accounts, he became erratic in his business dealings. Younger men within the company started challenging him, though he was but 38. Under increasing pressure, R.B. began to lose confidence. He was no longer able to charm upper management nor effectively consummate deals with clients. Finally, he was relieved of his job. By this time, he was in severe financial trouble and it seemed that no amount of hard work could extricate him from his plight. Unable to withstand further pressure and lacking support at home, R.B. committed suicide by asphyxiation.

Career Versus Family Demands

Work addicts, of the nature just described, experience conflicts to some extent because personal and family life interfere with their work. Many more managers and professional people experience conflicts because work and family place overlapping demands upon their time. Conflict occurs because the person wants to devote adequate attention to both family and work. Demands placed upon many managers can be excessive, but the individual—more often than he is willing to admit—can opt for a position of lesser responsibility. Frequently, this transition can be made with scaling down one's standard of living. "If you can't stand the heat, get out of the kitchen" is the cliché offered managers who complain about excessive work demands by one corporate director of personnel.

Managers and professional people, successful in their careers, frequently do not realize the psychological problems they create for their wives or girlfriends. Wives of successful husbands often develop feelings of anger and resentment toward their husbands because of their career involvement. Feelings of aloneness, boredom, and self-doubt are common to many women married to busy, involved executives.[43] Extramarital affairs are a frequent countermaneuver by the wife, jealous of her husband's work involvement. This behavior, if discovered, creates more conflict and stress for the husband.

Threats from Below

Many readers of this book pose a threat to the psychological well-being of the older generation of managers. Research conducted by my students suggests that younger men armed with modern management decision-making tools are perceived as a threat by managers above them in the organizational hierarchy. This feeling is cogently expressed by one 41-year-old financial manager:

> You aspire all your life to the mahogany paneled office. When you finally get close enough to taste success, they tear out the paneling and put a computer and a damn MBA in the space.

Harry Levinson candidly comments about the psychological stress younger people create for older executives:[44]

> *Generation*: What effect does the emphasis on youth play on the executive today?

> *Levinson*: It makes him as mad as hell. All adults are mad at youth because they have so much—so much money, so much sex, and so much fun. They don't understand the other side of youth. They are angry that they were born 40 years ago. They don't understand why kids don't laugh, why there is unhappiness today. They regret their lost youth and need help to understand today's youth and the emphasis on youth.

Intertwined with feelings of resentment toward youth is the widespread belief among executives that professional and managerial personnel of the future are effectively trained and educated. Mack Hanan contends that he knows of no chief executive who is not convinced that the managers of tomorrow will equal or surpass the performance of their most distinguished predecessors.[45] Older executives forced to compete with these younger people for key positions will be subject to more than a modicum of psychological stress.

The magnitude of this stress will vary with the level of emotional security felt by each executive. Middle-aged managers approaching obsolescence because of limited job knowledge and problem-solving ability will be subject to high stress. Few competent, knowledgeable executives have immediate worry about being replaced in the near future by a 23-year-old MBA graduate.

Middle-Aged Crisis

Stress directly traceable to having reached middle age and failed to achieve career goals is experienced by an unknown number of managers and professional people. "It's depressing to know that I'm no longer a young man with potential. I'm kind of a middle-aged nobody now," commented a laboratory group leader. Levinson uses age 35 as the entry point into middle age. By this age in life most men have enough data to make a realistic assessment of their success and failure pattern in life. The same author reports some research that provides insight into the middle-aged crisis:[46]

> Lee Stockford of the California Institute of Technology reports from his survey of 1,100 men that about five out of six men in professional and managerial positions undergo a period of frustration in their middle thirties and that one in six never fully recovers from it. Stockford attributes the crisis to a different kind of frustration: "This is the critical age—the mid-30's—when a man comes face to face with reality and finds that reality doesn't measure up to his dreams."

Machiavellianism and Job Strain

Behavioral scientists have in recent years conducted research about the ramifications of Machiavellianism in organizational life. According to a scale developed by R. Christie, people with a high Machiavellian orientation tend to manipulate others more, win more, and persuade others more than their counterparts with a low Machiavellian orientation.[47] Gary R. Gemmil and W. J. Heisler conducted research with 150 managers in a manufacturing firm, showing that Machiavellian orientation is positively associated with job strain.[48] Apparently, manipulating others in a work environment predisposes one to experiencing strain.

Here is an example of the relationship between Machiavellian orientation and job strain. In the research under discussion, a manager who responds "No" to question A, will probably respond "Yes" to question B:

A. I allow subordinates to participate in organizational goal setting.
B. I think somebody else may get the job for which I am directly in line.

PREVENTION OF DYSFUNCTIONAL STRESS

Stress in moderate amounts has positive consequences to individuals and the organization. Anxiety—the typical response to stress—in moderate amounts improves the performance of most tasks. One product manager pitted against another in competition to earn a larger share of the market may exhibit more imagination and drive than if such competition did not exist. Even at a physiological level, an element of stress prepares the body for elevated performance. Hopefully, the football quarterback will manifest some internal physiological changes to better prepare him for the rigors of the game. Dysfunctional consequences of stress, by definition, are stress reactions that have a negative impact on individuals and organizations.

Presented next are five broad strategies useful in preventing situations that breed dysfunctional stress: (a) practice good management, (b) create meaningful jobs, (c) modify organizational structure, (d) strengthen your personal qualifications, and (e) practice good mental health. These five strategies are neither exhaustive nor comprehensive. Almost any positive, constructive intervention by management, employees, stockholders, or consultants could result in reduced stress for some person somewhere in the organization. To cite one remote example, should an outside investor purchase three million dollars of stock in a small company, top management will automatically experience less stress in its role. Financial problems can reach stressful proportions; three million dollars is a powerful antidote for many problems.

Practice Good Management

Many of the sources of stress described in this chapter could be prevented by an appeal to "common sense" or generally accepted management principles. Research about the validity of management principles is in scant supply but, as shown by Rollin H. Simonds, they are still widely practiced by effective, on-going organizations.[49] Several volumes could be written about the application of good management principles in the reduction of stress. Two conceptual examples will suffice to illustrate how the application of sound management principles can reduce stress.

Stress reactions may occur when an individual has no control over people for whose work he is responsible—i.e., when his authority is not commensurate with responsibility. As mentioned earlier, the most casual observer of organizations will find many instances in which there is a serious gap between what a person is asked to accomplish and the authority given him to get it accomplished. Presumably, following the "authority–responsibility" principle would prevent many instances of stress.

Axiomatic to good personnel management is the placement of people in positions for which they are neither over- nor underqualified. Several of the sources of stress described above result from selection and placement errors. Mention was made of the stress that results when professional people are given assignments better suited to the qualifications of technicians or clerks. Adherence to elemental principles of selection would have avoided this problem and eliminated a source of stress.

Create Meaningful Jobs

Work has become an area in life in which most professional and managerial personnel seek satisfaction of higher level needs, as discussed in Chapter 2. "My managers expect more out of their jobs than they do out of their marriages" one company president humorously, yet insightfully, commented. Given such high expectations, frustration and stress result for many individuals when their work fails to satisfy higher level needs.

Resistance to the effects of certain forms of stress is likely to be higher when an individual is committed to his work. The product manager, for example, who has lived with his product from the concept to the distribution stage may be able to withstand adverse heavy travel and long hours because of his job commitment. In contrast, the computer operations manager may find irregular work demands stressful because he is continually working on "other people's problems."

Modify Organizational Structure

Subdividing a large complex organization into smaller entrepreneurial units is an extreme, albeit desirable, approach for enhancing work satisfaction of middle managers. One less grandiose alternative is the creation of task teams. These organizational subunits are often found helpful in raising morale and fostering a sense of identification with other team members. Hanan has recommended this approach in order that top management "make way for the new organization man."[50]

Stress can also be reduced through the simple expedient of modifying organizational structures that are inherently stressful. Ralph Fram's situation is illustrative:

> Fram is the district sales manager for a building materials company. Ten salesmen report directly to him; most of them require considerable guidance, training, and emotional support. Ralph began to feel that the demands of the job were more than he could handle. His primary complaint was about contradictory demands. As branch manager, he was expected to give final approval on all quotations given to customers, tend to minor administrative matters, and work with the salesmen—including visiting key customers. Fram lamented, "It's incredible. I just

127

can't get to my paper work. Planning and budgeting are just not possible. The salesmen and customers have to come first."

Stress impinging upon Ralph Fram was reduced by upgrading one of the salesmen to field sales manager. His responsibilities focused on the management of salesmen. Fram then functioned as the planner, controller, and organizer, while the field sales manager carried out the direct leadership role.

Few organizational problems lend themselves so readily to solution, but the principle illustrated here is crucial: Interaction patterns that create stress "interruptions" from salesmen while Ralph Fram was trying to accomplish his paper work should be modified to less stressful interaction patterns (the field sales manager perceives contact with salesmen as his primary responsibility rather than as "interruptions").

Strengthen Your Personal Qualifications

Countless managers and professional people remain under stress in their organizations because their options are limited. Those who complain bitterly about undercompensation, underutilization, and underappreciation cannot rightfully blame management for all their problems. Individuals placed under such stress have three alternatives: (a) wait for a transfer or promotion, (b) make a dramatic demonstration of worth to management, or (c) find a less stressful job in another company. Exercising these options, however, is not easy for everybody. In general, those individuals with the strongest qualifications have more options available to them. During a recession, for example, there are still some managers and professional people who voluntarily quit their jobs and find a more rewarding situation elsewhere.

Practice Good Mental Health

Dysfunctional effects of stress can be reduced or minimized to the extent that an individual has strong psychological adjustment. Managers and professional people sometimes neglect those practices in life that tend to improve personal adjustment and enhance mental health. Lawrence F. Shaffer and Edward J. Shoben, Jr., two psychologists, formulated a list of eight conditions for mental health that have withstood the test of time.[51] They are presented here in brief to provide some approximate guidelines for increasing resistance to stress. These principles do not invariably bring improved mental health to their adherents, nor are they easy to follow in the press of everyday activities.

1. *Good physical health* increases a person's resistance to both physical and psychological stress. The junior executive who is well rested, well fed, and obtains vigorous physical exercise can more readily cope with the "gaff" in his organization than his physically unfit counterpart.

2. *Accepting yourself* contributes markedly to good mental health. Managers who accept themselves can better accept subordinates. Self-acceptance does not infer a smug complacency (which blocks personal growth), but it does imply a realistic acceptance of one's own strengths and limitations. *Phoniness*, or self-deception, may increase a person's susceptibility to the negative effects of stress because of the mental energy required to maintain such a set of false beliefs.

3. *Maintaining a confidential relationship* is one of the most effective ways of both preventing and combating dysfunctional effects of stress and pressure. Discussing a stressful situation, such as a recent demotion you received with a person you trust, contributes to sound mental health. Confidantes (whether they take the form of wife, husband, friend, bartender, lawyer, or psychotherapist) play a vital role in helping a person combat anxiety and tension. Large numbers of business executives hire consulting psychologists primarily to function as sounding boards or sympathetic listeners.

4. *Constructive action must be taken* in order to overcome the effects of stress or eliminate its source. Admittedly, if a chemist feels grossly under-utilized in his job and is anxious because of it, he will derive some benefit from discussing his problem with a confidante; however, to deal effectively with the problem he must do something constructive. Presenting a concrete proposal to his superiors describing how his talents could be better utilized is one example of constructive action.

5. *Interaction with people* in addition to those with whom you are forced to interact at work tends to influence mental health in a positive direction. Placed in a group setting, people tend to be less preoccupied with their personal concerns. Managers and professional people who take the opportunity to interact with people without rehashing business problems are practicing good mental health.

6. *Creative experience* serves as another contributor to mental health. Each individual arrives at a personal definition of creativity, but one component is common to all creative experience. Vocational or avocational activities that provide the opportunity for an individual to choose the task and establish goals are creative in nature. Opportunities for creative experience do not abound in the life of every manager and professional; but each manager or professional can search out opportunities for creative input. Almost any nonautomated job in an organization can profit from an

innovative approach. Faced with declining rentals, a manager of an apartment complex offered present tenants a $25 prize for each referral that culminated in a signed lease. The manager in question was rewarded for his innovation by increased rentals and satisfaction in having produced a workable idea.

7. *Meaningful work* as a contributor to mental health is psychologically related to creative experience. As described earlier, many of the stresses faced in managerial and professional life could be prevented or alleviated by providing more people with opportunities for meaningful work.

8. *Using the scientific method* to solve personal problems is a generalized approach to coping with anxiety, tension, and stress.

> Judy Wilson, a personnel manager in a department store, decides that her present position inhibits her career development. Gradually she becomes preoccupied with this concern. First, she gathers data to carefully define the problem. For example, Judy asks management what her chances for advancement are in the store, and she investigates how much progress other women have made there. Second, Judy formulates the hypothesis that her store provides less opportunity for women than do other organizations in the area. Third, she discreetly canvasses the opportunities offered women in competitive stores. Her conclusion is that a job move is in order. Her campaign results in her obtaining the personnel director's position in the regional office of a casualty insurance company.

This section of the chapter has dealt primarily with approaches to preventing dysfunctional stress reactions and has only alluded to *curing* or treating the symptoms of stress. Two broad strategies for coping with stress reactions after they have occurred are (a) removing the person from the sources of stress and (b) treating the stress reaction chemically or psychologically. Psychiatry, clinical psychology, and psychiatric social work are the fields most directly concerned with the treatment of stress reactions; no attempt will be made here to capsulize that vast body of knowledge.

EXECUTIVE HEALTH IN PERSPECTIVE

Readers of this chapter should not conclude that managerial and professional life in organizations is inevitably hazardous to your mental and physical health. The opposite conclusion is more nearly correct. Undeniably, the knowledge worker is subject to a wide range of potential stress, but he or she has a higher probability of achieving good mental and physical health than people in general. Opportunities for a wide range of satisfactions and rewards exist at upper levels in organizations. Freedom from financial pressures alone has many positive side effects.

Dr. Harry J. Johnson, chairman of the medical board of The Life Extension Institute, contends that reports of tension and anxiety among business executives are greatly exaggerated. His conclusion is based on health examinations and interviews collected from about 25,000 executives a year at more than 700 different companies. About 87 percent of 2000 managers studied in 1958 and 1970 (not the same people) reported that they did not believe themselves to be working under abnormal pressures that created abnormal tensions. Based on both survey data and the approximately 1000 interviews he personally conducts annually, Johnson concludes:[52]

> From our experience we find no more evidence of tension in executives than run-of-the-mill people. Taxi drivers, for instance, suffer the same amount of tension or more from battling the Manhattan traffic. There is an exaggerated idea of the executive working under pressure. Executives are a healthy group.

RELATIONSHIP TO CORE PROPOSITIONS

The ideas contained in the preceding discussions about managerial and professional stress can be comfortably related to the framework for organizational behavior presented in this book.

Human Behavior

Reactions of human beings to stress is a well-researched topic of general and abnormal psychology. As suggested in the beginning of this chapter, the physiological changes that take place in the body under the influence of stress are approximately the same under a variety of stressful stimuli. Confronting a disaster in his business, the plant general manager will receive the same spurt of adrenalin that he receives when he faces a disaster at home.

One more illustration will suffice to emphasize the point that stress in organizational life follows generally accepted principles of human behavior. An ego threatened in organizational life will respond with the same defense mechanisms as an ego threatened in personal life. The woman rejected for a key promotion may rationalize to ease the pain, just as she might rationalize rejection by a lover.

Situational Nature

An understanding of stress and strain requires a careful scrutiny of the situation in which stress and strain occur. As observed earlier, reactions to stress are a function of the person's capacity to withstand stress and two situational factors: (a) the magnitude of the stress and (b) options available to the individual.

All of the factors described in the chapter section "Organizational Pressures" are situational factors that can create stress for individuals. Imagine the stress exerted on a person simultaneously subjected to the following pressures: (a) underutilization of abilities, (b) job insecurity, (c) exorbitant work demands, (d) interpersonal conflict, and (e) information stress.

Systemic Nature

Systems theory enhances a study of stress from at least two dimensions. First, the human body is a system. Even subjecting a person to a job he or she perceives as boring, results in a strain elsewhere in the system (e.g., migraine headache). Second, stress placed on one part of the organization (e.g., lowered sales) has ramifications in other parts of the system (e.g., cost cutting in staff departments).

The model reported in the beginning of this chapter (the relationship between individual and organizational stress) is a systems model. As specified by the model, organizational response to strain will change the organizational environment for the individual and thus create stress for the individual.

Structure and Process

Stress is sometimes created for organizational members by the interpretation (process) given to policies (structure). The chapter subsection entitled "Large Organization Pettiness" constitutes an example of how a rigid interpretation of company policy creates stress for people.

Pressure toward conformity is another issue related to the core proposition about the interaction between structure and process. Every organization has some formal policy about uniformity in behavior (e.g., office hours, vacations). The manner in which these policies are interpreted (process) may create more stress than the policies themselves (structure).

GUIDELINES FOR ACTION

1. An individual is probably under considerable stress when behavior patterns such as these manifest themselves: psychosomatic reactions (e.g., peptic ulcers), emotional disorders, alcoholism, drug abuse, excessive absenteeism, defensive tactics, and managerial obsolescence. Consultation with a psychiatrist or psychologist about such situations could prove beneficial for the individual and the organization.
2. Organizational members are less subject to harmful stress when:
    (a) proper utilization is made of their abilities,
    (b) threats of layoff or firing are not imminent,
    (c) sufficient authority is granted them to discharge their responsibilities,
    (d) work demands placed on them do not exhaust their physical and/or mental capacity,
    (e) intergroup and interpersonal conflict is kept within "reasonable" bounds,
    (f) "pettiness" (rigid interpretation and enforcement of minor rules) does not pervade the organization,
    (g) pressures toward conformity in thinking are not excessive,
    (h) job responsibilities and technical flaws do not breed stress,
    (i) work is perceived as relevant or "useful,"
    (j) concern for advancement and money does not reach obsessive proportion,
    (k) balance is achieved between work and family demands, and
    (l) the leadership style under which work is performed is "appropriate."
3. Organizational members will be in a better position to prevent stress reactions to the extent that they:
    (a) increase their options in life through commitment to self-development and self-improvement, and
    (b) practice habits and living patterns conducive to good mental health.

QUESTIONS

1. Identify and describe three sources of dysfunctional stress that exist where you work or attend school. Why doesn't someone recognize and do something constructive about this situation?
2. Think of the most stressful experience in your life. Describe the kinds of behaviors you exhibited in response to this stress.
3. Dave Nealon, a high school graduate, is the sales service manager of a large automobile dealership. Dave bitterly dislikes almost everything about his job and has recently developed a "nervous stomach" and migraine headaches. Jobs are scarce in his area; Dave has a wife and four children. What should he do about his stress situation?
4. Gordon Webster is a managing partner in a public accounting firm. His gross annual income is $38,500. What demands on his time can his firm legitimately make?
5. List five examples of organizational pettiness familiar to you. Why do people *really* object to the enforcement of these minor rules and regulations?

NOTES

1. The term professional in this context refers to members of skilled occupations whose education includes a minimum of a bachelor's degree. Thus, accountants, engineers, chemists, and some computer programmers are classified as professionals. Strauss and Sayles note that "Professional standing stems from unusual technical competence growing out of extended, prescribed training and often recognized in terms of special university degrees, licenses and certification." Quote from George Strauss and Leonard R. Sayles, *Personnel: The Human Problems of Management*, third edition. Englewood Cliffs, N.J.: Prentice-Hall, 1972, p. 57.
2. Jerome Steiner, "What Price Success?" *Harvard Business Review*, Vol. 50, No. 2, March–April 1972, p. 69.
3. Robert Tamarkin (editor), "The Frightening Problem of Executive Shock," *Generation*, Vol. 3, No. 3, March 1971, p. 68.
4. George J. Berkwitt, "The Revolt of the Middle Managers," *Dun's Review*, Vol. 94, No. 9, September 1969, p. 39.
5. Douglas T. Hall and Roger Mansfield, "Organizational and Individual Response to External Stress," *Administrative Science Quarterly*, Vol. 16, No. 4, December 1971, pp. 533–547.
6. Hans Selye, "Stress," *Psychology Today*, Vol. 3, No. 4, September 1969, p. 25.
7. Robert L. Kahn, "Stress from 9 to 5," *Psychology Today*, Vol. 3, No. 4, September 1969, p. 34.
8. Richard E. Dutton, "Industry's 2-Billion Dollar Headache—The Problem Drinker," *Personnel Journal*, Vol. 44, No. 6, June 1965, p. 303.
9. Robert D. Joyce, *Encounters in Organizational Behavior*. Elmsford, N.Y.: Pergamon Press, 1972, pp. 162–168.
10. Peter Benchley, "Office Junkies Plague Business," *Democrat and Chronicle*, Rochester, N.Y., March 26, 1972, Section C, p. 1, based on *Newsweek* article.
11. Robert H. Schaffer, "The Psychological Barriers to Management Effectiveness," *Business Horizons*, Vol. 14, No. 2, April 1971, pp. 17–25.
12. *Ibid.*, p. 20.
13. *Ibid.*
14. *Ibid.*, p. 21.
15. Tamarkin, *op. cit.*, p. 71.
16. An extensive discussion of managerial obsolescence is found in Andrew J. DuBrin, *The Practice of Managerial Psychology*. Elmsford, N.Y.: Pergamon Press, 1972, pp. 135–159.
17. Lewis E. Lachter, "Are You Considering a Second Career?" *Administrative Management*, Vol. 32, No. 4, April 1971, pp. 28, 32.
18. Readers should note that in organizational life one can be hired for numerous reasons. This psychologist could have been hired because of political pressures placed on the administration to conduct research.
19. Thomas J. Murray, "Peter F. Drucker Attacks Our Top-Heavy Corporations," *Dun's Review*, Vol. 97, No. 4, April 1971, pp. 38–41.
20. *Ibid.*, p. 39.
21. Tamarkin, *op. cit.*, p. 73.
22. Bob Stedfield, "Out-of-Work Engineers," *Machine Design*, Vol. 43, No. 4, April 29, 1971, p. 33.
23. Joyce M. Taylert gathered this quotation. Unpublished paper, Rochester Institute of Technology, 1971.
24. "The Rising Pressures to Perform," *Time*, July 18, 1969, p. 75.

25. George J. Berkwitt, "The Case of the Fragmented Manager," *Dun's Review*, Vol. 58, No. 7, June 1969, pp. 28–31.
26. *Ibid.*, p. 49.
27. Readers should note that work habits can be improved, thus relieving some of the pressures faced by the person in Berkwitt's case history. One widely used source for improving work habits is Peter F. Drucker, *The Effective Executive*. New York: Harper & Row, 1966.
28. Kahn, *op. cit.*, p. 35.
29. Harry Levinson, *Executive Stress*. New York: Harper & Row, 1970, p. 53.
30. Kahn, *op. cit.*, p. 37.
31. George J. Berkwitt, "Executives in Ferment," *Dun's Review*, Vol. 97, No. 1, January 1971, p. 25.
32. Tamarkin, *op. cit.*, p. 71.
33. William E. Perry, "Tomorrow Is Too Far Away," unpublished paper, Rochester Institute of Technology, 1971.
34. *Ibid.*
35. David R. Hampton, Charles E. Summer, and Ross A. Webber, *Organizational Behavior and the Practice of Management*. Glenview, Ill.: Scott, Foresman, 1968, pp. 358–366.
36. Lester M. Cone, Jr., "Toward a Theory of Managerial Obsolescence: An Empirical and Theoretical Study," unpublished doctoral dissertation, New York University, 1968, p. 171.
37. "The Generation Gap in the Corporation," *Time*, August 15, 1969, p. 70.
38. Judson Gooding, "The Accelerated Generation Moves into Management," *Fortune*, Vol. LXXXII, No. 3, March 1971, p. 101.
39. *Ibid.*
40. Levinson, *op. cit.*, pp. 93–102.
41. *Ibid.*, p. 98.
42. Albert Porter, Arthur F. Menton, and Seymour Halpern, "Hopkin's Syndrome: A Study of Compulsion to Work," *Business Horizons*, Vol. 13, No. 3, June 1970, p. 92.
43. Andrew J. DuBrin, *Women in Transition*. Springfield, Ill.: Charles C. Thomas, 1972, pp. 42–59.
44. Tamarkin, *op. cit.*, p. 71.
45. Mack Hanan, "Make Way for the New Organization Man," *Harvard Business Review*, Vol. 49, No. 4, July–August 1971, p. 138.
46. Levinson, *op. cit.*, p. 265.
47. R. Christie, *Studies in Machiavellianism*. New York: Academic Press, 1970.
48. Gary R. Gemmil and W. J. Heisler, "Machiavellianism as a Factor in Managerial Job Strain, Job Satisfaction, and Upward Mobility," *Academy of Management Journal*, Vol. 15, No. 1, March 1972, pp. 51–62.
49. Rollin H. Simonds, "Are Organizational Principles a Thing of the Past?" *Personnel*, Vol. 47, No. 1, January–February 1970, pp. 8–17.
50. Hanan, *op. cit.*, pp. 128–138.
51. Lawrence F. Shaffer and Edward J. Shoben, Jr., *The Psychology of Adjustment*. New York: Houghton-Mifflin, 1956, pp. 585–590.
52. "Myth: Bosses Are a Nervous Wreck," *Democrat and Chronicle*, Rochester, N.Y., November 26, 1972, Section C, p. 1.

5

Political Maneuvering in Organizations

Competence in your field, hard work, plus a few fortuitous circumstances (good luck) are necessary ingredients for success in organizational life. Success has also been characterized as a combination of good genes and good luck. Yet many competent, well-motivated people do not advance swiftly in their careers, nor do they receive acceptance for most of their proposals or programs. There remains another ingredient for achieving success in organizational life. *Political maneuvering*, in its various manifestations, is a set of behaviors required for career advancement or the acquisition of power within organizations; it is a ubiquitous aspect of organizational life that every organization member confronts at some time in his or her career. Three definitions are presented next to illuminate the type of behaviors connoted by the term *political maneuvering*:

1. *Politic,* according to a composite dictionary definition, refers to "sagacious in promoting a policy; ingenious in statecraft; shrewdly contrived, especially with regard to self-interest; expedient; pursuing one's ends with prudence rather than with principle; wisely adapted to attaining an end; crafty, artful."[1]
2. Company politics is the byplay that occurs when one man or a group of men want to advance themselves or their ideas regardless of whether or not those ideas would help the company.[2]
3. Political maneuvering is a broad concept that refers to miscellaneous actions by individuals that are directed more toward self-aggrandizement than toward the good of the company as a whole. Playing politics connotes a degree of deception and dishonesty.[3]

For purposes of this chapter, the term "political maneuvering" is defined as *those sets of behavior in addition to job competence, hard work, and fortuitous circumstances that are intended to accelerate one's career or to acquire additional power within an organizational setting.* According to this enlarged concept of political maneuvering, such behavior is not inevitably devious, dishonest, or deceptive.

Political maneuvering may be examined from another dimension by contrasting *political* and *social* approaches to resolving conflicts of interest. What does a manager do, for example, when his subordinates want to leave early for a softball game and his superior wants the department to work overtime on an emergency project? Bernard M. Bass notes that there are basically two approaches to resolving such conflicts of interest.[4] Political approaches are characterized by behaviors such as maintaining distance from subordinates, controlling the outflow of information, indulging in minor insincerities, and making superficial compromises. Social approaches, in comparison, are behaviors such as being open with subordinates, trusting them, and maintaining open lines of communication.

The Organizational Success Questionnaire was constructed by Bass to measure whether given individuals favor the political or social approaches as vehicles to success in organizations. Items in the scale illuminate the difference between political maneuvering and straightforward behavior. These are illustrated in Figure 5.1.

Moral judgments are required to differentiate between devious, unethical, and dishonest political maneuvering versus acceptable political astuteness in advancing one's position or career. For example, most people would classify as unethical the behavior of a manager who makes false statements about his competitor for a promotion in order to discredit the latter's ability. In contrast, the manager who turns down a transfer into a department where the competition is severe might merely be seen as exercising good judgment in managing his career. Common to the behavior of both is an element of political maneuvering.

This chapter discusses two broad categories of political maneuvering: (a) those political strategies directed specifically toward career advancement and (b) those strategies directed toward the acquisition of power.

WHAT CAUSES POLITICAL MANEUVERING?

Politically oriented behavior in organizations is ubiquitous. Few organizations exist in which all promotions and proposals are reviewed on the basis of merit alone. Two explanations are possible. People are either political in their personal values or organizations exert pressures on people that foster political maneuvering. There is more evidence and opinion to support the contention that a hierarchical organization creates a climate that

Political	Social
Withhold the release of information or time its release for when it will do the most good.	Level with others; be open, frank, and candid in their communications with others.
Act confidently when they are personally unsure about matters or when they lack relevant information.	Share in decision-making with their subordinates whenever possible.
Make political alliances with superiors and subordinates to foster and protect mutual interests.	Completely and openly commit themselves to a position or program.
Initiate actions which they are personally against but retard and delay carrying out the actions so that the actions are in progress but never completed.	Try to establish in advance mutual satisfactory objectives with others with whom they must work.
Maintain social distance; remain aloof, detached, uninvolved with others; always remain the boss when interacting with subordinates.	Foster mutual trust with others.
Openly compromise, yet privately divert or delay compromise plans so that their own aims will be pursued despite the stated compromise.	Arrange for their superiors and their subordinates to meet together to encourage group discussions among others above and below them in the organization with easy participation by all.

Figure 5.1 Political versus social approaches in resolving conflicts of interest. SOURCE: Bernard M. Bass, "How to Succeed in Business According to Business Students and Managers," *Journal of Applied Psychology*, Vol. 52, 1968, p. 258.

encourages its members to participate in political manipulations. Five forces and stresses that contribute to political maneuvering are described next.

First is the competition for power that is characteristic of all political structures.[5] Organizations are political structures because they provide a base for the development of executive careers and a platform for the expression of individual interests and motives. Large numbers of managers are competing for a small number of openings available at the top of the organizational pyramid. Executive success is measured to some extent by the accumulation of power and responsibility, thus intensifying the struggle for power in organizations.

Second is a basic distrust many people have of top management's ability to objectively measure the performance of subordinates. When managerial performance can be measured objectively, political maneuvering becomes less necessary. For example, if a scientist working for a pharmaceutical firm discovers a cure for leukemia, he does not need to participate in political maneuvering to achieve recognition. His results are apparent. In contrast, the vice-president of planning in a university has much less tangible output to show for his efforts. One feasible alternative to achieving recognition for his results might be political maneuvering. J. D. Batten and James L. Swab pessimistically observe that "Men engage in company politics because they believe that they can best achieve what they want in a devious, indirect, or underhanded way."[6]

Third is an underlying reason that helps to clarify why the performance of many managers is difficult to evaluate. According to research conducted by Eugene E. Jennings, the frequent job changing of managers makes it difficult for them to show depth in any one position.[7] Managers are often promoted or assigned a lateral position before the accomplishments of their prior positions have been forthcoming. Mobility of this kind heightens the need to impress and manipulate.

Fourth, as noted by Jennings in his research with top-level managers, is the tendency to push managers ahead so fast that they exceed their administrative skill.[8] Confidence suffers and these men begin to indulge in political tactics to compensate for what they feel might be substandard administrative performance.

Fifth is the gradual shift in leadership style and the nature of the executive role that has taken place in the last 15 to 20 years. Modern management thinking places a premium upon being democratic rather than autocratic. Managers, especially in large organizations, are no longer supposed to play the role of the boss whose "authority is not to be questioned."[9] Rather, they are supposed to be team players with a democratic approach to subordinates. Many managers find the shift from an autocratic to a democratic style uncomfortable. Their response is to appear democratic. One common tactic, according to Jennings, is to use committees, conferences, and informal groups as arenas for maneuvering and manipulating. (The reader must be cautioned at this point not to interpret this statement to mean that there are no legitimate and useful purposes served by committees and small, informal groups.)

Political maneuvering, in its manifold forms, is but one approach to career advancement. Merit, luck, and a complex of demographic factors also contribute to an individual's chances for promotion. John Rogers is six feet four inches tall, a White Anglo-Saxon Protestant, and a graduate of Yale University with a degree in Administrative Sciences. These *demo-*

graphic characteristics will represent assets to him in his attempts at career advancement in many business corporations. John Lorenzi is five feet six inches tall, an Italian Catholic, and a graduate of Center City Technical High School. These *demographic* characteristics will be to his disadvantage in achieving an executive position in a great many large business organizations. Mr. Lorenzi, however, might engage in *political maneuvering* by seeking employment in a company that has a demonstrated record of promoting people with similar demographic characteristics to positions of higher responsibility. Mr. Rogers might engage in political maneuvering by avoiding organizations that practiced reverse discrimination. One company in Buffalo, for example, has an unwritten bias against graduates of Ivy League schools. John Rogers would display political astuteness in managing his career by avoiding this company in Buffalo.

Prior to describing politically oriented career advancement strategies it will provide helpful background information to overview the total complex of factors that are related to promotion in business.

Race, Religion, and the Promotion of the American Executive, a research monograph prepared by Reed M. Powell, is a lengthy analysis of factors related to promotion.[10] Data were collected from 240 completed questionnaires gathered from managers in 40 business firms. In addition to questionnaire data, much information was collected at informal luncheons, cocktail parties, and spontaneous conversations. Readers are alerted in advance that most of the companies were apparently located in the geographic region around Columbus, Ohio, and data were collected in the mid- and late-1960s. Were the study conducted in the 1970s and in other regions of the country, the results might have been different. For example, many ethnic, racial, and sex barriers to promotion are gradually diminishing; regional differences in prejudices may also exist. None of the 17 factors related to promotion is labeled *political maneuvering* or *playing politics*, but several of them are clearly political in nature or have political undertones.

Managerial Capability

Performance, or ability, is still the number one factor related to promotion. Eighty-seven percent of the participants in this survey mentioned capability as being a necessary qualification for promotion. Organizations can best accomplish their objectives by appointing capable people to key positions—a finding that should come as no surprise to even the most politically oriented individual.

Personality

"An individual's acceptability to others and his capacity to be influential in the lives of his peers, superiors, and subordinates were stressed by the participants" as being important qualities for promotion. Ambition, aggressiveness, and drive was another part of personality stressed by over one-third of the managers in the study. Aggressiveness, it was pointed out, should not reach the point of offending others.

Informal Influences

"When considered in proper perspective it would be hard to find a factor more pertinent to advancement opportunities of an individual."[11] Over 50 percent of executives in the study commented on the importance of forming constructive relationships with people other than those individuals directly in their chain of command. Spending time with subordinates appeared to be a vast waste of time with regard to ascending the executive ladder. Associating with people at upper levels within the informal organization was seen as vital to the promotional process.

The Customer

"The customer is always right," according to an ancient business axiom. Powell's research indicated that the feelings and attitudes of key customers can exert influence over who receives or does not receive a promotion to top management.[12]

> In the rarified top-management atmosphere, concern over customer reaction becomes a guiding force for a number of the executives' decisions regarding such factors as the individual's appearance, his religion, race, etc.

The Government

Business organizations highly value the federal government as a customer. Because of the leverage exerted by the federal government this customer is considered a separate force in promotability. Significant government officials have the power to accelerate or curtail the career progress of a manager in a vendor (supplier) company. One participant in Powell's study reported an anecdote about an irate government representative who vowed he would destroy an engineer with whom he had had a verbal altercation. Because of the importance of this customer, the company felt compelled to remove the engineer from the project. According to others in the company, this engineer has been placed in a company "Siberia" since the incident.

Kinship

"Marrying the boss's daughter," despite its trite ring, still exerts some promotional influence. According to the research results, kinship relationships along either marriage or blood lines influenced promotion decisions. Promotional opportunities for the individual are enhanced when he (or, presumably, she) is a member of the board of directors, a substantial stockholder, or an officer of the company. For every four managers in the Powell study who regarded kinship as helpful to promotion, one regarded kinship as a hindrance.

Seniority

Experience with the company remains an important determinant of promotion. Over one-half the participants in the study viewed seniority as a direct influence, while one-third viewed it as an indirect influence. Not surprisingly, as managers progressed in their careers they assumed a more positive outlook on the value of seniority as a factor in promotability.

Physical State

Age, health, and appearance are all related to promotability. Candidates for promotion must neither be too young nor too old for promotion. Being too old is far more detrimental than being too young. Executive work is physically demanding, thus making good health an important factor to be taken into account at time of promotion. Even when an executive does not feel physically healthy, it was suggested by respondents that he attempt to appear physically robust. Height, weight, bearing, appropriate clothing, and "being clean cut" all can exert some influence upon one's eligibility for promotion. According to this research, the popular song that cautions "Long-haired, freaky people need not apply," has validity for executive positions in American business where public contact is critical.

Education

Advanced formal education is becoming an increasingly important qualification for elevation to top-management positions. The bachelor's degree has become an almost minimum requirement for an executive role, and the percentage of aspirants to top positions with masters or doctoral degrees is on the increase. Hal Higdon, in an article written for *Playboy*, estimates that 30 percent of company presidents hold doctoral degrees.[13] (Although this is undoubtedly an overestimate, it underscores the importance attached to formal education for promotion to executive positions.) Business administration was the type of background most highly regarded in this particular sampling of industrial and business organizations.

Influence of the Wife

Women exert an important influence on their husbands' careers. Lower level managers often need financial and emotional assistance from their wives. When a husband reaches a higher level, the woman must learn to manage the household with her husband being absent much of the time. Willingness on the wife's part to relocate also facilitates the husband's career. Once the husband reaches the upper organization ranks, the wife fulfills the additional role of social hostess both to company personnel and to customers.

In times of job change, the executive's wife is often interviewed. This practice appears more frequent in smaller towns where business-related socializing is a common practice. Such interviews are conducted for purposes of assessing the wife's (a) willingness to relocate (if it is an issue) and (b) her potential skill as a hostess. Wives who score poorly on these two criteria, could conceivably disqualify a husband for a management position.

The changing role of women in society is beginning to exert new pressures on upwardly mobile, married, male managers. Men are becoming more sensitive to the reality that success in their careers can create problems for their wives.[14] Many women resent the attention upwardly mobile men devote to their careers. This resentment creates another pressure on an individual that can detract from his on-the-job effectiveness.

Much of the literature about executives' wives in the past inferred that wives should adapt to the demands placed on a husband by his career.[15] As more women develop careers of their own outside the home, the wives' job situation will be given more consideration when promotional opportunities for the husband present themselves.

Community Influences

Attitudes of people within the community toward candidates for top management positions can exert an important influence on their promotability. Participation in professional organizations—both technical and managerial—was found to be an important factor in promotion. Membership in civic and charitable organizations such as the Kiwanis and Lions was also found to be a positive influence. Belonging to businessmen's social clubs carries prestige that can favorably influence a manager's career. Social contacts made possible through such clubs can be specifically helpful in accelerating one's career—clearly a political factor.

Political Identification

Being a Republican meets with more acceptance than being a Democrat, although the tendency is not as pronounced as in years past. Today, chief executives of several well-known corporations are ardent spokesmen for the Democratic Party. Executives in the Ohio State study conducted by Powell had negative reactions to individuals who identified with extremist organizations, either left or right. Membership in groups such as the John Birch Society, Americans for Democratic Action, or the American Civil Liberties Union was viewed as a negative factor in promotability, although no specific quantitative data are available on this topic.

Religion

Executives in this study perceived religion as an indirect positive influence and a direct negative influence in determining which individual receives a promotion. Elements of anti-Semitism were found throughout the research. Being Jewish was almost never found to be a help in gaining acceptance in the organizations studied. In vivid contrast, almost 92 percent of the respondents said being Jewish was a hindrance for vertical mobility. In some business organizations, however, being Jewish is a neutral or positive factor with regard to promotability. There are business organizations of substantial size in New York City where no company officer has a gentile name!

Racial and Ethnic Groups

An individual's race and/or his ethnic group profoundly influence his chances for promotion in the organizations studied by Powell. Despite much federal and state legislation to the contrary, it is well documented, for example, that being black has historically been a detriment to promotion. Research conducted by the *Harvard Business Review* in the early 1960s with almost 2000 managers indicated that 87 percent felt being Negro was harmful to advancement.[16]

	1940		1950		1960		1970	
	White	Black	White	Black	White	Black	White	Black
Professional and Technical	8	2.7	9	3.4	12	4.7	15	9
Proprietors, Managers, and Officials	9	1.3	10	2.0	12	2.3	12	3.5

Figure 5.2 Percentage of white and black knowledge workers in the United States. SOURCE: "Toiling at the Edge of the Economy," *Black Enterprise*, April 1971, p. 65. © Earl D. Graves Publishing Company, Inc., 1971.

By 1972, the number of blacks in middle- and top-management jobs in business organizations had substantially increased. Many organizations, according to informal observation, actively recruited blacks for management positions. *Black Enterprise*, a magazine "For black men and women who want to get ahead" presents some longitudinal data about the proportion of blacks in various job categories.[17] As noted in Figure 5.2, the proportion of black knowledge workers is gradually rising.

Despite these gains for blacks, considerable opinion exists that corporate racism is still a real problem. Black professional employees have told this writer that many blacks occupy "pseudo-management" positions; they are given managerial titles yet have no subordinates and no managerial authority. Stuart A. Taylor notes in a field study of the black executive that "In sixty percent of the cases the BAE (black American executive) is more qualified than his immediate superior."[18]

Refusal of a Promotion

When an executive is offered a promotion and refuses to accept the position, this refusal is detrimental to his future opportunities for advancement. (Politically astute individuals might want to ponder this finding.) Declining a promotion was regarded as a reflection on the judgment of those recommending and approving the promotion. Additionally, it was regarded by some executives as a lack of interest and ambition on the candidate's part. Research suggested that the individual who refuses a promotion, even for valid reasons, has a negative factor to overcome in his career.

Family Background

Executives tend to come from homes of executives and professional people. Rarely do they come from laborer, service worker, or other similar occupational backgrounds. As with other findings noted by Powell, this trend may be changing. Overall, American business is becoming increasingly democratic. (*See* Chapter 14, which deals with the future.) The wider availability of higher education has helped people of diverse socioeconomic backgrounds into corporate life.

Family background is often a determinant of manners and behavioral traits, which in turn can influence promotability. Powell records the following anecdote:[19]

> The President of one major firm was considering promoting one of the upper-middle level managers to a top-level position in the organization. In keeping with the importance of the position, the prospective candidate was invited to the president's home for dinner. At the end of the meal, pie was served. The candidate made the mistake of putting the tines (prongs) of the fork straight into the point of the pie instead of using the side of the fork. The president, appalled by this lack of sophistication, rejected the man with the comment that anyone so naive in his approach to such a simple matter as eating pie could certainly not be trusted to make important decisions.

Fortuitous Elements

Luck has a pervasive influence on the promotability of most people. For example, having the necessary qualifications at a time when a new division of the firm is seeking people can have a profound influence on one's career. Sudden removal of one's immediate superior is another classic example of fortuitous circumstance. Capable people must demonstrate their capability to others in the hierarchy; taking over the responsibilities of your boss is a unique opportunity.

CAREER-ADVANCEMENT STRATEGIES

Behavior to be described within the following categories manifests some degree of overlap. No assumption is made that the categorization to be presented next is scientifically precise. The major purpose of presenting this material is to help sensitize the reader to the varieties of political behavior managers exhibit in order to further their careers within organizations. Readers are free to reject or accept each strategy on ethical or moral grounds.

Focus on Mobility

Managers aspiring to top positions in their fields must accept frequent job changes, both within one company and from company to company, as the most probable route to accomplish this goal. Eugene Jennings feels that the mobility patterns of managers are systematic enough to warrant the science of mobilography.[20] The central figure in Jennings' studies is the *mobile hierarch*, a person who has moved from the bottom of the organization to the top without any family or marriage connections working for or against him. *Pure hierarchs* are those rare individuals who work their way up from the bottom of one company to its top. Thus, the management trainee who enters Chase Manhattan Bank at the age of 21 and becomes a Senior Executive Vice-President at Chase at the age of 47 is a pure hierarch. More frequently, the manager of today must plan his own moves, jumping from one company to another in order to achieve the vertical mobility he desires. According to Higdon, ". . . . in today's board rooms, the old-guard organization man is likely to be outwitted and outflanked by the crafty master of job jumping."[21] Various guidelines have been drawn to assist the manager in determining when it is time for him to *jump*. Several of these follow:

Richard E. Gleason has developed a set of milestones to help a manager decide if his career progress is satisfactory.[22] The first milestone occurs at age 25—the maximum age at which one should remain an individual performer. By age 30, the aspirant to executive success should have completed his tour of duty in first-level management. By age 35, he should have passed through the second level of management, such as a district sales management position. Managership of a broad corporate function (e.g., general sales manager or director of research and development) should take place by age 40. Upon reaching age 45, the successful executive should be a vice-president in charge of his own functional area. Personnel men, to cite one illustration, should be corporate director of personnel by age 45 if they are truly exceptional. Presidential responsibility, according to Gleason's milestones, should accrue to the executive by age 50.

Jennings has charted the various stages a mobile manager must pass through in his career if he is to qualify as a *mobile hierarch*.[23] These stages can also be interpreted as guidelines to judge one's progress through the corporate hierarchy. Stage one is the technical level (individual performer), encompassing such jobs as salesman, engineer, scientist, accountant, and personnel specialist. Stage two is the managerial level, beginning with the supervision of individual performers through managing managers to finally taking responsibility for running a corporate division. Stage three is the executive level, which is made up of the president, his immediate staff, and their immediate subordinates. All positions mentioned may be in either line or staff capacities.

According to Jennings, the *super-mobile* manager passes through stage one in zero to two years, stage two in eleven years, and stage three within eight years. The average age when made president for the super-mobile is 47.

Financial progress is another important way for a manager to measure his progress toward success in corporate life. Jennings has suggested that the man with considerable potential earns his age in salary. For example, during the period studied (the mid-1960s) a 34-year-old merchandising manager should be earning $34,000 per year. Fifty-year-old corporate officers, similarly, should be earning $50,000 per year in salary. There are obviously differences among types of organizations and industries. These figures have more applicability to industrial companies than to banks, insurance companies, or educational institutions.

Gleason suggests that the career man who plans his way to the top of the organization should double in salary every seven years.[24] Thus, the physicist who joined IBM in 1960 at $9000 per year should make $36,000 per year in 1974 as a middle manager!

What should the manager do who discovers that he is falling behind target in reaching some of these guidelines? The politically oriented answer is that he must judiciously job hop until he gains the forward momentum his career requires. Jennings espouses the idea that the mobile manager must have an 80–20 orientation toward most positions[25]—20 percent of any job counts for 80 percent of the learning. If the mobile manager can master the 20 percent and move on to another job, the learning curve is constantly rising. Mobile managers are also cautioned to stay in any one managerial assignment a maximum of 36 to 40 months. Failing to be promoted within this time frame is an indicator for the ambitious manager to begin searching for a new position.

Mobility can also be maintained by the practice of *strategic self-positioning*, as described by Auren Uris. This involves placing yourself in a job environment with considerable potential payoff for growth. Sensitivity to what constitutes a growth environment is of crucial importance. Uris quotes Eugene Thorpe, a highly paid executive in a textile firm:[26]

> When I was a salesman, I heard that my company was going in for a new line of synthetics. I pulled a few strings, got myself transferred to the division that eventually would handle the new product. When the division began to expand, I was in the catbird seat.

Another self-positioning strategy is to seek a transfer into a division of your company from which many upper level managers have risen in the past. For example, to the author's knowledge, few top-management positions are filled by people from the functions of personnel, quality control, or office services. In contrast, manufacturing, marketing, finance, and engineering are the conventional sources of executive talent. The mobile manager carefully studies the unique pattern of promotions for his company and/or his industry. Exceptions and individual differences always exist, but the prudent manager, at a minimum, avoids situations where there is a natural bias against his particular specialty in relation to promotional opportunities.

The reader should observe carefully that where (which functional specialty) the top executive comes from is frequently a reflection of the current needs of the company. During the 1960s, Ford Motor Company was particularly concerned about cost control; thus, top management at Ford typically rose through the financial end of the business. When Xerox Corporation began its ascent, advice about patent laws was vital to its survival. Sol Linowitz, a legal advisor to the company, was selected for a key executive position—in part because of his legal expertise.

In 1972, 37-year-old Arthur Taylor joined Columbia Broadcasting System as president.[27] According to an analysis by *Time*, CBS's prime need during that period was for financial expertise. Taylor had established an enviable reputation for financial management at both The First Boston Corporation and the International Paper Company.

Help Your Boss Succeed

One vital role of any subordinate is to help his immediate superior more effectively carry out his (the superior's) job function. To the extent that a subordinate helps his boss succeed, he is a valued subordinate. To the extent that the subordinate creates problems for his immediate superior, he is negatively valued by his superior. Aspirants to greater responsibility in any hierarchical organization must accept this basic premise of political strategy. Before transfers or promotions are given in almost any organization, a boss must give his approval.

Crucial subordinate is the label Jennings has provided for the individual who performs well in a crucial assignment upon which the superior's performance is dependent.[28] Assume that a business organization is receiving pressure from the community to donate generously to the Community Chest Fund. The subordinate who takes over this assignment and meets or surpasses the company quota will be viewed by the president as a crucial subordinate. The administrative assistant who carried out this function will have helped his boss succeed in a burdensome chore. Failure to meet the established charity quota could have resulted in an unfavorable image in the community.

Crucial subordinates are of two types: the complementary and the supplementary. Complementary crucial subordinates help the boss overcome his weaknesses. Should your immediate superior have difficulty in analyzing and preparing budgets and your expertise in this area is considerable, you could then complement his skills. If your boss is capable in working with budgets and you want to expand upon his strengths in this area, you might become a supplementary crucial subordinate.

Politically astute subordinates thus contribute whatever they can to assuring the success of those immediately above them in the hierarchy. What should a subordinate do when all these efforts fail? What is the recommended strategy when your boss has reached his ultimate level within the organization and will not leave until retirement? Political strategists recommend simply that you deftly search for a new position.[29]

Subordinates actively seeking transfers arouse some questions about their present manager's leadership capabilities. Efforts to leave a department may thus lower one's status with an immediate superior. Many members of large, complex organizations have found it prudent to locate a new position first before mentioning their desire for a transfer. The manager of the new department might then request that the "boxed-in" individual be transferred to his department.

Closely related to helping your boss succeed is providing him emotional support, both privately and publicly. Despite the positive climate that exists in many places today for openness and candidness in interpersonal relationships, superiors find it uncomfortable to be shown up in meetings by subordinates. Disagreements with superiors should be ironed out privately if the subordinate is concerned about the reputation he establishes with his boss.

Deliberate attempts to ingratiate oneself with the boss may seem old fashioned, transparent, and naive, but recent research evidence suggests they are still effective. *OBI Interaction: The Management Psychology Newsletter* reported some research results about *apple-polishing*, conducted by two industrial psychologists, Drs. Kipnis and Vanderveer. They remark, " . . . . the teacher who drops in for frequent chats with his department head or the junior executive who offers friendly greetings to his boss should win by a nose in the race for success . . . ."[30]

Circumstances in which apple-polishing is most likely to be effective were studied. Managers were studied under three sets of circumstances. Common to all three circumstances was an attempt by subordinates to curry favor with the boss. In some groups these workers were contrasted with pleasant but inept employees. In other groups the apple-polishers were paired with capable but abrasive colleagues. Group three was composed of the favor-seekers combined with employees who were neither hostile nor inept—just neutral.

Research results showed that superiors were prone to favor the apple-polishers when there was a hostile or disagreeable worker on the scene. Apple-polishing was significantly less effective when the other workers in the group were merely inept or neutral. Kipnis and Vanderveer note:

> .... the use of rewarding powers is influenced by the presence of a hostile problem worker. Not only were compliant workers given more pay raises, but they were also given more favorable performance evaluations when the hostile worker was present.

Editors of *OBI Interaction* cite illustrations of the career advancement consequences of currying favor with one's immediate superior. They present the following case as typical:[31]

> ... we recall the case of a service organization in which the top man worked with a small group of key executives. For the most part these were creative and uninhibited people. They spoke their minds; and the leader was often involved in abrasive confrontation. He boasted that he liked it that way; that this was the means of forging truly original effort. Did it bother him? No—"I have a tough skin."
>
> One member of the key group was different. He was single-mindedly compliant, praising and agreeing with the boss to a point that the situation became a standing joke. The leader participated in the joke. He would sardonically comment to his more volatile subordinates on the behavior of the apple-polisher.
>
> The service firm was acquired by a larger company. A reorganization was suddenly announced. And, lo and behold, the apple-polisher picked up all the apples. He was placed over his more abrasive and disbelieving colleagues. The leader's explanations were so feeble as to amount to scarcely more than rationalizations.
>
> Why? Drs. Kipnis and Vanderveer comment on similar behavior that they have observed: "One possibility is that the ... leaders may have felt personally threatened and uneasy over the hostile attitudes expressed by the noncompliant worker." No matter how much a manager may deny the fact, even to himself, disagreement can be perceived as a threat. And in a threatening situation the leader may tend to magnify the capabilities of the man whose presence is always smooth and soothing ... "a compliant individual may be most appreciated by a leader when there is an active vocal minority directly challenging the leader's decisions."

Find a Sponsor

Fundamental to successful political maneuvering is the ability to find an influential individual of higher rank than you in the organization to endorse your credentials for promotion. *Sponsors* must be found before vertical mobility can take place. *Visiposure* is the term developed by Jennings to describe the process by which ambitious organization members find adequate sponsorship. First, they must have the necessary visibility to see superiors. Some jobs exist in organizations that confine the individual's efforts to one department. For example, a young man in an aerospace company might be confined to a drawing board which would limit his contact with management to his immediate superior. Exposure occurs when one is seen by superiors. Visiposure is the combination of visibility plus exposure. Task force and committee assignments are highly valued by the upwardly mobile organization member because they provide the opportunity for visiposure.

Sponsors are sometimes called patrons, as suggested by Laurence J. Peter and Raymond Hull.[32] Patrons, according to the tenets of Peter and Hull, can pull one to greater heights in an organization. Satirically, these authors point out that being pulled up the organization is much more effective than exerting your own upward force, or push. The latter consists of such processes as hard work, competence, and self-development. Patrons, of course, must be motivated to sponsor an individual's career. To the extent that an individual is perceived as a crucial subordinate, his patron will continue to exercise pull. Losing a sponsor can precipitate a descent in a person's career as illustrated by the following situation:

> Randolph Foster was a planning specialist in an international corporation based in New York City. By age 27, he had worked himself into a key assignment as a special assistant to the vice-president of corporate planning at world headquarters. His sponsor, the vice-president of corporate planning, gave him a six-month assignment in the international division as an operations auditor. Foster's job was to overview problems and plans with key operating personnel from various overseas subsidiaries. Upon completion of this assignment, Randolph returned to headquarters. One week before his return, his sponsor was dismissed from the company.
>
> Foster was never even asked to report the results of his six-month investigation. The new executive in charge of corporate planning did not require the services of a special assistant. Foster's credentials were sent to corporate personnel. After one month of waiting for reassignment, he was offered an opportunity to work as a financial analyst at a company plant in Pittsburgh. Foster resigned, quite disgruntled about having lost forward momentum in his career.

Foster had another alternative depending upon how highly he was regarded by his sponsor. Sponsors frequently recruit to their new company crucial subordinates they have known from prior associations. The practice of a key executive moving to another company and then proceeding to recruit all or part of his executive team from his former company can be questioned on ethical grounds. Corporations have been known to examine carefully the legality of such practices. Nevertheless, the politically aware individual carefully assesses opportunities to follow his sponsor to another company.

Sponsors can sometimes be actively sought out to circumvent the blockage created by one's immediate superior. *Generation* reports a bold approach to seeking out a sponsor:[33]

> ... A young copywriter for a major ad agency, Arnie felt his work was being given short shrift by the copy supervisor, who Arnie thought was jealous of his superior talent.
>
> So Arnie (not his real name) went over the copy supervisor's head and struck up a friendship with the agency's creative director.
>
> In time, Arnie showed some of his copy to the creative director, who agreed that Arnie deserved more recognition. The creative director fired the copy supervisor and put Arnie in his place. The payoff: today, Arnie is the agency's creative director.

Manipulative approaches such as these are inherently risky. Managers who have been bypassed by a subordinate in the latter's attempt to find another sponsor typically seek revenge. Even the most politically naive individual recognizes the inherent danger in collecting enemies within an organization. (In Arnie's case the copy supervisor was fired, but in large organizations deposed individuals would more probably be transferred to another location within the organization.)

Exhibit and Obtain Loyalty

Despite the traditional ring to the term, *loyalty* to a supervisor and a company still elicits more promotions than disloyalty. Superiors feel more psychologically comfortable when they can rely upon a given subordinate to support the department in times of internecine warfare. Observers of organizational life are well aware that the high-level manager known to be looking for a position with a competitor company is best advised to take that new position. His present company will now question his loyalty and be less inclined to gear him for greater responsibility.

Extreme in form and ineffective in obtaining desired results is the *yes-man* variety of loyalty. According to Batten and Swab, the yes-man is agreeable to any suggestion or proposal because he wants to be liked.[34]

Strong managers are quick to detect such acquiescence and the yes-man syndrome becomes self-defeating.

Obtaining loyalty centers around forming alliances and coalitions with groups or individuals in the organization who have the power to influence your career. The palace revolt at Ford Motor Company in 1970 provides a legendary example of the importance of forming the right coalition. Semon E. Knudsen was brought to Ford as president after having served in a top-management position with General Motors. After less than two years at Ford, he was fired. Abraham Zaleznik provides an analysis of his demise:[35]

> .... While it is true that Henry Ford II named Knudsen president of the company, Knudsen's ultimate power structure depended on forming an alliance. The particular individual with whom an alliance seemed crucial was Lee Iacocca. For some reason, Knudsen and Iacocca competed for power and influence instead of using cooperatively a power base to which both contributed, as is the case with most workable coalitions. In the absence of a coalition, the alternate postures of rivalry and battle for control erupted. Ford ultimately responded by weighing his power with one side over the other.

Swim Against the Tide

Seeking out a nonconventional path to career success—swimming against the tide—might more properly be described as deft career planning than political maneuvering. E. A. Butler mentions the sales field as one approach to swimming against the tide.[36] According to his reasoning, a young man entering business in the 1970s is well advised to seek a direct sales position if vertical mobility is his goal. This is true for two crucial reasons. First, fewer college graduates of today apply for sales positions, thus creating more opportunities for the young man willing to sell. According to Butler ".... Now is the time for the really smart young man to enter sales. In a field of mediocrities, he will rocket to the top at double, triple the normal pace."[37] Second, despite its unpopularity among some college students, sales remains a vital business function in the modern business corporation. Sales is a stepping stone to managerial responsibility in many companies. As told to Butler by one sales-oriented executive, "Anybody can make the stuff. But it takes brains to *move* it."[38]

Careful observation is required to detect what constitutes "swimming against the tide" in any one industry for any one time period. During the late 1960s, the young man or woman intent on pursuing pollution control would have had a competitive edge. By 1970, however, the field had become glutted with people pursuing opportunities. Similarly, an oversupply of social workers has been predicted for the late 1970s because of the heightened social concern of college-age people. During the 1950s and 1960s, college-educated social workers were in short supply.

Discredit or Remove Others

Competition for promotion becomes intense enough in some organizations that outright attempts to discredit, remove, and even blackmail other individuals have been observed. This approach to advancing one's career has many different manifestations, all of which will appear unsavory to the ethically minded student or manager. Readers are also cautioned that such approaches may have legal implications. An extreme approach to discrediting another individual in an organization is illustrated by the following situation:

> A new man was brought into the marketing department of a midwestern company. Management provided others in the department with only a broad and loose description of the nature of this new department member's responsibilities. Several other older members of the department perceived him as a possible contender for a key spot within the department. These men hired a detective agency to find out everything about the individual's business and personal life. Any adverse information collected in this manner was then entered into conversation at social functions with company personnel.

Adverse information gathered about another individual within the organization is sometimes used for blackmail. One employee of an athletic equipment manufacturer found out that his immediate superior had falsified information on his federal income tax return. Knowing this information, he used it as leverage in obtaining favors from the boss, including a positive recommendation for promotion.

Vance Packard documents a number of devious strategies executives have used to protect their business reputations.[39] Occasionally, when rivalry for promotion is at its peak, an "outright operator" will backdate a memo to prove to the president that he was right and his rival wrong.[40] Another extreme reaction to competition Packard reports is the maneuverings of a vice-president of an Eastern company. "He kept a rival from attending an important executive meeting by plugging the carburetor of his automobile."[41]

Yet another aggressive action toward lessening the competition is easing the way for a threatening rival to be transferred away from your department. Making positive comments about the rival at various places in the organization can enhance his reputation, thus increasing the probability that another department will seek him out. Closely related in concept is the strategy described next:

> Bernie Stapleton, a personnel manager, learned that his boss, the corporate director of personnel, would be accepting early retirement within one year. Stapleton and one other personnel manager were logical contenders to replace the corporate director of personnel. Bernie felt his chances for obtaining the promotion were slightly less than those of his rival. In order to eliminate his competition, Bernie submitted the former's name to an executive search firm as a good candidate for any executive search assignments the firm might have for a personnel manager. The strategy worked. Bernie's rival was placed in another company and Bernie received the promotion he wanted.

Document Your Accomplishments

Positive comments made by other people, particularly when in written form, appear impressive to some people. Keeping *hero files* is the term given to this practice in the marketing division of a one billion dollar corporation.[42] Aspirants to greater responsibility made a deliberate effort to do simple things for other people with the expectations that the latter would write a memo thanking the former for his contribution. This memo then found its way to a hero file, which would be used to strengthen the individual's credentials for promotion or transfer. This practice, of course, is not too dissimilar from the older practice of collecting "To whom it may concern" letters praising an individual for his or her faithful job performance.

Empire building is another manifestation of documenting your accomplishments. One assumption underlying accumulating large numbers of people (whether or not they are needed to carry out the department mission) is that the size of a department is related to contribution. Managers making large contributions to the organization are then given prime consideration for positions of even greater responsibility. Empire building is thus encouraged when department size and contribution are seen as closely related by top management.

The empire builder reasons that his chances for promotion are in direct proportion to the size of his department. Similarly, the larger the budget he requires to run his department, the more impressive his function appears. Size of budget and number of people are easier to document than size of contribution to organizational objectives.

Again, it must be emphasized that career advancement encompasses much more than political maneuvering. The 17 factors mentioned earlier in the chapter all relate to promotability. Concentrated effort and self-development also contribute to upward mobility. Individuals who are well-prepared educationally, are competent, and well motivated do not have to rely heavily upon political maneuvering as a vehicle to promotion.

POWER-ACQUISITION STRATEGIES

Political strategies discussed so far have been directed more toward career advancement than toward power acquisition *per se*; the two are closely related. Career advancement usually proceeds more swiftly when one acquires additional power. Conversely, when you advance in your career you acquire more power. Empire building was discussed earlier as one political maneuver to facilitate vertical mobility. However, empire building is also one common method of acquiring additional power. The empire builder enlarges his power base even though it requires that members of his organizational unit involve themselves in unproductive work. A definition of politics offered by Alan N. Schoonmaker in his book, *Executive Career Strategy*, helps to explain why a discussion of political maneuvering in organizations should include a discussion of power acquisition:[43]

> "Politics" does not mean shirking work, apple polishing, or joining the right clubs; nor is it a legitimate excuse for not getting ahead (although many people use politics as an alibi). These things are part of politics, but politics is a much more general phenomenon that involves the distribution of power and strategies for obtaining and retaining it. Politics is always concerned with power, so the common expression "power politics" is both poor English and poor thinking. In other words, the name of the game is power.

Described next in this chapter are a variety of political maneuvers directed toward the acquisition of power. Readers interested in pursuing a sophisticated, broad analysis of power in organizations should consult *Power in Organizations*, the proceedings of an important sociology conference held at Vanderbilt University.[44] The present analysis deals with one specific aspect of this broad topic—"power grabbing."

Maintain Alliances with Powerful People

Fundamental to both career advancement and the maintenance of power in an organization is the formation of alliances with people who exert power themselves or influence others who exert power. Managers in many companies attempt to create a positive climate for acceptance of their ideas by maintaining cordial relationships with the president's secretary. Management consultants sometimes attempt to exert influence with line managers by inferring that they have a close working relationship with the chief executive officer. Thus, the line manager fears that he might lose influence with his ultimate superior if he fails to cooperate with the consultant.

Dramatic evidence of the importance of maintaining alliances with powerful people is found in one incident involving the Federal Bureau of Investigation. In this situation, the official who lost power also lost his job:[45]

> ... William C. Sullivan, 59, a top FBI administrator and agent for 30 years, is being forced to retire after a series of policy disputes with J. Edgar Hoover.
>
> While Sullivan was on sick leave Friday, his name was removed from his office door and the locks changed. Sullivan, who was once thought to be a likely successor to Hoover, 76, was not officially informed.
>
> The FBI said that Sullivan had been under intense pressure from Hoover to leave the bureau for months but that as late as 10 P.M. Friday, Sullivan was resisting the pressure and refusing to resign. . . .
>
> Sullivan's ouster was foreshadowed about six weeks ago when Hoover appointed W. Mark Felt over Sullivan into a newly created No. 3 post in the FBI just below the director and associate director Clyde W. Tolson, 71, Hoover's longtime righthand man.
>
> A former FBI official said Friday night that the downgrading of Sullivan's position was the tipoff that his days were numbered. "It's a technique the director has used for years," the official said. "You are bypassed and then ignored and, if you still don't get the idea, he just takes your name off the rolls."
>
> Justice Department sources said another cause of Sullivan's losing confrontation with Hoover was that the short, fiery Irishman had developed strong relationships with Atty. Gen. John N. Mitchell and other top Justice officials, apparently casting doubt on his loyalty to the director.
>
> The initial break between Sullivan and Hoover came during the early 1960's, ex-FBI sources said, when Sullivan argued that major domestic threat was no longer the U.S. Communist party USA, but rather the Ku Klux Klan's efforts to thwart civil rights advances in the South.
>
> "This advance was unfavorably received by the director, but Sullivan was persistent and actually made some gains in switching our emphasis," the source said. "But he lost the whole-hearted backing of Hoover after that and the gap between them widened as the years went by."
>
> Sullivan reportedly was the only top FBI executive addressed by his first name by Hoover in recent years. Sullivan is described as a favorite of Hoover's for years because of his intellectual approach to his duties.

Embrace or Demolish

Management and Machiavelli by Anthony Jay is an exciting historical and political analysis of the similarities between corporations and states.[46] Jay contends that many of Machiavelli's observations about power made in the

15th century are still valid. Some of these observations can be translated into power acquisition strategies. For instance, the following passage quoted from *The Prince* by Machiavelli provides guidelines for the conquest of smaller nations.[47]

> Upon this one has to remark that men ought either to be well treated or crushed, because they can avenge themselves of lighter injuries, of more serious ones they cannot; therefore the injury that is done to a man ought to be of such a kind that one does not stand in fear of revenge.

Jay then extrapolates this strategy to the situation of modern corporate takeovers:[48]

> The guiding principle is that senior men in taken-over firms should either be warmly welcomed and encouraged or sacked; because if they are sacked they are powerless, whereas if they are simply downgraded they will remain united and resentful and determined to get their own back.

As described in the preceding chapter, Machiavellianism in this form creates yet another source of stress in corporate life. An executive in an acquired firm may be the victim of an indiscriminate application of this strategy.

Divide and Rule

Ancient in origin, this well-known political strategy often has disastrous consequences for the organization in terms of teamwork and coordination. Underlying the use of this power tactic is the expectation that enemies will not unite forces and form a coalition to work against you. The dean of one college in a university, by an occasional remark, engendered controversy between the deans of two other colleges. His strategy was that he would gain in power in the eyes of the president because two of the other deans could not agree on overall university problems. Instead, they became engrossed in their personal disagreements. William H. Newman illustrates *divide* and *rule* with the situation of a chief engineer who hoped to strengthen his position by being the person with the balance of power among the senior executives.[49] Deliberately stirring up rivalry between the manufacturing and sales department was the strategy he chose to achieve the balance of power among the senior executives.

Manipulation of Classified Information

Power in most organizations accrues to the individual with access to vital information. Having access to such information, the politically astute manager can control others by manipulating this information.[50] For instance, the company controller can exert influence over others by advising them in advance about financial transactions in the company that could affect their department. Having shared such information with another executive in the organization, the controller is now owed a favor by the latter executive.

Robert Townsend, in his satirical yet insightful *Up the Organization*, cautions about the disadvantages of early release of information:[51]

> If you discovered how to eliminate air pollution for $1.50 per state, the worst way to accomplish it would be to announce your discovery. You'd be amazed at how many people would oppose your scheme. The best way, if you could stay alive and out of jail, would be just to start eliminating it, state by state.

Townsend further explains that preliminary announcement of your plans serves to unsettle potential supporters and to give opponents of your plan time to construct real and imaginary defenses.

Make a Quick Showing

Skepticism about changes can sometimes be overcome by the change agent first accomplishing something worthwhile on a minor problem. Newman cites the example of computer specialists first demonstrating the potential of electronic data processing to management by affecting economies in handling payroll or accounts receivable. Having demonstrated merit on such routine operations, they can gain acceptance of more elaborate programming tactics, which may take two years of preparatory work.[52] Once having enlarged the data processing facility, the manager in charge accumulates additional power.

Collect and Use IOUs

One vital source of power in organizations, Schoonmaker reasons, is the control of something that other people need such as information, money, or jobs. People higher ranking than you then need your cooperation and "you can use your power to bargain for favors, freedom, assignments, and even raises and promotions."[53] Power of this nature must be used subtly (with political astuteness). Schoonmaker recommends that the best way to use this power is to help people whenever you can, but to make it clear that you have done that person a favor. Later, when the need is critical, the IOU can be cashed. Here is a simple example of how an IOU was collected and used in a complex organization:

> A general foreman in a mill was advised by an executive that the latter's son was seeking summer employment. The general foreman

obliged by finding a job for the young man that both paid well and was physically safe in comparison to many other jobs in the mill. One year later, the foreman wanted to accumulate some vacation time in order to take an extended vacation. Although company policy discouraged accumulating vacation time, the executive who owed the foreman a favor was quite flexible in his interpretation of this policy.

Fabianism—Avoid Decisive Engagement

Acceptance of your ideas and the consequent acquisition of power is sometimes best accomplished by making gradual rather than revolutionary changes. Newman illustrates this principle with the situation of an executive who was brought into a company that had been coasting along well without new ideas for over a decade.[54] Instead of assuming his ultimate position of general manager immediately, he occupied the newly created position of sales promotion manager. This position provided him an opportunity to learn the business and make gradual suggestions for improvement. He carefully avoided clashes with the "old guard" and was patient about implementing his new ideas. Progress on many specific projects was slow, but eventually the new manager's power was enhanced because knowledgeable people remained with the organization and cooperation was sound.

Camel's Head in the Tent

According to the observations of Newman, sometimes a small beginning can be made when a total program would be unacceptable.[55] Step-by-step, the political power player wins his demands and gains power. One regional manager sought to develop his own group of staff services and rely less upon regional headquarters. Centralization of staff services was the current trend within his corporation, which led to his ideas being resisted. As a countermaneuver, this manager began by having his own employee training program developed because of what he insisted were "regional differences in types of people employed." The training program was successful, thus lowering resistance to his hiring a market planner to work exclusively on the problems of his region. Following this, the regional manager received authorization to hire consultants to help him with a variety of local problems. Ultimately, this "Camel's Head in the Tent" approach provided the regional manager with the autonomy he was seeking in the first place.

Things Must Get Worse Before They Get Better

Power in an organization is gained to the extent that a manager is able to implement programs emanating from his department. Considerable energy, effort, and time are often expended just to sell others on the value of a program or procedure. If the need for a change is not generally recognized, Newman points out that delay is sometimes wise even though the executive is convinced of the need for the action.[56] Thus, a systems manager who recognizes the need for a computer-based inventory of spare parts may have to wait until customer complaints about spare parts reach uncomfortable heights. Prior to the emergency situation, top management may be unwilling to invest money in a modern spare parts inventory control system.

Take Counsel with Caution

Norman H. Martin and John Howard Simms, in their classic analysis of the use of power by executives, suggest a strategy that is geared more toward preventing the erosion of power already acquired than toward acquiring power. The able executive, according to their reasoning, must be cautious about how he seeks and receives advice. Asking advice sometimes results in decisions actually being made by subordinates. The advice of Martin and Simms may seem out of keeping with today's emphasis on participatory management and shared decision making. Nevertheless, their suggestions must be carefully pondered before being ignored:[57]

> If an executive allows his subordinates to provide advice when he does not specifically call for it, he may find himself subject, not only to pressure, but to conflicting alignments of forces within his own ranks. A vague sort of policy which states, "I am always ready to hear your advice and ideas on anything," will waste time, confuse issues, dilute leadership, and erode power.

CAN POLITICS BE IGNORED?

Observers of political maneuvering in organizations agree on the importance of political behavior to success in organizational life.[58] To ignore politicking is to ignore an integral facet of organizational behavior. It would be equally naive to ignore such aspects of organizational behavior as the informal organization or the grapevine. Moral and ethical principles, however, dictate the extent and type of political maneuvering a given individual will practice in order to advance or acquire power. An ambitious person views the political maneuver of getting out from under a patron who has reached his plateau as an ethically sound procedure. In contrast, the same individual might be repelled by the political maneuver of backdating a memo to prove he was not to blame for a corporate blooper. The intent here is not to engage in the polemics of what is moral or immoral in organizational life but to underscore the importance of being sensitive to the ubiquitous nature of political maneuvering.

What weight should be given to "politics" as a factor in success? Arbitrarily, it is suggested here that *awareness of political factors* or *political astuteness* is one more component to be included in a multiple success factor already consisting of job competence, high motivation, and fortuitous circumstances. For example, however brilliant, hard working, and fortunate a junior executive at the Chevrolet Division of General Motors, it would be politically insensitive for him to drive a Volkswagen to the company parking lot.

Ardent believers in the merit system soft-pedal the importance of politically oriented behavior in the pursuit of career advancement. George Proxy (a pen name chosen by the author for fear of reprisal) in *How to Get Your Boss's Job* offers the following advice by one Harry G. Thayer as representative of this extreme position:[59]

> ... Forget yourself in your work. If your employer sees that you are more concerned about your own interests than about his, that you are fussy about getting credit for every little or big thing that you do, then you are apt to be passed by when a responsible job has to be filled ... Don't worry about how big an increase in your salary you can contrive to get. Don't let your mind dwell on money at all, if you can help it. Throw yourself, body, soul and spirit, into whatever you are doing ... The truth is that in every organization, no matter how large or small, someone is taking notice of any employee who shows special ability.

ANTIDOTES TO POLITICAL MANEUVERING

Political maneuvering, in excess, can have negative consequences to an organization with relation to productivity and morale. When political factors far outweigh merit, to cite one example, many effective employees may become disgruntled and quit. Fortunately, some evidence has accumulated that political maneuvering in organizations can be reduced to realistic proportions even if not eliminated. This evidence is discussed next.

Creating an Organizational Climate of Openness and Trust

This appears to be the most effective overall antidote to political maneuvering in the opinion of several writers.[60] Politically oriented behavior, at an underlying level, is probably a reaction to the fear of the consequences of revealing the truth about oneself. Most people in organizations probably fear the consequences of leveling about their true feelings and opinions with people above them in the hierarchy. Rare is the chemist, for example, who will tell his project leader that he feels the technical director of the company is technically incompetent. When organizational members do not fear the consequences of telling the truth they are more willing to be candid and nonpolitical.

Behavioral science techniques such as sensitivity training and organization development have had widespread application in industry for purposes of creating climates of openness and trust. When these ends are met, politically oriented behavior is reduced.[61]

Providing Objective Measurements of Performance

This is another palliative to political maneuvering. Chester Burger notes in *Survival in the Executive Jungle* that political situations result when an executive is evaluated using any measurements other than an objective method.[62] As discussed earlier, less need exists to engage in political maneuvering when a person's contribution can be measured directly.

Despite their psychological pitfalls, management-by-objectives or management-by-results systems should be helpful in reducing politically oriented behavior.[63] The sales manager who meets all his objectives under management by objectives has some factual data upon which to be promoted. Currying favor with his superiors then becomes a less influential factor in his promotion.

Nonpolitically Oriented Behavior on the Part of Top Management

This can serve as a subtle reminder that straightforward behavior is encouraged in the organization. Conversely, the frequent display of politically oriented behavior suggests to organization members that politicking is both necessary for survival and considered acceptable behavior. Examples set by top management often have a pervasive influence on the behavior of individuals at lower organizational levels. One management consulting firm was beset with problems of low morale, high turnover, and frequent disputes among its various divisions about allocation of personnel and other resources. Observers close to the scene felt that the political maneuverings of the president contributed to, if not caused, these problems:

> Roger Crowell, the president, was especially sensitive to the image he portrayed to present and potential clients and to personnel below him in the organization. When a visitor to the firm presented himself at the reception desk, he was asked to be seated and told, "Mr. Crowell will be with you shortly." Within several minutes the visitor would be escorted to a small anteroom outside Crowell's office. Here the visitor was usually required to wait 15 minutes before he could be seen by the president. Asked, by an internal staff member, why he used the anteroom, Crowell responded: "... To create the right impression of a dynamic, busy, consulting firm."

> Crowell employed another tactic to impress both outsiders and internal personnel. Conversations with visitors to his office were frequently interrupted by a buzz from his secretary. He would ritualistically pick up the phone, cup the receiver in his hand, and announce, "Excuse me, this is from Los Angeles" (the city would change from time to time). Soon it became well documented that the secretary was instructed to fabricate these phone calls.

> Part of Crowell's responsibility as president was to attract new business to the firm. During staff meetings he would report on the status of client development activities. At three consecutive staff meetings he made the point that although a particular company was "... quite interested in our firm working with them, I am not sure that theirs is the kind of problem we want to undertake." Staff members recognized that new business prospects were slim and that Crowell was either rationalizing or lying.

Meshing of Individual and Organizational Goals

This is perhaps the ideal antidote to political maneuvering.[64] When the goals, aspirations, and needs of employees can be met through their jobs, they tend to engage in behavior that will foster the growth, longevity, and productivity of their organization. TRW systems, an acknowledged leader in the application of behavioral science methods to work settings, feels they have minimized some aspects of politicking by merging individual goals with corporate aims. Project or *matrix* type organizations are established to accomplish company objectives. The essence of its contribution to meshing of individual and organizational goals is outlined by a TRW representative:[65]

With a wide range of work assignments to choose from, he can match his experience to his needs and goals. "The emphasis at TRW in career development is the creation of a climate that encourages self-actualization for the individual and the utilization of . . . self-actualization in terms of work for the company. . . ."

Job Rotation

This is sometimes helpful in minimizing political maneuvering. Assume that there is intense competition between two product managers within a food company. Each may waste company resources and time in fighting political battles. Should the two product managers switch assignments, they will be better able to understand each other's point of view and recognize the value of cooperation. Harold Rush provides a specific case of this antidote to political maneuvering.[66] Four vice-presidents were contenders for the presidency of a large oil company. Teamwork among the four men was poor. To cope with the problem, all four executives rotated jobs. For example, the manufacturing head became the sales vice-president and the sales vice-president took over the finance department. All four executives were rotated through the department twice in five years. Results observed by Rush included better teamwork, broadened backgrounds, and lessening of competition among the departments.

Several implications for policy making are suggested by the antidotes to political maneuvering mentioned above and by the chapter material in general. To the extent that some forms of political maneuvering are dysfunctional, policy should be formulated and implemented that minimizes such behavior. Four policies are thus suggested that should be helpful in minimizing political maneuvering.

First, programs of organization development (OD) should become an on-going part of attempts at organizational improvement. A variety of these programs are described in Chapter 13; for now it is sufficient to indicate their major intent. OD is designed to move organization members toward openness, frankness, and honesty in dealing with each other. Duplicity and deceit become less relevant forms of behavior in an organization successfully changed by OD.

Second, a system of management by objectives (MBO), or any other effective system of objectively measuring performance, should be integrated into company policy. As mentioned above, the need for political maneuvering is decreased when performance can be objectively measured. The manner in which MBO (or any other management system) is implemented heavily influences whether or not it will result in organizational improvement. For instance, Stephen J. Carroll, Jr. and Henry L. Tosi, Jr. concluded after a five-year study of MBO in the Black and Decker Manufacturing Company that[67]

> These data show the importance of organizational commitment to MBO. Managers must feel that the MBO program is important, that the company is serious about it.

Third, formal programs of career development and counseling should be made available to managerial and professional personnel. Few organizations pay more than scant attention to such concerns at this writing. Many managers and professional people resort to political maneuvering because they have limited awareness of more straightforward methods of career progression. Career planning would provide organization members with a more acute awareness of mobility routes within their organization. Additionally, it might provide employees with more valid data for deciding to remain in or leave their present organization. Many valuable managers and professional people are never told the organization's plans for them until they have already accepted a position with another organization!

Fourth, and related to career planning for individuals, the manpower planning function in most organizations could profitably be strengthened. Experiences could be designed for individuals that would help them grow in competence and stature and would simultaneously provide the organization with a more flexible cadre of managers and professionals. As already practiced in many complex organizations, job rotation (including assignment to temporary task forces) helps mesh individual and organizational goals. Meshing of this nature minimizes political maneuvering because people tend to deal in a straightforward way with institutions that provide them opportunities for growth and recognition.

RELATIONSHIP TO CORE PROPOSITIONS

Political maneuvering in organizations can be analyzed from the framework for organizational behavior presented in Chapter 1. The analysis that follows highlights how political maneuvering, similar to other phenomena studied in this book, relates to the four core propositions.

Human Behavior

Career advancement and power acquisition strategies both fit neatly into theories of human motivation. Simplistically, it might be said that both are expressions of the needs for power, accomplishment, and self-fulfillment. Political behavior takes place in order to gratify human needs. Equally important, it must be noted that political maneuvering in organizations gives one an opportunity to satisfy baser motives, such as gluttony, self-aggrandizement, and the expression of hostility toward others.

Some aspects of political maneuvering can be interpreted as a human response to frustration. Individuals who realize that their careers are not advancing swiftly enough on the basis of merit may experience frustration. In retaliation, they may resort to more devious methods of rising in the hierarchy.

Situational Nature

Political maneuvering does not take place in a vacuum. The extent to which organizational members manipulate to get ahead or grab for power is a joint function of individual and organizational characteristics. For instance, given a devious and distrustful person placed in an organization climate characterized by lack of trust, the inevitable result is political maneuvering. As discussed in the "Antidotes" section of this chapter, certain organizational practices, such as measuring people on the basis of result, tend to discourage people from "playing politics." In short, the situation is unfavorable for political maneuvering.

Systemic Nature

Political behavior in organizations is, in essence, the distribution of authority and power. Organizations, from this viewpoint, can be conceived of as power or political systems. As power is transferred and distributed throughout the system, certain functional and dysfunctional consequences result. To illustrate, when financial groups have too much power in an organization, it is conceivable that the quality of manufactured goods will suffer. The emphasis on cost control leads some managers to sacrifice quality. When marketing management retains too much control, profit margins may diminish because considerable sums are invested in product planning and promotion.

Organizations typically have some type of feedback mechanism to control inappropriate use of power and authority. Attitude surveys and other organization development approaches feed data back into the system to help determine if power and authority are being abused. Financial and operational audits also help to determine if power is being abused. Data from audits are fed back to management and (hopefully) appropriate adjustments to the distribution of power are made.

Structure and Process

Political maneuvering in organizations is related to aspects of both the formal and informal organization (or structure and process). Theoretically, if an organization had a perfect system of measuring the performance of people and then promoting them on the basis of merit, political maneuvering would be both unnecessary and futile. Similarly, if an organization were able to distribute power only on the basis of its relationship to overall organizational objectives, power acquisition strategies would be pointless. In the realities of organization life, systems of measuring and rewarding performance are less than perfect. The manner in which such systems are implemented (process variables) combines with the formal system to either encourage or discourage political maneuvering.

In sum, *how* a merit system is implemented and the nature of the merit system itself influence the degree of political maneuvering. Similarly, even a carefully drawn management-by-objectives system requires intelligent application. Misapplication (e.g., overrigid) of such a system encourages devious behavior.

GUIDELINES FOR ACTION

1. Success in organizational life requires job competence, hard work, fortuitous circumstances, and an awareness of political realities. In addition, there are many demographic characteristics that influence your promotability. Do what you can to improve your standing on all the promotion factors under your control.
2. Whether you decide to participate in or avoid political maneuvering, it will be useful for you to recognize when others are attempting to manipulate their way to power or advancement.
3. Mobility (experience in different jobs) has become a vital factor for achieving an executive position. Often the individual has to assume the initiative for acquiring mobility.
4. The single most important political strategy (in this author's opinion) is to help your immediate superior accomplish his job objectives.
5. Political maneuvering in organizations can best be kept to a minimum by creating an organizational climate of trust, openness, and candor. Confrontation is useful in disarming politicos.

QUESTIONS

1. You are the systems and procedure manager in a branch office of a commercial bank. The computer operations supervisor in your group informs you of an opening for a systems and procedures manager in the home office of a medium-

size bank. The position sounds ideal from your standpoint. How would you handle the situation?

2. Jerry Mitchell is 24 years old, short, intelligent, well motivated, and black. His undergraduate major is history, and he has just completed an MBA program. All Jerry's work experience has been of a part-time, nonspecialized nature. He states: "I want to become an officer in a big company." What career advice can you offer Jerry Mitchell?

3. Which are the three most ethical political maneuvers described in this chapter? Which are the three most unethical? On what basis did you make your judgments?

4. Based upon inputs you have received from this chapter and other information you may have available, how effective is that age-old strategy of "marrying the boss's daughter?"

5. Reread the FBI case presented earlier in this chapter. List all the career advancement or power acquisition strategies illustrated in this case history. Explain how each strategy is illustrated.

6. Are you an office politician? Insight about this matter can be obtained from completing a questionnaire prepared for *Nation's Business* by Eugene E. Jennings (reproduced here with permission).[68] Answers to these questions are found at the back of the book, on the page preceding the Index.

ARE YOU AN OFFICE POLITICIAN?

The test below will help you determine if you are among the one out of three business executives who have used power tactics to advance their careers. The statements were devised by Prof. Eugene E. Jennings and his fellow researchers at Michigan State University for use in their studies of executive behavior. The point of the test is to read the statements given, then mark each according to whether you tend to agree or disagree with it. Then turn to the answer page (p. 463) for an analysis of what your responses mean.

	Agree	Disagree
People will generally remember kindness longer than unkindness.	_____	_____
People generally look for opportunities to win favorable comparison over others.	_____	_____
People are generally unreliable when serving interests other than their own.	_____	_____
Many people will misrepresent themselves if they have a lot to gain and exposure isn't likely.	_____	_____
A man seeking to better himself in a chosen field should attempt to identify with those who have attained excellence.	_____	_____
The less people know about a person, the more they will respect him.	_____	_____
All men are both good and bad but at times it is wise to consider them more bad than good.	_____	_____
It is often advantageous to withhold information and to time its release.	_____	_____
One should tell the truth or not depending upon how others are affected.	_____	_____

	Agree	Disagree
One should not overly commit oneself except on basic issues of right and wrong.	———	———
One should know why people are one's friends.	———	———
An executive should be sure that subordinates rely solely on him.	———	———
It is wise never to let someone know that he has deeply offended you.	———	———
One should appear to believe that people are trustworthy.	———	———
One should personally select the subordinates upon whom one's success greatly depends.	———	———
Success is at times dependent upon being able to outguess what the other fellow will do.	———	———
It is oftentimes necessary to act boldly and swiftly in order to impress and disarm.	———	———
Friendship tends to blind one's critical faculties.	———	———
Words do not determine motives.	———	———
Bluffing is basic to gaining and maintaining a high reputation.	———	———
If one has to punish severely, it should not be spread out over a period of time.	———	———
Concessions should be more apparent than real.	———	———
It is much safer to be feared than loved by your subordinates.	———	———
One should not compete if one is not able to make a good showing.	———	———
It is necessary to keep some people in place by making them afraid of you.	———	———
Agreements should be made to commit the other person.	———	———
Loyalty of a new associate may be tested by suddenly giving him a lot of authority.	———	———
An executive should not allow subordinates to determine what matters are crucial.	———	———
Past promises need not stand in the way of success.	———	———
It is wise never to allow one's reputation to be fully tested.	———	———
If you have deeply offended another, you should not entrust him with important matters.	———	———
One should always keep in reserve some means of rewarding unexpected excellence.	———	———
One should not enter into a cooperative venture if one is going to risk personal advantage.	———	———
Sometimes it is important to appear ignorant in order not to be stampeded into action.	———	———

NOTES

1. This definition combines ideas expressed in *Webster's Seventh New Collegiate Dictionary* and *The Random House Dictionary of the English Language: The Unabridged Edition.*
2. Edward H. Hegarty, *How to Succeed in Company Politics: The Strategy of Executive Success.* New York: McGraw-Hill, 1964, p. iv.
3. Andrew J. DuBrin, *The Practice of Managerial Psychology.* Elmsford, N.Y.: Pergamon Press, 1972, p. 177.
4. Bernard M. Bass, "How to Succeed in Business According to Business Students and Managers," *Journal of Applied Psychology,* Vol. 52, No. 3, June 1968, pp. 254–262.
5. Abraham Zaleznik, "Power and Politics in Organizational Life," *Harvard Business Review,* Vol. 48, No. 3, May–June 1970, pp. 47–60.
6. J. D. Batten and James L. Swab, "How to Crack Down on Company Politics," *Personnel,* Vol. 42, No. 1, January–February 1965, pp. 8–20.
7. Eugene E. Jennings, *The Mobile Manager: A Study of the New Generation of Top Executives.* Ann Arbor, Mich.: University of Michigan Press, 1967.
8. Eugene E. Jennings, "You Can Spot Office Politicians," *Nation's Business,* Vol. 47, No. 12, December 1959, pp. 42–57.
9. *Ibid.,* p. 56.
10. Reed M. Powell, *Race, Religion, and the Promotion of the American Executive,* College of Administrative Science Monograph No. AA-3, Ohio State University, 1969.
11. *Ibid.,* p. 38.
12. *Ibid.,* p. 39.
13. Hal Higdon, "Executive Chess," *Playboy,* March 1971, p. 145.
14. Two recent sources about the stresses placed upon the wives of successful men are Andrew J. DuBrin, *Women in Transition.* Springfield, Ill.: Charles C. Thomas, 1972, pp. 42–59; and Joanne Triebal, "Your Wife: A Prisoner of Your Success?" *Industry Week,* June 26, 1972, pp. 29–32.
15. One article representing this point of view is Auren Uris, "Your Business is Her Business," *Nation's Business,* May 1970, pp. 73–76.
16. Garda W. Bowman, "What Helps or Harms Promotability," *Harvard Business Review,* Vol. 42, No. 1, January–February 1964, pp. 6–26.
17. "Toiling at the Edge of the Economy," *Black Enterprise,* April 1971, p. 65. © Earl D. Graves Publishing Company, Inc., 1971.
18. Stuart A. Taylor, "The Black Executive and the Corporation—A Difficult Fit," *mba,* January 1972, p. 91.
19. Powell, *op. cit.,* p. 46.
20. Mobilography in complete technical detail is found in the appendix to *The Mobile Manager* by Jennings, *op. cit.* A briefer introduction to the same material is found in a *Playboy* article by Higdon, *op. cit.*
21. Higdon, *op. cit.,* p. 150.
22. Richard E. Gleason, "Planning the Way to the Top," *Business Horizons,* Vol. 14, No. 3, June 1971, pp. 60–63.
23. Jennings, 1967, *op. cit.*
24. Gleason, *op. cit.*
25. Jennings, 1967, *op. cit.*
26. Auren Uris, *Turn Your Job into a Successful Career.* New York: Simon & Schuster, 1967.
27. *Time,* July 24, 1972, p. 67.
28. Jennings, 1967, *op. cit.*
29. E. A. Butler, "Corporate Politics—Monster or Friend?" *Generation,* Vol. 3, No. 3, March 1971, pp. 54–58, 74.

30. "Apple-Polishing Sometimes Pays Off," *OBI Interaction: The Management Psychology News-letter,* Vol. 1, No. 8, July 16, 1971, pp. 5–6, from Organizational Behavior Institute, 666 Fifth Avenue, New York, N.Y. 10019.

31. *Ibid.,* p. 5.

32. Laurence J. Peter and Raymond Hull, *The Peter Principle: Why Things Always Go Wrong.* New York: Morrow, 1969, pp. 56–58.

33. Butler, *op. cit.,* p. 56.

34. Batten and Swab, *op. cit.*

35. Zaleznik, *op. cit.,* p. 52.

36. E. A. Butler, *Move In and Move Up: A Guide to Making the Most Crucial "Life or Death" Decisions.* New York: Macmillan, 1970.

37. *Ibid.,* p. 32.

38. *Ibid.*

39. Vance Packard, *The Pyramid Climbers.* New York: McGraw-Hill, 1962.

40. "Backdating" in this context means writing a memo today but recording an earlier date.

41. Packard, *op. cit.,* p. 204.

42. E. Peter Schneider reported this practice in an unpublished paper, Rochester Institute of Technology, 1972.

43. Alan N. Schoonmaker, *Executive Career Strategy.* New York: American Management Association, 1971, p. 99.

44. Mayer N. Zald (editor), *Power in Organizations: Proceedings of the First Annual Vanderbilt Sociology Conference.* Nashville, Tenn.: Vanderbilt University Press, 1970. A briefer, classical article about the use of power by managers is Norman H. Martin and John H. Simms, "Thinking Ahead: Power Tactics," *Harvard Business Review,* Vol. 34, No. 6, November–December 1956, pp. 25–36, 140.

45. *Democrat and Chronicle,* Rochester, N.Y., October 3, 1971, p. 1.

46. Anthony Jay, *Management and Machiavelli.* New York: Holt, Rinehart and Winston, 1967.

47. *Ibid.,* p. 6.

48. *Ibid.*

49. William H. Newman, *Administrative Action: The Techniques of Organization and Management,* second edition. Englewood Cliffs, N.J.: Prentice-Hall, 1963. The section on strategic planning is found in David R. Hampton, Charles E. Summer, and Ross A. Webber, *Organizational Behavior and the Practice of Management.* Glenview, Ill.: Scott, Foresman, 1968, p. 635.

50. Packard, *op. cit.,* p. 205.

51. Robert Townsend, *Up the Organization.* New York: Alfred A. Knopf, 1970, p. 55.

52. Newman, *op. cit.,* p. 634.

53. Schoonmaker, *op. cit.,* p. 115.

54. Newman, *op. cit.,* p. 634.

55. *Ibid.,* pp. 634–635.

56. *Ibid.,* p. 639.

57. Martin and Simms (note 44), *op. cit.,* p. 28.

58. For example, see Butler, 1971, *op. cit.* and Packard, *op. cit. See also,* George Proxy (pen name), *How to Get Your Boss's Job.* New York: Grosset & Dunlap, 1968.

59. Proxy, *ibid.,* p. 127.

60. Batten and Swab, *op. cit.;* James C. Dwyer, "The Management Sandbox," *Personnel Journal,* Vol. 49, No. 10, October 1970, pp. 856–857; Rush, quoted in "Playing Office Politics or The Grab for Glory," *Industry Week,* Vol. 166, March 23, 1970, p. 25.

61. Rush, *ibid.* An important source of information about how organizations can be made more trusting and open is Chris Argyris, *Intervention Theory and Method: A Behavioral Science View.* Reading, Mass.: Addison-Wesley, 1970.

62. Chester Burger, *Survival in the Executive Jungle*. New York: Macmillan, 1964 (quoted in Rush, *op. cit.*, p. 25).
63. DuBrin, *The Practice of Managerial Psychology*, pp. 122–124, presents an analysis of some of these psychological pitfalls. For example, management-by-objectives systems often encourage people to focus on results and not on the methods they use to achieve these results. More extensive information on this topic is found in W. J. Reddin, *Effective Management by Objectives: The 3-D Method of MBO*. New York: McGraw-Hill, 1971.
64. The reader is referred to two classic treatments of this topic: Douglas McGregor, *The Human Side of Enterprise*. New York: McGraw-Hill, 1960; and Chris Argyris, *Integrating the Individual and the Organization*. New York: Wiley, 1964.
65. "Playing Office Politics," *op. cit.*, p. 30.
66. *Ibid.*, p. 29.
67. Stephen J. Carroll, Jr. and Henry L. Tosi, Jr., *Management By Objectives: Applications and Research*. New York: Macmillan, 1973, p. 45.
68. Jennings, 1959, *op. cit.*, p. 57. © 1959 *Nations Business*—The Chamber of Commerce of the United States. Reprinted by permission.

PART III

Small Groups

Preview

A substantial share of organizational behavior takes place within the context of small groups. This section of the text concentrates on those aspects of small group behavior that the author feels are crucial for understanding and predicting the behavior of people at work. Emphasis is again placed on information that has the most relevance for knowledge workers.

Information is presented about group relationships (including groups of two) that the knowledge worker will inevitably encounter. For instance, all knowledge workers will be exposed to the leadership style of a superior or will develop a leadership style of their own. Topics such as committees, task forces, leadership styles, communication barriers, and intergroup conflicts constitute the bulk of this section.

One important feature of this section is the applied nature of much of the information. Many ideas and concepts are presented that the reader can translate directly into the improvement of managerial skills. For example, most of the ideas discussed in Chapter 8 on coaching and counseling subordinates can be used as a check list to examine approaches currently used by the reader. Similarly, the suggestions for overcoming barriers to communication presented in Chapter 9 can be translated directly into the acquisition of new skills (provided that the reader is willing to expend the necessary time and effort).

6

Small Group Behavior

Organizations vary in size from owner-operated boutiques of two people to multidivision complexes of over 200,000 employees. Despite this wide range in size, much of the work in any organization takes place in the context of a small group. Work groups are the basic units or *modules* by which an organization can achieve its goals and objectives. An understanding of behavior in small groups is thus essential for an understanding of organizational behavior. Group dynamics, a major component of sociology and social psychology, is the field of study that attempts to explain small group behavior. *Group Dynamics*, a book by Dorwin Cartwright and Alvin Zander, is one authoritative source of information about this important field of knowledge.[1]

Later chapters in this section of the book examine specific aspects of small group behavior such as leadership, interpersonal communication, and intergroup conflict. For now, some general considerations about small groups and the behavior of people in them will be presented. In addition, attention will be directed toward two increasingly popular manifestations of group life in organizations—committees and temporary task forces. Every knowledge worker will have direct exposure to committees or task forces at some time in his or her organizational life.

WHAT IS A GROUP?

A definition of a group, offered by Edgar H. Schein, is appropriate here: "...any number of people who (1) interact with one another, (2) are psychologically aware of one another, and (3) perceive themselves to be a group."[2] All three aspects of this definition are useful in understanding the nature of a group. Five systems analysts conducting an internal consulting assignment constitute a group. Five systems analysts sharing an elevator ride cannot be considered a true group because they (1) do not interact with each other on the basis of their shared elevator experience, (2) probably have minimal psychological awareness of each other, and (3) do not perceive themselves as a group. Size also must be taken into consideration in defining a group. Two people, technically speaking, are sufficient to comprise a group. Beyond around 25 people, group members can no longer interact with each other on a frequent basis, and they begin to lose the *feel* of being a group. An *organization* is really an aggregate of many smaller groups.

Groups have been classified into many different types.[3] Formal groups are those deliberately created by the organization, such as a credit department. Informal groups arise in the organization but are not deliberately planned. Several people from different departments may gather together at lunch on an ongoing basis and discuss both social and work topics, thus constituting a group. Several behavioral scientists from different divisions within a large corporation may gather together periodically to discuss common concerns and to share techniques. Both situations illustrate the emergence of an informal group.

Schein subdivides informal groups using terminology developed by Melville Dalton.[4] *Horizontal cliques* are informal associations of organizational members of approximately the same organizational rank who work in the same general area. The group of behavioral scientists mentioned above fits into this category. *Vertical cliques* are groups composed of members from different levels within the same department (e.g., six people from marketing who meet together every Friday after work for a "rap session" at a nearby cocktail lounge). *Mixed cliques* are groups composed of people of different ranks, departments, and physical locations. According to Schein, mixed cliques arise to fulfill functional needs not taken care of by the formal organization. They are "private arrangements" made to circumvent normal channels. A mortgage coordinator may thus get a "quick reading" from his boss before going through the elaborate, formal procedure of processing a loan application.

The subject of formal versus informal work groups will be reintroduced later in the discussion of the dual leadership theory in Chapter 7. An understanding of leadership at the small group level requires a study of the difference between appointed and emergent leaders. Emergent leaders are those who serve as the leaders of informal work groups. As explained in the dual leadership theory, there are certain advantages to the organization and to the leader when the informal leader receives backing from the formal organization.

Groups have also been classified as those of stable versus unstable membership. This classification has gained in relevance because many organizations are moving toward dynamic and fluid structures characterized by groups of unstable membership. Warren G. Bennis describes these temporary groups as part of an *organic-adaptive* structure that is evolving in organizations that operate under conditions of rapid technological change and growing environmental turbulence.[5] He forecasts such temporary groupings as a key feature of organizations of the future, where problems may be solved by groups of relative strangers. According to Bennis, unstable membership should not impair organizational performance. This position contrasts with the theorizing of Rensis Likert about small groups. As analyzed by B. D. Fine:[6]

> In an organization lacking stable face-to-face work groups, group-oriented methods of supervision would be difficult if not impossible to apply, and interpersonal communication and influence would consequently decline. Capacities for decision making, performance goal setting, motivation, and group loyalty, would decrease, followed eventually by a drop in the levels of end-result variables such as productivity, earnings, satisfaction, and mental health.

Fine conducted a long-term study with over 700 members of an oil refinery to compare the relative superiority of stable and unstable work groups. His data suggested that unstable work group membership does not necessarily impair a department's functioning. Workers in temporary groups are able to contend with the absence of more enduring work relationships without a major disruption of organizational processes.

Groups may also be described according to their psychological climate. For instance, some groups have more team spirit and more intimacy among members than do other groups. (Information in Chapter 11 about organizational climate is also applicable to understanding the climate of small groups.)

A FRAMEWORK FOR UNDERSTANDING SMALL GROUPS

The combined efforts of several behavioral scientists, shown in Figure 6.1,[7,8] have produced a useful frame of reference for understanding small groups. At a minimum, this framework dramatizes the complexity of small group behavior. Any one of the seven classes of variables depicted in Figure 6.1 (group composition, group structure, task and environment, group process, group development, task performance, and effects on group members) has been the subject of extensive study by behavioral

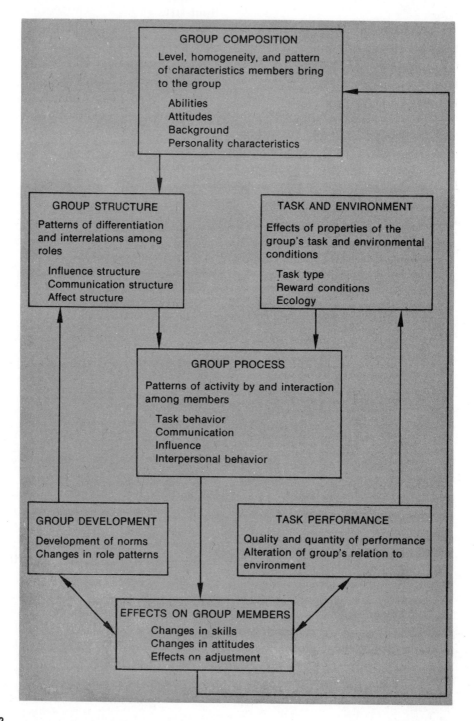

scientists. A brief description of how this framework might be applied to an actual group will illustrate its meaning.

A group consisting of seven management consultants (MCG) is assigned the task of studying the operating efficiency of a governmental agency. Important aspects of MCG's *composition* include the abilities, attitudes, educational backgrounds, and personality characteristics of its members. For example, the group will be more homogeneous if all members have an operations research background. The *group structure* will be a function of both what roles the various members play and how these various roles interrelate. For example, MCG will operate differently if one member acts as a disseminator of messages throughout the group than if all group members have equal access to information.

The *task and environment* also influence group behavior. For instance, if MCG is given minimum cooperation and is seen as a threatening influence to agency welfare, it will have a difficult time accomplishing its mission. *Group process* refers to the actual ongoing workings of the group. For instance, one process is how the members actually go about conducting their study of operational efficiency.

Over time, there is evidence of *group development*. To illustrate, the group will probably decide what amount of work constitutes a "fair share." *Task performance* primarily concerns itself with "how well the group is doing" in accomplishing its mission. Its effectiveness and efficiency will influence its reputation (and viability). Group life has *effects on group members*. At a minimum, members of MCG will develop some new work-related skills including improved ability to participate in teamwork.

A second important characteristic of this framework is that it encompasses a systems view of small group behavior. Three sets of variables—*group composition, group structure,* and *task and environment*—can be viewed as input variables. Continuing with the systems analogy, next comes the *group process* or the central workings of the group. Outputs are the consequences or results of the group's behavior: *group development, task performance,* and *effects on group members*. Eventually these outputs in turn become inputs. For example, the group composition actually changes as the group members become more skilled.

Figure 6.1 A framework for understanding small groups. SOURCE: William G. Scott and Terence R. Mitchell, *Organization Theory: A Structural and Behavioral Analysis.* Homewood, Ill.: Richard D. Irwin and Dorsey Press, 1972, p. 114 (Modification of a figure presented by Joseph E. McGrath in *Social Psychology.* New York: Holt, Rinehart and Winston, 1964, p. 114).

A PRACTICAL THEORY OF SMALL GROUP BEHAVIOR

Small group behavior has been studied from many theoretical perspectives in addition to the systems framework just presented. The sociological perspective of George C. Homans has endured as one useful approach to understanding the social structure of the group.[9] Homans' analysis explains such phenomena as (a) why some people are disliked by other group members, despite a normal personality structure, and (b) how favorable interaction with a person we dislike may lead to viewing him or her more favorably.

Four basic elements underly Homans' analysis of small group behavior: (1) *activity*—the operations people perform within the group, (2) *sentiment*—the feelings and attitudes of people, (3) *interaction*—the communications they carry on, or actual "traffic patterns" with each other, and (4) *norms*—the standards or values they uphold. In addition, Homans distinguishes between external and internal systems within the group. *External* systems deal with how the group can survive in the outside environment. For instance, how might an operations research group justify to top management that it is valuable to the organization? *Internal* systems is group behavior that is an expression of the sentiments that group members develop toward one another as a function of working (or playing) together.

Activities, sentiments, and interactions are mutually interdependent. To illustrate, assume that a black member is added to a management team in which substantial anti-black prejudice exists (sentiments). His job title is controller (activity). Generated by his formal activity or role, the black manager has considerable *interaction* with the white managers; he provides financial advice to other members of the management team. As his advice proves worthwhile (favorable interaction), attitudes toward him become less prejudiced (favorable sentiments). In short, activity has influenced interaction, which in turn influences sentiment.

Homans' analysis was later developed into a concept of social exchange; interaction between people is an exchange of material and non-material goods.[10] Stated in the popular jargon of organizational life, "Do me a favor today and I'll return it tomorrow." The curious expression "There is no such thing as a free lunch" also explains the subtleties of social exchange.

Although Homans' analysis should not be considered an all-encompassing theory of small group behavior, his research has provided support for such common sense hypotheses as the following:[11]

1. The more frequently persons interact with one another, the more favorable will be their sentiments toward one another.
2. People who interact with each other frequently are more like one another in their activities than they are like people with whom they interact less frequently.
3. Group members higher in rank tend to originate and receive more interaction than do members of lower rank.

WHAT FUNCTIONS DOES A GROUP PERFORM?

Work groups, both formal and informal, serve a variety of useful functions to both individuals and organizations. Their resistance to extinction alone would suggest that groups perform a number of constructive purposes.

Assistance in Accomplishing Tasks

Work groups are usually formed by the organization in order to achieve specific tasks.[12] Heart transplants cannot be performed without the combined effort of a smooth-running medical team within the operating room. An aerospace company cannot prepare a proposal for designing and building a flight simulator without the combined efforts of a number of specialists working closely together. Aside from these formal arrangements, many informal arrangements within the group are functional in terms of accomplishing tasks. Management cannot plan in advance for every possible contingency; some gaps are inevitable. Informal arrangements stemming from the work groups help fill in the gaps. For instance, informal arrangements may be made among a group of design engineers to assist each other with complicated design problems. The end result is equipment design of higher technical integrity than if such informal arrangements did not exist.

In short, groups of people working together can often accomplish more than the same number of people working alone. Synergy—a term that has come to mean that the group accomplishes more than the sum of its parts—probably comes about because of the sharing of ideas and the feedback on these ideas that takes place in a cohesive group.

Satisfaction of Psychological Needs

Based upon this author's observations, many people receive most of their work-related satisfactions from group interaction. One example is the college professor whose high point of the day is having coffee with other faculty members and students. Many managers secretly dislike analytical tasks such as planning and budgeting. Job satisfaction to them derives from formal and informal meetings where interaction with people is the primary work activity. Many people dislike positions that are basically devoid of group contact. Some salesmen, insurance claims adjusters, field auditors, and the like sometimes find these positions unsatisfactory because they have a minimum of contact with an enduring work group. Schein has presented an incisive analysis of the psychological functions groups can fulfill for their members. Groups can provide:[13]

1. *An outlet for affiliation needs.* Almost every person needs some friendship, support, and love.

2. *A source of emotional support to group members.* Work groups and therapy groups alike provide members with reassurance and support. When a group member of a cohesive group feels emotionally despondent (down), he or she can rely on the group for some temporary bolstering. Salesmen can complain about customers to the work group; lawyers can vent their frustrations about clients to partners; and case workers can find a sympathetic ear from other case workers when they discuss problems involved in handling agency clients.

3. *A means of coping with a common enemy.* In recent years, white-collar groups have been more attuned to collective action in voicing their complaints about work. People feel more secure when they collectively discuss strategy; collective action is a more powerful mechanism than individual action.

Work groups, of course, also provide some dysfunctions to both the individual and the organization. Strong informal groups can limit productivity by establishing agreed upon maximum levels of performance. For instance, in one research organization an ambitious new member was told "Around here we do not push ourselves too hard" when he appeared to be generating an exceptional amount of work. Individuals with strong needs for independence are usually frustrated by the process of being pressured to adhere to the customs and mores of both the informal and formal work groups.

GROUP PRESSURES TOWARD CONFORMITY

Conformity to group pressure is an emotionally laden topic in organizational life. Members of large organizations, in particular, have been accused of needless conformity in thinking, dress, and living habits. A best-selling book of the 1950s, *The Organization Man*, by William H. Whyte, Jr., is an indictment of some of the conforming practices of knowledge workers in large organizations.[14] As noted in Chapter 4, pressures toward conformity still create strain for some organization members.

Influences the group exerts on members toward conformity have been of long-standing interest to social psychologists. As documented in the widely quoted experiments conducted by Solomon Asch, some people will change their opinions about highly objective matters (such as the relative length of two lines) in the face of group pressures.[15] Asch brought together groups consisting of one genuine subject and various numbers of other subjects who were actually confederates of the experimenter. These confederates were told beforehand to deceive the genuine subject by unanimously agreeing on the "wrong answer" in a series of visual judgments. About one-third of the genuine subjects gave judgments distorted in the direction of the false group consensus. The implication of these and similar experiments for small group behavior outside of a laboratory setting is that groups can generate pressure toward conformity in thinking.

Good, Bad, and Unchallenged Conformity

Conformity, similar to any other complex behavioral phenomenon in organizational life, can be functional or dysfunctional. Another aspect of conformity should also be taken into consideration in attempting to understand it. Some acts of conformity go unchallenged by most people because the conformity required creates no conflicts. Examples of "good," "bad," and "unchallenged" conformity are presented next.

Functional conformity. All computer programmers in one company agree to use the same machine language despite individual preferences. This saves time and money and makes training new programmers a less arduous task. Another example is that all members of the Miami Dolphins football team agree to wear the same uniform. Teammates and fans can then make more accurate identification of the players in the field. Conformity of this nature also may have some positive effect on *esprit de corps.* Conformity to health and safety regulations is yet another example of functional conformity.

Dysfunctional conformity. Four women band together to form an advertising agency. They agree to "play it safe" with their first few clients and present a unified front about advertising campaigns and art work. As part of the unified front, they are careful not to disagree with each other in the presence of a client or client prospect. One client prospect with a potentially sizeable account decides not to use their agency after hearing their presentation. His argument is: "Why should I pay for four people, when I am only getting the thinking of one?" Another example of dysfunctional conformity would be if members of a brokerage firm took a group position on several stocks; all agree to make the same buy or sell recommendation for the same stocks. A given stock may represent a sound investment for most people but not for a few other people in terms of their own unique situation. Conformity to a group norm thus penalizes a minority.

Unchallenged conformity.   A wide variety of minor aspects of behavior and thinking reflect conformity of this nature. People wear clothing to work, typists agree to use black ink, salesmen do not swear at customers, psychiatrists to not laugh at patients, bills are sent out the first of the month, only cash is accepted from customers at bowling lanes, and people say "Good Morning" even on bad mornings! For these and a myriad of other behaviors, people conform in an automatic manner and offer very little resistance to group expectations. It might be argued that if conformity of this nature did not take place, the results could be dysfunctional. What would happen if on a given day one member of a small group did *not* wear clothing to work and salesmen *did* swear at their customers? Conformity to group pressures obviously plays an important role in keeping an organization running smoothly.

Individual Differences in Conformity

People vary widely in their willingness or need to conform to group pressures. Common sense and casual observation would suggest that independently minded and talented people show a smaller likelihood of conforming to group pressures than do dependent and untalented people. A well-known series of studies conducted by Richard S. Crutchfield provides strong support for this statement. More than 450 persons participated in a "group pressure situation" in which they were influenced to change their personal judgments about experimental tasks by the groups. Included in the sample were military officers, college students, and medical students. A correlational analysis of a wide variety of personality and intellectual measures with conformity scores revealed the following characteristics of the person who is able to withstand group pressure and remain independent:[16]

1. intelligence, as measured by standard mental tests;
2. originality, as manifested in thought processes and problem solving;
3. "ego strength," that is, the ability to cope effectively despite stressful circumstances;
4. self-confidence and absence of anxiety and inferiority feelings;
5. optimal social attitudes and behavior such as tolerance, responsibility, dominance, and freedom from disturbed and dependent relationships with other people.

People who readily succumb to group pressures—high conformists—are characterized as ranking much lower on these dimensions of behavior. For example, a person characterized as intellectually average, unoriginal, low in ego strength and self-confidence, and having dependent and disturbed relationships with other people, would probably be a conformist (perhaps out of self-protection!).

Situations that Foster Conformity

Individuals show wide variations in conformity to group norms, and situations also show some variation in the extent to which they encourage or precipitate conformity. Under conditions of crisis or danger, for example, conformity to group norms is highly probable. Should a small group of people be stranded in a cabin during a snowstorm, they will readily accede to the group norm of not venturing outside unless accompanied by another member of the group.

A set of experiments conducted at the University of Michigan provides some relevant information about the conditions under which people will most probably accept performance goals established by the group and/or the leader. (Adhering to performance goals is one measure of conformity.) Abraham K. Korman notes that according to these research results, susceptibility to a social norm as a determinant of work performance increases with:[17]

1. *The ambiguity of the situation.* When people are not certain of what is expected of them they become somewhat dependent upon whatever norms of behavior might be available.

2. *The necessity of going along with the group for goal achievement.* Six people on a product team are willing to adhere to group norms of conduct when it becomes apparent that they are technologically dependent upon one another. For example, team members are willing to adhere to rules and regulations with regard to computer usage if they need computer time to complete a project.

3. *Decreased self-confidence of the individual.* As mentioned earlier, people low in self-confidence are receptive to conforming to group norms of conduct.

4. *The appropriateness of the goals being offered the individual.* When group goals mesh with individual goals, people are quite willing to adhere to group standards of performance. For instance, a law firm might maintain the group productivity norm of having all lawyers bill an average of 65 percent of their time to clients. Members of the firm will probably accept this norm because this level of billing will place them at a desired level of income.

Considerable sentiment exists that some organizations encourage conformity, while others place more emphasis on individuality. Critics of large organizations frequently cite the uniformity in dress and behavior of employees of these companies. One reason that large organizations breed conformity is that a host of rules, regulations, procedures, and customs accumulate in the process of the growth of an organization. Early in their history, most organizations are less in need of formal procedures. More emphasis on formal structure (and therefore conformity to rules and regulations) appears to be an inevitable consequence of large organizational size.[18]

What are the penalties for violating the informal rules imposed by the work group? Social ostracism and withholding emotional support are the two most widely applied forms of punishment. They are described in the case illustration of Perry Bomrad, an insurance underwriter, presented in Chapter 8 in connection with organizational punishments.

EFFECTIVE WORK GROUPS

An identification of the characteristics that differentiate between effective and less effective work groups would be of profound theoretical and practical significance. Identifying these properties would provide more knowledge about small group behavior and would also make for improved functioning of organizations. *Effectiveness* must be measured from at least two perspectives—productivity and satisfaction. As mentioned earlier, two crucial functions of a group are to accomplish tasks and to provide for the psychological satisfaction of group members. Often the same characteristics of a group that facilitate output also facilitate job satisfaction. For instance, a group that provides emotional support to members may foster creativity and allow for the satisfaction of higher level needs. At other times the same characteristics of a group may enhance productivity while diminishing satisfaction, or vice versa. Sometimes a cohesive group, for example, will lead to high member satisfaction but low productivity.

Size

Effective work groups come in different sizes. The optimum size of a work group, as one would suspect, depends upon the nature of the task to be performed. All things being equal, smaller groups are less subject to problems of coordination, but certain qualifying conditions must be considered. In a straight "additive" task, such as accountants preparing income tax returns, each new worker can produce additional units. In tasks where coordination among group members is essential, productivity is dependent upon the most or least competent worker. As noted by William G. Scott and Terence R. Mitchell, in the former case, an increase in size increases the chances of getting a competent individual.[19] Unfortunately, increased group size also increases the probabilities of adding an incompetent person to the group.

The old adage "too many cooks spoil the broth" has relevance for understanding effective work groups. Studies suggest that as group size increases a point of diminishing returns is reached whereby coordination becomes quite difficult and productivity decreases. This is often true when the group size exceeds five people. Alan C. Filley and Robert J. House note that the negative effects on coordination are most marked when the task involves no clear and objective criterion for judging the quality of performance.[20]

Cautiously, the observation is offered that a group of five, six, or seven members is the most effective size for accomplishing tasks of a general nature (e.g., devising a campaign strategy for a local candidate). Paul A. Hare observes that a group of five is most effective, in part because of three characteristics.[21] First, no deadlock is possible with an odd number of group members. Second, a group member does not feel deviant being in the minority, as he or she would in an even smaller group. Third, a group of five is large enough for members to shift roles easily. Summarizing an array of evidence, Philip B. Appelwhite notes: "The trend toward an optimal size of about five or seven is clear, but the 'proof' is lacking."[22]

The safest generalization about group size, as mentioned at the outset of this discussion, is that group size is contingent on the situation. Key situational variables are: (a) amount of coordination required among members—with less coordination required, the group can be larger, (b) task complexity—larger groups are better equipped to handle more complex tasks, (c) urgency of the problem—all things being equal, smaller groups accomplish their mission more quickly.

Emotional Support

One important purpose of a group is to provide emotional support to group members. It follows logically that effective groups are those that do in fact provide support to members. Support of this nature can take the form of verbal encouragement for ideas expressed, listening to a group member's problems, or even providing technical assistance.

Rensis Likert has developed a list of 24 characteristics of an effective work group. Common to almost all of these characteristics is the element of support provided to group members. Three of these 24 characteristics are sufficient to illustrate the principle that an effective work group is supportive:[23]

> The group is eager to help each member develop to his full potential. It sees, for example, that relevant technical knowledge and training in interpersonal and group skills are made available to each member.
>
> All the interaction, problem-solving, decision-making activities of the group occur in a supportive atmosphere. Suggestions, comments, ideas, information, criticisms are all offered with a helpful orientation. Similarly, these contributions are received in the same spirit. Respect is shown for the point of view of others both in the way the contributions are made and the way they are received. . . .
>
> The supportive atmosphere of the highly effective group stimulates creativity. . . . The group attaches high value to new, creative approaches and solutions to its problems and to the problems of the organization of which it is a part. The motivation to be creative is high when one's work group prizes creativity.

Group Cohesiveness

Groups in which members share strong mutual attraction toward one another allow for high member satisfaction but are not necessarily the most productive. Group cohesiveness contributes to increased productivity provided that the goals of the group are aligned with those of management. When the group norm does not favor the goals of management, decreased productivity is the result. Stanley E. Seashore demonstrated that cohesive work groups are high in productivity when group members have high confidence in management. When confidence is low, productivity also tends to be low.[24]

Experimental evidence collected some years ago by Stanley Schacter and his associates helps explain these relationships. Results of their research indicate that group cohesiveness acts as a determinant of whether or not the individual will go along with the group with respect to task performance. Members of cohesive groups tend to accept group goals whether they reflect high or low productivity.[25]

Cooperation Versus Competition

The reward structure given to a group is instrumental in determining whether group members become cooperative or competitive. When people are paid according to individual output they tend to compete among themselves. When group rewards are given, cooperation is the normal result. Scott and Mitchell caution management to match the reward structure to the degree of interdependence inherent in the task:[26]

> To introduce what is traditionally called a competitive system (high differential reward) when employees are dependent upon each other may very well decrease performance instead of increasing it. To make sure that everyone gets the same compensation on a task where employees work and contribute independently may hinder effectiveness.

This admonition was based on an analysis of 24 studies comparing cooperative and competitive groups presented by L. Keith Miller and Robert L. Hamblin.[27] These authors suggested that the concept of cooperation versus competition might fruitfully be understood from two dimensions—interdependence and differential reward. Interdependence refers to the degree to which group members are dependent upon each other to complete a task. An airplane crew would illustrate a highly interdependent situation. Differential reward refers to the degree to which individual effort is compensated. Differential rewards can be classified as high versus low, and so might degree of interdependence, as shown in this contingency table prepared by Scott and Mitchell in their reanalysis of data provided by Miller and Hamblin.[28]

		INTERDEPENDENCE	
		High	Low
DIFFERENTIAL REWARD	High	1	3
	Low	2	4

Miller and Hamblin noted that productivity would be lower (group effectiveness would be less) in situations 1 and 4 than in 2 and 3. Expressed verbally, productivity tends to be low when (a) group members are given quite different rewards for their output, yet they are dependent on each other to get out the work; (b) group members are not given different pay for different output, yet they are not particularly dependent on each other to accomplish their tasks. Readers may observe that this analysis corroborates statements made in Chapter 2 about motivation. People tend to be better motivated (expend more job effort) when reward is matched to output. Productivity, following this logic, would tend to be high in situation 3 where people work independently and rewards are based on individual contribution.

Scott and Mitchell reviewed two studies which suggest that the above analysis applies equally well to the satisfaction dimension of work group effectiveness. For example, situation 2 produces more satisfaction than situation 1. In situations where team members are highly interdependent they prefer not to receive differential compensation.

Homogeneous Versus Heterogeneous Composition

Again, the demands of the situation exert a profound influence upon the realities of organizational behavior. Sometimes groups composed of people of different opinions and abilities lead to high effectiveness, while in other situations homogeneous groups are the most effective. Evidence for this conclusion is supported by a variety of laboratory experiments reviewed by Bernard M. Bass.[29]

Homogeneous groups tend to be the most productive under three conditions: First, when the task is relatively simple and a variety of resources are not needed to complete the task (e.g., a group of accountants preparing the payroll). Second, when considerable cooperation is required to complete a task, homogeneous groups are effective because there is less conflict and competition in such groups. Third, where a chain of reactions is required of a group (e.g., a group of statisticians making pension calculations), group homogeneity is helpful because the group is no better than its poorest member.

Three conditions can also be identified under which heterogeneous groups tend to be the most productive. First, heterogeneous groups are well suited to completing complex tasks because of the diversity of opinion and capability in such groups. Second, when a speedy solution has potentially unfavorable consequences, a heterogeneous group has merit.

Homogeneous groups tend to work more rapidly because of the congruence of opinion. Bass notes that a heterogeneous jury takes longer to reach a decision, thus allowing for a more intensive analysis of the testimony. Third, where creativity is required, groups of dissimilar people have the advantage. Varied resources tend to enhance creativity.

As mentioned with respect to group size, there is probably an optimum balance of homogeneity versus heterogeneity for each task. If group members are too heterogeneous, their difficulties in interacting smoothly with each other may inhibit productivity. Conversely, if the group is too homogeneous, agreement is reached too readily and the resources of the group are sparsely utilized.

Trust and Confidence

A major premise of the organization development (OD) movement is that when mutual trust and confidence exist among group members the group tends to be productive. One section of Chapter 12 discusses methods of bringing about trust and confidence and also some of the evidence about the effectiveness of these approaches. Schein observes that only when groups achieve mutual trust and confidence are they more effective than individuals in solving problems and making decisions.[30] Groups in which distrust and suspicion exist are often counterproductive. The defensive behavior of people in such groups detracts from dealing with underlying or fundamental issues. For instance, when a small task force established to investigate customer complaints expends much effort in blaming each others' departments (rather than establishing confidence in each other) the ensuing defensiveness may hamper problem solving.

Leadership Style

Effective work groups are characterized by a leadership style appropriate to the particular group situation. Leadership style is a major topic by itself and is given separate treatment in the next chapter. Several theories of leadership underscore the interaction of leadership style and characteristics of the group. Fred Fiedler's contingency model of leadership, for example, contends that work group effectiveness can be predicted if the interactions among three variables are studied: (a) type of group task, (b) the position of the leader in the group, and (c) the orientation of the leader toward group members.[31] To illustrate briefly, given a structured task (e.g., erecting a building), a leader with a strong position in the group is likely to produce good results provided he is more task than people oriented.

COMMITTEES

One major manifestation of small group behavior in organizational life is the committee. All but the smallest organizations make use of committees, and large organizations make the most frequent use of them. Despite their widespread criticism and the many popular jokes about their ineffectiveness, committees appear to be a permanent part of complex organizations. Committees are difficult to eliminate in organizations that make any pretense at using democratic approaches to management. One university appointed a committee to study the advisability of using the committee system for reaching so many decisions!

The concept of *committee* is imprecise. A multitude of small groups are included under this general concept. Filley and House interpret a committee as a "... special type of meeting, characterized by a limited membership, a specific task or goal, a designated leader, and an explicit or implicit plan of action."[32] Harold Koontz and Cyril O'Donnell take an even broader view of a committee:[33]

> Whether referred to as a committee, board, commission, or team, its essential nature is the same, for the committee is a group of persons to whom, as a group, some matter is committed.

An important characteristic of committees is that they are superimposed upon an already existing organizational structure. Committees are consequently perceived as a choice assignment or additional burden, depending on the committee member's basic motivation and/or the importance attached to the committee by the organization.

Readers interested in examining some of the empirical evidence about the functioning of committees should consult the appropriate chapter of *Managerial Process and Organizational Behavior* by Filley and House.[34] Attention in this chapter is focused on a few selected aspects of committees including a look at how some companies are led by a committee rather than a single president. A comprehensive overview of the use of committees as part of the organizing function of management is found in *Principles of Management* by Koontz and O'Donnell.[35]

Advantages of Committees

Mention of committees or committee work evokes a negative reaction from most people who have worked in organizations. Nevertheless, a useful purpose will be served by overviewing some of the advantages and disadvantages of committees. Recognizing these negative and positive features will help direct the reader toward more appropriate use of the committee method of management. Advantages of committees can be summarized around nine points.[36]

Pooling of intellectual resources.   One major justification for using the committee method of accomplishing organizational tasks is that "two heads are better than one." One person—the alternative to using a committee—simply may not have the intellectual resources at his or her disposal to arrive at an optimum (or superoptimum) solution to the committee task. Pooling of resources increases the probability of finding such a solution.

Diffusion of responsibility.   Koontz and O'Donnell note that committees are widely used because of the fear of delegating too much authority to a single person. Committees are a vehicle for attempting to diffuse or share responsibility among a group of people. The use of a board of directors illustrates a committee approach to preventing one person—the chief executive officer of the organization—from having too much responsibility and power.

Representation of interested groups.   The committee method of organizing is a convenient one for allowing a range of interested people to provide their input into a common concern. Should a county decide to promote industrial development in its area, many people might wish to make a contribution or at least be heard. For instance, representatives of local industry, the school systems, and county government might wish to participate.

Coordination of plans and policies.   Committees allow for almost automatic coordination of activities. Every committee member present is immediately informed of new developments and what actions need to be taken. A related advantage is that suggestions for improvement or modification of plans can be made on-the-spot within the committee meeting.

Efficient communication of information.   Underlying the coordination advantage of committees is the fact that messages can be communicated efficiently in a committee meeting. All interested parties receive information directly from the transmitter in a face-to-face interaction. This allows for *transactional* communication (*see* Chapter 9 about interpersonal communications), which helps clarify potential misunderstandings and misinterpretations.

Commitment through participation.   Committees are a practical way of managing in a democratic manner. Members at different levels in the organization have an opportunity to participate in plans and policies that will later affect them quite directly. Frequently, this participation is crucial in gaining commitment to organizational goals. Churches and academic institutions, when faced with the need for recruiting a new executive, typically form a search committee composed in part of organizational members. Parishioners and faculty members, it is anticipated, will be more responsive to the new administrative head. In this author's observation, participation only leads to commitment when people who serve on such committees *volunteer* to serve. Being forced to serve on a committee typically leads to resentment and resistance rather than commitment.

Avoidance of action. Management sometimes has a legitimate need to delay action on a problem. A committee is a useful vehicle for postponing action. For instance, if management feels pressed to take action about alleged sound pollution from its machinery, a committee can be appointed to "study the problem." By the time the committee is ready to make a recommendation, management may be in a better financial position to take corrective action on the pollution problem. (The reader is free to make his or her own value judgment about this use of a committee.)

Satisfaction of social needs. As noted earlier in this chapter, an important function of small groups in organizations is to provide for the satisfaction of a variety of psychological needs. Committees perform admirably in fulfilling this function. Cynically, it might be observed that part of the motivation for forming many committees is to help organizational members overcome their feelings of loneliness. Many people occupying administrative positions in both profit-seeking and service-rendering organizations cannot find enough constructive activity to fill their workdays. Pangs of loneliness often arise out of such unfulfilled time. Scheduling a committee meeting is a socially acceptable antidote to this type of loneliness.

Management development. Assignment to a committee can provide valuable developmental experience to people seeking managerial assignments or those already occupying such positions. Benefits of this nature accruing from committees include practice in improving face-to-face communication skills, exposure to different points of view, an opportunity to be recognized by people from diverse places in the organization, and the broadening that stems from working on a problem outside of your specialty area.

Disadvantages of Committees

Disadvantages of a committee can be summarized around five points.[37] (This is not to imply that committees have nine advantages and five disadvantages.)

Misallocation of human resources. Committees are notorious for consuming large numbers of manhours. The real cost of any meeting is difficult to estimate, in part because of the workings of Parkinson's Law in reverse. Assume that five executives averaging $25 per hour attend a two-hour meeting; it is specious reasoning to conclude that this committee meeting cost $250. According to the reverse of Parkinson's Law, these executives will accelerate their pace that day to compensate for the time devoted to the meeting. Nevertheless, unless a committee is highly productive, an undetermined amount of important work goes undone while employees congregate in meetings. One indirect dysfunction of meetings is that for many people they are demotivating and energy consuming. Many people feel uncreative and intellectually drained after leaving a meeting. In short, there is some unmeasurable opportunity cost associated with potentially effective people attending committee meetings.

Indecision. A striking disadvantage of committees is that they are typically indecisive. Committee meetings are characterized by participants ventilating their feelings, discussing tangential issues, and engaging in soliloquies meaningful only to themselves. Attempts at coming to agreement on even minor matters are often countered with an alternative suggestion from one member of the group. Indecision of this nature, as mentioned earlier, is an advantage if management's objective is to postpone committing itself on a given issue.

Compromise at the least common denominator. In order to placate everyone in the group, a compromise decision is often reached which does not confront the real issue or solve the underlying problem. A solution of this nature is termed a "least common denominator" because it represents the one point on which everyone can agree. A committee in a business organization was assigned the task of choosing a development program for middle management. After considerable debate, agreement could be reached on only one type of program—a series of five lectures on "principles of management." Although this program did not have a negative impact on the organization, it avoided confronting some of the real problems facing middle management. Programs of more immediate relevance, such as one dealing with problems of intergroup conflict, were discarded as being "too controversial."

Responsibility not pinpointed.   Committee decisions are group decisions; no one person then feels full responsibility for any decisions reached. As noted by Koontz and O'Donnell, "Since no one can practically or logically feel accountable for the actions of the group, no individual feels personally responsible for his action within it."[38] Correspondingly, there is a limited amount of recognition that can be derived from participating in a committee decision.

Sham democracy.   Committees, in practice, are frequently used as manipulative devices to create the impression that participative management has taken place. In these instances of "sham democracy," the committee chairman knows beforehand the decision he wants the committee to reach. After the inevitable debate that takes place in a committee, members are willing to accept any reasonable decision provided that it promises to bring the committee to a close. (Readers may object that this statement is overly cynical of the committee function. Skeptics are encouraged to observe the restlessness and boredom that takes place in so many committees. Some members are willing to accept almost any rational decision in order to return to their normal work functions.)

Another variation of sham democracy is for the chairman to sit back and allow lengthy discussion on crucial points. He then emphasizes in a summary statement those points that support his point of view. All participants may not agree with the decision, but they receive some satisfaction from knowing that their opinion was heard.

Conditions Favoring the Use of Committees

An important conclusion to be drawn about committees is that, similar to most phenomena of organizational life, they are neither completely advantageous nor disadvantageous. Used properly, committees make an important contribution to organizations. The advantages and disadvantages of committees noted above provide some hints about the proper use of committees. Next are several conceptual guidelines for effective use of committees.

1. *Committees work most effectively when they have the properties of effective work groups in general.* As discussed earlier, this includes such considerations as optimum size, optimum mix of heterogeneous versus homogeneous group membership, emotional support to members, trust and confidence, and an appropriate system of rewards.

2. *The committee chairperson should be directive and task oriented in his or her behavior, but not necessarily authoritarian.* As noted in a *Harvard Business Review* survey, ". . . the problem is not so much committees in management as it is the management of committees."[39] Considerable empirical evidence and common sense underscore the importance of an effective leader for productive committee functioning. Filley and House note that although the task orientation is crucial, the chairperson or someone else must take care of the social-leadership role as well.[40]

3. *The committee chairperson should encourage constructive ideas by sharing power and acting as a collaborator with members.* George M. Prince (founder of synectics—a method for enhancing creativity, discussed in Chapter 3) notes that in most meetings the superior makes many statements that inhibit creative responses from group members. Learning to be more accepting of ideas from participants tends to spur on creativity. Considerable skill is required to modify or resist suggestions from the group without inhibiting creativity or further contributions. Prince suggests that concerns and flaws be noted as subproblems to be worked on in order to keep the group's energy focused on building a solution. Here is a sample interchange of this approach:[41]

> *Mr. A*: You know, if we decentralize our manufacturing, we could cut shipping costs.
>
> *Manager*: Decentralizing would do some nice things for us. It would save on shipping and it would give us smaller, faster-moving manufacturing units. Another thing I like about the idea is that it would break up this huge, centralized operation and spread responsibilities in the organization. (Having acknowledged the value in Mr. A's thinking and revealed some of his values too, the manager shifts to his own concerns.) I have some problems here to consider—how to decentralize without any capital expense, for one. Another is how to retain both economies of scale and the advantages of small plants.

4. *Committee members should be technically and personally qualified to serve on the committee, and they should also have an appropriate interest in serving.* As obvious as this principle sounds, it is frequently violated in organizational life. Many people are appointed to committees who either cannot or do not wish to make a contribution. Some people are technically knowledgeable about the subject matter under discussion but lack the face-to-face communication skills necessary to be an effective participant. Often communication skills can be acquired in training programs or by serving on committees of lesser importance. One company president's analysis of the technical and personal qualifications for committee membership is relevant here:[42]

Committee members should be selected on the basis of their knowledge, their responsibility, and their interest in the areas in which the committee is to function. They should bring knowledge and information to the committee; . . . they should be interested, active participants. To my way of thinking, the appointment of a man to a committee for the sole purpose of conferring some sort of status on him, or building his ego and prestige, is a bad move.

OFFICE OF THE PRESIDENT: RUNNING A COMPANY BY COMMITTEE

One of the most exalted functions served by a committee is to actually run a company. Ernest L. Molloy, the former president and chief executive officer of R. H. Macy and Company, states the justification for these high-level committees: "I've become convinced that the office of the president is too much for one man."[43] Sentiments of this nature have moved a number of corporations in recent years to rely on a team rather than one individual as chief executive officer. The *Office of the President* consists of two to five executives who share responsibility for major corporate decisions. Usually each member of the team has his particular area of expertise, but theoretically all have equal power.

Towers, Perrin, Forster and Crosby, a management consulting firm, on the basis of a study concluded in 1971, found that about 45 American corporations use the Office-of-the-President arrangement in which participation in top decision making is recognized on a formal basis.[44] Many other corporations, however, share top-level decision making on an informal basis. Well-known organizations using the Office-of-the-President concept, or a version similar to it, include Macy, Grace, Ampex, General Electric, TRW, Caterpillar Tractor, Bausch and Lomb, and Borden.

The Office of the President offers two important advantages to the organization that has the financial resources to fund such an arrangement. First, major decisions facing the organization receive input from several senior executives. By way of example, the company president facing the decision of merging with another company may benefit from and need the suggestions of other key executives. Second, the Office of the President allows for unusually effective coordination. Almost immediately, two or more key executives know "who will be responsible for what."

One subtle and somewhat minor advantage of the Office of the President is that under this arrangement the president feels somewhat less lonely and isolated. Charles D. Flory has noted that presidents acting alone in their capacity lack peers with whom they can exchange ideas and socialize.[45] The Office of the President automatically provides the chief executive officer with several peers or confidantes.

Disadvantages of the Office of the President can also be noted. First, as found in most partnerships, the arrangement only works if the individual personalities mesh or "groove." Charles D. Dickey, Jr., shortly after being appointed as chief executive officer of Scott Paper Co., was asked by *Business Week* what he thought of the Officer-of-the-Chairman technique his predecessor had tried. He replied:[46]

> You use this sort of organization when the people and personalities in top management lend themselves to it, but it's an awkward way to do business.

Second, there is inevitably some confusion about which member of the top-level executive team is responsible for what decision. This is particularly true because many decisions at the top cut across traditional functional lines. Decisions about laying off personnel, to cite an illustration, fall neither strictly into the province of financial nor personnel executives. Marshall Lewis, another Scott executive, commented:[47]

> Inevitably there's some confusion about who's in charge of what. I'm not quite sure if the Office of the President is a way of making decisions or avoiding them. It creates an uncertainty down the line....

Third, and of a less serious nature, some individuals at lower levels in an organization perceive Office-of-the-President assignments (aside from the original president) as reserved for senior executives being "kicked upstairs." This author has heard more than one middle manager protest that executive staff assignments are reserved for individuals no longer capable of running an operating unit.

TEMPORARY TASK FORCES

Temporary task forces are small groups of individuals called together to solve a problem or explore and develop a new idea for an organization. Conceptually, a temporary task force is similar to a committee, but two important points of distinction can be drawn: (a) members of a temporary task force usually work together full time until their assignment is completed, while most committees meet periodically during their life span; and (b) the task force often has more decision-making power than a committee, although this point will have many exceptions.

Members of a temporary task force are chosen on the basis of their presumed expertise and ability to complete a mission. These groups frequently disregard organizational rank. For example, the task leader may be an employee of lower rank in his formal organizational unit than one or two members who report to him in the task force. Cost reduction or profit improvement teams exemplify the task force grouping. Care is taken to gather team members from different units of the organization to increase the likelihood that their recommendations will be viewed as objective.

Management consulting firms rely heavily on task forces to solve client problems. A task force of consultants devotes full time on a temporary basis to studying a specific client problem. For example, one aerospace company, faced with declining business, hired a consulting firm to help it decide the feasibility of subleasing one-half of its manufacturing space. This task force was headed by a member of the consulting firm, but it included employees of the aerospace company.

Task forces to solve problems that lie outside the scope of normal operational patterns are not new, but they are gaining in popularity. Behavioral scientists have noted the positive motivational value of such arrangements. Team members can readily identify with the mission of the group. It is predicted that temporary task teams will be more widely utilized in organizations of the future.[48]

One key advantage of the temporary task force to the organization is its superior problem-solving capability.[49] Task force members can be chosen strictly on the basis of competence for solving the problem at hand. From the individual's standpoint, assignment on a task force can give him the exposure and visibility necessary for career advancement (as developed more fully in Chapter 5). Temporary task forces, however, also have their disadvantages or "sensitive" aspects as outlined by Vernon R. Averch and Robert A. Luke, Jr.:[50]

1. Choosing people on the basis of competence rather than seniority creates some hurt feelings and bruised egos. When an individual is chosen for a valued task assignment, and his superior is not chosen, relationships with the superior may become strained. (The more insecure the superior, the more magnified the problem.)

2. Full time is often required for the task force assignment, thus detracting from the team member's normal job. Should the temporary task force become prolonged, the team member may find that his regular job is now being filled by someone else. Searching for a new position may become mandatory, similar to the plight of many project managers.

3. Interpersonal skills of a greater magnitude than most people possess may be required in the temporary task force arrangement. Rapport among strangers has to be built in a truncated period of time. Technically competent but interpersonally unsophisticated individuals fail

because they require considerable time to establish trust and confidence with others.

4. Top-level executive support is required at the various stages of the task team's life. Without such support it may be difficult to obtain data needed for the study, thus wasting organizational resources.

5. Costs of the task force effort must be determined beforehand to avoid the embarrassment of the task force that spends more company money than it saves.

6. Considerable sensitivity is required to implement findings of the temporary task force. Averch and Luke note that the task force report usually suggests changes. Those immediately affected by the proposed changes will probably be asked to alter their customary style of marketing, advertising, or operating their department. An outsider making such broad recommendations to a manager is usually perceived as a threat. Assume that you were the national sales manager and a task force recommended that the company switch from using salesmen to a direct mail-order approach to marketing. How threatened would you feel? Circumventing such resistance is best accomplished by allowing people to participate in changes that will later involve them.

RELATIONSHIP TO CORE PROPOSITIONS

Small group behavior fits readily into the basic framework for organizational behavior presented in Chapter 1. Several of these relationships to the core propositions have been included in the main body of this chapter. A few additional illustrative relationships are presented next.

Human Behavior

Attitudes and behavior of people in small groups are best understood in the light of general principles of human behavior. For example, knowledge obtained from the study of individuals is helpful in interpreting the behavior of people in small groups. First, the research evidence about individual differences in propensity to conform helps to explain why some people readily succumb to group pressures while others remain more independent. In general, more intelligent, original, and confident people show a smaller likelihood of being high conformers. Second, the popularity of both formal and informal groups in organizations can be attributed partially to the wide range of psychological needs satisfied by groups. Among these are an outlet for affiliation needs and a source of emotional support. Groups also reduce anxiety for members by giving people an opportunity to discuss common problems with each other and, if needed, to defend against a common enemy.

Situational Nature

Small group behavior provides pointed examples of the situational nature of organizational behavior. Work group effectiveness is a function of a complex of situational variables. For instance, work groups can be larger when the task is additive in nature; creative, complex tasks require a more heterogeneous group; and when emotional support is provided to group members creativity may be enhanced. Providing economic rewards to group members also illustrates the situational nature of small group behavior. When a competitive system (high differential rewards) is introduced into a work group where group members are dependent upon each other, the result may well be decreased performance. Conversely, if each group member receives equal compensation on a task where employees work and contribute independently, output may also be hindered.

Systemic Nature

Each small group has some properties of a self-contained system, even though each group is linked to at least one other group in the organization. Among the many systemic properties of small groups are the following: (1) Each group has its own communication net or pattern of communication. (2) An individual group requires the proper balance of people for effective functioning. Should a group be too homogeneous or too heterogeneous an imbalance may occur that hampers group effectiveness. (3) Each group member has some kind of impact upon every other member. Replacing one member of a group with another person (one element of the system) can have a pronounced influence on the psychological climate within the group. (4) Behavior patterns and traits exhibited by the leader are a vital mediating influence on the output of the small group system. When a leader is not sufficiently task oriented, productivity will usually be low. However, when the leader becomes too task oriented, he or she runs the risk of becoming a restraining influence on the group and thus inhibiting the creativity of group members.

Structure and Process

Small groups in organizations provide yet another example of how the formal and informal organization (structure and process) interact. Within most small groups, each member is assigned a formal role. In a systems and procedures group one person might be assigned the task of developing systems and procedures for office work. Other group members are assigned different formal roles. Despite this differentiation in formal roles, people assigned to developing other types of systems will probably provide the "office systems" person useful suggestions about his project. Suggestions of this nature constitute part of the informal system that is created within an organization to fill in the gaps created by the formal system. People have their structured roles, yet providing informal assistance to one another is an important part of the *process* by which tasks are accomplished in an organization.

GUIDELINES FOR ACTION

1. If you require considerable emotional support and frequent technical assistance in problem solving, you will probably be more effective working in a group than by yourself.
2. You will be better able to resist conformity to group pressures if you develop some unique talents of your own. Self-confident, talented people have less need to conform than do self-confident and less talented people.
3. In forming a group to accomplish a given task, begin with five persons with slightly different backgrounds and appoint an effective leader. This is the most widely applicable type of group.
4. Committees can be an effective method for accomplishing tasks provided that (a) action is taken to see that they have the properties of an effective work group, (b) the chairperson is task oriented, (c) the chairperson encourages constructive ideas by sharing power and acting as a collaborator with members, and (d) committee members are qualified to serve.
5. Should it be your responsibility to convey the recommendations of a temporary task force to organizational members who will be affected by them, use sensitivity and tact. (Yet do not distort the true intent of your message.)

QUESTIONS

1. Would you derive more satisfaction from membership in a temporary or stable group? What factors underly your decision?
2. Would you prefer to work in an individual or a team effort? Why?
3. State five of your specific behaviors which suggest that you conform and five which suggest that you do not conform to group standards.
4. Think of any one group in which you are now or once were a member. Evaluate its effectiveness according to the criteria for effective work groups presented in this chapter.
5. Have you ever belonged to a committee that produced tangible results? What factors seemed to be responsible for bringing about these positive results?

NOTES

1. Dorwin Cartwright and Alvin Zander, *Group Dynamics: Research and Theory*. New York: Harper & Row, 1968.
2. Edgar H. Schein, *Organizational Psychology*, second edition. Englewood Cliffs, N.J.: Prentice-Hall, 1970, p. 81.
3. Peter Weissenberg, *Introduction to Organizational Behavior: A Behavioral Science Approach to Understanding Organizations*. Scranton, Pa.: Intext Educational Publishers, 1971, p. 344.
4. Schein, *op. cit.*, p. 84.
5. Warren G. Bennis, *Changing Organizations*. New York: McGraw-Hill, 1966, p. 12.
6. B. D. Fine (now named Dov Eden), "Comparison of Work Groups with Stable and Unstable Membership," *Journal of Applied Psychology*, Vol. 55, No. 2, April 1971, p. 170.
7. William G. Scott and Terence R. Mitchell, *Organization Theory: A Structural and Behavioral Analysis*, revised edition. Homewood, Ill.: Richard D. Irwin and Dorsey Press, 1972, pp. 113–114.
8. Joseph E. McGrath, *Social Psychology: A Brief Introduction*. New York: Holt, Rinehart and Winston, 1964, p. 114.
9. George C. Homans, *The Human Group*. New York: Harcourt, Brace, 1950.
10. George C. Homans, "Social Behavior as Exchange," *American Journal of Sociology*, Vol. 62, May 1958, pp. 597–606.
11. Michael S. Olmsted, *The Small Group*. New York: Random House, 1959, p. 106.
12. David R. Hampton, Charles E. Summer, and Ross A. Webber, *Organizational Behavior and the Practice of Management*. Glenview, Ill.: Scott, Foresman, 1968, p. 277.
13. Schein, *op. cit.*, pp. 84–85.
14. William H. Whyte, Jr., *The Organization Man*. Garden City, N.Y.: Doubleday-Anchor, 1956.
15. One good synthesis of these experiments is found in David Krech, Richard S. Crutchfield, and Norman Livson, *Elements of Psychology: A Briefer Course*. New York: Alfred A. Knopf, 1970, p. 479.
16. *Ibid.*, pp. 479–482.
17. Abraham K. Korman, *Industrial and Organizational Psychology*. Englewood Cliffs, N.J.: Prentice-Hall, 1971, p. 60.
18. Hampton, Summer, and Webber, *op. cit.*, pp. 186–187.
19. Scott and Mitchell, *op. cit.*, p. 121.
20. Alan C. Filley and Robert J. House, *Managerial Process and Organizational Behavior*. Glenview, Ill.: Scott, Foresman, 1969, p. 290.
21. Paul A. Hare, *Handbook of Small Group Research*. New York: Free Press, 1962, pp. 243–244.
22. Philip B. Appelwhite, *Organizational Behavior*. Englewood Cliffs, N.J.: Prentice-Hall, 1965, p. 81.
23. Rensis Likert, *New Patterns of Management*. New York: McGraw-Hill, 1961. Chapter on "The Nature of Highly Effective Work Groups" reproduced in David A. Kolb, Irwin M. Rubin, and James M. McIntyre (editors), *Organizational Psychology*. Englewood Cliffs, N.J.: Prentice-Hall, 1971, pp. 163–175.
24. Cited in Schein, *op. cit.*, p. 61.
25. Cited in Korman, *op. cit.*, p. 59.
26. Scott and Mitchell, *op. cit.*, p. 123.
27. L. Keith Miller and Robert L. Hamblin, "Interdependence, Differential Rewarding, and Productivity," *American Sociological Review*, Vol. 28, No. 5, October 1963, pp. 768–778.
28. Scott and Mitchell, *op. cit.*, p. 123.
29. Bernard M. Bass, *Organizational Psychology*. Boston: Allyn & Bacon, 1965, pp. 204–209.
30. Schein, *op. cit.*, p. 95.

31. Fred E. Fiedler, *A Theory of Leadership Effectiveness.* New York: McGraw-Hill, 1967.
32. Filley and House, *op. cit.,* p. 321.
33. Harold Koontz and Cyril O'Donnell, *Principles of Management,* fourth edition. New York: McGraw-Hill, 1968, p. 377.
34. Filley and House, *op. cit.,* Chapter 14.
35. Koontz and O'Donnell, *op. cit.,* Chapter 18.
36. Points one through seven are based on a comprehensive analysis by Koontz and O'Donnell, *ibid.,* pp. 379–383. Points eight and nine are based more specifically on my personal observations.
37. Points one through four are based on Koontz and O'Donnell, *ibid.,* pp. 383–385. The last point reflects my personal observations.
38. Koontz and O'Donnell, *ibid.,* p. 385.
39. Cited in Filley and House, *op. cit.,* p. 326.
40. *Ibid.,* p. 344.
41. George M. Prince, "Creative Meetings Through Power Sharing," *Harvard Business Review,* Vol. 50, No. 4, July–August 1972, p. 53.
42. Rollie Tillman, Jr., "Problems in Review: Committees on Trial," *Harvard Business Review,* Vol. 38, No. 3, May–June 1960, p. 171.
43. Reported in *Democrat and Chronicle,* Rochester, N.Y., November 14, 1971, Section C, p. 1.
44. *Ibid.*
45. Charles D. Flory (editor), *Managers for Tomorrow.* New York: New American Library, 1965, p. 74.
46. *Democrat and Chronicle, op. cit.,* Section C, p. 1.
47. *Ibid.,* Section C, p. 5.
48. Mack Hanan, "Make Way for the New Organization Man," *Harvard Business Review,* Vol. 49, No. 4, July-August 1971, p. 138.
49. Vernon R. Averch and Robert A. Luke, Jr., "The Temporary Task Force: Challenge to Organization Structure," *Personnel,* Vol. 47, No. 3, May–June 1970, p. 16.
50. *Ibid.,* pp. 22–23.

7

Leadership Styles

Successful organizations consistently differ from ineffective organizations in one respect—the former are characterized by dynamic and effective leadership.[1] Recognition of this generalization is one crucial impetus underlying the vast amount of writing and research about leadership. No other single topic, except for work motivation, has received as much attention in the organizational behavior literature. Leadership is the process of influencing people to achieve desired objectives, either their objectives or those of the leader. By definition, leadership must take place within the context of a group. Leading, as most readers recognize, is but one vital aspect of the managerial process; controlling, planning, organizing, and innovating constitute the balance of a manager's job.[2] Additionally, non-managers can exercise leadership in organizational settings. Informal leaders—those without official sanction from the organization—emerge in many settings.

Having overviewed a few general comments about leadership style, the major issue of this chapter can be confronted. *What constitutes an effective leadership style? Ample research evidence and logical analysis indicate that an effective leadership style is one that adapts to the unique demands of a given situation.* Contrary to opinions frequently expressed in the business and trade literature, behavioral scientists have rarely expressed the opinion that one style of leadership is best for all situations. The late Douglas McGregor, to cite the most common example, is interpreted by his critics to imply that Theory *Y* is the universally recommended leadership style. Closer examination of his writing, however, indicates that Theory *Y* is in reality a plea for management to select a leadership style which is most appropriate for each situation.[3]

Additional support for the concept that effective leadership is adaptive comes from a recent review of the literature about two dimensions of leadership behavior—consideration and initiating structure (defined later in this chapter). Based upon an analysis of approximately 45 studies, Peter Weissenberg and Michael J. Kavanagh conclude:[4]

> ... situational factors, and subordinate's perceptions, as well as the attitudes and personality of the leader, must be considered when attempting to achieve an "ideal" leadership climate.

Leadership theories and other approaches to understanding leadership presented in this chapter are based on the concept that leadership is *adaptive*; effective leaders respond to the demands of the situation. All other theories of leadership are considered to have less application to organizational behavior. Adaptive theories of leadership do not imply that characteristics of the leader, such as *charisma*, are not important. Certain leadership situations are best served by a dynamic, charismatic leader.

Each leadership theory presented is selected to some extent on the basis of its potential practical application to organizational settings and its contemporary nature. Readers are encouraged to relate each description of leadership style to their present or prospective leadership roles.

LEADER TRAITS AND LEADERSHIP SITUATIONS

Prior to 1949 most psychological studies of leadership attempted to isolate traits which would reliably differentiate leaders from nonleaders and effective leaders from ineffective leaders. Review of exhaustive amounts of literature on leadership suggests that there are few traits which consistently make these kinds of differentiations. Ralph M. Stogdill, in a widely quoted survey of leadership studies, indicated that only the traits of intelligence, scholarship, dependability and responsibility, social participation, and socioeconomic status consistently differentiate leaders from nonleaders.[5] In contrast, Cecil A. Gibb several years later concluded that "the numerous studies of personalities of leaders have failed to find any consistent patterns of traits which characterize leaders."[6] Negative results such as these are in part attributable to combining leadership studies from varying situations, each of which probably has different leadership demands. For example, combining a study assessing the personal traits of athletic coaches with a study assessing the personal traits of big business leaders will probably be inconclusive. Leadership studies that make assessments of leaders in comparable situations are more likely to reveal characteristics that differentiate between more effective and less effective leaders.

Despite many negative research results about leadership traits, it is difficult to convince observers of managerial behavior or managers themselves that there are no psychological differences between effective and ineffective leaders. Long-range, large-scale research conducted by Edwin E. Ghiselli and his associates indicates that some traits are related to effective managerial performance. Ghiselli concludes, based upon studies of managers in a variety of industrial organizations, that important to managerial success are the traits of intelligence, supervisory ability, initiative, self-assurance, and perceived occupational level.[7]

Intelligence

Individuals with high intelligence have a higher probability of being effective leaders and of rising higher in management, up until a certain crucial point. Managers who fall among the top 2 or 3 percent of the population in intelligence have a smaller probability of being successful managers than those immediately below them (in measured intelligence). Ghiselli notes:[8]

> It is possible that those individuals at the very extreme high levels of capacity to deal with abstract ideas and concepts do not find in managerial activities the intellectual challenge they need.

This conclusion is supported by the present author's experience that individuals who score at the very top in intelligence tests are better suited, from an interest standpoint, for work that deals more heavily with ideas than with people. Leadership positions, in general, deal more with interpersonal relationships than with analytical or abstract work.

Supervisory Ability

Ghiselli defines this trait behaviorally—"effective utilization of whatever supervisory practices are indicated by the particular requirements of the situation."[9] As would be expected on logical grounds, this type of behavior was found to be positively related to occupational level. Higher level managers have better supervisory ability than lower level managers, and effective higher level managers score higher on supervisory ability than their less effective counterparts. Supervisory ability, in short, represents the most important trait for managerial success of the five traits reported by Ghiselli.

Initiative

As defined by Ghiselli, this characteristic has a motivational and a cognitive component. The first aspect involves taking action without stimulation and support from others. Problem finding and opportunity finding (as explained in Chapter 3) are related to the second aspect. People with initiative are able to see courses of action and implementation that are not readily apparent to others. Scores on Ghiselli's test of initiative are positively correlated with both performance ratings and management level. Not surprisingly, initiative was found to be highly valued at the upper two levels of management (president and vice-president), but not at the bottom two (first- and second-level supervisors).

Self-Assurance

The extent to which an individual perceives himself to be effective in dealing with the problems that confront him proved to be another important leadership trait. Ghiselli's concept of self-assurance is conceptually identical to self-confidence—long considered a vital leadership trait. In the words of Ghiselli:[10]

> As with the other managerial traits, as one proceeds from the lower occupational levels to the higher ones there is a greater and greater amount of self-assurance manifested by the personnel at those various levels. There is a substantial distinction between lower and middle management, but also between middle and upper management. Highly placed executives are outstanding in the confidence they have in themselves.

Perceived Occupational Level

Individuals who see themselves as belonging to a high occupational level tend to be more proficient in their work and also tend to engage in higher level managerial work. The converse explanation is also plausible. Proficiency in a job, or the act of performing high-level responsibilities, elevates one's occupational self-perception.

Individuality

Ghiselli contends that differences between leaders and nonleaders his research reveals may all be based upon a substratum of individuality and its corollary—the desire for self-realization through creative activity. According to his findings, those managers who displayed the greatest individuality in managerial behavior tended to be among the best managers. Nonconformity—individuality in social behavior—is not at issue in Ghiselli's work. Successful managers were those who went about their work in a more individualized, unique manner.

This key research and opinion about leadership, then, demonstrates that some traits or characteristics can be isolated that are important for leadership in a variety of organizations. This evidence in support of the trait theory of leadership does not dismiss the value of situational theories of leadership. An up-to-date conception of leadership requires an integration of the trait and situational approaches. Figure 7.1 illustrates how leader traits and leadership situations are both important in making practical decisions (e.g., selection and placement) in organizations. This conception of leadership is explicitly or implicitly used by almost every professional engaged in making selection decisions about managers. The professional assessor asks, "What leadership situation (job description, organizational climate, and so forth) is this person being considered for?"

Situation Cluster A and Situation Cluster B are two sets of situations that presumably would require similar leaders. (The reader is cautioned that

Situation Cluster	Situation Cluster
A	**B**
University English Department	Highway construction team
R&D Laboratory	Vocational school gym class
Advertising boutique shop	Timber clearing team
Folk music band	Explosives department
Constellation of Desirable Leader Traits	Constellation of Desirable Leader Traits
High technical competence	Average technical competence
Permissiveness	Dogmatism
Sensitivity to people	Sensitivity to people
Flexibility	Firmness
Consultative	Unilateral
Concern for detail	Concern for detail

Figure 7.1 Illustrative relationships between leadership situations and leader traits.

the following analyses about Cluster *A* and Cluster *B* are based upon logic and the author's impressions gathered in organizations; they are not based upon specific research.) For example, the four situations listed in Cluster *A* will all be staffed with creative people (with the exception of clerical and support staffs). Although the technical knowledge required for effective leadership of each of these groups may differ, the personal characteristics may be quite similar.

According to the framework presented in Figure 7.1, a leader of each of these groups would have to be technically competent (creative people are quite adamant about being supervised by leaders of some demonstrated technical competence), reasonably permissive, sensitive to people, flexible, consultative, and would have to show some concern for detail. This latter characteristic is important because creative people usually prefer that somebody else take care of their administrative detail. Characteristics in addition to the six mentioned may also be required for effective leadership in Situation Cluster *A* (and in *B*); this is an illustrative, not exhaustive, list of traits.

Leadership situations described in Situation Cluster *B* differ considerably from those in Cluster *A* with respect to organizational climate. All may require a leader who provides considerable structure and is quite mindful that standard procedures are closely followed. Permissiveness with respect to safety precautions, to cite an obvious illustration, could have fatal consequences in an explosives manufacturing department or in a logging operation. High school gym classes and construction teams also require a firm leader. This same degree of firmness might have negative consequences in the situations contained in Cluster *A*.

Generalizing, it is postulated that leadership situations can be grouped into clusters based upon the predominant characteristics of those situations. (The discussion of organizational climates contained in Chapter 11 provides more information about this topic.) Each situation within that cluster requires approximately the same kind of leader with respect to personal characteristics. An undefined number of personal characteristics, however, are important in every leadership situation. Sensitivity to people, or *insight*, to cite an illustration, is undoubtedly a universal leadership requirement.

CONTINGENCY THEORY OF LEADERSHIP EFFECTIVENESS

The situational nature of leadership is presented with the most precision by the research of Fred E. Fiedler.[11] Fiedler's contingency model suggests that task-oriented leaders (those who concentrate on tasks that the group is supposed to perform) are more effective when the leadership situation is very favorable or very unfavorable. Relations-oriented leaders (those who give more emphasis to the interpersonal requirements of the leadership job) are more effective in situations of intermediate favorability. Attention is devoted next to explaining this basic statement of Fiedler's theory.

Contingency theory of leadership effectiveness suggests that leadership is an influence process where the ease or difficulty of exerting influence is a function of the favorableness of the group task situation for the leader.[12] Three commonly acknowledged determinants of favorability are leader–member relations, task structure, and position power. For example, the most favorable situation for a leader would be when a highly popular leader leads his group through a very structured, well-defined task, and he has considerable power. Should a well-liked corporation president walk around the plant giving out Christmas bonuses, he would be in a highly favorable leadership position. In contrast, a hostile (poor leader–member relations) third-level (low power) manager attempting to initiate a safety campaign (low task structure) would be in an extremely unfavorable leadership situation. Fiedler classifies each group situation by taking actual measures of leader–member relations, task structure, and position power. Once these are accomplished, the leadership situation is classified as belonging to one of eight possible combinations of these three variables, as

	Favorable				Unfavorable		
	I	II	III	IV	V	VI	VII	VIII
Leader–Member Relations	G	G	G	G	Mp	Mp	Mp	Mp
Task Structure	Str	Str	Ust	Ust	Str	Str	Ust	Ust
Leader Position Power	St	W	St	W	St	W	St	W

Code: G=good, Mp=moderately poor.
Str=structured, Ust=unstructured.
St=strong, W=weak.

Figure 7.2 Favorability of eight different leadership situations. (*Explanatory note*: The above classifications are measures of three critical leadership variables: (a) leader–member relations, (b) task structure, and (c) power of leader in the position.) SOURCE: Walter Hill, "A Situational Approach to Leadership Effectiveness," *Journal of Applied Psychology*, Vol. 53, No. 6, December 1969, p. 513.

shown in Figure 7.2. Cells I and VIII, the extreme points, have already been described.

Empirical data underlying Fiedler's theory are considerable, but tests of his theory sometimes produce nonsignificant results.[13] Nevertheless, an important practical contribution of the contingency theory is that it helps sensitize the leader or prospective leader to the importance of situational factors in attempting to achieve goals. To illustrate, the leader might ask, "What needs to be done to make this leadership situation favorable so that I can carry out my mission?"

MANAGERIAL GRID STYLES

The most widely quoted taxonomy of leadership styles is that contained in the Managerial Grid of Robert R. Blake and Jane S. Mouton.[14] Perhaps 500,000 managers throughout the world have participated in Managerial Grid training programs or facsimiles of them put together by management development personnel. Chapter 13 describes the Grid in some detail with respect to its application in organization development. (Some readers may find it helpful to read that material first and study the actual Grid.) Attention now is directed to the five key leadership styles highlighted by the Grid. They will be repeated in Chapter 13 (Organizational Change) from a slightly different perspective.

Leadership styles in the Grid system are classified according to one's rating on two key dimensions of leadership behavior: concern for people and concern for production. These two dimensions are extensions and popularizations of the concepts of *initiating structure* and *consideration* stemming from a long series of studies conducted at Ohio State University. "Production emphasis" and "people emphasis" are both rated on a one to nine scale. Concern for production is rated on the horizontal axis of the Grid. Concern for people is rated on the vertical axis. Verbally, these leadership stereotypes can be described as follows:

Impoverished (1, 1)

Leader exerts minimum of effort to get work accomplished. He concerns himself very little with people or production. This style of leader is basically lazy and uninvolved and reflects withdrawal. Illustrative here is the middle manager in a large bureaucratic (governmental or private) organization waiting out his retirement date.

Country Club (1, 9)

Leader gives considerable attention to the needs of people, but minimum concern to task accomplishment. This behavior leads to a comfortable, friendly, and relaxed work atmosphere where nobody "makes waves." During the early 1960s, many government contract "think tanks" were run in this manner.

Task (9, 1)

Leader achieves efficiency in operations by arranging conditions of work in such a way that human elements interfere to a minimum degree. Feelings and attitudes of subordinates, within reason, are kept from interfering with productivity. First-level supervisors in canning factories often adapt this leadership style.

Middle-of-the-Road (5, 5)

Leader maintains adequate organization performance and morale. Mediocrity is perpetuated but things keep "perking along." Probably most managers consciously or unconsciously utilize this leadership style.

Team (9, 9)

Leader is able to elicit high productivity from a committed and dedicated group of subordinates. Goals of the organization and the people are successfully *integrated*. Leaders of this type are rare. Talented leaders and talented subordinates (in this author's opinion) are required for these ideal conditions to occur. Small, technically sophisticated businesses are often characterized by a pulling together of management and employees. All members of the team are both happy and productive.

3-D THEORY OF LEADERSHIP

William J. Reddin has developed an elaborate theory of leadership that adds the dimension of effectiveness (achieving the output requirements of the position or reaching goals) to the dimensions of task (concern for production) and relations (concern for people).[15] Central to his theory is the situational nature of leadership; no one leadership style is good or bad. What is relevant is the appropriateness of a given style to the situation (followers, technology, organizational climate, etc.) at hand. For example, should you have the unenviable leadership assignment of erecting a house in 30 days, you would probably have to behave in an autocratic, demanding, and insensitive manner. In order to accomplish your mission you might adversely affect long-term relationships with employees and suppliers; however, in terms of the exigencies of the situation, your leadership style would be adaptive. Readers seeking full knowledge of the 3-D theory of leadership should consult Reddin's *Managerial Effectiveness*, which, in addition to describing leadership styles, provides an elaborate framework for adapting style to circumstances.[16] Figure 7.3 presents the 3-D theory in graphic form. Central to the 3-D theory of situational management is an eight-style typology of leader behavior. These eight styles, similar to Fiedler's contingency model, result from eight possible combinations of task orientation, relationships orientation, and effectiveness. Verbally, these eight styles are portrayed as follows:[17]

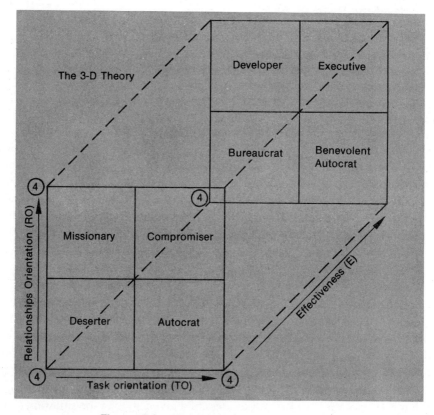

Figure 7.3 The 3-D theory of leadership.

Four of these styles are less-effective; they are: DESERTER, MISSIONARY, AUTOCRAT, COMPROMISER.

Deserter. A manager who is using a low Task Orientation and a low Relationships Orientation in a situation where such behavior is inappropriate and who is therefore less-effective. Seen as uninvolved and passive.

Missionary. A manager who is using a high Relationships Orientation and a low Task Orientation in a situation where such behavior is inappropriate and who is therefore less-effective. Seen as being primarily interested in harmony.

Autocrat. A manager who is using a high Task Orientation and a low Relationships Orientation in a situation where such behavior is inappropriate and who is therefore less-effective. Seen as having no confidence in others, as unpleasant, and as being interested only in the immediate job.

Compromiser. A manager who is using a high Task Orientation and a high Relationships Orientation in a situation that requires a high orientation to only one or neither and who is therefore less-effective. Seen as being a poor decision maker and as one who allows various pressures in the situation to influence him too much. Seen as minimizing immediate pressures and problems rather than maximizing long-term production.

The four parallel more-effective styles are: BUREAUCRAT, DEVELOPER, BENEVOLENT AUTOCRAT, EXECUTIVE.

Bureaucrat. A manager who is using a low Task Orientation and a low Relationships Orientation in a situation where such behavior is appropriate and who is therefore more-effective. Seen as being primarily interested in rules and procedures for their own sake, and as wanting to maintain and control the situation by their use. Often seen as conscientious.

Developer. A manager who is using a high Relationships Orientation and a low Task Orientation in a situation where such behavior is appropriate and who is therefore more-effective. Seen as having implicit trust in people and as being primarily concerned with developing them as individuals.

Benevolent Autocrat. A manager who is using a high Task Orientation and a low Relationships Orientation in a situation where such behavior is appropriate and who is therefore more-effective. Seen as knowing what he wants, and knowing how to get it without creating resentment.

Executive. A manager who is using a high Task Orientation and a high Relationships Orientation in a situation where such behavior is appropriate and who is therefore more-effective. Seen as a good motivator who sets high standards, who treats everyone somewhat differently and who prefers team management.

PATH–GOAL THEORY OF LEADERSHIP

Robert J. House has formulated a theory of leadership effectiveness that builds upon the research underlying the Managerial Grid, the 3-D theory of leadership, and expectancy theories of motivation.[18] In general, this new formulation can be interpreted as an explanation of the effects of leader behavior on subordinate satisfaction, motivation, and performance. A major contribution of the path–goal theory of leadership effectiveness is its ability to specify some of the situational *moderators* (conditions) for effective leadership. A full understanding of this comprehensive, abstract, and potentially useful theory can only be achieved by a concentrated study of its original statement.[19] An abridgement and simplification of some of the major aspects of the path-goal theory are presented next; it receives considerable attention here because it contains important concepts about leadership effectiveness.

Theoretical Background

Sociologists have identified two major dimensions of leadership behavior—*instrumental* and *social–emotional* or *expressive*. Conceptually, they are quite similar to the task versus relations distinction mentioned earlier in this chapter. Psychologists uncovered the same dimensions of leadership behavior, calling them *initiating structure* and *consideration*. Popularized by the Managerial Grid theory of leadership, these dimensions have been the subject of extensive behavioral science research.

Initiating structure is used to describe the degree to which the leader initiates structure for subordinates by activities such as assigning specific tasks, specifying procedures to be followed, scheduling work, and clarifying expectations of subordinates. Traditional management functions such as planning, organizing, and controlling are aspects of initiating structure. *Consideration* describes the degree to which the leader creates an environment of emotional support, warmth, friendliness, and trust by engaging in such behaviors as being friendly and approachable, looking out for the personal welfare of the group, keeping the group abreast of new developments, and doing small favors for the group.[20]

Field research has indicated that leaders high on structure are generally rated highly by superiors and have higher producing work groups than leaders who score lower on this dimension. Leaders rated high on consideration tend to have more satisfied employees than those less considerate. Research evidence about the relationship between initiating structure and subordinate satisfaction is complex and mixed. Studies about this topic have revealed some situationally based findings.[21]

1. Initiating structure is frequently resented by unskilled and semiskilled employees and contributes to dissatisfaction, grievance, and turnover.

2. Employees in large groups have a more favorable attitude toward structure than do employees in small groups.

3. Among high-level employees initiating structure is positively related to satisfaction, performance, and perceptions of organizational effectiveness, but negatively related to role conflict and ambiguity.[22]

The path–goal theory of leader effectiveness attempts to integrate such discrepant findings by use of an expectancy theory model (discussed in more detail in Chapter 2). In review, expectancy theory posits that whether or not an individual will engage in a specific behavior is a function of (a) his expectations that the behavior will result in a specific outcome and (b) the sum of the valences—that is, personal utilities or satisfactions that he or she derives from the outcome.

Central to the path–goal theory is both a formulation and a formula, as quoted directly:[23]

> ...the individual makes probability estimates with respect to two linking points connecting behavior with its outcomes, and subjectively places values on the outcomes. The magnitude of these probability estimates indicates the degree of path instrumentality of his behavior for work-goal accomplishment and valence. This formulation can be expressed in the following formula:

$$M = IV_b + P_1 \left[IV_a + \sum_{i=1}^{n} (P_{2i} EV_i) \right] \qquad i = 1, \ldots, n,$$

where: M = motivation to work;

IV_b = intrinsic valence associated with goal-directed behavior;

IV_a = intrinsic valence associated with work-goal accomplishment;

EV_i = extrinsic valences associated with work-goal accomplishment;

P_1 = path instrumentality of behavior for work-goal attainment;

P_{2i} = path instrumentalities of work goal for extrinsic valences.

Leader behavior is related to all the independent variables in this formulation. For example, the leader helps determine what external rewards should be associated with work–goal accomplishment, (EV_i) in the formula. Also, through personal behavior the leader can provide support for the subordinate's efforts, thus increasing the probability that the subordinate's effort will result in work–goal attainment, P_1.

Propositions to the Theory

The preceding research and theory underly four general propositions that help explain the relationship between leader behavior, or roles, and effectiveness (in terms of motivation, satisfaction, and performance).

1. Leaders perform a motivational function by increasing personal pay-offs to subordinates for achieving work goals, and by making the path to pay-off smoother. Clarifying the path, reducing road blocks and pitfalls, and increasing opportunities for satisfaction en route are behaviors that make the path smoother.
2. The leader's behavior will exert positive motivational effects to the extent that it reduces role ambiguity or makes possible the exercise of externally imposed controls. (Externally imposed controls are considered motivational by some because they help relate reward to effort.)
3. Attempts by the leader to clarify path–goal relationships will be seen as redundant by employees if the work system already carefully defines the path–goal. Under these conditions, control may increase performance, but it will also result in decreased satisfaction.
4. Leader behavior aimed at need satisfaction of subordinates will increase work performance if such satisfaction increases the net positive valence (attractiveness) of goal-directed effort.

Illustrative Empirical Research

These four propositions led logically to a series of eight research hypotheses, three of which were tested with 200 office employees of a heavy equipment manufacturing company: (1) Leader initiating structure will be positively related to subordinate satisfaction. (2) Leader initiating structure will be negatively related to subordinate role ambiguity. (3) The variance in role ambiguity will account for the relationship between initiating structure and subordinate satisfaction.

A situational rationale is offered for these hypotheses. Since the employees in this study were engaged in high-level clerical administrative work, much of their time would be devoted to ambiguously defined tasks. A leader who reduced ambiguity and therefore increased the clarity of path–goal relationships would increase employee satisfaction.

Questionnaire measures were taken of initiating structure, job satisfaction, and role ambiguity. For the latter two scales, respondents were asked to indicate the degree to which statements were true or false on a seven-point scale ranging from one (very false) to seven (very true). Next are four sample items: the first two measure satisfaction, the second two measure role ambiguity.

> The pay I receive for my work.
> The dignity with which I am treated.
> I feel certain about how much authority I have.
> I know exactly what is expected of me.

All three hypotheses received statistically significant but modest support. It was particularly noteworthy that the relationships between structure and satisfaction are not significant when the influence of role ambiguity is partialled out. House notes that his findings might have been more dramatic if the employees were involved in more highly ambiguous work.[24] Combined with two other studies, these findings led to the overall conclusion that among high occupational groups leader initiating structure was generally related to subordinate satisfaction and performance. House accounted for these relationships in terms of variance in subordinate role ambiguity, which was negatively correlated with initiating structure. Apparently, knowledge workers prefer a clear definition of their job responsibilities, which helps them attain work-related goals!

DUAL LEADERSHIP THEORY

Amitai Etzioni, an organizational sociologist, has developed a situational conception of leadership style that helps explain how the organization can influence leadership effectiveness. His dual leadership theory emphasizes the effects of power and authority on leadership behavior. Leadership is defined by Etzioni as the "ability, based on the personal qualities of the leader, to elicit the followers' voluntary compliance in a broad range of matters."[25] When only a narrow range of matters is involved, referring to matters of minor importance, *influence* rather than leadership is exercised.

A central concept in the dual leadership theory is the distinction between expressive and instrumental roles. Etzioni notes that task-oriented groups will achieve higher performance and member satisfaction when the group commands both instrumental and expressive leaders. Further, while these two kinds of leadership might be carried out by one person (a "great man") they tend not to be. Finally, when two people carry out the two leadership roles, mutual support is required for effective leadership of the group. The dual leadership theory stands in contrast with prevalent theories that expect leadership to be provided by one person.

The dual leadership theory is applied to small groups in complex organizations by adding the concept of power. A contingency table helps explain these sets of relationships, as shown in Figure 7.4.

According to this four-way conception, an individual ("actor" in Etzioni's term) may have only positional power or formal status, in which case he or she is referred to as an "official." When the person has only broad personal influence, he or she is called an "informal leader." A combination of positional and personal power makes a person a "formal leader."

225

	Positional Power	
	Yes	**No**
Yes	Formal Leader	Informal Leader
Personal Power		
No	Official	Follower

Figure 7.4 Dual leadership in complex organizations. SOURCE: Amitai Etzioni, "Dual Leadership in Complex Organizations," *American Sociological Review*, Vol. 30, 1965, p. 694.

Finally, a "follower" is a person who has neither personal nor positional power.

Three critical issues underly the application of the dual leadership proposition to small groups in complex organizations: (a) whether both instrumental and expressive leadership are provided for, (b) whether they are mutually supportive, and (c) how and to what extent the leadership is backed by organizational power. Etzioni makes this crucial analysis:[26]

> A group in an organization where both types of leadership are exercised by informal leaders—persons without organizational positions—will be very different from a group where both types of leadership are exercised by formal leaders—persons in organizational positions—or a group where one type of leadership is provided by an occupant of an organizational power position while the other is not.

An important implication of the dual leadership theory is that the organizational location of expressive and instrumental leadership affects three aspects of organizational behavior.

Degree of Organizational Control over the Group

When an organization has instrumental and expressive leaders who hold power—and are accepted by the informal group—it will have good control over participants. Underlying this implication is the notion that informal leaders tend to be less loyal to the organization than are formal leaders.

Degree of Collaboration Between the Two Kinds of Leaders

In general, collaboration between instrumental and expressive leaders is more likely to occur when both of the leaders hold organizational positions, or when neither does, than when only one of them holds an organizational position.

Power Relations Between the Two Kinds of Leaders

Granting more power (e.g., higher rank and salary) to an instrumental leader than an expressive leader will shift the emphasis of the small group toward instrumental activities. That is, if the instrumental leader is given more power by the organization, his (or her) group will tend to be more task oriented. Organizational power, and position in the hierarchy, thus becomes a more important variable than personal characteristics in understanding leadership effectiveness.

The dual leadership theory, at Etzioni's own admission, is essentially a set of carefully deduced propositions that await empirical verification. An important implication of these propositions for leadership style is that structural and technological, as well as psychological, factors mediate leadership behavior. For instance, an intelligent, well-motivated person will behave weakly in a leadership role if he or she is not given appropriate organizational support in terms of prestige and power.

LEADERSHIP STYLE AND PRODUCTIVITY

Productivity is an important, but not exclusive, goal of organizational leadership. Outputs such as worker satisfaction, morale, and long-range development of people are other legitimate goals of supervision and leadership. All these outputs, or dependent variables, follow the same situational perspective advanced in this chapter. Effective leadership (whether effectiveness is measured in morale or productivity) is a function of choosing the leadership style appropriate to a specific situation. Paul Hersey and Kenneth H. Blanchard, in their up-to-date analysis of empirical research about leadership in organizations, conclude that "different leadership situations require different leader styles."[27]

Researchers at The University of Michigan's Institute for Social Research have provided an important historical base for exploring the relationship between leadership style and productivity. An important conclusion reached, based upon work with clerical and production workers, was that supervisors of high-producing units behaved differently than those of low-producing units. Among the differences in style noted were that supervisors of productive groups in comparison to their lower producing counterparts were: (a) more emotionally supportive of subordinates, (b) more likely to play a *differentiated role*—plan, regulate, and coordinate the activities of subordinates, but not become directly involved in work tasks, and (c) more likely to exercise general rather than close or "tight" supervision.[28]

Later research by the Institute shed new light on the complexity of the relationships between leadership style and productivity. Robert Dubin has prepared a critical synthesis of some of the research on this topic reported by Robert L. Kahn.[29] One group of employees in a large life insurance company was managed in an employee-centered style; another comparable group was managed in a production-centered style. Contrary to expectations, both groups showed a significant increase in productivity. However, the employee-centered leadership style produced an increase in favorable attitudes toward the supervisors and the company. In contrast, the production-centered group showed a marked decrease in favorable attitudes toward supervision and management. Reporting on research conducted with 20,000 employees in a firm manufacturing earth moving equipment, Kahn concluded that foremen with the best production records were both production and employee centered. (Readers will recognize that research of this nature underlies the Managerial Grid approach to understanding leadership presented earlier.)

Rather than leave this situational perspective of leadership with the weak conclusion that "the situation will tell you which leadership style to choose," it is worth mentioning two key situational variables—level of technology and occupational level of the worker.

Technological determinants of the optimum leadership style, as revealed by the research of Joan Woodward in England, have already been overviewed in Chapter 1. In brief, the more a production process resembles a unit or batch technology, the greater is the probability that a leadership style characterized by general supervision will lead to high productivity.[30] Conversely, the more a production process resembles a continuous-production system, the greater the probability that a leadership style characterized by close supervision will be optimum.

Logical analysis and insights gathered directly in organizations indicate that most people working in professional level occupations produce the best under conditions of participative leadership.[31] In short, a leadership style that allows for the satisfaction of higher level needs—among people who are trying to satisfy these needs—leads to high productivity. Professional people seek leaders who are simultaneously task and people oriented.

DETERMINANTS OF LEADERSHIP STYLE

What determines which leadership style a person will select for himself or herself? Considerably more attention has been paid by writers about leadership to describing styles of leaders than to searching for answers to this more basic question. Knowing why a person has adapted a particular leadership style is a matter of practical concern. Attempts to change leadership style might be more effective if the reasons underlying the adaptation of a particular style were known. For example, if a manager chooses a "relations-oriented" leadership style because he feels this is what the organization really wants, his perceptions about the organization will have to be changed before his leadership style will change.

The basic personality structure with which an individual enters the leadership situation exerts a profound impact upon the leadership style he chooses. Personality, in turn, is influenced by an entire lifetime of experiences. It represents the consistent manner in which a person relates to the world, or that person's unique *style*. Education, training, early childhood experiences, and relationships with key people in life are but some of the forces shaping personality. Placed in a leadership situation, an individual's natural tendency is to pursue a leadership style that is compatible with his current personality structure. Two vignettes are presented next to illuminate the influence of personality structure upon leadership style.

Paul Feldman is a warm, accepting, likeable, and pleasant individual. When disagreements with his wife surface, he typically takes an apologetic stance. According to his wife, Paul will counter her dissatisfaction with a statement such as, "I can see how you feel that way. If I were in your shoes I would probably also be angry at me. What can I do to make it up to you?" Paul has difficulty in disciplining his children. He felt uneasy about administering physical punishment to his children when they were younger. All three children receive lavish allowances even though they fail to perform the agreed-upon chores to receive the allowance. Mr. Feldman, by occupation, is the owner of a scientific instrument company, employing about 300 people. He is less permissive with employees than with his children, yet his leadership style must be characterized as moderate concern for production and high concern for people. The union considers him a "pushover," and employees from all levels in the company call upon him to discuss personal problems, particularly those relating to finances. Paul's closest advisors have urged him to adapt a less permissive approach to managing the company. His response is insightful in its simplicity: "What else can I do? I love people."

Stuart Daniels is a cold, perfectionistic, and aggressive individual. He is married to a woman who defers to him in every marital disagreement. She contends, "I hate to upset Stu, he thinks he is always right and he usually is. He feels that he is the head of household and I guess he is." Daniels describes his two children, one boy and one girl, as being "good little soldiers" who toe the line when it is necessary. By occupation, Mr. Stuart Daniels is the business manager of a university. He insists that department secretaries defend in writing why they purchase a particular brand of office supplies, particularly when lower priced substitutes can be purchased. Shortly after arriving on the job, he wrote a memo urging the clerks and secretary within his department to comply strictly with official hours, including the lunch break. A secretary within his department asked to be dismissed one hour early every Thursday afternoon to take a data processing course. After three days of deliberation, he responded in writing: "Your request for time off has been denied. It is not within the charter of this department to subsidize the formal education of its employees. Consider this matter closed." Daniel's leadership style could properly be characterized as high concern for tasks and low concern for relations.[32] One member of the department describes his style less academically: "He's a first-rate creep!"

The assumptions a manager makes about people are considered by the late Douglas McGregor and his disciples to be a major determinant of his leadership style. For those readers not already familiar with the assumptions made about people by the ubiquitous Theory X–Theory Y, they are presented here as condensed by John J. Morse and John W. Lorsch:[33]

Theory X assumes that people dislike work and must be coerced, controlled, and directed toward organizational goals. Furthermore, most people prefer to be treated this way, so they can avoid responsibility.

Theory Y—the integration of goals—emphasizes the average person's intrinsic interest in his work, his desire to be self-directing and to seek responsibility, and his capacity to be creative in solving business problems.

Should a marketing manager harbor Theory X assumptions about salesmen, he might attempt to motivate them with the following set of management practices and behavior:

We have established sales quotas for each of you. Each year your quota is reached, the company will pay for a five-day trip for you and your wife. This will be in addition to your normal vacation. If you meet your quota for five consecutive years, you are almost guaranteed a permanent position with our company. Salesmen who are unable to meet their quota for three consecutive quarters will probably not be invited back for a fourth quarter.

In contrast, should a marketing manager harbor Theory Y assumptions about salesmen, he might attempt to lead them in the following manner:

You and your sales managers will get together on establishing sales quotas for each year. If you achieve your quotas you will receive extra money. High performance as salesmen is one important factor in being considered for a management assignment. Another important part of your job besides selling is to keep our product-planning group informed about changes in consumer demand. Many of our new products in the past stemmed directly from the suggestions of salesmen.

The leadership style adapted by the chief executive officer of an organization influences the leadership style of his subordinates. First-hand observers of organizational behavior are amused by the willingness of many subordinates to conform to the leadership style of their superiors. Conformity to the leadership style prevalent above varies to some extent with the ego strength and emotional security of the individual manager. Weaker, less secure managers more readily search for a leadership style that will meet with approval from above. Managers at Micro Devices Inc. of Sunnyvale, California, are known to manage with a carefree, loose, and free-wheeling style, all within the framework of hard work. They are willing to gamble on a new idea. Certain aspects of their behavior are undoubtedly influenced by the leadership style of their colorful president, Jerry Sanders. As abridged from *Electronic News*:[34]

"Guys think I'm cocky and brash, and I guess I am, but it's because I am always forward looking."

When Mr. Sanders was bumped out of the marketing vice-presidency of Fairchild late in 1968 by the incoming Hogan regime, not many industry observers would have tagged him as presidential timber. "My failure to make it with Les Hogan had to be a matter of style," he admits. And it was precisely the free-wheeling Hollywood style of this one-time aspirant for a film-acting career that seemed to militate against his ever becoming the top dog in any company.

Sanders assumed the presidency of Micro Devices as if to the mantle born, worked and drove furiously as he made AMD shape up into one of the hottest new companies around.

"My greatest strength is also my greatest weakness," Mr. Sanders says, getting back to that ego. "It drives me to succeed—I'm hung up on achieving. I've spent my life setting goals, but the gratification pales quickly, so I'm always setting impossible goals, and I take it all very personally."

Mr. Sanders' people-handling technique is a combination of prodding and motivating. "I'm a real believer in behavioral science, and I believe that most people can do better than they normally do," he said. "So I maintain an environment of sustained urging. And I'm a hypocritical sonofabitch concerning anything that is short of excellence."

Even though some of his one-time associates might find it difficult to believe, today Jerry Sanders is leading his team as a team man. "Today no one guy can do everything. This is the age of the specialist," he says. "My skill has been to recognize experts, and to get them to work together. You've got to take care of those guys, and make them feel important."

Ideally, the demands of the situation should be the primary determinant of leadership style, as implied throughout this chapter. For example, a normally consultative, permissive leader may be required to shift toward a more unilateral, directive leadership style when his group is confronted with an emergency situation. Under the threat of survival (economic or physical) many ordinarily independent individuals become quite dependent upon direction from above. The perceptive leader thus adapts his style to fit the exigencies of the situation. Support for this statement is found in Fred Fiedler's review of over 50 studies covering a span of 16 years. His analysis revealed both directive, task-oriented leaders and nondirective, human relations-oriented leaders are successful under some conditions.[35]

IMPROVING YOUR LEADERSHIP STYLE

Improving leadership style has become an important goal of many management development programs. Sensitivity training, the Managerial Grid, and the 3-D theory of managerial effectiveness in practice are approaches to leadership development. Readers interested in an overview of management development concepts and methods might consult *The Practice of Managerial Psychology.*[36] Leadership seminars and training programs usually include some attempt to provide insight into leadership style and assistance in making actual changes in behavior (if they are found to be desirable or necessary). Improving leadership style has become a widespread activity in the United States, Canada, Great Britain, and other countries throughout the world. The nature, relevance, and commercial appeal of such activities is suggested by an American Management Association brochure describing their course, "Management Style and Self-Directed Change."

Do you really know how you are coming across to your subordinates? your fellow managers? your boss?

The impact that you have on others can make or break you! It isn't easy to find out what your people *really* think of you—because they'll never tell you. But your subordinates show you every day in actions that are far more meaningful than words.

Your effectiveness as a manager is reflected in the productivity of your people. And if you're not getting the results you want, it's quite possible that your staff is responding unfavorably to some element in your management *style*.

But what is your management style? It's a composite of all the approaches and techniques that characterize your dealings with people—and problems. It's your own way of getting things done—and since a management style develops gradually with experience, your methods are by now used almost unconsciously.

And *there's* the danger. As your management style evolves, you tend to slip more and more into patterns—habitual ways of operating that may limit your ability to deal with new situations. Even if you think your methods "always work pretty well," you can't afford to be satisfied. You could be in a rut that is diminishing your managerial effectiveness.

To provide you and other experienced managers with the opportunity to assess your own management style—and explore ways to enhance your managerial effectiveness—AMA offers this challenging course, MANAGEMENT STYLES AND SELF-DIRECTED CHANGE.

Feedback about present leadership or management style is an essential ingredient to most programs of leadership development. Forms of feedback include scores on structured questionnaires that attempt to measure leadership style and feedback from other seminar participants. The *Leadership Opinion Questionnaire*, distributed by Science Research Associates, is one such standardized questionnaire. Each participant receives a score for both consideration (human relations orientation) and structure (task orientation). Forty items of the following kind constitute the questionnaire (presenting an item verbatim jeopardizes the reliability of a published test):

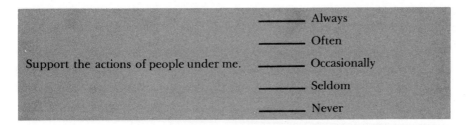

Support the actions of people under me.
_____ Always
_____ Often
_____ Occasionally
_____ Seldom
_____ Never

Feedback of a more emotionally charged nature comes from fellow participants in a leadership development seminar. Typically, toward the conclusion of such a seminar each participant takes his turn on the *hot seat*. All other participants level with him about his impact on them. (This author has seen managers become pale as they sit on the hot seat awaiting their feedback.) One leadership development program used at a large corporation borrows heavily from the Managerial Grid seminars. Their approach to providing feedback about leadership style is well-structured, yet representative of management-style workshops:

> *Purpose*:   To offer constructive criticism to each group member which will aid in each person's personal growth.
>
> *Procedure*:   Your group task is to provide feedback in terms of constructive criticism for each member of your group. Be as open and candid as possible. The following are some suggested elements which you may wish to consider as you discuss the observed behavior of each member.
>
> (a) Decisions (d) Emotions (temper)
> (b) Convictions (e) Humor
> (c) Conflict (f) Effort
>
> • The elements of discussion must be aimed at aiding the individual in his development.
> • We suggest you allow a specific period of time, 25–30 minutes should be ample.
> • The subject is to remain silent as the group discusses his behavior. It is imperative, however, that he remain in the room even though he is not to participate. He may ask questions for clarification only after the discussion is completed.
> • There is no time limit for the completion of this task except that you must finish in time to attend class tomorrow morning at 8:30 a.m.
>
> To assist you, we have provided a summary of a typical discussion. It is not judged as good or poor. It *is not* intended to be a model. It is for your reference only.
>
> "He approached decision making in an authoritarian yet innovative manner. He has wide perception. He is quick, determined, and is sometimes perceived in an intolerant, and argumentative way. His humor is quick and purposeful. He initiates conflict and thrives on it. When he is faced with conflict, he initially responds with a bull-dozer approach, but if reproached, he may become touchy and withdrawn. He approaches all problems in a vigorous manner. We judge his managerial style to be (9,1) dominant and (1,1) back up."
>
> Needless to say, the information that is exchanged is of a highly confidential nature and should not be discussed after the group meeting under any circumstances!

What evidence has accumulated that leadership styles can be improved or even changed by such programs? Sensitivity training—one commonly used approach to improving leadership style—has resulted in more effective leadership performance in some situations, less effective performance in others, and in many cases has had no impact on leadership performance. Negative results can occur because sensitivity training may encourage *con-*

sideration, while more emphasis upon *structure* may be called for in a given situation. An intricate, technical review of approximately 100 studies about the effects of T-group training through 1968 has been presented by John P. Campbell and Marvin D. Dunnette.[37] Chapter 13 of this book (*Fundamentals of Organizational Behavior*) summarizes some more current data about the utility of laboratory training. Few of these studies, however, focus specifically on the question of improvement in leadership style.

Changes in leadership style stemming from any type of leadership development program, sensitivity training included, have a low probability of enduring unless (a) the participant is motivated toward change and (b) the organization climate permits the manager to use what he or she learns. Research about leadership training has paid too little attention to this critical variable of motivation. An oft-repeated shibboleth is that all development is self-development. In practice this means that the leader who wants to develop a more adaptive leadership style must use the insights he or she gathers in a leadership seminar as prods for establishing change goals. Thus, the leader who learns in a sensitivity training experience that he or she turns off subordinates because of poor listening should make an almost daily effort to listen more attentively to subordinates. Without this persistent *self-monitoring,* permanent changes resulting from leadership training are unlikely to be forthcoming.

Another key determinant of the permanency of any benefits forthcoming from leadership training is frequency of exposure. Perhaps 50 managers have told this author, "Yes, that leadership seminar had some good effects on our group, but after two months, everybody went back to his old habits." If an organization sees leadership development as a desirable end, multiple exposures over time to such seminars constitutes the necessary means.

Fred E. Fiedler offers some empirical evidence based on his contingency model to explain why many attempts at improving leadership effectiveness fail to produce positive results. In a recent analysis, Fiedler conceptualizes that leadership training increases the favorableness of situations rather than changing the individual. His data suggest that the same type of leadership training and experience apparently increases the effectiveness of some and decreases the effectiveness of other managers. Underlying this curious phenomenon could be factors such as the following:[38]

> That some individuals decrease in performance as a result of increasing experience and training should not surprise us. Many men get bored, arrogant, or slipshod when the task becomes too easy or structured; they need the constant challenge to perform at their best. Others need continuity and routine.

RELATIONSHIP TO CORE PROPOSITIONS

Leadership, as much or more so than other topics explored in this book, follows the framework for organizational behavior described in Chapter 1.

Human Behavior

Leadership is a very human process, governed by principles of human behavior. For example, the psychology of individual differences governs many aspects of leadership behavior. First, as described earlier in this chapter, a person's basic personality structure is a key determinant of the leadership style he or she will choose. Dogmatic and rigid people will tend to lead others in a dogmatic and rigid manner, even if the situation calls for another leadership style. Second, individual differences among people influence the style of leadership to which they can best adapt. To illustrate, self-confident, emotionally secure people need a minimum of structure and direction from their superiors. Less confident and secure people may need more structure and reassurance from their superiors. Third, individual differences in psychological traits such as intelligence and emotional control contribute to leadership effectiveness. Leaders may not necessarily be "born" or "made," but certain inherited and acquired traits influence leadership behavior.

Situational Nature

Leadership, as expounded throughout this chapter, is situational; any study of leadership or leadership style must be cognizant of the situation in which leadership takes place. Paul Hersey and Kenneth H. Blanchard provide a formula to represent the situational nature of leadership: ". . . the leadership process is a function of the *leader*, the *follower*, and the *situation*, $L = f(l, f, s)$."[39]

Systemic Nature

Selected aspects of leadership fit neatly into a systems framework. At the broadest level of abstraction, leadership can be conceptualized as an influence process that provides input into the total organizational system. This input (leadership) influences or mediates employee behavior. Effective leadership increases employee output, while ineffective leadership may actually decrease output. Systemic consequences of leadership can also be analyzed at a much lower level of abstraction. Whenever a leader exerts influence over one group member, intended and unintended consequences occur for other group members as illustrated by this industrial example:

One division general manager was forced by his job to spend about one week per month away from his office. He appointed his manager of planning as the acting general manager during his absences. Behind his decision was the feeling that the planning manager could be spared more readily for this assignment than other members of his staff. Unfortunately, the manufacturing manager interpreted this action to mean that the manager of planning was the division general manager designate. The manager of manufacturing, who aspired toward the general manager position, became discouraged and sought job opportunities in another company.

Structure and Process

Leadership involves a constant interaction between structure and process. In order to effectively lead his group, a manager must be mindful of the formal aspects of his job. He must conduct performance appraisals, administer salaries, and interpret policy, among many other required behaviors. Effective leadership, however, also requires that the leader be sensitive to initiate behaviors that go beyond those contained in his job description. Observe how one branch manager in a casualty insurance company supplemented the formal part of his job (structure) with sensitivity to its informal demands (process).

One of a branch manager's formal responsibilities in this company (as in most) is to furnish leads to new salesmen. This branch manager noted that one of his newer salesmen had not consummated an actual sale after one month's tenure on the job. Merely assigning leads and training the recruit in insurance was not producing results. Upon receiving the next legitimate inquiry about insurance coverage, the branch manager called the new man into the office and offered the following bit of inspiration: "Look, Tiger, I don't care how you do it, but here is a piece of business we need badly. Just bring this S.O.B. home." Apparently this forceful intervention worked (or at least was not harmful); the salesman did make his first sale.

GUIDELINES FOR ACTION

1. If you want your organization to prosper, find a sharp, dynamic, and effective leader.
2. Several leadership traits and behaviors are important for success in a wide variety of leadership situations. Four of these traits are somewhat amenable to development: supervisory ability, initiative, self-assurance, and individuality.
3. A task-oriented, decisive leadership style works best when the work to be performed is of a repetitive, uncomplicated nature and group members are of average work motivation; for example, leading a group of production workers.

4. A relations-oriented, permissive leadership style works best when the work to be performed is of a nonrepetitive, complicated nature and subordinates manifest high work motivation; for example, leading a small group of creative people.
5. Effective leaders, within limits, adapt their leadership style to the requirements of the situation. In order to accomplish this you would have to understand the task to be performed, the subordinates, and the variation in management style acceptable to top management.
6. Don't expect to make dramatic changes in your leadership style by simply attending a leadership workshop for these reasons: (a) Much of your leadership style is determined by your basic personality structure. (b) You must be strongly motivated to change. (c) You must carefully monitor your behavior over a period of time to bring about lasting changes.

QUESTIONS

1. What kind of group are you best equipped to lead? Why?
2. List three characteristics or traits of people that you think are *unrelated* to leadership effectiveness in most situations.
3. What type of leadership style should a woman running a beauty salon utilize? Relate your conclusion to leadership theory.
4. Describe two situations in which you think a "Benevolent Autocrat," as defined by Reddin in his 3-D theory, would be effective.
5. Assume you are a mail room supervisor in a large company. Your manager informs you that your operation will now be staffed with trainees recruited from the hard-core unemployed. What assumptions do you make about these people, and how will these assumptions influence your leadership style?

NOTES

1. Paul Hersey and Kenneth H. Blanchard, *Management of Organizational Behavior*, second edition. Englewood Cliffs, N.J.: Prentice-Hall, 1972, p. 67.
2. This represents one commonly accepted formulation of the management process. An eclectic overview of this topic is presented by R. Alec Mackenzie, "The Management Process in 3-D," *Harvard Business Review*, Vol. 47, No. 6, November–December 1969, pp. 80–87.
3. Saul W. Gellerman, *Management by Motivation*. New York: American Management Association, 1968, pp. 231–232.
4. Peter Weissenberg and Michael J. Kavanagh, "The Independence of Initiating Structure and Consideration: A Review of the Evidence," *Personnel Psychology*, Vol. 25, No. 1, Spring 1972, p. 127.
5. Ralph M. Stogdill, "Personal Factors Associated with Leadership: A Survey of the Literature," *Journal of Psychology*, Vol. 25, 1948, pp. 35–71.
6. Quoted in Alan C. Filley and Robert J. House, *Managerial Process and Organizational Behavior*. Glenview, Ill.: Scott, Foresman, 1969, p. 398.
7. Edwin E. Ghiselli, "Managerial Talent," *American Psychologist*, Vol. 18, No. 10, October 1963, p. 635. Copyright The American Psychological Association.

8. *Ibid.*, p. 637.
9. *Ibid.*, p. 638.
10. *Ibid.*, p. 639.
11. Fred E. Fiedler, *A Theory of Leadership Effectiveness.* New York: McGraw-Hill, 1967.
12. Walter Hill, "A Situational Approach to Leadership Effectiveness," *Journal of Applied Psychology,* Vol. 53, No. 6, December 1969, p. 513.
13. *Ibid.*, pp. 513–517.
14. Robert R. Blake and Jane S. Mouton, *The Managerial Grid.* Houston: Gulf, 1964.
15. William J. Reddin, *Managerial Effectiveness.* New York: McGraw-Hill, 1970.
16. *Ibid.*
17. William J. Reddin, "Managing Organizational Change," *Personnel Journal,* Vol. 48, No. 7, July 1969, p. 503.
18. Robert J. House, "A Path Goal Theory of Leadership Effectiveness," *Administrative Science Quarterly,* Vol. 16, No. 3, September 1971, pp. 321–338.
19. *Ibid.*, p. 321.
20. *Ibid.*, pp. 321–322.
21. *Ibid.*, p. 322.
22. John R. Rizzo, Robert J. House, and Sidney E. Lirtzman, "Role Conflict and Ambiguity in Complex Organizations," *Administrative Science Quarterly,* Vol. 15, No. 2, June 1970, pp. 150–153.
23. House, *op. cit.*, pp. 322–323.
24. *Ibid.*, p. 328.
25. Amitai Etzioni, "Dual Leadership in Complex Organizations," in Donald E. Porter, Philip B. Appelwhite, and Michael J. Misshauk, *Studies in Organizational Behavior and Management,* second edition. Scranton, Pa.: Intext Educational Publishers, 1971, p. 327.
26. *Ibid.*, p. 329.
27. Hersey and Blanchard, *op. cit.*, p. 107.
28. Arnold S. Tannenbaum, *Social Psychology of the Work Organization.* Belmont, Calif.: Wadsworth, 1966, p. 74.
29. Robert Dubin, "Supervision and Productivity: Empirical Findings and Theoretical Considerations," in Walter Nord (editor), *Concepts and Controversy in Organizational Behavior.* Pacific Palisades, Calif.: Goodyear, 1972, pp. 524–525.
30. Cited in *ibid.*, p. 537.
31. John B. Miner, *The Management Process: Theory, Research and Practice,* New York: Macmillan, 1973, p. 348.
32. It would be justifiable also to characterize Stuart Daniels as a poor manager who neglects his responsibilities for developing people.
33. John J. Morse and John W. Lorsch, "Beyond Theory Y." *Harvard Business Review,* Vol. 48, No. 3, May–June 1970, p. 61.
34. Reprinted by permission—*Electronic News,* October 18, 1971, pp. 1, 12. Copyright Fairchild Publications, Inc., 1973.
35. Fiedler, *op. cit.*, p. 247.
36. Andrew J. DuBrin, *The Practice of Managerial Psychology.* Elmsford, N.Y.: Pergamon Press, 1971, pp. 55–86.
37. John P. Campbell and Marvin D. Dunnette, "Effectiveness of T-Group Experiences in Managerial Training and Development," *Psychological Bulletin,* Vol. 70, No. 2, August 1968, pp. 73–104.
38. Fred E. Fiedler, "Predicting the Effects of Leadership Training and Experience from the Contingency Model," *Journal of Applied Psychology,* Vol. 56, No. 2, April 1972, p. 118.
39. Hersey and Blanchard, *op. cit.*, p. 68.

8

Improving
Subordinate Performance

Larry Barnes works as a systems analyst in a big company; he is the "Individual in the Organization" depicted in Figure 8.1. Impinging upon Larry are multiple forces aimed at improving his performance. Larry's superior exerts personal influence on him via coaching, motivating, and persuading. Peers want Larry to perform better in order to elevate group output. His company has an elaborate personnel system designed to improve individual performance. Among these

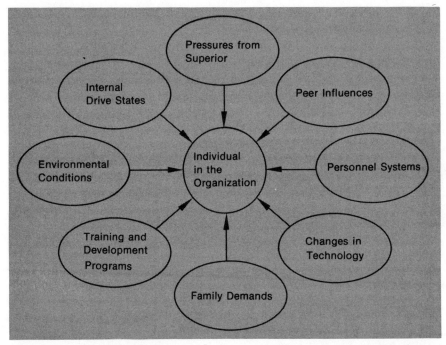

Figure 8.1 Factors potentially influencing the individual in the organization toward improved performance.

are a wage and salary plan, a management-by-objectives program, and a physical fitness program sponsored by the company recreational league. Changes in technology also prod Larry toward acquiring new knowledge in order to keep up with the demands of his job. (His company has just decided to convert to a new generation of computers.) Larry's wife is an upwardly mobile person who urges him to earn a sizeable salary increase. Larry's company assigns him to participate in a variety of training and management development programs, all having the ultimate purpose of improving his work output.

Larry Barnes is also subject to two forces aimed at improving his performance which cannot be attributed in any direct manner to his company or family. First, general environmental conditions such as inflation or recession may goad him on toward improvement. Inflation creates an urge to improve job performance merely for the sake of staying even with an escalating cost of living. Recessionary forces might prod Larry toward improved performance because the more valuable employees tend to be retained during layoffs. Second, internal drive states, such as needs for self-fulfillment, may force Larry toward improved performance.

Focus in this chapter is on but one aspect of the vortex of forces urging people toward improved performance—influence of the leader. Specifically, the role of the leader in carrying out such processes as coaching, counseling, rewarding and punishing individuals, and building group cohesiveness will be examined. Many of the ideas and practices involved in improving the performance of groups, or the individuals composing them, are essentially *motivational techniques.* Motivating people, in its broader context, has been explored in Chapter 2.

ESTABLISHING IMPROVEMENT GOALS

Elaborate systems have developed in recent years to assist organizational members in improving their performance. Management by objectives, for example, is an organization-wide system of management in which every manager and staff person, from the board of directors to individual workers, establishes performance targets. It is anticipated that the process of setting goals and measuring progress toward these goals will raise the level of performance in an organization.

The positive motivational effects of allowing subordinates to participate in decision making may in some measure be attributable to goal setting. Participating in the decision-making process usually requires that employees establish goals to which they commit themselves. For instance, a group of house painters may decide that three days will be required to paint a four-bedroom colonial house. Psychologically, this means that the painters have set a personal target of three days to accomplish the job. Having a specific goal to aim at may be as important as the motivational impact of sharing in decision making.

Approaches to improving individual or group performance to be discussed in this chapter all require that specific improvement targets be established. In addition, the individuals whose performance is to be improved must *desire* to improve.

FRAMEWORK FOR COACHING AND COUNSELING

An important direct influence process available to the manager intent upon improving subordinate performance is day-by-day coaching or counseling. Counseling or coaching strategies to be discussed in this chapter are those most applicable to the healthy, well-integrated, effective knowledge worker. Discussions about managerial intervention in problems of alcoholism, emotional disorders, and drug addiction similarly fall outside the scope of this chapter. *The Management of Ineffective Performance* by John B. Miner is still the most comprehensive overview of counseling with ineffective employees.[1] Readers interested in learning about the counseling process in general might consult *The Psychology of Counseling* by Edwin C. Lewis.[2]

Counseling and coaching are similar but not identical processes. Counseling involves more listening than does coaching. Another important distinction is that the feelings of the person being helped are involved more in counseling than in coaching. How an individual *feels* about a given situation is always explored in a counseling session. Felix M. Lopez, Jr. draws a more rigorous differentiation between coaching and counseling. Counseling involves the longer term development of the individual, while coaching deals with present job performance. Lopez states:[3]

> The supervisor's function is to coach, not counsel. The proper object of *coaching* is to improve present job performance; the proper object of *counseling* is the realization of potential. The former emphasizes *doing*, the latter, *becoming*. In helping a person "become," many factors besides job performance are considered—native ability, previous background and experience, personality, attitudes toward and opportunities in a specific occupational field, in a particular company—factors with which the supervisor is not expected to be familiar. If the supervisor attempts to counsel rather than coach, he will indeed do exactly what some critics accuse him of doing: "play God."

Improving subordinate performance by on-the-spot coaching about work-related behavior is justified by at least two principles of learning: (a) feedback on performance is closely related to the time at which the performance takes place, and (b) tasks are learned through active practice, rather than passive listening or observing. In the coaching process, the manager functions in the manner of a tennis coach or ski instructor. An error or room for improvement in the work of a subordinate is brought to the latter's attention as soon as feasible. For instance, the chairman of a statistics department walked by the classroom in which a faculty member was lecturing about probability sampling. The chairman noted that the professor was delivering most of his lecture with his face pointed toward the blackboard. While facing the blackboard the professor could not respond to the facial grimaces of his students; i.e., he was shutting out feedback on how well (or poorly) his lecture was being received. Rather than waiting for a year-end performance appraisal, the chairman openly discussed the faculty member's approach with him that afternoon. Not being overly sensitive to criticism, the professor interpreted the criticism as constructive and made the necessary modifications in his teaching approach.

Counseling and coaching by managers, whether related or structurally different processes, can both be considered management *interventions.* *Counseling and coaching can have helpful, neutral, or harmful consequences to people.* The following situation that took place in a casualty insurance company is probably not atypical.

> Leon Potzka, a 27-year-old insurance underwriter, asked for a conference with his manager to discuss his job situation. Leon told his boss that he was becoming bored with underwriting and wished to inquire about job opportunities elsewhere in the company. His manager suggested that Leon apply for a sales position. This recommendation was based on the observation that (a) Leon "looked like a salesman," and (b) his underwriting experience would give Leon the technical knowledge necessary for selling insurance. Leon failed dismally as a salesman and left the company discouraged and disappointed. Counseling from his manager had a negative impact upon his career.

Counseling in this instance failed because, as a later psychological evaluation revealed, the manager gave Leon advice based on incomplete information. Leon had a favorable external appearance but lacked the self confidence necessary to confront people in a sales situation. If the manager had merely listened and not given advice, the counseling would probably have had neutral or even positive consequences.

The conditions under which coaching or counseling by a superior are likely to have positive, neutral, or negative consequences to the person counseled are summarized in Figure 8.2. A similar set of *conditional variables* could be developed for most managerial interventions.

Examined next are some specific observations about the counseling aspects of a manager's role. They are based more on practice than theory or research.

COUNSELING IN PRACTICE

A psychological consulting firm distributed a pamphlet entitled "The Manager is a Counselor."[4] Asked his reaction to the material, one textile executive replied: "It just doesn't fit our business. We have no time to counsel employees. Either they measure up or find a job elsewhere." Despite this not atypical sentiment, the counselor role of a leader is inescapable, particularly if subordinate performance is to be improved. People inevitably make some mistakes, and they are less likely to repeat these mistakes under the influence of counseling than chastisement. Counseling, according to James P. McSherry and Charles N. Newstrom, is a legitimate managerial activity defined as:[5]

> ... simply a way of talking with people to enhance the chance of achieving mutual goals and of generating within subordinates a greater desire to take responsibility for their own growth and their own performance.

Counseling, in the context of the superior–subordinate relationship has five important elements. These are reviewed next with a special emphasis on improving work performance.

1. *Counseling is grounded in a belief in man's capability for growth.* Managers, and the subordinates whose work performance they are trying to improve, must believe that improvement is possible. Admittedly, many aspects of work performance cannot be improved through counseling. The young woman with an IQ of 100 probably will never be able to debug scientific computer programs. In contrast, a young woman with an IQ of 125, whose first advertising campaign for a product fails dismally, can probably be counseled about her mistakes. If a manager does not believe that people can change in a positive direction, only surface attention will be devoted to counseling subordinates.

2. *Counseling demands respect for the individual.* Basic respect for the individual is paramount for counseling to be carried out effectively. Counseling implies that another individual has the right to express his or her opinion,

Consequences		
Positive	**Neutral**	**Negative**
Organizational climate encourages development. Superior is skillful coach who wants to help. Subordinate identifies with superior. Coaching is seen as important part of job responsibility. Superior and subordinate examine their relationship. Coaching sessions are held frequently.	Superior only intervenes in trivial matters, or only at times of performance review. Does not perceive coaching as vehicle for development. Does not care if subordinate develops.	Superior perceives subordinate as threatening rival. Coaching approaches demotivate subordinate. Coaching perceived as vehicle for reprimand. Mistakes are not tolerated.

Figure 8.2 Conditions under which superior–subordinate coaching can have positive, neutral, or negative consequences.

even if the counselor disagrees. Even the mere process of listening intently to subordinates conveys the feeling that what they have to say is important. A basic conviction of counselors states: convey belief and faith in another individual's capacity to improve and that individual will improve. Encouragement is a potent motivational device.

3. *Counseling rests on trust and leveling.* One method of leadership development is to enhance the willingness of people to deal openly with each other. This skill is essential to a counseling-type relationship. Subordinates should neither be deluged with praise nor overwhelmed with criticism about their shortcomings. McSherry and Newstrom illustrate the set of attitudes indicative of a sound counseling-type relationship with a subordinate:[6]

> When you add up all of my strengths and weaknesses, I'm already an important member of the team. It is vital to me and to the organization that I become a better member of the team.

4. *Counseling requires understanding.* An authentic counseling relationship with subordinates requires a heavy degree of understanding. The manager who is functioning effectively as a counselor communicates an understanding of subordinates' perceptions, feelings, and attitudes. For example, the branch manager of a consumer credit company might state to a collection agent who has been grumbling about his work:

> "I know you have one of the most difficult jobs in the company. It's rough when you have to practically grab people by the arm to make collections. I know this upsets you. Every manager had to go through the same aggravation in order to work his way up in the company."

Understanding, in large measure, means communicating acceptance of another person's strengths and weaknesses. When a subordinate (or any other person) recognizes that he is accepted, he becomes less defensive. Lowered defensiveness, in turn, establishes the necessary precondition for change (and improvement) to take place.

5. *Counseling develops insight.* Listening to subordinates tell you about their problems and level with you about yourself (if you are a manager) provides you with insight about human behavior. Portions of the insight emerge because a counseling relationship requires setting aside preconceived notions about people. In the process of improving subordinate performance, a manager can make some improvements of his own. One illustration is the situation of a manager listening to a subordinate review his fears about presenting a marketing forecast to the company president. In the process of listening to his subordinate's fears, the manager may obtain

more insight into his own apprehension about making the same type of presentation.

IDENTIFICATION WITH A SUPERIOR

Coaching subordinates effectively requires that a manager develop some of the counseling skills alluded to in the preceding section of the chapter. Above all, a manager must be able to confront subordinates about their mistakes in an open, interested, and nonhostile manner. Once a manager develops appropriate counseling and coaching skills, other barriers have to be overcome before the opportunities for subordinate growth and development can be maximized. These barriers concern factors that inhibit or block the subordinate from *identifying* with his superior, as described by Harry Levinson.[7]

Levinson notes that a major factor in the psychological growth of people is the opportunity to identify with other individuals who have more experience, skill, and power. This requires that the subordinate to be developed has continued personal contact with his superior in relationships that facilitate identification. The latter is facilitated by a superior who grants affection, encouragement, and the freedom to express feelings; conditions that are similar to a counseling relationship. Five barriers to identification found in business organizations and cited by Levinson are discussed next.[8]

Lack of Time

Superiors often limit coaching to annual appraisal sessions. They place low priority on counseling and coaching activities because the reward system in their organization rarely provides tangible rewards for time spent in developing subordinates. Manager performance is more likely to be evaluated on the basis of traditional measures such as profits, cost savings, and developing new markets.

No Mistakes Allowed

Emphasis in American industry is on close to perfect performance. This emphasis leads to close supervision and many measurements of performance leading to feelings of not being trusted. These feelings in turn make the process of identification difficult.

Dependency Needs Rejected

Even strong subordinates have occasional needs to depend on a strong leader. When superiors reject legitimate dependency needs of subordinates, the process of identification is inhibited.

Rivalry Is Repressed

Most superiors are loathe to admit to themselves or particularly to their subordinates that they have some concerns about being dethroned by their subordinates. (The present author notes that strong managers, at least at the conscious level, contend that they welcome strong subordinates; many organizations refuse promotion to a manager who has not identified an adequate replacement. Levinson's point, then, appears to be more characteristic of weak managers.) Concerns about being dethroned, if not brought to the surface, can interfere with the superior making objective appraisals of the subordinate and, in turn, can cause the subordinate to reject the superior's appraisal of him. One way in which the subordinate might retaliate against a harsh evaluation is to reject promotion and the superior, thus destroying possible identification.

Relationship Is Unexamined

Identification is fostered to the extent that the superior and subordinate examine the nature of their relationship—a practice that is infrequently carried out. The subordinate must be permitted to express to the superior his feelings about what the superior is doing in the relationship and what the subordinate would like the superior to do to enhance task accomplishment. Examination of the relationship might also include open discussion of hostility and anger between superior and subordinate.

PERFORMANCE APPRAISALS AND IMPROVEMENT

Performance appraisal is a formal way of recording and documenting the job performance of individuals at all levels in an organization. Few large organizations exist today—including industrial, business, education, and governmental institutions—which do not utilize some system of evaluating and recording worker performance. Winston Oberg recently summarized the array of purposes underlying performance appraisal systems:[9]

- Help or prod supervisors to observe their subordinates more closely and to do a better coaching job.
- Motivate employees by providing feedback on how they are doing.
- Provide back-up data for management decisions concerning merit increases, transfers, dismissals, and so on.
- Improve organization development by identifying people with promotion potential and pinpointing developmental needs.
- Establish a research and reference base for personnel decisions.

Despite these lofty goals, performance appraisal systems frequently fail to meet their most important objective—improving individual and/or organizational performance. Goals of performance appraisals related to administrative matters, such as providing data for wage and salary compensation, are easier to attain. Later in this section of the chapter, the conditions under which performance appraisal is most likely to improve performance or develop people will be explored. Next is an overview of the far-ranging criticisms behavioral scientists and management theorists have launched against performance appraisal systems and methods. These criticisms serve as a helpful background for understanding how performance appraisal can serve as a vehicle for influencing subordinate performance in a positive direction.

1. *Performance appraisal programs demand too much time from managers.* Many managers complain that properly conducting performance appraisals consumes an inordinate amount of their time. A performance review session in which the superior and subordinate show major disagreement can consume half a workday. The problem of time consumption is more critical for supervisors than for higher level managers. Many first-line supervisors have upwards of 25 subordinates. In order to make accurate appraisals of every member of their unit, extensive amounts of time would have to be invested in observing their actual work performance.[10] (Some management theorists, of course, might argue that this is precisely what a manager should be doing.) Several large business organizations have computer based "tickler files" that remind managers when each subordinate is due for a performance review.

2. *Many performance appraisal programs force managers to rate personality characteristics and traits of people; a task for which they feel ill prepared, and therefore tend to resist.*[11] Another manifestation of "playing God," according to many managers, is having to rate subordinates on traits such as "intelligence," "initiative," "loyalty," and "leadership skill." Judging traits of this nature is a subjective process that is done with only moderate accuracy by even experienced psychologists and psychiatrists. Objections to rating

the traits of people have given impetus to the widespread use of results-oriented rather than person-oriented appraisal systems (to be discussed later in this chapter).

3. *Performance standards vary widely among different managers and different departments within the same organization.* Some managers rate more stringently than others and some departments have a higher proportion of competent people. (Students will recognize the same problem with academic grading systems. Some professors are tougher than others!) As a consequence of these varying standards among departments and raters, persons subject to less competition or lenient ratings can receive higher appraisals than equally or more competent peers.[12]

4. *Performance appraisals often measure variables that are unrelated to job success.* Charles L. Hughes notes that ". . . performance appraisals in most companies are irrelevant to the job."[13] To illustrate, a research scientist might be rated partially on the basis of the number of scientific articles he or she publishes. Scientists who publish frequently, however, may be no more (or less) effective in contributing technical ideas that actually result in new products or product improvement.

5. *Performance appraisal may contribute to or reinforce the dependency needs of people.* Chris Argyris observes that the appraisal process may make the subordinate even more dependent upon the superior. He states:[14]

> I am perplexed as to how many writers "prove" the importance of "merit rating" or "evaluation" programs by citing people's need to know. These data may simply show how dependent the subordinates are and how well the programs are institutionalizing the dependence.

6. *Performance appraisals of a traditional nature can lead to defensive, inferior performance that varies directly with the amount of criticisms used by the person conducting the appraisal.* These problems led researchers at General Electric to conclude that, among other modifications, criticism should be eliminated from performance appraisal.[15] An important secondary finding of the GE studies was that only those employees with a high degree of self-esteem appear to be stimulated by criticism to improve their performance.[16]

7. *Performance appraisals act as a deterrent to the coaching or counseling-type relationship that should ideally exist between superior and subordinate.* Appraisal interviews tend to place the superior in the role of a judge reading a "verdict" to the subordinate; this runs counter to the equally important role of teacher and coach. Defensiveness about hearing criticism from the boss may lead to a reluctance on the part of the subordinate to accept counsel from the superior.

How might performance appraisals be used to improve subordinate performance? On the positive side, some evidence has accumulated that under the proper conditions the manager can use the appraisal method as a useful, direct influence process. Ronald J. Burke and Douglas S. Wilcox conducted field research about characteristics of effective employee performance review and developmental interviews.[17] Key results of their study will be combined next with observations from practice to provide a list of eight critical factors for effective performance appraisal. The first four of these factors stem from combined inputs from the field and the literature research conducted by Burke and Wilcox. Factors five through eight are based on the author's observations in organizations.

1. *High levels of subordinate participation in the appraisal and development process.* As implied under the discussion, "The Manager is a Counselor," job performance counseling is but one special application of counseling in general. Individuals being counseled (in this situation, subordinates) must make some discoveries for themselves and reach some of their own decisions about their own behavior. Effective job performance interviews are characterized by extensive listening on the superior's part. Antithetical to a high level of subordinate participation would be extensive advice given by the superior. A research chemist (known to his boss to be having marital problems) mentions in the performance appraisal session that recently he has experienced difficulty in concentrating on his work. Observe a counseling versus an advice-giving approach to this problem:

> *Counseling*: Perhaps we could talk about why you are having difficulty concentrating on your research problems.

> *Advice Giving*: The reason you cannot concentrate is because you have marriage problems. I think you and your wife should see a marriage counselor, then you would be able to concentrate on your work.

2. *The superior conveys a helpful and constructive attitude to the subordinate.* Threats to the self-esteem of subordinates increase their defensiveness, which leads to negative attitudes toward the appraisal process and consequently lowers the probability that positive changes in job performance will be forthcoming. Threats to self-esteem can be lessened by using positive rather than negative motivators. Positive motivation includes listening, giving recognition for legitimate accomplishments, permissiveness, and offering assistance. Negative approaches include blaming, lecturing, advice giving, paternalism, and domination of the interview. The reader is cautioned

that a minority of people—those with either negative self-images or those who have grown up under a climate of fear—respond best to negative motivators. Some people actually *enjoy* being punished in their daily living. (Readers interested in abnormal psychology might ponder the personality dynamics of the sexual masochist.) Billy Turner, a young stockbroker, laments to his superior that his last five recommendations have lost money for customers. Positive or negative motivators might be applied in this manner:

Positive Motivator: Let's review why you recommended these five purchases. Maybe we can find a trend.

Negative Motivator: I know why this has happened. You were the guy who thought the training program was too theoretical. If you had listened more carefully this would never have happened.

3. *Specific goals to be achieved by the subordinate in the short run are mutually set by superior and subordinate.* Earlier in this chapter the caveat was offered that goal setting is crucial for all methods of improving subordinate performance. Research about performance appraisals has consistently emphasized the value of specific goal setting. Burke and Wilcox's investigation revealed that goal setting via group decision can have strong influences on an individual's later performance. Prior research has also shown that:[18]

... the setting of specific goals in the development interview resulted in over twice as much improvement in performance than did a discussion of general goals or criticisms without reference to specific goals.

What is the difference between a specific versus general goal in terms of actual job behavior? Assume that a director of highway safety is being reviewed; here is a statement of an improvement goal he might establish in both general and specific terms.

General: Take appropriate action to improve highway safety in our county.

Specific: Decrease serious automobile accidents by ten percent or more during the next twelve months. Also, identify the ten most critical accident spots in the highway system.

4. *Job problems are solved which may be hampering subordinate's current job performance.* Superior and subordinate should team together to take a "problem-solving approach" to performance improvement. Both members of the superior–subordinate team have a personal involvement in the subordinate improving job performance, and the superior has a good

vantage point from which to assist. A willingness on the superior's part to accept the possibility that problems may lie within the man or be external to him suggests that the man is not necessarily being blamed for what has gone wrong. The General Electric Company has adopted a work planning and review program which centers around solving job-related problems rather than attempting to correct personal deficiencies in people.

How might a manager intervene in a problem that was hampering the performance of his work group or one of its members? One business machines company launched a new product that differed markedly from its current product line, both in terms of its technology and potential market. Despite these differences, the corporation decided to market the new product with the existing sales force. Faced with meager sales, the product manager blamed some of his poor results on not having a separate sales force. His superior investigated the problem and a decision was made to develop a separate sales force for the new product. (Results from this decision might be described as "encouraging" rather than outstanding.)

5. *Salary discussions are not held during performance appraisal.* People are emotional about money. Discussions of salary adjustment will preoccupy an individual once they are introduced into a performance review session. Should money be discussed early in the interview and the result is unsatisfactory for the subordinate, little else will register during the balance of the interview. Should money be discussed at the end of the interview, the person being appraised will be too anxious to concentrate on what transpires before the financial discussion. Salary increases favorable to the individual are sometimes interpreted as an indication that no further work improvement is really necessary. Salary reviews regarded as unfavorable (including the absence of an increase) engender resentment and inhibit future job performance improvement.

What time interval should exist between salary and performance reviews? Curiously, some companies that have separated salary and performance reviews have returned to discussing money and performance ratings in the same session. Evidence about the optimal time interval between both types of review is difficult to obtain. For readers willing to accept a casual observation about these matters as helpful, a time lag of about two months (with performance discussed first) seems appropriate. In this way money is seen as related to performance, but performance reviews are not interpreted as being exclusively salary reviews.

6. *Managers with the appropriate skills and personal characteristics are better able to bring about job-related improvements than those lacking the appropriate skills and personal characteristics.* Managers require training in basic skills re-

lated to performance appraisal such as interviewing. Without proficiency in interviewing, managers feel uncomfortable in conducting performance appraisal interviews. They may avoid the situation or do a perfunctory (or sometimes inept) job. There is reason to believe that some personality structures are basically unsuited to performing the coaching or counseling function. Managers who fundamentally believe that employees should not be provided help and counsel, fit this category. Managers with limited insight into human behavior also have difficulty counseling subordinates toward improved job performance. Other personal characteristics of the superior that might inhibit the developmental aspects of performance appraisal include hostility and inflexibility. Here is a hostile statement a mining supervisor in Canada made to one of his mechanical engineers during a performance appraisal:

"This is my performance review of you. You remind me of a pimple on my backside. I know you are there and I find you annoying but you're not important enough to do anything about!"

7. *Job improvements selected as goals lie within the individual's capacity to change.* This is an obvious but sometimes overlooked principle. Managers can only expect subordinates to make improvements in areas where they have the appropriate experience, education, intelligence, or personality characteristics to make such changes. No matter how effective a superior may be in the role of counselor, he cannot help a subordinate become a more intelligent individual. Even when the person being appraised sets the improvement goal, it should be set at a level that stretches him or her as an individual, but is not so difficult to attain that only frustration ensues.

Determining what goals lie within or beyond the capability of an individual (or group) requires considerable thought. An individual's own estimate of what he or she can do and that person's past performance are both helpful bits of information. Sudden, dramatic spurts in performance are rare rather than frequent. For example, if a feature writer for a newspaper had been completing ten usable stories per month, it might be realistic for her to increase her performance to an average of 12 or 13. A goal of 20 might lie beyond her productive capacity.

8. *The performance appraisal provides the opportunity to evaluate both the person and his or her results.* Opinion and sentiment have accumulated in the United States and Great Britain over the last decade that results rather than people should be evaluated during a performance appraisal session. According to a results-oriented system of appraisal, whether a district sales manager is loyal, self-confident, aggressive, friendly, and orderly is of

minor consequence. What is of consequence is the profitability of his district and other business results he has been achieving.

Management by Objectives

MBO is the most widely known approach to measuring performance in terms of attainment of specific objectives.[19] Targets and goals are often used as synonyms for objectives, particularly in business and industry. Primary school, secondary school, and college teaching is now sometimes measured by the attainment of specific behavioral objectives. MBO, in its most complete form, goes beyond a method of appraising performance. Broadly conceived, it is an elaborate system of management that can take up to three years to completely install. Key to a pure management-by-objectives program is a system of management that defines individual manager responsibilities in terms of corporate objectives. Managerial behavior, not manager personality, is measured. Positive behavior is that which leads to the attainment of organization goals. Lopez has summarized the common elements in most MBO programs into a four-step procedure.[20]

Establishing organization goals. Considerable portions of this activity are carried out by top levels of management. These goals can be quite broad and may encompass business, community, and societal goals. Determination is then made about what must be accomplished by divisions or units in order for organization goals to be met.

Establishing unit objectives. Unit heads then establish objectives for their units, and this proceeds down the line. Objectives must always be compatible with (or, more specifically, designed to assist) the goals and objectives of the next higher unit. If, for example, a corporate goal were to produce a higher quality product, the manager of quality control might need to design instrumentation to more effectively detect variations from quality standards, or he might help in establishing quality criteria.

Individual commitment. Individuals down the line must be committed to both objectives of higher level units and their own objectives. According to Lopez:[21]

> ... individual commitment depends upon the opportunity to participate in the establishment of objectives, understanding of the value of the organization goals, and identification and involvement with them. This commitment is attainable only after a series of consultative interviews among all levels of management.

Reviewing performance.   Each member of the management team has a performance review to complete the first cycle. Performance can fall below, meet, or surpass stated objectives. Manager and subordinate discuss why negative deviations from objectives exist, and plans for improvement are specified. Ideally, these improvement plans are mutually developed. New objectives are then set for the next rating period.

Despite their logical appeal as an approach to performance appraisal, these MBO systems have the potential of being sterile from a psychological viewpoint. People in organizations recognize that promotions are based not only upon attaining results at one level, but also upon what higher management thinks of the total person. Well-motivated individuals have some interest in how well they have performed in their current position, but have an even stronger interest in learning about their prospects for additional responsibility. Two district sales managers could have performed equally well in terms of meeting their objectives, but one is considered a candidate for a regional sales manager position and the other is not. In the judgment of the company, one man does not have the interpersonal skills nor the planning ability to be effective at the next level of responsibility. These intellectual and interpersonal limitations, however, do not prohibit him from performing satisfactorily at the district manager level.

PUNISHING PEOPLE TO IMPROVE PERFORMANCE

An assumption tenaciously held by society (sometimes in the face of contrary evidence) is that punishment is a useful method of controlling human behavior. Punishment is thus administered to people whose behavior has deviated from acceptable norms (e.g., law breakers are sent to prison). Threats of punishment for violating laws are used as control mechanisms (e.g., the threat of a prison sentence is used to deter criminal acts). Punishment in organizations is similarly levied against those who violate organizational rules (some employees are "docked" for unexplained personal absences). Threats of punishment are also used as control mechanisms (e.g., executives in some companies are told that they will be subject to dismissal if they purchase company stock on the basis of inside information). Less frequently, punishment is used with the expectation that it will lead to improved work performance. Employers hopefully are more concerned with achieving organizational objectives than with retribution or controlling behavior *per se.* The present discussion will describe several types of punishment in organizations and simultaneously examine effective approaches to administering punishment.

Criticism

Considerable self-control is required for a manager not to criticize a subordinate when he or she commits an error. The urge to criticize is a natural reaction to the mistakes of others. Criticism, however, is only moderately effective in evoking improved performance.

Haim G. Ginott provides suggestions for administering criticism to teenagers that also provide insight into superior–subordinate relationships.[22,23]

Don't attack personality attributes. A restaurant owner notices that one of his waitresses orders a disproportionately small number of alcoholic drinks. (Other waitresses serving approximately the same number of customers order more drinks from the bar.) The owner might attack her personality by stating, "Doris, the reason you get so little drink business is that you are so passive. I think you are afraid of customers." Following the tenets of Ginott, the owner might state, "Doris, I think you could increase the volume of your drink orders if you would ask people if they wish to order another round."

Don't criticize character traits. A manager in an advertising agency notices that one of her layout artists is completing too few layouts to meet the informal standards set for the position. The artist's character traits could be criticized in this fashion: "Lois, you are the laziest, most unproductive person we've ever had on this job. If you don't get more ambitious soon, we won't be able to use you." Focus could be placed upon Lois' work rather than her character using this approach: "Lois, you are not turning out enough drawings to keep up the requirements of your job. If the number of drawings you complete per month cannot be increased, we won't be able to keep you."

Deal with the situation at hand. Confronted with a business crisis, many managers will lash out to criticize the person most immediately responsible for the crisis. Dr. Ginott advises coping with the problem at hand rather than attacking the person, as illustrated by this situation:

> Six days before payday, the payroll supervisor in a medium-sized company rushed into his superior's office to announce that the payroll department had quit *en masse.* Nobody else in the company was trained in the techniques and procedures of the payroll department. It appeared that the payroll could not be processed in time. Considerable restraint on the controller's part was required not to retort, "You absolute knucklehead. You are so far from being a manager it's pitiful. Don't

you know what the hell is going on in your department?" Instead the controller dealt with the situation at hand. He replied, "This certainly is a mess. You must be upset and quite worried about the ramifications of this problem. Let's you and I sit down right now and work out an emergency plan. Later we can figure out a way to avoid repetition of this problem."

Ostracism from the Group

Punishment administered by group members in the form of social rejection can be as influential as punishment administered from above. Depending upon the strength of an individual's need for social acceptance, he may improve his performance simply to avoid ostracism from the group. Originally observed as a process taking place within small groups at the production and clerical levels, social ostracism also exists among professional and technical workers. Work groups inevitably develop some objective or subjective criteria to judge acceptable performance. Productivity below this level places the individual in jeopardy of being rejected from the group (psychologically more than physically). Higher level productivity is less likely to result in social alienation among professional workers. Punishment in the form of social rejection is demonstrated by the situation of a casualty insurance underwriter.

> Perry Bomrad completed fewer cases than any other member of his six-person work unit. In addition to individual performance appraisals, his insurance company instituted a "group productivity factor" that could provide up to a five percent bonus provided an agreed-upon level of output was reached. Perry Bomrad completed forty percent fewer cases per week than any other member of his underwriting department. Perry soon found himself subject to the following group rejections. First, his advice was never sought about technically difficult cases. Second, the group no longer asked him to join them for lunch. Third, when he placed second in the company bowling tournament, other members of the group made only passing mention of his accomplishment.

> Unfortunately, Perry resigned, and the effectiveness of these social pressures in improving his performance cannot be determined.

Administrative Punishments

Managers within organizations often use administrative power to punish subordinates. Generally, it is anticipated that such punishment will spur the individual to improved performance. The value of penalties and threats as motivational devices, however, is questionable as described in Chapter 2 on motivation. Penalties and threats rarely *turn people on*; more probably, they turn people away from identifying with the organization. Described next are three possible forms of administrative punishment meted out by management.

Demotion is a form of punishment more frequently exercised at upper than middle or lower levels of management. Poor performance is negatively rewarded by placing the guilty individual in a position of lesser responsibility. One corporate manager of planning was demoted to a branch manager position because he was perceived as being too abrasive to top management. After he "mellowed" (in the eyes of top management) he was promoted back to a position in company headquarters.

Assignment to an undesirable task is a subtle form of organizational punishment. Managers in large organizations are sometimes reassigned to a less desirable position at the same level of responsibility as a mild form of reprimand. Many organizations have their "corporate Siberias" to use for such purposes. Administrators in universities (in this author's perception) sometimes use committee assignments as a punitive measure. Committee assignments typically remove college teachers from the two prime sources of need gratification in their roles—teaching and research. Few professors volunteer for committee work, and they interpret committee assignments as a mild form of punishment. Prestigious professors sometimes refuse to accept such assignments, again attesting to the negative motivational value of college committee assignments.[24]

Firing is next to the ultimate punishment an organization can administer to its member. (The ultimate punishment is to make negative comments about an individual in response to reference checks.) Firing as a form of punishment may in rare instances have some therapeutic value for the individual; he is confronted with the consequences of his poor performance and thus may profit from the experience. The organization that fires the individual, however, fails to capitalize on any improvements in performance that might be forthcoming from the firing.

The "Red-Hot-Stove Rule"

How might a superior inflict discipline (a euphemism for punishment) without engendering resentment from subordinates and simultaneously provide a constructive learning experience? The "red-hot-stove rule," formulated by the late Douglas McGregor and popularized by George Strauss and Leonard R. Sayles, is offered as a logically sound suggestion.[25] Receiving discipline, according to this rule, should be analogous to touching a hot stove. "When you touch a hot stove your discipline is *immediate*, with *warning*, *consistent*, and *impersonal*."[26]

> Ed Maxwell, a purchasing agent, works for an electronics company whose major customer is the United States Government. Recognizing the image of scrupulous integrity the government prefers to find among its suppliers, Maxwell's company established a rule forbidding purchasing agents to accept gifts from suppliers. It was reasoned that if the government learned that ——————— Electronics was influenced by personal favors in its purchasing policies, its prices on products to the government would reflect this subjective type of purchasing.

> Ed Maxwell, it was discovered, accepted two tickets to the Super Bowl game from a supplier. *Immediately* after learning of this transaction, Maxwell's superior called him into the office to discuss the situation. (Unhappily, this occurred on the Monday after Super Bowl Sunday.) Maxwell received *immediate* punishment; he was told to send a check to his supplier for the legitimate price of the Super Bowl tickets. In addition, an official reprimand was inserted in his personnel files. *Advance warning* was received by Maxwell. Every quarter a policy statement was sent to the purchasing department about the "no gifts" policy. *Consistency* is involved because the last purchasing agent caught accepting a gift from a supplier was required to return it (a case of scotch). *Impersonality* is always difficult to convey in a disciplinary situation, but Maxwell's superior did make an effort to criticize him for having accepted a gift, not for being dishonest.

GROUP COHESIVENESS AND IMPROVED PERFORMANCE

Approaches to improving subordinate performance discussed so far have emphasized working with the individual within the group as opposed to working with the group itself. Performance, however, can also be enhanced under some circumstances by strengthening teamwork or group cohesiveness.[27] The circumstances under which group cohesiveness leads to improved performance are tied closely to the group's attitudes to and feelings about the organization. Cohesive groups that are also angry and hostile to management serve to lower organizational performance. In contrast, cohesive groups that identify with the goals of management are a force for high levels of performance. Robert L. Kahn, a person long identified with the study of work groups, makes the following research-based comment:[28]

We now recognize that a highly cohesive group can motivate its members to work toward whatever the group has defined as its goal. If the group has accepted higher productivity as its goal, then its members will be high producers. But if the group is hostile to management, then its cohesiveness will be a most effective means of reducing and restricting productivity of its members.

Group cohesiveness, as the term implies, relates to the internal strength of the group. A closely knit, mutually supportive, well-meshed group of people constitutes a cohesive group. Cohesiveness comes about primarily because of the attraction that the group has for its members. Attractiveness of the group, in turn, is related to two broad sets of conditions:[29]

1. Properties of the group such as its goals, programs, size, type of organization, and position in the community. Small, high status groups, such as the Boston Celtics, for example, tend to be cohesive.
2. Psychological needs of the individual for affiliation, recognition, security, and emotional support that can be provided by group membership. Groups composed of highly independent and resourceful people are usually low on cohesiveness. The physics faculty at a prestigious university would represent one such example.

Given the aim of improving work group performance, managers (team leaders) can achieve this end to some extent by building group cohesiveness. Essentially, this involves making the group an effective source of need gratification. Henry Clay Smith and John H. Wakeley have developed a set of guidelines for encouraging teamwork among work groups supported by William C. House's analysis of group cohesiveness and organization performance.[30] Several of Smith and Wakeley's guidelines are presented next as they might apply to the situation of enhancing cohesiveness among a group of construction engineers.[31]

Stop Assignments at the Group Level

Project engineers might seek assignments for members of the firm that involve the coordinated efforts of three or more engineers. This would be preferable to a series of "lone wolf" assignments.

Fit the Team Together

Teams selected for compatibility tend to form the most cohesive units— an obvious principle that is infrequently capitalized upon in organizational life. The engineering firm might ask individual engineers to name the four other engineers they would most prefer to work with on a job assignment. These preference ratings could then be used as a basis for team assignments.

Encourage Interaction on the Team

Tasks that require cooperation and coordination provide optimum conditions for interaction. Periodic staff meetings are essential for maintaining group cohesion when many of the group members disperse during normal working conditions. Construction engineering firms and other varieties of consulting firms often regard staff meetings as an investment necessary to maintain some semblance of group cohesiveness.

Stabilize the Team

Turnover among group members is a corrosive force with respect to group cohesiveness. (Additionally, costs of retraining and recruitment are considerable.) Consulting engineering firms often resort to financial incentives as a method of discouraging turnover. It is anticipated that money will compensate for the discomforts of heavy travel and tight schedules.

Let the Group Decide

Professional level workers in general are quite receptive to participating in decision making about both technical and administrative matters. The mere process of the consulting engineers conferring together about relevant concerns (e.g., what other kinds of jobs should the firm bid on) would contribute to teamwork. Job satisfaction, another contributor to teamwork and cohesiveness, would also tend to be enhanced by shared decision making.

STRUCTURAL AND TECHNOLOGICAL FACTORS

Another important way in which a leader can help subordinates improve performance is for the former to contribute to the resolution of structural and technological problems that could be inhibiting task accomplishment. Stated differently, there are frequently factors outside the control of a worker at any occupational level that could be blocking optimum performance. The fourth point about improving performance appraisals mentioned in this chapter touched on this concept. The discussions about faulty work flow design in Chapter 4 and changing the organizational structure in

Chapter 13 also concern the relationship between structural and technological factors and performance. For now, these topics will be examined from a different perspective.

Structural factors include authority relationships. Company representatives are sometimes given substantial formal authority in order to facilitate task accomplishment. For instance, many sales personnel are assigned symbols of formal authority in excess of their actual duties in order to provide them more "power" with customers. Many salesmen bearing a business card with titles such as "Territorial Manager" or "Regional Vice-President" are in fact salesmen with limited formal authority inside their own company. Top management assumes (or hopes) that such elevated formal status will increase customer acceptance and thus influence sales results in a positive direction. Similarly, the discussion of the dual leadership theory in the previous chapter underscored the importance of organizational position (power) in mediating leadership effectiveness.

William Foote Whyte's classical studies of the restaurant industry provided some of the earlier insights about the relationship between structural factors and job performance.[32,33] Among the many examples gathered by Whyte and his research team was the importance of avoiding the work flow situation in which waitresses "shout orders" at bartenders or countermen.[34]

> One bartender and one counterman not only enjoyed their work but were considered by waitresses to be highly efficient and pleasant to deal with. Both of them had independently worked out the same system of handling the job when the rush hour got underway. Instead of handling each order slip in turn as it was handed to them (thus responding to each individual waitress) they would collect several slips that came in about the same time, lay them on the counter before them, and fill the orders in whatever order seemed most efficient. For example . . . he would make up all the "Martinis" at once before going on to the next drink.

One general foreman failed to meet his semi-annual objectives because he was unable to find machine operators who "could read the sizzle," thus illustrating the importance of technological factors. According to this general foreman, one of the key machines in his plant was antiquated to the point that only one or two artisans could keep it running properly. Experienced hands would know when the machine temperature was optimum by the sound of the sizzle when a finger wet with saliva was placed against that machine. Inexperienced people assigned to this machine were unable to use such a sensitive feedback mechanism. As a resolution of the problem, top management consented to replace the machine with a newer model that could be operated by simply following written directions.

RELATIONSHIP TO CORE PROPOSITIONS

Improving the work performance of people can be viewed from the perspective of the four core propositions contained in our framework for organizational behavior. Readers may have noted some of these relationships at various places in the chapter.

Human Behavior

Behavioral improvements of almost any kind follow the principles of human learning. Many of the comments made in this chapter about enhancing performance are related to learning theory. Assume that a manager wanted to help a subordinate improve his or her planning skills. Principles of learning such as *goal setting, motivation,* and *reinforcement* should be applied to this coaching situation. The subordinate should set specific, realistic goals. His or her level of motivation should be high in order to enhance the learning process. The subordinate might want to know how improved planning would lead to increased opportunities for satisfaction of his or her higher level needs. An adequate schedule of reinforcements will also be desirable. Improved planning should lead to some tangible or intangible reward. For instance, better planning should lead to more accomplishment on the job or to more financial compensation.

Situational Nature

Counseling and coaching, as with other approaches to improving subordinate performance, will be effective to the extent that the situation is favorable. Figure 8.2 is basically a situational analysis of the conditions under which superior–subordinate coaching can have positive, neutral, or negative consequences. For example, coaching or counseling will most probably facilitate work improvement when the organizational climate encourages development and when the superior is a skillful coach who wants to help.

Systemic Nature

Performance appraisal methods, when properly applied, fit into an overall plan or system. Management by objectives, for example, is usually considered a system of management, rather than an isolated method. Ideally, proper implementation of an MBO system leads to improvement in individual and organizational performance. This improvement begins by translating the goals of top management first into unit and then into individual objectives. Performance reviews constitute an important link in the system. As goals and improvement are made, the MBO system is regenerated by the establishment of new objectives.

The systemic property of improving subordinate performance can be illustrated at a slightly higher level of abstraction. Subordinates who achieve substantial improvements in their performance frequently become dissatisfied with their present levels of responsibility and/or income. Subtle pressures are then created on management to find these "improved" individuals newer responsibilities. Minor reverberations throughout the organizational system are then created. The transfer of any one employee results in several realignments unless a new position is created.

Structure and Process

Douglas McGregor has pointed out that formal procedures (structure) for increasing employee motivation work best when combined with an informal behavior pattern (process) to match.[35] Performance appraisal systems result in employee improvement when they are implemented by a superior with certain key attitudes. For example, counseling works best when the manager doing the counseling believes in the dignity and worth of the individual. The manager who conveys a sincere belief in a subordinate's capacity to grow is likely to help bring about improved performance with an appraisal system. In this situation, managerial attitude has interacted with a formal procedure to produce good results.

GUIDELINES FOR ACTION

1. In attempting to improve the work performance of subordinates, pay careful attention to establishing specific improvement goals.
2. Counseling with subordinates about their mistakes is a legitimate managerial function. Effective managers are also effective counselors.
3. Performance appraisal systems should be used as vehicles for improving employee performance in addition to their more traditional role of reviewing salary and recording performance.
4. Criticism should be levied against the actions or job behavior, not the personality attributes or character traits, of people.
5. Provided that the work group identifies with the goals of management, steps taken to enhance group cohesiveness will also result in improved performance.

QUESTIONS

1. What forces do you feel are impinging upon you to improve your work (or school) performance?
2. What techniques does your present boss (or the last one you had) use to improve employee performance? How do these techniques compare to those discussed in this chapter?
3. How open would you be in "examining your relationship with your boss?" For example, assume you thought you were more technically competent than he; how would you handle the situation?
4. State three forms of organizational punishment used in any organization with which you are familiar.
5. Provide an example of a cohesive group, hostile to management. What effect did or would this situation have upon organization performance?

NOTES

1. John B. Miner, *The Management of Ineffective Performance.* New York: McGraw-Hill, 1963.
2. Edwin C. Lewis, *The Psychology of Counseling.* New York: Holt, Rinehart and Winston, 1970.
3. Felix M. Lopez, Jr., *Evaluating Employee Performance.* Chicago: Public Personnel Association, 1968, p. 112.
4. James P. McSherry and Charles N. Newstrom, "The Manager is a Counselor," in Charles D. Flory (editor), *Managing Through Insight.* New York: New American Library, 1968, pp. 181–191.
5. *Ibid.*, p. 183.
6. *Ibid.*, p. 185.
7. Harry Levinson, "A Psychologist Looks at Executive Development," *Harvard Business Review*, Vol. 40, No. 5, September–October 1962, pp. 69–75.
8. *Ibid.*
9. Winston Oberg, "Make Performance Appraisal Relevant," *Harvard Business Review*, Vol. 50, No. 1, January–February 1972, p. 61.
10. *Ibid.*, p. 62.
11. Alva F. Kendall and James Gatza, "Positive Program for Performance Appraisal," *Harvard Business Review*, Vol. 41, No. 6, November–December 1963, pp. 153–154.
12. Oberg, *op. cit.*, p. 62. For a lengthy analysis of errors of leniency and departmental differences, *see* Joseph Tiffin and Ernest J. McCormick, *Industrial Psychology*, fifth edition. Englewood Cliffs, N.J.: Prentice-Hall, 1965, pp. 244–249.
13. Charles L. Hughes, *Goal-Setting — Key to Individual and Organizational Effectiveness.* New York: American Management Association, 1965, p. 45.
14. Chris Argyris, *Integrating the Individual and the Organization.* New York: Wiley, 1964, p. 106, footnote 27.
15. Abraham K. Korman, *Industrial and Organizational Psychology.* Englewood Cliffs, N.J.: Prentice-Hall, 1971, p. 300.
16. Herbert H. Meyer, Emanuel Kay, and John R. P. French, Jr., "Split Roles in Performance Appraisal," *Harvard Business Review*, Vol. 43, No. 1, January–February 1965, p. 123.

17. Ronald J. Burke and Douglas S. Wilcox, "Characteristics of Effective Employee Performance Review and Development Interview," *Personnel Psychology*, Vol. 22, No. 3, Autumn 1969, pp. 291–306.

18. *Ibid.*, p. 302.

19. Useful references about the MBO system are: John W. Humble, *Management by Objectives in Action.* New York: McGraw-Hill, 1971; George S. Odiorne, *Management by Objectives.* New York: Pitman, 1965; Peter F. Drucker, *The Practice of Management.* New York: Harper & Row, 1954; Stephen J. Carroll, Jr. and Henry L. Tosi, Jr., *Management by Objectives: Applications and Research.* New York: Macmillan, 1973.

20. Lopez, *op. cit.*, pp. 227–229.

21. *Ibid.*, p. 228.

22. Haim G. Ginott, *Between Parent and Teenager.* New York: Avon, 1971, p. 77.

23. Eugene H. Fram, "Child Psychology Applied to Management Development," paper in process, Rochester Institute of Technology, 1972.

24. Committees in academic departments also serve many other purposes. Aside from their contribution to the democratic process, they relate to the power structure in the department or college.

25. George Strauss and Leonard R. Sayles, *Personnel: The Human Problems of Management,* third edition. Englewood Cliffs, N.J.: Prentice-Hall, 1972, pp. 267–268.

26. *Ibid.*, p. 267.

27. William C. House, "Effects of Group Cohesiveness on Organization Performance," *Personnel Journal*, Vol. 45, No. 1, January 1966, pp. 28–33.

28. Quoted in *ibid.*, p. 29.

29. *Ibid.*, p. 30.

30. *Ibid.*, pp. 28–33.

31. Henry Clay Smith and John H. Wakeley, *Psychology of Industrial Behavior*, third edition. New York: McGraw-Hill, 1972, pp. 94–102.

32. William Foote Whyte, "The Social Structure of the Restaurant," in Donald E. Porter, Philip B. Appelwhite, and Michael J. Misshauk, *Studies in Organizational Behavior and Management*, second edition. Scranton, Pa.: Intext Educational Publishers, 1971, pp. 582–595.

33. William Foote Whyte, *Human Relations in the Restaurant Industry.* New York: McGraw-Hill, 1948.

34. Whyte, "Social Structure," *op. cit.*, pp. 589–590.

35. Douglas McGregor, *The Human Side of Enterprise.* New York: McGraw-Hill, 1960, pp. 61–75.

9

Interpersonal Communications

Communication is the basic process by which everything between people happens in an organization. Broadly conceived, the study of organizational behavior *is* the study of interpersonal communications. For example, communication is the process by which leadership is executed and subordinate performance improved. Communication, in the context used here, refers to the transmission of information between and among people in organizations; emphasis here is on face-to-face communication. Without delimiting the concept of communications, our discussion would encompass topics such as advertising, public relations, annual reports, television, telephone, radio, readability formulas, and public speaking. Information about the fundamentals of communications processes can be found in *The Psychology of Communication* by Jon Eisenson, Jeffrey Auer, and John V. Irwin, or *Managerial Psychology* by Harold Leavitt.[1]

THE UNIVERSAL COMMUNICATIONS PROBLEM

Communications problems among organization members plague almost every organization.[2] Formal analyses of organizational problems frequently identify the presence of communications breakdowns. Even organizations whose business is communication (e.g., IBM, AT&T, ITT, and RCA) are not exempt from communications problems. Communications breakdowns persist despite the advances in mechanical and electronic methods of transmitting information. Underlying the persistence of these problems is the inescapable truth that most messages are eventually communicated between people in a face-to-face encounter. For instance, the regional Internal Revenue Service manager may learn from a computer print-out that frequent errors in interpreting a new tax clause are being committed. Actions to be taken by subordinates about these errors, however, will probably be communicated in a small group meeting.

Illustrations of the communications problem that plagues so many organizations are legion. Three examples are provided next to illuminate the problem.

The director of community affairs (public relations) at an eastern university requested permission to hire an administrative assistant on the basis of a heavy workload. His superior, the provost, carefully reviewed the situation and agreed that an administrative assistant would be justified from the standpoint of workload. Budgetary considerations, he cautioned, would still weigh heavily in his thinking. Whenever the director of community affairs met with the provost in the normal course of events, the latter did not take the initiative to mention hiring an administrative assistant. In response to a direct question about the topic, the provost would reply, "The matter is being given careful consideration." Next, the director of public relations took to writing memos about the disposition of the case. Finally, one year later, the provost mentioned casually, "This is a tough year for the school financially. Bring up your manpower needs again next year."

Johnnie Carter was the manager in charge of concessions for a football stadium. One month prior to the conference opening game he made specific assignments about ordering supplies for the season. One man was to order food, one souvenirs, one programs, and so forth. Two hours before kickoff the refreshment stands began to be set up for the crowd. A hungry worker accidentally discovered that frankfurter rolls were nowhere to be found in the stadium. The man in charge of food planning could only respond, "I'm sure I told the bakery the right date. It's not my fault."

Brighton Tool Company arranged a trade show exhibit to feature a recently developed numeric control system designed to have a major impact on the machine tool industry. The company president thought the trade show would be a sound advertising investment. Brochures were printed, material for the booth was purchased, and even a trade show model was hired. Two weeks before the exhibit opened the manager of manufacturing announced to the president, "As I told you one month ago, this damn thing will not be ready for shipment for the spring show. I'm not Superman, and none of my people can walk on water."

Why do communications breakdowns take place so often? Perhaps there is a reason even more fundamental than the barriers to communication (presented later) generally cited by communications theorists. One potential reason is that people simply either do not wish to or refuse to communicate.[3] Another fundamental reason might be the self-protective behavior of people. Subordinates do not communicate bad news to their superiors for fear of recrimination. Superiors, in turn, have hidden fears about the consequences of rejecting subordinates' demands and are hesitant to communicate a "no" to a request from a subordinate.

Managerial behavior that discourages open communication is another fundamental reason underlying the breakdown of communications. Managers who reinforce subordinates' fears that communicating bad news leads to recrimination serve to perpetuate a closed system of communication. For example, a manager might respond to unfavorable news with the statement, "I think you are blowing that problem all out of proportion." Although such a response is not strongly negative, the employee in question will probably develop some inhibitions about bringing unfavorable news to his or her superior.

COMMUNICATION IS TRANSACTIONAL

Effective face-to-face communication is *transactional*.[4] Person *A* may send messages to Person *B* to initiate communications, but *B* must react to *A* to complete the communications loop; a transaction between two or more people must take place. One reason written messages frequently fail to achieve their purpose is that the sender of the message cannot be sure what meanings are attached to its content. Face-to-face transactions help clarify meanings. Harold Leavitt, based upon both research and first-hand experience, has drawn some interesting contrasts between one-way and two-way (transactional) communication.[5]

1. *Speed* can be accomplished more readily with one-way communication. For example, a manager might call a staff meeting, announce his directive, and leave. Only 15 minutes have been consumed of his executive time. Transactional communication might have taken three hours. Readers who have served on committees acutely recognize the time consumed by group discussions. In the long range it is quite possible that the time advantage of one-way communication will be lost. One-way messages have a lower probability of acceptance than two-way messages.

2. *Appearance* of one-way messages is more impressive. One-way directives appear business-like and official. The manager above might have entered the conference room, made the announcement that there will be a 15 percent reduction in personnel, and left the room. During a war, military officers feel compelled to operate in this manner because of the exigencies of time and the importance of "military bearing."

3. *Covering up of mistakes* is easier with one-way communication. In the words of Leavitt, "Then the sender will not have to hear people implying or saying that he is stupid or that there is an easier way to say what he is trying to say."[6]

4. *Protection of one's power* is more readily accomplished with one-way than two-way communication. When mistakes occur (an inevitable part of organizational life), the sender can justify to himself that he delivered the appropriate message, but the intended receiver did not listen. When mistakes occur in transactional communication, the sender shares the blame, but it is also much more probable that the intended message will be communicated.

5. *Simplification of managerial life* is better accomplished with one-way than two-way communication. Once communication becomes transactional, the manager must deal with the feelings, attitudes, and perceptions of his subordinates. Similarly, the subordinate must deal more directly with people when he or she attempts transactional communication. For instance, it is much simpler to write your company president a letter of complaint than to confront him with your dissatisfactions.

6. *Planfulness, orderliness, and systemization* characterize one-way communication. Managers (and college professors) who carefully rehearse the material they want to present to subordinates (or students) can have well-organized staff meetings (or classes). Transactional communication is much sloppier. It is difficult to predict what embarrassing questions the receiver will ask when you solicit questions and opinions.

7. *More valid* communication is possible with the two-way approach. It allows for more accurate transmission of facts and, from a systems standpoint, allows for feedback and correction. A subtle result of transactional communication is that authoritarian leadership behavior is difficult to maintain. Shared authority is one consequence of the transactions that take place. Value judgments are required to determine if shared authority—democratic leadership—is "good" or "bad." Material presented earlier about leadership style suggested that a more crucial issue is whether democratic leadership is appropriate or inappropriate in a given situation.

William V. Haney, influenced by the earlier Leavitt studies, gathered some experimental evidence about the differences between unilateral and bilateral communication.[7] For experimental purposes bilateral communication was defined as a "... transactional format in which the sender receives and decodes an indication of his relative success in terms of the receiver's comprehension of the content and intent of the sender's message."[8]

Four hundred people participated in the study, distributed among 18 heterogeneous groups, including business students, police administrators, management trainees, civil service administrators, and business executives. One person in each group occupied the role of "communicator." Participants were informed that the experiment would involve first unilateral, then bilateral communication.

The experimental task was to reproduce as accurately as possible a drawing (shown in Figure 9.1) which was to be communicated verbally by the sender. Subjects had to estimate—without the aid of a watch—the elapsed time of each transmission. During the unilateral phase the communicator faced away from receivers and was instructed not to emit any nonverbal cues. Haney notes that the communication format was not unlike that of a radio. Immediately after transmission of the message, recipients were asked to record answers to a series of questions:

1. Were you frustrated, unhappy, tense, etc. with the fact that you were unable to communicate back to the sender—to ask questions, to make comments, offer suggestions, etc.?

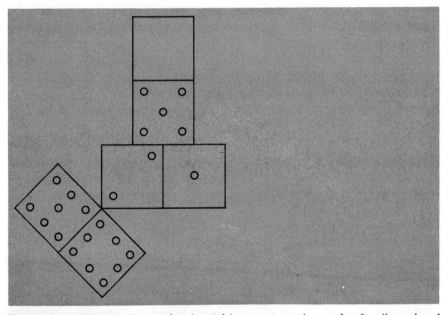

Figure 9.1 One experimental task used in a comparative study of unilateral and bilateral communication. SOURCE: William V. Haney, "A Comparative Study of Unilateral and Bilateral Communication," *Academy of Management Journal*, Vol. 7, No. 2, June 1964, p. 129.

2. Are you reasonably confident that you interpreted the message (i.e., reproduced the drawing) correctly?
3. What is your estimate to the nearest minute of the time elapsed during the transmission?

During the bilateral phase, the restrictions placed upon the communicator remained the same. Recipients, however, were now permitted to ask questions, make comments, recommend methods of attack, and so forth. After transmission of the message only the second and third questions were asked because it was assumed by the experimenter that asking about frustration in response to transactional communication was not relevant.

Among the experimental results, based both on factual data and experimenter impressions, were that bilateral communication in comparison to unilateral communication: (a) generates much less frustration, (b) is more accurate, (c) generates more confidence in the receiver that he or she is correct, (d) promotes more willingness to decide and act on the basis of information, (e) tends to obviate the potential morale problem that stems from having to act when confidence is low, (f) requires more time, and (g) will tend to be effective and constructive to the extent that the sender and receivers remain open and nonthreatened by the communications experience.

Unilateral communication, also as noted by Leavitt, is more advantageous when (a) the message becomes familiar and routinized between sender and recipient and (b) orderliness, apparent tranquility, and the suppression of emotional reactions by recipients are required.

AN INTERPERSONAL COMMUNICATION PROCESS MODEL

Communications between people is a complicated process. One simplified model of the basic interpersonal communication process will be presented now. (*See* Figure 9.2.) Later in this chapter, two other models are

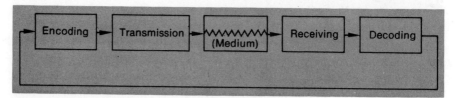

Figure 9.2 An elementary model of the interpersonal communication process.

presented: a schematic model to explain barriers to communications and a more advanced verbal model to illustrate the systemic nature of interpersonal communications.

Communication between two people can be conceptualized as a process involving the following sequence of events: encoding, transmitting over a medium, receiving, and decoding.[9,10] Elementary knowledge of systems suggests that such a process is cyclical; upon decoding a message, the receiver in turn sends out a message. Figure 9.2 schematically represents these relationships. Verbally, they can be illustrated by the situation of a clothing company executive, Vera, who thinks that her leading stylist, Jules, should develop something more "daring" for the forthcoming season.

Encoding begins when Vera feels the *need*, based on mediocre sales projections, to influence business in a positive direction. She goes through the process of *encoding* a message—perceives her experiences and formulates a series of symbols for expressing them. As expressed by William V. Haney, "The 'code' part of *encoding* is important for 'code' as we are using it as a system of *symbols* and a symbol is something that *stands* for *something else*."

Transmission takes place next. Vera has encoded her message and she must deliver it to Jules. Her past experience with Jules tells her that he prefers spoken to written communications. Vera also knows from her experience that Jules is sensitive to criticism, and therefore must be approached diplomatically. The opening comment she plans is "Jules, I want you to give free rein to your creative mind in this assignment." As Vera encodes, neural impulses are sent from the brain to the abdominal muscles for air power, the larynx for phonation, and the articulator organs ((tongue, glottis, lips, and jaw). Vera is now *transmitting*. As Haney explains:[11]

Transmitting what? Words? Thoughts? Ideas? Feelings? The message? No—vibrations—compressions and rarifications of molecules in the air.

Vera's message is transmitted over a *medium*. Spoken messages are transmitted over air. Other modes of transmission include speaking, writing, gestures, and telephones. Vera's vibrations now reach Jules' hearing organs. Technically speaking, these vibrations are physical stimuli which are relayed to the brain via an intricate set of processes in the form of neural impulses.

Decoding is both a neural and psychological process. Jules converts the impulses sent to his brain into symbols and the symbols into meaning. A complex set of variables including his intelligence, personality characteristics, and past experiences with Vera (or other authority figures, particularly those who are female) mediate his responses to these neural impulses. Intervening variables discussed later in relation to barriers to communication would also apply to the decoding process. Haney notes that if communication has been successful, the decoding by the receiver matches the encoding by the sender.[12]

Finally, the interpersonal communication process incorporates another systemic property because the decoder then encodes and transmits. Jules formulates a message to send to Vera. Perhaps, "Do you mean to imply that I have not been giving free rein to my creativity lately?" An important form of interpersonal communication—the dialogue—has begun.

INTERPERSONAL COMMUNICATION STRUCTURES

Another important aspect of interpersonal communications is their structural properties. An individual's ability to communicate is influenced to some degree by his or her vantage point in the group or organization. For instance, an industrial engineer by virtue of his constant interaction with both management and workers receives communications from both groups. Few people in any one organization can be kept informed on all important matters. Roberto Michels notes that these few people ". . . who occupy critical communication points emerge as leaders who make decisions that affect others."[13]

Behavioral science research has provided support for the idea that the person in a favorable position to receive and disseminate information will probably emerge as a leader and problem solver. Figure 9.3 illustrates two opposite types of small group structures in which much of this research has been conducted. Under the "wheel" arrangement, one person sits at the communications hub; all messages must be sent through that person. Under the "all-channel" arrangement, everyone could communicate with everyone else.

Dramatic differences in decision-making effectiveness were related to a person's position in the communications network. As reported by David R. Hampton, Charles E. Summer, and Ross A. Webber, whether decisive or indecisive, the man at the hub emerges after repeated problems as the leader and decision maker.[14] Even if a group member had very good personal leadership characteristics, the communications advantage held by the person at the hub gave him decision-making power.

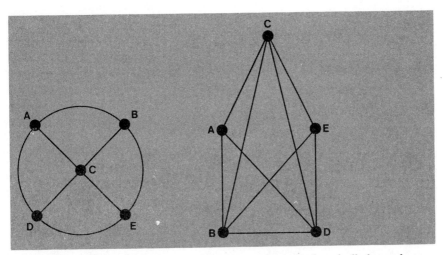

Figure 9.3 Two communications networks: wheel and all-channel.

The all-channel network provides more information about the nature of organizations than about communications. Problem solving is quite difficult when the communication channels become too complex. Everyone attempts to communicate with everyone else and disorganization is the result. Groups that begin as all-channel inevitably appoint a leader (or allow the emerging leader to assume that role) in order to get problem-solving tasks accomplished. Even though highly centralized groups offer the advantage of allowing for efficient problem solving, they are not without some psychological disadvantages. Harold Leavitt draws the following conclusion based on extensive research in this area:[15]

> Highly centralized groups may often be used for their consistency with general organizational designs, their speed, and their controllability; but they are also used as psychological defense devices to protect superiors' "weaknesses" from being exposed to subordinates and vice versa.

Information about the dimensions and characteristics of individual communications networks within the business organization structure has been gathered by A. K. Wickesberg.[16] His study thus provides valuable information about the application of communications theory to a live organizational setting, particularly at the managerial and professional level. Ninety-one business people in the University of Minnesota's Executive Master of Business Administration program recorded all oral and written communications, transmitted or received, for five individual days scattered over a five-week period. Thirty-five business organizations were represented. Participants were equally divided between managers and non-managers. No superior–subordinate or other communications pairs were included in the sample.

Daily communication logs included information about (a) the purpose of the communication, (b) whether written or oral, (c) the amount of time taken for each entry, and (d) to whom or from whom the communication was transmitted or received. Each participant also furnished the researcher with a company organization chart. An examination of the communications data suggested that they fit logically into five different categories or purposes: (a) information received or disseminated, (b) instructions given or received, (c) approval given or received, (d) problem-solving activities, and (e) nonbusiness related communications or "scuttlebutt."

Wickesberg arrived at several conclusions based on both quantitative and qualitative analyses. Each of his conclusions provides some insights about aspects of organizational behavior that transcend the patterning of communications networks within a sampling of midwestern business organizations.

First, the extent of the total communications network is more complicated than revealed by the formal organizational structure, span of control, or superior–subordinate relationships. A substantial number of horizontal and diagonal contacts among people were found, which existed outside of formal role prescriptions. For instance, a company controller might be receiving some of his most valuable input from a field sales manager even though the two have no *formal* relationship.

Second, the concept of manager should be expanded to include all individuals performing managerial (administrative) functions, whether or not these individuals have people formally reporting to them. The communications data revealed that managers and nonmanagers alike performed such activities as planning for, implementing, and controlling activities assigned to them. (Experienced sales personnel among our readers will recognize this caveat. Salesmen are often advised that their real position is that of territory manager!)

Third, resource allocation based exclusively on power structures described by formal role prescriptions is ". . . no longer sufficient in meeting the demands produced by increasing levels of technology and higher levels of member competence."[17]

An important overall conclusion to this section about communication structures within organizations is that the study of these networks is capable of providing an array of insights into broader aspects of organizational behavior. To illustrate further, Arthur M. Cohen reached some important conclusions about the problem-solving behavior of people in organizations based on a series of communications networks studies:[18]

> Give people a rigorous training in the kinds of problems that they will have to solve within a fairly structured training framework. Provide them with institutional supports for developing stable and efficient work procedures. Then, reduce the constraints of the work structure and give them the opportunity to develop on their own the kinds of work procedures that are best for solving problems. Under these conditions . . . possible avenues for organizing for work in new situations will be better explored and utilized than would be the case otherwise.

TECHNOLOGY AND INTERPERSONAL COMMUNICATION

The level of technological sophistication in an organization can influence interpersonal communication patterns among its members. As technology advances, two somewhat contradictory forces are exerted upon those engaged in specialized activities. First, people become more interdependent as technology and specialization advance. Interdependency, in turn, facilitates certain formal and informal communications with people. For instance, a marketing executive may need more interaction with his or her marketing researcher because of advanced techniques alluded to in company marketing research reports. At a minimum, advanced technology often forces people to ask each other questions about technical matters. Discussions about technical problems, in turn, may lead to an increase in nontechnical or nonbusiness interpersonal contacts. Second, as technology advances specialists often develop an in-group comraderie based on a common jargon and professional interests. "In-grouping" of this nature tends to diminish interpersonal communications with people from different specialties.

High technology combined with project or team forms of organizational structuring can facilitate interpersonal communications. Simply stated, if an organizational task is sufficiently complex to warrant a team effort, you will have more opportunity to talk to others about work and nonwork topics. One of the major satisfactions many knowledge workers derive from project assignments is the opportunity to exchange ideas with (and learn from) peers.

Research conducted by Richard L. Simpson provides some specific information about the influence of mechanization (one aspect of technology) on interpersonal communication in formal organizations.[19] The major thrust of his research was to demonstrate that communications tend to proceed

279

horizontally across organizations, rather than vertically as suggested by traditional theory. In practice, lines of authority are broken as people proceed to accomplish organizational tasks. An important hypothesis emerged from Simpson's research that helps to explain the influence of technology on communications: *A critical variable in the direction of communication is the degree of mechanization of the work process.*

Interviews about communication patterns were conducted with the eight supervisors in the spinning department of a synthetic textile mill: a general foreman at Level *A*, a shift foreman and a supervisor at Level *B*, and five foremen at Level *C*. Each supervisor was asked how many work-related contacts he had with every other supervisor. The experimenter asked:[20] "About how often do you talk with ——————— on business? Don't include times when you just say hello or pass the time of day, just the contacts needed to get your work done. . . . What kind of things do you talk about with him?"

A tabulation of the direction of the responses, combined with an analysis of their content, revealed that communications of the first-line foremen were mainly horizontal because of the mechanized nature of the work. For example, in the spinning department few instructions were necessary. Only in a department called "bobbin stores," where work was dependent upon coordination with another department, were frequent contacts between the foremen and his superiors crucial. Situations calling for joint problem solving also brought about horizontal communication. One filament foreman explains his lateral communications with the other filament foreman:[21]

> We get together on a lot of problems. If a machine is acting up, or labor is short and we have to make sure all the machines are properly covered, we talk things over. Things are coming up all the time that we have to work out together.

Simpson concludes his case research with a useful and logical hypothesis about the influence of technology on interpersonal communications: Mechanization reduces the need for vertical communications (or close supervision) because the machine—not the foreman—sets the work pace for employees. In contrast, automation (the extreme of mechanization) increases the need for vertical communication in order to cope with the frequent and serious machine breakdowns. Parenthetically, it must be added that highly efficient machines—whether the product of high or low technology—reduce the need for vertical communication.

BARRIERS TO COMMUNICATION[22]

Messages sent from Person *A* to Person *B* (or to a group of persons) are rarely received by those people in exactly the form intended by Person *A*. Barriers exist that complicate the process of communication.[23] Systems theory, as illustrated in Figure 9.4, provides a framework for understanding what transpires when messages are communicated. *Input* consists of messages—spoken or written—as sent by the receiver. A host of variables or conditions shape the ultimate *output* of the message. Intervening variables may be related to (a) the receiver, (b) the sender, or (c) the environment. For instance, (a) the receiver might be a group of hostile people, (b) the sender might have poor communication skills, and (c) the organizational climate might be one of distrust and suspicion. This list of intervening variables should be considered illustrative, not exhaustive.

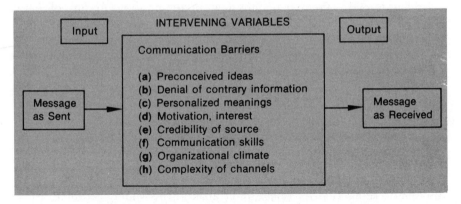

Figure 9.4 Barriers to the communications process.

Preconceived Notions

"People hear what they expect to hear" is perhaps an overused cliché, yet it concisely explains a major barrier to communication. This same principle explains why people so frequently state: "I've heard that message before." Perhaps they are only *receiving* the same message as they received before.

During a period of declining sales, a company president made five consecutive monthly announcements of the need for "belt tightening." Made during staff meetings, the announcements concluded with a specific recommendation about reducing the work force. The president concluded the sixth speech with a general statement that a need for keeping a tight belt still existed, but he did not make specific recommendations for layoff. Unfortunately, the engineering manager thought he heard the president call for more cuts in staff. Two more engineers were laid off. Shortly thereafter the mistake was rectified and both engineers agreed to return to work, but the embarrassment value of this mistake was high.[24]

Denial of Contrary Information

Messages that conflict with information already accepted as valid by the receiver are often rejected or denied. (This phenomenon is one key aspect of behavior known as *cognitive dissonance.*)

> During a management development seminar attended by managers from several different organizations, a manager from Company *A* accused Company *B* of being anti-Semitic. The manager from Company *B* said, "There are many Jews in key positions in our company, and I think I can prove it." The representative from Company *A* replied, "You're just covering up for your company." Company *B*'s representative brought an annual report to the seminar the following week and confronted his antagonist with the observation that four of the sixteen company officers listed in the annual report had Jewish *names.* The man from Company *A* replied, "That evidence doesn't count. You still don't know if they *are* Jewish."

Personalized Meanings

Words have different meanings to different people. An entire discipline—semantics—has been built around this widely accepted aspect of communications. *Semantics* can be defined simply as the study or science of meaning. S. I. Hayakawa, a well-publicized semanticist (and later college administrator), offers a more complex definition of semantics:[25]

> (1) In modern logic, the study of the laws and conditions under which signs and symbols, including words, may be said to be meaningful; semiotic; and (2) the study of the relation between words and things; later extended into the study of the relations between language, thought and behavior, that is, how human action is influenced by words, whether spoken by others or to oneself in thought; significs. The word was originally used to mean (3) in philology, the historical study of changes in the meanings of words; semasiology.

A brief case illustration follows that shows how the various meanings people attribute to the same word or phrase can create problems in organizational life.

The president of a large manufacturing company was quoted in the local newspaper as saying, "Technical competence is not dead in our society and this will be shown in our company. I see an increasing emphasis for us upon technical competence." During the next several weeks, small group discussions were held in individual departments to discuss the implications of this statement. A perceptive personnel manager recorded some of the different *meanings* attached to the phrase "technical competence."

Engineers, in general, were encouraged because they interpreted "technical" to refer to engineering as opposed to administration, manufacturing, or marketing. One engineer stated, "At last, the importance of our efforts to the company is being recognized."

According to a manufacturing manager, some production workers were upset by the president's statement. They interpreted it to mean that higher productivity levels would be needed to obtain the same wage rates. (This was a nonunion shop.)

Two members of the management training program felt the statement implied that younger administrative employees might be cut, because the company was shifting away from administrative work and toward technical work.

The industrial nurse (who overhears many concerns of employees when they visit the company medical facility) commented that the public statement was interpreted as an early warning of an impending layoff. According to this interpretation, poor performers—those considered by the company to be technically incompetent—were in jeopardy of losing their jobs.

Motivation and Interest

It is difficult to get through to a person who is not interested in what you have to say. Salesmen confront this phenomenon in everyday work life. If receivers are not motivated to accept the messages sent by the sender, the communication loop will probably remain incomplete.

A junior executive was told by his boss that the United Fund was looking for volunteer workers and the latter would qualify. Six months later, during performance appraisal, the junior executive was asked by his boss why he had not contributed his time to community affairs. He replied, "I didn't know of any suitable openings." Working for the United Fund was of such low interest to the junior executive that the message sent by his boss about this topic did not register.

Credibility of the Source

Messages often do not register with receivers because the sender is not trusted. *Incredible* messages are literally those not believed to be true! Senders of messages, in order to be credible, have to earn such a reputation over an extended period of time. Reputations of low credibility, however, can be earned in a much shorter period of time. Sometimes class stereotypes create a mental set that the sender of messages must overcome. Professional politicians, for example, must work hard to establish themselves as a credible source of information because of stereotypes that a politician is an individual of low credibility.

> An owner of a food wholesaling company had developed a bonus incentive plan for all employees. The size of profit participation varied with both seniority and job level. More senior and higher level employees were to receive the highest bonus. Each year for three consecutive years at Christmas time, the owner made an impassioned plea to employees about the importance of patience on their behalf. His analysis of industry trends revealed that the food business was in a temporary profit squeeze, but prospects for the next year were indeed bright. After the third consecutive "poverty speech" (backed up by miniscule bonuses) most of the capable employees joined competitors. At this point almost no employee believed the owner and, those who had a choice, left.

Communication Skills

Substantial individual differences exist in the ability of people to communicate, representing yet another intervening variable influencing the transmission of messages from sender to receiver. Some differences in communication skills are attributable to education and training, while others stem from more basic personality characteristics. For instance, articulate, persuasive, and confident people communicate more effectively.

Communications effectiveness is influenced by subtle aspects of personality such as sensitivity about the *timing* of messages. Poor timing is exemplified by the managers who relay important instructions to employees on the Friday afternoon before a holiday. By that time most people will be shifting their attention away from work and toward vacation. Good timing, in contrast, is exemplified by the department manager who asks for new funds after information has been released that the company has achieved its financial objectives for the year. Under these circumstances the department manager's superior is more likely to listen to his proposition.

Receivers of messages also manifest individual differences. Some people are better listeners than others by virtue of education, training, personality characteristics, or physical characteristics (e.g., level of hearing acuity). Personal conflicts may also serve as a barrier to developing listening acuity. Anxious people sometimes are too preoccupied with their personal problems to pay an appropriate amount of attention to messages from other people. People placed under considerable organizational stress may also show some decrease in listening acuity.

Organizational Climate

The atmosphere or "personality" of an organization (the subject matter of Chapter 13) also influences the extent to which a message is received. Messages sent in an organization where a high degree of trust and openness exist have a higher probability of being received than those sent in a climate of distrust and defensiveness. Another aspect of organizational climate affecting the communication of messages relates to the formality versus informality of orders and requests. In some organizations formal orders must be issued to accomplish all but routine tasks.

> The chief administrator of a hospital told his head nurse he wanted the wards readied for an impending state inspection. Later that week an inspection team did visit the hospital. Among the irregularities noted in the hospital were dirty linen stored in closets and bags of food stored in the refrigerator reserved for pharmaceuticals. After the inspection report noted these "demerits," the chief administrator demanded an explanation from the head nurse. Her defense was, "I felt that if anything you wanted done was important, you would put it in writing. I guess I didn't take your comment seriously."

Complexity of Channels

All things being equal, communications efficiency decreases with the number of "baffles" information must pass through before reaching its intended receiver.[26] This partially explains why face-to-face communication works more effectively in small than in large organizations. Direct channels can be more readily used in small organizations because fewer layers of management have to be penetrated. For instance, if a small company president has information he wishes to relay to a middle manager, he will probably feel no qualms about violating the chain of command by speaking directly to the manager in question. Large, complex organizations have heightened communications problems by the very nature of their complexity. In short, more face-to-face communications take place in small organizations.

COPING WITH BARRIERS TO COMMUNICATION

Despite the barriers to communication present in every organization, the situation is not hopeless. Many messages do get through to the receiver as intended, and many barriers to communication can be circumvented. Simply developing an awareness that such barriers exist is an important starting point in coping with them. Strauss and Sayles note that a wide variety of research confirms the validity of considering communications as both a psychological and technical problem.[27] Approaches to coping with the psychological factors that distort messages are emphasized here. Technical aspects of communications encompass such wide-ranging considerations as voice audibility, type size, and noise pollution.

Recognize Receiver's Frame of Reference

One unifying point contained in Figure 9.3 is that the receiver's point of view must be factored into the transmission of messages. Effective communicators intuitively empathize with their intended listeners. Frames of reference resist change. Recognition of this proposition implies that the sender of messages will have to work patiently at changing any aspect of another individual's frame of reference. *Preconceived ideas* and *denial of contrary information* (variables (a) and (b) in Figure 9.4) constitute part of a person's frame of reference. An apartment building owner learned to cope with these variables after an initial frustration:

> Roy Drake, a dentist, purchased a four-unit apartment building. Dr. Drake visited his new property the Sunday following the house closing. Each tenant was given the following message: "I'm glad to be the new owner of this building. I think you will all find me to be a very fair landlord. I am too busy with my dental practice to knock on your door every month and collect rents. Around the first of each month please send me your rent. Please try and call me only in an emergency. As I said, I'm a very busy person."
>
> By the tenth of the month only one tenant had mailed in the rent. Roy Drake was concerned enough to telephone each delinquent tenant. Each tenant explained in essence that a landlord is supposed to collect rent in person. (Their preconceived notion about the role of a landlord hindered them from receiving the message that rents should be

mailed.) Within ten more days, two tenants had still not mailed their rent. Another set of telephone calls was required to collect the two remaining rents.

Next month, Drake was forced to repeat the process of making follow-up telephone calls to collect the rent. Finally he hit on a mechanical aid to cope with the tenants' sturdy frame of reference. Drake, under counsel from his real estate broker, gave each tenant a set of stamped, addressed envelopes in which to mail their rent each month. He also hand delivered these envelopes to each tenant and patiently explained that the rules of the game had changed. Tenants would now be responsible for mailing their rental payments to him.

Collection of rents from this point forward, within reason, did not require personal visits by the new landlord; the new system worked. It had failed at first, not because the tenants were "deadbeats," but because the dentist underestimated the power of his tenants' preconceived notions about the role of a landlord.

Utilize Feedback

Systems theory indicates that communications are complete only when the sender receives feedback that the message has been received as intended. Feedback "... refers to the ability of certain complex machines (technically, systems) to check on their own performance and to correct it if necessary—often called cybernetics."[28] Individuals communicating to each other can receive both verbal and nonverbal feedback. (Nonverbal communication is explored later in this chapter.) Written messages afford much less opportunity for feedback. Considerable emotion and feeling has to be elicited from a written communication before a written response is made voluntarily. (Think of how strongly you would have to feel before voluntarily responding to a memo in writing.)

Managers who ask subordinates or colleagues how they feel about a given message are rare. Yet feedback will provide the manager clues about the acceptance of his message. Brief, straightforward questions such as the following are helpful in eliciting feedback about the reception of a message:

How do you feel about my statement?

What do you think?

Tell me how what I have said has come across to you.

Do you see any problems with what we have talked about?

Failing to elicit verbal feedback about other peoples' reactions to a message paves the way toward misunderstanding or sometimes a breakdown in communications. When receivers are timid, shy, or afraid, additional effort must be invested in eliciting feedback. The unfortunate situation of one new car dealer illustrates how failing to receive feedback can impair organizational performance:

> Under pressure from his superior, the owner of a new car franchise called his sales force together for a meeting. According to company statistics, this agency was not selling its share of higher priced, "loaded" models. A disproportionate number of their sales were coming from the lowest priced model in that manufacturer's line. The agency head attempted to motivate his sales force with this message:
>
> "We are all falling down in our jobs. We are letting customers walk out of here with the cheapest, most inexpensive models on the floor. You know, I know, and Detroit knows that the profits come from the fancier models loaded with accessories. From now on anyone who sells only cheapies will be penalized by three hours of floor time per week. If there is anyone working for me who doesn't want to make more money let me know right now. If you do what I tell you, you'll make more money, I'll make more money, and Detroit will be happy."
>
> This message had a dysfunctional impact on organizational performance. Total agency sales decreased in the following month. Underlying the disproportionate emphasis on lower priced car sales was the current climate of economic uncertainty in the town's largest employer. New car purchasers were unwilling to spend more money than absolutely necessary to purchase a new automobile. Even worse, several of the salesmen, recognizing the current economic pinch, were offering rebates to new car purchasers. ("You buy a car from me and I'll send your wife $25 as soon as I get my commission.") Attempts to sell higher priced models in the current economy resulted in some customers leaving the showroom discouraged and annoyed.

Nonverbal communication also serves as a vital source of feedback about how effectively a message is being communicated. Popularized in recent years by Julius Fast's *Body Language,* nonverbal communication refers to the multitude of cues in addition to language that people use to communicate.[29] Essentially, these cues refer to aspects of behavior more subtle than punching someone in the arm or grabbing him by the lapels. Frequently observed nonverbal messages include directing gaze away from another person to communicate lack of interest, holding the mouth open to communicate enthusiasm (or passion), and placing one's hand on the chin to indicate careful consideration of another person's comments.

Observing nonverbal cues is useful in providing insight into how the receiver feels about a message. Nonverbal signs may be at variance with the content of a person's reaction to a message. For example, a manager might ask a programmer if he or she feels confident in debugging an important program. "Yes, I'm confident" might be the verbal response, but a hand tremor and a speech stammer suggest otherwise. Feedback of this nature would serve as a signal to the manager that he should volunteer to provide assistance in the more difficult portions of the assignment.

An industrial organization lagged behind competitors in new product development. One antidote selected by the president was to appoint a new product committee composed of representatives from a diagonal slice of the company. Chaired by the executive vice-president, the next highest ranking member was the vice-president of engineering. Lowest in organizational rank among committee members was an inspector from the electronics assembly area. Following is a list of some of the nonverbal cues communicated by committee members and tentative interpretations of these cues. (High degrees of subjective reasoning are required to interpret body language.)

Member *A* yawned. He felt many of the ideas being generated had been suggested many times in the past. Furthermore, as he verbally communicated later, not everybody on the committee was qualified to serve.

Member *B*, a new product planner, tapped his fingers and shuffled his feet. The fact that this meeting was necessary implied to some extent that he was not doing his job—a situation that raised his anxiety level.

Member *C* maintained a smile even during the more somber moments of the meeting. She was the only female engineer in her department and was enjoying the opportunity to demonstrate her capability to a cross section of the organization. Her smile did not necessarily imply total acceptance of all the ideas brought forth in committee.

Member *D* occupied the chair closest to the chairman. During the meeting he inched his chair even closer to the chairman. At a minimum, this implied an acceptance of the chairman and perhaps an attempt to curry favor with him.

Member *E* directed his gaze away from the committee chairman whenever tentative assignments were thrown out to the group such as, "We need someone to review in the trade magazine what new products using our technology have been brought out in the last several years." *E* does not want to take individual responsibility for any subproject, yet would not be willing to confront the chairman with this attitude.

Reinforce Words with Action

Verbal statements of intent represent but a beginning to the communications process. Statements of policy or intended actions become credible only after management (or anyone else) has established the reputation of backing up words with action. Following through on the behavior suggested by a written or spoken message decreases the "credibility gap" and helps establish a climate of trust. This elementary principle is frequently violated in the pressures of organizational life.

> One publicly held corporation issued a policy statement that the corporation would place more emphasis on participative management. To demonstrate the seriousness of this intent, a New Ventures Committee was established with representatives from all key functional areas of the business. A stated purpose of this committee was "to assist top management in making decisions about new ventures which could shape the destiny of the organization." Three months later it was announced that the corporation was negotiating to be acquired by a large electronics firm. No one on the New Ventures Committee was asked his opinion about the desirability of such a course of action. Future policy statements by the corporation were met with considerable skepticism.

Reinforcing words with actions helps to circumvent three barriers to communication discussed earlier. First, the credibility gap is narrowed. Second, an organizational climate characterized by trust is fostered. Third, it encourages interest in spoken or written communications because they are perceived as vital and meaningful.

Use Appropriate Language

"Written communications should be as intelligible and readable as possible" states a widely accepted principle of good communication. Every reader can think of at least one example where a written or spoken message lost (or alienated) its intended receiver because of its complexity. Exhortations about the importance of clear communications overlook one subtle consideration that deserves mention. *Appropriate* language is perhaps more important than *simple* language (although simple language is usually appropriate). Oversimplified messages can be interpreted as condescending and therefore may engender resentment. Well-read patients sometimes resent the simplified messages given to them by physicians. Physicians, of course, are concerned that the use of medical terminology would not be comprehensible to the average patient, and therefore seek the lowest common denominator of language.

Avoid Speeches and Lectures

Effective communication is transactional, as cautioned earlier. Attempting to communicate with people on-the-job by lecturing or making speeches to them violates this principle. Responding to the cues sent out by the listener is difficult when the sender is intent upon conveying his or her entire message. Additionally, when an individual or group is not mentally *set* to hear a speech or lecture (perhaps in a staff meeting) such behavior on the sender's part may evoke irritation or resentment on the receiver's part. An example from the sales field illustrates the importance of avoiding speechmaking when two-way communication is called for.[30]

> A young man embarked upon a career in the ethical pharmaceuticals field. He was given a training program to prepare him for demonstrating tranquilizing drugs to physicians. On one of his early sales calls, he was accompanied by one of the senior men in the territory, "an old pro" with a successful sales record. The new salesman entered the waiting room of a general practitioner with a busy schedule. He and the older salesman were kept waiting one hour before the doctor was able to see them. The old pro let the trainee take the initiative and decided to observe the interaction between the sales trainee and the doctor. The young man introduced himself and quickly launched into a seven-minute lecture on the advantages of his firm's tranquilizing drug. He quickly lost rapport with the physician. The busy doctor was visibly squirming and losing patience. At this point, the experienced salesman decided things had gone too far and that it was his responsibility to save the situation. He leaned over, looked directly at the physician and said, "Doctor, do you have any patients who worry so much they are failing at their work?" The doctor was taken by surprise but immediately perked up and said, "Sure I do. Is that what this young man is talking about?"

TRANSACTIONAL ANALYSIS

Popularized by two best selling books (*Games People Play* and *I'm OK—You're OK*), transactional analysis has become one of the most frequently mentioned behavioral science concepts.[31] Transactional analysis (TA) is simultaneously a theory of behavior, a method of psychotherapy, and an approach to improved human relations and better self-understanding. This new development in interpersonal communications deserves mention here because it offers some promise of helping people to interpret human behavior in organizations. Readers interested in understanding the basics of TA should consult an original source.[32] A brief overview and one organizational application of this popular development in behavioral science is sufficient for the scope of this chapter.

TA, as the name implies, analyzes transactions that take place between and among people. This approach to interpersonal relations confronts people with the intellectual fact that they are responsible for what happens in the future, no matter what has happened in the past. The late Eric Berne, founder of TA, proposed three active elements in each person's makeup: the Parent, the Adult, and the Child (P-A-C). Closely related to the psychoanalytic terms, ego, id, and superego, they are conditions of the mind. The Parent (superego) personifies the "don't's" and a few "do's" that are imbedded in a person's psyche. The Child (id) represents spontaneous emotion (e.g., life should be filled with sex and other forms of fun). Both Parent and Child must be kept in proper relation to the Adult (ego) who performs a reality function by integrating feeling with experience. According to the Adult, there is a time and a place for everything. According to Thomas A. Harris, the popularizer of TA, its goal[33]

> ... is the strengthening and emancipation of the Adult from the archaic recordings in Parent and Child to make possible freedom of choice and the creation of new options.

Transactional analysis has four key life positions that are essentially attitudes toward oneself and others: They are (1) I'm not OK—You're OK (the anxious dependency of the immature that leads to feelings of depression); (2) I'm not OK—You're not OK (the give-up or despair position that in extreme cases leads to schizophrenia); (3) I'm OK—You're not OK (the criminal position that hints of paranoid thinking); (4) I'm OK—You're OK (the response of the mature adult and the only response that is intrinsically constructive).[34]

Games that people play represent a key ingredient of transactional analysis and also provide fruitful tools of analysis for understanding organizational behavior. Descriptively, a game is "... a recurring set of transactions, often repetitious, superficially plausible, with a concealed motivation; or, more colloquially, a series of moves with a snare or 'gimmick.' "[35] Emotionally healthy as well as sick people play games both in and outside of organizational life. Among the games played are: "Ain't it Awful," "Confession," "I Am Bigger," "If It Weren't for You I Could," "Kick Me," "Mine Is Better Than Yours," "Now I've Got You, You S.O.B.," and "So's Your Old Man."[36] Described next is a case history of "Indigence," a game played between a case worker and a welfare client, as analyzed by a student of Eric Berne.

"Indigence" is a complement to "I'm Only Trying to Help You" ("ITHY"), which relates to the attitude held by some professional people-helpers that clients or patients are ungrateful and disappointing. "Indigence" is played with equal competence by the social worker and client, both of whom earn their livings by playing it.[37]

> Ms. Black was a social worker in a government subsidized welfare agency. An important aim of the agency was the economic rehabilitation of indigents; in practice this meant finding them jobs. Official reports usually stated that clients were making progress, but very few of them were actually "rehabilitated." Ms. Black, from her training in game analysis, began to suspect that the agency was playing games ("I'm Only Trying to Help You") with clients. She sought to confirm or deny her suspicions by making a field inspection.

> She asked her own clients from week to week how many job opportunities they had actually investigated. Ms. Black found that very little genuine effort was being devoted to job hunting. Sometimes the token efforts clients did make had an ironic quality:[38]

>> For example, one man said that he answered at least one advertisement a day looking for work. "What kind of work?" she inquired. He said he wanted to go into sales work. "Is that the only kind of ad you answer?" He said that it was, but it was too bad that he was a stutterer, as that held him back from his chosen career.

> Learning that she was asking clients these types of questions, Ms. Black's supervisor reprimanded her for putting "undue pressure" on her clients. Despite the reprimand, she decided to fulfill her mission of rehabilitating at least some of her welfare clients. Concentrating on able-bodied people who did not appear to have a legitimate reason to continue receiving welfare, Ms. Black talked over the games "ITHY" and "Indigence." When clients were willing to concede the point, Ms. Black said that unless they found jobs she was going to terminate their welfare funds and refer them to a "different type of agency." Several clients almost immediately found employment, but they were indignant at her attitude and, in retaliation, some wrote letters of complaint to her superior.

> Ms. Black's supervisor reprimanded her on the grounds that, although her former clients were working, they were not "really rehabilitated." The meaning of this latter term was not clarified and she was again admonished about putting undue pressure on clients.

Eric Berne noted that in this agency there was a tacit agreement between the worker and the client which read as follows:[39]

> W: "I'll try to help you (providing you don't get better)."
> C: "I'll look for employment (providing I don't have to find any)."

According to game analysis, if a client broke the agreement by getting better, the client would lose welfare benefits (and have to work) and the agency would lose a client. If a professionally responsible case worker steered the client into finding work, the agency would bear the brunt of the client's complaints, and these complaints might come to the attention of higher authorities. As long as both client and agency obeyed the implicit rules, both received what they wanted. The client received his or her welfare benefits and the agency had an opportunity to "reach out" and collect interesting case material for staff conferences.

Humanitarian minded (or at least noncynical) readers may find comfort in these qualifying comments made by Berne:[40]

> First, "Indigence" as a game rather than a condition due to physical, mental, or economic disability, is played by only a limited percentage of welfare clients. Second, it will only be supported by social workers who are trained to play ITHY. It will not be well tolerated by other workers.

COMMUNICATION, PRODUCTIVITY, AND SATISFACTION

Effective communications within an organization should not be an end in itself. Improved interpersonal communications should lead to improvements in productivity and/or job satisfaction. Common sense and an array of opinion would suggest that communication is related to productivity. Even the most casual observer of organizational behavior recognizes that many organizational problems stem from communication breakdowns. (Breakdowns in communications, it could be further argued, may stem from root causes such as poor morale.) Jack R. Gibb reports that surprisingly little research exists to support or deny the widely held assumption that communication and productivity are positively related.[41] Research evidence does exist, however, about the relationship between communications and job satisfaction.

Ronald J. Burke and Douglas S. Wilcox investigated how openness of communication between superior and subordinates influenced the job satisfaction of 150 female telephone operators.[42] This aspect of face-to-face communication was measured by two questions:

> How free and open are you in communicating your feelings and ideas about your job and your job situation with your immediate superior?
>
> How free and open is your immediate superior in communicating to you?

Job satisfaction was measured by a lengthier questionnaire. Results of the study were encouraging for proponents of open communication. In general, the greater the openness of either superior or subordinate (or both), the greater the degree of subordinate satisfaction with (a) the company, (b) the job, (c) the climate for personal growth, (d) the presence of a helping relationship, and (e) the supervisor. Presumably, openness of communication is also related to worker morale for a variety of occupations in a variety of organizations.

RELATIONSHIP TO CORE PROPOSITIONS

The processes involved in interpersonal communications in organizations fit logically into our overall framework for organizational behavior. Many of these relationships have already been woven into the body of the chapter; a few more will be highlighted in the next several paragraphs.

Human Behavior

Interpersonal communication obviously takes place among people; as such, it follows the principles of human behavior. An understanding of selected aspects of human behavior precedes an understanding of why some messages fail to register with people. For example, the concept of *selective perception* helps to explain why an individual will respond to some messages and not to others. People tend to receive those messages they find nonthreatening, and not receive threatening messages. Thus, the 56-year-old mechanical engineer may not *hear* the engineering vice-president state that the company is shifting from a mechanical to an electronic technology.

Similarly, the concept of cognitive dissonance helps to explain why some important messages are not received by people. According to this well-known social psychological principle, people prefer not to hold ideas or beliefs that are mutually incompatible. Incompatibility of this nature makes people tense, and ways are found to reduce the tension. Many employees in a company may deny the presence of economic indicators that they will not be receiving a year-end bonus. Thoughts of a zero bonus may be incompatible with some already-planned purchase, and with a fundamental belief in the inevitability of a Christmas bonus.

Situational Nature

Interpersonal communications have a distinct situational nature, as suggested by Figure 9.4, "Barriers to the Communications Process." The intervening variables shown in this figure can also be interpreted as variables in the environment that influence the process of communications.

When these situational variables (or factors) are favorable, the message has a high probability of being received. The analysis presented under the heading, "Coping with Barriers to Communication," is essentially a list of suggestions for making these situational variables more favorable. Specifically, a message would have a relatively high probability of being received under the following conditions:

(a) the receiver's frame of reference is taken into account
(b) feedback from the receiver is utilized
(c) words are reinforced with action (i.e., the sender of the message is perceived as a *credible* person over time)
(d) appropriate language is used in communicating the message
(e) speeches and lectures are avoided (i.e., communication is transactional rather than unidirectional).

Systemic Nature

Interpersonal communications processes within an organization are most appropriately viewed as communications systems. A communications network in an organization can be considered its *nervous system.* All information is transmitted through this system. Many systems models have been proposed to explain the communications process that takes place within an organization. A basic system model of communications presented by William G. Scott and Terence R. Mitchell illuminates the systemic nature of the flow of information within organizations.[43]

> The model shows that for communication to exist both a sender and a receiver are necessary. Additionally, communication in this model relies on a *closed* circuit, requiring both the elements of downward passage of information and understanding feedback to be present.... the model is indeed a first approximation.

> The circuit model is quadratic, symmetrical, and continuous. It is quadratic in that four elements are basic to it; it is symmetrical because information emitted by the sender (ideally) is balanced by understanding evidenced by the receiver; and it is continuous because it portrays communication as an undisrupted interchange between the sender and receiver.

Structure and Process

In every organization both formal (structure) and informal (process) communications channels exist. Probably no organization could function effectively (or at all!) if an informal communications system did not fill in the gaps created by the formal system. The *grapevine* is the best-publicized vehicle of transmitting information along informal channels. Grapevines are sometimes dysfunctional. For example, untrue and disruptive rumors may be transmitted by the grapevine. Grapevines can also be functional. A president may communicate via formal channels the company's intent to upgrade the quality of customer service. Official notices may be sent to lower level managers and the company newspaper may contain a feature about the importance of customer service. However, when the informal processes (the grapevine) suggest that the company president "really means it this time" the message is likely to get across. Thus, formal and informal (structure and process) mechanisms interact to bring about a change in organizational behavior.

GUIDELINES FOR ACTION

1. Communication problems among members undoubtedly exist in your organization. Identify those you can and attempt to solve them. Their solution will probably improve both productivity and job satisfaction.
2. Practice two-way rather than one-way communication if you are concerned about getting your message across.
3. An important general suggestion for improving your communications with others is to understand their frames of reference before composing or delivering your message.
4. While delivering your message, ask for verbal feedback and be sensitive to nonverbal cues about how your message is getting across.
5. An important determinant of the effectiveness of your communications is your credibility. You will be perceived as credible to the extent that your behavior reinforces your words.
6. Effective speaking, writing, and listening skills are a valuable asset to a knowledge worker in any organization.

QUESTIONS

1. What symptoms of a communication problem can you identify within the organization with which you are most familiar?
2. How would you rate your ability to communicate with others in face-to-face situations? What evidence do you have to support your rating?
3. How effective are you in receiving messages? What evidence do you have to support your opinion?
4. What nonverbal cues do members of a basketball (or football) team convey to each other during a game?
5. Comment on the "communications effectiveness" of this chapter.

NOTES

1. Jon Eisenson, Jeffrey Auer, and John V. Irwin, *The Psychology of Communication*. New York: Appleton-Century-Crofts, 1963; Harold Leavitt, *Managerial Psychology*, second edition. Chicago: University of Chicago Press, 1964, pp. 138–152, 218–251.
2. Andrew J. DuBrin, *The Practice of Managerial Psychology*. Elmsford, N.Y.: Pergamon Press, 1972, pp. 172-173.
3. Personal statement from Todd Bullard, a political scientist and college executive; and William O'Donnell, "The Real Problem in Communications," *Personnel Journal*, Vol. 46, No. 1, January 1967, p. 51.
4. Later in this chapter a description of *transactional analysis* will be presented.
5. Leavitt, *op. cit.*, pp. 141–150.
6. *Ibid.*, p. 144.
7. William V. Haney, "A Comparative Study of Unilateral and Bilateral Communication," *Academy of Management Journal*, Vol. 7, No. 2, June 1964, pp. 128–136.
8. *Ibid.*, pp. 129–130.
9. William V. Haney, *Communication and Organizational Behavior*, revised edition. Homewood, Ill.: Richard D. Irwin, 1967, Chapter 5.
10. Another process model of human communication is Franklin Fearing, "Toward a Psychological Theory of Human Communication," *Journal of Personality*, Vol. 22, 1953–1954, pp. 73–76.
11. Haney, 1964, *op. cit.*, p. 154.
12. *Ibid.*, p. 158.
13. Cited in David R. Hampton, Charles E. Summer, and Ross A. Webber, *Organizational Behavior and the Practice of Management*. Glenview, Ill.: Scott, Foresman, 1968, p. 189.
14. *Ibid.*, p. 190.
15. Leavitt, *op. cit.*, p. 241.
16. A. K. Wickesberg, "Communications Networks in the Business Organization Structure," *Academy of Management Journal*, Vol. 11, No. 3, September 1968, pp. 253–262.
17. *Ibid.*, p. 262.
18. Arthur M. Cohen, "Changing Small Group Communication Networks," *Administrative Science Quarterly*, Vol. 7, No. 1, March 1962, pp. 443–462.
19. Richard L. Simpson, "Vertical and Horizontal Communication in Formal Organization," *Administrative Science Quarterly*, Vol. 4, No. 3, September 1959, pp. 189–196.
20. *Ibid.*, p. 192.
21. *Ibid.*, p. 194.
22. This discussion of barriers to communication is heavily influenced by the ideas of George Strauss and Leonard R. Sayles, *Personnel: The Human Problems of Management*, third edition. Englewood Cliffs, N.J.: Prentice-Hall, 1972, pp. 205–224.
23. Leon C. Megginson, *Personnel: A Behavioral Approach to Administration*. Homewood, Ill.: Richard D. Irwin, 1972, p. 603.
24. This example may not represent a pure case of "preconceived notions." Under a more open organizational climate, the engineering manager might ask the president directly what he (the president) wanted accomplished.
25. S. I. Hayakawa, "Semantics, General Semantics, and Related Disciplines," in S. I. Hayakawa (editor), *Language, Meaning, and Maturity*. New York: Harper, 1954, p. 19. For a recent advanced treatment of the field of semantics, *see* Danny D. Steinberg and Leon A. Jakobovits (editors), *Semantics: An Interdisciplinary Reader in Philosophy, Linguistics and Psychology*. New York: Cambridge University Press, 1971.
26. Strauss and Sayles, *op. cit.*, p. 214.
27. *Ibid.*, p. 217.

28. *Ibid.*, p. 221.
29. Julius Fast, *Body Language*. New York: M. Evans, distributed in association with Lippincott, 1970.
30. Andrew J. DuBrin, "Salesmen: Manipulative or Insightful," *The Management Psychologist*, Series 3, No. 9, January 1968 (Copyright, Roher, Hibler & Replogle), pp. 12–13.
31. Eric Berne, *Games People Play*. New York: Grove Press, 1964; Thomas A. Harris, *I'm OK—You're OK*. New York: Harper & Row, 1969.
32. In addition to Berne and Harris, a recommended source is Muriel James and Dorothy Jongeward, *Born to Win*. Reading, Mass.: Addison-Wesley, 1972.
33. Harris, *op. cit.*, book jacket.
34. In addition to Harris, *op. cit., see* a review of *I'm OK—You're OK* by Webster Schott, "How to be Happy Though Adult," *Life*, August 11, 1972, p. 20.
35. Berne, *op. cit.*, p. 48.
36. Harris, *op. cit.*, pp. 274–275 (Index).
37. Berne, *op. cit.*, pp. 147–150. Reprinted by permission of Grove Press, Inc. Copyright © 1964 by Grove Press, Inc.
38. *Ibid.*, p. 148.
39. *Ibid.*, p. 149.
40. *Ibid.*, p. 150.
41. Jack R. Gibb, "Communication and Productivity," in Walter Nord (editor), *Concepts and Controversy in Organizational Behavior*. Pacific Palisades, Calif.: Goodyear, 1972, p. 372.
42. Ronald J. Burke and Douglas S. Wilcox, "Effects of Different Patterns and Degrees of Openness in Superior–Subordinate Communication on Subordinate Job Satisfaction," *Academy of Management Journal*, Vol. 12, No. 3, September 1969, pp. 319–326.
43. William G. Scott and Terence R. Mitchell, *Organization Theory: A Structural and Behavioral Analysis*, revised edition. Homewood: Ill.: Richard D. Irwin and Dorsey Press, 1972, p. 144.

10

Intergroup
Conflict

"I refuse to have purchasing tell our department what parts we should buy and where to buy them," said the engineering manager.

"I would rather tackle my toughest customer than put up with the rigmarole I have to go through to get something special out of manufacturing," said the industrial salesman.

Both the engineering manager and the industrial salesman are expressing statements symptomatic of conflict between groups. As such, they are responding to an omnipresent part of organizational life. Conflict, technically defined, refers to a situation in which a person must make a choice between two incompatible goals. If one goal is achieved, the other goal cannot be acquired. Conflict, in the context used here, refers to the opposition of persons or forces that gives rise to some tension. Skirmish, battle, strong disagreement, internecine warfare, and clash are all terms that refer to the type of behavior implied by the word *conflict*. In contrast, *balance* is a term that refers to a state of harmony and contentment, or the absence of antagonistic strains within an organization.[1] Behavioral scientists view balance as a remote possibility in an organization of people (even within the confines of a family). Conflict is an inevitable result of almost any kind of complex social interaction.

This chapter completes the discussion of small group behavior by examining intergroup conflicts from several viewpoints. What are the sources (or causes) of intergroup conflict? How might intergroup conflicts be classified? What kinds of intergroup conflicts actually take place? How might conflict be channeled into constructive ends?

A SYSTEMS MODEL OF INTERGROUP CONFLICT

Intergroup conflict, like most aspects of organizational behavior, can be profitably viewed from a systems perspective. Figure 10.1 presents a systems model of intergroup conflict that incorporates most of the key variables to be discussed in this chapter. The underlying thesis is that intergroup conflict can be helpful or harmful, functional or dysfunctional, depending upon the mechanisms used by the organization to handle conflict. When intergroup conflict (in at least some degree) is viewed as inevitable, and it is *managed* properly rather than suppressed, it may lead to positive outcomes for the organization and its members. In contrast, when intergroup conflict is inadequately handled (mismanaged) it leads to dysfunctional outcomes.

Dysfunctional outcomes of intergroup conflict generate more conflict, as shown in Figure 10.1. For instance, if one subgroup in an organization distorts goals by offering staff services whether or not they are needed by the organization, more conflict is generated. One group distorting goals may provoke other groups to engage in similar behavior. Other staff groups may feel the need to engage in similar self-protective behavior in order to survive.

The specific variables contained in the systems model of intergroup conflict will be described shortly under appropriate chapter subheadings. In overview, the inputs to the systems model are sources of conflict, eight of which are discussed in this chapter. The intervening variables are mechanisms for dealing with intergroup conflict, which may be arbitrarily classified as "adequate" versus "inadequate." A later discussion of traditional versus behavioral science approaches to conflict resolution describes several variables belonging to each category. Outputs to the systems model are functions and dysfunctions of intergroup conflict. To illustrate, one functional outcome of a conflict between marketing and manufacturing might be the development of accurate marketing forecasts to simplify production scheduling.

The systems model of intergroup conflict developed here is also applicable to understanding other types of conflicts. The content of the conflict may change, but the systems analogy should remain valid. An analysis of social conflict developed by Alan Fox illustrates how conflict at even the societal level can be functional:[2]

> ... Manifest conflict is seen as having a constructive contribution to make towards what is defined as a "healthy" social order. Given the appropriate institutions of regulation and control, the overt and active manifestation of conflict resolves discontents, reduces tensions, clarifies power relations and adjusts social structures accordingly, creates at least as many solidary groupings as it divides, and embodies the principles of self-determination essential to a free society.

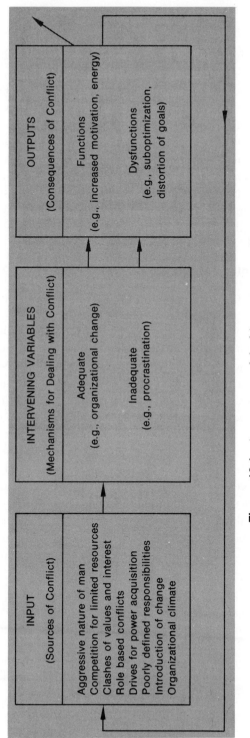

Figure 10.1 A systems model of intergroup conflict.

INPUT (Sources of Conflict)	**INTERVENING VARIABLES** (Mechanisms for Dealing with Conflict)	**OUTPUTS** (Consequences of Conflict)
Aggressive nature of man Competition for limited resources Clashes of values and interest Role based conflicts Drives for power acquisition Poorly defined responsibilities Introduction of change Organizational climate	Adequate (e.g., organizational change) Inadequate (e.g., procrastination)	Functions (e.g., increased motivation, energy) Dysfunctions (e.g., suboptimization, distortion of goals)

SOURCES OF CONFLICT

A large number of potential sources of conflict exists in organizational life. Caution must be exercised in speaking about *causes* of conflict. All conflict is ultimately caused by the feelings people have when their desires or goals cannot be achieved. For instance, one occupational group might be dissatisfied with wages and seek unionization in order to bargain for higher wages. The *source* of conflict here is a difference of opinion between management and that working group about what constitutes satisfactory wages. The cause of conflict is that group's subjective feelings about being underpaid. When feelings lead to action, conflict will probably occur.

Aggressive Nature of Man

Evidence and opinion abound that many human beings have underlying aggressive tendencies seeking outward expression. Wars, hockey games, bull fights, homocide, suicide, and child battering provide telling evidence that man is at least in part an aggressive and hostile animal. *On Aggression,* a widely acclaimed book by Konrad Lorenz,[3] and *The Naked Ape* by Desmond Morris[4] are both intensive treatises about the aggressive side of living organisms. Given this hypothesis—that man is aggressive and seeks expression of these aggressive impulses—it follows that organizations are sometimes used as arenas for the expression of conflict.

Aggressiveness is sometimes expressed in physical combat between groups such as the demonstrations at national political conventions and bombings by extremist groups. Aggressive impulses can be satisfied in a more socially acceptable manner by intergroup conflicts conducted at a verbal level. In short, some conflict in organizations stems from the normal need of some people to find outlets for their aggressive impulses. Note the aggressive and hostile undertones to the following situation of intergroup conflict:

> A financial executive had just returned from an important meeting with representatives from manufacturing. Based upon some encouraging projections of increased sales, the latter requested funds for plant expansion. Prior to the meeting, the financial staff assigned to this problem had determined that the company could not afford plant expansion at this time. During the meeting, the financial executive made a persuasive appeal for his point of view. He reflected upon the meeting:

"We sure nailed those bastards to the wall. I loved the expression on their faces when Jim pointed out the holes in the marketing forecast. They know they have to play ball with us from now on to get what they want."

Competition for Limited Resources

People working in complex organizations are faced with the perpetual struggle of acquiring enough money, material, and manpower to accomplish their mission. Few organizations are in a position to provide all organizational units a "blank check" to pursue their aims. Management is thus forced to allocate resources according to the criterion of contribution to organization effectiveness. Intergroup conflict arises when various groups compete to win their share of these limited resources.[5,6] One financial vice-president of a prominent American corporation stated that a crucial part of his job was to "... do a better job of dividing up the corporate pie in order to overcome some of the gluttony that has developed around here over the years."

Conflict becomes particularly intense when the viability of a staff group is threatened because it loses out in competition for funds. For example, it is not uncommon for a staff group to be so devoid of resources that it is unable to function in a useful manner.

> During an austerity campaign, a large machine tool manufacturer decided to cut back on all programs that were not "vital to the profitability of the firm." The management training department was reduced from five to two people—the director and his assistant. All their training programs for the year requiring travel or outside speakers were canceled. One management development program that dealt with interpreting company policy was allowed to remain; and this was to be conducted in the company cafeteria. In effect, this gave the director and his assistant virtually nothing to do for the upcoming year. Shortly, the director and his assistant came into conflict with the sales service department. The training director reasoned that the customer training offered by the sales service department should really be a functional responsibility of his department. Ultimately, the company president intervened and gave the training director and his assistant some special assignment in minority group hiring.

Another scarce resource groups and individuals compete for is top management's time. Few executives have enough time to schedule meetings with everyone who requests a share of their time. Executive secretaries often act as buffers to prevent their bosses from being inundated with appointments. Lower level managers gain in stature to the extent that they win out in competition for top management time.

Clashes of Values and Interests

Considerable conflict in organizations comes about simply because the values and interests of various subgroups differ. Union and management conflict represents the most readily understandable example of this basic phenomenon. A business corporation may announce publicly that profits and sales have established a new record. That same year they might contest with labor their ability to grant a new round of wage increases. Labor interprets this behavior as both an inconsistency and a lack of interest in the economic welfare of employees. Management feels justified in arguing against a wage increase. From their viewpoint such an increase would decrease earnings per share and make the company a less attractive investment opportunity for potential stockholders. Differences between personal and reference groups, attitudes between management and labor also underlie conflict between these two groups. D. E. Zand and William E. Steckman conducted an experiment with 180 union members and practicing managers, which showed that such attitudes are a powerful determinant of personal positions taken in grievance disputes.[7]

Conflicts that sometimes take place between older and younger workers can be conceptualized as a special case of incongruence between two different value systems. These differences are most apparent when bureaucratic or paternalistic organizations complain about the problems they are having in trying to "understand" younger employees. Many of their actions are interpreted by management as acts of disloyalty, impatience, and lack of interest in their work. Younger people in turn view themselves as being identified with their professional group, eager to perform work of relevance, but unwilling to perform routine clerical chores.

Interdepartmental or *interfunctional* conflicts constitute a good example of how differences in values or interests breed conflict. The difference in points of view between marketing and manufacturing illustrates this principle. Customers are best satisfied when they are offered a variety of products and can anticipate delivery of these products in a short time span. Marketing, in its attempt to please customers, presses manufacturing to meet these demands. Manufacturing, in contrast, can perform its function best when products are standardized, volume is predictable, and variety is limited. Manufacturing thus accuses marketing of submitting to unprofitable customer demands that only serve to clutter up production schedules.

Conflict that so frequently takes place between engineering and manufacturing also illustrates how differences in values might underlie a dispute. Engineers value technical sophistication and careful engineering. "Good" products from their standpoint are those with good technical integrity; i.e., the parts work and they work for long periods of time. Manufacturing entertains slightly different values. Their mission is to produce a product at the least possible cost (within the limits of safety and customer acceptance). Manufacturing thus accuses engineering of attempting to design products that "will last for 50 years, but that customers cannot afford." Engineering accuses manufacturing of attempting to manufacture products of such limited durability that the company reputation will suffer.

Role-Based Conflict

Intergroup conflict sometimes surfaces because different groups occupy different roles that are inherently antagonistic to each other.[8,9] Building inspectors, for example, are in frequent conflict with landlords because of their differences in role. In order to justify their existence, building inspectors must find at least some illegal defects in the conditions of buildings. Basically their role involves monitoring the judgment and opinion of landlords (who feel they are offering the public safe and proper living conditions). When a building inspector notes irregularities, the landlord must spend money and time in order to make his building comply with city or state regulations. Many instances exist in which landlords and building inspectors coexist in a spirit of cooperation. Role-based conflict has the highest probability of emerging when the landlord attempts to offer substandard housing to the public.

"Built-in conflicts" is the term William H. Newman, Charles E. Summer, and E. Kirby Warren use to describe role-based conflicts.[10] Many jobs in complex organizations create conflict by design. Industrial engineering departments represent one organizational function that inherently experiences many intergroup conflicts. Industrial engineers are charged with the responsibility of improving the ways in which other groups go about their work. Management in a sporting goods company may decide, for example, that the present method of manufacturing skis contains too many hand operations; more of the process could be automated or at least machine produced. Engineers are then asked to study the present method of ski making and later suggest areas for improvement. Theoretically, if the manager in charge of ski manufacturing were performing his job perfectly, no improvements in the process would be warranted. Should the industrial engineer make recommendations for change, the production manager must automatically cope with several problems:

1. manage the resistance toward change expressed by subordinates (as discussed in the next chapter);
2. attempt to maintain production quotas while the new machinery is being introduced;
3. look for potential sources of job dissatisfaction because some of the opportunity to satisfy the "craftsman instinct" will be lost from the ski-maker's position;
4. convince himself and subordinates that the quality of skis will not diminish with the introduction of this new labor-saving machinery.

Financial analysts find themselves in frequent intergroup conflicts because their role, in the eyes of many others, represents a policing function. "I'm the cop around here. I blow the whistle when somebody is spending too much money," said one company controller. One budget analyst, during a job satisfaction interview, made the following comment about his role:

> I'm getting a lot of kicks out of my job this year. I've become sort of a hero in financial circles around here lately. I found a hole big enough to drive a truck through in the cost estimates of that new product line. I proved to be right. I know people in manufacturing hate my guts. I don't care. I'm not getting paid to be liked. Besides that, I don't hold any grudges when people dislike me. I can only look good when they look bad.

Drives for Power Acquisition

Intergroup conflict also arises from the very human tendencies toward greed and gluttony. (Strategies designed to bring power to groups have been discussed in Chapter 5.) Empire building and internecine warfare are both manifestations of political maneuvering that breed intergroup conflict. One example here will suffice to reintroduce the topic of political maneuvering as a source of conflict:

> An industrial manufacturer arrived at a new insight about its sales force. Based on the increasingly sophisticated nature of the company's products—they had escalated from small adding machines to such complicated devices as desk top computers—it was decided that salesmen were to reflect a new image. They were no longer to be salesmen

in the old-fashioned connotation of the term. Salesmen were now to act in the role of business consultants who managed their territories and provided business systems advice to customers and prospective customers. Making the transition to this role would involve considerable upgrading in skills and knowledge. Training and development for this new role was to be provided internally by the company. This decision precipitated a curious display of intergroup conflict.

Hearing of this contemplated move by the company, the employee training department manager began busily preparing proposals to submit to his manager that documented plans for taking on this substantial assignment. Simultaneously, the management development department took up the same task of vying for this new assignment. When the training and development managers learned of each other's quest for power acquisition, they defended their respective positions more vigorously. Eventually they both resorted to discrediting each other's position with statements such as the following:

Training Manager: Our role has always been to provide specific job-related skills to employees of this company. Much of the activities carried out by the development department is not useful for actual on-the-job performance.

Development Manager: We are in the business of teaching sophisticated things to higher level employees of this company. The training department is best suited for teaching skills to lower level workers. It would lower the image of our new sales force if you let the training department do the job.

(Plagued by the pettiness of these two groups, top management resolved the situation by forming a new department—Sales Development and Training.)

Poorly Defined Responsibilities

The illustration just presented indicates that conflict may emerge when two organizational units compete over new responsibilities. Intergroup conflict stemming from disagreements about who has responsibility for on-going tasks is an even more frequent problem.[11,12] Newcomers to organizations are often struck by the ambiguity that exists about job responsibilities. Few organizations make extensive use of job descriptions to periodically update the job descriptions that do exist. (Furthermore, it is the rare manager or employee who consults his or her own job description.) Managerial and staff jobs by their very nature are difficult to tightly structure around a job description. Academic as well as other organizations are prey to the intergroup conflict that arises from poorly defined responsibilities.

————————— Polytechnical Institute added an MBA program to its offerings. Among the required courses in the program was "Economic Thought." One year later, the Dean of the College of General Studies heard about this course in basic economics. He wrote a memo to the Dean of the College of Business formally protesting the fact that the College of Business was teaching a basic course in economics. According to his reasoning, economics is a social science subject that comes under the jurisdiction of the College of General Studies (whose mission is to provide for the general education of all students on campus). The business dean protested in return that only the College of Business faculty could successfully apply economic theory to the realities of the business world.

Introduction of Change

Change, as described in Chapter 11, is an important source of stress in organizational life. Change can also breed intergroup conflict.[13] Acquisitions and mergers, for example, encourage intergroup conflict, competition, and stress (as noted in Chapter 4). When one organization is merged into another a power struggle often exists between the acquiring and acquired company. An attempt is usually made to minimize conflict by laying out plans for power sharing before the acquisition or merger is consummated. Frequently, the acquired company is given representation on the board of directors of the acquiring company. Nevertheless, power struggles are difficult to avoid.

One manufacturer of high volume, relatively low-priced toys acquired a company that made "creative," low volume, high-priced toys for children. Shortly after the acquisition the old and new company were involved in intergroup conflict. The parent company insisted that the new company work toward increasing its volume and decreasing its unit price for products. Management of the new company insisted this could not be done and still preserve its unique image. Ultimately, the parent company attempted to resolve the conflict by dissolving the acquired company and merging its product line into already-existing facilities of its own. Within a two-year period after the acquisition almost all the creative people (toy designers, etc.) and management of the acquired company left.

Organizational Climate

An organization's character, personality, or *climate* is sometimes a contributor to or a source of intergroup conflict. Recent observations by Alonzo McDonald, a management consultant, indicate that intense and frequent conflict among members of top management sets a tone that contributes to conflict at lower levels in the organization. According to the McDonald analysis, conflict is infectious:[14]

> As contagion spreads, even distant departments are soon infected with pettiness, personal rivalries linked to different leaders and arbitrary rulings of little logic or importance.

Intergroup conflict can also be related to the amount of psychological distance organizational units maintain from each other. Gordon G. Darkenwald, Jr. concluded on the basis of an extensive study of organizational conflict in colleges and universities that medium amounts of *differentiation* breed the most conflict.[15] Differentiation is defined as "the degree to which the sub-units within each school have boundaries, interests, and functions separate from the other units in the institution." Chairmen of academic institutions with medium differentiation found themselves in less decision-making conflict with the central administration. Negotiating faculty salaries exemplifies one area in which intergroup conflict might occur.
In short, this study has collected some evidence that when professional groups are very much or very little distant psychologically from the administration intergroup conflict is minimal. When the boundary between the two groups is of medium permeability, intergroup conflict tends to be highest.

CONSEQUENCES OF INTERGROUP CONFLICT

Intergroup conflict can be functional or dysfunctional to individuals and organizations. Earlier studies of conflict within organizations focused upon the negative impact of conflict. An awareness has developed in recent years that conflict can also serve useful ends. The opinion of many behavioral scientists about this topic is that an optimal level of conflict exists for every situation. Conflict of a lesser magnitude is dysfunctional (e.g., a feeling of lethargy may develop that inhibits creativity and productivity). Conflict in excess of this theoretical optimum level is also dysfunctional (e.g., organizational members may waste time and money in fighting their petty battles).

Functional consequences of intergroup conflict include the following:[16]

1. Dissociating elements in a situation may be removed and unity may be reestablished. In common parlance, "A good fight helps clear the air." After open expression of conflict, the combatants may feel closer to each other.
2. After conflict, new leadership may be brought to the organization because the former leaders may be found unsuitable under the pressures of conflict. This is a rare, albeit important, function of intergroup conflict.
3. Old goals may be modified or replaced by more relevant goals as a result of the conflict. Engineering, for example, after having fought with manufacturing about price considerations, may decide to place less emphasis on precision in design.
4. Conflict may become *institutionalized.* After several incidents of intergroup conflict, outlets may be established "so that people can 'blow off steam' without damaging the structure of the organization." *Executive rap sessions*—informal group discussions between members of management and employees—is one contemporary approach to the institutionalization of conflict.
5. Motivation and energy available to complete tasks may be increased under the influence of intergroup conflict. In short, conflict "revs up" the opposition.
6. Conflict may increase innovation because of the greater diversity of viewpoints and a heightened sense of necessity.
7. Each group member may develop increased understanding of his own position because conflict forces people to articulate their views and to bring forth all supporting arguments.
8. Groups may achieve greater awareness of their own identities.
9. Intergroup conflict may satisfy the aggressive urges inherent in so many people.

Dysfunctional consequences of conflict include the following:

1. The mental health of some combatants in the conflict may be adversely affected. Intergroup conflict must be considered another organizational pressure capable of precipitating emotional stress reactions in some people.
2. Intergroup conflict of a highly intense nature usually results in misallocation of organizational resources. People waste company time and money in carrying out their internecine warfare. For instance, even the "poison pen" and "P.Y.A." memos written in the

heat of interdepartmental conflict consume time and slight amounts of money.

3. Suboptimization of parts of the system occurs when disputants in the conflict push their own positions to the extreme. Literal compliance with rules and regulations illustrates this phenomenon of suboptimization. Several years ago air traffic controllers were in dispute with their management about salary and working conditions. They expressed their dissatisfaction by strictly adhering to every airplane landing and takeoff regulation in vogue at the time. A slowing down of air traffic almost to the point of a standstill was the result.

4. The distortion of goals, according to Newman, Summer, and Warren, is the most detrimental effect of conflict.[17] People "play games" instead of pursuing their assigned mission. In this manner a credit department in dispute with a sales department might stretch its imagination to find poor credit risk indicators among new customers found by the sales force.

Figure 10.2 provides a two-dimensional typology of intergroup conflict. In addition to the helpful–harmful (functional–dysfunctional) aspect,

Type I (Functional–Substantive)

Two product departments in a pharmaceutical company compete to develop a cologne for adolescent girls. Despite duplication of effort, a product gets to market that proves to be successful.

Type II (Dysfunctional–Substantive)

The financial and manufacturing departments come into conflict about purchasing an expensive piece of machinery. A compromise is reached by purchasing a less expensive machine that proves to be inadequate for the purpose. Money is wasted and productivity is not improved.

Type III (Functional–Personal)

The auditing and advertising department have long-standing "bad blood" between them. Auditing forces the issue by accusing the advertising department of fraudulent practices. Irregularities in use of expense accounts are discovered and these practices are then corrected.

Type IV (Dysfunctional–Personal)

The kitchen staff in a hotel distrust and dislike the owners. One evening, as a prank, they serve stale bread and over-salted soup. Many guests check out of the hotel and the head chef is fired.

Figure 10.2 A typology of intergroup conflict.

another aspect of conflict is added—mostly substantive versus mostly personal. Substantive conflict refers to technical or administrative concerns (e.g., our department is better equipped than yours to handle planning for that new product). Personal conflict refers to animosities and jealousies that involve deep-rooted personal feelings and attitudes. Personality clashes fall into this category. One example of a conflict involving *personal* issues comes from a hospital setting. In this hospital the departments of neurology and neurosurgery were in continuous dispute. Underlying their differences was the neurologists' feeling that they possessed the more sophisticated knowledge, while neurosurgeons received considerably more prestige, status, and income. From the standpoint of neurosurgery, neurology was conducting a campaign to "put down" the professional skills of the neurosurgeon.

As shown in Figure 10.2, this two-dimensional typology of conflict provides a four-way classification of conflict situations. An advantage of this four-way schema is that it provides the manager with tentative answers to two crucial questions about any conflict situation:

1. Should this conflict be resolved? Generally an attempt should be made to resolve only dysfunctional conflict.
2. If the answer to the first question is affirmative, another question is posed. How difficult will this conflict be to resolve? In general, personal conflicts (particularly those of long-standing duration) are more difficult to resolve than substantive conflicts. This is true because feelings have to be worked through before resolution can take place. (Conflict resolution will be discussed later in this chapter.)

Every conflict situation, if analyzed properly, can be classified as belonging to Type I, II, III, or IV. An example of each type is presented in Figure 10.2. To illustrate, the intergroup conflict situation involving two departments trying to design a better product is classified as Type I. Despite some misallocation of resources, the net effect of this substantive conflict is to improve organizational performance.

REDUCING INTERGROUP CONFLICT

Destructive intergroup conflict often needs to be resolved to prevent further problems within the organization.[18,19] Conventional approaches to such reduction of conflict will be overviewed next. Later in this chapter more sophisticated approaches to dealing with conflict—behavioral science intervention and techniques to capitalize on conflict—will be explored.[20]

Compromise is perhaps the most frequent mechanism by which individuals and groups attempt to settle conflict. Top management often serves as the *umpire,* allocating resources for groups when they are unable to settle their conflicts. It is assumed that both sides will be placated if each receives partial fulfillment of its demands. When opposing sides in a conflict have to compete for some resource that is in limited supply, compromise solutions are looked upon with favor. In large industrial organizations, budgets for improvements of physical facilities are often submitted to the corporate financial group by decentralized groups for the former's approval. Facilities *A* and *B* might submit a combined budget that equals twice what the corporate group feel can be expended for capital improvements for the coming fiscal year. The decision is made to give each facility exactly half its demands along with a statement of the necessity of such a decision. It is anticipated that both sides will perceive the logic behind the allocation of funds and conflict will be avoided or reduced if it has already surfaced.

Compromise of this nature is often *suboptimal.* Most managers may be satisfied with the bargain reached, but it does not penetrate the real issue—funds should be invested in such a manner as to maximize return on investment. Careful study of the situation might reveal that Facility *A* is in the better position to capitalize on physical improvements. Allocating Facility *A* all the available funds will do the corporation the most good, but it will precipitate poor cooperation and antagonism from Facility *B.* Rather than dealing constructively with this antagonism from *B,* conflict is avoided by partially satisfying both sides.

Third-party judgment includes such conflict resolution approaches as arbitration, legislation, and the imposition of the will of a common superior. The last approach is the more usual in the settlement of conflicts between departments. In such a situation, two managers who have reached an impasse on an issue of significance to both ask their common superior to listen to both sides of the argument and then give his decision as to which side has the most defensible position. When the common superior makes this decision the group that has lost in this win–lose situation is unlikely to be psychologically committed to the decision. From the standpoint of the psychological processes involved, this approach to conflict resolution is not much different than a parent deciding who is right when two children fight over the possession of one toy.

Procrastination is a subtle and usually unproductive method of resolving conflict. Rather than working toward the resolution of a conflict situation, opposing parties will delay action with the expectation that an environmental change or *fate* will resolve the differences. The special risks department of an insurance company might be in continuous conflict with the sales department about risk acceptance and rejection. Recognizing that the sales manager will be retiring within three years, the manager of special risks elects to wait for this date before having the situation resolved. Another alternative he sees is to request that both sides obtain a final policy ruling from the company president, but there is an even chance that he will be voted down. He opts to wait three years and hopes that the new head of sales will be more underwriting-oriented in business philosophy.

Ignoring the demands of others in order to resolve conflict is a variation of the procrastination theme. The underlying psychology here is that no decision will arouse less conflict than a rejection of another person's or department's demands. The director of engineering may receive a carefully documented presentation from one of his supervisors that additional draftsmen are needed to provide assistance to the engineers. He recognizes that this is an issue of considerable concern to the supervisor, but he also recognizes that employment of additional draftsmen is not within his budget. His attempt at conflict resolution is to table the request with the expectation that perhaps the supervisor will forget the matter. Avoided in this approach is the underlying issue of why the company does not see fit to honor this request.

Peaceful coexistence is an approach to conflict resolution that simply suppresses disagreement and emphasizes commonalities. Parties in conflict decide it is better for the organization to avoid overt displays of disagreement. The consequences of open conflict are strenuously avoided. Cooperation between groups is good on the surface, but rarely do they collaborate in such a way as to maximize their joint potential. Union–management relations in companies with a history of no strikes are often examples of peaceful coexistence. Unwritten agreements dictate that the company maintain a permissive approach toward work standards in return for industrial peace. Both sides may have important issues that could be resolved, but they fear the alleged consequences of facing these problems. Headquarters and division relationships sometimes take on the characteristics of peaceful coexistence. The division unit may have grievances it feels need resolution but the prospects of being listened to by headquarters seem remote. Significant operating problems at the division level are covered over. Exposure of these problems, it is felt, will lead to misunderstanding and chastisement rather than resolution of the real problem.

Changing the organizational structure, a topic explored at length in Chapter 13, is another approach used by organizations to resolve intergroup conflict.[21] Reorganization can help resolve conflict by (a) allowing for the settling of conflict at lower levels in the organization and (b) by eliminating organizational special interest groups.

One justification sometimes offered for decentralization is that it creates a greater number of common bosses than would be possible under centralization. Intergroup conflicts can then be settled at a lower level within the organization. According to this reasoning, if a billion dollar company were divided into traditional functional divisions such as marketing, manufacturing, engineering, etc., all disputes between different functions, even at the lowest level, would have to be settled by the company president. Thus, if a district sales manager were in conflict with a production control manager about delayed shipment on some spare parts, their conflict would go unresolved unless they went to the president.

In the situation just described, only one person—the president—would be the common boss for large numbers of managers. Under decentralization, organizational units are smaller and more common superiors are available to help settle intergroup and interpersonal conflict.

Grouping organizational activities into teams rather than functional units helps resolve some types of intergroup conflict. Small cohesive teams may come into conflict with other units outside their own team, but they are less likely to be in conflict among themselves. Instead of identifying with one department, individuals identify with the entire project. (Positive morale consequences of teams have already been mentioned in Chapter 4.)

Surgical teams and airplane crews illustrate how "compound groups" tend to minimize conflict.[22] Conflicting pressures still exist, but the critical need for cooperation and constructive face-to-face relations overrides vested interests.

Liaison groups or *intermediaries* are sometimes used to assist in reducing intergroup conflict. (One might argue that there are usually severe organizational problems present when liaison groups are needed. Nevertheless, as organizations have become more complex, the use of liaison groups has increased.) Two departments that would be in conflict if they interacted with each other on a daily basis ("We get along just fine if we don't have to live with each other") are separated and a messenger mediates between them. One justification offered for this liaison position is that one person is needed who can "speak the language" of both groups. For instance, some organizations use "demand analysts" to translate manufacturing requirements to marketing, and marketing requirements to manufacturing. An important advantage of the intermediary is that he is perceived as not having a vested interest in either group. One disadvantage for the liaison person is that he falls prey to the possibility of feeling like a "corporate eunuch." His power is derived from the inability of other people to effectively manage their differences, but he has no real power of his own.

317

Game Theory and Conflict Resolution

An understanding of some of the strategic aspects of conflict resolution by traditional methods has been furthered by game theory. Joe Kelly notes that game theory attempts to formulate rules of behavior that optimize outcomes by considering the utilities and probabilities of various outcomes to each player.[23] Underlying game theory is the assumption that the players behave rationally. For instance, each side understands why it and the other side are choosing a particular preference. Game theory is a complex subject and its scope can best be appreciated by consulting an original source.[24,25]

An elementary, but popular, manifestation of game theory is the two-person zero-sum game. As implied by the name, the sum total of wins and losses in this game is zero. If Side A wins $1000, B correspondingly loses $1000. Similar to intergroup conflict situations in organizations, each side intends to limit the winnings of the other to the smallest possible quantity. Both sides attempt to minimize their losses and maximize their gains. Game theory has a jargon all of its own. For example, both sides seek to maximize their security levels—defined as the minimum amount received from any choice.

An essential difference between zero-sum (or similar games) and conflict situations outside the laboratory, is the availability of information to each side. Groups or individuals in conflict typically are more "closed" than "open." They reveal only what they consider essential to strengthen their strategy. Both sides in nonlaboratory settings often act on the basis of what they imagine to be the other side's preferences. Wage negotiations in union–management conflict situations often proceed on this basis. Management does not reveal how large an increase it is willing to pay until the final moments of negotiation. Labor, similarly, waits until the final moments to reveal how small an increase it is willing to accept.

BEHAVIORAL SCIENCE INTERVENTION IN CONFLICT

Behavioral scientists in recent years have contributed their skills to the resolution of intergroup conflict within organizations. Central to their various approaches is helping both groups in conflict confront the underlying problem and then resolve it. Traditional approaches to conflict resolution, as just described, tend to avoid or smooth over underlying issues. Helpful overviews of behavioral science approaches to conflict resolution are found in the Organizational Development series edited by Warren G. Bennis, and in *The Practice of Managerial Psychology.*[26] A description of one behavioral science method of conflict resolution is sufficient for the purposes of this chapter.

Image exchanging (or corporate mirrors) is the name given to one elaborate approach to the resolution of conflict between groups. Parties to the conflict come to learn how they are perceived by the other group; this exchanging of images provides understandings and insights that hopefully lead to problem solving. Edgar H. Schein summarizes a representative format for image exchanging developed by Robert R. Blake.[27]

1. Each group prepares its self-image and its image of the other group. Groups are encouraged to write down whatever they feel or think; consensus is not mandatory. Images can be described by sentences or merely in adjectives.
2. Each group assigns a representative who presents these images to the other group. Exchanging of images provides each group data about how it is perceived by the other group and how the other group perceives itself.
3. Both groups then meet separately to discuss what kind of behavior might have led to the image formed by the other group.
4. The conclusion reached about each group's own behavior is exchanged with the other group and jointly discussed.
5. In the final stage, specific action plans are developed that are designed to reduce the discrepancy between each group's self-image versus the image held by the other group. Usually plans cannot be developed to reduce all of the discrepancies. A realistic goal is for both groups to develop methods of relating to each other which will reduce conflict and increase cooperation.

Presented next is a condensed description of image exchange activity between two groups in conflict—a headquarters personnel group and a division personnel group of the same large organization. The images exchanged portray a pressing need for improved communication and enhanced mutual respect between two groups.

1. Division personnel's image of headquarters personnel.
    (a) Too academic and theoretical. They spend time on projects that are of no help to us.
    (b) They are mainly interested in keeping people happy.
    (c) They have no rapport with first-line management.
    (d) One-way communicators. They enjoy collecting information but are hesitant to provide information.

(e) Bright and intelligent. They keep up with new developments in the field.

(f) Basically politicos. They find out what top management is interested in, and pursue those projects.

(g) Highly paid in comparison to their contribution.

2. Division personnel's image of itself.
   (a) In tune to the realities of the business world; practical minded.
   (b) We help the corporation turn in a profit.
   (c) We have good rapport with first-line supervision.
   (d) We show some impatience for getting things accomplished.
   (e) Through our efforts the company is able to keep going.
   (f) Our operation is lean in terms of manpower.
   (g) We require very little guidance or help from headquarters in order to keep going.

3. Headquarters personnel's image of division personnel.
   (a) A bit narrow minded in their approach. Automatically dismiss the value of new approaches.
   (b) Limited appreciation of company-wide problems.
   (c) Difficult to satisfy. They ask for help, but often refuse to listen when it is given.
   (d) Too identified with line management, which makes them subjective in their viewpoint.
   (e) They dislike integrating their activities with corporate objectives.
   (f) Nice, hard-working guys who play an important role in the company.
   (g) Probably a good place for a professional personnel man to get field experience.

4. Headquarters personnel's image of itself.
   (a) Skillful at utilizing new approaches and techniques for the good of the company.
   (b) Broad and progressive in our thinking.
   (c) We prevent division people from thinking of only their problems.
   (d) We undertake activities and programs that are designed to meet corporate objectives.
   (e) Sometimes our thinking is a little too sophisticated for division people to understand.
   (f) We are stretched pretty tight in terms of getting to everything that we are charged with accomplishing.
   (g) Our contribution to the corporation is much greater than most people realize.

Illustrative of the kind of action plan for improvement that can be developed is the treatment of point "a" of division personnel's image of headquarters personnel. The issue of the headquarters group working on projects of limited interest to the division unit came about because several times headquarters sent to the field a detail statement in writing of its plans for a new personnel program requiring implementation, without any previous informal word about the project. Twice, when these field programs were announced, the division group had been in need of assistance in quite different areas of personnel services to their management. This placed the field personnel people in the position of being perceived as uncooperative by headquarters because of their limited enthusiasm for the new project and as ineffective by line management because they were not solving the personnel problems most vexing to line management. An action plan was then developed whereby headquarters personnel would periodically consult with division personnel to determine what problem areas they (division) felt required assistance by headquarters. These requests would then be balanced against demands from top management for corporate-wide services and the judgment of the headquarters personnel staff as to what programs they felt a headquarters group should involve itself in. The emerged plan was helpful in modifying perceptions originally held at the time of image exchanging.

1. Division's image of headquarters personnel as: being too academic and theoretical. They spend time on projects that are of no help to us; being basically politicos. They find out what top management is interested in, and pursue those optics; having no rapport with line management.
2. Headquarters' image of division personnel as: having limited appreciation of company-wide problems; being too identified with line management, making them subjective in their viewpoint; disliking to integrate their activities with corporate objectives.

CAPITALIZING ON CONFLICT

Coping with or reducing intergroup conflict is often a necessary part of a manager's job. Recent thinking suggests an even more challenging role for the manager—capitalizing on conflict. Astute managers are sometimes able to use conflict as a constructive, creative force. In this manner conflict becomes functional to the organization. Behavioral science is not yet sophisticated enough to provide the manager or staff person with a lengthy checklist of how to capitalize on conflict. As a temporary substitute, several strategies that appear promising will be discussed. More important than a descriptive list, however, is the realization that conflict is a natural, inevitable part of organizational life that is potentially capable of becoming an asset to organizational functioning.

Make Creative Use of Crisis

Crisis inevitably brings about some conflict between groups or people. The astute manager is sometimes able to capitalize on this turmoil and strengthen the organization as a result. Organizations, like people, tend to gain in maturity and viability once they have overcome a crisis. Joe Kelly illustrates how this phenomenon works.[28]

> In the creative use of crisis, the effective executive welcomes uncertainty and plans for its exploitation, if not its creation. An example of this is provided by the experience of a British manufacturing company which reacted to the government's introduction of a payroll tax by grasping the chance to reorganize and rationalize its product lines, so that each factory was charged with the making of one component instead of two.
>
> What is significant about this case is not only that the company subsequently had the tax and a bit more refunded to it, but also that the chief executive grabbed at the chance to make dramatic organizational changes which he had been mulling over for some time. In other more tranquil circumstances, such changes would have been subject to considerable and sustained negotiations both in the front office and in the work councils.

Foster Constructive Levels of Tension

Behavioral scientists have recognized for many years that human productivity is best when an optimum level of tension and anxiety is present. Under the influence of minimal tension, most people are not sufficiently "revved up" to perform at their best. Severe degrees of tension and anxiety, however, immobilize (or at least impair the productivity of) most people. Similarly, conflict in moderate doses is functional to organizations and individuals. Positive consequences of intergroup conflict discussed earlier are all contingent upon an optimum level of conflict. In short, in an organization where very little conflict exists it may be necessary to introduce conflict in order to capitalize on the advantages of conflict. Kelly notes that scientists tend to be the most productive when conflict elements in their work are present, provided there also exists an abundant supply of stability, confidence, and security. Critical feedback from competitive colleagues is one productive source of conflict. One manager in a hospital setting introduced intellectual conflict into his group in order to enhance its productivity.

A chief psychiatrist held weekly staff conferences to which all members from each professional discipline on the staff were invited: psychiatry, clinical psychology, psychiatric social work, registered nursing, and occupational therapy. Diagnostic conferences about one or two inpatients were conducted at each meeting. Conflict was introduced by allowing representatives from each discipline to fully describe how they perceived the patient in terms of behavior, attitudes, ability to function, and primary problem. Psychiatrists were discouraged from claiming unchallenged professional prerogatives in making diagnoses. Clinical psychologists were discouraged from claiming that their diagnostic tests provided "scientific evidence" of a particular diagnosis. Social workers were discouraged from making the statement that they had exclusive knowledge about the "real life" behavior of the patient. Breaking down these traditional professional prerogatives created more than a modicum of conflict. In one conference, for example, the occupational therapist vigorously challenged the psychiatrist's judgment that a particular patient was psychotic.

After a year of experience with this system, it became apparent that this type of conflict had two functional consequences: (a) diagnostic statements were more lucid and specific than in the past and (b) more effective treatment programs were implemented because the inputs of several disciplines were actually being used in developing a treatment regimen for each patient.

Introject a Control Unit

A widely practiced approach to introducing conflict into an organization in order to improve organizational performance is the creation of a special purpose staff group. The function of this group is to provoke other groups into some desired course of action. Conflict is built into such a situation from the outset. Departments in contact with such a group recognize that extra demands will be placed upon them by yet another staff group. During the 1970s some company presidents established units to promote the employment of blacks. A major function of the "minority employment coordinator" is to insure that operating people adhere to corporate philosophy (and state and federal legislation) in hiring blacks.[29] Without this checking and cajoling by the specialized unit, many organizations were falling behind target in their minority employment hiring.

Consumer product companies, in recent years, have sometimes placed women in high-level positions to serve as "consumer watchdogs." Specialists of this nature are given the responsibility of representing the voice of the consumer to the corporation. Conflict is built-in, but the end result is

323

presumably a product more acceptable to both the consumer and the *consumerists.*

Another modern development in organizational life serves to enhance organizational performance by introducing conflict—quality assurance.

> One well-known consumer appliance manufacturer had amassed evidence that both small and large appliances were of less than adequate quality. Prestige they had acquired in earlier years (and a heavy advertising budget) helped sustain sales, but their quality reputation was beginning to suffer. Borrowing from the aerospace industry, a large quality assurance department was established whose mission was to be responsible for product quality at every stage of its life. (Quality control, in contrast, relates mostly to inspecting for manufacturing defects.) Quality assurance personnel were given free rein to "bug" research engineers about products of the future, challenge advertising on unsubstantiated claims, discuss repair problems with dealers, challenge the manufacturing inspection methods, and even argue with financial people about funding for quality programs. Given such a broad charter, the unpopularity of quality assurance people spread rapidly. Operating people, in large numbers, felt the "quality freaks" were usurping their functions.

> Despite these protests, introjecting a quality assurance group paid dividends to the organization (and to the consumer). Product quality, as measured by fewer customer complaints and product failures, did increase.

RELATIONSHIP TO CORE PROPOSITIONS

Intergroup conflict can be analyzed from the perspective of the four core propositions contained in our basic framework for organizational behavior. Several of these relationships have already been commented on at various places in the chapter. Again, the purpose of this analysis is to help the reader integrate information into an overall framework. No attempt is made to review all possible relationships between intergroup conflict and the four core propositions.

Human Behavior

Intergroup conflict in organizations is but a special case of conflict in general. Basic psychological knowledge about conflict processes helps to understand the nature and consequences of intergroup conflict. Three illustrations of this proposition follow. First, conflict is a normal aspect of social intercourse and it is therefore not surprising that intergroup conflict takes place in organizations. Second, conflict precipitates aggressive behavior in most people. Therefore, when two departments are in conflict it is understandable that they will sometimes seek aggressive ways of settling their dispute. Conflict also leads to escape. Some people, following this principle, will quit an organization rather than persevere in a conflict situation. Third, conflict is a source of stress and will therefore produce strain (reactions to stress) in many people. Psychosomatic reactions and other forms of emotional disorder can thus be precipitated by intergroup conflict in organizations.

Situational Nature

Intergroup conflict is another aspect of organizational behavior that is situational in nature. Situational variables have an important influence on the type and severity of intergroup conflict. An analysis reported in *The Journal of Conflict Resolution* of many studies of interparty conflict concludes that situational variables affect conflict behavior.[30] Three of these situational variables are (a) magnitude of the incentive, (b) type of communication opportunity, and (c) opponent's strategy. To illustrate, when the stakes are high and the opportunity for one group to communicate with another is good, intergroup conflict might be higher than under conditions of low stakes and limited communication. Additionally, when one opponent employs an unethical strategy (e.g., "hits below the belt" by falsifying reports), this will tend to enhance conflict.

Systemic Nature

Intergroup conflict should also be viewed from a systems standpoint. Earlier in this chapter it was mentioned that conflict at the top of an organization adversely affects other parts of the organization. Groups in conflict precipitate consequences at other places in the organizational system. Should the professional and administrative personnel in a hospital be engaged in intergroup conflict, it would not be unforeseen for patient care to suffer. Earlier, mention was made of the *suboptimization* that occurs within the system when resources are misallocated in order to conduct interdepartmental conflicts. For example, if the loan department in a bank wished to "get even" with top management they could find ways of literally complying with virtually every loan regulation. This would disqualify so many loans that the bank would miss out on some opportunities for profitable loans.

Structure and Process

One significant source of intergroup conflict relates to the roles certain occupational groups are assigned. Budget analysts, for example, are placed in a role whereby they naturally conflict with the operating groups whose budgets they must review in the normal course of their work. The amount of conflict emanating from this formal role, however, is a function of the process by which it is carried out. Should the budget analysts develop the reputation of being helpful staff advisors on financial matters, their formal role will generate a minimum of intergroup conflict. Conversely, if this formal auditing role (structure) is carried out in a punitive and spying way (process), conflict among the financial and operating groups will be intensified.

GUIDELINES FOR ACTION

1. Conflict is an inevitable part of organizational life; it cannot be avoided or ignored. Instead, you must learn how to cope with or capitalize on conflict.
2. Conflict in moderate amounts can be useful in improving the quality of creative performance, and in "keeping people on their toes intellectually."
3. Despite its several advantages, conflicts must be resolved when it becomes dysfunctional. The primary dysfunctional consequence of conflict is that it wastes time, money, and other resources.
4. The essence of resolving conflict is to confront the underlying issue and then take a problem-solving approach.
5. One practical and feasible approach to capitalizing on conflict is for a staff group to prod the performance of various departments throughout the organization on a specialized mission or task.

QUESTIONS

1. What is the most pronounced intergroup conflict in the place you work (or school you attend)? Does it appear to be based on substantive or personal issues?
2. Assume you are the general manager of a business How would you know what intergroup conflicts exist in your organization?
3. The Paris Peace Talks conducted over the Viet Nam War fell short of expectations as a method of conflict resolution. What would you speculate is the basic reason for the shortcomings of these meetings?

4. Describe three positive consequences that have emerged from conflict in your life.
5. Write down what you think would be the probable results if the instructor in this class and the students "exchanged images."

NOTES

1. William G. Scott and Terence R. Mitchell, *Organization Theory: A Structural and Behavioral Analysis*, revised edition. Homewood, Ill.: Richard D. Irwin and Dorsey Press, 1972, p. 179.
2. Alan Fox, *A Sociology of Work in Industry*. London: Collier–Macmillan, 1971, p. 145.
3. Konrad Lorenz, *On Aggression*. New York: Harcourt, Brace & World, 1966.
4. Desmond Morris, *The Naked Ape*. New York: Dell, 1969.
5. John B. Miner, *The Management Process: Theory, Research, and Practice*. New York: Macmillan, 1973, p. 395.
6. Joseph A. Litterer, *The Analysis of Organizations*. New York: Wiley, 1965.
7. D. E. Zand and William E. Steckman, "Resolving Industrial Conflict—An Experimental Study of the Effects of Attitudes and Precedent," *Proceedings of the 21st Annual Winter Meeting of the Industrial Research Association*, 1969, pp. 348–359.
8. George Strauss, "Tactics of Lateral Relationships: The Purchasing Agent," *Administrative Science Quarterly*, Vol. 7, No. 2, September 1962, pp. 161–186.
9. George Strauss, "Workflow Frictions, Interfunctional Rivalry, and Professionalism: A Case Study of Purchasing Agents," *Human Organization*, Vol. 23, No. 2, 1964, pp. 137–149.
10. William H. Newman, Charles E. Summer, and E. Kirby Warren, *The Process of Management: Concepts, Behavior, and Practice*, third edition. Englewood Cliffs, N.J.: Prentice-Hall, 1972, p. 190.
11. Miner, *op. cit.*, p. 403.
12. J. V. Baldridge, *Power and Conflict in the University*. New York: Wiley, 1971. This reference includes many instances of intergroup conflict stemming from "loose lying responsibilities."
13. Fox, *op. cit.*, p. 143.
14. Alonzo McDonald, "Conflict at the Summit: A Deadly Game," *Harvard Business Review*, Vol. 50, No. 2, March–April 1972, p. 60.
15. Gordon G. Darkenwald, Jr., "Organizational Conflict in Colleges and Universities," *Administrative Science Quarterly*, Vol. 16, No. 4, December 1971, pp. 407–412.
16. The first four consequences come from Scott and Mitchell, *op. cit.*, pp. 191–193: the second five come from Richard E. Walton, *Interpersonal Peacemaking: Confrontation and Third-Party Consultation*. Reading, Mass.: Addison-Wesley, 1969, p. 5.
17. Newman, Summer, and Warren, *op. cit.*, p. 199.
18. Joe Kelly, *Organizational Behaviour*. Homewood, Ill.: Richard D. Irwin and Dorsey Press, 1969, pp. 536–540.
19. William G. Scott, *The Management of Conflict*. Homewood, Ill.: Richard D. Irwin and Dorsey Press, 1965.
20. An overview of traditional and behavioral science conflict resolution approaches is found in Robert R. Blake, Herbert A. Shepard, and Jane S. Mouton, *Managing Intergroup Conflict in Industry*. Houston: Gulf, 1964.
21. A technical and theoretical treatment of this topic is found in Paul R. Lawrence and John W. Lorsch, *Organization and Environment: Managing Differentiation and Integration*. Boston: Graduate School of Business Administration, Harvard University, 1967.
22. Newman, Summer, and Warren, *op. cit.*, p. 201.

23. Kelly, *op. cit.*, pp. 520–525.
24. T. C. Schelling, *Strategy of Conflict.* Cambridge, Mass.: Harvard University Press, 1966.
25. R. D. Luce and H. Raiffa, *Games and Decisions.* New York: Wiley, 1957.
26. Andrew J. DuBrin, *The Practice of Managerial Psychology.* Elmsford, N.Y.: Pergamon Press, 1972, Chapter 9.
27. Edgar H. Schein, *Process Consultation: Its Role in Organization Development.* Reading, Mass.: Addison-Wesley, 1969, pp. 71–72. Warren G. Bennis is the editor of this series.
28. Joe Kelly, "Make Conflict Work for You," *Harvard Business Review*, Vol. 48, No. 4, July–August 1970, p. 106.
29. Newman, Summer, and Warren, *op. cit.*, p. 199.
30. Daniel Druckman, "The Influence of the Situation in Interparty Conflict," *The Journal of Conflict Resolution*, Vol. 15, No. 4, December 1971, p. 547.

PART IV

Organizations

Preview

Total organizations rather than individuals or small groups are the *primary focus* of this section. The term primary focus is given special attention because it is difficult to draw clear-cut distinctions between organizations and the groups of people composing them. Organizations are essentially aggregates of a large number of smaller groups. Chapter 13 deals with bringing about changes in organizations, yet many of these changes are initiated at the individual and small group level. For instance, an assumption is made that if small groups of people in organizations learn to deal more openly and honestly with each other the total organization will become more effective.

Chapter 11 presents a difficult to measure yet highly significant aspect of organizational behavior—organizational climate. This entire chapter might be construed as an attempt to document the intriguing notion that organizations, like people, have unique personalities of their own.

Chapter 12, "Management of Individual and Group Change," could fit logically into this section or the previous section about small groups. It represents a transitional topic between groups and organizations. Ideas presented about principles of attitude change in Chapter 12 might have been included in Chapter 13 on organizational change. In addition, the modular unit for organizational change is the small group and perhaps even the individual. When organization changes are introduced the manager must cope with resistance to change by dealing with people one at a time or with small groups.

Organizational Climate

Gil Benson, an accountant, expressed his reaction to the company he recently joined: "What a difference. First Realty is a smooth-running, well-manicured outfit. It's go, go, go, and everybody knows where they're going. My job at Business Investment Associates was a disaster. It was push, push, push, but the company was headed straight downhill. Everything was a crisis."

Benson was intuitively recognizing that organizations have personalities. Every organization has some properties or characteristics possessed by many other organizations; however, each organization has its own unique constellation of characteristics and properties. *Organizational climate* is the term used to describe this psychological structure of organizations. Climate is thus the "feel," "personality," or "character" of the organization's environment. Garlie A. Forehand and B. Von Haller Gilmer, in their keystone article about organizational environment, use the term organizational climate to refer to:[1]

> ...the set of characteristics that describe an organization and that (a) distinguish the organization from other organizations, (b) are relatively enduring over time, and (c) influence the behavior of people in the organization.

Broadly conceived, all of organizational behavior revolves around considerations of climate. To contain discussion of organizational climate within realistic limits, this chapter will provide some answers to the following questions: What factors and forces determine the climate of a given organization? How is organizational climate diagnosed? How might the organizational climate influence individual motivation? What impact does organizational climate have on the behavior of individuals? What are some behavioral differences between the characteristics of successful and unsuccessful organizations? How might I apply knowledge about organizational climate to my own career? (*See* the Guidelines for Action section.)

A FRAMEWORK FOR VIEWING ORGANIZATIONAL CLIMATE

Organizational climate, similar to most topics explored in this book, is a complex set of interrelated variables. A framework for ordering knowledge about organizational climate is presented in Figure 11.1. All components of the framework are discussed separately at later points in this chapter. The general framework approximates a systems model with one important exception—intervening or mediating variables are not incorporated. One could argue that the determinants of climate listed as input variables are actually mediating variables for organizational effectiveness. For instance, the basic inputs to an organizational system are people, money, and material. Mediators such as leadership style and company policy influence organizational effectiveness.

Input variables in this framework are forces that shape or determine organizational climate. For instance, a new company (defined by the variable "life stage of organization") enjoying high profits ("economic conditions") will have a different climate than an old company incurring financial losses. Many other variables in addition to those mentioned in Figure 11.1 contribute to organizational climate. Explored here are only variables presumed to be primary determinants.

Organizational climate in turn influences many aspects of organizational life such as the motivational level of some employees and work productivity. Dependent variables of this nature are labeled "proximate outputs" because, although tangible outputs, they in turn help determine other variables. According to the theoretical position taken here, these proximate outputs influence the "ultimate output"—organizational success or lack of success. As explained later, organizational success itself is a multidetermined concept.

DETERMINANTS OF CLIMATE

The uniqueness of each organization is determined (or caused) by a variety of interacting and overlapping forces. Virtually every topic mentioned in this book must in some small way influence organizational climate. Introducing five politically oriented middle managers into a company, as a case in point, would probably create enough impact to give a political flavor to the company environment. To develop the idea that organizational behavior is a function of the interaction of many forces, the influence of eight such forces will be described.

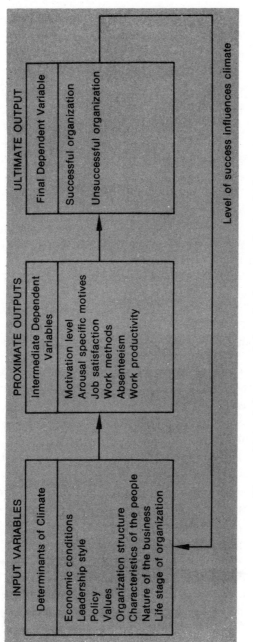

Figure 11.1 A framework for viewing organizational climate.

Economic Conditions

Organizations develop different "feels" according to their position on the economic cycle. In times of prosperity—when budgets are loose rather than tight—companies and other organizations are more adventuresome. Risks into new ventures and new programs are more readily taken because money is in more ready supply. Visitors to district offices of the Internal Revenue Service are struck by the austere working conditions. Faded green walls, dark green, aged file cabinets, and metal top desks all contribute to a feeling of constriction and bleakness. Economic conditions—perpetually tight control over expenditures—have dictated such modest physical surroundings.

Tight budgets also contribute to an air of caution and conservatism within an organization. Few managers are willing to suggest new programs of potential merit when mandates from above call for tight control over expenses. Thus, the underwriting manager in an insurance company voted "no" to conducting research about youthful drivers that might have benefited his company in the long range. In times of prosperity, management's willingness to invest money in new programs contributes to an organizational climate of elan and high risk taking.

Leadership Style

Approaches utilized by managers to lead subordinates (described in Chapter 7) exert a key influence on the climate of an organization. One well-known industrial corporation has a research and development management team that is perceived by many of its members as showing "high concern for production and low concern for people." In common with most R&D efforts, the majority of their work is conducted on a project basis. This combination of production-oriented management and project organization produces some interesting reactions to the organizational climate. One electrical engineer comments:

> What an atmosphere of bad news. Most of us would quit if there were other jobs around (note—data collected in 1972). When we are finished with one project, no one asks us what we would like to do next. We are shunted around like migrant workers. You never know what's coming next. On my last assignment, I had a high-level clerical job with a fancy title. This place is really unprofessional, but there is nothing I can do about it now.

Leadership style at the top of the organization is more influential in shaping climate than leadership style practiced below. Managers below the chief executive officer predictably adapt leadership styles and practices they feel are "in vogue" at the time. One illustration will suffice to explain this widely noted phenomenon of organizational life.

Larry McHugh was the newly elected president of an old line manufacturing company in Cleveland. Larry held an MBA from the Graduate School of Industrial Administration at Carnegie-Mellon. He was intellectually and emotionally committed to giving subordinates an important share in the decision-making process. Within six months after his arrival, those staff members reporting directly to him recognized that they would now be consulted when a decision involved matters about which they might have useful information.

Gradually this consultative style of management filtered down into the organization. Within one year production workers were commenting that "someone finally thought they had something to say." (Parenthetically, it must be noted that consultative supervision was met with some suspicion at lower levels in the organization. One worker complained to his union steward that he was being "manipulated" by his boss!)

Later in this chapter the effect of leadership style on organizational climate will be examined within the context of the interrelationship among leadership style, organizational climate, and motivation.

Policy

Another important determinant of the climate of an organization are its policies. Written and unwritten policies serve as guidelines to managerial action. Policy thus dictates *what* to do in a given situation, but not *how* to do it. Implementation of these policies over a period of time plays a key role in shaping perceptions about the organization. Visualize how each of the following three policies plays a role in shaping organizational climate.

Company *A* supplies batteries to automobile manufacturers. Demand for their product is highly variable. Sales are directly affected by changes in demand for automobiles. In order to protect profit margins, Company *A* has had a long-standing policy of laying off personnel when sales decline and recalling employees when sales again increase. This policy contributes to both a widespread lack of identification with the company and an atmosphere of uneasiness about the future. Management frequently accuses employees of holding back on output in order to smooth out gyrations in the work load. From an economic standpoint management may be fully justified. One executive of the company reasons, "If we did not adjust payroll to meet sales, the company would fold and nobody would have a job." Economic justification, however, is not the issue under consideration. This incident is cited to illustrate how one personnel policy affects organizational climate.

Company *B* manufactures a line of expensive hand tools, such as ratchet wrenches and small power drills. Theft of these tools became widespread, leading to several embarrassing and uncomfortable incidents. Twice in a one-month period, security guards found tools in the trunks of employee automobiles. Another time, a small set of wrenches fell out of a woman's blouse as she was walking through the cafeteria. Searching for an antidote to thievery of this nature, management instituted a policy of having all manufacturing employees pass through a magnetized theft-detection system upon leaving the plant. Management reasoned that "innocent employees had nothing to fear." Losses due to pilfering became negligible; changes in climate were also observable. Attitudes of resentment toward the security system became pronounced and, according to the director of labor relations, employee morale decreased. Company employees were often asked by other townspeople how they liked being "frisked" on the way home. A long-range complicated research effort will be required to determine if the loss in negative attitudes that resulted from the detection policy was compensated for by the decrease in theft.

Company *C* is engaged primarily in lending money to individuals. Loans are not secured by real property such as furniture, appliances, or automobiles. Company policy dictates that the maximum interest be charged for loans, and that an attempt should be made by each loan officer to encourage borrowers to refinance loans once they have established a satisfactory repayment record. This policy of charging maximum legal interest influences organizational climate in several ways. First, the clientele established are those individuals who have difficulty borrowing money at more modest rates. Customers thus begrudgingly use the services of Company *C*, and infrequently are warm feelings shared between customer and company official. Second, loan officers are encouraged to firmly remind customers about the penalties of default on their loans. Treating customers in this manner adds further to a tense climate. Third, charging maximum interest rates leaves many people in the organization to question Company *C*'s social conscience. Few employees of Company *C* experience feelings of pride in mentioning the name of their employer to acquaintances.

Values

Ideals and beliefs that a person or organization considers important are termed *values*. After all available objective data have been collected, management decisions often are reduced to a question of values. Germane here is the situation of the movie theater owner who refused to run "X" rated movies, despite their high income yield in his town. Factual information unequivocally indicated that most motion picture films with other ratings yield slim profit margins. This owner's values (whether they be described as civic minded or puritanical) led him to arrive at a decision that he felt was morally sound though unprofitable from a business standpoint. Values are subtle and intangible, but they constitute important ingredients of an organizational climate. Three vignettes illustrate this relationship between values and climate.

Company *D* places a high value on providing for the welfare of people. Employees receive a much higher share of profits than the industry average. Managers are requested to visit any employee hospitalized with a serious accident or illness. Employees or dependents of employees who give birth to children receive flowers. Those who lose their jobs are provided free counseling services to help them find suitable employment. Paternalistic values illustrated by these practices have helped contribute to an organizational climate characterized as "warm," "friendly," and "helpful."

Company *E*, a publisher, places a high value on prestige and technical leadership. One biology journal they publish receives high recognition among scholars, but is no longer self-supporting. Earnings from more profitable books and journals are used to subsidize this prestigious journal. Advisers to the publisher have recommended that this journal be discontinued because of its drain on company profitability. Top management, however, feels that prestige in the scientific community is a paramount consideration. Values of this sort have contributed to an organizational climate characterized by "haughtiness," "refinement," and "self-respect."

Company *F* places a high value on creating opportunities for disadvantaged minority groups. Another organizational value held by the company is the importance of cooperation and lack of conflict. Recruiting and training large numbers of minority group members has precipitated two sources of conflict in the organization. First, many foremen complained to management about the difficulty they were experiencing in implementing the policy of hiring and retaining minority group members. Employees of high seniority, for example, often argued that the newcomers were being given preferential treatment. This created stress for production foremen which they, in turn, passed along to higher management. Secondly, approximately ten hard-core minority group members were assigned to clerical areas of the company but given no specific assignment. Representatives of their group lodged a complaint about this situation to management.

Top management was thus faced with a clash in organizational values; social conscience versus a desire for cooperation and harmony. Confronted with this realization, top management reasoned that the value of social concern was stronger (ranked higher) than the desire for minimum conflict. Adhering to this ranking of values, the company decided to intensify rather than diminish the minority group program. Continued conflict about this issue, in some degree, was considered inevitable but a climate was established whereby top management was seen as *credible*. In the face of conflict they persevered in the pursuit of previously announced values.

Organizational Structure

The manner in which an organization is designed or structured can influence the attitudes and behavior of organizational members. Such attitudes are an important contributor to the perceptions people form of the organizational climate. Two markedly different company situations will illustrate this phenomenon.

Company *G* is a venerable commercial bank. Organization is almost purely by functional departments; e.g., commercial loans, data processing, and investments. Ten layers separate tellers from the president, and organizational members are given elaborate titles to convey their rank. Predictably, these manifestations of classical organizational design contribute to a climate of "rigidity," "traditionalism," and "caution."

Company *H* is a real estate investment firm. Organization is based on the project being investigated at the time. For example, the firm organized a project to market some New Mexican land to buyers throughout the United States. Another project was established to investigate the feasibility of erecting a large-scale shopping center in a semirural area. These mercurial project arrangements contribute to a climate characterized as "free form," "loose," and "adventuresome." (Admittedly the nature of the business—commercial banking versus real estate investment—affects climate to a stronger degree than does organizational structure. However, the importance of structure cannot be dismissed.)

Characteristics of the People

Organizational climate can be profoundly influenced by the psychological and demographic characteristics of its personnel. Organizations with a heavy component of older, less well-educated, and less upwardly mobile employees, will have a different psychological climate than an organization with many more younger, highly educated, and ambitious employees. The perceived average chronological age of employees is one aspect of an organization that is frequently commented on by job candidates and new-comers. Presumably, younger people perceive an organization with a young management team as having a "dynamic" climate.

Nature of the Business

An influential determinant of organizational climate is an organization's basic business or mission. A visitor to a meat packing company would per-ceive a different organizational climate there than if he or she visited an insurance company of comparable size. The nature of the business is not an isolated variable; it influences many other organizational characteristics such as policies, characteristics of the people, and leadership style. For instance, the meat packing company in question will require a different mix of employees than would the insurance company.

Life Stage

An organization's location on its life cycle is yet another determinant of its organizational climate. Companies, for example, generate a different "feel" in their infancy than in adulthood. Younger organizations tend to be less formal and smaller. Mature organizations tend to be more formal and larger; growth usually requires time. Life stage thus affects size and struc-ture, which in turn influence climate. Younger organizations also show greater promise of rapid growth, which also influences organizational climate.

An important summary point about determinants of organizational cli-mate is that most of them are interrelated. A few key variables might ac-count for most of what is claimed to be *organizational climate.* Degree of formal structuring might be one such key variable. Tightly structured or-ganizations influence such variables as policy, leadership style, and to some extent characteristics of the people (some personality types refuse to work for a tightly structured organization). Nature of the business, as suggested earlier, might be another key variable. To illustrate, a phosphate mine will inevitably have a different type of climate than would an advertising agency.

DIAGNOSIS OF ORGANIZATIONAL CLIMATE

Approaches to *diagnosing* or measuring organizational climate fall into two general categories: the formation of subjective judgments or the collection of objective indices. Diagnosis or measurement of human personality may similarly be grouped into these two categories. Diagnosis of organizational climate, however, has been undertaken much less frequently than the diagnosis of human personality. Formal attempts to measure aspects of organizational climate appear to date back to the research conducted by John K. Hemphill and Charles M. Westie of Ohio State University in the late 1940s. The dimensions of organizational climate arrived at by their research are described below in the section "Contrasting Hotel Climates."

Subjective Reactions

Descriptions and vignettes of organizations presented so far in this chapter have all been based on subjective or intuitive observations. By way of illustration, Rochesterians have long called the Eastman Kodak Company, "Mother Kodak." Such a label reflects a subjective reaction of many individuals that this company provides emotional and financial support to its members. Similarly, labels such as "aggressive" or "paternalistic" organization are based on subjective or intuitive (but not necessarily inaccurate) evaluations of an organization. Saul W. Gellerman has provided some provocative categories for ordering these subjective or judgmental observations. His categories consist of four company personalities: (a) paternal, passive; (b) paternal, aggressive; (c) impersonal, passive; (d) impersonal, aggressive.[2] The meaning of such company personality types is illustrated by a description of an *impersonal, aggressive* company.[3]

> ... This company made paints and varnishes, and also went for the do-it-yourself market in a big way. Salesmen were chosen for their aggressive manner and were schooled in hard sell tactics. District managers kept close tabs on their men and were instructed to keep the pressure on at all times.
>
> Salesmen could (and did) make a great deal of money, but the personal touch was missing. Bonus checks arrived at their homes by mail without even a note from the home office executives. The men seldom had contact with anyone in the company other than their immediate superior; once the initial training was over, the men who judged their performance did so from afar. Some men became demoralized by the absence of management interest and accepted jobs with other firms (sometimes at a financial loss).
>
> The men who survived were a very hard-boiled breed—independent to a fault. Through them the company earned a reputation for relentless competitive

pushing. Turnover was fairly high, but the company looked upon this as an effective winnowing-out process that corrected its hiring mistakes and gradually filled its ranks with hardy veterans who neither wanted nor needed management to take a personal interest in them.

Objective Indices

Organizations can also be described by the results of paper and pencil measures. "Organization personality tests" of these types, however, are still subjective in one important sense. Organizational members report their subjective reactions to a large number of questionnaire items. Complex statistical analyses are then applied to the data. In the final analysis, any categorization of organizational climate is based on a substratum of human impressions. Figure 11.2 is a sampling of the nature of these research questionnaires which provide objective indices of organizational climate.

Please circle the number that indicates how you feel about each of the following statements. Number 1 means the highest agreement, while number 7 means the strongest disagreement. Number 4 means you neither agree nor disagree with the statement. Please answer every question, even if you are not sure about the way you feel on that topic.

1. Managers in my organization insist on high production.

| 1 | 2 | 3 | 4 | 5 | 6 | 7 |

Agree strongly   disagree strongly

2. It is difficult to form a close relationship with most managers in my organization.

| 1 | 2 | 3 | 4 | 5 | 6 | 7 |

Agree strongly   disagree strongly

3. People in this organization really pull together when the chips are down.

| 1 | 2 | 3 | 4 | 5 | 6 | 7 |

Agree strongly   disagree strongly

4. We spend too much time around here shuffling papers.

| 1 | 2 | 3 | 4 | 5 | 6 | 7 |

Agree strongly   disagree strongly

5. The days around here seem very long.

| 1 | 2 | 3 | 4 | 5 | 6 | 7 |

Agree strongly   disagree strongly

Figure 11.2 Questionnaire items used to measure organizational climate.

Questionnaires of this type vary from about 30 to 200 questions. Many of the questionnaire items are really measuring similar feelings and attitudes. Correlation coefficients are computed between the responses to each item and every other item to measure the degree of interrelationship. Various forms of *factor analysis* are then applied (usually with the assistance of a computer) to determine what factors or dimensions the questionnaire is really measuring.[4] Assume as one case in point that the questionnaire contained 100 items. These 100 items might in fact be measuring only ten different thoughts or attitudes. For example, the following two items might really be tapping the same idea:

Management really cares about us as individuals.

Management believes in the dignity of people.

Dimensions of organizational behavior as revealed by factor analysis of an organizational climate questionnaire are amply illustrated by Frank Friedlander and Newton Margulies.[5] These researchers modified the Organizational Climate Description Questionnaire, which contains 64 descriptive statements about an organization. Respondents express strong agreement to strong disagreement with each item on a seven-point scale. Factor analysis of this questionnaire has suggested the existence of eight dimensions. Factors one through four are climate dimensions relating to the *behavior of nonmanagerial personnel*:[6]

1. *Disengagement* describes a group which is "going through the motions"; a group that is "not in gear" with respect to the task at hand.
2. *Hindrance* refers to those feelings by members that they are burdened with routine duties and other requirements deemed as busy work. Their work is not being facilitated.
3. *Esprit* is a morale dimension. Members feel that their social needs are being satisfied, and, at the same time, they are enjoying a sense of task accomplishment.
4. *Intimacy* refers to members' enjoyment of friendly social relationships. This is a dimension of social need satisfaction not necessarily associated with task accomplishment.

Climate dimensions 5 through 8 refer to *aspects of managerial behavior* as contrasted to aspects of group member behavior just described:[7]

5. *Aloofness* refers to management behavior characterized as formal and impersonal. It describes an "emotional" distance between the manager and his subordinates.
6. *Production Emphasis* refers to management behavior characterized by close

supervision. Management is highly directive and insensitive to communication feedback.

7. *Thrust* refers to management behavior characterized by efforts to "get the organization moving." This behavior is marked by attempts to motivate through example. Behavior is task-oriented and viewed favorably by members.

8. *Consideration* refers to behavior characterized by an inclination to treat members as human beings and to do something extra for them in human terms.

Organizational psychologists question the extent to which such dimensions of climate can be reliably measured. Measurement of human personality, of course, is also subject to error. Assuming that dimensions of the kind cited above are reliable, the diagnosis of organizational climate is facilitated. Accurate dimension scores would create the opportunity to make comparative descriptions of organizations in the following manner:

> Company *A* is characterized by people who simply go through the motions of their work. They are hindered in their work performance by an overload of busywork. Members feel that their social needs are being thwarted and that they do not enjoy a sense of task accomplishment. Friendly social contacts are almost nonexistent. Managers in the company are quite formal and impersonal. Management supervises closely, is highly directive, and insensitive to opinions from below. Management attempts to get the organization moving forward, but does so in an insensitive manner.

> Company *B* is characterized by people who mesh in getting things accomplished. Minimum time is wasted on busywork. Morale is high because people's social needs are being met. There is ample opportunity to form rewarding social contacts. Managers are generally informal and personal. Supervision is more often general than close. Management exerts considerable effort to move the organization forward and, in the process, treats people in a considerate and sensitive manner.

ORGANIZATIONAL CLIMATE AND MOTIVATION

Logically, it can be concluded that the organizational climate in which a person works can influence his or her motivation. Two researchers at the Harvard Business School, George H. Litwin and Robert A. Stringer, Jr. conducted a lengthy set of experiments that, among other findings, support this notion.[8] The far-reaching implications of such a finding justify summarizing the essentials of this research.

Definition of Concepts

Motivational patterns in the Litwin and Stringer experiment were measured in terms of three specific motives: (a) *need for achievement* (*n* Achievement, as described in Chapter 2), defined as the need for success in relation to an internalized standard of excellence; (b) *need for affiliation* (*n* Affiliation), defined as the need for close interpersonal relationships and friendships with other people; and (c) *need for power* (*n* Power), defined as the need to control or influence others. The strength of these motives was measured by content analyses of responses to projective tests. Two important situational determinants of motivation must be evaluated in order to understand these motives. First, *expectancy* refers to the subjective probability of need satisfaction or frustration (refer back to the discussion of expectancy theory contained in Chapter 2). Second, *incentive* value is the amount of satisfaction or frustration the person attaches to the outcome of a situation.

Organizational climate is defined in this research as "... *the summary of the total pattern of expectancies and incentive values that exist in a given organizational setting.*"[9] Stated differently, organizational climate in this context refers to the *kind* and *amount* of need satisfaction the person is getting from the environment. Six specific dimensions, as measured by a 31-item questionnaire, are used to analyze organizational climate:[10]

1. *Structure*: the feeling the workers have about the constraints in their work situation; how many rules, regulations, and procedures there are.
2. *Responsibility*: the feeling of being your own boss; not having to double check all your decisions.
3. *Risk*: the sense of riskiness and challenge in the job and in the work situation.
4. *Reward*: the feeling of being rewarded for a job well done; the emphasis on reward versus criticism and punishment.
5. *Warmth and support*: the feeling of general "good fellowship" and helpfulness that prevails in the organization.
6. *Conflict*: the feeling that management isn't afraid of different opinions or conflict; the emphasis placed on settling differences here and now.

Experimental Design

Different organizational climates were created by instructing the leaders of three different simulated business organizations to use different leadership styles as described below. Each company had 15 members plus a president. A careful attempt was made to match all three companies in every other variable but leadership style. For instance, factors such as nature of the task, physical location, and the sex, age, and motivational patterns of employees were matched for all three groups. An abridged description of the experimental activities is as follows:[11]

> Each simulated business operated in a 100-seat classroom. The work involved the production of miniature construction models of radar towers and radar-controlled guns of various kinds from "Erector Set" parts. A typical product was comprised of from 30 to 50 parts. The businesses had three major tasks and three corresponding, functional departments—production, product development, and control (or accounting). The president appointed people to each department, selected department managers, and was responsible for establishing job specifications and operating procedures. . . .

> The experiment was conducted over a two-week period, comprising eight actual days of organizational life. The work day averaged about six hours. During the course of the experiment, daily observations were made and periodic readings were taken using questionnaires and psychological tests. These data were used to provide feedback to the presidents indicating to what extent they were achieving the intended leadership styles.

The president of Organization A was instructed to place strong emphasis on the maintenance of a formal structure; to run a "tight organization." Roles were rigidly prescribed to company members. A conservative approach was taken to the essential task of the group. Reliable and consistent quality were given higher value by management than was product innovation. The experimenters predicted this "power-related" climate would induce worker reaction against the formal structure and that job satisfaction would be low.

The president of Organization B was instructed to maintain a loose, informal structure. His role was to emphasize friendliness, cooperation, group loyalty, and teamwork. Group decision making was used at every level of the simulated company. Encouragement and assistance were used in lieu of punishment and threats. The experimenters predicted that job satisfaction and morale would probably be high under this "affiliative climate" but that efficiency in accomplishing tasks would only be moderate.

High productivity was emphasized by the president of Organization C. People were encouraged to set their own goals; creativity and innovation were supported by management. Feedback on performance was given frequently in order to encourage competition. Excellent performance was rewarded by recognition and approval as well as promotion and pay raises. Teamwork was encouraged by emphasis on competition against an external standard. The experimenters predicted that this "achieving" organizational climate would facilitate personal involvement, commitment, high productivity, and an interest in setting even higher goals.

Impact on Motivational Pattern

Systematic variation of leadership style (which induced variation in organizational climate), as hypothesized, did have an arousal effect on the three key motives or needs.[12] Organization A aroused a high level of power motivation, which was still activated at the second measurement point taken at day five. Organization B aroused a moderately high level of affiliation motivation which was also maintained throughout the measurement period. Organization C aroused a high level of achievement motivation which actually increased during the period of measurement.

Another major finding was that the induced organizational climates did not reduce the strength of any motive. For example, organization A (power-related) did not result in a reduction of n achievement, although it was hypothesized that such a reduction of motivation would take place.

Experimentally minded readers should recall that members of the three organizations were matched with respect to initial levels of the motives under study. Such an experimental control makes tenable the interpretation that the difference in motivation levels are a result of the impact of the leadership styles and the climates they induced. Equally important, it should be noted that the experimentally induced organizational climates affect motives in *that particular situation.* Measurements taken one month later and in a neutral situation revealed that participants tended to return to their usual motivational pattern.[13]

ORGANIZATIONAL CLIMATE AND BEHAVIOR

Attempting to understand how organizational climate affects the behavior of organizational members is almost as far-reaching a task as attempting to explain how environment affects behavior. The earlier discussion of determinants of organizational climate is closely related to the present discussion of climate and behavior. For example, organizational policy (one determinant of climate) has a decided influence on behavior in its own right. Strictly enforced policy, to cite one extreme case, may encourage low risk-taking behavior. The present discussion of climate and behavior will concentrate on information not woven into discussion at other points in the book.

Descriptions of the impact of climate on behavior make the implicit assumption that both organizational climate and human behavior can be reliably measured. There is room for considerably more precision in both kinds of measurements. Nevertheless, there is still value in working within the constraints imposed by available measuring devices. Four separate examples will be presented of how organizational climate affects the behavior of people in organizations.

Contrasting Hotel Climates

Before delving into climatic differences between the Alpine and Vanguard hotels, a discussion of how these differences might be measured is warranted. Hemphill and Westie have empirically developed a set of organizational dimensions that have withstood the test of time. These 13 dimensions of group or organizational functioning, as summarized by Carroll L. Shartle, are as follows:[14]

1. *Autonomy* is the degree to which a group functions independent of other groups and occupies an independent position in society. It is reflected by the degree to which a group determines its own activities, by its absence of allegiance, deference and/or dependence relative to other groups.

2. *Control* is the degree to which a group regulates the behavior of individuals while they are functioning as group members. It is reflected by the modifications which group membership imposes on complete freedom of individual behavior and by the amount or intensity of group-derived government.

3. *Flexibility* is the degree to which a group's activities are marked by informal procedures rather than by adherence to established procedures. It is reflected by the extent to which duties of members are free from specification through custom, tradition, written rules, regulations, codes of procedure, or even unwritten but clearly prescribed ways of behaving.

4. *Hedonic Tone* is the degree to which group membership is accompanied by a general feeling of pleasantness or agreeableness. It is reflected by the frequency of laughter, conviviality, pleasant anticipation of group meetings, and by the absence of complaining.

5. *Homogeneity* is the degree to which members of a group are similar with respect to socially relevant characteristics. It is reflected by relative uniformity of members with respect to age, sex, race, socio-economic status, interests, attitudes and habits.

6. *Intimacy* is the degree to which members of a group are mutually acquainted with one another and are familiar with the personal details of one another's lives. It is reflected by the nature of topics discussed by members, by modes of greetings, forms of address, and by interactions which presuppose a knowledge of the probable reaction of others under widely differing circumstances, as well as by the extent and type of knowledge each member has about other members of the group.

7. *Participation* is the degree to which members of a group apply time and

347

effort to group activities. It is reflected by the number and kinds of duties members perform, by voluntary assumption of non-assigned duties and by the amount of time spent in group activities.

8. *Permeability* is the degree to which a group permits easy access to membership. It is reflected by absence of entrance requirements of any kind, and by the degree to which membership is solicited.

9. *Polarization* is the degree to which a group is oriented and works toward a single goal which is clear and specific to all members.

10. *Potency* is the degree to which a group has primary significance for its members. It is reflected by the kind of needs which a group is satisfying or has the potentiality of satisfying.

11. *Stability* is the degree to which a group persists over a period of time with essentially the same characteristics. It is reflected by the rate of membership turnover, by frequency of reorganizations, and by the constancy of group size.

12. *Stratification* is the degree to which a group orders its members into status hierarchies. It is reflected by differential distribution of power privileges, obligations, and duties and by asymmetrical patterns of differential behavior among group members.

13. *Viscidity* is the degree to which members of the group function as a unit. It is reflected by absence of dissension and personal conflict among members, by absence of activities serving to advance only the interests of individual group members, by the ability of the group to resist disrupting forces, and by the belief on the part of the members that the group does function as a unit.

Given these definitions as a reference point, two resort hotels, the Alpine and Vanguard are rated on a one to seven scale on each one of these dimensions as shown in Figure 11.3. Using an elementary form of profile analysis, the climate of both hotels will be characterized according to their three highest and three lowest scoring dimensions. Hotel Alpine is thus high on Flexibility, Intimacy, and Stability but low on Control, Homogeneity, and Permeability. Translating these labels into the behavior implied by their definitions, the Alpine has an informal, loose set of work regulations, close personal relationships among employees, and low turnover. The hotel is quite selective in adding new employees at all levels in the organization. Hotel employees make little attempt to regulate each other's behavior and they reflect a wide range of personal backgrounds.

Organizational climate at the Alpine exerts a positive influence on the attitudes of most organizational members. Job satisfaction is high and this in turn produces positive behavioral consequences. Turnover is low among the administrative staff (even among managers the hotel *wants* to retain), and managers take the initiative to recruit friends into the organization.

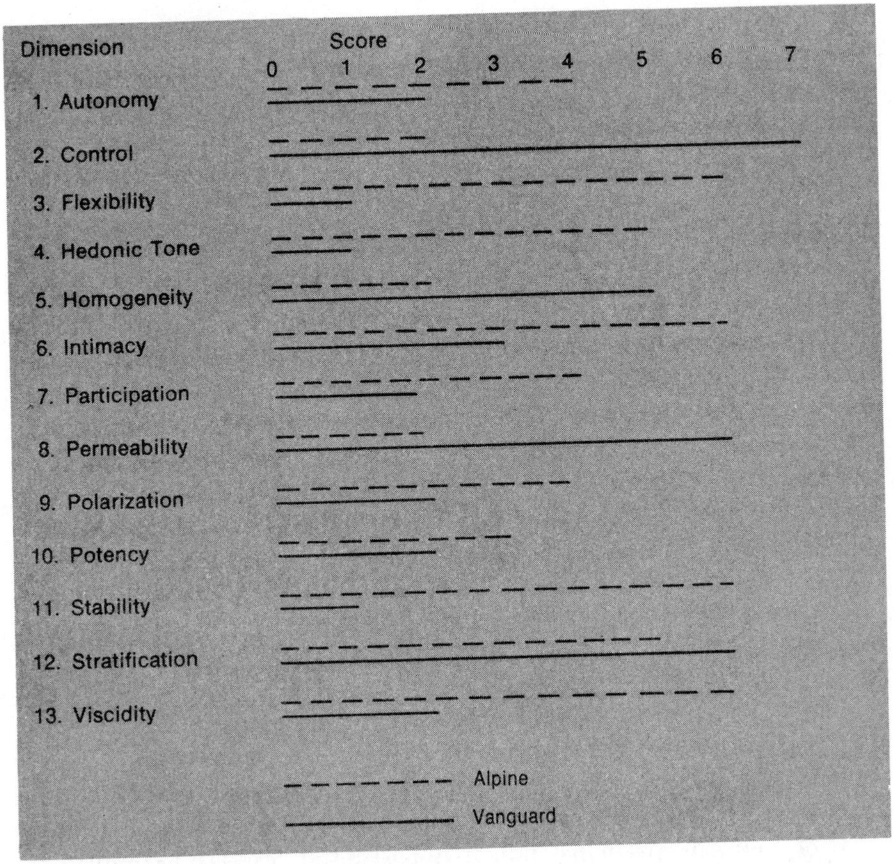

Figure 11.3 Organizational climate of two hypothetical resort hotels.

Schools of hotel administration encourage their graduates to work at the Alpine.

In contrast is the organizational climate at the Vanguard. Hotel Vanguard is high on Control, Permeability, and Stratification, but low on Flexibility, Hedonic Tone, and Stability. Behaviorally, much control is exerted over organizational members, minimum selectivity is exercised in bringing new employees into the hotel, and there is a rigid status differential among people at different levels in the hotel (e.g., kitchen help are forbidden to walk through the lobby at any time, while waiters have this privilege). Tight rules, regulations, and procedures govern employee behavior and a somber, unhappy atmosphere pervades the work force. Reorganizations are frequent and job satisfaction at the Vanguard is low and reflect in high turnover and a difficulty in obtaining help even when economic conditions are good. Schools of hotel administration caution their graduates about working conditions at the Vanguard.

Organizational Climate and Production Work

Research conducted at Non-Linear Systems, Inc., a rapidly changing organization in the electronics industry, supports the situation presented about the two resort hotels. Friedlander and Margulies conducted a study with 91 rank-and-file and four managerial personnel at Non-Linear Systems that, among other findings, demonstrated the relationship between organizational climate and work satisfaction.[15] Organizational climate had a greater impact on attitudes toward interpersonal relationships than toward other areas of work satisfaction. For example, organizational climate had a very small effect on attitudes toward advancement opportunities. *Esprit* (roughly a feeling that social needs are being satisfied) was the dimension of organizational climate most closely related to job satisfaction.[16] Surprisingly, in this study, *Aloofness* and *Production Emphasis* (*see* the definitions presented earlier) were not related to job satisfaction.

Contrasting Climates in the Department of Commerce

Researchers sometimes have to simulate live conditions in order to study complicated phenomena. N. Frederickson used such an approach to systematically study variations in organizational climate, as reported by John P. Campbell *et al.*[17] Two-hundred sixty middle managers working for the state of California participated in an in-basket test designed to simulate the chief of field service of the Department of Commerce. (The in-basket approach gives each participant a sampling of the kind of problems he or she might face in the actual job situation. Frequent use is made of telephone calls, memos, sudden orders from the boss, and so forth.)

One experimental condition involved the general prevalence of "rules and regulations." Half the subjects were led to believe that the Department of Commerce encouraged new ideas, innovation, and creative problem solving. Instructions were that rules existed but that they could be broken if they prevented work from getting accomplished. In contrast, the other half were told that a very valuable set of rules had been built up over the years and that they should only be broken under extreme circumstances. The second experimental condition concerned the closeness of supervision. Subjects were told that either the organization preferred a subordinate's work to be closely supervised or that subordinates should be allowed to work out details for themselves (general supervision).

One major finding of the experiment was that the work output of people is more predictable in an innovative than in a rules-oriented climate. Consistency of organizational climate also influenced the output of participants in the exercise. Consistent climates predictably led to consistent work output.

Frederickson later reanalyzed his data to arrive at another valuable conclusion. Participants in the in-basket exercises were found to use different work methods under different climate conditions.[18]

> For example, in the In-basket under the climate conditions permitting more freedom, administrators dealt more directly with peers, while in restrictive climates, they tended to work through more formal channels.

The relevance of this study to students of organizational behavior is that it documents a major premise of this book: *the organization can and does influence the work behavior of its members.*

Organizational Climate and the Hard Core

The power of organizational climate to influence work behavior is dramatically illustrated by research conducted with hard-core unemployed (HCU).[19] Frank Friedlander and Stuart Greenberg examined the relationship between job performance and seemingly important variables among a large group of predominantly male, black, lowly educated individuals who were unemployed prior to an AIM-JOBS Program in Cleveland. These variables were biographic/demographic data (e.g., length of prior employment), measures of attitudes toward work, including job motivation, and measures of the organizational climate in which the HCU was placed and employed. Organizational climate, as measured by the amount of psychological support the HCU felt he received, alone was related to job performance:[20]

> ... the work effectiveness and behavior of the HCU depends predominantly on the social climate in which he is placed and works. Increasing the supportiveness of this climate seems to be a major avenue for increasing the HCU's performance and retention.

Friedlander and Greenberg note that their findings are not unique. Research conducted on JOBS NOW in Chicago indicates that such variables as age, education, IQ, marital status, police record, or length of previous employment are unrelated to job performance of hard-core unemployed.[21]

> ... the sole factor that differentiated successful from unsuccessful HCU persons at statistically significant levels was the degree of support within the immediate organizational context in which the HCU was placed. The retention rate for "high support" organizations was 82% while that for "low support" organizations was 28%....

ORGANIZATIONAL CLIMATE AND PRODUCTIVITY

Further evidence about the relevance of organizational climate stems from field research conducted by the Institute of Social Research under the direction of Rensis Likert.[22] One interpretation of the results of these studies is that the organizational climate stemming from a *participative group* style of management facilitates higher productivity. Systems 4 is the symbolic name Likert uses to identify this behavioral science-based system of management. An appreciation for the nature of the climate generated by Systems 4 management can be achieved by noting ten of its characteristics, as measured by the Profile of Organizational Characteristics:

1. Superiors have complete confidence and trust in all matters involving subordinates.
2. Subordinates feel completely free to discuss things about the job with superiors.
3. Personnel at all levels feel real responsibility for organization's goals and behave in ways to implement them.
4. Considerable communication exists with individuals and groups.
5. Superiors know and understand problems of subordinates.
6. Very substantial cooperative teamwork is present throughout the organization.
7. Employees are involved fully in all decisions related to their work.
8. Goals, except in emergencies, are usually established by means of group participation.
9. Quite widespread responsibility for review and control exists. Lower units at times impose more rigorous reviews and tighter controls than do top management.
10. Controls are used for self-guidance and for coordinated problem solving and guidance rather than punitively.

Likert and his colleagues have gathered data from several different companies supporting the inference that an organizational climate fostered by a Systems 4 type management facilitates high productivity. Quantitative evidence from this inference has been found both directly and indirectly. The nature of the management system (and indirectly the organizational climate) in all studies was measured by a questionnaire. More objective indices were used to measure productivity.

Direct evidence of the relationship between Systems 4 management and productivity was obtained in a garment manufactory. In this plant of 800 employees, management was trained in group participative (Systems 4) methods of management. Other complex changes, such as improved work flow design, also were implemented, thus making it impossible to estimate precisely increases in production which can be attributed to change in the management system alone. A "reasonable estimate" was obtained by using an index based on changes in the earnings of hourly workers. As explained by Likert:[23]

> This method of measuring productivity improvement eliminates the effect of changes in technology, since the hourly earnings are based on piece-rate payments. Whenever changes occur in the work or the method, the job is retimed on the basis of the new job content, and new rates are set.

Changes in the management system from approaches such as "exploitive–authoritative" to participative group led to substantial increases in productivity. For one two-year period under study the productivity increase was 26 percent. During the same general time period, total manufacturing costs decreased by about 20 percent.

Indirect evidence for the relationship between climate and productivity stems from the most highly productive plant in "one of the most successful plants in the United States." The system of management in this plant was compared to the system of management used in a sampling of prestigious American business organizations. According to the questionnaire results, the middle and upper levels of management in the highly productive plant see the management of their plant resembling Systems 4 to a significantly greater extent than do managers in the comparison group. An inference drawn here is that the system of management (and concomitant organizational climate) contributed to this high level of productivity. A reciprocal interpretation, however, that high levels of productivity allowed for a Systems 4 style of management, cannot be readily dismissed.

SUCCESSFUL VERSUS UNSUCCESSFUL ORGANIZATIONS

Organizational climate can be conceptualized from yet another dimension: organizational success versus failure. The same aspect of organizational life might be viewed from the perspective of *healthy* versus *pathological* organizations; however, the concept of success versus failure lends itself more readily to an operational dimension than does health versus pathology. Distinct differences exist between the psychological climates of successful organizations versus unsuccessful organizations.

At the present state of the art of organizational measurement, organizational success can be considered to lie on a continuum. On one extreme lies the successful organization; on the other extreme lies the unsuccessful organization. Most organizations lie somewhere in between these two end points.

Organizational success is a complex notion that takes into consideration economic and psychological factors. At a minimum, a successful organization must make a profit (or stay within its budget if it is a nonprofit organization) and simultaneously provide satisfaction to its members. An illuminating study by Hal Pickle and Frank Friedlander makes a beginning attempt to provide an empirical base for judging organizational success.[24]

What is the relevance of research about organizational success to considerations of organizational climate? First, it should be recognized that organizational success is another possible determinant of organizational climate. Climate can then be better understood if something is known about an organization's health. Second, research of this nature illustrates that these somewhat abstract dimensions of organizational climate can be measured if systematic efforts are applied. Third, this research illustrates that even such a precise sounding concept as *organizational success* is in reality multifaceted. Fourth, it provides some empirical evidence about how an interface with the outside environment might influence one contributor to or determinant of organizational climate. Organizational success is the determinant under study in this research.

Management success, reason Pickle and Friedlander, must be judged by the ultimate criterion of organizational success. But organizational success is an elusive concept that must take into account the perceptions of all those people who have traffic with that organization. To cite a well-known illustration, a chemical company with a 25 percent return on invested capital would not be considered totally successful if that same firm polluted surrounding waters. Seven "parties-at-interest" all have a say in determining organizational success: owners, customers, suppliers, employers, community members, and local, state, and perhaps federal governments. Successfully fulfilling societal needs, argue the authors, is the criterion by which to measure organizations. This multiple measure of the successful organization is schematically illustrated in Figure 11.4.

Pickle and Friedlander chose to study 97 small businesses because they were primarily interested in studying the degree to which manager ability and personality affect the success of an organization (an issue not of concern in this chapter). "In large organizations, a variety of additional factors would undoubtedly attenuate the importance of the characteristics of any one manager, even though he might be at the highest level."[25] Multiple

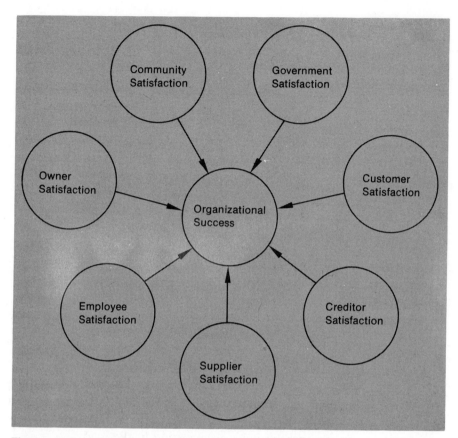

Figure 11.4 Schematic model of the organizational–societal interactions. (Adapted from Hal Pickle and Frank Friedlander, "Seven Societal Criteria of Organizational Success," *Personnel Psychology*, Vol. 20, No. 2, Summer 1967, p. 166.)

methods were used to determine the degree to which the seven parties-at-interest were satisfied with each business.

Owners of each of the 97 business organizations were administered a questionnaire by the interview method. Owner satisfaction was measured in two broad categories:[26]

(1) financial satisfaction, including dollar amounts, return on investment, return on hours of work, profit relative to other organizations, previous financial record, and growth potential;
(2) nonmonetary satisfactions, including enjoyment and pride in ownership.

Customers were also surveyed by administering a questionnaire during an interview. The respective business was rated by 15 to 25 customers per business on a five-point scale on each of the following features:[27]

1. Location,
2. Quality of goods and services,
3. Variety of offering,
4. Quantity available,
5. Appearance of establishment,
6. Hours,
7. Days open,
8. Knowledge of product,
9. Availability of fashion,
10. Speed of service,
11. Prestige,
12. Merchandise display,
13. Various customer services,
14. Satisfaction of complaints,
15. Parking,
16. Advertising,
17. Dependability,
18. Various employee factors,
19. Price,
20. Sales techniques,
21. Congestion—inside and outside, and
22. Air conditioning.

Employees were all administered the SRA Employee Inventory, a standardized job-satisfaction questionnaire. A total of 513 inventories were completed by employees, representing an average of 5.29 employees per organization. This approach made possible computing an average job-satisfaction score for each business organization in the study.

Supplier satisfaction was measured in three different categories: (1) supplier's cost of filling orders for the business, (2) organization's record of meeting its financial obligation to the supplier, and (3) organization's record of stability in the continuity of its relationship with the supplier. Close to 52 percent of the 403 questionnaires mailed to suppliers were completed and returned.

Creditor satisfaction with each company in the study was measured via statistical information gathered during interviews with banks, retail merchant associations, and Dun & Bradstreet. Reliability in paying bills was the obvious factor being measured.

Community satisfaction was determined by taking measurements in three different areas: (a) support of organizations in the community, (b) support of charities and schools, and (c) participation in political activities. Information about these topics was elicited by administering questionnaires to the 97 managers as part of a structured interview.

Governmental satisfaction with the 97 companies was measured indirectly. Owners of each company completed a questionnaire about their relations with federal, state, and local governments. Questionnaire items concerned communication with state and federal officials, the support given to lobbying groups, questioning by Internal Revenue Service officials about income tax returns, penalties paid on taxes, or reprimands by tax officials. The intent of these items was to reflect the degree to which the company carried out its explicit and implicit responsibilities with governmental agencies.

Interrelationships among all seven satisfaction scores were then determined by computing correlation coefficients. Intercorrelations among the satisfactions of the seven "parties-at-interest" are shown in Figure 11.5. (A coefficient of 1.00 would indicate that two scores are perfectly related in a positive direction. Conversely, a correlation coefficient of −1.00 would indicate that a perfect negative relationship exists. For example, supply and demand are negatively correlated according to classical economic theory. Coefficients of around zero indicate a chance or random relationship between two scores.)

One important conclusion to be reached from the interrelationship among these scores is that the satisfaction of the seven parties-at-interest is not completely independent; there is some degree of positive relationship among many of the scores. The moderate relationships found among the satisfaction scores also suggest that an organization's ability to satisfy one party-at-interest does not necessarily suggest that other parties-at-interest

Party-at-Interest	Community	Government	Customer	Supplier	Creditor	Employee
Owner	0.23*	−0.12	0.37†	0.14	0.00	0.25*
Community		0.16	0.04	0.16	0.14	0.22*
Government			−0.09	0.11	0.20*	−0.07
Customer				0.17	0.23*	0.23*
Supplier					0.08	0.17
Creditor						0.08
Employee						

*Indicates that a relationship of this magnitude could only have occurred five times in one hundred by chance.

†Indicates that a relationship of this magnitude could only have occurred one time in one hundred by chance.

Figure 11.5 Intercorrelations of satisfactions of seven parties-at-interest with 97 business firms. (Adapted from Hal Pickle and Frank Friedlander, "Seven Societal Criteria of Organizational Success," *Personnel Psychology*, Vol. 20, No. 2, Summer 1967, p. 171.)

will be satisfied. In short, the successful organization must make specific attempts to satisfy the demands of diverse groups.

RELATIONSHIP TO CORE PROPOSITIONS

At several places in the following analysis a relatively high level of abstract thinking will be required to follow the relationship between organizational climate and the core propositions.

Human Behavior

Understanding principles of human behavior assists in understanding organizational climate. Drawing the analogy between human personality and organization personality is helpful in appreciating the meaning of the concept, *organizational climate*. To illustrate, both individual personality and organizational climate are relatively enduring attributes. Considerable force (e.g., drugs, psychotherapy over a protracted period of time, or a traumatic life experience) is required to significantly change personality. Similarly, a dramatic change in management, products, services, or profitability or an unusually effective program of organization development would be required to change a given organizational climate.

Organizational climate emphasizes the total *subjective* impact of an environment on people. In order to comprehend the implications of the concept "organizational climate" it would therefore be necessary to know something about human attitudes and feelings (two key components of a subjective impact).

Situational Nature

Experiments conducted by Litwin and Stringer, described in this chapter, illustrate the situational properties of organizational climate. Particularly relevant here was the finding that the motivational pattern of people can be demonstrably influenced by the situation in which they are functioning. For instance, given an organizational climate that is characterized by power-oriented leadership, power drives of individuals will be intensified. Extrapolating these findings to the realm of casual observation, placing a normally kind and gentle person in a hostile and threatening environment will activate his or her underlying aggressive and hostile impulses. Readers with battlefield (or football, or hockey) experience can probably attest to this observation.

Systemic Nature

Organizational climate can also be viewed from a systems perspective. Several approaches to isolating the dimensions (or characteristics) of organizations were described earlier. These characteristics are usually interdependent; at a minimum they are intercorrelated as shown by correlational analysis. Two hypothetical examples using the dimensions described under "hotel climates" will help to explain these interdependencies:

1. Increasing the *intimacy* (familiarity among members) of a group would probably have an impact on other dimensions of group behavior. For instance both *hedonic tone* (general feeling of pleasantness or agreeableness among group members) and *participation* (the degree to which members of a group apply time and effort to group activities) would probably show an increase along with the changes in *intimacy*.

2. Increasing group *homogeneity* (member similarity with respect to socially relevant characteristics) would probably precipitate increases in *stability* (the group persisting over time) and *polarization* (the degree to which a group works toward a single goal that is clear and specific to all members).

Structure and Process

Elements of organizational climate serve as another illustration of the interaction between structure and process that is characteristic of organizational behavior. As described earlier, organizational climate is a function of (determined by) a number of variables; some of these are structure-related, while others are process-related. The interaction between (or combination of) some of these variables is responsible for many aspects of organizational climate. One structure-related variable is the type of organizational structure used to carry out the objectives of the organization. Certain structures, such as a multilayered hierarchy, tend to breed a climate characterized as formal. The type of leadership style (a process-related variable) predominating the organization also influences the nature of the organizational climate. However, the combined influence of organizational structure and leadership style is a more influential determinant of climate than either variable (organizational structure or leadership style) alone.

To help make the above abstraction more concrete, consider this illustration: The combination of a high task-oriented, low relations-oriented leader and a multilayered, hierarchical structure will probably produce a "stiff, formal" climate. Combining the same structure with a low task-oriented, high relations-oriented leader, will probably produce a climate of moderate "stiffness" and formality.

GUIDELINES FOR ACTION

1. Should you have a choice, work in an organizational climate that fits your individual characteristics. For example, if you like to innovate, select an organization or unit of an organization that encourages innovation.
2. The most practical way for you to measure organizational climate is to make careful observations of the organization around you and informally question others about their reactions to the organization.
3. Organizational climate should be taken seriously; the "right" climate can increase your job satisfaction, while the "wrong" climate can decrease your job satisfaction.
4. If you wish to determine whether a climate is sick or healthy, check the attitudes of as many parties-at-interest as you can. Healthy financial status alone does not make for a healthy organization.

QUESTIONS

1. Rate the organization most familiar to you on the dimensions described on page 344. What general conclusions can you reach about your organizational climate?
2. Describe how a policy of "promotion based mostly on seniority" might affect organizational climate.
3. Attempt to compare the organizational climate of a state penitentiary with that of a state mental hospital. What similarities and differences do you see?
4. Using organizational dimensions discussed in this chapter, describe the climate of a "third-rate, dog-eat-dog" business establishment.
5. Describe how profits might influence organizational climate and also how organizational climate might influence profits.
6. What do you think could (or should) be done to change the type of climate generated by the policies described in Companies A, B, and C (see the "Policy" subsection under "Determinants of Climate").

NOTES

1. Garlie A. Forehand and B. Von Haller Gilmer, "Environmental Variation in Studies of Organizational Behavior," *Psychological Bulletin*, Vol. 62, No. 6, December 1964, p. 363.
2. Saul W. Gellerman, *People, Problems and Profits.* New York: McGraw-Hill, 1960 (reported in B. Von Haller Gilmer, *Industrial Psychology*, second edition. New York: McGraw-Hill, 1966, pp. 58–60). Used with permission of McGraw-Hill Book Company.

3. *Ibid.*, p. 59.
4. Readers unfamiliar with the concepts of correlation or factor analysis will find these topics amply treated in most books about psychological statistics, statistics for the behavioral sciences, or quantitative decision making for business. One suggested source for correlational analysis is Joan Welkowitz, Robert Ewen, and Jacob Cohen, *Introductory Statistics for the Behavioral Sciences.* New York: Academic Press, 1971. Readers seeking comprehensive information about factor analysis should consult Stanley A. Mulaik, *The Foundations of Factor Analysis.* New York: McGraw-Hill, 1972.
5. Frank Friedlander and Newton Margulies, "Multiple Impacts of Organizational Climate and Individual Value Systems upon Job Satisfaction," *Personnel Psychology,* Vol. 22, No. 2, Summer 1969, pp. 171–183.
6. *Ibid.*, p. 174.
7. *Ibid.*, p. 174.
8. This experiment is described in extensive detail in George H. Litwin and Robert A. Stringer, Jr., *Motivation and Organizational Climate.* Boston: Division of Research, Harvard Business School, 1968. Reproduced by permission of the publisher. A concise analysis of the same material is George H. Litwin, "Climate and Motivation: An Experimental Study," in Renato Tagiuri and George H. Litwin (editors), *Organizational Climate: Explorations of a Concept.* Boston: Division of Research, Harvard Business School, 1968, pp. 169–190. Note: The latter article also appears in David A. Kolb, Irwin M. Rubin, and James M. McIntyre (editors), *Organizational Psychology.* Englewood Cliffs, N.J.: Prentice-Hall, 1971, pp. 109–122 .
9. Cited in Kolb *et al.*, p. 111.
10. *Ibid.*
11. Litwin and Stringer, *op. cit.*, pp. 94–97.
12. *Ibid.*, pp. 121–123.
13. *Ibid.*, pp. 127–131.
14. Carroll L. Shartle, *Executive Performance and Leadership.* Englewood Cliffs, N.J.: Prentice-Hall, 1956, pp. 63–65. ©1956 Reprinted by permission of Prentice-Hall, Inc.
15. Friedlander and Margulies, *op. cit.*, pp. 171–183.
16. *Ibid.*, p. 177.
17. John P. Campbell, Marvin D. Dunnette, Edward E. Lawler, III, and Karl E. Weick, Jr., *Managerial Behavior, Performance, and Effectiveness.* New York: McGraw-Hill, 1970, pp. 400–402.
18. Cited in *ibid.*, p. 402.
19. Frank Friedlander and Stuart Greenberg, "Effect of Job Attitudes, Training, and Organization Climate on Performance of the Hard-Core Unemployed," *Journal of Applied Psychology,* Vol. 55, No. 4, August 1971, pp. 287–295.
20. *Ibid.*, p. 293.
21. *Ibid.*
22. Rensis Likert, *The Human Organization.* New York: McGraw-Hill, 1967, pp. 13–46.
23. *Ibid.*, pp. 36–37.
24. Hal Pickle and Frank Friedlander, "Seven Societal Criteria of Organizational Success," *Personnel Psychology,* Vol. 20, No. 2, Summer 1967, pp. 165–178.
25. *Ibid.*, p. 167.
26. *Ibid.*, p. 168.
27. *Ibid.*, p. 169.

Management of Individual and Group Change

Change is inevitable in organizational life and the rate of change is accelerating. Gradually or swiftly, the process of change confronts almost every individual in his work and personal life. Heraclitus, the philosopher, recognized the inevitability of change with the following comment made in the year 217: "All things are in process and nothing stays still . . . You could not step twice into the same river." A modern day social commentator, Alvin Toffler, notes that all things are in reality processes that are in a continuous state of flux; the state of "un-change" does not exist.[1]

Concentration in this chapter is on the management of change at the individual and group level. Change is further examined in the following chapter from a different perspective—how changes are purposely brought about in total organizations. Another aspect of change was examined in Chapter 7—how changes in leadership style are brought about through management development. An array of subdisciplines within behavioral science deal with change.[2] Among these are psychotherapy, counseling, management development, and organizational development. The present chapter thus deals only with selected aspects of change.

One major assumption underlies all comments about change made in the following pages. Any changes introduced into one organizational unit have ramifications in other parts of the organization. One example will suffice to illustrate this "domino-like" phenomenon. Should management decide to significantly improve one department (e.g., allow people more responsibility, income, or opportunities for advancement), people in other departments will not let this go unnoticed. Managers in rival departments will be forced to handle employee requests for transfer to the new, "more glamorous" department. Similarly, other department managers will seek improvement opportunities for people in their departments. The reader can probably imagine a variety of subtle changes taking place in other parts of the organizational system because one department receives special attention.

Understanding the nature of change and how it affects people contributes to an understanding of human behavior in organizations. Diverse aspects of organizational behavior such as managerial obsolescence, some labor strikes, and many instances of voluntary turnover owe much of their origin to people's reaction to change.

A TAXONOMY OF CHANGE

What is change as it relates to organizational behavior? Figure 12.1 represents one step toward a systematic framework for classifying changes that take place within an organization. The taxonomy presented here was developed because of its assumed practicality and relevance for a wide range of organizations. Change in this taxonomy is divided into three types: (a) change in technology or nature of the business, (b) change in organizational structure or policy, and (c) personnel change. Some changes are difficult to classify neatly. For example, an organizational change might involve a change in structure and considerable shifts of personnel. Each type of change is then classified as having high or low impact. Severity of change theoretically represents a continuum from zero impact to highest impact.

SEVERITY OF CHANGE	TYPE OF CHANGE		
	Technology or Business	Structure or Policy	People
High Impact	**1.** Processes automated. "Business" of unit changes. Shift from mechanical to electrical design.	**2.** New incentive plan. Function to be phased out of organization. Work flow changed from purpose to process.	**3.** Unit head replaced. One-half of unit quits. Opposite leadership style is implemented.
Low Impact	**4.** More powerful computer installed. Unit provides one more service. Power tools substituted for hand tools.	**5.** Lunch hour changed. Unit reports to new place on organization chart. Organization changes name.	**6.** One person added to large unit. Poor performer is fired. Draftsman or secretary is added.

Figure 12.1 A taxonomy of some changes taking place within an organizational unit. (*Note*: These cells constitute only a sampling of changes that take place in organizational life.)

"High impact" and "low impact" are thus end positions on the continuum, not discrete categories.

What criteria are used to determine if a given change has a high or low impact? Research evidence about the relative impacts of specific changes on people is unavailable and would be difficult to obtain. For now a logical analysis based on direct familiarity with organizations must suffice as a basis for rating the impact of a given change. Three such criteria are:

(a) total number of people affected—the more people affected, the higher the impact;
(b) ramification in terms of the number of activities touched by the change—high-impact changes involve many more activities than do low-impact changes; and
(c) investment in resources—high-impact changes involve more substantial investments in time, money, machines, material, and people.

A third dimension could justifiably be added to this taxonomy. Changes in each of the six cells might be also described as functional or dysfunctional. Some changes, whether they are of high or low impact, help the system adapt (functional changes) while other changes of high or low impact are harmful to the system (dysfunctional changes). A systems model of change, presented in the following section, explores this concept further.

Cells 3 and 5 of Figure 12.1 will be explained in detail to assist in interpreting the Taxonomy of Change. The same interpretive approach can be applied to the remaining four cells in the Taxonomy. Readers should recognize that these cells constitute only a sampling of the population of changes that are present in organizational life.

Three relatively high impact changes involving personnel are mentioned in Cell 3 of the Taxonomy. The first situation mentioned is one in which the head of an organizational unit is replaced. In most organizations this brings about many changes in the operations of the unit. Subordinates must now rebuild (or in some cases avoid) the relationship they had established with the former superior. Many newly appointed managers will mandate changes merely for the sake of asserting their leadership. Informal work patterns that have developed are now subject to review and scrutiny. For example, one person within the department may have unofficially functioned as the number two man upon whom the former had relied for advice. The new superior may not wish to perpetuate this pattern. Standards of work performance may now also be raised or lowered by the new head (within the limits of his authority). Employees within the department who aspired to the department head may be disgruntled because they were confronted with the fact of being passed over. Poor performers within the department may experience elevated levels of apprehension about the prospects of a "new broom sweeping clean."

Half of a unit quitting at the same time—the second situation mentioned in Cell 3—also has a high impact. Productivity would probably be severely curtailed and the morale of the remaining workers will probably suffer. One advertising agency experienced the high-impact personnel change of five of the six account executives leaving simultaneously. Three years later the agency still had not recovered its former vitality. The dual loss of accounts and personnel made a comeback all but impossible.

A reversal of leadership style—the third situation in Cell 3—also has a heavy impact on organizational behavior. Shifts in leadership style may stem from the replacement of a leader or dramatic changes in the leader himself. For instance, it is not uncommon for an authoritarian leader to overcompensate and become an overly permissive leader as a result of leadership training. Subordinates encountering this situation usually have difficulty in coping with the situation. Some workers come to doubt the credibility of their changed leader. They might interpret being asked their opinion as a manipulative ploy. In time an opposite leadership style may be accepted, but the initial impact is severe.

Three changes in structure or policy of relatively minor impact are mentioned in Cell 5. Changing the policy about lunch hours has a relatively low impact on a department. Should the lunch hours be shortened, a few complaints will be forthcoming, but most mature people will make the necessary adjustments. Lengthening the lunch hour, similarly, has a low impact. A few people may feel elated at first, but such elation will be short lived. In general, the majority of managerial and professional people adjust their lunch break to fit their workload, and policies on this matter go unnoticed.

Large complex organizations have a passion for organizational changes. Quite often *to whom* (what person or department) a particular unit reports (e.g., public relations) will have a relatively low impact on workers within the department. People writing annual reports will be performing the same responsibilities whether their department reports to the vice-president of personnel or to the executive vice-president. The department head, however, may have major concern about the *power* of his unit as defined by the level to which the unit reports.

Changing the name of an organization—the third situation mentioned in Cell 5—has a negligible impact on most people within the organization. For example, changing the name of the American Standard and Sanitary

Corporation to American Standard may have helped disidentify that company with urinals, but people within the organization hardly noticed the change. Changes in letterheads and advertising may have the long-range impact of modifying the organizational climate, but the short-range impact is negligible.

A SYSTEMS MODEL OF CHANGE

A complex set of variables enters into the change process at the individual, group, or organizational level. Systems theory can be used to provide a useful framework for understanding the interrelationships among these variables. Figure 12.2 presents a basic model of this nature. Many of these variables—particularly those considered intervening variables—are discussed later in this chapter and in Chapter 13, which deals with change at the organizational level.

Inputs to the system are any attempts to bring about changes. Arbitrarily, attempts at change can be classified as stemming from direct influence techniques by management or from technology. Whether these changes have a positive (functional), neutral, or negative (dysfunctional) impact on the organization is a function of a large number of *intervening variables*. Variables of this nature mediate acceptance or rejection of such changes. Similarly, they also influence the nature of the consequences that will be forthcoming from the changes. For instance, no matter how technologically sound a proposed change, if the organization is too inflexible to accept change, neutral or negative consequences are likely to be forthcoming from the change.

The concept of "organic versus mechanistic" organization is an all-encompassing intervening variable that warrants separate mention. In addition to individual and group sources of resistance, certain structural features, role prescriptions, and values influence the receptivity of an organization to change. Developed originally by Tom Burns and G. M. Stalker in a study of 20 British electronics firms, they have recently been reformulated by John B. Miner.[3]

Organic organizations—those that have found it easy to adapt to changing environmental demands—have these characteristics:[4]

1. A close and direct relationship between individual role prescriptions and organizational goals.
2. Continual redefining of role prescriptions through the discussions with others.

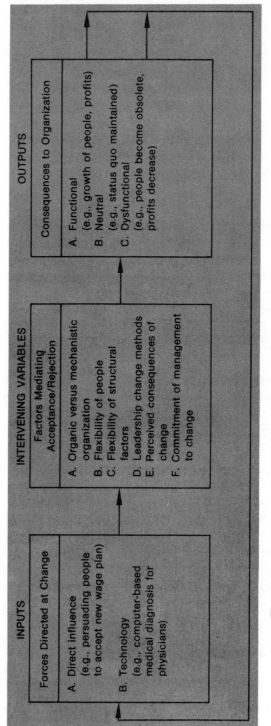

Figure 12.2 A systems model of change at the individual, group, and organizational level.

3. Rejection of the "it's not my responsibility" response as an excuse for failures.
4. The substitution of a broad sense of commitment to organizational goals in place of the inducements-contribution contract as a basis for work effort.
5. The presence of information and knowledge at various points in the organization network as appropriate to the task.
6. Stress on horizontal as opposed to vertical communication, and consultation rather than demand; hierarchy is minimized.
7. Strong commitment to task rather than maintenance goals, coupled with a status system which is often related to relevant outside reference groups.

Mechanistic organizations—those that resist change by their very nature—displayed opposite tendencies. One characteristic of mechanistic organizations not mentioned in connection with organic organizations is of particular interest to professionals. In general, members of mechanistic organizations formed close ties to their employer and his values rather than to outside reference groups such as a profession.[5]

EFFECTS OF CHANGE ON PEOPLE

Change affects different people in different ways. The specific impact of change is a function of (a) the magnitude and type of change and (b) the person's capacity to tolerate change. Losing one's wife and job within a one-month period, for example, would have negative effects on almost any man. In contrast, a change of lesser magnitude, such as being demoted, might precipitate hurt feelings in one person but be welcomed by another. Reactions to change can be major or minor, diffuse or focused, and psychological or physiological.

Stress Reactions

Future Shock, a best-selling book by Alvin Toffler delivers the central message that[6]

... there are discoverable limits to the amount of change that the human organism can absorb, and that by endlessly accelerating change without first determining these limits, we may submit masses of men to demands they simply cannot tolerate. We run the high risk of throwing them into that peculiar state that I have called future shock.

Limits to work-related change people can endure have not been researched, but reactions to other life changes have been measured. Toffler reports the development of a Life-Change Units Scale that provides some objective data about the relative impact of different changes. Thousands of men and women in the United States and Japan ranked various changes with respect to the impact these changes had on people. Widespread agreement was found as to which changes require major adjustment and which are comparatively unimportant. High-impact changes included items such as losing a spouse or being laid off from a job (and unable to find a new one). Low-impact changes included items such as moving to a new home or taking a vacation.[7] There are, of course, individual differences with respect to the impact of changes. For many people, moving into a new home is a traumatic experience involving a host of major and minor adjustments.

What happens when a person encounters changes ranked quite high on the Life-Change Units Scale? Not surprisingly, stress reactions similar to those described in Chapter 4 (e.g., psychosomatic disorders and emotional illness) are the result. Research data on this topic are strikingly clear; high rates of change and high rates of illness show a strong positive correlation.

Even among a physically healthy population—3000 sailors—the finding was true. Sailors in the top ten percent of Life-Change Scores turned out to suffer from one-and-a-half to two times as much illness as those in the bottom ten percent. Toffler hypothesizes that the curious phenomenon of one spouse dying shortly after his or her spouse had died is one more example of how people succumb to the stress of change.

Stress reactions resulting from rapid changes in the context of work can be quite severe, including cardiac difficulties. Milder stress reactions can also occur when the work group environment contains *too little* change. Energetic, eager individuals face the prospects of becoming restless, bored, listless, and frustrated when the work situation is devoid of "action."

Resistance

People resist change, particularly when the impending change threatens their financial or emotional security. Improvements in job efficiency, as a case in point, are usually resisted because the worker feels that a more efficient method of performing his job will make his personal contribution less important. When a person's unique contribution to the job is less important, that person can be replaced by a less-experienced (and lower-paid) employee. Described next is a sampling of ways in which people at work react to change with resistance.

Passive–aggressive behavior, or "expressing hostility through inaction" is one frequently observed form of resistance, as illustrated by the following two anecdotes:

> Spencer Ford, a professor of mechanical engineering, received a memo from his chairman indicating that the department was seriously considering changing the text used in the basic mechanical engineering course. Professor Ford had mixed feelings about the contemplated switch. On the positive side, a new book might be more current; on the negative side, this switch would require a substantial increase in preparation time. One month later Professor Ford attended a department meeting called to discuss the change in books. Asked his opinion, Ford replied: "I have no thoughts on the topic. I haven't had time to read the new text. Do what you want."

> Jim Brainard was a supervisor in a dairy plant. The company installed an automated ice cream making machine which, when fully implemented, would allow for a sharp reduction in personnel—a consequence that clashed with Jim's humanistic values. Three days after the installation of the machine, a group of executives from the home office scheduled a visit to observe the new ice cream machine. Embarrassingly, something went wrong with the machine that day. The "shut-off" control failed. Ice cream in three different flavors spewed out over the machine. A person could have stood knee deep in cream for a three-foot radius around the machine. Horrified, the plant superintendent (who served as tour guide for the visiting executives) demanded an explanation from Jim Brainard. "What was I supposed to do? Nobody gave me instructions on how to disengage an automatic ice cream machine."

Resentment is another common manifestation of resistance to change. According to George Strauss and Leonard R. Sayles, this resentment comes about primarily because change necessitates more orders from and control by management.[8] Instruction on how to comply with new changes, unfortunately, take on the form of orders. The following case history involving salesmen and a secretary describes how a simple administrative change can evoke strained interpersonal relationships and resentment:

> Ramsey Safe Company elected to carefully control expenditures for toll calls. Under a new procedure, salesmen would be required to submit monthly reports indicating all long distance business calls they made the preceding month. Each call was to be followed by a notation explaining why each call was made; specifically to whom and for what purpose. Toll calls were to be made, with rare exceptions, only to customers, customer prospects, and, in rare instances, suppliers. Salesmen resented the additional piece of paper work required by this

control procedure. Stronger resentment, however, was soon to follow. Characteristically, the sales manager's secretary—the person responsible for collecting this information—would ask for clarification on many of the reports. One of her more poignant phrases was: "Should this call you made on ————— be classified as business or personal?" Salesmen resented being controlled by a secretary because they felt she had lower occupational rank than they had.

Direct aggressive behavior is the most dramatic approach to resisting change. Resignation, absenteeism, requests for transfer, and sabotage can all represent manifestations of resistance to change. An MBA student who worked for several years on the assembly line of a major automotive plant reports the following case example of aggressive resistance to change:

> You should have seen what happened in that plant. The company decided to automate the plant for this new automobile to the fullest extent possible. As it worked out, the whole plant looked like some kind of science fiction, so few people were needed to run the line. As you can imagine the union and the workers didn't go for this maneuver by management. All of a sudden these new ————— started coming off the line all screwed up. Upholstery was slashed with knives, exterior paint was scratched, bulbs were missing from tail lights, and hinges were missing from some doors. Everybody said management wouldn't get away with automating the hell out of a plant, and the workers were proving it.

Labor strikes might also be conceived of as large-scale direct aggressive behavior symptomatic of resistance to change. However, this generalization requires some narrowing. First, the majority of strikes are a response to changes *desired* by labor, not changes made by management. Second, the implication should not be drawn that all strikes are unwarranted or that all changes suggested by management are constructive. Labor leaders have on occasion called a strike to force changes in physically harmful working conditions. Attempts to organize migrant farm workers reflect a strike of this nature.

Welcoming Change

Pessimistic responses to change have been the center of attention so far. Many changes taking place in organizations are welcomed by managers and individual workers. Change is usually welcomed if people perceive the change as enhancing their well-being. Rare would be the circumstances under which people resist salary increases, extended vacation, pretty secretaries, or handsome office boys. Eugene Falk, an industrial engineer and assistant production manager, has provided information about the introduction of physical changes in the composing room of a medium-size newspaper:[9]

> Close to $200,000 was authorized to completely revamp this old-fashioned composing room. Carpeting was provided not only for the floors but for the columns as well. Complete climate control was instituted, whereas in the past the room was not air conditioned. Acoustical tile was installed. Even office landscaping was generously applied. According to our standard productivity measures, production increased dramatically. Printers who were accustomed to dressing in a "workingman's motif" now came to the composing room in jackets and ties. Absenteeism was down, and people appeared more cheerful. Morale increased so much that measuring the change would be belaboring the obvious. Many of the printers and their supervisors mentioned they now had much more respect for their jobs. Nobody believed when I requested the money for these changes that so much could be accomplished simply by modifying working conditions.

The above comments were recorded six months after physical working conditions had been improved. Similar changes in morale and productivity were not forthcoming from the control group—a comparable composing room in the same organization. Even if these improvements in morale and productivity were a function of the Hawthorne Effect (difference might have been attributable to the fact that management paid extra attention to employees), it does not dismiss the notion that some change is welcomed. ·

Just as some families enjoy the process of relocation (admittedly they are in the minority), some work groups like change for its own sake. During the 1960s teams of scientific and technical personnel migrated from one Southern California aerospace company to another, depending upon which company received the latest major government contract. Some members of these teams welcomed relocation of this type as a fringe benefit of their profession.

ATTITUDES AND ATTITUDE CHANGE

The management of change implicitly involves coping with people's attitudes toward change. In the following sections of this chapter we will examine why people resist change, what types of change people resist, and methods to reduce resistance to change. In addition, we will examine methods of encouraging some types of changes—those dealing with technological innovation. A brief inquiry into the nature of attitudes and attitude change is essential to avoid an oversimplification of this fundamental topic in organizational behavior. Overcoming resistance to change, for example, is but a special case of attitude change.

What is an Attitude?

An attitude, as defined by Abraham K. Korman (and many others), is a type of affective reaction, either pleasant or unpleasant, which a person may have toward some object in his or her environment.[10] According to John P. Campbell and his associates, an attitude has at least three components.[11] First, the *cognitive* component refers to the knowledge or intellectual beliefs that an individual might have toward an object. For instance, a market researcher might have accumulated considerable factual information about statistics (particular methods, tests of significance, etc.). Second, the *feeling* or *affective* component refers to the emotions connected with that object. The market researcher in question might basically dislike statistical analysis due to some unpleasant experiences in college associated with statistics. Third, the *behavioral* component refers to how a person acts. This market researcher might make negative statements about statistical methods or avoid their use in his reports.

How Do You Change Attitudes?

Thousands of studies have dealt with this topic from a variety of perspectives. Almost any text in social psychology contains a chapter about the complexities of attitude change.[12] Assume that a 29-year-old female accountant is appointed manager of accounts payable in a hospital, replacing a male manager who has retired. She has appropriate education and experience for the position. Reporting to her are five male accountants and bookkeepers, ages 44, 46, 47, 51, and 56. Assume also that her subordinates have negative attitudes toward being supervised by someone younger and/or female. This situation will be used to explain the nature of five different methods of attitude change. Attitude change in organizational settings usually is brought about by using a combination of these methods.[13]

Communication of additional information. Management would need to add to the base of intellectual knowledge these men have about the capabilities of female managers. Department members should be apprised that Ms. X has appropriate credentials for the position, perhaps including the vital item of information that she is a Certified Public Accountant. Information should also be provided that radical changes in the working procedures of the department are not anticipated (if this is true). Working with the new manager will provide some concrete evidence about her competence.

Approval and disapproval. Rewards and incentives should be reasonably related to desired changes in attitudes. To the extent that department members display more positive attitudes toward being managed by a female, they should receive rewards. Perhaps mention of "cooperation with the management" should be included in the performance appraisal. Should the value of the reward (e.g., salary increase) exceed the value of maintaining an original attitude (resistance to being supervised by a female), changes in attitude, and perhaps behavior, are likely to be forthcoming. Displays of negative attitudes toward the new manager should be countered with disapproval. Withholding of cooperation might be met with withholding of a portion of an anticipated salary increase.

Group influences. One effective method of attitude change would be for group members with negative attitudes toward female supervision to interact with group members with positive attitudes toward female supervision. Under the case illustration given, this might involve encouraging the first "convert" to enter into informal discussion about the topic with co-workers. Group influences are likely to be the strongest if the informal leader changes his attitudes toward the concept of being managed by a young woman.

Being induced to engage in discrepant behavior. In laboratory studies subjects have been asked to assume the attitudes of persons with opposite viewpoints. Engaging in such discrepant behavior often brings about changes in attitude. The organization development technique of *image exchanging*, described in the following chapter, capitalizes on this concept. Department members in the situation under consideration will be required to engage in behavior contrary to their attitude. For instance, they will find it necessary to at least approach their new manager with administrative problems. Assuming that these problems are handled in a manner satisfactory to her subordinates, gradual shifts in attitude may take place.

Adapt change methods to individual differences. Few work groups are monolithic in their attitudes. Of the five men, one or two may be much less rigid in their attitudes than the other three. These individual differences should be taken into account. To further illustrate, one of the five men might be a highly defensive person who must be approached gradually and cautiously. Another person might be quite open himself and can be confronted directly about his attitudes toward being supervised by a female manager much younger than himself.

WHY PEOPLE RESIST CHANGE

Some types of change are resisted by some people in some situations. When change is resisted in the context of work it is usually resisted for reasons important to the person or group potentially affected by the changes. Both economic and emotional factors underlie resistance to change as suggested by the analyses of several writers.[14] Joseph Tiffin and Ernest J. McCormick have developed a conception of resistance to change that parallels closely an *expectancy theory* of motivation (refer back to Chapter 2). People develop subjective hunches about whether change will be harmful or helpful to them and base their attitude and behavior accordingly. In the words of Tiffin and McCormick:[15]

> The prospect of some change in an individual's situation typically brings about some speculation—vague or definitive—as to the *nature* of various possible consequences (outcomes) to him; as to the *probabilities* of the various outcomes; and as to the *values* (plus or minus) of the various possible outcomes. If these tend to add up to the strong likelihood of probable gains to the individual, he would adopt a favorable attitude regarding the change. If these add up to the strong likelihood of loss to the individual, he would be inclined toward resisting the change. And, if . . . he is left in a state of considerable *uncertainty* about the possible outcomes he might tend toward taking a dim view of the whole affair.

Economic Reasons

Money weighs heavily in the considerations of people; particularly for those who feel they lack sufficient funds to comfortably meet all their expenses. Changes that pose the possibility of lowering a person's income directly or indirectly are thus resisted with force. Economically based resistance to change is common not only to production workers and salesmen; executives have been known to complain about or openly resist changes in executive compensation packages that have the potential of decreasing their earnings:

> All employees at the middle levels of management and above in a kitchen supplies manufacturing company participated generously in a

company profit-sharing plan. During one highly profitable year, no member of the management team made less than $27,000. Earnings of people below these levels of management were modest by general industrial standards. The year following this management bonanza, the company was bought by a larger organization. One of the first changes implemented was a new company-wide compensation plan that narrowed the difference between managers and employee salaries. In practice this meant that the incomes of nonmanagers would be elevated, while the average manager bonus would be substantially reduced. Managers bitterly complained that their "motivation was being destroyed," and several years later were still suggesting a return to the original compensation system.

Professional people, also, are not exempt from resisting change, at least in part, for economic reasons. Developed in recent years, "do-it-yourself-divorce-kits" provide the purchaser with a flow chart of activities that enables a person to obtain a divorce without engaging the services of an attorney. Lawyers, individually and in concert, have vociferously denounced this change in the traditional way of obtaining a divorce. A genuine desire to protect the public interest may underlie some of this resistance to change, but much of the resistance appears to be economically based. (A substantial portion of a general law practitioner's income is derived from divorce proceedings.) The efforts of lawyers to block the passage of no-fault automobile insurance lends itself to an identical analysis.

Fear of the Unknown

Confronting the unknown makes most people somewhat anxious and each significant change in the work situation carries with it an element of uncertainty. Contemplates the engineer: "What might happen if I relocate to Vermont for the company? Will my family like it? Suppose I get laid off, then we will probably have to relocate again." Uncertainty is involved not so much in the change itself, but in the *consequences* of the change. Consequences of almost any change are difficult to predict with scientific precision. For example, a newly appointed scientific director of a consumer products company made the following policy statement: "Too much of our research and development dollar has been put into research. Our needs for the near future are to develop some products that can be swiftly brought to the marketplace." Many scientific personnel would feel "up-tight" about the potential consequences of this policy decision, even though no one consequence is absolutely certain. Among the anxiety-provoking potential consequences are these:

1. Company scientists and engineers who enjoy basic research can anticipate a loss in job satisfaction.
2. "Blue sky" thinkers will be either transferred or fired.
3. Research scientists will suffer a diminution in power in comparison to
   development types. When a development engineer needs additional
   help, research engineers will be assigned to his project.

Fear of the unknown experienced by an individual's family about the
consequences of change can contribute to that individual's uneasiness.
For example, a homemaker obtained a job as a mutual fund saleswoman.
Her husband, a dentist, was anxious about the ramifications of this
change on the family welfare. Her school-age children also expressed apprehension about the shift in their life style. Family anxieties in turn influenced the woman to express concern about her ability to manage her new
dual role in life.

Threats to Interpersonal Relationships

"How to Deal with Resistance to Change," a classic article by Paul R.
Lawrence, contends that employees really do not resist technical change.
What they do resist is the change in their human relationships that generally accompanies technical change. Organizational changes (as described in
the next chapter) have the most dramatic effect on breaking up established
patterns of interpersonal relationships. Changes in machines also usually
bring about some personnel shifts necessitating the formation of new working relationships. Professional personnel as well as production and clerical
workers sometimes resist change because of its effect upon their fixed pattern of interpersonal relationships.

Tony Placito was an internal financial consultant on the corporate staff
of a multidivision organization. His pattern of operation was to visit
about 15 plants to advise them about financial matters such as implementing new financial systems. One day a new directive was issued relating to company travel. All trips to company installations were to be
avoided unless they involved an emergency problem. This cost-cutting
maneuver meant that Tony Placito would now become a "backroom
financial analyst," rarely visiting operating personnel. His primary
media of communication would now be letters and telephone calls.
Tony protested to management that he could not carry out his job
effectively via long distance. He felt that his real contribution to the
company stemmed from the quality of interpersonal relationships he
had established with general managers and financial people in field
installations. In his absence they would no longer seek his advice, and

his contribution to the company would dwindle. Tony resisted this policy change by management in large measure because many of the rewards from his job stemmed from the warm working relationships he had established with people. Conducting financial analyses had become a distant second in terms of job satisfaction.

Inconvenience

". . . understandable is the resistance to change that threatens to make life more difficult" state Strauss and Sayles.[16] Change, for whatever merits it possesses, inevitably brings about some inconvenience, and very few people (except those who enjoy playing the martyr role) welcome personal inconvenience. Company relocation is perhaps the ultimate act of imposing inconvenience upon employees. Obtaining a new operator's license, selling and buying a home, reregistering children in school, buying new draperies, and establishing working relationships with a new secretary are but among a sampling of the inconveniences an executive faces in relocating. Even those who quit rather than relocate face the inconvenience of finding new employment. To circumvent the inconveniences of relocation, some people refuse promotions. One higher level manager sold life insurance and another opened a bicycle sales and service store rather than contend with the changes involved in relocation. Neither manager was opposed to change itself. Both were willing to change occupations, but neither was willing to endure the inconvenience of relocation.

REDUCING RESISTANCE TO CHANGE

Adaptation to change is a characteristic that weighs heavily in an organization's chances for survival. As stated by H. Igor Ansoff in his predictions about the future: "In the modern world adaptive change is a requirement for survival, and innovative change a condition for success."[17] Coupling this observation with the idea that many people resist change, the ability of a manager to reduce resistance to change is magnified in importance. Approaches to reducing change discussed next are based on fundamental knowledge of how humans behave in organizations, rather than specifically on the results of large-scale research investigation.

Select Positive People

A basic but infrequently mentioned principle is that resistance to change can be reduced by selecting as employees those individuals least likely to resist change. Implementing such a principle takes one into the field of personnel selection—a complex set of considerations that lie beyond the scope of this book.[18] Generalizing, those people least resistant to change are people who benefit from most changes. Upwardly mobile, capable, intelligent, and self-confident people tend to welcome most types of change. Age itself is not inevitably related to this positive orientation toward change. Older people, in general, resist change more than their younger counterparts, but many exceptions exist. Many younger people resist change, while many older people are heavily change-oriented.

Flexibility is another synonym for a positive orientation to change. This aspect of behavior is pervasive. Employees who are flexible about relocation are more probably the same individuals who will show flexibility in accepting changes in work methods, fellow employees, and management. In short, the manager who is able to fill his or her department with flexible individuals will have the best chances of managing change. One corollary is that resistance to change can be reduced by replacing (transferring or firing) inflexible with flexible employees. (Note that this approach is not recommended from a humanistic standpoint but its effectiveness cannot be readily dismissed.)

Avoid Coercive Tactics

Resistance to change is often lowered by the expedient of coercing the people involved into accepting the change. Strauss and Sayles term this approach *overcoming* resistance, in contrast to *reducing* resistance.[19] Threatening to fire a manager if he refuses to relocate, suspending a waitress until she consents to wearing a new topless uniform, or reducing a salesman's pay until he complies with completing a new form required by the company are all examples of coercive tactics. The primary effectiveness of these power tactics is short range. Many employees will endure changes or other inconveniences in the short range to protect their economic security while they seek employment elsewhere.

Another drawback of using coercive tactics to reduce resistance to change is that these tactics may increase covert resentment and tension. Assume that a technical products company decides that each chemist no longer requires one full-time laboratory technician to assist him. Chemists may argue that management is wrong; the proper ratio of chemist to technician is one to one. Management then declares that any chemist unwilling to accept a 50 percent reduction in the technician staff is invited to leave the company. Chemists who feel adamant about this issue will perceive the management policy of "like it or leave it" as a coercive tactic.

Resentment will accumulate and resistance to change may manifest itself in subtle areas such as diminished creative output. Added to covert resistance is the accumulation of tension and strained feelings about the technician layoff. In short, resistance to change has been suppressed through coercion, but dysfunctional consequences have taken place.

Provide Valid Information

When resistance to change stems from fear of the unknown, valid information about the scope and content of the forthcoming changes will help reduce resistance. Valid information in this context refers to information about the changes that later proves to be essentially correct. It is difficult for management to accurately predict all the ramifications of a given change, but major distortions of the truth must be avoided. Should the information presented about forthcoming changes prove to be invalid the credibility gap will hamper future communications. Reducing resistance to change by the presentation of valid information is illustrated by the experience of a heavy equipment manufacturing company in closing down a plant.

> Capital Equipment Corporation, based on extensive financial analyses, concluded that it would be economic to phase out its Jersey City plant and simultaneously expand its facility in Charlotte, North Carolina. The president and the Jersey City plant general manager jointly chaired a conference with plant management. Personnel were told that all supervisors and technical personnel would be given the opportunity to transfer to the southern plant after the phase out. It was also carefully spelled out that phasing out the plant, according to industry-wide experience, could take anywhere from three months to one year; bonuses would be awarded for a swift phasing out of plant operations. Within two weeks, the personnel manager was authorized to review with each interested employee details about company policy on reimbursement of relocation expenses. In addition, the company authorized one round trip to Charlotte for each interested supervisor or technical person and his or her spouse.

> Observers of this plant shut down were impressed by the ease with which this complicated mission was accomplished. Other factors may have contributed (e.g., a long history of positive human relations), but the presentation of valid information about the changes (especially the bonus and the invited transfers) appeared to play a key role in overcoming resistance to change.

Minimize Social Changes

Resistance to change can be softened if social relationships important to the individual are not disrupted by the change, following the logic of Paul R. Lawrence mentioned earlier. Some types of change, such as relocation, inevitably result in social changes unless an entire organization is relocated. Other types of change provide more opportunity for keeping established interpersonal relationships intact despite a change in technology or policy. The situation of one medium company shows how social relationships can be kept intact, despite major changes in policy.

> Eastern Scientific Corporation was a venerable supplier of laboratory equipment and chemicals to schools, hospitals, and industrial companies throughout its region. Company salesmen made periodic visits to customers and 90 percent of the sales went to a group of the same established customers. Selling, in this context, consisted primarily of taking orders from a lengthy catalog. Based upon advice received from a management consultant who studied the situation, Eastern Scientific decided to make a drastic shift in its method of distribution. Outside selling was to be replaced by an enlarged and improved inside sales departments. The new procedure was carefully explained to the customers, and most seemed to prefer ordering by mail or telephone than having to spend time with the salesman who visited their premises. Salesmen, many of whom had been calling on the same customers for years, felt that the personal bonds they had built up with customers would be broken. Considerable resistance was expressed about now becoming "inside order takers." The company devised a simple plan to avoid disruption of these valued social relationships. Four out of the six outside salesmen were retained. Each was assigned as a service representative to his old list of customers (plus a share of the other unassigned customers). Key to the service representatives' job was to provide customers an outlet for complaints, answer special questions, and visit customers under unusual circumstances.

> After a short period of time, these four salesmen welcomed their new positions. They had retained some contact with old social ties and had a less physically demanding job (important because of the advanced age of these salesmen). Profits were increased because approximately the same sales volume was retained minus the cost of two salesmen and most of the travel expenses.

Avoid Preoccupation with Technology

Staff specialists, more than any other occupational group within an organization, confront resistance to change. Resistance to the suggestions of staff specialists comes from above and below. First, the staff person must overcome the resistance of higher management to have his program initiated. Second, the resistance of people at the operating level must be overcome in order to have the changes implemented. Lawrence claims that many of these resistances might be lowered if staff people would concentrate more on observing the reactions of people and less on their own methods, techniques, and purposes. People affected by changes are more concerned about these effects than upon the technical features of the change method or the change agent.[20] Next is an account of how one industrial engineer encountered resistance to change because of his self-preoccupation.[21]

> An industrial engineer undertook to introduce some methods changes in one department with the notion firmly in mind that this assignment presented him with an opportunity to "prove" to higher management the value of his function. He became so preoccupied with his personal desire to make a name for his particular techniques that he failed to pay any attention to some fairly obvious and practical considerations which the operating people were calling to his attention but which did not show up in his time-study techniques. As could be expected, resistance quickly developed to all his ideas, and the only "name" that he finally won for his techniques was a black one.

The interpretation should not be drawn from the above material that the majority of staff specialists are insensitive to the human factors crucial to the acceptance of their programs. In this writer's experiences, most industrial engineers see themselves as part-time applied behavioral scientists who must deal more with people than with things or ideas.

Make Changes Tentative

Finality has a mild shock effect upon many people. Reversible changes are more palatable to most people than irreversible changes. Sales strategists are well aware of this aspect of human behavior. Typewriter salesmen often suggest that a customer simply try their brand for a period of time. Should the result prove satisfactory, the customer can then purchase the typewriter—but still with a return allowed policy. Situations do not abound where changes can be made on a tentative basis. The installation of major equipment, the reduction in a work force, or the redefinition of a department's function are all changes difficult to reverse. Strauss and Sayles give two reasons why allowing employees to go along with a change on a tentative, trial basis helps to reduce resistance to change: (a) employees can test their own reactions and obtain more facts about the new situation; and (b) a tentative change helps "unfreeze" attitudes and encourages people to think objectively about the proposed change.[22]

> The vice-president of administrative services in an insurance company, on the basis of information fed him from below, suggested a major change in secretarial services for all but the first two levels of management. Instead of having private secretaries, or even sharing secretaries, all work would now be funneled into a secretarial pool. Anticipated benefits from this new procedure from the company standpoint were (a) a steadier, more even flow of work for secretaries, and (b) fewer secretaries and typists would be needed, thus bringing about a cost savings. Reactions to these changes were at first quite negative. Middle managers made such varied claims as: "Only a private secretary can read my handwriting," and "this is the last step in depersonalizing this outfit." The vice-president of administration then slightly altered his policy. Managers were encouraged to try the secretarial pool system on a trial three-month basis. If the system proved to be inefficient and cumbersome, a return to the decentralized typing and secretarial services would be made.
>
> Resistance to this change did lower after about one month of experience. Managers found that they now spent less time dealing with personnel problems and that the quality of work (the secretarial pool included a "quality control" function) improved. Petty status problems about who shared a secretary versus who had exclusive access to one were also minimized.

Use Shared Decision Making

Axiomatic to lowering resistance to change is to allow people to participate in the changes affecting them. The underlying dynamics of this situation are uncomplicated. When an individual or group of individuals contributes ideas to a proposed change, disapproving or resisting that change later is the equivalent of disagreeing with oneself. Caution must be drawn, however, about the universal applicability of shared decision making as an approach to reducing resistance to change. Participation of this type works best when management is relatively indifferent to what the group decides. For example, top management may not care how middle management improves profitability, so long as profitability is changed for the better. Strauss and Sayles note that when a group finds participation in decision making foreign to its way of life, participation will not work effectively; in turn, resistance to change will not be lowered.[23] In addition, a small minority of people prefer to avoid any responsibility for decision making.

Readers may recognize that shared decision making might be viewed as a composite of some of the approaches to reducing resistance already discussed. For instance, allowing for tentative changes provides people with an opportunity to exercise decision-making authority about the change—they can ultimately reject the change. Selecting positive people almost insures that shared decision making will transpire. Enthusiastic workers welcome the opportunity to assist in decision making and may volunteer to bring about constructive changes within their work groups.

Management consultants, both internal and external, rely heavily on the potency of shared decision making in lowering resistance to change. Organizational planning represents one case in point. In most studies conducted prior to recommending organizational changes, managers and employees are asked their opinion about what changes should be made. Often the final report to top management consists largely of an integration of the ideas for restructuring suggested by individuals further down in the organization.

Use Economic Incentives

Obviously, money is still important to most people in any organization. Many of their fears about change stem from a concern that the contemplated change will reduce their personal income. Changes that promise to increase the income of people affected will usually be endorsed with enthusiasm. Changes that threaten to reduce individual income will be protested with vigor. In rare situations where management can guarantee that the proposed changes will not reduce income, resistance to change will correspondingly be reduced.

MANAGING TECHNOLOGICAL INNOVATION

Emphasis in the preceding section has been placed on reducing or preventing resistance to change. Approaches such as providing economic incentives for accepting change have an almost *defensive* quality. A major challenge facing management is to also develop a climate that actually encourages change and innovation before resistance sets in. *Offensive* strategies may be called for in such situations. Donald A. Schon underscores the importance of technological innovation in describing it as the "lifeblood of the firm," a contention shared by perhaps thousands of businessmen.[24] Technological innovation must also be considered a major force in creating new markets.

Organizational behavior, as a body of knowledge, has not provided definitive answers as to what managerial practices encourage technological innovation. Nevertheless, Donald R. Schoen (not to be confused with the writer just mentioned) has provided some fruitful information about encouraging technological innovation based on a review of literature and his consulting experience.[25] The five propositions presented next stem from the conclusions he presents about the management of technological innovation.

1. *Many people resist technological innovation, despite stated attitudes to the contrary.* Schoen observes that in every organization, forces for stability exist that work against innovation. Management must recognize these forces and deal with them in a positive manner instead of treating them as "annoying aberrations." Methods of reducing resistance to change discussed earlier in the chapter are also germane here. Many tangible reasons exist as to why so many people resist technological innovation. When significant technological change takes place in an organization, many machines, people, and customary ways of doing things automatically become obsolete. Donald A. Schon provides an analysis of the underlying negative attitudes many people have toward innovation:[26]

> Technical innovation is dangerous, disruptive and uncertain. It is the enemy of orderly, planned activity. It changes everything about the business we are in. It hurts. Let us talk about it, study it, espouse it—anything but do it!

2. *Flexibility in organizational structure and leadership styles may be required to encourage innovation.* Evidence is lacking about what specific type of organization, structure, or leadership style is consistently the most effective in encouraging technological innovation. Some research exists that suggests the need for flexibility in organization patterns. Tom Burns and G. M. Stalker reported the results of 20 studies in England concerned with the relationship between technological innovation and organizational system. A positive correlation was found between ". . . success in technological innovation and the adoption of an 'organic' (as opposed to 'mechanistic') system of organization."[27]

As reported in Chapter 2, Jack R. Gibb notes that the wrong type of leadership climate can reduce the need for creative expression. According to Gibb, managers release creativity by acting in a trustful and open manner. Defensive behavior, in contrast, tends to inhibit creative expression. He summarizes some evidence that creativity in organizations has actually been increased in a variety of ways. Among these is the use of sensitivity training to encourage greater openness, more free communication, and the sharing of creative ideas:[28]

> The evidence is indirect and inconclusive, but highly suggestive, that this increased openness has an accelerating effect upon productive creativity within the organization.

3. *Innovators, entrepreneurs, product champions, or other similarly committed individuals are essential to innovation in organizations.* At several points throughout this text, attention is focused on the importance of the well-motivated, creative individual. Such a person is the basic building block of innovation in organizations. (Chapter 3 on decision making described the psychological makeup of creative people.) Schoen notes the widespread endorsement for the belief that innovation is dependent upon individuals committed to ideas. Even in large, complex organizations, successful inventors tend to be obsessed with the importance of their ideas. Hearings from a Senate subcommittee that dealt with innovation are cited by Schoen to corroborate his conclusion:[29]

> Expert witnesses were asked to provide background on how innovation takes place. Many of them devoted much of their testimony to describing the tenacity with which inventors pushed their ideas to fruition. Included were Richard Walton and the shrink-proofing of knitted goods, Samuel Ruben and the mercury battery, and Chester Carlson and xerography.

4. *Significant innovations are likely to stem from sources outside the organization.* Documentation of this conclusion about technological innovation is substantial. A Commerce Department panel study lists 33 significant contributions of 20th century independent inventors. Most of these were translated into commercial successes by larger organizations. A 30-year study of innovations by DuPont indicates that a greater number came from outside than inside that organization. Independent inventors usually do not have at their command the financial or manpower resources necessary to translate inventions into a marketable product. Of greater behavioral importance is the question, "Why do disproportionately few technological inventions take place in large organizations?"

One possible answer to this question comes from Robert Schlaifer.[30] He implies that some breakthrough ideas go unnoticed because they are competing for management attention with other, less innovative ideas or projects. James R. Bright suggests that the basic function of most R&D

departments appears to be development and product improvement rather than basic or pure research. Emphasis is placed on more certain short-term gain, rather than on the "uncertain, long-term revolution." Individual inventors are willing to take bigger, long-term risks. Bright also notes:[31]

> Sources of ideas are not necessarily found in the logical places. This means that an explicit recognition-appraisal effort or system is needed to find these new ideas and to give them an open-minded consideration.

5. *Significant technological innovations will most probably take place in organizations where top management is committed to innovation in both words and action.* Schoen notes that this conclusion is more implicit than explicit in the literature of technological innovation. Upper levels of management are almost always involved in any radical innovation that takes place, whether the project is large, medium, or small. In general, it can be concluded that the proper management of innovation requires attitudes of commitment, experimentation, and a willingness to take risks. A commitment of this nature also requires substantial financial support. Venture capital and entrepreneurial thinking are both required to carry an innovative idea to the marketplace.

MANAGERIAL AND PROFESSIONAL OBSOLESCENCE

What happens when a manager, professional, or technical person is unable or unwilling to accept change? Obsolescence—that situation where a once-capable manager or professional person loses some of his or her former effectiveness—is usually the result. According to some fragmentary data, it has been estimated that approximately ten percent of managerial and professional people are obsolete to the point that their job performance suffers. An extensive discussion of obsolescence is available elsewhere.[32,33,34] Sufficient for now is an overview of obsolescence from the standpoint of its underlying factors, treatment, and prevention.

Factors Underlying Obsolescence

Managerial and professional obsolescence stem from a broad range of individual, organizational, and environmental factors. Many of the individual responses to stress discussed in Chapter 4 are also factors that predispose one toward becoming obsolete. Among these are emotional and physical disorders, alcoholism, and drug addiction. Even without the influence of stress some people become obsolete. Certain personality traits and behavioral characteristics predispose one toward obsolescence. Included here are a decrease in work motivation, limited intelligence for the demands of a job, rigid attitudes, limited physical energy, and advanced chronological age. However, there is no linear relationship between age and obsolescence. Some managers and professional people become obsolete in their early thirties, while others play an active and dominant role in their organizations up until, and sometimes beyond, retirement.

People become obsolete within the context of an organization. The case of Roger Wingate illustrates how the combination of personal problems and being disappointed by an employer can combine to precipitate obsolescence.

> Roger Wingate, age 37, is the manager of internal operations (the "cage") at a small brokerage firm. His job performance has been rated satisfactory, but the managing partner informs him that a new manager is being brought into the firm as director of administration, to whom Roger will report. Roger and his wife have six children. A week after learning he has been passed over for promotion, Roger's wife is involved in an automobile accident. The medical prognosis is that his wife will live but she will be immobilized for approximately six months.

> Roger exhibits changes in his work behavior. He fails to communicate vital information to his boss. The content of his written reports are difficult to interpret. Two female supervisors reporting to Roger resign from the firm, complaining of poor treatment from their boss. According to their testimony, Roger has taken to criticizing them publicly about taking excessive coffee breaks and tolerating inadequate performance on the part of their subordinates. He calls a staff meeting and threatens to fire "anybody else who thinks first of himself and last of the firm." Roger's atypical behavior is further brought to the attention of the firm when he writes a letter to the manufacturer of the company's computer. This letter describes what he considers to be "malicious sales practices"; specifically, that they have sold his firm a computer with capabilities well beyond the firm's needs.

Organizations must share some responsibility for managerial and professional obsolescence. Through its policies and practices the organization can foster obsolescence of some of its members. Three such influences will be mentioned here to provide some preliminary insight into the relationship between organizational variables and obsolescence.

Promotion of individuals into positions beyond their capabilities. This phenomenon constitutes the basis for the widely mentioned

Peter Principle: "In a hierarchy every employee tends to rise to his level of incompetence."[35] From our viewpoint, *The Peter Principle* should more correctly state: In every organization where sophisticated systems of promoting individuals are not utilized, some individuals will be elevated to positions beyond their capability. Organizations that rely on the most up-to-date internal selection systems will also commit occasional over-promotions because no selection system is error free.

Narrow work assignments. Managerial and professional work assignments can be sufficiently narrow to contribute to obsolescence in two important ways. First, over-specialization in one task can contribute to a narrowness of outlook which makes an individual poorly equipped for broader assignments in the future. Second, task specialization can lead to boredom, apathy, indifference, and perhaps other symptoms of job challenge loss. These attitudes in turn manifest themselves as a decrease in former effectiveness.

Inappropriate leadership climate. Working under a manager with a leadership style inappropriate to the situation can contribute to obsolescence by blocking intellectual and professional growth. Simply stated, it is difficult to prevent becoming obsolete when you work for a manager (or managers) over a long period of time who inhibits your development. An inappropriate leadership style has been shown to dampen motivation and growth.[36]

Factors external to individuals and organizations can also contribute to managerial and professional obsolescence. Sudden shifts in the preferences of consumers, clients, students, or any user of products or services can suddenly obsolete individuals. A trade institute that specializes in teaching drafting might be forced to drastically reduce the number of these courses because many engineering drawings are now produced through automation.

H. Bedrosian has illustrated how an environmental shift contributed to managerial obsolescence.[37] When the banking industry changed swiftly from a "wholesaler" of money to a "retailer," new managerial capabilities in data processing and marketing were needed. Emphasis changed from a managerial group made up basically of technicians to a group required to manage data processing technicians (in new branch operations to serve the retail business). This new orientation in work patterns obsoleted many managers, many of whom were passed over for promotion or placed into positions of lesser responsibility.

Interventions in Obsolescence

In some instances the process of managerial or professional obsolescence is reversible or arrestable. Ideally, remedial measures taken in a given case of obsolescence would be specifically related to the contributing or underlying factors. If a manager becomes obsolete because of having been overshadowed by an authoritarian boss, a rigorous program of "independence training" might reverse the obsolete behavior pattern. In practice, remedial measures taken are usually more general and less tied to specific etiological factors.

Interventions helpful in dealing with obsolescence can be classified under two broad approaches: *job change* and *developmental programs*. Reliance on both approaches is more likely to bring about change than reliance on either. For example, a manager whose managerial style is appropriate for his present position might be reassigned to another position with different leadership demands. In this new position he might attend a Managerial Grid training seminar to gather more insight into different leadership styles.

Among the several types of job changes is firing. Proponents of firing an obsolete manager have observed that such an action shocks a person into understanding the impact of his or her mistakes. Another point of view is that firing a person without offering some genuine corrective measures has two important disadvantages. First, it is humiliating for the fired person. Second, responsibility for handling the obsolete person is only transferred from the organization that fires the person to another organization that eventually hires him or her.

Prevention of Obsolescence

Prevention of managerial obsolescence may be more effective than intervention after the process of obsolescence has already begun. Because managerial and professional obsolescence is multidetermined, its prevention would require attention to a wide range of individual characteristics and organization practices. Individuals have substantial responsibility for preventing their own obsolescence, but there are certain organizational programs, practices, procedures, and values that can help minimize the frequency and severity of managerial and professional obsolescence. Scientifically sound approaches to the selection, performance measurement, and development of managers and professionals represent an important starting point in this direction. Combining these approaches with an attempt to measure and modify organizational practices that stifle (prevent self-fulfillment of) individuals would further decrease the severity and frequency of such obsolescence. An *organic* organization, as described earlier, should be helpful in preventing obsolescence stemming from an inability to accept change. Robert J. House has described an ideal climate for management development that, if attainable, would probably also prevent many instances of managerial and professional obsolescence. These ideal environmental conditions are quoted directly:[38]

1. Managers at all levels in the organization understand the overall objectives of the business.
2. The basic principles, intentions, values, assumptions and beliefs of top management and each manager's superior are communicated and understood.
3. The particular functions or activities of each member of the organization are clearly understood by that member and by those with whom he deals.
4. Responsibility and authority have been delegated to the extent that each manager is challenged by his responsibilities and has the opportunity to make decisions and mistakes and to profit from these mistakes through guidance from his superiors.
5. Control and accountability have been established so that each manager has adequate information and guidance for periodical review of both his own and his subordinates' performance.
6. Current managerial practices do not conflict with the intent or prescriptions of the management development program.
7. Managers are willing to make the necessary commitment to change, to coach their subordinates, and to learn new skills themselves.
8. The informal organization and the personal beliefs and attitudes of nonmanagerial employees do not conflict with the objectives of the development effort.
9. Top management has the confidence of the members of the organization and it is viewed as a good place to be employed.
10. The members of the organization are not experiencing anxieties resulting from such factors as punitive leadership practices, role conflict, role ambiguity, or excessive job pressures.

RELATIONSHIP TO CORE PROPOSITIONS

Managing change can be viewed from the perspective of the four core propositions about organizational behavior presented in the first chapter. An illustrative set of these relationships is provided next.

Human Behavior

Practicing the management of change requires an understanding of many principles of human behavior. The following are among the relevant principles of human behavior: (1) Change is a source of stress and resultant strain. (2) People manifest wide individual differences in their response to change. (3) In order to reduce a person's resistance to change, that person's attitudes toward change must first be modified. Managing technological innovation also requires an understanding of human behavior. For instance, it is well recognized that creative, innovative people are the force underlying technological innovation. Whatever psychological "facts" management has about innovative, entrepreneurial people will be helpful in encouraging innovation. One such tentative "fact" is that most creative people resist too much structure in their environment.

Situational Nature

The management of change is quite situational in nature. Whether a given change introduced into an organization will be resisted or accepted is a function of many variables in the situation. Such variables constituted the subject matter of two sections of this chapter, "Why People Resist Change" and "Reducing Resistance to Change." Situational variables determining whether or not innovation is likely to take place were discussed in the section called, "Managing Technological Innovation." To illustrate, a change introduced into an organization will probably be accepted if the *situation* is such that (a) people perceive the change as benefiting them, (b) most of the people in the organization unit affected are flexible, (c) coercive tactics are avoided, (d) valid information is provided, (e) social changes are minimized, (f) economic incentives for accepting the changes are provided, and so forth.

Systemic Nature

As stated in the introduction to this chapter, "Any change introduced into one organizational unit has ramifications in other parts of the organization." This systemic nature of organizational change is vividly apparent when a technological innovation is introduced. Adjustments throughout the system have to be made to adapt to the new technology. Many machines, processes, and people may become obsolete. Donald A. Schon provides a telling account of changes in the organizational system precipitated by the replacement of a natural material by a synthetic.[39]

The established technology will be rendered obsolete. Men who have built up craft skills over decades will suddenly find their skills irrelevant to the new problems. Production will change from batch processing of materials to a continuous chemical process... It may be necessary to double or triple the volume of sales at lower prices, in order to keep the company's net profit constant... New salesmen, and new forms of technical service to sales, will be required.

Structure and Process

Technological innovation illustrates one way in which structure and process interact with respect to the management of change. Frequently, an innovative, entrepreneurially minded person develops a breakthrough idea outside of a large organizational setting. (Some companies literally begin with a "garage and an idea.") The innovative *process* leading to a marketable product has begun, but the process must be supported by the *structure* of a large organization. As ideas go from conception to development to manufacturing they must be nourished along by a host of policies, procedures, and budgets. Great ideas interacting with efficient organization result in end products useful to society. A delicate balance exists between structure and process as they relate to innovation. Flexibility in organizational structuring (including policies, procedures, spans of control, and so forth) is necessary to enhance creativity and innovation; however, an undisciplined organization may not be efficient enough to carry a good idea through to the product stage.

GUIDELINES FOR ACTION

1. You have no alternative but to learn how to manage change. Change is inevitable and the rate of change seems to be accelerating.
2. A person complaining vehemently about the amount of change he or she is exposed to might be suffering a stress reaction to change. Tread lightly in exposing that person to any more changes.
3. If a subordinate of yours exhibits passive–aggressive behavior in response to change, your best antidote is a "rap session" with that person about his or her behavior. One good conversation opener is "What about this job makes you unhappy?"
4. Few people would resist change if (a) they benefited economically from the change, (b) most consequences of the change were spelled out in advance for them, (c) their interpersonal relationships at work were undisturbed, and (d) inconveniences were kept to a minimum.
5. If, as a staff person, you wish to bring about changes in your organization, emphasize paying attention to the concerns of people you are paid to help. Focus less on your personal aggrandizement, methods and techniques.

QUESTIONS

1. Based on what you have observed personally or learned from the popular media, what types of change are the most often resisted by employees? What accounts for this resistance?
2. Do you know anyone who suffers from "future shock"? Describe that situation as fully as you can.
3. Describe two high-impact changes you have been subjected to in your lifetime. Why did they have such a high impact?
4. Is your general tendency to resist or welcome change? What evidence have you used to arrive at your conclusion?
5. Several times in American history, the Equal Rights Amendment that provides equal rights for men and women has been resisted. What factors account for this resistance to change?
6. An organization wishes to hire people for key positions who will show flexible attitudes toward change. What kind of information about people might be predictive of their attitudes toward change?

NOTES

1. Alvin Toffler, *Future Shock*. New York: A Bantam Book published by arrangement with Random House, Inc., 1971, p. 20.
2. A current scholarly book about change is William C. Lewis, *Why People Change; the Psychology of Influence*. New York: Holt, Rinehart and Winston, 1972.
3. Tom Burns and G. M. Stalker, *The Management of Innovation*. London: Tavistock, 1961; John B. Miner, *The Management Process: Theory, Research, and Practice*. New York: Macmillan, 1973.
4. Miner, *op. cit.*, p. 270.
5. *Ibid.*, p. 268.
6. Toffler, *op. cit.*, p. 326.
7. *Ibid.*, pp. 330–331.
8. George Strauss and Leonard R. Sayles, *Personnel: The Human Problems of Management*, third edition. Englewood Cliffs, N.J.: Prentice-Hall, 1972, p. 246.
9. Research project conducted by Eugene Falk, Rochester Institute of Technology, 1972.
10. Abraham K. Korman, *Industrial and Organizational Psychology*. Englewood Cliffs, N.J.: Prentice-Hall, 1971, p. 258.
11. John P. Campbell, Marvin D. Dunnette, Edward E. Lawler, III, and Karl E. Weick, Jr., *Managerial Behavior, Performance, and Effectiveness*. New York: McGraw-Hill, 1970, p. 263.
12. One recommended source is Goodwin Watson and David W. Johnson, *Social Psychology*, second edition. Philadelphia: Lippincott, 1972.
13. Points 1, 2, 3, and 4 come from an analysis by Campbell *et al.*, *op. cit.* Point 5 is added by the present author.
14. Strauss and Sayles, *op. cit.*, pp. 242–250; Joseph Tiffin and Ernest J. McCormick, *Industrial Psychology*, fifth edition. Englewood Cliffs, N.J.: Prentice-Hall, 1965, pp. 424–431; Paul R. Lawrence, "How to Deal with Resistance to Change," *Harvard Business Review*, Vol. 32, No. 3, May–June 1954, pp. 49–57.
15. Tiffin and McCormick, *op. cit.*, p. 425. Reprinted by permission of Prentice-Hall. Inc., Englewood Cliffs, N.J.

16. Strauss and Sayles, *op. cit.*, p. 243.
17. H. Igor Ansoff, "A Strategic Plan for the Graduate School of Management," Vanderbilt University, 1968 (Mimeo), p. 1.
18. One excellent overview from a conceptual and methodological point of view is Korman, *op. cit.*, Chapters 8. 9, and 10.
19. Strauss and Sayles, *op. cit.*, p. 251.
20. Lawrence, *op. cit.*, p. 53.
21. *Ibid.*, p. 54.
22. Strauss and Sayles, *op. cit.*, p. 257.
23. *Ibid.*, p. 254.
24. Donald A. Schon, *Technology and Change.* New York: Seymour Lawrence book published by Delacorte Press, 1967, p. xvi.
25. Donald R. Schoen, "Managing Technological Innovation," *Harvard Business Review*, Vol. 47, No. 3, May–June 1969, pp. 156–168.
26. Schon, *op. cit.*, p. 43.
27. Burns and Stalker, *op. cit.*, p. 158.
28. Jack R. Gibb, "Managing for Creativity in the Organization," in Calvin W. Taylor (editor), *Climate for Creativity.* Elmsford, N.Y.: Pergamon Press, 1972, p. 29.
29. Cited in Schoen, *op. cit.*, p. 161.
30. Quoted in *Ibid.*, p. 166.
31. James R. Bright (editor), *Technological Forecasting for Industry and Government.* Englewood Cliffs, N.J.: Prentice-Hall, 1968, p. 381 (cited in Schoen, *op. cit.*).
32. Andrew J. DuBrin, *The Practice of Managerial Psychology.* Elmsford, N.Y.: Pergamon Press, 1972, Chapter 6.
33. Lester M. Cone, Jr., "Toward a Theory of Managerial Obsolescence: An Empirical and Theoretical Study," unpublished doctoral dissertation, New York University, 1968.
34. F. C. Haas, "Executive Obsolescence," AMA Research Study 90. New York: American Management Association, 1968.
35. Laurence J. Peter and Raymond Hull, *The Peter Principle: Why Things Always Go Wrong.* New York: Morrow, 1969, p. 26.
36. M. Scott Myers, "Conditions for Manager Motivation," *Harvard Business Review*, Vol. 41, No. 1, January–February 1966, pp. 58–71.
37. H. Bedrosian, "Managerial Obsolescence in Banking," in H. Lazarus and E. K. Warren (editors), *The Progress of Management.* Englewood Cliffs, N.J.: Prentice-Hall, 1968, pp. 277–279.
38. Robert J. House, *Management Development: Design, Evaluation, and Implementation.* Ann Arbor: Bureau of Industrial Relations, University of Michigan, 1967, pp. 53–54.
39. Schon, *op. cit.*, p. 67.

13

Organizational Change

Change is an inevitable part of organizational life. Organizations described as "static" are in fact subject to gradual rather than zero change. Shifts in attitudes of consumers, technological breakthroughs, and demands from diverse groups in society are a sampling of the forces that underlie organizational change. The preceding chapter discussed strategies and processes for coping with change at essentially the individual and group level. The present chapter investigates a broader aspect of change.

Organizational change in the context used here is a *planned and deliberate attempt to modify the functioning of a total organizational system or one of its major components* in order to bring about increased effectiveness. Change of this type can be initiated by organizational members or external change agents. Excluded from consideration here are changes created by forces such as fire, bombings, sabotage, strikes, lockouts, or government decree. For example, the Food and Drug Administration learned that a line of children's sweaters was highly flammable. The clothing manufacturer in New York City responsible for merchandising this line was forced to discontinue production, creating drastic organizational changes such as decreasing the number of employees and adversely affecting the company image. This type of change lies beyond the purview of this chapter.

Four major ways of modifying organizational functioning, to be discussed in this chapter, are:

(a) realigning executives—"changing the people in the boxes," or "playing musical chairs";
(b) structural changes —"rearranging the boxes on the chart";
(c) changing the technology—changing the methods by which work is accomplished, such as installing a management information system or switching from mail order to direct selling; and

(d) organization development—using behavioral science techniques to create a climate of increased trust and openness among organizational members. Considerably more attention will be devoted to this approach to change than the above three in keeping with the behavioral science orientation of this book.

ORGANIZATIONAL CHANGE STRATEGIES

The four methods of modifying organizational functioning just mentioned can also be conceptualized as strategies for bringing about change. Other organization and management theorists have used different categories for identifying the several approaches to facilitating organizational improvement. To further illustrate the complexity of this topic, behavioral science methods of organizational change themselves have been entered into an elaborate classification scheme—the D/D Matrix (to be described at the end of this chapter).

Harold J. Leavitt has developed a typology of organizational change quite similar to the one presented in this chapter.[1] According to Leavitt, organizational change can be accomplished by three approaches: (a) *the structural*, in which change is brought about by modifying the formal organization; (b) *the technological*, which focuses on the problem-solving mechanisms used by the organization such as work measurement techniques, communications systems, and computers; and (c) *the humanistic*, which changes organizations by bringing about changes in organization members.

William F. Glueck developed an empirical classification of change strategies, based on a survey conducted in 58 business organizations.[2] Organization specialists in organization departments were questioned about their job duties in terms of the extent to which they performed certain activities. For instance, they rated the importance of activities such as the following to their department:

Organization, Procedures, Policy Manuals, and Directories

Analyze information system and improve internal communication

Changing the organization's work climate

Training for better group or team development

Two different approaches to the work of organization specialists emerged from an analysis of questionnaire responses, the Organization Development Approach and the Organization Planning Approach. (Many readers will recognize that large organizations familiar to them have departments with these labels. However, the functions performed by such departments may not coincide with the labels.)

Glueck notes that departments using the Organization Development Approach assume that organizations can be changed effectively only ". . . if you attempt to study and influence the people and the organization structure of the firm."[3] For instance, one specialist claimed he changed the whole organizational structure and work environment of his firm. His approach included reducing the number of levels in the hierarchy and training workers to make decisions by themselves. The latter was done to reduce the number of managers and staff people required to assist workers.

In contrast, the Organization Planning Approach departments attempt to influence the organization structure and work environment of the firm by modifying formal structure alone. Glueck observes: "They change reporting relationships, but do not attempt to change the attitudes or behavior of the people concerned."[4] Organization specialists of this type do not dismiss the importance of human factors; they simply feel such activities are not part of their function.

A MODEL FOR THE MANAGEMENT OF ORGANIZATIONAL CHANGE

Before delving into the implementation of change strategies, it is helpful to take a systematic overview of the change process. In the preceding chapter a systems model was presented to assist in understanding the circumstances under which a given change is likely to be functional, neutral, or dysfunctional. Now a useful sequential model developed by James H. Donnelly, Jr., James L. Gibson, and John M. Ivancevich is presented to provide a framework for understanding the complete change cycle that takes place in organizations.[5] Both change models help illuminate different aspects of the change process and could be applied with only minor modification to individuals, groups, or total organizations. Principles of change apply equally well to individuals, groups, and organizations. Chris Argyris has even questioned the distinction often drawn between individual and sociological variables in his book *The Applicability of Organizational Sociology*.[6] A mature understanding of organizational behavior requires the simultaneous comprehension of individual, small group, and large group (organizational) variables.

The Donnelly, Gibson, Ivancevich model shown in Figure 13.1 will be explained in condensed but sequential form. Several of its components

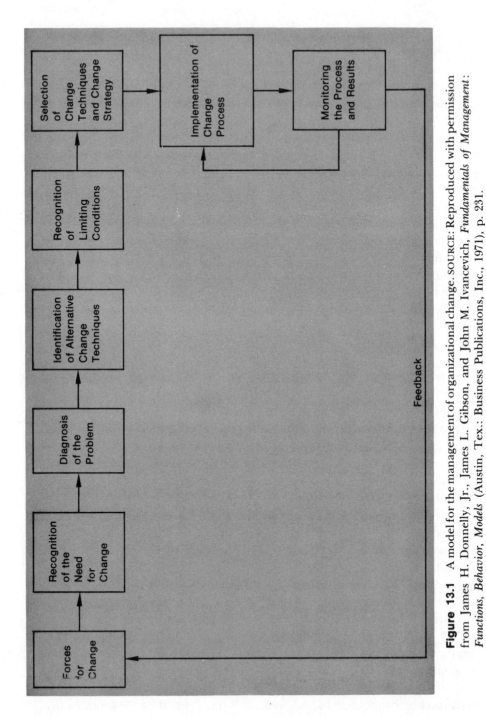

Figure 13.1 A model for the management of organizational change. SOURCE: Reproduced with permission from James H. Donnelly, Jr., James L. Gibson, and John M. Ivancevich, *Fundamentals of Management: Functions, Behavior, Models* (Austin, Tex.: Business Publications, Inc., 1971), p. 231.

overlap with information contained elsewhere in this book. One key assumption underlying this model is that forces for change continually act upon the organization. Despite the omnipresence of forces for change, a constant state of flux ("organizational chaos") is not necessarily desirable, but neither is stagnation. The manager (or other change agent) thus must develop the sensitivity to recognize the need for change and/or stability. As discussed in Chapter 12, organizational change must be introduced in such a way that resistance is minimized. The eight steps Donnelly and his associates use to explain the management of change are described next.

Forces for Change

A variety of external and internal forces move the organization toward change. External forces might include stockholders and the public. Internal forces can stem from processes or people. Machine failure or the creative suggestions of employees can initiate the change process.

Recognition of the Need for Change

Astute managers recognize the need for change before disaster descends upon the organization. Feedback control data such as inventory reports or machine failure are examples of the kind of information that can signal the urgency of change.

Diagnosis of the Problem

The decision-making model presented in Chapter 3 provides a behavioral viewpoint of how organizational problems might be diagnosed. Axiomatic to the resolution of any problem is a careful diagnosis of the underlying problem. Thus, the decline in profitability of a railroad might not be traceable to a nonchalant attitude on the part of railroad employees; the crucial issue might be technological or cultural. People prefer alternative modes of transportation. Donnelly and his associates note that the objectives of this stage can be described by three questions:[7]

What is the problem as distinct from the symptoms of the problem?

What must be changed to resolve the problem?

What outcomes (objectives) are expected from the change, and how will such objectives be measured?

Identification of Alternative Change Techniques

As amplified throughout this chapter, organizations can be changed via strategies that focus upon structural, technological, or human factors. In keeping with the core propositions, it must be noted that structure, technology, and people are interdependent. For instance, giving field personnel new cars (technology) and more responsibility (structure) will influence their attitudes (people).

Recognition of Limiting Conditions

Change agents must be realistic. Forces within the organization may limit the type of change strategy or the change method utilized. For instance, an organization characterized by a high degree of distrust and suspicion among members may not be *ready* for a full-fledged program of organizational development (described later). Alan C. Filley and Robert J. House note in an analysis of management development programs that the formal organization must be compatible with proposed changes.[8] Assume that a company had a policy of full employment. The implementation of a change in technology that reduced the work force would be incompatible with this policy.

Selection of Change Techniques and Change Strategy

According to a formulation by Larry E. Greiner, change strategy lies along a power continuum.[9] Unilateral authority is at one extreme, delegated authority at the other extreme, and shared authority in the middle. An example of unilateral authority would be an edict from top management telling people lower in the organization what needs to be changed and how to implement the change. Shared approaches follow the consultative or participative approach to management. Employees are asked their opinions and attitudes about both the nature of a problem and recommendations for its solution. Delegated authority turns over complete authority to subordinate groups.

Greiner observes that strategies that emphasize shared decision making have the highest probability of leading to constructive organizational change. One of his reasons is that shared authority tends to minimize resistance to change. Unilateral approaches almost create resistance, while delegated approaches may fail to provide people the structure and guidance people may want from management. (Organizational members sometimes complain that "management is lazy" when they relinquish complete authority.)

Implementation of Change Process

At this stage management faces the challenge of implementing a change that seems advisable. To illustrate, management might decide that a project form of organization is best for accomplishing the objective of decreasing turnover among professional personnel. Donnelly and his associates observe that implementation has two dimensions—*timing* and *scope*. Timing relates to selecting the appropriate point in time to initiate the change. "Now" might not be the best time to restructure the organization because several other changes in the organization are already taking place. Scope refers to selecting the appropriate scale or magnitude of the change. Should the company in question convert all activities of professional personnel to project teams or should restructuring begin on a more modest scale?

Monitoring the Process and Results

Feedback is furnished in this phase to both the implementation phase and the forces for change. Feedback information tells management how well the changes are being received. Change is self-perpetuating because the change process creates new problems, which themselves may require new changes. For instance, the project form of management may automatically create some surplus managers, thus creating a new organizational problem that requires attention.

EXECUTIVE REALIGNMENT

Management clings tenaciously to the assumption that improvement in organizational functioning can be brought about swiftly by replacing key executives. Considerable merit underlies this assumption. The chief executive officer and his immediate staff profoundly influence the policies and direction of an organization. Effective executives even exert a positive motivational impact on subordinates. Factors beyond any one individual's control, however, also influence the effectiveness of an organization. New York City, to cite one mammoth example, continues to suffer from many of the same problems despite changes in the administration. University presidents resign with alarming frequency when they realize that many of the problems besetting the university are beyond their control. Realignment of the top management team has failed to bring about improvement in the functioning of several railroads. Although an imperfect approach to improving organizational functioning, replacing executives is widely practiced. *Business Week* has a section called "Executive Suite," which regularly reports on executive changes in major corporations. One complicated example of "executive musical chairs" involves two well-known truck manufacturers. Readers of this case history might want to check current annual reports of both White Motor Corp. and Mack Trucks, Inc. to determine if this realignment of executives brought with it the intended financial gains.[10]

Truck makers swap managers.

As White Motor Corp. and Mack Trucks, Inc. scramble to regain the heavy-duty truck market share lost in the past decade to Ford and General Motors, the personnel battle lines now appear clear: White Motor will be headed by ex-GM executives, and Mack by ex-White Motor brass.

Last week Henry J. Nave, who a week before had left the White Motor presidency, was named president of Mack, which is the most profitable subsidiary of Signal Cos., Inc. Nave will report to Mack Chairman and Chief Executive Zenon C. R. Hansen, who was a White Motor executive vice-president from 1958–1965. Mack was acquired by Signal in 1967 after dodging a tender offer from White Consolidated Industries, Inc., a conglomerate headed by still another former White Motor executive, Edward S. Reddig.

To complete the irony, Nave's attempt to merge ailing White Motor into White Consolidated made him an outsider last year after the Justice Dept. shot down the merger and the board brought in Semon E. "Bunkie" Knudsen as chairman, with the chief executive title that Nave had held.

Heir apparent. Hansen, 62, indicates that Nave, 58, will probably be his successor in three years. Hansen expects to bring the company to $1-billion sales by then. "I've been working 16 to 18 hours a day, which is too much," he says. "We have a top staff and we needed a man between me and that staff." Nave, however, like Hansen, has a sales background. Nave's inexperience in production and finance was considered a problem at White Motor.

"They're opposites," says an executive who served both. "Hansen is a bulldog extrovert and Nave reserved." James R. Berdell, an analyst with Los Angeles-based Mitchum, Jones & Templeton, Inc., says: "There was a communications problem between Hansen and the corporate office" that he thinks the move will solve.

Nave's departure just about finishes Knudsen's housecleaning at White Motor. Only a month before, Harry D. Weller, group vice-president for trucks, who had also been courted by Mack, departed. "I hadn't had 20 minutes with Knudsen in six months," says Weller. Knudsen will not name a president soon, but engineering whiz James G. Musser, Jr. 37, a Knudsen protege and now White Motor's engineering vice-president, is a strong candidate.

Replacing one company president with another is a popular method of bringing about organizational change. This method of organizational change assumes that the president is responsible for many of the company's problems. For example, in the case history to be presented next it was decided that Bell & Howell lacked good product development. A search was conducted for a company president with a demonstrated record of success in product development. When the company president resigned, he was replaced by this new executive. Again, the reader is asked to check current information to see if the executive realignment achieved its purpose:[11]

He'll put snap into Bell & Howell.

With no pun intended, a Boston investment fund manager sharply criticizes Bell & Howell Co. whose products include cameras, as being the company that "never got a product that would click big." This week, the task of making B&H products click in the marketplace fell to a new man, Donald N. Frey, who was named chairman and chief executive officer.

Frey, an ex-Ford Motor executive and until last week president of General Cable Corp., relishes the task. Working at General Cable, he says, was "a lot of fun and we made some important changes," but he has hungered to get back into consumer markets, a taste he developed at Ford.

"I like consumer goods," he explains, "and B&H has a lot of them," ticking off cameras, tape recorders, slide projectors, cassettes, and hi-fi equipment. Such products account for about a quarter of B&H's sales.

And Frey, a Ph.D.metallurgist from the University of Michigan, is quick to add: "B&H products all involve high technology, and I'm a technologist at heart."

In his first official act, Frey went to Pasadena, Calif., early this week to sit in on a periodic corporate review of B&H's new products. His early participation in such activities is hardly surprising since his specialty at Ford was product development. He played a key role in the birth of the highly successful Mustang and was Ford's group vice-president for product development when he left three years ago.

Frey says his appearance at the review, a procedure established by his predecessor, Peter G. Peterson, who resigned last month, is "symbolic." Chicago-based B&H "lives on product development technology," he says.

Slim pickings. But Bell and Howell has had difficulty in translating its expertise to the marketplace. The company is broadly diversified—photographic equipment, business machines, educational training equipment, and electronics instruments—but it cannot claim a lion's share of any big markets as can Eastman Kodak, for example, in the film business. In its runner-up position, B&H bumps up against not only Kodak in photographic equipment but such stalwart competitors as Xerox and 3M in the copier and duplicator fields.

The company has a strong position in home-movie equipment, but that market is threatened by Polaroid, now developing an instant home-movie system. Ironically, B&H now manufactures Colorpak cameras under contract to Polaroid.

Since 1968, one of B&H's biggest troubles has been in its electronics business. Defense and aerospace work has declined, and an expected "space-age technological fallout" of consumer products has proven more difficult to achieve than first thought.

There have been other problems as well. At best, the company will probably break even on a contract to supply movie systems to Pan American aircraft. It has also taken some lumps in developing videotape systems, although they show "good promise."

Last year, thanks to a strong fourth quarter, profits were up slightly from 1969, to $11-million, on about the same sales, nearly $298-million. Both years trailed 1968's record $12.5-million earned on sales of $281-million.

Thin margin. With pressure on profit margins, Peterson two years ago launched a sweeping cost-cutting and consolidation program. It included dropping some 1,500 employees, mostly in the electronics area, where B&H has sold off some small operations. "The big thing going is tightening-up on costs," says Ralph Kaplan, a securities analyst at Oppenheimer & Co. "Their 7% pretax margin on sales is too low."

"What B&H needs," adds an analyst for a big mutual fund, "is more successes like they scored with their 35-mm slide cube projector." The projector features a plastic magazine, hardly bigger than a large ice cube, that will hold 65 slides. Introduced about a year ago, it has been a big seller. And that, no doubt, is just the kind of product sales development that Don Frey likes best.

CHANGING THE ORGANIZATIONAL STRUCTURE

"Organizational change," in its most typical connotation, implies a restructuring of the organization. Changing the organizational structure, in the context used here, is but one method of attempting to improve functioning of the organization. Many reorganizations that take place are done so with the intention of capturing the unique advantages of another form of organizational grouping. Typical here is the situation of a large, centralized organization that decentralizes in order to capitalize on the advantages of teamwork and self-control that frequently occurs in smaller, decentralized units. Another illustration is the assignment of a product manager to supervise a product once that product appears to have good market potential. It is anticipated that the small product might be neglected in a large functional organization.

Reorganization has become epidemic in industry. D. Ronald Daniel, a consultant in the area of organizational planning, estimates that . . . "one major restructuring every two years is probably a conservative estimate of the current rate of organizational change among the largest industrial corporations."[12] He also notes that reorganizations are common practice in both American and international businesses. Forces behind such frequent reorganizations include the following:[13]

(1) The pressures of competition on margins and profits have put a premium on efficient organization structure. Overlapping departments are being combined, product divisions consolidated, and marginal units eliminated.

(2) The booming internationalization of business has compelled more and more companies to supplant export departments by international divisions, to establish regional management groups, and to restructure corporate staffs.

(3) Mergers and acquisitions have generated strong pressures for reorganization in parent companies as well as in newly acquired subsidiaries. (Note that in the early 1970's the increase in mergers and acquisitions has decelerated.)

(4) New developments in technology—such as the advanced management information systems made possible by recent progress in EDP hardware and software—often require new organizational arrangements to realize their ultimate potential for improving corporate performance.

(5) Last, but not least, sheer growth is compelling many companies to amend time-honored organizational arrangements in order to cope with volume increases of as much as 20% a year.

Recognizing the inevitability of organizational restructuring, Daniel then describes several guidelines for reorganization based on his personal experiences (and those of his management consulting firm).

Success Requirements

Every enterprise has a unique set of "make or break" factors. These success requirements are illustrated by the importance of a strong dealer organization in automaking. Colleges of business, to cite another example, in order to prosper must cater to the difficulties people employed full time have in attending class. Most MBA programs thus offer courses at night in locations accessible to businessmen. The relationship between success requirements and organizational restructuring is demonstrated by the case history of a cement company.[14]

> A functionally structured cement company decided, after analyzing its success requirements, that the importance of transportation economies and local market contacts demanded a region-by-region approach to the business. The company restructured itself into geographic divisions with local profit accountability. Its return on investments has already improved markedly in the two years since the shift.

Objectives and Plans

Although their importance seems self-evident, notes Daniel, many companies neglect incorporating the objectives and future plans of the enterprise into organizational changes. Often the formulation of new plans and objectives will dictate the type of reorganization required. One situation at General Foods illustrates this principle:[15]

> ... General Foods determined several years ago to greatly strengthen its trade franchise. To help achieve this basic objective, the company adopted a new organizational concept. It consolidated the physical distribution and order-taking activities of all its product divisions in a single Distribution Sales Service Division. This move has greatly facilitated the attainment of GF's trade franchise objectives.

After taking into consideration both the success requirements of a business enterprise and its objectives and plans, reorganization must still work within limits imposed by certain realities.

Range of "Givens"

Careful organizational planning might suggest an ideal structure for an enterprise but certain "givens" or "reality factors" may make that ideal structure unattainable. Manpower resources represent one such given that may serve as a constraint on establishing the ideal reorganization. Experienced and competent people have to be available to fill the posts created by organizational changes. Daniel provides the following case history to illustrate this point:[16]

> A multibillion-dollar company wanted to structurally separate top-level policy making and day-to-day administration, but found it could not do so because of a shortage of executive talent. After considering and rejecting the possibility of outside recruiting, the chairman and the president decided they would have to share both roles until three group vice-presidents could be developed within the company. Four years later, the shift was successfully made, and operations were explicitly assigned to the group vice-presidents.

Adherence to Organizational Principles

After the organization has been restructured on paper, experience suggests that the new design be compared against commonly accepted principles of organization. Old saws such as "responsibility should be commensurate with authority" and "each man should report to only one superior" can be useful guidelines. Project and product organizations are somewhat in violation of this principle, yet are widely used forms of organization. Daniel comments that where the structure is at odds with the principles, the reasoning behind the structure should be examined for possible weaknesses. "Where weaknesses are discovered, the structural arrangement is reconsidered: where none are found; it is of course allowed to stand."[17]

Another "principle of organization" that has received less mention than those above is worth noting. Reorganizations often result in the cumbersome one-over-one-over-one arrangement. Specifically, after an organization reshuffle, one executive might be left with only one manager reporting to him. He becomes squeezed into the role of passing messages back and forth between his subordinate and his superior. Such an organizational arrangement is not only poor for the intermediary's morale, but it often leaves him with no important function to perform for the organization. Frequently, within a short period of time, the executive in the middle is considered superfluous.

Management Philosophy

Organizational changes stemming from restructuring should be consonant with existing management philosophy. Changes made during reorganization may not work if they lack consonance with management attitudes and values. This is a subtle but important point. Decentralizing units, for example, will not enhance organizational effectiveness if top management is reluctant to allow division managers freedom to operate. Daniel makes this comment:[18]

> A division manager I talked with recently put it more pungently. "The form and substance of this corporation are out of whack," he said. "On the surface, you'd think we had autonomous product divisions. But the way the man upstairs wants to run things, our divisionalized setup is a fiction."

Mutual adjustment of corporate philosophy and organization structure is necessary for reorganizations to be highly effective. Without such meshing, much of the effort expended in changing reporting relationships and reshuffling personnel is wasted.

CHANGING THE TECHNOLOGY

Changing the technology of an organization has far-reaching effects in areas that lie outside the processing or manufacturing of goods. Technology is but one vital input in a total system composed of people, technology, and material objects. Almost any manufacturing plant, mill, or office that has been partially or totally automated would serve as a valuable case history about the impact of technology on organizational change. One such case history will be reported at length here to illustrate the organizational implications of automation.

Otis Lipstreu and Kenneth A. Reed conducted a two-year study of a 1200-employee baking plant undergoing a transition from an old mill-type plant to a new, highly automatic facility.[19] Information about the effects of change were studied using a variety of techniques: first-hand observations, interviews, attitude surveys, and analyses of personnel statistics. Actual changes that could be attributed to automation will be described in the next several paragraphs.

Reduced Supervisory Levels

Widespread is the belief that automation reduces the number of layers of management. Observations made toward the end of the two-year study period were that the first level of supervision was soon to be eliminated but the inevitable had not yet occurred. Spans of control had been reduced, and first-line supervisors[20]

... weren't needed since the production superintendent could perform easily their general oversight duties. The other tasks could be handled functionally by general maintenance technicians, whose duties overlapped those of the supervisors.

Increased Supervisory Responsibility

Under the influence of automation, it became apparent that the potential implications of any one mistake were increased. Although supervisors might have fewer people reporting to them, the consequences of human error were multiplied because of the speed of the line and the tremendous cost of breakdowns. Lipstreu and Reed note that prior to automation supervisors had more time to correct errors. The increased speed of the line and the restricted mobility of machine operators reduced opportunities to avoid substantial scrap by early detection of production difficulties. As a consequence, supervisory tension increased.

Increased Supervisory Interdependency

Another interesting implication of automation is that supervisors on the same level become more dependent on each other to accomplish their tasks. Each supervisor becomes an even more crucial link in the chain. The researchers point out, however, that increased interdependency sometimes increases rather than decreases conflict, particularly when pressures for production are high.

Increased Ratio of Supervisors to Workers

Automating a plant almost inevitably increases the number of supervisors in comparison to the number of nonsupervisors. The most vivid example of the accelerating supervisory ratio took place in the baking and
mixing department (the area experiencing greatest technological change).
Before automation, approximately 70 employees were supervised by a
foreman and an assistant foreman. After automation, these two supervisors
plus an additional assistant foreman supervised 25 men. "So, in this one
department a 35:1 ratio has become roughly an 8:1 ratio."[21]

Logical and profit-oriented factors, Lipstreu and Reed point out, contributed to changes in the ratio. Among these was a rearrangement of
machine layout. Workers were in some instances spread out among three
floor levels after the changes. It then became physically difficult for one
supervisor to be in contact with many workers.

Increased Proportion of Indirect Labor

Automation usually brings about an increase in the number of employees who are not directly involved in the production process. Systems
analysts, production planners, and maintenance personnel are three examples of *indirect* workers. The baking plant's ratio of indirect labor to total
plant work force changed from 1 to 6.73 before the change, to 1 to 4.12
after the change.

Reduced Size of Work Teams

Automation of operations dramatically reduced the size of work crews
and work teams in the baking plant. Much of the work was now accomplished by machine monitors. Helpers were reduced in number or eliminated entirely. Team work was only required when machines broke down.
As a corollary, many workers were now involved in individual work. This
led to feelings of isolation among workers, which in turn created morale
problems. According to morale survey results, workers objected to the lessened time available for talking with fellow workers.

Restricted Freedom of Movement

Popular belief about automation suggests that automating an operation
provides the worker with freedom to roam from his machine because it
runs "automatically." The baking plant experience was more nearly the

opposite. After automation, machine tenders were assigned to monitor one or more machines within a limited area. During the debugging phases (approximately nine months) machine tenders felt compelled to stay close to the machines because of frequent breakdowns, and the normal human tendency to override the controls of a new machine (as a new driver tends to oversteer an automobile).[22]

Past the debugging phase of automation, an illusory degree of freedom occurred. Workers could move a short distance out of orbit, but the negative consequences of neglecting the machine were substantial. "... any failure to observe alertly the various gauges could have resulted almost instantaneously in serious product loss and/or costly machine damage."[23]

Breaking Up of Worker Cliques

Automation characteristically brings about a new arrangement of the interactions among workers. Reduction in personnel, interdepartmental transfers, and different spatial arrangement of machines are some of the factors breaking down the preautomation informal organization. Conceivably, new informal groups will emerge after the new work arrangements have become solidified, but in the interim many workers are left with a feeling of isolation. Observations made in one specific department are cogent:[24]

> In the Mixing Department, two unauthorized free-time periods enjoyed by employees both in the morning and evening had been eliminated, reducing the amount of interaction time by almost 20 minutes per day. Some of the machine monitors told us they seldom saw some of their old friends with whom they formerly enjoyed regular contact. Women in the non-automated areas reported even more dissatisfaction.

Shift Toward Centralization of Authority

Experience dictates that automating a production system moves some control away from the plant level and toward a centralized authority in order to capitalize on benefits from the new technology. At the baking plant, authority for product planning and scheduling was centralized. Product decisions were then evaluated in terms of the capacity of the total system, rather than one plant. A clear intent was to unify (and perhaps avoid duplication of effort) the entire system. Lipstreu and Reed note the following statement from a company brochure: "When the Unification Program is completed, the System as a whole will operate in much the same way as any one of our Divisions is operating."[25] One interesting consequence of unification was the transfer of the president to the home office as a senior vice-president of the system. He was replaced by an acting resident manager accompanied by a centralization of functional control in the home office.

Impact of Computers on Organizations

Effects of computer technology on organizational behavior have been the subject of several large-scale empirical studies.[26] *The Impact of Computers on Organizations* by Thomas L. Whisler is a book-length analysis of the widespread ramifications of computers on a variety of companies in the life insurance industry.[27] A sampling of his major findings will be reported here to provide another illustration of how changes in technology bring about changes in both organizational behavior and other variables (such as job content), which in turn influence behavior (e.g., increase level of motivation).

Organizational structure is influenced by computer technology in several important ways. One conclusion drawn by Whisler was that if computers were removed from the companies and they attempted to maintain the same quality of service to customers, 60 percent more clerical personnel, 9 percent more supervisory personnel, and 2 percent more managerial personnel would be required. At lower levels in the organization, the span of control declined, and it remained unchanged at higher levels. More directly related to organizational structure was a shift toward functionalization or centralization of some activities. In one instance a company regrouped its two "premium and commission accounting departments" into two functional departments.[28]

Decision making, as would be expected, was broadly influenced by computer technology. Decision making moved to higher levels in organizations and was increasingly quantified and rationalized. The primary impact was at the middle levels of management. Top-management decision making showed little change except that substantial new problems of inflexibility in decision making resulted from computer use. Another dysfunction noted by Whisler was that, although the use of computers stimulated ideas for change, the cost of implementing such changes greatly increased.[29]

Authority and control is influenced by computer technology in life insurance organizations in very significant ways. Computers increase the centralization of control and take over certain aspects of controlling human behavior. An implication of the latter is a tightening of control or discipline of individual behavior at lower levels in the organization. Explained one company official: "Humans are not accustomed to having their work audited under conditions allowing no margin for error."[30]

Job content was influenced by the use of computers, but its impact was a function of job level. Clerical jobs tended to become more routinized, while the job of the first-line supervisor tended toward enlargement or enrichment. An underlying explanation of these differences offered is that the focus of computer systems in the life insurance industry (at the time of the study) is still at the level of clerical jobs. Attendant changes such as consolidation of functions and the retraining of personnel have enlarged the activity scope of first-line supervisors. No trends were evident about the enlargement of managerial jobs.[31]

Interpersonal communication patterns, another aspect of job content, were influenced by computers in two contrasting ways. After a computer system is well entrenched and systems are running smoothly, interpersonal contact diminishes. Where computer systems are in the process of development, the result is to increase the flow of interpersonal communication.

Skill levels were heavily influenced by computer technology, particularly at the clerical levels. In general, skills were upgraded but approximately one-third of clerical jobs showed a downgrading. Skill levels were relatively uninfluenced at the top-management levels.

ORGANIZATION DEVELOPMENT[32]

Organization development is the name given to a variety of behavioral science approaches directed toward improving organizations in the direction of more open and honest communication among individuals and groups of individuals. Essential to organization development is the acquisition of self-critical attitudes toward present policies, procedures, and behavior patterns. Members of the developed (or changed) organization are hopefully open, explicit, and direct in their dealing with each other.

The scope and potential impact of organization development are reflected in the following definition presented by Warren G. Bennis, an influential figure in the organization development movement:[33]

> *Organization development* (OD) is a response to change, a complex educational strategy intended to change the beliefs, attitudes, values, and structure of organizations so that they can better adapt to new technologies, markets, and challenges, and the dizzying rate of change itself. Organization development is new and still emerging, only a decade old, so its shape and potentiality are far from granted and its problems far from solved. Yet it holds promise for developing the "real knowledge" about our post-modern world.

Organization development can be achieved by a variety of methods and techniques. Approaches to resolving conflict described in Chapter 10 can rightfully be called OD techniques because they enable an organization to resolve behavioral problems that are negatively affecting some part of its overall functioning. Three widely practiced approaches to organization development will receive attention here: sensitivity training, the Managerial Grid, and team development meetings. Readers interested in acquiring more depth about OD theory and practice might consult the Addison-Wesley Series on Organization Development edited by Warren G. Bennis. Slightly more advanced is a treatment by Chris Argyris, *Intervention Theory and Method.*

Readers are cautioned that not all activities given the label "organization development" refer to the type of activities described in the following pages. Many industrial organizations, for example, have organization development units within the personnel department that may or may not conduct OD. Some of these departments are essentially involved in manpower planning and related concerns.

Sensitivity Training

Sensitivity training is a widespread, well-known, and controversial technique of manager and organization development. Probably few readers are unfamiliar with the idea of sensitivity training or closely related interaction techniques such as encounter groups. Such techniques have received widespread attention in professional and business journals, movies, television, magazines, and daily newspapers. Variants of encounter groups have even included a technique whereby participants gather together nude in a large swimming pool. Encounter groups have proliferated in schools, churches, and civic groups. The present discussion concerns the application of sensitivity training to improving organization effectiveness. It would be artificial not to intermix the role of sensitivity training in manager development with its role in organization development: the two are closely related. Organizations cannot be developed without developing managers in the process.

Sensitivity training is also referred to as laboratory training, T-group, or laboratory education. Technically, the T-group is a specialized aspect of sensitivity training whereby the learning that takes place stems from people to people interaction rather than via the dissemination of behavioral science principles by a lecturer. Verbal descriptions of T-group activity fail to fully communicate the essence of what transpires in practice. Such descriptions are imprecise because much of the activity transpiring during the experience relates to emotion and feeling, not intellect. An analogy can be drawn to the difficulty in verbally communicating the feelings concomitant to skydiving, skiing down a steep hill, or hitting a hole-in-one. Mechanical and physical aspects of these athletic experiences can readily be described, but the actual feelings of exhilaration (or fear) are difficult to communicate. This discussion of sensitivity training will focus on the processes involved, its purposes, and its effectiveness. Attention will also be given to qualifications of the T-group leader, characteristics about an individual or organization that could have a bearing on the effectiveness of sensitivity training, and ethical considerations.

Processes. Sensitivity training focuses on feelings, attitudes, and perceptions, not on the acquisition of formal knowledge. Confrontation and emotional arousal are characteristic of the T-group. Most sensitivity training laboratories include some component about behavioral science principles, but these are supplementary to the central events of the laboratory. Behavioral science areas that might be lectured about include leadership, motivation, communication, and group dynamics. Often participants are assigned reading material as preparation for the laboratory experience.

T-groups vary in size, duration, and composition. Size of the groups vary from about six to fifteen members with eight to ten being considered typical. Duration of the laboratories can be anywhere from a long weekend to four weeks. T-groups, however, frequently are conducted at one-week intervals for three- or four-hour periods; e.g., every Monday from 1:00 p.m. to about 5:30 p.m. for five weeks. The T-group is sometimes conducted as a total immersion experience with little time off from the activity, except for meals and sleep. Such "marathon groups" are more popular with private individuals than public organizations. Location of sensitivity training is usually in an informal atmosphere away from the normal distractions of family and work—either in a hotel setting or in a rural retreat. In this author's experience, T-groups proceed more effectively when people sit on floors rather than around a table or on chairs.

T-groups can be conducted with strangers, coworkers, or people from different parts of the same total organization (e.g., representatives of different departments). Using sensitivity training for organization development usually dictates that participants be members of the same organization. It is anticipated that, as a result of the experience, organization members will later function more smoothly as a team. Earlier applications of sensitivity training to business and industry emphasized sending managers to "stranger" groups.

Each T-group has a leader who is typically an organizational or clinical psychologist. On rare occasions, people with no training or certification in psychology or psychiatry conduct T-groups. As the discussion of sensitivity training progresses, it will become apparent that this is a questionable procedure. The role of the leader is to serve as a catalyst to group interaction. He or she is a change agent, not a lecturer, in this role. Leaders attempt to guide the group toward the most beneficial learning experiences. Some leaders quickly drop their leadership role and become group members, including confronting others and welcoming confrontation about themselves. The personality style and sensitivity of the leader can have an important bearing on the productiveness of the group, whether the leader joins the group or remains aloof.

Informality, permissiveness, and lack of structure characterize the group meetings. There is no specific agenda to be covered and no fixed rules in the T-group. Emphasis is on expression of feelings and attitudes. Group members share their personal feelings and reactions about each other with each other. Free expression of feelings and confrontation are encouraged. According to Alfred J. Marrow:[34]

> Experience has shown that the lack of structure heightens the sensitivity of the participants to one another's behavior and enables them to become aware of their own insensitivities and distortions.

Throughout the sessions there is continuous feedback. Participants come to learn how they are perceived by other people and are able to compare these perceptions with their self-perceptions. When one approach to relating to another individual does not achieve the desired result, the participant is free to try another and observe the difference in the reactions of coparticipants. As the laboratory progresses, members become more *sensitive* to their own feelings and the feelings of others. Several examples follow of the kind of confrontation of feedback that can take place during a laboratory experience.

> A management development specialist attended a T-group. After the fourth day he shared with the group his feeling that he was not achieving much acceptance from other group members. ". . . you fellows talk to me and are nice to me, but I'm really not one of the group." Another member replied: "Allan, I'll tell you why. You're really here as a spy. Your occupation is to develop managers and you're just here to observe us as if you were the teacher and we are the pupils. If you would stop observing us and really participate, maybe we would like you better."
>
> After the sixth hour in the life span of one T-group, an irritated group member decided to confront the leader. "This foolish meeting has

been going on all day and you haven't told us one item of information worth anything. We're all busy executives whose companies have paid quite a sum for us to come here. You sit there with a stupid look on your face and all we hear is this patter from the group members. Is that what we came for?" Another group member replied: "George, you're a pretty impatient fellow, but at least we now know what you think of us. According to you, what the rest of us have to say is just patter."

John M. devoted extensive time during his laboratory experience to questioning the real importance of each man's occupation or contribution in the world outside the T-group. He then began to even question the value of education in particular. A fellow group member confronted him with a feeling that was supported by the group members: "John, I get the impression you are a professional critic. I don't mind, nor do I think anybody else minds, your complaining about everything other people are proud of but what is your contribution? Don't just tell us things are dark. Light a candle."

Feedback to T-group participants is occasionally of a less spontaneous and more formalized nature. As a supplement to the continuous confrontation some laboratory sessions require that each participant be placed on a *hot seat* and be apprised of the impact he has made on the other group members during the laboratory. The multiple feedback session occurs toward the end of the laboratory session. Participants, for example, are asked to provide five positive and five negative adjectives descriptive of the individual being confronted. Recipients of these adjectival descriptions thus do not feel they are alone in receiving negative comments. Some kind of group consensus is required in order to arrive at ten final adjectives. A scribe or recorder might then present this group description to each individual as a permanent record of the experience. Experience suggests that the choice of negative adjectives presented to the participant about himself are rarely perceived as humiliating or shocking. This may be partially explained by the fact that the hot seat experience comes toward the end of the sensitivity training session and by then members have learned how to receive feedback about themselves in a constructive manner. Positive adjectives presented tend to be truisms, descriptive of many well-integrated individuals. Following is the list of adjectives received by a manager of administrative services at the end of his T-group experience:

Positive	*Negative*
intelligent	hip shooter
friendly	poor listener

Positive	*Negative*
energetic	tries to impress people
cooperative	wants his way
aggressive	disorganized

Anxiety is another characteristic feature of T-groups. The ambiguity of the situation plus the frequent confrontation and feedback are undoubtedly the primary contributors to the heightened anxiety of participants. For many people, the felt anxiety contributes toward making sensitivity training a meaningful experience. For a small number of people, the anxiety evoked is more than they can comfortably handle. An individual's natural predisposition toward feeling anxious determines to a large extent how anxious he will feel when placed under the stresses of sensitivity training.

Purposes. Sensitivity training has many stated purposes, goals, and objectives, some of which seem to overlap. The broadest purpose of sensitivity training is to increase the interpersonal competence of participants and increase the effectiveness of their organizations, as implied in the title of Chris Argyris's important work about this method: *Interpersonal Competence and Organizational Effectiveness.*[35] Interpersonal skill acquired in sensitivity training should go well beyond the kinds of skill that might be acquired from a Dale Carnegie course, which concentrates more on superficial aspects of behavior. Laboratory education is geared toward the acquisition of insight or learning about oneself and others in depth. Another broad goal or terminal behavior anticipated from a successful laboratory experience is for individuals to learn more constructive ways of dealing with feelings of their own and those of other people. Our listing of sensitivity training goals is based on the conceptualizations of those professionals who conduct sensitivity training activity. Individuals entering into a laboratory experience may express their expectations in fundamental and simplistic terms such as: "I would like to learn more about myself" or "I would like to improve my skills in dealing with people." Robert Tannenbaum and his associates formulated a list of goals for sensitivity training that is still relevant:[36]

1. *Greater self-understanding.* An opportunity is provided for participants to achieve insight into their conflicts, feelings, defenses, and impact upon people. Every T-group participant should acquire knowledge about how he or she is seen by others.
2. *Understanding others.* Sensitivity training provides an appropriate psychological climate for people to observe, study, and react to each

other. Participants often learn to reconsider long-held stereotypes they hold about people.

3. *Insight into group processes.* Laboratory sessions place considerable emphasis on how groups operate. The process of what is happening is often more important than the content of what is being said. Members learn that there is something happening in the group that transcends the sum of individual personalities involved.

4. *Recognizing the culture.* Sensitivity training is said to assist individuals in obtaining a greater sensitivity into the character, style, or feel of their own organizations. This is roughly synonymous with learning to perceive the organizational climate.

5. *Developing specific behavioral skills.* New understandings and insights without specific behavioral skills to accompany them are of limited value. Many neurotic individuals, for example, know what they do wrong in their relationships with people and perhaps why they do it, but persist in their self-defeating behavior patterns. It is anticipated that, in addition to the acquisition of insight, sensitivity training can help participants develop such specific skills as listening, interviewing, praising, criticizing, and communicating verbally and nonverbally (e.g., gestures, posture, frowns).

Many of the goals of sensitivity training lie in the direction of producing changes in the individual's behavior or attitudes. This does not necessarily imply that most laboratory participants will undergo profound or dramatic behavioral changes. Saul W. Gellerman indicates that participation in a T-group experience is not designed to make a person into a new man:[37]

> The real purpose of sensitivity training is much more subtle than behavior changes: it is to acquaint people with the process of self-discovery and make that process attractive enough to initiate the practice and repetition that can turn it into a habit.

Potential hazards of sensitivity training. Screening and preparation of participants for sensitivity training is a controversial and important matter. Screening of participants has received attention by psychologists because scattered anecdotal evidence has been accumulated that some individuals are psychologically harmed by the rigors of sensitivity training. Psychological harm to participants, in this author's opinion, has been much more frequent in community and educational settings than in industrial settings. In the former settings sometimes too little attention is paid to qualifications of the trainer or characteristics of the participants.

Self-discovery makes most people anxious, and some individuals are more upset by this process than others. Discovering how others really react toward and feel about you can also be an emotionally distressing experience to individuals of modest ego strength. Opponents of sensitivity training have cited cases where individuals have required hospitalization and extensive psychiatric care as a result of their T-group experience. Sometimes the emotional disturbance has a sudden onset during the laboratory process. Specific cases of psychotic episodes of this kind, however, are rare. There is a paucity of evidence as to how many people have been harmed by sensitivity training. It will be even more important for the future to know what specific kinds of personality structure are liable to disintegrate under the stress of a laboratory experience. Several general principles and guidelines can be drawn about screening people for T-groups, until specific evidence is accumulated:

1. As in most manager development experiences, the strongest and most competent individuals are likely to benefit the most from sensitivity training. Psychologically strong individuals have the flexibility and wherewithal to capitalize on the newly acquired insights and modes of behavior that emanate from the group experience. Conversely, individuals with the least viable strengths are likely to benefit least from T-groups. Argyris has stated that sensitivity training should not be conducted with people at the lowest supervisory levels.[38]
2. Managers with histories of psychiatric illness, and also those whose present adjustment appears tenuous, should not be considered candidates for sensitivity training. According to Argyris, there have been four nervous breakdowns among 10,000 sensitivity training participants, all of whom had previous psychiatric histories.[39]
3. Individuals whose self-image is grossly discrepant from their image as perceived by others may need this kind of defense for psychologically important reasons and thus could be harmed by being stripped of these defenses. Rarely does our self-image coincide with the way we are perceived by others, but some individuals are almost delusional about how they are perceived by others—these are the individuals for whom sensitivity training is contraindicated.
4. Individuals with heightened sensitivity to personal criticism may not be ready for sensitivity training. Once they have obtained some preliminary insight into their inability to profit from negative feedback, they are likely to benefit from the laboratory experience.

Many individuals selected for sensitivity training by their organizations may have no prior awareness of what the process entails. Some may be anticipating a series of lectures on principles of human relations and leadership, particularly because some training laboratories use general titles such as "Leadership Seminar." Preparation for the laboratory experience should include a mention of the voluntary nature of the experience, plus some statement of the purposes and the process. Sensitivity training participants often receive some behavioral science literature to study before entering the formal sessions. This is another kind of preparation and is not to be confused with giving individuals advance notice on the kind of experience they are likely to encounter. An obvious principle of preparing people for an emotional experience such as sensitivity training is not to practice deception about the purposes. One general manager told his five department heads that they were all to report to a particular hotel for a four-day seminar on improving company communications. When the department heads arrived, they discovered that the kind of communications referred to was the development of openness and trust among each other. The general manager had seen fit to practice deception in order to expose his key people to a method of learning to be less deceptive in their dealings with each other.

Qualifications of the trainer. This is a major consideration in sensitivity training because of the heavy emphasis on emotional learning that takes place. Sensitivity training is a powerful tool, and is not a recommended procedure for individuals without appropriate skills and knowledge. Appropriate skills and training are difficult to specify, because there is no formal university curriculum that certifies individuals as sensitivity trainers, nor is sensitivity training a professional discipline by itself. It is a highly specialized technique practiced by professionals. A conservative approach would be to allow only certified psychologists with some background in clinical and social psychology to conduct sensitivity training. Clinical skills are infrequently called into play in a laboratory session, but when they are necessary their presence can have a major impact on the mental health status of an individual who might be faltering under the strain of the experience. The leader should be alert to any cues that a group member is exceeding his tolerance limits for the pressures inherent in the confrontation.

T-group trainers should derive most of their professional satisfactions from contributing to the growth of individuals and groups. The emphasis should not be on diagnosing what group members are like once their facades have been lifted. Focusing on personality diagnosis obscures the real goals of the laboratory experience.

Organizational climate. Appropriateness of organizational climate is another factor that must be weighed before managers attend sensitivity training. The values propagated in the laboratory experience should also be endorsed in the *back home* situation, or much of the learning is wasted. New modes of behavior and attitudes are quickly forgotten if they are not reinforced in the work situation. Candidness, openness, or leveling with others is a mode of behavior encouraged in sensitivity training. It is anticipated that the manager attending the T-group will level with superiors, subordinates, peers, and himself once he leaves the group. This kind of frankness is welcomed in a few organizations, but not in all. Occasionally, participants interpret the permissive atmosphere as an indication that tactfulness and diplomacy are unnecessary in a business environment, whether or not this is an intended result. An incident was reported in the *Wall Street Journal* about a woman, who, after attending a sensitivity training course, developed the courage to tell her superiors that she was tired of their procrastination about accepting her ideas, and then resigned to take a comparable job elsewhere.[40] The author of this article was describing the negative consequences of sensitivity training, but it is also possible that such a move may have been advantageous in terms of the woman's career development.

Managers who have had a successful laboratory experience often learn to value listening to others and allowing them to make decisions. This approach to management works well in many organizational environments, but may not work with a group of subordinates who are not prepared to make decisions by themselves.

One implication to be drawn from incidents relating to the difficulty of transferring modes of behavior learned during sensitivity training to the job setting is that more than a few isolated managers from one organization should attend sensitivity training. If organization effectiveness is to be enhanced, and sensitivity training is a proper vehicle for such enhancement, then changes in behavior should begin at the top of an organization. Organization development begins at the top and works its way down. People are more likely to adopt modes of behavior that are directly or indirectly rewarded by their superiors. Managers find it easier to deal openly and honestly with their subordinates if they are dealt with openly and honestly by their superiors.

Effectiveness of sensitivity training. Controversy in the professional and business literature surrounds this subject.[41] Considerable information has been collected in the form of both stated opinions and experimental studies with regard to the effectiveness of sensitivity training. Opinions about the positive effects of sensitivity training can be summarized as follows:

1. It is the best method yet developed by behavioral scientists for producing beneficial and lasting changes in people.
2. Habits of self-examination lead to improved interpersonal relationships for participants, both on the job and at home.
3. Achieving a higher sense of self-confidence and self-satisfaction is possible; that alone is worth the time and effort devoted to the training.
4. It is possible through this technique to build an organization whereby the goals of the individual and the organization are integrated.
5. Through this method people learn to deal openly, honestly, and frankly with one another, which sets the stage for individual and organizational development.

Opinions about the negative effects of sensitivity training can be summarized as follows:

1. It forces many individuals to undergo a personality-humiliating and anxiety-provoking experience from which they might not recover.
2. It strips some people of defenses they badly need and provides them with nothing to replace these defenses.
3. It encourages behavioral modes that are acceptable in the laboratory but unacceptable in most organizational settings.
4. Any benefits accrued from the experience are so short lived as to make the experience a waste of time and money.
5. It encourages and subtly coerces individuals into revealing aspects about themselves that constitute an invasion of privacy, thus harboring later resentment in participants.

Experimental evaluations of the effectiveness of sensitivity training have demonstrated both negative, positive, and neutral results. Conflicting results are likely to be found when any psychological technique is subjected to research investigation, and it is to the credit of sensitivity trainers that they have researched their own work. Robert J. House has prepared a scholarly review of research studies about the effects of T-group's education both on the participant's characteristics and his job behavior.[42] Broadly interpreted, we can conclude from House's review that sensitivity training can produce either helpful or harmful changes in the individual and in his job behavior. Helpful personal changes documented by research include improved listening skills, more supportive behavior toward other people, less need to be dependent on others, and less demand for subservience from others. Research evidence about the negative effects of sensitivity training centers around the possible incompatability between the values reinforced in the T-group and those rewarded in a participant's organization back home. Additionally, the management strategy encouraged in sensitivity training might lead to poor results in terms of leadership effectiveness. There is research evidence, for example, that managers attending sensitivity training become more considerate in their behavior to subordinates, but simultaneously feel less need to impose structure upon members' group activities. High leadership effectiveness in most organizations, in contrast, is characterized by high concern for both consideration and structure.

Research has been recently conducted that questions whether T-group training can enhance organizational effectiveness. Reed M. Powell and John F. Stinson involved 75 college seniors and MBA students in a management simulation game. Participants were told that they would receive grades based on their simulated company's profitability and increase in stock price. The basic experimental design was as follows:[43]

> At the end of one simulation year (four decision periods), the fifteen companies were broken into three groups, two experimental and one control. The companies in the groups were matched on the basis of accumulated gross profit during the first simulation year. Five of the companies participated in the laboratory training as family groups. Members of the five other companies participated in stranger groups, training members of other work groups. The remaining five companies acted as a control group and received no training.

T-group experience was more structured than the type of sensitivity training described so far, but more like Robert R. Blake's Managerial Grid seminars (to be described next in this chapter). Results of these experiments were contrary to some popular ideas about organizational development. One major finding was that family group training resulted in less task accomplishment than the stranger-trained group or the control group. More disheartening was the finding that leaders trained in either family or stranger groups tended to *abdicate the leadership role.* They decreased significantly in both task-oriented and relationship-oriented leader behavior! Should these findings be replicated outside the laboratory with experienced managers, the implications for organization development would be grim. This, of course, does not discredit the value of sensitivity training for purposes such as exploring attitudes and feelings or acquiring self-insight.

Based on the opinions expressed and the research alluded to so far, tentative conclusions can be reached about the most appropriate and ethical use of sensitivity training. Beneficial effects are most likely to occur to the individual and the organization when the following conditions are met:

425

(a) participants are carefully screened and prepared, with an emphasis on group members being competent and emotionally healthy individuals;

(b) training leaders have appropriate psychological training and skills;

(c) sensitivity training begins at the top of an organization and works its way downward; and

(d) leadership or management strategy encouraged in the T-group is encouraged in and suitable to the participants' organizational environment back home.

Ethical considerations. One of the complex issues here concerns whether or not any individual should be asked to subject himself or herself to a procedure that could conceivably increase his or her anxiety to an unmanageable extent. Emphasis on preselection of participants, careful preparation of the goals and methods of T-groups, and the voluntary nature of the experience are steps in the direction of guarding against ethical violation. Another ethical issue frequently mentioned in regard to sensitivity training is one of invasion of privacy. Privacy would certainly be violated if the statements made during the T-group were reported back to management without the participant's awareness. Provided that statements made in sensitivity training are not used to form evaluative judgments about individuals, and individuals are free to speak or not to speak during the sessions (as is the usual case), invasions of privacy would appear to be at a minimum.

The Managerial Grid

Sensitivity training has led to other group approaches to development. The most widely known of these approaches is the Managerial Grid, developed by Robert R. Blake and Jane S. Mouton.[44] A distant off-shoot of sensitivity training, the Grid technique is designed to accomplish far more than the development of individual managers. Exponents of this approach regard it as a far-reaching method that integrates individual, team, and organization development. Essentials of the Grid will be summarized here. Interested readers are referred to the original work of Blake and Mouton in order to comprehend the complexities of this method. The Grid technique assumes that it is possible for managers and the organizations of which they are members to maximize both production and concern for human values organization and individual goals are compatible and congruent rather than diametrically opposed. People can be both productive from a cost-accounting viewpoint and fulfilled from a psychological viewpoint.

Beginning in the early 1960s, the Managerial Grid has achieved widespread application in the United States, Canada, Europe, and other countries. Full-scale implementation of the Managerial Grid within an organization requires a long-term commitment by line management and staff specialists. In its pure form the Grid is a six-phase approach to organization development designed to take place over a period of two to five years. Initially, individual managers are developed, followed by team development. This leads in logical fashion to creating conditions for improved communications and problem resolution between groups within the organization. Next, a long-range strategic business model for improving the organization is established and implemented. A key phase, which begins early in the OD project, involves diagnosis, evaluation, and critique. Phase 1 (Managerial Grid laboratory—seminar training) has had a substantial impact on popular management thinking and jargon and thus will receive separate mention here.

Early in Grid training, attention is focused on the fact that production and people are interdependent. Notions that management behavior must be classified as one extreme or another (e.g., permissive versus authoritarian, strict versus lenient) are seriously questioned. A major goal of this phase is:[45]

> ... for managers to study and to understand the Managerial Grid in a concrete and personal way so that they can replace intuitive assumptions and habits with sound thinking for getting work done in a manner that generates mutual confidence and respect.

Unlike sensitivity training, line management conducts the Grid seminar. Aside from studying the Managerial Grid, activities include participating in structured experiments that provide insight into how interpersonal relationships affect task accomplishments and results. Participants in any one seminar are chosen by a diagonal slice method in order to represent different levels within the organization. No one, however, participates in the same group with his usual supervisor, subordinates, or peers.

Feedback in the seminar focuses on each individual learning his management style, both as perceived by himself and by others. In this system, management style is more a function of the assumptions a manager makes about people and not strictly a function of his "fixed" personality characteristics. Management style is described according to location on a grid, as illustrated in Figure 13.2. The horizontal axis indicates concern for production, while the vertical axis indicates concern for people. Concern ranges from a minimum of one to a maximum of nine.

There are four possible extremes on the grid. A manager with low concern for people and production is described as (1, 1). This type of manager

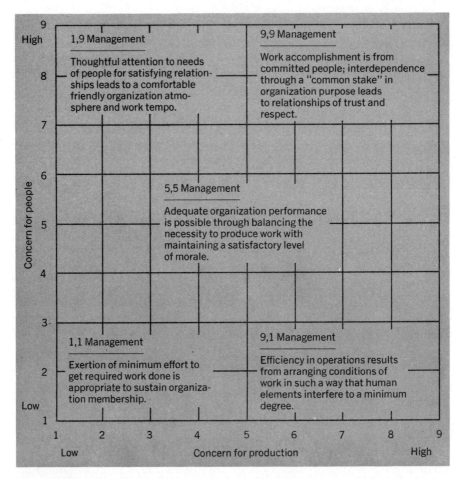

Figure 13.2 The Managerial Grid ®.Scientific Methods, Inc. (From *The Managerial Grid* by Dr. Robert R. Blake and Dr. Jane S. Mouton. Houston, Tex.: Gulf Publishing Company, 1964, p. 10. Reproduced with permission.)

has surrendered—production will be limited because it is assumed people don't want to work and there is little reward in work accomplishment with others. In the upper left-hand corner of the grid is the (1, 9) management style—minimum concern for production but maximum concern for people. A basic management assumption underlying this style is that pressing for production is incompatible with the basic needs of people. Additionally, it is assumed that if people are made comfortable and secure in a warm way production will take care of itself. Conflict is avoided or smoothed over by not pressuring people. Diagonally across is the (9, 1) management style—maximum concern for production and minimum concern for people. This management style also assumes that people basically resist production, but unlike (1, 9) the manager exerts heavy pressure and controls on people to try to get high production.

In the upper right-hand corner of the grid is the (9, 9) manager who strives to maximize production and concern for people. He assumes that people are basically mature and responsible and, if given rewarding work to which they are committed, maximum production will result. He basically believes that the needs of the organization and its members are compatible. The middle of the grid describes the (5, 5) management style characterized by intermediate concern for production and people. This management style also assumes that there is a conflict between the needs of people and production; he resolves this conflict through splitting such as compromise and similar measures.

These grid points have been presented in some detail because of the impact they have had on modern management thought. Many managers today characterize their management styles by using grid terminology. Perhaps a major contribution of Blake and Mouton's work is that they have graphically illustrated what insightful managers and behavioral scientists have known for a long time. Many people at all levels in the organization take pride in being high producers. Although many managers today use grid terminology, it is likely that too many of them perceive themselves as (9, 9) in philosophy, but in practice they behave quite differently.

Effectiveness of the Managerial Grid approach to organization development has not been widely researched probably because of its comprehensive and long-term nature. Two aspects of the Grid system probably underlie its helpfulness in an organizational setting. It forces management to carefully examine its own organizational problems and it is based on established group dynamics theory. Blake and Mouton present a chapter that documents the contribution made by their organization development program to a plant of 2400 employees. Results reported are impressive, but not based on an experimental approach. Among the improvements stemming from implementing the Grid system were increases in profitability, more cooperative intergroup relationships, and reduced interpersonal friction. On the individual level, some people were observed to have displayed increased individual effort and creativity, which apparently enhanced their job satisfaction.

Additional information about the effectiveness of the Managerial Grid approach to organization development is presented in extensive detail in a *Harvard Business Review* article.[46] Quantitative measures were obtained indicating that the Grid system used with 800 employees had a positive impact on (a) productivity and profits, (b) managerial practices and behavior, and (c) attitudes and values.

Team Development

Organization development specialists have increased their emphasis on working with intact "family" or "cousins" groups. Focus is on creating a more cohesive and effective team. Sensitivity training and the Managerial Grid also are geared toward the development of teams. *Team development* (or team building) in the present context refers to OD activity with work teams at top and middle levels of an organization. These are team development approaches other than sensitivity training and the Managerial Grid. Approaches to the development of groups at the top organizational level are also applicable to working with teams further down in the organization.

The growth of team development approaches has received impetus by both perceived negative and positive features of actual T-groups. On the positive side, T-groups have brought attention to the importance of working with groups of managers rather than exclusively with managers in isolation as a vehicle for development. Additionally, T-groups and the other facets of sensitivity training have underscored the importance of administrators dealing openly and honestly with one another. On the negative side, if groups are to be developed, a method has been sought that would minimize some of the potentially upsetting kind of feedback that transpires in the T-group. Also, criticism has been made of sensitivity training that the content of the sessions is too far removed from actual work problems. Team development meetings have the potential of capitalizing on the strengths of the T-groups, while minimizing the possible disadvantages. Brief procedural descriptions are presented next of two approaches to team development: (a) a general model directly familiar to the author and (b) the team building approach used at TRW Systems (an approach widely referred to by OD practitioners).

General model. Periodic meetings are established with the president, his staff, and an internal or external OD consultant. Meetings are held in a conference room on company premises rather than in a cultural island atmosphere. Meetings are more group-centered than leader-centered. There is sometimes an agenda and sometimes not. Typical agendas include topics such as:

What is good or bad about the way we communicate with each other?

How can we be more effective as an organization?

Does each of us know what we are actually supposed to be doing?

Do we really understand what's happening in the organization below us?

Similar to the T-group, there is confrontation and feedback among group members, but certain restrictions are placed on the kind of leveling that takes place. The leader encourages members to focus on job-related behavior rather than personal characteristics in their feedback to each other. Honesty and frankness is encouraged, but comments that might lead to dysfunctional consequences are discouraged. An example of the same feeling expressed first in terms of an individual's personal characteristics and then more in terms of its job consequences is illustrated in the statements made by the head of marketing to the head of manufacturing:

> *Personal Characteristics*:   Ed, you are so darned indecisive that you're ineffective. I have to worry more about you than I worry about the customers. I'm convinced that until you learn to make a decision, you'll never be a strong executive.
>
> *Job Behavior*:   Ed, there is one thing you're doing that makes it very difficult for me to properly run the marketing end of the business. When one group presents some plans to manufacturing, it takes too long to get a commitment. We have to keep our customers waiting while you decide whether or not manufacturing can meet our demands. If we could get decisions sooner from you, and if the decisions you made were firm commitments, we could do a much better job of serving customers.

The organization development specialist can play an active or passive role, depending upon how the group sessions are progressing. He might provide an interpretation of what process he observes is happening to the group, interject behavioral science theory, or guide the group back toward productive topics. There is a tendency for some groups to gravitate toward "shop talk" about relatively minor matters. If this occurs, the uniqueness of the team effectiveness meeting is lost. Management teams may be encouraged to continue the meetings without the consultant if the consultant feels they have the skill for such self-development and if the meetings appear to be contributing to organizational improvement. Emphasis is placed on every member of the group being present at every meeting and avoiding interruptions unless crises or emergencies develop.

Team building at TRW Systems. Under the direction of Sheldon A. Davis, an OD specialist, TRW Systems has established an elaborate program of team building.[47] The rationale and overall purpose of this program closely follow the general model of team development just described. One important specific purpose at TRW, however, is to achieve "effective behavioral coupling between technical specialists." In popular language, this means achieving better collaboration and less competition among people from different technical disciplines. Team building sessions are used with long-standing teams or with newly formed teams. Project teams are frequently established at TRW, as with other aerospace companies, thus increasing the opportunity to apply team building methods before teams develop ineffective patterns of interpersonal relationships. Team building at TRW is considered a long-range activity, and intact teams return periodically for additional OD activity. A condensation is presented next of Davis' description of the mechanics of team building at TRW Systems.

Initially the team manager calls a staff meeting introducing the OD consultant as someone who is going to work with the team, and says something like this: "I'd like to do some team building, and our agenda is going to be 'how can we improve our effectiveness?' I think there are some issues we need to deal with, including my own behavior as a leader, so let's try this out."

Prior to exploring the "effectiveness question" with the whole team, the consultant will interview each member of the team for half an hour or an hour. Generally the data collected by the consultant are considered public. That is, everyone understands that when the group meeting begins, he is going to feed back what he thought he heard in the interviews—the kinds of problems the individual team members identified, were concerned about, and would like to see discussed.

Davis prefers "personalizing the feedback"—being specific about identifying who raised what issue, except on those few points where the person being interviewed doesn't want to be identified. At the first team building meeting, the consultant reviews the major themes contained in the interviews. Usually themes dealing with the leadership approach of the top man are discussed first. (Unless the formal leader is emotionally involved, team building will fail!) The discussion may go like this:

"What sort of issues might relate to the top man? Well, they can be relatively mechanical ones like: How frequently does he see individuals on the team? How often does he have staff meetings? Are they long enough? Too long? Or there can be issues relating to the decision-making process that the leader uses: Do people feel involved? Do they feel he is constantly deciding important things without really involving or consulting with his people? ... There can be issues with respect to how he handles conflicts."

Issues of peer relationships are frequently discussed. For example, the issue of how much trust exists in the group is a popular one. Someone may feel that someone else is spending considerable energy trying to look right so he can get promoted. "There can be issues between people regarding their styles of operating with one another. Some people, for example, are so aggressive in making a point that they turn other people off." What the consultant is trying to do in a gross sense is to place issues that people have almost discussed out on the table and face them squarely.

In presenting interview data, the consultant is trying to get the team members to really hear each other and to understand the issues in a relatively nondefensive way. He tries to prepare the top man to be nondefensive, and lets him set the example. For instance, if the style in which the top man conducted staff meetings were criticized, his reply should be something like this: "All right, go on, what you don't like about them. I'd really like to understand what you don't like and to suspend judgment for the moment."

The consultant strives to help team members realize that there are alternatives to present ways of functioning. Should a person be told that he or she is overly aggressive, he or she might begin to think about other ways of responding to colleagues. "Or take a group of engineers each of whom is responsible for a different subsystem on a certain project. There's constant conflict among them, everything is getting done painfully, and maybe 40 percent of their energy is going into fighting one another, and only 60 percent into engineering. Maybe it turns out from the discussion that everyone is assiduously avoiding some of the trade-offs that have to be made if the system as a whole is to work. A candid facing of that issue leads to an alternative way of behaving, and the energy balance goes to 10 percent fighting and 90 percent engineering. That's an enormous shift—not a complete one but fewer arguments get escalated, there is less yelling, and the hardware flows faster." After examining internal team functioning, the group often then focuses on intergroup relationships. With prodding by the consultant, they may ask themselves a very important introspective question: "Are we a part of the problem we're talking about?" To illustrate, soon after condemning people in manufacturing, maybe someone will say, "You know, we've received a bunch of contract changes on that project recently, and maybe we're switching priorities on those guys too often. Maybe we should send someone down to find out whether that is contributing to their problems." According to Davis, this suggestion indicates that the group has made a big step forward in the team building process.

After the last stage of this initial exposure to team building, a determined effort is made to develop written action items. Who is going to do what and when is spelled out clearly to avoid the team building sessions from becoming only discussion groups. Action items vary widely in content but may include such diverse activities as increasing the frequency of staff meetings or working out a specific problem with manufacturing.

Effectiveness of team development meetings. OD approaches of this type are capable of contributing to the resolution of a wide range of problems that might not have been resolved as efficiently without the presence of these meetings. In addition to resolving problems, team development can also contribute to growth and development functions. Potential contributions of team effectiveness meetings include:

(a) resolving work barriers or specific disagreements between two or more members of the group;
(b) resolving interdepartmental conflict, at least at the top level;
(c) helping members of the group clarify their individual responsibilities in relation to one another;
(d) assisting in the development of sensitivity to how one's behavior and management style is perceived by others with whom one works on a regular basis;
(e) creating a climate for the improvement of communications in other group efforts such as staff meetings; and
(f) providing an appropriate setting for the establishment of organizational improvement goals.

In evaluating the contribution of team development, one subtle advantage must be given some consideration. There is a miniscule chance that deleterious effects to the individual or the organization will be forthcoming from these meetings. Confrontation and anxiety are not present to the extent of the T-group, thus minimizing the risk of overreaction to the experience. The feedback climate created minimizes the danger of making statements about one another that will create disunity or incompatibility in the life outside the meetings.

Research directly applicable to evaluating the effectiveness of team development meetings, as defined here, is difficult to isolate. Experiments conducted by Frank Friedlander with intact work groups and organizational training laboratories are relevant and show promising results.[48]

Friedlander compared the effects of four- to five-day organizational training laboratories on certain aspects of group functioning. Four work groups
in a research and development organization were compared to eight work
groups in the same organization that did not receive the same training.
Group sessions concentrated on the identifications of problems and developing plans for their resolution. This kind of work-related activity is
more typical of team development meetings than T-groups. Changes in
behavior were measured by a questionnaire especially designed to measure
areas of group functioning that were known to be problem areas as perceived by the group.

Overall, it was demonstrated that meaningful improvements in effectiveness of work groups can result from participation in organizational training laboratories. Specific problem areas that improved were group effectiveness, mutual influence among group members, and personal involvement or participation of group members in the meetings. Those problem
areas that did not manifest changes as a result of the group training
laboratories were leader approachability, intragroup trust, and the evaluation of group meetings. Broadly interpreted, Friedlander's research supports the notion that having managers face common problems in a group
setting is a defensible and worthwhile procedure. This does not mean,
however, that all organization development meetings will inevitably
strengthen an organization or its members as individuals.

Organization Development in Overview

The technology of organization development continues to grow. Reflecting the proliferation of OD methods and approaches, Blake and Mouton
have formulated the D/D Matrix (organization diagnosis and development). This new matrix summarizes 25 different change efforts carried out
by OD practitioners.[49] Five different types of interventions are applied to
five different units of change or settings. These five units are (a) individual,
(b) team, (c) intergroup, (d) organization, and (e) society. The five different
interventions require explanation.

A *cathartic* intervention enters into contact with the feelings, tensions,
and subjective attitudes that block a person and prevent him or her from
performing at peak effectiveness. Allowing a manager to "blow off steam"
about his or her resentment about the company would be an example of a
cathartic intervention at the *individual* setting.

A *catalytic* intervention involves entering a situation and adding something that assists in transforming the situation into something actually

different from the original. Catalytic intervention at the *team* setting was described earlier under "Team Development," the most widely practiced form of organization development.

A *confrontation* type of intervention forces a person to look at an existing situation and formulate some ideas about revamping the *status quo.* Confrontation at the *intergroup* unit of change was described under "Behavioral Science Intervention in Conflict" in Chapter 10. Riots initiated by students and other groups might loosely be classified under the confrontation type of intervention.

A *prescriptive* type of intervention involves an outside consultant telling the client organization what course of action should be taken to bring about constructive change. An expert is introduced to the organization; after he makes his assessment of the problem, he *tells* management what he thinks should be done. When a consulting firm recommends changes in organizational structuring for a client, it is employing a prescriptive approach at the *organization* setting.

A *principles, models, or theories* type of intervention is based on the assumption that:[50]

> ... deficiencies of behavior or performance can be resolved best when people responsible for results use relevant principles, theories or models in terms of which they themselves can test alternatives, decide upon and take action, and predict consequences. It is an approach which emphasizes intervention by concepts and ideas rather than by people.

B. F. Skinner, perhaps the world's best known contemporary behavioral scientist, has used this intervention approach at the *societal* unit of change on the basis of his book, *Beyond Freedom and Dignity.*[51] Skinner's theories for improving society are touched on in Chapter 14, which is about the future.

RELATIONSHIP TO CORE PROPOSITIONS

Organizational change, as with the other chapter topics contained in this book, can be viewed from the perspective of our basic framework for organizational behavior. Knowledge workers attempting to change (not "switch") organizations will have to deal directly with the implications of the four core propositions.

Human Behavior

Attempts at organizational change in any form should be cognizant of individual reactions to change. Many of these observations were presented in Chapter 11. One important principle worth repeating here is that individuals show wide variation in their receptiveness to change. Flexible, secure individuals will accept change more readily than will less flexible and less secure individuals. Approaches to organization development sometimes fail because some of the participants in the OD activity are not psychologically prepared to accept the experience. For instance, a highly defensive suspicious person might be ill-advised to attend a team building workshop until he or she is better able to cope with confrontation.

Situational Nature

The topic of organizational change is useful in illustrating the situational nature of organizational behavior. Executive realignment was mentioned as one method of bringing about organizational change. Instances have been observed where a series of executives or other managers have failed in the same position. Consecutive failures by seemingly qualified people suggest that the *situation*, not the individual executive, is at fault. The situation might be marked by technical or human problems of such magnitude that the executive in charge is destined to fail. For instance, some political scientists and newspaper writers have argued that anyone would fail in the role of mayor of New York City.

Organization development is another approach to organizational change that is situational in nature. Cautions were noted earlier that the effectiveness of OD is a function of certain situational variables. For instance, if the leadership climate in an organization is such that openness and trust are discouraged, OD approaches have a small likelihood of bringing about constructive changes.

Systemic Nature

The systemic nature of organizational change was illustrated in the case history of technology changes brought about in a baking plant undergoing a transition from an old mill-type plant to a new, highly automatic facility. Ramifications occurred throughout the entire organizational system. Three of these changes brought about by automation were: (1) Supervisors had more responsibility thrust upon them because the consequences of any one mistake were multiplied. (2) Supervisors became more interdependent under the new system and more interpersonal conflict manifested itself. (3) Established cliques were severed, with the result that many workers now felt socially isolated.

Structure and Process

Organizations are viewed by some writers as sociotechnical systems; both social and technical aspects of the organization must be considered in understanding organizational change. The term "technical" in this context includes many structural factors such as layout, procedures, policies, controls, and formal structural authority. "Social" factors include many process factors such as the interaction pattern among people, motivational level, and informal group structure.

Social and technical factors (or process and structural factors) interact to bring about organizational change. For example, if an organization decided to elicit an increased number of ideas for improvement from its employees, the combination of more emotional support for suggestions, plus organization policies and procedures that supported new ideas, might be necessary to achieve these changes.

GUIDELINES FOR ACTION

1. Whatever method you might choose to improve organizational functioning, patience is required. Organizational change in the direction of improvement is a slow and gradual process.
2. Should you become a key executive in an organization, recognize that you will be a prime target for those in pursuit of organizational change. Widespread is the belief that organizational change is most swiftly accomplished by replacing executives.
3. Changes in the technology of an organization (or one of its components) will create both desirable and undesirable side effects. One of your responsibilities as a manager is to detect and effectively manage these side effects.
4. In reorganizing a company or department, look for its unique "success requirements," and then adapt the organizational structure to them.
5. If you and your colleagues behave less defensively and more openly about problems, you would capitalize on many of the benefits that might be forthcoming from formal OD methods.

QUESTIONS

1. Assume that an organization development specialist suggested that he conduct T-group sessions within your organization. What information about him would you like to know before you authorized his conducting the groups?
2. Mention three approaches to organizational improvement you have heard about that are *not* mentioned in this chapter. Should they have been included?

3. "Young people are so open and candid today that soon there will be nothing left for OD specialists to do." Discuss this statement.
4. Can a manager really have high concern for people and production? Do you feel these goals are compatible in the real world of business and industry?
5. What kind of evidence would you need to determine if replacing a company president would enhance organizational effectiveness?

NOTES

1. Harold J. Leavitt, "Applied Organizational Change in Industry: Structural, Technological and Humanistic Approaches," in James G. March (editor), *Handbook of Organizations.* Chicago: Rand McNally, 1965, pp. 1144–1168.
2. William F. Glueck, "Applied Organization Analysis," *Academy of Management Journal*, Vol. 10, No. 3, September 1967, pp. 223–234.
3. *Ibid.*, p. 230.
4. *Ibid.*, p. 231.
5. James H. Donnelly, Jr., James L. Gibson, and John M. Ivancevich, *Fundamentals of Management: Functions, Behavior, Models.* Austin, Tex.: Business Publications, 1971, Chapter 12.
6. Chris Argyris, *The Applicability of Organizational Sociology.* Cambridge, England: University Press, 1972, p. 67.
7. Donnelly *et al., op. cit.*, p. 236.
8. Alan C. Filley and Robert J. House, *Managerial Process and Organizational Behavior.* Glenview, Ill.: Scott, Foresman, 1969, pp. 423–434.
9. Larry E. Greiner, "Patterns of Organization Change," *Harvard Business Review*, Vol. 45, No. 3, May–June 1967, pp. 119–130.
10. *Business Week*, January 29, 1972, p. 25, reproduced with permission.
11. *Business Week*, February 20, 1971, pp. 28–29, reproduced with permission.
12. D. Ronald Daniel, "Reorganizing for Results," *Harvard Business Review*, Vol. 44, No. 6, November–December 1966, p. 96.
13. *Ibid.*, p. 97.
14. *Ibid.*, p. 100.
15. *Ibid.*, p. 101.
16. *Ibid.*, p. 102.
17. *Ibid.*, p. 103.
18. *Ibid.*
19. Otis Lipstreu and Kenneth A. Reed, "A New Look at the Organizational Implications of Automation," *Academy of Management Journal*, Vol. 8, No. 1, March 1965, pp. 24–31.
20. *Ibid.*, p. 25.
21. *Ibid.*, p. 26.
22. *Ibid.*, p. 28.
23. *Ibid.*
24. *Ibid.*
25. *Ibid.*, p. 30.
26. Two important examples include Ida Russakoff Hoos, "When the Computer Takes Over the Office," *Harvard Business Review*, Vol, 38, No. 4, July–August 1960, pp. 102–112; and James A. Vaughan, Avner M. Porat, and John A. Haas, *FDIC Study of the Impact of Computers and EDP on Managerial and Organizational Behavior in Small to Medium-Sized Banks.* Pittsburgh: University of Pittsburgh Press, 1968.
27. Thomas L. Whisler, *The Impact of Computers on Organizations.* New York: Praeger, 1970.
28. *Ibid.*, p. 63.

29. *Ibid.*, p. 93.

30. *Ibid.*, p. 115.

31. *Ibid.*, p. 132.

32. Major portions of the information presented here about organization development are based on the author's treatment of this topic in *The Practice of Managerial Psychology* (Elmsford, N.Y.: Pergamon Press, 1972). OD has become a field of practice and knowledge within itself and new techniques and theory continue to emerge. Readers seeking more intensive knowledge about OD are referred to the following current sources of information: Chris Argyris, *Intervention Theory and Method: A Behavioral Science View.* Reading, Mass.: Addison-Wesley, 1970; Chris Argyris, *Management and Organizational Development: The Path from XA to YB.* New York: McGraw-Hill, 1971; C. L. Cooper and I. L. Mangham (editors), *T-Groups: A Survey of Research.* New York: Wiley, 1971; Robert T. Golembiewski and Arthur Blumberg (editors), *Sensitivity Training and the Laboratory Approach: Readings About Concepts and Applications.* Itasca, Ill.: F. E. Peacock, 1970; Harry Levinson with Janice Molinari and Andrew G. Spohn, *Organizational Diagnosis.* Cambridge, Mass.: Harvard University Press, 1972.

33. Warren G. Bennis, *Organization Development: Its Nature, Origins, and Prospects.* Reading, Mass.: Addison-Wesley, 1970, p. 2.

34. Alfred J. Marrow, *Behind the Executive Mask.* New York: American Management Association, 1964, p. 31.

35. Chris Argyris, *Interpersonal Competence and Organizational Effectiveness.* Homewood, Ill.: Richard D. Irwin and Dorsey Press, 1962.

36. Robert Tannenbaum, Irving R. Wechsler, and Frederick Massarik, *Leadership and Organization: A Behavioral Science Approach.* New York: McGraw-Hill, 1961.

37. Saul W. Gellerman, *Management by Motivation.* New York: American Management Association, 1968, p. 263.

38. Cited in Robert J. House, *Management Development: Design Evaluation, and Implementation.* Ann Arbor, Mich.: Bureau of Industrial Relations, 1967, p. 70.

39. *Ibid.*

40. B. E. Calame, "The Truth Hurts," *Wall Street Journal*, July 14, 1969, p. 1.

41. There is a growing literature on the effects of sensitivity training. A thorough, but moderately technical, review of this nature is Marvin D. Dunnette and John P. Campbell, "Laboratory Education: Impact on People and Organizations," reprinted in Walter Nord (editor), *Concepts and Controversy in Organizational Behavior.* Pacific Palisades, Calif.: Goodyear, 1972.

42. Robert J. House, "T-Group Education and Leadership Effectiveness: A Review of the Empiric Literature and a Critical Evaluation," *Personnel Psychology*, Vol. 20, No. 1, Spring 1967, pp. 1–32.

43. Reed M. Powell and John F. Stinson, "The Worth of Laboratory Training: Impact on Leadership and Productivity," *Business Horizons*, Vol. 14, No. 4, August 1971, p. 91.

44. Robert R. Blake and Jane S. Mouton, *The Managerial Grid.* Houston: Gulf, 1965.

45. *Ibid.*, p. 267.

46. Robert R. Blake and Jane S. Mouton; Louis B. Barnes and Larry E. Greiner, "Breakthrough in Organization Development," *Harvard Business Review*, Vol. 42, No. 6, November–December 1964, pp. 133–155.

47. Sheldon A. Davis, "Building More Effective Teams," *Innovation*, Number 15, 1970.

48. Frank Friedlander, "The Impact of Organizational Training Laboratories Upon the Effectiveness and Interaction of Ongoing Work Groups," *Personnel Psychology*, Vol. 20, No. 3, Autumn 1967, pp. 289–307.

49. Robert R. Blake and Jane S. Mouton, *The D/D Matrix.* Austin, Tex.: Scientific Methods, Inc., 1972.

50. *Ibid.*, p. 18.

51. B. F. Skinner, *Beyond Freedom and Dignity.* New York: Alfred A. Knopf, 1971.

PART V

The Future

Managers and Organizations
of the Future

Fundamentals of organizational behavior have been examined in the preceding 13 chapters. An attempt has been made to discuss information crucial to the understanding of human behavior in organizations. In this chapter several emerging trends are examined that could have a profound impact on the behavior of people in organizations over the next 30 years. To the extent that forecasting of broad societal trends can be done reliably (i.e., that the *futurists* are somewhat legitimate as seers), these trends will be an important part of organizational life in the year 2000.

Discussions about the future, similar to those about sex, automobiles, or money, are of inherent interest to many people. Aside from appealing to the reader's desire for intellectual excitement, a discussion of the future is eminently practical. A glimpse into the future provides some approximate guidelines for career development, life planning, and coping with organizations. It is both difficult and discouraging to gear one's life toward an unknown environment. Individuals who make accurate predictions about the future are at an obvious advantage. For example, in the late 1950s a machine accounting instructor forecast that community colleges would soon be teaching courses in electronic data processing. Capitalizing on this prediction, he devoted all of his free time for a nine-month period to preparing a basic text in data processing for community colleges. First to hit the market, his book provided enough royalties in two years to give him the capital he needed to pursue the type of life he wanted.

TOP MANAGEMENT ELITE

Several years ago, the present author synthesized some predictions about the impact of high-speed information processing on the number and nature of managerial jobs.[1] Shortly after these predictions were prepared for publication, J. G. Hunt and P. F. Newell (a management professor and his student, respectively) published an article which coincidentally provided survey information about the accuracy of these trends.[2] These earlier forecasts will be presented first, followed by feedback on their accuracy and any necessary modifications in terms of new evidence.

Prediction

There is a convergence of opinion that advances in the processing and analyzing of information will have a profound impact on the nature of tasks carried out by middle and top managers in the organization of the future. Computer technology will make it possible for a small cadre of individuals within one organization to conduct many of the planning activities and other creative functions that are now shared by members of middle management. According to the widely quoted forecasts of Harold Leavitt and Thomas L. Whisler made in 1958, middle-management jobs in the 1980s will become more structured and simultaneously top-level managers will assume an even larger proportion of the creative functions.[3] Middle-management positions, on this basis, will become divided into two broad classifications. Members of middle management selected for more creative positions will move upward in status and will be eligible for entrance into the top echelon of planners and thinkers. Members of middle management not selected for creative assignments will find themselves in lower status positions, highly programmed and structured in nature. This latter phenomenon will not be too different psychologically from the craftsmen earlier in the century who were forced to work as assemblers on a production line because the creative aspects of their job were removed by advances in industrial engineering. The *top management elite* are likely to have the interpersonal and entrepreneurial skills of today's successful managers. Out of necessity, they will also possess the analytical and problem-solving skills of the operations research or staff specialist of today.

Computer technology will thus change the nature of jobs carried out by middle managers, rather than displace them. Some jobs may become more complex and others more simple, but the number of positions available should not necessarily be reduced. There will perhaps be a more pronounced dichotomy between jobs that require systems *design* and those that require systems *implementation*.

Feedback and Updating

Computer technology, according to some mixed evidence gathered by Hunt and Newell, has influenced both the nature and number of middle-management jobs. Although computers have not caused wide-scale un-employment among middle managers, fewer middle managers are required to accomplish more work.[4]

> For example, a report by the American Foundation on Automation and Employment (AFAE) found that the volume of business at Metropolitan Life soared 75% since the first computer was installed in 1954, while the number of middle managers has hardly increased.

The business recession which began in approximately 1970 also influenced the decline in the proportion of middle managers. According to informal reports, many managers who were laid off in the height of the business decline were not rehired when sales volume returned to former levels. Partially because of advances in data processing, it was relatively easy for organizations to "close ranks" and operate efficiently with fewer administrative personnel.

As of this writing, corporations are still not run by a handful of "super-brains sitting in front of computer consoles"[5] but some managerial jobs are becoming more complex, while some jobs are becoming more pro-grammed. Underlying this apparent discrepancy is the observation of Leavitt and Whisler that the particular function carried out by a manager most likely determines the extent and direction of change in his job duties. As referenced by Hunt and Newell, here are two opposite situations:[6]

> 1. In all companies where there had been a change (as a result of using computers) there was an expansion of the responsibilities of middle managers and an increase in the necessary job qualifications. With the advent of computers, middle managers spent more time on such functions as communication, interpretation, and counsel. These jobs require more analytical and planning ability, more judgment and greater communications skills. Repetitious, routine aspects of their jobs decreased or disappeared.

> 2. ... the buyer in a purchasing department has typically used his personal judgment in deciding such things as what vendor to use. Now, models run through the computer can determine decisions of this type, as a result of which one highly important part of the buyer's job has been taken out of his hands.

Predictions made about the impact of computers on middle-manager decision making might be truer today if it were not for middle-management resistance to change. Based on 35 interviews with business, government, and university spokesmen, the AFAE notes that many middle managers voice skepticism about the potentialities of the computer and resist its encroachment into new areas.

Predictions about the future of managers and organizations inevitably confront the issue of whether computer programs can be developed to replace human judgment, thus displacing many knowledge workers.

Current thinking, as summarized by William J. Stevenson, indicates that computers will continue to perform functions humans cannot perform with equal skill. Conversely humans will continue to perform functions in which they have a natural advantage over computers such as exercising judgment.[7]

Heuristic decision-making models, as originally developed by Herbert A. Simon and Allen Newell, show the greatest promise of exhibiting humanoid thinking.[8] Martin K. Starr notes that heuristic models utilize logic, common sense, and past experience to diagnose an environmental pattern and provide a prescription for its treatment.[9] The heuristic approach can thus be used to simulate the decision-making pattern of human beings in the system. Among its advantages are reliability, speed, and the capacity to cope with more data and larger systems than is otherwise possible. Starr notes that heuristic analysis, despite its suitability for dealing with repetitive decision making, is not particularly applicable to long-range problems. Human judgment will continue to make a major contribution to organizations of the future.

Robert M. Fulmer recently collected some opinions about the management of tomorrow from a group of distinguished senior management professors (all Fellows of the Academy of Management).[10] Opinions were mixed on almost every topic. In reference to the future plight of middle managers, one dominant theme was that the computer will assist middle managers to perform more and better work. Harold Koontz, one of the panelists, estimated that perhaps 5 to 15 percent fewer middle managers will be required in the future.

In conclusion, there is a discernible trend toward a fewer number of middle managers performing a workload formerly handled by a larger number of managers. More of their work is of a specialized, creative nature.

FLEXIBLE ORGANIZATIONAL STRUCTURES

Spurred on by the acceleration of change, structures of future organizations will be more flexible and more diverse. The dominant form of organization will be the project or task team, because of its ability to meet the demands of change. Organizational structuring will be increasingly given more consideration as an independent variable in accounting for organizational health and viability.

Decline of the Pyramid

Based on the predicted thinning out of middle-management jobs owing to computer technology, it has been predicted that the organization chart of the future will become heavy at the top and bottom. Soon the overall shape of the organization will resemble an hourglass or a football vertically balanced on a bell. (There will still remain large numbers of people performing tasks at the bottom of the organization.) Following the "football on a bell" organizational structure will be a flattened structure. A survey of predictions about future organizational shapes indicates:[11]

> The organization will be rearranged along the actual flow of information, with a reduction in the number of departments accompanied by a reduction in personnel within these departments. Management as we think of it today will disappear in time. The only form of management that will remain in the future organization will be the computer experts and the analysts who can control the computer information-coordination system.

Even among those management theorists who think the pyramid will remain, opinion is expressed that a changing organizational form is a possibility. The panel of management professors mentioned earlier predicts a modification of the pyramid to facilitate information flow between comparable levels of different departments.[12]

Organizational Theory and Management Practice

Two scholars in the field of management and behavioral theory, Alan C. Filley and Robert J. House, contend that the knowledge area of "organizational taxonomy" will influence organization shapes of the future.[13] According to this barely emerging body of knowledge, the classification schemes presently used are ineffective in distinguishing between optimum structures for different purposes. A more sophisticated approach to classifying organizations (a new taxonomy) will enable management to design the best structure for each situation. Organizational theory will be applied directly to the solution of many perplexing management problems. Filley and House present a concise illustration of how research-based knowledge might be applied in this manner:[14]

> ...the appropriate form of organizational structure depends on the production technology and external environment. When the environment and technology are stable and predictable, the traditional pyramidal organization appears to work best. Where the product is customized and the environment is unpredictable, a loose, nonhierarchical organization appears more appropriate.

Organizational Structure and the Youth Culture

Another manifestation of flexibility in shaping organizations of the future is the prediction by Mack Hanan that organizations will make some concessions to the interests of youth. According to Hanan, the "new organization man" is best described as a *corporateur*.[15] This paradoxical breed of manager is not entrepreneurial or adventuresome enough to start his own business, but he still wants more excitement than most middle-management jobs might provide. Corporateurs prefer that the organization provide the capital to satisfy their entrepreneurial urges. Three varieties of decentralization are now being used by a few large organizations for this purpose: *divisional incorporation, subsidized start-ups* of new businesses, and *venture task teams*. Entity decentralization of this kind, it is predicted by Hanan, will be more popular in the future.

Divisional incorporation holds some promise to satisfy the entrepreneurial urges of but a handful of upper-middle managers. Under this system, division managers become division presidents. General Foods and Houdaille Industries are two corporations that use the division president title. Although given most of the prerogatives of a president, the corporateur still must mesh division objectives with those of the parent corporations. For example, he usually must strive to meet parent corporation ideas about an adequate return on investment.

Subsidized start-ups of new businesses provide corporateurs a unique opportunity to launch and maintain new businesses. Corporations investing in these new businesses sometimes do so with the intent of acquiring them once they have grown to a size considered worthy of acquisition. Younger people with strong entrepreneurial urges are attracted to organizations that invest in small outside businesses. Several well-known corporations are becoming involved in these subsidies:[16]

> For example, Boise Cascade, Coca-Cola, General Electric, and Union Carbide are among the companies which have been investing in small, outside businesses. In these companies, and also in others, such as DuPont, Mobil Oil, and International Paper, there is a growing awareness that many of their new breed are "men with ideas" for new businesses whose subsidization can return profits.

Venture task teams represent the most alluring form of organizational structure to young people. Task teams of this type are exploring and entering into new business ventures, usually of a small or medium-size nature. One corporate director of development quoted by Hanan describes the excitement of venture task teams:[17]

It's been electrifying. Every bright young manager in the company wants to be a venture leader. They tell me they're jumping at the chance to manage something pretty much on their own—something new, where they can start from scratch and build it themselves. If we let them, we'd have almost every product manager in the company running a venture.

The temporary nature of venture task teams has important motivational consequences; it provides the "new organization man" with the diversity and meaningful work he seeks. Corporateurs given these choice assignments benefit from being exposed to a variety of management styles. The organization receives the additional benefit of being able to observe the task team member perform under a variety of pressure circumstances.

MORE POWER TO THE PEOPLE

As documented by research cited in Chapter 5, managerial positions in most large business organizations have been populated largely by White Anglo-Saxon Protestant males. Present trends point toward an upsurgence of individuals in managerial positions emanating from a broader base of religious, ethnic, and sex backgrounds. Catholics, Jews, Blacks, and females are on the rise in organizational life. Federal and state legislation has been an important impetus behind a more democratic approach to selecting people for key managerial positions (particularly in business organizations that serve as federal contractors). The Women's Liberation Movement and the Black Awareness Movement are two additional forces that have served to weaken the supremacy of the male WASP in managerial positions.

At this writing members of the Black Awareness Movement would argue that many promotions of Blacks to key corporate positions merely reflect tokenism. One observer noted that many Blacks are given the title of manager but in fact have no subordinates and no managerial responsibilities. A more moderate view would argue that the appointment of a Black person as the president of Michigan State University or as a board member of General Motors is indeed a "large token" that will set the pace for many similar appointments in the future. Perhaps the best example in 1972 was the situation of Elizabeth Duncan Koontz, as abridged here from *Women's Wear Daily*.[18] (Situations are subject to sudden change in organizational life. On December 12, 1972, the resignation of Koontz was accepted by President Richard M. Nixon.)

Libby's Been Liberated a Long Time

WASHINGTON—Elizabeth Duncan Koontz, one of the 90 women in the Federal Government who make more than $28,000 a year delights in exploding myths.

As head of the Labor Department's Women's Bureau for three years and the newly named deputy assistant secretary to coordinate all federal programs involving women, Ms. Koontz is the top black woman in government...

She credits her office as switching government sentiment toward support of the equal rights constitutional amendment. She testified in its support, and her office provided much of the background material for others who appeared to win Congressional approval.

(Her view of women's role in government:)

"They should be at the top, certainly in the cabinet and there's no reason why there shouldn't be a woman vice-president. I think the country is ready for it. The trouble is that there is not a woman who has been able to obtain the experience necessary in what is essentially a man's world."

Although the illustration of Ms. Koontz is derived from government, not business, the trend is still noteworthy. Historically, federal and state governments have preceded business organizations in providing equal opportunity for minority group members.

MANAGERS OF TOMORROW

Individuals who occupy managerial positions in large and medium-sized organizations are gradually shifting toward the self-image of a professional person. This shift in orientation from nonprofessionals to professionals (or from locals to cosmopolitans) will probably move more swiftly in the future, particularly if the late 1970s and early 1980s prove to be a period of economic well-being. During times of economic malaise, managers become less concerned with professional status and more concerned about economic security.

Professionalism among the newer breed of managers is reflected in the emphasis placed on "institutionalizing" the MBA. Two magazines at this writing capitalize on the need of MBAs to consider themselves professional (or at least distinct from other groups): *Master of Business Administration* and *The MBA Executive*. Emphasis in the former magazine is on highly readable, interesting features about matters of concern to young professionals and managers. *The MBA Executive* concentrates more on trade information such as employment opportunities and wage scales for MBAs.

Perhaps the most specific evidence that management is emerging into a profession is provided by the Certified Administrative Manager (CAM) designation. Robert F. Pearse noted in 1972 that CAMs broke professional ground; ten men and one woman were awarded the Certified Administrative Manager designation by the Professional Accreditation Commission of the Administrative Management Society. As described by Pearse:[19]

> Each of the 11 candidates had to meet five program standards designed to measure their "professionalism" and pass a five-part examination aimed at measuring the individual's knowledge of the skills, concepts, and fundamentals of administrative management. It is also required that each C.A.M. have at least two years' management experience and high standards of personal and professional conduct. Finally, evidence of the individual's leadership and communicative ability is submitted, reviewed, and approved by the commission, which is made up of leading administrative managers and educators.
>
> ... On any exam day, a candidate may take a maximum of any two of the first four parts, covering personnel management, financial management, control and economics, administrative services, and systems and information management. The fifth part of the exam is an in-depth management case problem, which the candidate has 30 days to complete.

The professionalization of the new breed of managers is reflected in his new self-image and value system. Eugene E. Jennings, the most active writer about these matters, observes that this shift in values is reflected in attitudes toward vertical mobility (refer back to Chapter 5 for an extensive discussion of this topic). A review of a recent book by Jennings, *Routes to the Executive Suite*, cogently summarizes how younger managers of today (and tomorrow) are more identified with their careers than with their organizations.[20]

> Loyalty, conformity, self-sacrifice, long and faithful service, company oriented—these are the criteria conventional wisdom subscribes to as controlling the route of the executive aspiring for the top positions in his company. To reach them, he must submerge himself completely in the corporation, and accept implicitly its internal and external codes of conduct.
>
> An obsolete model, says the author of this book. The decade of the Sixties marked the end of the era of the loyalty ethic and corporation domination of the individual, and the beginning of the individual-managed, career-centered period. The technological explosion of the Sixties, unheralded economic affluence, an exponential rate of change, triggered this development. The corporate maze is still a jungle, but now survival has psychological, rather than managerial overtones. The struggle is to survive emotionally, to preserve and enhance one's identity or ego.
>
> The individual, rather than the corporation, is in the driver's seat. Not for him, any longer, the patient years of waiting for the top echelon to retire or die. The

"open sesame" now to advancement, is mobility, managed and timed by the employee. Mobility places a premium upon individuality, independence, self-assertiveness. The self-sacrificing man recedes into the limbo of legend. The cult of personality becomes deemphasized. What counts in the race toward the Olympian heights, is competence and performance.

Despite this emphasis on career mobility by the manager of today and tomorrow there is a strong countervailing attitude developing against *geographic* mobility. *Business Week* recently collected some evidence and opinion indicating that an increasing number of young executives refuse relocation if it is perceived as interfering with family welfare and the "good life." In reference to relocation, Harry Levinson notes:[21]

> People are asking themselves, "What am I going to get out of it?" The sentiment goes along with hippies questioning life styles, kids questioning their parents.

Antirelocation sentiment has also developed from a popularization of the notion that geographic moves can have an adverse impact on psychological welfare. Alvin Toffler notes in *Future Shock* that executive mobility is detrimental to healthy family life and can also adversely affect the political, religious, and educational structures in communities. *A Nation of Strangers* by Vance Packard is a book devoted almost exclusively to the negative effects of relocation on people.[22]

The reader is cautioned that not all behavioral scientists believe relocation is inevitably dysfunctional. Herbert J. Gans, a sociologist at M.I.T., takes exception to the conclusions reached by Packard.[23] Among the counter arguments he notes is that many families readily establish friendly relations with new neighbors and make new friends with persons they find compatible. Gans further notes that ". . . where strangers come together to create a new life, rates of loneliness and pathology are low and satisfaction is great."[24]

EXPLORATIONS IN NEW VALUES

A gradually shifting value system will influence organizations of the future in many more ways than those already mentioned in this chapter. Ian H. Wilson, a *futurist*, notes that "shifts in people's basic values may be the single most important element in forecasting the environment in which organizations and people will operate in the future." This conclusion stemmed from a survey of futurist thinking conducted by the Business Environment Section of General Electric. Business organizations of the future may be confronted with a variety of consequences stemming from this exploration in new values:[25]

1. Technology will force a democratization of our industrial system. The management system must be restructured to "encourage experiment, flexibility and variety."
2. Growing importance will be attached to the formulation of explicit goals. Planning and goal-setting increase in importance as they increase in difficulty, largely because the greater variety of options among which choices must be made.
3. The set procedures of a bureaucratic management, and the power of administrators, will alike be weakened in face of employee pressures for variety, challenge and responsibility in their daily tasks.
4. Employees will insist on greater participation in management, will judge an organization on their assessment of how it assists or hinders them in their self-fulfillment needs.
5. Attitudes toward work will change. There will be more leisure, longer vacations, extended weekends, shorter working hours, more part-time workers. The Protestant ethic that hard work is highly honorable will become less important.
6. There will be less concern about future security (company insurance and pensions) in favor of immediate earnings and fringe benefits.
7. In industry, there will be further decentralization of responsibility and authority, accompanied by greater centralization of control through computerized data gathering.
8. Economic efficiency as an end in itself will be downgraded when it conflicts with individual dignity and standards of social justice.

Several of these predictions are trends that are already visible in corporate life. Recently, *The Wall Street Journal* featured a story documenting the shift taking place toward less formality in executive work habits. They found, among other things, that there are executives who run company operations from home or yacht, wear informal clothes, sleep late, and do push-ups in the board room.[26]

Fred D. Barton, the chairman and president of Fre Bar Inc., illustrates this trend toward revamping traditional notions about executive life and work habits:[27]

> ... The company, a maker of auto radiator leak and rust preventatives and other automotive supplies, is based in Holly, Mich., a small town about sixty miles north of Detroit. But the 63 year old chief executive runs it from a spacious home on the windward side of Oahu Island in Hawaii.

Mr. Barton says he keeps in touch with his company by telephone every day, giving orders and getting reports from his associates. He gets a copy of the company's balance sheet every month and a list of corporate expenditures every week. "I get a list of any checks written anywhere," he says.

About seven times a year, Mr. Barton goes to Holly, sometimes for as long as a week, to check up on things.

What type of manager will be needed to cope with these changed values? Tomorrow's manager will have to be even more adaptive (responsive to the situation) than he or she is today. Harlan Cleveland, the president of the University of Hawaii, has examined the environment in which the manager of tomorrow will operate and reports how he thinks the new manager will have to behave in order to cope with the new breed of worker and the changing times.[28] A dominant conclusion reached by Cleveland is that unresponsive and authoritarian managers will have considerable difficulty in operating in tomorrow's climate.

Managers of today using yesterday's value system are already having difficulty in coping with "the decline of the work ethic." Young people (and a growing number of older people) are shying away from heavy emotional commitment to work. As nonprofessional workers in increasing numbers opt for shorter working weeks and longer vacations, professionals and managers may follow suit. Leisure activities—tennis, skiing, and camping, to name a few—are gaining in both popularity and prestige. In this author's opinion, the most telling evidence about the desire for a "better life" is the increasing number of managers who refuse promotions to offices located in congested metropolitan areas.

SCIENTIFIC CONTROL OF BEHAVIOR

As the quest for effective use of resources intensifies, organizations of the future may make more extensive use of psychological techniques of behavior control.[29] A technology has already been developed that is dramatically more effective than nonsystematic approaches in controlling the behavior of people toward desired ends. Some of these applications of the psychology of learning have already been applied in organizations. Few readers of this book, for example, have not been exposed to some type of programmed learning—a technique stemming directly from the research about learning conducted by B. F. Skinner. Teaching machines, however, are only a precursor to a behavior technology of more far-reaching application.

Behavior modification—the precise name for techniques of applying reinforcers to shape behavior—has been practiced with gratifying success in the solution of a variety of problems. Individuals with specific phobias have learned to overcome their fears. Elementary school children have accelerated their learning rate. Patients in mental hospitals who have been impervious to drugs, psychoanalysis, or staff authority sometimes become alert and healthier when each good behavior wins a token that can be spent for candy or desired freedom.[30] A systematic application of reinforcers at Emery Air Freight Corporation illustrates how behavioral science technology can be used to control behavior.[31]

> Around the worldwide offices and terminals of Emery Air Freight Corp. the password these days is "positive reinforcement." For hundreds of Emery employees, that academically pretentious term, identified with controversial Harvard psychologist B. F. Skinner, has taken on a precise meaning. They are getting a daily feedback on how their work measures up to company goals and standards, many of which they have helped to set themselves. And they are receiving praise and recognition for improved performance. In effect, Emery is applying Skinner's theory that behavior can be affected by positive rewards.
>
> Although this sounds like an obvious, elementary principle for any well-managed operation to follow, many companies ignore it. For Emery, it has become the key element in a new performance improvement system based largely on Skinner's ideas. That system has saved the company an estimated $2-million over the past three years.
>
> The system was set up by Vice-President Edward J. Feeney, 44, who joined Emery as a freight agent in 1950 after graduation from Northwestern University. By 1966, Feeney had worked his way up to assistant vice-president for sales. His interest in applying Skinner's techniques to management problems began with a training program. Feeney was disillusioned with the results of traditional sales training methods, which consisted of courses that used movies on generalized selling techniques or evangelical lectures from supersalesmen. He felt that the courses were often irrelevant in the field. So he armed himself with a tape recorder and trekked across the U.S. to analyze hundreds of Emery selling situations.
>
> *Teaching salesmen.* His trip convinced him that sales calls had to be made more productive and induced him to assemble a programmed-learning course that each Emery salesman now completes on his own. It is a carefully engineered, step-by-step program, with frequent feedback questions and answers to let the salesman know how he is doing. The course contrasts with movies and lectures in which, Feeney says, the salesman is unable to gauge what he has learned. The aim is to get the customer on each sales call to take some kind of action indicating that he will use Emery services. Significantly, in 1968, the first full year after the new course was launched, sales jumped from $62.4-million to $79.8-million, a gain of 27.8%, compared with an 11.3% rise the year before.

In designing the new sales course, Feeney became intrigued with some of Skinner's behavioral science experiments. Skinner designed some of the first teaching machines and is the author of the current best-seller, *Beyond Freedom and Dignity.* He contends that to change behavior—to make an employee more productive, for example—one has to manipulate the environment, such as the work situation itself. Many conventional training techniques center on the somewhat mystical process of what happens within an individual—involving such factors as attitude, motivation, or sensitivity, which Skinner and his followers say cannot be measured. "To talk about those things is to deal with symptoms of behavior, not causes," grumbles Feeney.

A fundamental Skinner principle is that behavior can be engineered, shaped, or changed by a carefully controlled system of rewards—a process that he calls "positive reinforcement." In an industrial setting, this means devising ways of letting an individual employee regularly learn how well he is meeting specific company goals, and rewarding performance improvement—chiefly through frequent praise and recognition. But such reinforcement, Skinner contends, should always be positive. In contrast with "carrot and stick" management approaches, Skinner believes that punishment for such things as poor performance can only produce negative results. It is much more efficient, he argues, to shape behavior by rewarding positive results.

Coddling. Some critics consider such an approach to be namby-pamby. Others see sinister implications in any behavioral engineering, objecting that it could lead to a totalitarian society. Feeney, who has had such reactions even within the company, rejects the criticism. "It works," he says, citing improved profits and performance and what he considers greater contentment on the part of employees who know they are doing a good job.

The results of Emery's new sales training course convinced Feeney that some Skinner theories might be put to work in other company areas. He soon met consultants and personnel executives from companies such as AT&T, American Can, Ford, Upjohn, United Air Lines, Addressograph-Multigraph, Connecticut General Life, and Warner-Lambert, who were equally interested in applying Skinner's ideas to business situations. They have since formed the Training Research Forum, which meets every two months at a plush Long Island conference center called Harrison House to swap ideas.

Feeney has been particularly intrigued by techniques developed by Praxis Corp., a Skinner-inspired group of Manhattan-based consultants. Praxis has come up with a system to audit performance deficiencies and to pinpoint areas where performance improvement would produce the greatest payoff to profits.

Shortly after the results from the new sales course began to come in, Feeney was promoted to head Emery's marketing services. Still eager to apply Skinner techniques to other Emery operations, he persuaded the company's top brass to let him take the company's customer service department under his wing for an experiment.

Self-improvement. That department had set a goal of responding to customer queries within 90 minutes. When employees and supervisers were polled, most thought that they were doing this nine times out of 10. But a study soon showed that they were meeting the goal only 30% of the time.

The obvious solutions—hiring more personnel or launching a special training program—were rejected in favor of a simple feedback system of daily checklists. Operators ticked off on their sheets whether each call had been answered within 90 minutes. Performance improvement was greeted with praise and recognition from supervisors. If there was no improvement, the employee was told, "At least you've recorded your performance honestly," while being reminded of the goal.

Performance in the first test office went from 30% of standard to 95% in a single day. The system has now been extended to all Emery customer service offices, and, after three years, performance still averages 90 to 95%. "In Chicago, they're trying to go us one better," says Gerald A. Connors, senior vice-president and general manager. "Their goal is to respond to all customers queries in 90 minutes—and to have all the requested answers. They're setting a much higher standard for themselves than if we told them what they should be doing."

Feeney has since been named to head a special five-man Systems Performance Div., which is ferreting out other company areas where his techniques to increase productivity could be applied. But selecting new targets has presented problems. "Any organization tends to react to situations that are irritants," says Feeney, "but doing something about them may or may not have a payoff." So he set out to do a careful performance audit, the kind suggested by Praxis, to determine where correction of performance deficiencies would boost profits the most.

Container use.   That area, to Emery's surprise, turned out to be the company's highly touted containerized shipment operation. Emery had been increasing the use of containers—combining many smaller packages into a single shipment—at an impressive rate each year. The company had been convinced that containers were being used about 90% of the time that they could be used. But Feeney found that the actual figure was more like 45%. Since Emery's largest single cost item is air freight—some $50-million a year—increased use of containers would cut costs substantially.

Again, Feeney felt that training was not the answer. Most of the workers on the loading dock knew how and when to use containers. The problem was mostly one of poor feedback. Employees did not know how they were actually performing, and they were only vaguely aware of the impact that container use had on company profits.

As he had with customer service, Feeney devised a simple checklist to let each employee determine for himself how well the goals were being met. At the same time, supervisors and regional sales managers applied positive reinforcement in the form of praise and recognition for performance improvement. The results: Container use throughout the country jumped from 45% to 95%. And in more than 70% of the offices, the increase came in a single day.

More important, performance has remained at this high level for nearly two years. In the few cases in which feedback was temporarily interrupted because of, for example, managerial changes, performance slumped more than 50%, only to rise rapidly again when feedback was resumed. Cost reduction from this program was initially pegged at $650,000 a year, but in October alone, record savings of $125,000 were chalked up.

Feeney's group is currently involved in a performance audit of Emery's overall dock operations and a special program for route drivers. Feeney is also talking with freight division executives from five major airlines about using Emery's system in their operations.

To some, Emery's approach—the success of which depends on telling employees they are doing a good job—seems overly simplistic and idealistic. But Emery believes that it has hit on a unique way to link such theoretical ideas as work measurement, management by objectives, job enrichment, productivity and profit improvement, and participative management into a practical program that pays off.

Beyond Freedom and Dignity, B. F. Skinner's best-selling manifesto about the need for and technology of behavior-shaping techniques, has been the subject of passionate controversy.[32] Religious leaders and other humanists have bitterly denounced Skinner's ideas. Spiro T. Agnew made a public address condemning both *Beyond Freedom and Dignity* and its author. What underlies these objections to more effective control of the behavior of people in organizations and society?

Environment Is Overemphasized

Key to Skinner's theory is that behavior is shaped by what transpires in a person's environment. Reinforcers, not internal states of man, thus determine behavior. Advancing this position automatically dismisses the importance of values, beliefs, and feelings. Concepts such as *love, hate, loyalty*, and *desire* are given almost no importance in comparison to objective determinants of behavior such as positive and negative reinforcers. People then do not "resist temptation" because of religious belief but because the particular schedule of rewards and punishments they have been exposed to has taught them to avoid that particular stimulus (temptation). Skinner urges that a true science of behavior can exist only when man is no longer regarded as a self-determining organism:[33]

> We need a technology of behavior, but we have been slow to develop the science from which we might draw such a technology. One difficulty is that almost all of what we call behavioral science continues to trace behavior to states of mind, feelings, traits of character, human nature, and so on. Physics and biology once followed similar practices and advanced only after discarding them.

Humanism and Behavior Control Conflict

Behavior modification was considered by *Psychology Today* in 1971 as the second fastest growing movement within psychology.[34] "Behavior mod," because of its effectiveness, is spreading in popularity. Humanism—that aspect of psychology concerned with the feeling side of people—is gaining in popularity at an even faster rate. Sensitivity training, encounter groups, and OD (organization development) are all examples of the recent emphasis in society on human feeling. Behavior mod and humanism also conflict to a mild degree in the elementary school classroom. Humanists are concerned with the free expression and emotional development of children, while behavior modifiers are more concerned about improving the efficiency of children's learning.

In short, the renewed interest in humanism with its emphasis on feelings and emotions conflicts with the "hard-nosed" discipline of behavior modification. (In its defense, behavior modification can be applied to the healthy development of emotional expression. Constructive emotions can be given verbal rewards while destructive emotions can be given negative or zero reinforcement.)

Manipulation Is a Dirty Word

Behavior mod, by its very nature, is an attempt to effectively manipulate behavior toward desired ends. In the air freight company case described above, employee behavior was manipulated toward improved performance in reaching company goals. Manipulation of this type brings about shouts of "Big Brother," "Brave New World," and "Shades of 1984" from many people. A secretary working in the reception area of a psychological counseling center stated to her boss that she objected to being manipulated. Asked, "Manipulated in what way?" she replied: "Instead of telling me that I'm wrong or stupid, you just grin and say 'Mmh.' I know you're doing something to me, but I'm not sure what."

Who Will Control Behavior Technologists?

Underlying almost all objections to an effective method of controlling behavior is the fear that the *wrong people* will gain control. "Who designs and administers the environmental contingencies that control behavior?"[35] What would happen if an elite group of behavioral scientists banded together to modify the behavior of people toward destructive ends? Who controls the controllers?

Skinner conceptualizes that his ideal state is like a cybernetic system.[36] Controllees have a reciprocal influence on the controllers. A system of reinforcers that eventually *harms* rather than helps people will be self-defeating. Positive reinforcers then become negative reinforcers.

Employees who are reinforced to work harder will continue to work hard only if rewards from working hard are indeed rewards, not punishments. Should increased productivity lead to layoffs and lower pay (undesired consequences or punishments), the behavior that led to such undesired consequences will be changed by the controlled themselves.

Even the most ardent antibehavior mod, antibehavioral scientist can see major flaws in how society is presently conducting itself. Violent acts of aggression and destruction of private property and the public environment constitute a dismal sample of the negative consequences of nonmodified behavior in society. Returning our attention to the first statement in our exploration of organizational behavior, scientific control of behavior at least holds some promise of making organizations "less screwed up."

GUIDELINES FOR ACTION

1. If you want to become part of the "top management elite," begin developing your conceptual and analytical skills now.
2. The prospects of not developing in this direction appear to lie in occupying a fairly dull, repetitive job (should you work in a large organization).
3. Future opportunities for younger organization members to participate in exciting task force assignments appear bright; however, only a handful of talented people will enjoy the luxury of receiving these assignments.
4. If you are a male or female, Black or White, non-WASP, feel somewhat optimistic about having equal opportunities in business organizations. Many older prejudices are diminishing.
5. Learning how to apply positive and negative reinforcers to subordinates may be a required skill of managers of tomorrow.

QUESTIONS

1. How do you feel about the predictions that middle managers will be in less demand in organizations of the future?
2. Do you consider a junior executive with an MBA degree to be a professional person? What criteria do you use to determine if a given occupation is a "profession"?
3. What do you feel are the prospects of any major corporation having a Black female president within the next ten years? Explain the basis for your conclusion.
4. How accurate do you feel the prediction is that in the future, "The Protestant ethic that hard work is highly honorable will become less important?" Discuss.
5. How would you feel about being subjected to the "scientific control of behavior"?

NOTES

1. Andrew J. DuBrin, *The Practice of Managerial Psychology*. Elmsford, N.Y.: Pergamon Press, 1972, pp. 285–287.
2. J. G. Hunt and P. F. Newell, "Management in the 1980's Revisited," *Personnel Journal*, Vol. 50, No. 1, January 1971, pp. 35–45.
3. Harold J. Leavitt and Thomas L. Whisler, "Management in the 1980's," *Harvard Business Review*, Vol. 36, No. 6, November–December 1958, pp. 41–48.
4. Hunt and Newell, *op. cit.*, p. 39.
5. Quote from Peter Redwood, a manager of management science.
6. Hunt and Newell, *op. cit.*, p. 40.
7. Personal communication from William J. Stevenson.
8. Herbert A. Simon and Allen Newell, "Heuristic Problem Solving: The Next Advance in Operations Research," *Operations Research*, Vol. 6, No. 1, January–February 1958, pp. 1–10.
9. Martin K. Starr, *Production Management: Systems and Synthesis*, second edition. Englewood Cliffs, N.J.: Prentice-Hall, 1972, p. 136.
10. Robert M. Fulmer, "Profiles of the Future (The Management of Tomorrow)," *Business Horizons*, Vol. 15, No. 4, August 1972, pp. 5–12.
11. Hunt and Newell, *op. cit.*, p. 37.
12. Fulmer, *op. cit.*, p. 9.
13. Alan C. Filley and Robert J. House, "Management and the Future," *Business Horizons*, Vol. 13, No. 4, April 1970, p. 14.
14. *Ibid.*, p. 15.
15. Mack Hanan, "Make Way for the New Organization Man," *Harvard Business Review*, Vol. 49, No. 4, July–August 1971, p. 132.
16. *Ibid.*
17. *Ibid.*, p. 133.
18. "Libby's Been Liberated a Long Time," *Women's Wear Daily*, reprinted in *Democrat and Chronicle*, Rochester, N.Y., May 14, 1972, Section E, p. 4.
19. Robert F. Pearse, "Certified Professional Managers: Concept into Reality?" *Personnel*, Vol. 49, No. 2, March–April 1972, pp. 30–31.
20. Eugene E. Jennings, *Routes to the Executive Suite*. New York: McGraw-Hill, 1971, reviewed by Harry Seligson in *Personnel Psychology*, Vol. 25, No. 1, Spring 1972, pp. 178–180.
21. Quoted in *Business Week*, October 28, 1972, p. 114.
22. *Ibid.*, pp. 113–114.
23. Herbert J. Gans, "Vance Packard Misperceives The Way Most American Movers Live," *Psychology Today*, September 1972, pp. 24–28.
24. *Ibid.*, p. 28.
25. "General Electric Looks Ahead," *Personnel Journal*, Vol. 50, No. 7, July 1971, p. 566.
26. "Out of the Rut," *The Wall Street Journal*, May 12, 1971, p. 1. Reprinted with permission of *The Wall Street Journal*.
27. *Ibid.*
28. Harlan Cleveland, *The Future Executive*. New York: Harper & Row, 1972.
29. One such program already available that utilizes entertaining and content-oriented comic strips integrated with semiprogrammed conceptual material is Dale M. Brethower, *Behavioral Analysis in Business and Industry*. Kalamazoo, Mich.: Behaviordelia, 1972.
30. T. George Harris, "All the World's a Box," *Psychology Today*, Vol. 5, No. 3, August 1971, p. 35.
31. "New Tool: Reinforcement for Good Work," *Business Week*, December 18, 1971.

32. B. F. Skinner, *Beyond Freedom and Dignity.* New York: Alfred A. Knopf, 1971.
33. *Ibid.,* as printed in *Psychology Today,* Vol. 5, No. 3, August 1971, pp. 3, 37.
34. Harris, *op. cit.,* p. 33.
35. William G. Scott and Terence R. Mitchell, *Organization Theory: A Structural and Behavioral Analysis,* revised edition. Homewood, Ill.: Richard D. Irwin and Dorsey Press, 1971, p. 392.
36. *Ibid.*

ANSWERS TO QUESTIONS ON OFFICE POLITICIANS

A political type of executive would agree with all the statements in the test. Dr. Jennings says that if you did not mark "agree" to the statements cited, this indicates a *less* than uniform disposition on your part to use of power tactics than a typical business politician would use. Self-appraisal is the keynote, Dr. Jennings explains. He adds: "If you agree with all of the statements, be sure to check to see if your reasons for agreeing are the same or different than those covered in the article on power tactics" (*Nation's Business*, December 1959, p. 52).

Name Index

Agnew, S. T., 458
Ansoff, H. I., 379, 396
Appelwhite, P. B., 28, 191, 208, 239
Argyris, C., 175, 251, 267, 399, 415, 419, 421, 439, 440
Asch, S., 187
Auer, J., 269, 298
Averch, V. R., 204, 205, 209

Baldridge, J. V., 327
Barnes, L. B., 440
Bass, B. M., 6, 28, 38, 68, 138, 139, 173, 194, 195, 208
Batten, J. D., 140, 154, 173, 174
Bedrosian, H., 390, 396
Behling, O., 42, 68
Benchley, P., 134
Bennis, W. G., 181, 208, 318, 415, 440
Berkwitt, G. J., 104, 115, 117, 134, 135
Berne, E., 292, 293, 299
Blake, R. R., 218, 239, 319, 327, 425, 426, 428, 429, 435, 440
Blanchard, K. H., 227, 236, 238, 239
Blumberg, A., 440
Bobbitt, H. R., 42, 68
Bowman, G. W., 173
Brethower, D. M., 461
Bright, J. R., 387, 388, 396
Bruns, W. J., 102
Bryant, C. D., 34, 67
Bullard, T., 298
Burger, C., 165, 175
Burke, R. J., 252, 253, 268, 294, 299
Burns, T., 367, 386, 395, 396
Butler, E. A., 155, 173, 174

Calame, B. E., 440
Campbell, J. P., 15, 38, 49, 69, 88, 101, 235, 239, 350, 361, 374, 395, 440
Carrol, S. J., 168, 175, 268
Cartwright, D., 179, 208
Christie, R., 125, 135
Clarkson, G. P. E., 95, 102
Cleveland, H., 454, 461
Cohen, A. M., 278, 298
Cohen, J., 361

Cone, L. M., 101, 120, 135, 396
Cooper, C. L., 440
Crutchfield, R. S., 188, 208

Dalton, M., 180
Daniel, D. R., 406, 407, 408, 409, 439
Darkenwald, G. G., 311, 327
Darley, J. G., 54, 69
Davis, G. A., 88, 101
Davis, S. A., 432, 440
DeCoster, D. T., 102
Dickey, C. D., 203
Donnelly, J. H., 399, 400, 401, 403, 439
Drucker, P. F., 8, 10, 28, 82, 101, 112, 134, 135, 268
Druckman, D., 328
Dubin, R., 228, 239
DuBrin, A. J., 28, 68, 102, 134, 135, 173, 175, 239, 298, 299, 328, 396, 461
Dunnette, M. D., 38, 68, 88, 101, 235, 239, 361, 395, 440
Dutton, R. E., 134
Dwyer, J. C., 174

Eden, D., 208
Eisenson, J., 269, 298
Emory, W., 72, 73, 101
Etzioni, A., 225, 226, 227, 239
Ewen, R., 361

Falk, E., 373, 395
Fast, J., 288, 299
Fearing, F., 298
Fiedler, F. E., 17, 195, 209, 216, 217, 218, 235, 239
Filley, A. C., 79, 101, 191, 196, 201, 208, 209, 238, 402, 439, 447, 461
Fine, B. D., 181, 208
Fitzpatrick, S., 63, 69
Flory, C. D., 53, 69, 202, 209, 267
Follett, M. P., 16, 28
Forehand, G. A., 331, 360
Forrester, J. W., 7, 28
Fox, A., 302, 327
Fram, E. H., 268
Frederickson, N., 350, 351

French, J. R. P., 267
French, W. L., 69
Friedlander, F., 342, 350, 351, 354, 355, 357, 361, 434, 435, 440
Friedman, A., 69
Fulmer, R. M., 446, 461

Gans, H. J., 452, 461
Gatza, J., 267
Gellerman, S. W., 63, 69, 238, 360, 420, 440
Gemmil, G. R., 125, 135
Ghelardi, M., 121
Ghiselli, E. E., 53, 69, 213, 214, 238
Gibb, C., 212, 386, 396
Gibb, J. R., 55, 69, 90, 102, 294, 299
Gibson, J. L., 399, 400, 439
Gillis, J., 101
Gilmer, B. V. H., 331, 360
Ginott, H. G., 258, 268
Gleason, R. E., 148, 149, 173
Glueck, W. F., 398, 399, 439
Gold, M., 87, 101
Golembiewski, R. T., 440
Gooding, J., 135
Goodman, P. S., 69
Gordon, W. J. J., 88, 101
Greenberg, S., 351, 361
Greiner, L. E., 402, 439, 440

Haas, F. C., 396
Haas, J. A., 439
Hagenah, T., 54, 69
Hall, D. T., 104, 105, 134
Halpern, S., 123, 135
Hamblin, R. L., 193, 194, 208
Hampton, D. R., 29, 67, 119, 135, 174, 208, 276, 298
Hanan, M., 127, 135, 209, 448, 461
Haney, W. V., 272, 273, 298
Hare, P. A., 208
Harris, T. A., 292, 299
Harris, T. G., 46, 68, 461, 462
Haskell, R. J., 28
Hayakawa, S. I., 282, 298
Hegarty, E. H., 173
Heisler, W. J., 125, 135
Hellriegel, D., 29
Hemphill, J. K., 340, 347
Hersey, P., 227, 236, 238, 239
Hershey, G. L., 10, 28
Herzberg, F., 33, 41, 42, 43, 45, 54, 59, 68, 69
Higdon, H., 144, 148, 173

Hill, W., 28, 217, 239
Homans, G. C., 184, 208
Hoos, I. R., 439
House, R. J., 68, 79, 101, 191, 196, 201, 208, 209, 221, 238, 239, 268, 392, 396, 402, 424, 439, 440, 447, 461
House, W. C., 262
Hughes, C. L., 251, 267
Hull, R., 153, 174, 396
Humble, J. W., 268
Hunt, J. G., 444, 445, 461

Irwin, J. V., 269, 298
Ivancevich, J. M., 399, 400, 439

"J" (author), 76
Jaastad, K., 88, 101
Jakobovits, L. A., 298
James, M., 299
Jay, A., 159, 160, 174
Jennings, E. E., 140, 147, 148, 149, 150, 153, 173, 175, 451, 461
Johnson, D. W., 395
Johnson, H. J., 131
Jongeward, D., 299
Joyce, R. D., 107, 134

Kahn, R. L., 116, 134, 228, 261
Kapell, H., 39, 68
Kast, F. E., 10, 20, 21, 28, 29
Kavanagh, M. J., 212, 238
Kay, E., 267
Kelly, J., 3, 23, 28, 29, 318, 322, 327, 328
Kendall, A. F., 267
Kipnis, D., 151, 152
Klemme, H., 109
Knudsen, S. E., 155, 404
Kobayashi, S., 64, 65, 69
Kolasa, B. J., 13, 28
Kolb, D. A., 208, 361
Koontz, H., 196, 197, 200, 209, 446, 449, 450
Korman, A. K., 189, 208, 267, 374, 395, 396
Krech, D., 208

Lachter, L. E., 110, 134
Lawler, E. E., 38, 62, 68, 69, 361, 395
Lawrence, P. R., 327, 378, 382, 395, 396
Lazarus, H., 396
Leavitt, H., 269, 271, 272, 274, 277, 298, 398, 439, 444, 461
Levinson, H., 113, 122, 124, 135, 248, 267, 440, 452

Lewin, K., 6, 267
Lewis, E. C., 243
Lewis, M., 203
Lewis, W. C., 395
Likert, R., 181, 192, 208, 352, 353, 361
Linowitz, S., 150
Lipstreu, O., 410, 439
Lirtzman, S. E., 239
Litterer, J. A., 327
Litwin, G. H., 343, 358, 361
Livingston, J. S., 101
Livson, N., 208
Lopez, F. M., 243, 256, 267, 268
Lorenz, K., 304, 327
Lorsch, J. W., 230, 239, 327
Luce, R. D., 328
Lugo, J. C., 12, 28
Luke, R. A., 204, 205, 209

"M" (author), 76
McClelland, D. C., 33, 45, 46, 47, 68
McCormick, E. J., 267, 376, 395
McDonald, A., 311, 327
McGrath, J. E., 183, 208
McGregor, D., 39, 55, 68, 69, 175, 211, 230,
    260, 266, 268
McGuire, J. W., 10, 12, 28, 34, 36, 37, 67, 68
McIntyre, J. M., 208, 361
McSherry, J. P., 245, 247, 267
Mackenzie, R. A., 238
MacKinnon, D. W., 85, 86, 101
Mackworth, N. H., 81, 101
Mangham, I. L., 440
Mansfield, R., 104, 105, 134
March, J. G., 97, 101, 102
Margulies, N., 342, 350, 361
Marrow, A. J., 417, 440
Martin, N. H., 163, 174, 175
Maslow, A. H., 33, 39, 41, 43, 45, 68, 89, 90,
    101
Massarik, F., 440
Mayo, E., 5
Megginson, L. C., 298
Menton, A. F., 123, 135
Metcalf, H. C., 28
Meyer, H. H., 267
Michels, R., 276
Miller, L. K., 193, 194, 208
Miner, J. B., 28, 48, 69, 239, 243, 267, 327,
    367, 395
Misshauk, M., 28, 239
Mitchell, T. R., 20, 29, 49, 69, 98, 101, 102,

183, 191, 193, 194, 208, 296, 299, 327, 462
Mitchell, V. F., 69, 79, 97
Mockler, R. J., 16, 28
Molinari, J., 440
Molloy, E. L., 202
Morrell, R. W., 73, 101
Morris, D., 304, 327
Morse, J. J., 230, 239
Mouton, J. S., 218, 239, 327, 426, 428, 429,
    435, 440
Mulaik, S. A., 361
Murray, T. J., 112, 134
Myers, C. A., 16, 28
Myers, M. S., 64, 69, 396

Nader, R., 21
Newell, A., 446, 461
Newell, P. F., 444, 445, 446
Newman, W. H., 5, 28, 73, 82, 87, 101, 160,
    174, 307, 327, 328
Newstrom, C. N., 245, 247, 267
Niland, P., 72, 73, 101
Nixon, R. M., 449
Nord, W., 239, 299, 440

Oberg, W., 249, 267
Odiorne, G. S., 268
O'Donnell, C., 196, 197, 200, 209
O'Donnell, W., 298
Olmsted, M. S., 208
Osborn, A. F., 87, 101

Packard, V., 156, 174, 452
Paster, I., 64
Pearse, R. F., 10, 28, 451, 461
Perry, W. E., 135
Peter, L. J., 153, 174, 396
Pickle, H., 354, 355, 357, 361
Pigors, P., 16, 28
Pollay, R. W., 76, 101
Porat, A. M., 439
Porter, A., 123, 135, 239
Porter, D. E., 11
Powell, R. M., 140, 173, 425, 440
Prince, G. M., 201, 209
Proxy, G., 164, 174

Rados, D. L., 94, 102
Raiffa, H., 328
Reddin, W. J., 175, 219, 220, 239
Redwood, P., 461
Reed, K. A., 410, 439

Reeser, C., 28
Rizzo, J. R., 239
Roethlisberger, F. J., 5
Rosen, L. S., 96, 102
Rosenzweig, J. E., 10, 20, 21, 28, 29
Rubin, I. M., 208, 361
Rush, H. M. F., 167, 174

Sanders, J., 231, 232
Sayles, L. R., 49, 50, 68, 69, 134, 260, 268,
    286, 298, 371, 379, 380, 395, 396
Schacter, S., 193
Schaffer, R. H., 108, 109, 134
Schein, E. H., 24, 29, 179, 180, 208, 319, 328
Schelling, T. C., 328
Schelsky, H., 84, 85
Schlaifer, R., 387
Schneck, R. E., 96, 102
Schneider, E. P., 174
Schoen, D. R., 386, 387, 396
Schon, D. A., 385, 393, 396
Schoonmaker, A. N., 158, 161, 174
Schott, W., 299
Schwartz, H. A., 28
Scott, W. G., 20, 29, 69, 79, 97, 98, 101, 102,
    183, 191, 193, 194, 208, 296, 299, 327, 462
Seashore, S. E., 192
Seligson, H., 461
Seyle, H., 106, 134
Shaffer, L. F., 128, 135
Shartle, C. L., 347, 361
Shepard, H. A., 327
Sherwin, D. S., 35, 68
Shoben, E. J., 128, 135
Simms, J. H., 163, 174
Simon, H. A., 97, 102, 446, 461
Simonds, R. H., 126, 135
Simpson, R. L., 279, 280, 298
Skinner, B. F., 436, 440, 454, 455, 456, 457,
    462
Slocum, J. W., 29
Smith, H. C., 262, 268
Spohn, A. G., 440
Stalker, G. M., 367, 386, 395, 396
Starr, M. K., 28, 95, 102, 446, 461
Steckman, W. E., 327
Stedfield, B., 113, 134
Steinberg, D. D., 298
Steiner, J., 103, 134
Stevenson, W. J., 446, 461
Stinson, J. F., 425, 440
Stockford, L., 125

Stogdill, R. M., 212, 238
Strauss, G., 49, 50, 68, 69, 134, 260, 268, 286,
    298, 327, 371, 379, 380, 395, 396
Stringer, R. A., 343, 358, 361
Summer, C. E., 5, 28, 29, 67, 73, 82, 87, 101,
    118, 135, 174, 208, 276, 298, 307, 327, 328
Swab, J. L., 140, 154, 173, 174

Tagiuri, R., 361
Tamarkin, R., 134, 135
Tannenbaum, A. S., 239, 419
Tannenbaum, R., 440
Taylert, J. M., 134
Taylor, A., 150
Taylor, C. W., 146, 396
Taylor, D. W., 72, 73, 101
Taylor, F. W., 5, 27
Taylor, S. A., 146, 173
Telly, C. S., 69
Thayer, H. G., 164
Tiffin, J., 267, 376, 395
Tillman, R., 209
Toffler, A., 363, 369, 395, 452
Toren, P., 19, 39, 68
Tosi, H. L., 169, 175, 268
Townsend, R., 161, 174
Triebal, J., 173

Uris, A., 149, 173
Urwick, L., 28

Vanderveer, B. A., 151, 152
Vaughan, J. A., 439
Vroom, V. H., 42, 49, 68, 69

Wakeley, J. H., 262, 268
Walton, R. E., 327
Wanous, J. P., 38, 68
Warren, E. K., 5, 28, 73, 82, 87, 101, 307, 327,
    328, 396
Watson, G., 395
Webber, R. A., 29, 67, 119, 135, 174, 208,
    276, 298
Wechsler, I. R., 440
Weick, K. E., 15, 38, 68, 361, 395
Weissenberg, P., 208, 212, 238
Welkowitz, J., 361
Wernimount, P. F., 19, 39, 63, 69
Westie, C. M., 340, 347
Whisler, T. L., 413, 439, 444, 461
Whittaker, J. O., 101
Whyte, W. F., 264, 268

Whyte, W. H., 187, 208
Wickesberg, A. K., 277, 278, 298
Wigdor, L. A., 68
Wilcox, D. S., 252, 253, 268, 294, 299
Wilson, I. H., 452
Winter, D. G., 47, 68
Wolf, M. G., 43, 45, 59, 68, 69

Wolfle, D., 101
Woodward, J., 7, 28, 228

Zald, M. N., 174
Zaleznik, A., 155, 173, 174
Zand, D. E., 10, 28, 306, 327
Zander, A., 179, 208

Subject Index

Absenteeism, 108
Acceptance of change, 372–373
Achievement motivation, 45–47
Adaptability lags, 11
Administrative Management, 110
Advice giving, 252
Affiliation needs, 186
Aggressiveness and change, 372
Aggressiveness in man, 304–305
Alcoholism, 107–108
American Civil Liberties Union, 145
American Management Association, 232
Americans for Democratic Action, 145
Antidotes to political maneuvering, 164–168
    job rotation, 167
    matrix organization, 166
    meshing of goals, 166
    objective performance measurement, 165
    openness and trust, 165
    policy implications, 167
    top management example, 165–166
Anxiety, 107, 285, 419
The Applicability of Organizational Sociology, 399
Apple polishing, 151–152
Appointed leader, 180
Asch studies on conformity, 187
Assumptions about people, 230–231
Attitudes, attitude change, 373–376
    approval and disapproval, 375
    definitions, 374
    discrepant behavior, 375
    group influences, 375
    individual differences, 375–376
    provide additional information, 374–375
Authority
    and control, 413–414
    computer influence, 413–414
    dual leadership theory, 225–227
    in leadership, 225–227
    insufficient, 114, 126
    vs. responsibility, 126
Automation, 409–414
Automation and communication, 414

Baking plant study, 409–412
Balance, 301

Barriers to communication, 281–286; *see also*
    Coping with barriers to communication
    anxiety, 285
    channel complexity, 285–286
    cognitive dissonance, 282
    communication skills, 284–285
    credibility of the source, 284
    denial of contrary information, 282
    motivation and interest, 283
    organizational climate, 285
    personalized meanings, 282–283
    preconceived notions, 281–282
    semantics, 282–283
    systems framework, 281
    timing of messages, 284
Behavior modification, 454–460
    control of technologists, 459–460
    controversy about, 458
    environmental emphasis, 458
    vs. humanism, 458–459
    manipulation, 459
    reinforcers, 455
Behavioral science; *see also* Organizational
    behavior
    company wide application, 64–65
    definition, 3
    intervention in conflict, 318–321
Behavioral skill acquisition, 420
Bell & Howell, 405–406
Beyond Freedom and Dignity, 436, 456, 458
Bilateral communication, 271–274; *see also*
    Transactional communication
Black Awareness Movement, 449
Black Enterprise, 146
Blacks
    management opportunities, 145–146
    power in organizations, 449
Blue-collar workers, 34, 122
Body Language, 288
Brainstorming, 87–88
Budget control, 114
Bureaucrat, 220, 221
Business characteristics, 339, 407
Business recession, 445
Business Week, 34, 202, 403, 452

Cadet Dry Cleaners, 72
Career advancement, 32, 140–141
Career advancement strategies, 147–157
  apple polishing, 151–152
  backdating memo, 156
  crucial subordinate, 150–151
  discredit or remove others, 156–157
  document your accomplishments, 157–158
  eighty–twenty job orientation, 149
  emotional support to boss, 151
  empire building, 157
  exposure, 153
  find a sponsor, 152–154
  help boss succeed, 150–152
  hero files, 157
  loyalty, 154–155
  manipulative approaches, 154, 156–157
  measurements of progress, 148–149
  mobility, 147–150
  mobilography, 147–149
  sales positions, 155–156
  strategic self-positioning, 149
  swim against the tide, 155–156
  transfer rival, 156–157
  visibility, 153
  visiposure, 153
Career planning, 168
Career reorientation, 109–110
Career vs. family demands, 123–124
Case study
  alliances in F.B.I., 159
  behavior modification, 454–458
  career reorientation, 109–110
  executive realignment, 404, 405–406
  interpersonal communication, 270
  introduction of change, 310
  managerial obsolescence, 389
  motivation of individual, 59–61
  overcommunication, 291
  poorly defined responsibilities, 310
  problem finding, 81–82
  words vs. action, 290
  work obsession, 123
Centralization of authority, 412–413
Certified Administrative Manager, 451
Change, 363–439; *see also* Individual and group change, Organizational change
Changing the organizational structure, 406–408
  decentralization, 406
  growth impact, 407

  internationalization of business, 407
  management philosophy, 409
  mergers and acquisitions, 406
  objectives and plans, 407–408
  organizational principles, 408–409
  profit margins, 407
  range of givens, 408
  success requirements, 407
  technological developments, 407
  underlying forces, 406–407
Changing the technology; *see* Impact of technological change
Charisma, 212
Coaching; *see* counseling
Coercive tactics, 380–381
Cognitive dissonance, 282
Columbia Broadcasting System, 150
Committees, 119, 196–203
  advantages and disadvantages, 196–200
  avoidance of action, 198
  commitment by participation, 197–198
  communicating information, 197
  compromise, 199–200
  coordination of plans and policies, 197
  diffusion of responsibility, 197
  favorable conditions, 200–201
  indecision, 199
  lack of responsibility, 341
  management development, 198
  misallocation of resources, 199
  nonverbal communication example, 289
  office of the president, 202–203
  pooling of intellectual resources, 197
  representation of interested groups, 197
  satisfaction of social needs, 198
  sham democracy, 200
  ubiquitous nature, 196
Communications, 65, 269–299; *see also* Barriers to communication, Coping with barriers to communication, Interpersonal communications, *selected topics under* Communications
Communication networks; *see* Communication structures
Communication process model, 274–276
  decoding, 275–276
  encoding, 275
  medium, 275
  need, 275
  transmitting, 275
Communication skills, 284–285, 290–291
Communication structures, 276–279

Communication structures, (cont.)
  decision-making effectiveness, 276–277
  formal pathways, 278
  influence on leadership, 277
  informal pathways, 278
  problem solving, 277
  wheel and all-channel networks, 276–277
  Wickesberg studies, 277–278
Company relocation, 379, 452
Competition in conflict, 305–306
Complementary crucial subordinate, 151
Compound groups, 317
Compromise, 315
Computers
  decision making, 413, 445–446
  dysfunctions, 413
  impact on managerial work, 444–446
  influence on skill level, 414
Computers and behavior; see Impact of
  technological change
Conflict, 301–328; see also Individual conflicts, Intergroup conflict, Conflict resolution
  consequences, 311–314
  definition, 301
  interdepartmental conflict, 301–328
  sources, 304–311
Conflict resolution, 314–321
  change organization structure, 316–317
  compound groups, 317
  compromise, 315
  corporate mirrors, 319
  decentralization, 317
  executive rap sessions, 312
  game theory, 318
  image exchanging, 319–321
  liaison groups, 317
  peaceful coexistence, 316
  political vs. social approaches, 139
  procrastination, 315–316
  third-party judgment, 315
Conflict sources (causes), 304–311
  aggressive nature of man, 304–305
  built-in conflict, 306–307
  clashes in interests, 306–307
  clashes of values, 306–370
  competition for resources, 305–306
  differentiation, 311
  introduction of change, 310
  older vs. younger workers, 306
  organizational climate, 311
  poorly defined responsibilities, 309–310

  power drives, 308–309
  role differences, 307–308
Conformity, 186–190
  conducive situations, 189–190
  encouragement toward, 189–190
  individual differences, 188–189
Conformity pressures, 118–119, 186–187
Confrontation in T-group, 417–419
Conglomeration, 112–113
Consideration, 218, 222, 233, 235, 343
Conspicuous leisure, 37
Contingency theory of leadership effectiveness, 17, 216–218, 235
Control unit, 323–324
Coping with barriers to communication,
  286–291
  appropriate language, 286
  feedback utilization 287–288
  nonverbal feedback, 288–289
  receiver awareness, 286
  receiver's frame of reference, 286–287
  reinforcement, 290
  speeches and lectures, 291
Corporate eunuch, 112
Corporate mirrors, 319
Corporateur, 448
Counseling, 243–247
  belief in growth, 245
  vs. coaching, 243–244
  conditional variables, 245, 246
  consequences to individual, 244
  definition, 244
  development of insight, 247–248
  five key elements, 245–248
  respect for individual, 245–246
  trust and leveling, 247
  understanding, 247
Creative Management, 64
Creativity, 84–90
  architects, 85
  brainstorming, 87–88
  characteristics of creative people, 85–86
  creative experience, 129–130
  human system, 89–90
  methods of improvement, 86–89
  overcoming perceptual blocks, 87
  self-discipline, 89
  synectics, 88–89
Credibility of information, 284
Criticism of subordinates, 258–259
Crucial subordinate, 150–151
Custom, 24, 117

Customers, 355–356
Cybernetics, 287, 459

The DD Matrix, 398, 435–436
Decentralization, 317, 406
Decision characteristics, 79–80
Decision making, 71–102
  adequacy of available information, 75
  behavioral aspects, 71–102
  big vs. little decisions, 72
  clarification of the problem, 82–84
  computer influence, 413, 445–446
  context of problem, 83–84
  coping with ambiguity, 93
  decision characteristics, 79–80
  Decision-Making Schema, 74
  education, 75
  emotional factors, 76–77
  entrepreneurial attitude, 76
  evaluation of outcomes, 72, 93–94
  experience, 75
  finding creative alternatives, 72, 84–89
  flow conception, 72–73
  gap between desired and actual, 83
  heuristic models, 446
  information overload, 96–97
  input, 73
  insight, 76
  intelligence of decision maker, 75
  intermediate causes of problem, 82
  intuition, 76
  making the choice, 72, 92–93
  management science, 95
  optimum decision, 80–81
  organizational policy, 98
  organizational system, 89, 97–98
  pediatricians, 73
  perfectionism, 75–76
  personality characteristics of decision maker, 75–76
  problem finders, 82
  problem finding, 80–82
  process conception, 72–73
  processes involved, 73–74
  quantitative decision making, 95–96
  rational analysis of alternatives, 90–91
  reliable information, 75
  repetitive decision making, 94–95
  root causes of problem, 83
  satisficing decision, 80
  serendipity, 77–78
  shared, 384–385
  stages, 78–79
  suboptimum decision, 80
  superoptimum decision, 79
  uncontrollable factors, 77–78
  values in, 92
  weighing alternatives, 72, 90–92
Decision-Making Schema, 72–94
Definition of responsibility, 309
Denial of problems, 108
Democratic Party, 145
Demotion, 260
Demotivation, 56, 59–61
Determinants of leadership style, 228–232
  assumptions about people, 230–231
  personality structure, 229–230
  situational demands, 232
  style of top official, 231–232
Determinants of organizational climate, 332–339
  characteristics of people, 338–339
  economic conditions, 334
  leadership style, 334
  life stage, 339
  nature of the business, 339
  organizational structure, 338
  policy, 335–336
  values, 336–338
Developmental programs, 391
Diagnosis of organizational climate, 340–343
  factor analysis, 342
  impersonal, aggressive company, 340–341
  objective indices, 341–343
  questionnaire method, 341–343
  subjective reactions, 340–341
Differentiation and conflict, 311
Dimensions of organizational climate, 340, 342–343, 344, 347–348
Distortion of goals, 313
Divisional incorporation, 448
Drug addiction, 107–108
Dual leadership theory, 225–227
Dun & Bradstreet, 356
Dun's Review, 112
Dysfunction of computer, 413

Economic conditions, 334
Economic factors in change, 376–377, 385
Economic incentives, 62–64, 385
Effective work groups, 190–195
  cohesiveness, 192–193
  cooperation vs. competition, 193–194

Effective work groups, *(cont.)*
  differential rewards, 193–194
  emotional support, 192
  homogeneous vs. heterogeneous, 194–195
  leadership style, 195
  size, 191–192, 411
  trust and confidence, 195
Electronic News, 231
Emergent leader, 180
Emery Freight Corporation, 455–458
Emotional disorders, 106
Empire building, 157
Employee-centered leadership, 288
Entrepreneurial behavior, 45–46, 79, 387
Entrepreneurial skills, 444
Equity theory, 48, 50, 63
Ethics in sensitivity training, 426
Ethnic groups, 145–146, 449
Executive; *see also* Manager, Management
  Black, 146
  education, 143–144
  general level of health, 130–131
  performance measurement and mobility, 140
  routes, 148–150, 451–452
  underutilization of abilities, 111–112
Executive Career Strategy, 158
Executive flameout, 108
Executive musical chairs, 404
Executive rap sessions, 312
Executive realignment, 403–406
Expectancy theory, 48–50, 376
Experimental design, 345
Expressive leadership, 222, 226

Factor analysis, 342
Fear of unknown, 377–378
Federal Bureau of Investigation, 159
Feedback; *see also* Systems, Model
  communication barriers, 287–289
  communications process, 274
  decision making, 93–94
  in organization development, 417–418, 427, 432
  organizational change, 400, 403
  performance appraisals, 249–257
Feelings of isolation, 412
Financial analyst role conflict, 308
Firing people, 260, 391
First Boston Corporation, 150
Flexible people, 379–380

Forces for change, 401
Ford Motor Company, 150, 154
Formal groups, 180, 226
Formal organization, 24
Formal vs. informal leader, 225–226
Fortune, 121
Friedlander and Greenberg study of hard-core unemployed, 351
Frustrated ambitions, 121–122
Fundamentals of Organizational Behavior, 235
Future, 443–462
  behavior modification, 454–460
  Certified Administrative Manager, 451
  divisional incorporation, 448
  entrepreneurial skills, 444
  human judgment, 446
  impact of computers, 443–446
  managerial decision making, 444–446
  managers needed, 446, 450–452
  organization structures, 446–449
  organization theory and management practice, 447–448
  power to the people, 449–450
  professional managers, 450–452
  scientific control of behavior, 454–462
  subsidized start up new businesses, 448
  top management elite, 443–446
  values, 452–454
  venture task teams, 448–449
  work ethic, 454
  youth culture, 448–449, 454
Future Shock, 369, 452
Futurists, 443, 452

Games in transactional analysis, 292–294
Games People Play, 291
Game theory, 317
General Adaptation Syndrome, 106
General Electric, 251, 453
General Foods, 408
General Motors, 155
General Motors, Lordstown, 34
General systems theory, 20–21
Generation, 104
Geographic mobility, 452
Good management practices, 126–127
Group behavior, 179–209
Group, 179–209; *see also* Effective work groups
  activity, 184
  appointed leader, 180
  Asch studies, 187

Group, (contd.)
  cohesiveness, 192–193
  committees, 196–203
  composition, 183
  definitions, 179–180
  development, 183
  effectiveness, 190–195
  dyfunctional conformity, 187–188
  dysfunctions, 186
  emergent leader, 180
  emotional support, 186
  environment, 183
  external systems, 184
  formal, 180, 185
  framework for understanding, 181–183
  functional conformity, 187
  functions performed, 185–186
  horizontal cliques, 180
  influence on attitudes, 375
  informal, 180, 185
  interaction, 184–185
  internal systems, 184
  norms, 184
  office of the president, 202–203
  penalties for nonconformance, 190
  pressures toward conformity, 186–190
  process, 183
  sentiment, 184
  social exchange, 184
  stable membership, 181
  structure, 183
  synergy, 185
  task, 183
  task performance, 185
  team spirit, 181, 187
  temporary task force, 203–205
  theory of small group behavior, 184–185
  types, 180
  unchallenged conformity, 188
  unstable membership, 181
  vertical cliques, 180
Group cohesiveness, 192–193, 261–263
  assembling the team, 262
  group assignments, 262
  group decision, 263
  methods of encouraging teamwork,
    262–263
  needs of members, 262
  and performance, 261–263
  properties of the group, 262
  stabilizing the team, 263
  team interaction, 263
  underlying factors, 261

Group Dynamics, 179
Group dynamics, 179
Group functions, 185–186
  affiliation needs, 186
  emotional support, 186, 198
  need satisfaction, 186, 198
  task accomplishment, 185
Group norms, 184
Group participation, 197–198
Growth factors, 41

Haney communication studies, 272–274
Hard-core unemployed, 351
Harvard Business Review, 145, 201, 429
Herzberg's motivation–hygiene theory,
  41–43
Heuristic models, 446
Honor system, 65
Horizontal cliques, 180
Horizontal communication, 280
Hot seat in T-group, 418
Housewife syndrome, 35
How to Get Your Boss's Job, 164
Human behavior principles, 13–15
  decision making, 98–99
  individual and group change, 393
  intergroup conflict, 324–325
  interpersonal communications, 295
  leadership, 236
  motivation, 66
  organizational change, 436–437
  organizational climate, 358
  performance improvement, 264
  political maneuvering, 168–169
  small groups, 205–206
  stress, 105–106, 131
Human judgment, 446
Hybrid expectancy model, 49

I.O.U., 161–162
Ideal organizational climate, 392
Identification with superior, 248–249
  dependency needs, 249
  no mistakes allowed, 248
  repression of rivalry, 249
  superior–subordinate relationship, 249
  time constraints 248
Illusion, 108
I'm OK—You're OK, 291
Image exchanging, 319–321
Impact of change, 364–367, 369–373
The Impact of Computers on Organizations,
  413

Impact of technological change, 409–414
  authority and control, 413–414
  centralization of authority, 412–413
  computer influence, 413–414
  decision making, 413
  freedom of movement, 411–412
  indirect labor proportion, 411
  job content, 414
  organization structure, 413
  size of work team, 411
  span of control, 411
  supervisory independency, 410
  supervisory levels, 410
  supervisory ratio, 411
  supervisory responsibility, 410
  worker cliques, 412
Impersonal–aggressive company, 340–341
Improving your leadership style, 232–235;
  see also Organization development
  American Management Association
    program, 232–233
  effectiveness of programs, 234–235
  hot seat, 418
  Leadership Opinion Questionnaire, 233
  management style, 233
  necessary conditions, 235
Improving subordinate performance,
  241–267
  coaching and counseling framework,
    243–245
  effective use performance appraisals,
    249–256
  group cohesiveness, 261–263
  identification with superior, 248–249
  improvement goals, 242–243
  management by objectives, 256–257
  motivational techniques, 242
  performance appraisals, 249–256
  principles of learning, 244
  punishment, 257–261
  role of leader, 242
  structural and technological factors,
    263–264
Indirect labor, 411
Individual commitment, 256
Individual conflicts, 120–125
  blocked routes, 122
  career vs. family demands, 123–124
  change in social status 122
  frustrated ambitions, 121–122
  irrelevant work, 120–121
  Machiavellianism, 125
  middle-aged crisis, 125

symbolic deprivations, 122
  threats from below, 124
  work obsession, 122–123
Individual differences, 375–376
Individual and group change, 363–395
  attitudes, 373–376
  economic factors, 376–377, 385
  fear of unknown, 377–378
  impact, 364–365, 369–373
  inconveniences, 379
  inevitable nature, 363
  managerial and professional obsoles-
    cence, 388–392
  organic vs. mechanistic organization, 367,
    369
  organization structure change, 365–366
  reasons for resistance, 376–379
  reducing resistance to change, 379–385
  systemic nature, 363
  systems model, 367–368
  taxonomy, 364–367
  technological changes, 364
  technological innovation, 385–387
  threats to interpersonal relationships,
    378–379
Individuality, 214–216
Industrial and organizational psychology,
  4, 6
Informal groups, 180, 226
Informal organization, 23–25; see also Dual
  leadership theory, groups
Information overload, 96–97
Information stress, 117–118
Initiative, 214
Innovation
  sources, 387–388
  work environment for, 11, 55
Inputs; see Systems, Models
Instant expert, 118
Institute for Personality Assessment Re-
  search, 85
Institute of Social Research, 352
Instrumental leadership, 222, 226
Integration of goals, 166–167
Intelligence in decision making, 75
Intelligence in leadership, 213
Interdepartmental conflict, 306; see also In-
  tergroup conflict
Interfunctional conflict, 306–307; see also
  Intergroup conflict
Intergroup conflict, 301–328
  balance, 301
  behavioral science intervention, 318–321

Intergroup conflict, (*cont.*)
  consequences, 311–313
  constructive tension levels, 322–323
  constructive use, 321–323
  control unit function, 323–324
  creative use, 322
  functional analysis, 313–314
  mechanisms for handling, 302
  mental health, 312
  organizational pressure, 115
  resolution, 314–321
  sources, 304–311
  substantive vs. personal, 313–314
  systems model, 302–303
  typology, 313–314
Intergroup conflict consequences, 311–314
  distortion of goals, 313
  dysfunctional, 312–313
  functional, 312
  suboptimization, 313
Interpersonal communications, 269–299
  barriers, 281–286
  bilateral communication, 271–274
  breakdown, 269–270
  computer effects, 414
  coping with barriers, 286–291
  Haney studies, 272–274
  nonverbal communication, 288–289
  one-way messages, 271–272
  process model, 274–276
  and productivity, 294–295
  reasons for problems, 270–271
  and satisfaction, 294–295
  speed, 271
  structures, 276–279
  technological influences, 279–280
  transactional analysis, 291–294
  transactional nature, 271–274
  unilateral communication, 291–294
  universal problem, 269–271
  valid communication, 272
International Paper Corporation, 150
International Telephone and Telegraph, 21
Interpersonal Communication and Organizational Effectiveness, 419
Intervening variables; *see* Model, Systems theory
Intervention Theory and Method, 415
Interventions in obsolescence, 391
Introduction to Behavioral Science for Business, 13

Introduction of change, 310
Inventors, 387

Job content, 42, 414
Job design, 119–120
Job enrichment, 6, 46, 56
Job insecurity, 112–113
Job relevance, 120–121
Job rotation, 167–168
Job satisfaction, 38–39
Job satisfaction and productivity, 38–39
John Birch Society, 145
Journal of Conflict Resolution, 325

Knowledge worker, 8–11
  conformity, 118–119
  decision making, 72
  definition, 9–10
  topics of concern, 10–11

Laboratory education; *see* Sensitivity training
Law of the situation, 16
Leadership, 211–238; *see also* Leadership style
  adaptive style, 211–212
  autocrat, 221
  benevolent autocrat, 221
  bureaucrat, 221
  characteristics of effective style, 211
  charisma, 212
  collaboration, 226
  compromiser, 221
  consideration, 218, 222, 233, 235, 343
  contingency theory, 216–217, 235
  country club style, 219
  definition, 211, 225
  deserter, 221
  desirable traits for situation, 215–216
  determinants of style, 228–232
  developer, 221
  differentiated leadership role, 227
  dual leadership theory, 225–226
  effective style, 219–221
  effective vs. ineffective leaders, 213–215, 219–221
  emotional support by leader, 227
  employee-centered, 228
  executive, 221
  expressive, 222, 225
  favorability of situation, 217–218
  formal vs. informal, 225–227
  formula for path–goal theory, 222

Leadership, (*cont.*)
general vs. tight supervision, 227
impoverished style, 218
improving your style, 232–234
individuality, 214–215
instrumental, 222, 225
initiating structure, 218, 222, 233, 235, 343
initiative, 214
intelligence, 213
leader–member relations, 217
Managerial Grid styles, 218–219
middle-of-the-road, 219
missionary, 221
moderators, 222
participative style, 228
path–goal theory, 221–225
perceived occupational level, 214
position power, 216–217, 225–226
power, 225–226
relationship to productivity, 227–228
role ambiguity, 224–225
situations, 212, 215
structural factors, 276
supervisory ability, 213
task, 219
task-structure, 217
team, 219
technological determinants of style, 228
3-D theory, 219–220
training, 232–234; *see also* Organization development
traits, 212–216
University of Michigan studies, 227–228
Leadership climate, 120, 390
Leadership moderators, 222
Leadership Opinion Questionnaire, 223
Leadership style, 25, 211–238; *see also* Leadership
effective work groups, 195–196
exploitive–authoritative, 353
inappropriate style, 120, 390
organizational climate, 334–335
participative-group, 352
and productivity, 227–228
systematic variation, 345
technological innovation, 386
Leadership training, 232–234; *see also* Organization development
Leisure, 36–37
Liaison groups, 317
Life Change Units Scale, 369–370
Life Magazine, 36

Line organization, 10
Lipstreu and Reed study of technological change, 409–413
Litwin and Stringer study of organizational climate and motivation, 343–346
Luck, 137, 147

The MBA Executive, 450
MBA programs, 407
Machiavellianism, 125, 159
Machine Design, 113
Mack Truck, Inc., 404
R. H. Macy, 202
Management
commitment to innovation, 388
computer impact on job, 413, 443–446
creative management, 64
interventions, 224–225
motivational impact of behavior, 62–64
negative policies, 35
philosophy, 409
principles, 12
professional, 11, 451
replacement, 403–406
success, 354
tasks, 11
top elite, 443–446
Management: A Modern Approach, 95
Management by Machiavelli, 159
Management by objectives, 256–257
common elements, 256
individual commitment, 256
organization goals, 256
political maneuvering, 165, 167–168
psychological pitfalls, 257
reviewing performance, 257
unit objectives, 256
Management development, 198; *see also* Organization development
Management elite, 443–444
The Management of Ineffective Performance, 243
The Management Psychology Newsletter, 151
Management science, 95
Management simulation game, 425
Management stresses, 103–135; *see also* Stresses in managerial and professional life
Management Styles and Self-Directed Change, 233
Manager; *see also* Management, Managerial achievement motivation, 46

Manager, (cont.)
coping with change, 330, 363–396
coping with future, 454
decision making, 71–102
development of subordinates, 64
efficiency vs. effectiveness, 82
expanded concept, 278
entrepreneurial training, 47
future managers, 450–452
geographic mobility, 452
motivational consequences of behavior, 62–65
motivations, 53, 58
self-image, 451
use of penalties, 59, 257–258
promotability survey, 141–147
proportion of work force, 9
role of communicator, 287
super-mobile, 148–149
value system, 452
"The Manager is a Counselor," 245, 252
Managerial Effectiveness, 220
Managerial Grid, 218–219, 426–430
effectiveness studies, 430
feedback to participants, 427
impact on management thought, 427
phases, 427
styles represented, 218–219, 427–429
Managerial Process and Organizational Behavior, 196
Managerial and professional obsolescence, 388–392
developmental programs, 391
environmental factors, 390
firing, 391
ideal climate, 392
inappropriate leadership climate, 390
interventions, 391
job change, 391
narrow work assignments, 390
organic adaptation, 392
organic organization, 392
overpromotion, 389–390
The Peter Principle, 390
prevention, 391–392
underlying factors, 388–390
Managerial Psychology, 269
Managerial stress, 103–135
Maslow's theory of motivation, 39–41
Master of Business Administration, 450
Matrix organization, 166
Meaningful jobs, 127, 130

Mechanistic organizations, 369
Mental health and conflicts, 312
Mental health principles, 128–130
confidential relationship, 129
creative experience, 129–130
good physical health, 129
interact with people, 129
meaningful work, 130
scientific method, 130
take constructive action, 129
Mental set, 75, 82
Mergers and acquisitions, 407
Methods of attitude change, 374–376
Middle-aged crisis, 125
Middle management work, 445–446
Minnesota Mining Company, 78
Mobile hierarch, 148
Mobility drive, 103
Mobilography, 148
Model
change, 367–368, 399–403
communication barriers, 281
communication process, 274–275
decision making, 72–73
equity theory, 47
hybrid expectancy, 49
individual and group change, 367–368
intergroup conflict, 301–304
leadership, 222
management of organizational change, 399–403
organization development assumptions, 435–436
organization subsystems, 20
organizational behavior, 14
organizational change, 400
organizational climate, 332
organizational–societal interactions, 355
path–goal expectancy, 50
small group analysis, 181–183
stress, 105
superior–subordinate counseling, 246
Work Motivation Schema, 51
Model of organizational change
change techniques, 402
diagnosis, 401
forces for change, 401
implementation, 403
limiting conditions, 402
monitoring the results, 403
recognition of need, 401
shared decision making, 402

Model of organizational change, (*cont.*)
    strategy, 402
Money, 62–64; *see also* Salary
Motivating Economic Achievement, 47
Motivation and communication, 283
Motivation to work, 33–69
    accomplishment, 46
    achievement motivation, 45–47, 344
    activation of needs, 57–58
    alienation, 35
    case history, 59–61
    commitment, 35
    consequences of managerial behavior,
        62–65
    conspicuous leisure, 37
    creative management, 64
    creativity, 55
    demotivation, 56
    entrepreneurial behavior, 46
    equity theory, 48, 63
    excape from work, 36–47
    expectancy theory, 48–59
    growth factors, 42
    Herzberg's motivation–hygiene theory,
        41–43
    hybrid expectancy model, 49
    idiographic nature, 53
    insatiable needs, 58
    job content factors, 41–42, 44–45, 56
    job context factors, 41–42, 44–45, 56
    job motivation, 43
    leisure, 36–37
    life value, 35–36
    managerial motivation, 53, 58
    Maslow's theory of motivation, 39–41
    money, 62–64
    motivated employee, 52
    motivation vs. satisfaction, 38–39
    motivational cycle, 51
    motivators, 42
    need deficits, 40
    occupational level theory, 54
    organizational climate, 54–55, 343–346
    path–goal analysis, 50
    penalties and threats, 59
    reward for hard work, 37
    salary, 44
    sources of gratification, 54–56
    sources of need gratification, 45
    task-oriented behavior, 52, 57
    Theory X and Theory Y, 39, 230
    ungratified needs, 43, 59

    Wolf's need gratification theory, 43–45
    work as calling, 35
    work as punishment, 34–35
    Work Motivation Schema, 51–59
Motivational pattern, 344
Motivational techniques, 242
Motivators, 42

The Naked Ape, 304
A Nation of Strangers, 452
Need for achievement, 45–48, 344
Need for affiliation, 344
Need for power, 344
Neurotic behavior, 107
Newsweek, 108
Nonconformity, 453
Non-Linear Systems, Inc., 350
Nonverbal communication, 288–289

Objectives and plans, 407–408
Obsolescence; *see* Managerial and profes-
    sional obsolescence
Occupational level theory, 54
Office landscaping, 7
Office politics; *see* Political maneuvering
Office of the president, 202–203
    advantages, 202
    disadvantages, 203
Old Testament, 34
On Aggression, 304
One-over-one-over-one, 409
One-way communication, 271–274; *see also*
    Unilateral communication
Organic organization, 367–368, 392
Organization; *see also selected topics*, Organi-
    zational behavior
    communications, 11
    development (OD), 414–436
    goals, 256
    life stage, 339
    subsystems, 20
    success requirements, 407
    successful vs. unsuccessful, 353–358
Organization development (OD), 5,
    414–436; *see also* Sensitivity training,
    Managerial Grid, Team development,
    Conflict resolution
    conflict resolution, 314–321
    definitions, 414
    Managerial Grid, 218–219, 426–430
    overview, 435–436
    political maneuvering, 165, 167

Organizational development, (cont.)
  sensitivity training, 415–426
  team development, 430–435
  variety of approaches, 414, 435–436
OD interventions, 749–750
  cathartic, 435
  confrontation, 436
  prescriptive, 436
  principles, models, theories, 436
  societal, 435
The Organization Man, 87
Organization theory, 4
  behavioral approach, 5
  management practice, 447–448
  operations research, 6
  rationalistic–model approach, 5
  scientific management, 5
Organizational behavior; see also specific
    topics
  computer impact, 7
  conceptual framework, 13–24
  definitions, 3
  determinants, 17
  dimensions, 36
  equation for, 17
  fields excluded, 12–13
  industrial engineering, 7
  industrial and organizational psychology,
    6
  interdisciplinary nature, 3–8
  introduction to, 3–29
  knowledge worker, 9–10
  organization theory, 5
  principles of human behavior, 13–15,
    65–66, 98–99, 131, 168–169, 205–206,
    236, 265, 295, 324–325, 358, 393, 436–437
  relationship to other fields, 3–8
  situational nature, 15–19, 66, 99, 132, 169,
    206, 236, 265, 295–296, 325, 358, 393, 437
  structure and process, 23–25, 66, 99–100,
    132, 170, 206, 237, 266, 296–297, 326,
    359–360, 394, 438
  systemic nature, 19–23, 66, 99, 169, 206,
    236–237, 265–266, 296, 325–326, 359,
    393–394, 437
Organizational change, 397–440
  computer impact, 413–414
  definition, 397
  executive realignment, 403–406
  four methods, 398–399
  humanistic, 398
  model, 399–403

organization development (OD), 414–436
  OD in overview, 435–436
  organization planning, 399
  strategies, 398–399
  structural, 398, 406–409
  technological, 398, 409–414
Organizational climate, 331–361; see also
    Determinants of organizational cli-
    mate, Diagnosis of organizational cli-
    mate
  behavior, 346–353
  communication, 285
  conflict, 311
  definition, 331, 344
  diagnosis, 340–343
  determinants of climate, 332–339
  dimensions, 340, 342–343, 344, 347–348
  exploitive–authoritative, 353
  framework, 331
  motivation, 54–55, 343–346
  productivity, 352–353
  sensitivity training, 422–423
  simulation, 345
  situational nature, 346
  successful vs. unsuccessful organizations,
    353–358
  System 4 management, 352
Organizational climate and behavior,
    346–351
  contrasting hotel climates, 347–350
  Department of Commerce, 350–351
  hard-core unemployed, 351
  production work, 350
Organizational Climate Description Ques-
    tionnaire, 342
Organizational control, 226
Organizational openness and trust, 165, 195
Organizational pettiness, 117
Organizational policy, 98
Organizational pressures, 110–120
  conflicts, 115–116
  conformity, 118–119
  conglomeration, 112
  exorbitant work demands, 115
  faulty job design, 119–120
  inappropriate leadership style, 120
  information stress, 117–118
  insufficient authority, 114
  job insecurity, 112–113
  large organization pettiness, 117
  role ambiguity, 116
  technical problems, 119–120

Organizational pressures, *(cont.)*
  uncertain professional status, 113–114
  underutilization of abilities, 111–112
Organizational principles, 408–409
Organizational structure, 22, 97
  change, 406–409
  computers, 413
  conflict reduction, 316–317
  decline of pyramid, 447
  flexible arrangements, 446–449
  job pressures, 119
  organic-adaptive, 181
  organizational climate, 338
  reduction of stress, 127–128
  venture task teams, 448–449
  youth culture, 448–449
Organizational Success Questionnaire, 138
Organizational system, 97
Organizational taxonomy, 447
Ostracism from group, 259
Outputs; *see* System models

Participative group management, 352
Participative leadership, 228, 352, 402
Parties-at-interest, 354–357
Passive–aggressive behavior, 370–371
Path–Goal theory of leadership, 221–225
Patron, 153
Pay and Organizational Effectiveness, 62
Penn Central, 21
Perceived occupational level, 214
Perfectionism, 75
Performance appraisal, 249–257; *see also*
  Management by objectives
  criticisms, 249–252
  constructive attitude, 252–253
  defensiveness about, 251
  dependency needs, 251
  deterrent to coaching, 251
  distrust by subordinates, 139–140
  feasible changes, 255
  goals, 250
  mutual goal setting, 253
  performance standards, 251
  personal characteristics required, 254–
  255
  positive vs. negative motivators, 252–253
  purposes, 250
  rating of traits, 250–251
  relationship to success, 251
  results vs. person, 255–256
  salary discussions, 254

  skills required, 254–255
  solving job problems, 253–254
  subordinate participation, 252
  time demands, 250
Personal characteristics, 338–339
Personal conflict, 314
Personality, 142
Personality characteristics, 75–76
Personality in decision making, 75–76
Personality structure, 228–229
Personalization, 85
Personnel Administration, 16
Personnel changes, 364–366
Personnel Psychology, 6
The Peter Principle, 390
Pettiness in organizations, 117
Physical appearance, 143
Physicians, 114
Physiologic response to stress, 106
Pickel and Friedlander study of organiza-
  tional success, 354–357
Plan of the book, 25–27
Playboy, 144
Playing politics, *see* Political maneuvering
Policy, 335–336
Political astuteness, 315–316
Political maneuvering in organizations,
  137–175
  antidotes, 164–168
  awareness of political factors, 164
  career advancement strategies, 147–158
  career planning, 168
  causes, 138–140
  competition for power, 139
  definitions, 137–138, 158
  factors related to promotion, 141–147
  ignoring politics, 163–170
  manpower development, 168
  measurement, 138
  organization development, 165, 167
  Organizational Success Questionnaire,
  138
  political approaches to conflict resolution, 138–139
  power-acquisition strategies, 158–163
  relationship to democratic management,
  140
Politicization, 85
Pollay decision-making experiment, 76
Portfolio Selection, 95
Positive vs. negative motivators, 253
Powell survey of promotability, 141–147

Power, 225–227
Power-acquisition drive, 308–309
Power-acquisition strategies, 158–163
  alliances, 158–159
  Camel's head in tent, 162
  collect IOU's, 161–162
  divide and rule, 160
  embrace or demolish, 159–160
  Fabianism, 162
  Machiavellianism, 159–160
  make a quick showing, 161
  manipulate information, 160–161
  take counsel with caution, 163
  things must get worse, 163
Power diffusion, 449
Power in Organizations, 158
Power structures, 278
The Practice of Managerial Psychology, 319
Preconceived notions, 281–282
Preoccupation with busywork, 109
Prestige suggestion, 47
Prevention of dysfunctional stress, 125–130
  create meaningful jobs, 127
  modify organization structure, 127–128
  practice good management, 126–127
  practice good mental health, 128–130
  strengthen personal qualifications, 128
The Prince, 160
Principles of Management, 196
Problem finders, 81
Problem finding, 80–84
Problem solving, 279
The Process of Management, 5, 73
Procrastination, 315–316
Product champions, 387
Production-centered leadership, 288
Production work study, 350
Productivity and communication, 294–295
Professional, definition, 134
Professionalism in business, 10–11, 451
Professional status, uncertain, 113–114
Professionalization of management, 450–452
Profit margins, 407
Promotability factors, 141–147
  community influences, 144–145
  customer influences, 142
  education, 143–144
  ethnic group, 145
  family background, 146–147
  government, 142–143
  informal influences, 142

  kinship, 143
  managerial capability, 141
  marrying boss's daughter, 143
  personality, 142
  physical state, 143
  political party, 145
  racial groups, 145
  refusal of promotion, 146
  religion, 145
  seniority, 143
  wife influences, 144
Psychological growth, 248
Psychological tests, 86
Psychology; *see* Behavioral science
The Psychology of Communication, 269
The Psychology of Counseling, 243
Psychology Today, 46, 458
Psychosomatic disorders, 105, 106
Psychotic behavior, 107
Punishment in organizations, 257–261
  administrative punishments, 259–260
  attacking personality attributes, 258
  criticism, 258
  criticism of character traits, 258
  dealing with situation, 258–259
  demotion, 260
  firing, 260
  ostracism from group, 259
  Red Hot-Stove Rule, 260–261
Pure hierarch, 148

Quantitative decision making, 95–97

Race, Religion, and the Promotion of the American Executive, 141
Reality factors, 408
Red Hot-Stove Rule, 260–261
Reducing intergroup conflict; *see* Conflict resolution
Reducing resistance to change, 379–385
  coercive tactics, 380–381
  economic incentives, 385
  selection of people, 379–380
  shared decision making, 384–385
  social changes, 382
  technological preoccupation, 383
  tentative changes, 383–384
  valid information, 381
Reinforcers, 460
Religion, 145
Repetitive decision making, 94–95
Republican Party, 145

Resistance to change, 370–372
Response to change, 369–373
  conditional variables, 369
  direct aggressiveness, 372
  Life Change Units Scale, 369
  passive–aggressiveness, 370–371
  resentment, 371
  resistance, 370–371
  stress reactions, 369
  welcoming change, 372–373
Responsibility vs. authority, 408
Role ambiguity conflict, 116
Role ambiguity in leadership, 225
Role conflict, 307–308
Role prescriptions, 278
Routes to the Executive Suite, 451

SRA Employee Inventory, 356
Salary, 43; *see also* Money
  compensation policies, 62
  discussion in performance review, 254
  job context factor, 43
  progression, 149
  relationship to performance, 43, 63
  relief of discomfort zone, 62
Satisfaction and communication, 294–295
Scientific management, 5
Scientific method, 130
Scott Paper Company, 203
Selection of people, 379–380
Self-aggrandizement, 137
Self-assurance, 214
Self-discipline, 89
Self-esteem threats, 252
Self-understanding, 419
Semantics, 282–283
Seniority, 143
Sensitivity training, 5, 415–426
  anxiety, 419
  behavioral skills, 420
  confrontation, 416
  duration of group, 416
  effectiveness, 423–426
  ethical considerations, 426
  feedback to participants, 417–418
  hot seat, 418
  insight into groups, 420
  member composition, 416
  potential problems, 420–422
  precautions, 420–423
  processes, 416–419
  proper organizational climate, 422–423

  purposes, 419–420
  qualifications of leader, 422
  recognizing the culture, 420
  self-understanding, 419
  size of group, 416
  structure, 417
  trainer qualifications, 422
  T-group, 416
  understanding others, 419
The Sensuous Man, 76
The Sensuous Woman, 76
Serendipity, 77–78
Shared decision making, 384–385, 402
Simulation of organizational climate, 354
Situational nature of organizational behavior, 15–19
  decision making, 99
  individual and group change, 393
  intergroup conflict, 325
  interpersonal communications, 295–296
  leadership, 211, 236
  motivation, 66
  organizational change, 437
  organizational climate, 358
  performance improvement, 265
  political maneuvering, 169
  small groups, 181–183, 206
  stress, 132
Situational theory of management, 16
Size of work group, 191–192, 411
Skill levels, 414
Social changes, 382
Social conscience, 337
The Social Dimensions of Work, 34
Social exchange, 184
Social responsibility, 121
Social status change, 122
Societal conflict, 302
Sociology; *see* Behavioral science
SONY Corporation, 64
Span of control, 410
Stock purchase, 95
Strategic self-positioning, 149
Strategy for organizational change, 399–403
Stress reactions, 105–110
  alcoholism, 107
  career reorientation, 109–110
  defensive behavior, 108–109
  denial, 108
  drug addiction, 107
  emotional disorder, 107
  executive flameout, 109

Stress reactions, (*cont.*)
  general adaptation syndrome, 106
  illusion, 108
  physiological response, 106
  preoccupation with busywork, 109
  psychosomatic disorders, 106–107
  psychotic behavior, 107
  xenophobia, 109
Stress reaction to change, 369–370
Stresses in managerial and professional life,
    103–135
  absenteeism, 108
  anxiety, 107
  capacity for stress, 105
  individual conflicts, 120–125
  magnitude of stress, 105–106
  model, 104–105
  neurotic behavior, 107
  organizational pettiness, 117
  organizational pressures, 110–120
  overall perspective, 130–131
  prevention of dysfunctional stress,
    125–130
  stress vs. strain, 104
  today vs. yesterday, 104
Structural concepts, variables, 7–8, 66, 98,
    113, 119–120, 127, 241, 259, 263–264,
    276–279, 309–310, 317, 323, 338, 390,
    406–409, 413, 446–449
Structure; *see* Initiating structure
Structure and process interaction, 22–25
  decision making, 99–100
  individual and group change, 394
  intergroup conflict, 326
  interpersonal communication, 296–297
  leadership, 237
  motivation, 66
  organizational change, 438
  organizational climate, 359–360
  performance improvement, 266
  political maneuvering, 170
  small groups, 206–207
  stress, 132
Structural and technological factors in per-
    formance, 263–264
  antiquated machine, 264
  authority relationships, 264
  dual leadership theory, 225–226
  Whyte's restaurant studies, 264
Suboptimization, 313
Subsidized business start ups, 448
Substantive conflict, 313–314

Successful organizations, 211
Successful vs. unsuccessful organizations,
    353–358
  community satisfaction, 356
  creditor satisfaction, 356
  customer satisfaction, 355
  governmental satisfaction, 357
  owner satisfaction, 355
  relationship to climate, 353
  supplier satisfaction, 356
Super-mobile manager, 148
Superior–subordinate relationship, 248–249
Supervisory ability, 213–214
Supplementary crucial subordinate, 151
Survival in the Executive Jungle, 165
Symbolic deprivations, 122
Synectics, 88–89
System; *see also* Organizational behavior,
    Systems theory, Model
  dysfunctions, 19
  functions, 19
Systems 4 management, 352
Systems model; *see* Model, Systems theory
Systems theory, 19–23
  communication of messages, 274–276,
    281–286, 296
  cybernetics, 287
  decision making, 72–78, 99
  feedback, 287
  individual and group change, 367–369,
    393–394
  interaction of subsystems, 20
  intergroup conflict, 301–304, 325–326
  interpersonal communication, 296
  leadership, 236–237
  motivation, 66
  organizational change, 399–400, 437
  organizational climate, 359
  performance improvement, 265–266
  political maneuvering, 169–170
  small group behavior, 181–183, 206
  stress, 132
  total human system, 89–90

TRW Systems, 432–435
Task forces, 11, 203–205
Team building; *see* Team development
Team development, 429–434
  comparison with sensitivity training, 430
  confrontation and feedback, 431
  effectiveness, 434–435
  feedback, 431

Team development, (*cont.*)
  general model, 430–431
  long-range nature, 432
  TRW case history, 432–435
Technical problems, 119
Technological change, 385–388
Technological developments, 394
Technological innovation, 385–388
  entrepreneurs, 387
  inventors, 387
  leadership style, 386
  management commitment, 388
  offensive strategy, 385
  organization structure, 386
  sources of innovation, 387
  underlying resistance, 386
Technological obsolescence, 21
Technological preoccupation, 383
Technologists, 7
Technology and communications, 279–280
  automation, 280
  facilitation of communication, 279
  horizontal communications, 280
  interdependency of people, 279
  mechanization influence, 280
  vertical communication, 280
Technology and leadership style, 228
Temporary task force, 11, 203–205
  advantages, 204
  disadvantages, 204
  management consulting firms, 204
Theory of small group behavior, 184–185
Theory X and Theory Y of McGregor, 39,
  55, 211, 230
Third party judgment, 315
Threats to interpersonal relationships,
  378–379
Threats from subordinates, 124
3-D theory of leadership, 219–221
T-group; *see* Sensitivity training
Tight organization, 345
Time, 115, 150
Timing of messages, 284
Towers, Perrin, Forster, and Crosby, 202
Transactional analysis, 291–294

adult, 292
child, 292
games, 292–294
Games People Play, 291
I'm OK—You're OK, 291
"I'm Only Trying to Help You," 292
"Indigence," 292
parent, 292
Transactional communication, 271–274
Typology of intergroup conflict, 313–314

Understanding others, 419
Underutilization of abilities, 13–14
Unilateral communication, 271–274
University of Michigan Leadership studies,
  227–228
Up the Organization, 161

Validity of information, 381
Values, 336–338, 452–454
Values in conflict, 306–307, 338
Venture task teams, 448
Vertical cliques, 180
Vertical communication, 280

Wall Street Journal, 423, 453
WASP (White Anglo-Saxon Protestant),
  140, 449
Western Electric, 5
Whyte's restaurant studies, 264
Wickesberg communication experiments,
  277–279
Wife, 144
Wolf's need gratification theory, 43–45
Women's changing role, 144
Women's liberation movement, 449
Women's Wear Daily, 449
Work demands, 115
Work ethic decline, 454
Work Motivation Schema, 51–59
Worker cliques, 412

"Yes man," 154

Xenophobia, 109

LET'S ROCK

IGNEOUS ROCKS

CHRIS OXLADE

Heinemann
LIBRARY

Chicago, Illinois

H www.heinemannraintree.com
Visit our website to find out
more information about
Heinemann-Raintree books.

To order:

☎ Phone 888-454-2279

💻 Visit www.heinemannraintree.com
to browse our catalog and order online.

Edited by Louise Galpine and Diyan Leake
Designed by Victoria AllenNorth Mankato, MN
Illustrated by KJA artists
Picture research by Hannah Taylor
Originated by Capstone Global Library Ltd
Printed and bound in the United States of America,
North Mankato, MN

14 13 12
10 9 8 7 6 5 4

Library of Congress Cataloging-in-Publication Data
Oxlade, Chris.
   Igneous rocks / Chris Oxlade.
      p. cm. — (Let's rock)
   Includes bibliographical references and index.
   ISBN 978-1-4329-4679-1 (hb)
   ISBN 978-1-4329-4687-6 (pb)
   1. Rocks, Igneous—Juvenile literature. 2. Petrology—Juvenile
literature. I. Title.
   QE461.O95 2011
   552'.1—dc22   2010022201

052012
006707RP

Acknowledgments
The author and publisher are grateful to the following for
permission to reproduce copyright material: Alamy Images
p. 5 (© Phil Degginger/Jack Clark Collection); © Capstone
Publishers p. 29 (Karon Dubke); Corbis pp. 11 (Martin
Rietze), 15 (Reuters/Ho), 26 (Alberto Garcia); istockphoto
p. 10 (© Diego Barucco); Photolibrary pp. 4 (Andoni Canela),
13 (Peter Arnold Images/Robert Mackinlay), 16 (The Travel
Library/Adam Burton), 18 (imagebroker.net/Egmont Strigl),
19 (imagebroker.net/Christian Handl), 20 (Superstock/
Hidekazu Nishibata), 21 (Francesco Tomasinelli), 23 (Susanne
Palmer); Science Photo Library pp. 12 (Tony Camacho), 14
(Oar/National Undersea Research Program); shutterstock p. 17
(© Josemaria Toscano).

Cover photograph of the Giant's Causeway, Northern Ireland,
reproduced with permission of Photolibrary (Superstock/
Richard Cummins).

We would like to thank Dr. Stuart Robinson for his invaluable
help in the preparation of this book.

Every effort has been made to contact copyright holders of
any material reproduced in this book. Any omissions will
be rectified in subsequent printings if notice is given to
the publisher.

CONTENTS

What Are Igneous Rocks?.......................... 4

What Is Inside Earth?.............................. 6

How Are Igneous Rocks Made?................ 10

What Types of Igneous Rock
    Are There?.................................... 16

What Do We Use Igneous Rocks For?....... 20

Do Igneous Rocks Last Forever?............... 22

Are We Harming Igneous Rocks?.............. 26

Make Your Own Sugar "Lava"!.................. 28

Glossary.. 30

Find Out More....................................... 31

Index... 32

Rock roles
Find out about the work involved in the study of rocks.

Science tip
Check out our smart tips to learn more about rocks.

Number crunching
Discover the amazing numbers in the world of rocks.

Biography
Read about people who have made important discoveries in the study of rocks.

Some words are printed in bold, **like this**. You can find out what they mean by looking in the glossary on page 30.

WHAT ARE IGNEOUS ROCKS?

Red-hot **lava** blasts out of a **volcano's** crater. It flows down the volcano's sides in a glowing river. Eventually it cools down, stops flowing, and becomes solid, forming new rock. Rock made when **molten** rock cools is called igneous rock. Igneous rock is one of the three types of rock that make up Earth. The other two types are **sedimentary rock** and **metamorphic rock**.

INSIDE ROCKS

All rock, not just igneous rock, is made from materials called **minerals**. Igneous rocks are made from a mixture of different minerals, but some other rocks are made from just one mineral.

This is the Kilauea volcano in Hawaii.

Minerals themselves are made up of **atoms**. In all minerals, the atoms are arranged neatly in rows and columns. Materials with atoms arranged like this are called **crystals**, and they are easy to see in igneous rocks.

Igneous rock is being made all the time. It is also being destroyed all the time. This is part of a process called the **rock cycle**. In this book we follow the journey of igneous rock through the rock cycle.

This mineral is microcline feldspar, which is common in an igneous rock called **granite**. It is also known as Amazon stone.

WHAT IS INSIDE EARTH?

Rocks are all around us all the time. Mostly they are underneath us, because Earth is a giant ball of rock. If you dig down deep enough anywhere, you will eventually come to solid rock. This is part of a rocky skin that covers Earth called the **crust**.

UNDER THE CRUST

The crust sits on top of very hot rock below. This hot rock forms a layer thousands of miles deep, called the **mantle**. When rock rises from the mantle, it melts. This is the source of **molten** rock that forms igneous rocks.

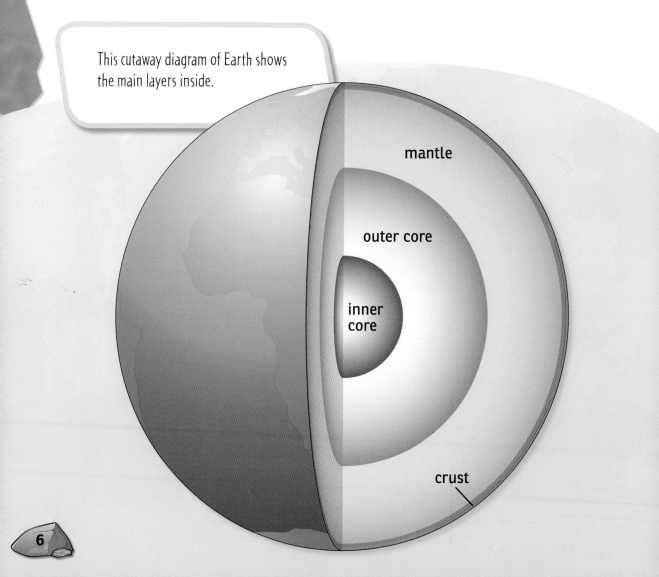

This cutaway diagram of Earth shows the main layers inside.

mantle

outer core

inner core

crust

THE ROCK CYCLE

The rocks in Earth's crust are constantly changing. During the **rock cycle**, igneous rocks and other rocks are made either deep underground or at Earth's surface. Some rocks (which can be igneous, **sedimentary**, or **metamorphic**) are destroyed when they are forced down into the mantle. Others are worn away at the surface.

The rock cycle is a slow process. Igneous rocks can form in a few hours when **lava** spews from a **volcano** and cools, but they can take millions of years to make their journey around the rock cycle before they are finally destroyed.

The crust is very thin compared to Earth's other layers. It is thinner under the oceans than under the continents.

Layer	Thickness
crust under the continents	25 to 90 kilometers (15 to 56 miles)
crust under the oceans	6 to 11 kilometers (4 to 7 miles)
mantle	2,900 kilometers (1,800 miles)
outer core	2,300 kilometers (1,430 miles)
inner core	1,200 kilometers (745 miles)

THE CRACKED CRUST

Earth's crust is cracked into many enormous pieces called **tectonic plates**. The edges of the plates, where the plates meet each other, are called **plate boundaries**. Most igneous rocks start their journey at these boundaries.

WHAT HAPPENS AT PLATE BOUNDARIES?

At some boundaries the two plates move slowly away from each other. At other boundaries the two plates move slowly toward each other. When two plates move apart, hot rock from the mantle below melts and rises up to fill the gap in the crust. Where two plates move toward each other, one plate is often pushed under the other and into the mantle. Eventually the rocks inside it get hot enough to melt, forming new molten rock that rises up into the crust above.

Here, two tectonic plates are moving apart under an ocean. The rise made by new rock is called a mid-ocean ridge.

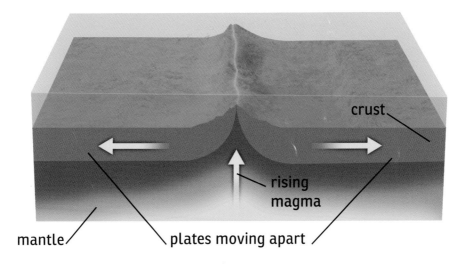

crust

rising magma

mantle

plates moving apart

At both types of boundary, the molten rock that moves into the crust goes on to make new igneous rocks. Molten rock also rises into the crust at places called **hot spots**. Hot spots are areas of very high temperature under the plates.

Biography

Alfred Wegener (1880–1930) was a German scientist. In 1911 he discovered that fossils in rocks that were thousands of miles apart on opposite sides of oceans appeared to match each other. This showed Wegener that the continents we know today were once joined together, but then drifted apart. Today, we know that this happens because Earth's crust is cracked into tectonic plates that are constantly moving.

Here, two plates are moving toward each other. The sinking plate melts, creating molten rock that rises upward to make volcanoes.

volcano

crust

mantle

magma produced as plate melts

HOW ARE IGNEOUS ROCKS MADE?

The **molten** rock that rises into Earth's **crust** at the edges of some **tectonic plates**, and at **hot spots** in the plates, is called **magma**. The journey of igneous rock begins when the magma cools and becomes solid. As it cools, **crystals** of **minerals** grow in it. This happens on Earth's surface, under the sea, and also deep underground in the crust.

Rock roles

A **geologist** is a scientist who studies how rocks are made, how they change, and how they make up Earth. Geologists do many different jobs, some of which involve igneous rocks. For example, some study marine geology, which includes tectonic plates, and some study volcanoes (see page 15).

Igneous rocks on Mount Etna, in Italy, formed when magma cooled.

A fountain of lava blasts from Stromboli, an Italian volcano. The rocky cone is made from cooled lava.

IGNEOUS ROCKS ON THE SURFACE

Sometimes rising magma finds its way to the surface, where it forms **volcanoes**. As soon as magma comes out of a volcano, it is called **lava**. At some volcanoes the lava is runny. It flows away from the volcano and gradually cools. When it solidifies, it stops flowing and forms new igneous rock. At other volcanoes the lava is thick. When the volcano erupts, the lava gets blasted to tiny pieces, which make ash when they cool. Some volcanoes produce both runny lava and ash. Any igneous rock made on the surface at volcanoes is called **extrusive rock**.

FLYING ROCKS

Lava that flows across the ground builds up layers of new igneous rock. But bits of lava thrown into the air often solidify before they land, forming lumps of new igneous rock. Big lumps of lava that solidify in the air are called **volcanic bombs**. Big bombs sometimes break open when they land, spewing out lava that is still runny. **Cinders** are small chunks of rock (about the size of grapes) that solidify in the air. They are full of holes made by gas bubbles.

ROCK FROM ASH

Volcanic ash is formed when magma is blasted apart by gas. It is made up of tiny bits that look like broken glass. When ash settles to the ground, it forms layers. The deep layers of ash slowly turn to rock.

Archaeologists dig at the ancient Roman city of Pompeii, which was buried under ash from the nearby volcano Vesuvius.

Half Dome, in California's Yosemite National Park, formed when magma cooled underground.

IGNEOUS ROCKS UNDERGROUND

Some igneous rocks begin their journey around the **rock cycle** under the ground. They form when magma rises into the crust but cannot get to the surface. The magma cools slowly underground to make new igneous rock. Igneous rocks made underground like this are called **intrusive rocks**.

THE LARGEST LAVA FLOWS

These are some of the biggest eruptions of lava we know about. The eruptions lasted hundreds of thousands of years.

Area	Date (million years ago)	Amount of lava (million km³ *)
Ethiopia	31	about 1
Deccan, India	66	more than 2
Antarctica	176	0.5
Karoo, South Africa	183	more than 2
Siberia, Russia	249	more than 2

* A km³ (cubic kilometer) is an amount 1 km (0.6 mile) wide, 1 km (0.6 mile) high, and 1 km (0.6 mile) deep.

13

ARE THERE VOLCANOES UNDER THE SEA?

Many volcanoes erupt under the sea. In fact, there are more volcanoes under the sea than on land, and most igneous rock forms under the sea. The boundaries where tectonic plates move apart are normally on the seabed. Volcanoes form all along these boundaries as magma rises upward from the **mantle**. The rock cools quickly in the water, forming new igneous rocks. Earth's crust, which lies under all the world's oceans, is made mostly from igneous rocks that have formed under the sea.

These are lumps of pillow lava, which forms when lava from under the seabed cools quickly in the water.

IGNEOUS ROCK ISLANDS

Sometimes volcanoes grow up from the seabed. These underwater mountains are called seamounts. Sometimes they get so tall that they break the surface, forming new islands, such as Surtsey, near Iceland. This can happen above **plate boundaries** or over **hot spots**. The Hawaiian Islands are the tops of giant volcanoes.

Rock roles

A volcanologist is a scientist who studies volcanoes. Volcanologists try to understand why volcanoes erupt. They record eruptions, they study igneous rocks made during eruptions, and they try to predict when eruptions are likely to happen. It is one of the most dangerous rock roles because volcanologists often visit erupting volcanoes!

Ash blasts into the air as a volcano erupts just under the sea surface near the island of Tonga in 2009.

WHAT TYPES OF IGNEOUS ROCK ARE THERE?

We can divide igneous rocks into two groups—**intrusive** and **extrusive rocks**. Here you can see some of the most common extrusive and intrusive igneous rocks.

Granite is a very common igneous rock. It is an intrusive rock. There are several different sorts of granite, which come in different colors, such as white, pink, and gray. The colors are made by the different **minerals** in granite, which are mostly quartz, feldspar, and mica.

Other common intrusive rocks are gabbro (normally a very dark color), porphyry and pegmatite, which both have some large **crystals** of minerals in them, and dolerite, which is dark colored and has medium-sized **grains**.

This granite outcrop in England is known as Saddle Tor. It has been left exposed as softer rock around it has been worn away.

Basalt is a very common extrusive igneous rock. It is a dark-colored rock made from solidified **lava**. Some types of basalt have gas-filled holes inside. Other common extrusive rocks include rhyolite, which is light colored and made from thick, sticky lava, and andesite, which has small crystals.

The famous Giant's Causeway in Northern Ireland is made of basalt, which cracked into columns as it cooled down.

Identifying igneous rocks

Most igneous rocks have crystals of different minerals that you can see. The crystals interlock with each other (which means they are tightly packed together). Igneous rocks are normally hard, and they never contain **fossils**. Use the table here to help to identify igneous rocks.

Rock	Grain size	Color
granite	coarse	light
gabbro	coarse	dark
pegmatite	very coarse	light and dark
basalt	fine	dark
rhyolite	fine	light
andesite	fine	medium

CRYSTALS IN IGNEOUS ROCKS

In intrusive rocks, such as granite, the crystals of minerals are normally large enough to see. This is because the **magma** cools slowly, which gives time for the crystals to grow. We say that these rocks are coarse-grained. In extrusive rocks, such as basalt, the grains are normally too small to see. That is because the magma cools quite quickly on Earth's surface, and crystals do not have time to grow large. We say that these are fine-grained rocks.

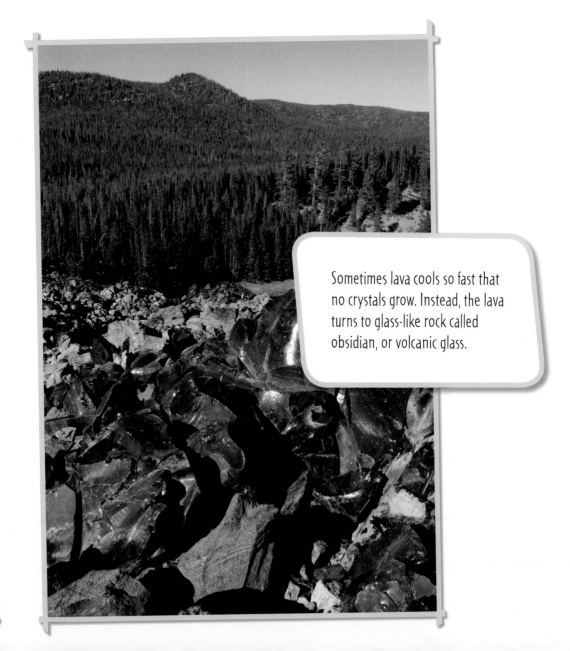

Sometimes lava cools so fast that no crystals grow. Instead, the lava turns to glass-like rock called obsidian, or volcanic glass.

ROCKS FROM FLYING LAVA

Volcanic bombs are made of common rocks, such as basalt and andesite. Small pieces of lava blasted into the air at high speed cool very quickly. Most turn to **volcanic** ash. Some form pumice, which is full of air bubbles, like honeycomb, and is so light that it floats in water. Tuff is light-colored rock made from layers of ash. Some tuff contains lumps of pumice.

Science tip

All the rocky planets and moons in the solar system have **crusts** made mostly of igneous rocks. If you do not live in a volcanic area of Earth, these igneous rocks are hard to find. But you can take a look at the Moon (with binoculars is best). The dark areas of the surface are huge craters flooded with igneous rock.

Meteorites are lumps of igneous rock from space that hit Earth. This meteorite was found in Namibia, in Africa.

19

WHAT DO WE USE IGNEOUS ROCKS FOR?

Where igneous rocks make up the landscape, such as around **volcanoes** and on **volcanic** islands, they are used for building the walls of houses and walls around fields. **Cinders** are common in volcanic areas and are used to make road and path surfaces.

The colorful **crystals** in **granite** make it a tough but beautiful decorative material. The granite is often cut and then polished to make the crystals shine. Granite is used to clad (cover) buildings and to make sculptures, kitchen and bathroom countertops, decorative tiles, and ornaments.

Pumice is used for making many things, from building blocks and concrete to toothpaste and cosmetics. Some igneous rocks are sources of **minerals**, gems, and metals. For example, some pegmatites also contain crystals of beryl and garnet.

Nearly 2,000 years ago, Roman engineers built the dome of the Pantheon in Rome from lightweight concrete made with pumice stone.

IGNEOUS ROCKS IN THE PAST

People have made use of locally available igneous rocks, such as basalt and cinders, for thousands of years. Some of the giant stones at Stonehenge, an ancient site in England, are dolerite, an igneous rock. In ancient Mexico, the Aztecs used obsidian, which breaks into sharp pieces, to make cutting tools.

Science tip

You might live in a volcanic area of the world where igneous rocks are common. If not, look for igneous rocks in your home, your backyard, and your neighborhood. Granite and gabbro are commonly made into countertops. You might find pumice in the bathroom, obsidian in ornaments, and basalt in tiles and cobblestones.

Houses built from lumps of black igneous rock are a common sight on the Azores, a group of volcanic islands in the Atlantic Ocean.

DO IGNEOUS ROCKS LAST FOREVER?

Now we have reached the final stage of the journey of igneous rocks. How long do igneous rocks last? Basalt made where **tectonic plates** are spreading apart on the seabed may last for nearly 200 million years, but basalt made from **lava** flows may be **eroded** quite soon. But whatever happens to igneous rocks, they do not last forever. Eventually they are destroyed or changed into other rocks.

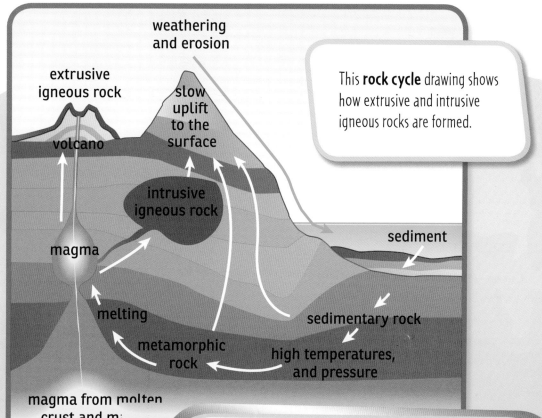

weathering and erosion

extrusive igneous rock

slow uplift to the surface

volcano

This **rock cycle** drawing shows how extrusive and intrusive igneous rocks are formed.

intrusive igneous rock

sediment

magma

melting

metamorphic rock

sedimentary rock

high temperatures, and pressure

magma from molten crust and m

Biography

James Hutton (1726–1797) was a Scottish geologist. After working as a chemist and a farmer, Hutton began studying rocks. He came up with the theory that rocks are constantly being made and destroyed, and that this has been going on for millions of years. He was one of the first geologists to realize that new rocks are formed at volcanoes.

DESTRUCTION AT THE SURFACE

Some igneous rocks finish their journey at Earth's surface. They are worn away by processes called **weathering** and **erosion**. Weathering is how rocks are broken up by the effects of weather. An example is ice weathering, where water falls into cracks in rocks. The water then freezes and expands, which breaks up the rock. Erosion is how the rock broken up by weathering is carried away by flowing water, the wind, and gravity. Flowing water and **glaciers** also break up rock by scraping it away. So, weathering and erosion break igneous rock into tiny pieces.

These **volcanic** rocks are being eroded on the coast of Iceland. The beach is made of broken-up rock.

DESTRUCTION UNDERGROUND

Some igneous rocks end their journeys underground, in Earth's crust. At **plate boundaries**, where two plates are moving toward each other, igneous rocks under the oceans are pushed down into the mantle, where they melt. Some of the molten rock may rise to the surface again, forming new igneous rock.

IGNEOUS TO METAMORPHIC

Sometimes igneous rocks are changed by extreme heat and immense **pressure**. They turn into new rocks called metamorphic rocks. Extreme heat comes from magma flowing close to the rocks. Immense pressure happens where rocks are squeezed, normally when tectonic plates crash into each other. For example, **granite** becomes gneiss (pronounced "nice") when it is put under huge pressure.

Here, two tectonic plates are colliding under the ocean. The rock in the plates is melting as it is forced into the mantle.

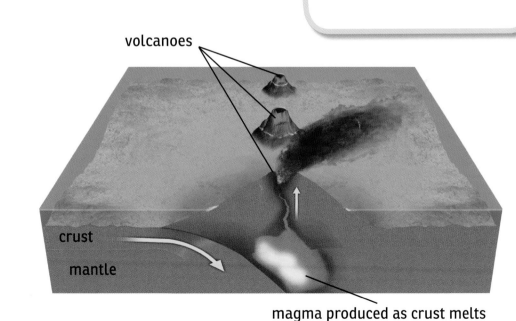

volcanoes

crust

mantle

magma produced as crust melts

HOW DO WE KNOW HOW OLD ROCKS ARE?

To find out how long ago samples of igneous rocks were formed, geologists date the samples. The main way of dating igneous rock is called radiometric dating. It relies on the fact that, over time, some types of **atom** change into other types. This process is called radioactive decay. The amount of various types of atom in a sample is measured to figure out the age.

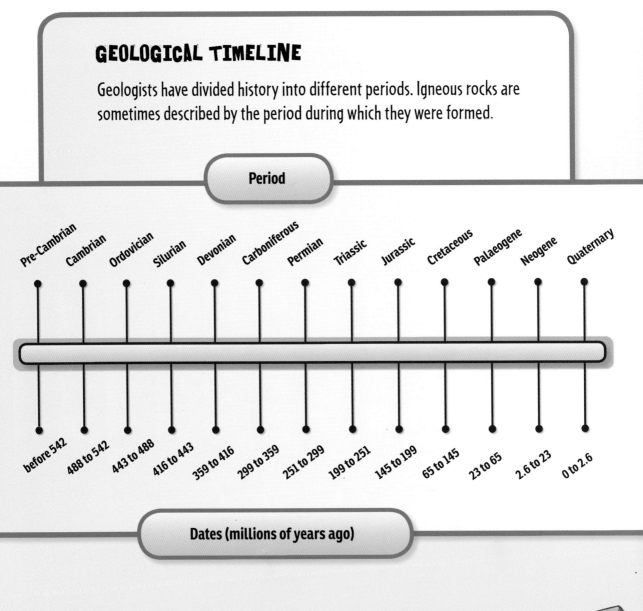

GEOLOGICAL TIMELINE

Geologists have divided history into different periods. Igneous rocks are sometimes described by the period during which they were formed.

Period

Pre-Cambrian Cambrian Ordovician Silurian Devonian Carboniferous Permian Triassic Jurassic Cretaceous Palaeogene Neogene Quaternary

before 542 488 to 542 443 to 488 416 to 443 359 to 416 299 to 359 251 to 299 199 to 251 145 to 199 65 to 145 23 to 65 2.6 to 23 0 to 2.6

Dates (millions of years ago)

ARE WE HARMING IGNEOUS ROCKS?

People have been using igneous rocks for tens of thousands of years, and these rocks are still an important resource for us. However, we destroy the rocks when we take them from the ground. Where they are near the surface, we dig them out at **quarries**. Quarrying itself creates noise and dust **pollution**, which can cause breathing problems for local people. Quarrying also destroys animal and plant **habitats**.

No matter how much quarrying we do, we will not stop the **rock cycle**, because it happens on a massive scale. However, we should take care of Earth's rocks as much as we can, as they are part of our natural environment.

We cannot stop the rock cycle! Its immense power is demonstrated by the eruption of Luzon, a volcano in the Philippines, in 1991.

JOURNEY'S END

Our journey through the life of igneous rocks is complete. The journey began in the hot rock of the **mantle**. The rock melted and rose upward into Earth's **crust**. If it reached the surface it formed a **volcano**, making **lava** and ash. If the **molten** rock did not get to the surface, it cooled slowly, forming igneous rock inside the crust.

New igneous rocks are being made all the time, and old igneous rocks are being destroyed all the time. These changes are part of the rock cycle. The rock cycle has been going on since Earth was formed 4.5 billion years ago, and it will continue for billions of years to come.

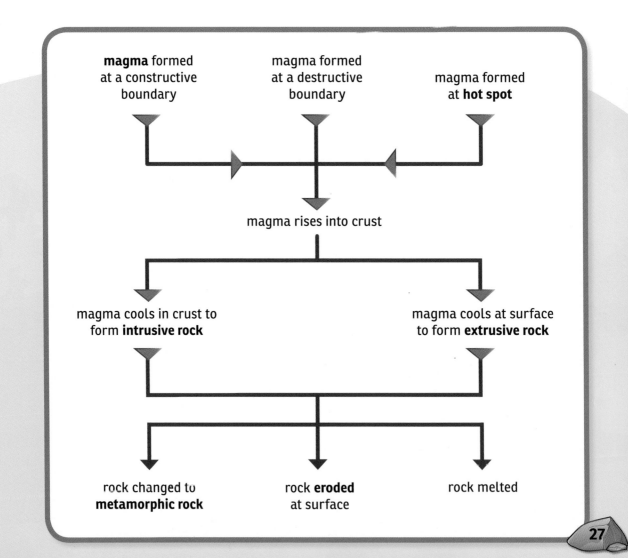

magma formed at a constructive boundary

magma formed at a destructive boundary

magma formed at **hot spot**

magma rises into crust

magma cools in crust to form **intrusive rock**

magma cools at surface to form **extrusive rock**

rock changed to **metamorphic rock**

rock **eroded** at surface

rock melted

MAKE YOUR OWN SUGAR "LAVA"!

Here is a simple experiment that will help you to understand the journey of igneous rocks we have followed through this book. Before you try the experiment, read the instructions, prepare the materials you need, and prepare an area where you can work.

Ask an adult to help you with this experiment.

YOU WILL NEED:
- granulated sugar
- a wooden spoon
- a saucepan
- a plate
- a tablespoon
- heatproof oven mits.

WHAT TO DO:

1. Put two heaped tablespoons of sugar in a saucepan.

2. Gently heat the pan on the stove. Keep stirring the sugar until it melts. (It will turn brown when it does.)

3. Carefully pour some of the **molten** sugar onto a cold plate.

4. Tip the plate to make the sugar flow, and watch what happens. The sugar will cool and become solid quite quickly.

The molten sugar is like **lava**. (Remember that lava is the molten rock that comes from a **volcano** onto Earth's surface.) Like lava, it flows very slowly, rolling over itself as it goes. The sugar "lava flow" slows down as it cools. It soon gets hard, just as lava turns into new igneous rock.

GLOSSARY

atom smallest particle of chemical matter that can exist

cinder grape-sized piece of igneous rock made when lava is blasted into the air from a volcano

crust rocky surface layer of Earth

crystal piece of material in which the atoms are organized in neat rows and columns

diamond type of valuable mineral forming the hardest crystals on Earth

erode wear away

erosion wearing away of rocks by flowing water, wind, and glaciers

extrusive rock igneous rock formed when lava cools on Earth's surface

fossil remains of an ancient animal or plant found in sedimentary rock

geologist scientist who studies the rocks and soil from which Earth is made

glacier slow-moving river of ice that flows down from a mountain range

grain pattern of particles in a rock (the particles can be crystals or small pieces of rock)

granite common intrusive igneous rock

habitat place where an animal or plant lives

hot spot area of high temperature under Earth's plates

intrusive rock igneous rock formed when magma cools underground

lava molten rock that comes out of a volcano onto Earth's surface

magma molten rock below Earth's crust

mantle very deep layer of hot rock below Earth's crust

metamorphic rock rock formed by the action of heat or pressure

mineral substance that is naturally present in Earth, such as gold and salt

molten melted

plate boundary place where one tectonic plate meets another

pollution harmful substances that are realeased into the air, water, or soil.

pressure force or weight pressing against something

quarry place where large amounts of rock are dug out of the ground

rock cycle constant formation, destruction, and recycling of rocks through Earth's crust

sedimentary rock rock made when tiny pieces of rock or the skeletons or shells of sea animals are buried underground and compressed

tectonic plate one of the giant pieces that Earth's crust is cracked into

volcanic describes a rock made at a volcano, or an area where volcanoes erupt

volcanic bomb big lump of lava that solidifies in the air

volcano opening in Earth's surface where magma escapes from underground

weathering breaking up of rocks by weather conditions such as extremes of temperature

FIND OUT MORE

BOOKS TO READ

Faulkner, Rebecca. *Igneous Rock* (Geology Rocks!). Chicago: Raintree, 2008.

Pipe, Jim. *Earth's Rocks and Fossils* (Planet Earth). Pleasantville, N.Y.: Gareth Stevens, 2008.

Walker, Sally M. *Rocks* (Early Bird Earth Science). Minneapolis: Lerner, 2007.

WEBSITES

See animations of how rocks are formed at this website of the Franklin Institute: **www.fi.edu/fellows/fellow1/oct98/create**

Find lots of information about rocks and minerals, as well as links to other interesting websites, at this site: **www.rocksforkids.com**

PLACES TO VISIT

American Museum of Natural History
Central Park West at 79th Street
New York, New York, 10024-5192
Tel: (212) 769-5100
www.amnh.org
Visit a large and fascinating collection of rocks, minerals, fossils—and dinosaurs!

The Field Museum
1400 S. Lake Shore Drive
Chicago, Illinois 60605-2496
Tel: (312) 922-9410
www.fieldmuseum.org
See fascinating exhibits of rocks, minerals, and fossils from around the world.

Yosemite National Park Half Dome, northeastern Mariposa County, California
www.nps.gov/yose/planyourvisit/halfdome.htm
You can take a hike up this granite dome, which formed when magma cooled underground.

INDEX

andesite 17, 19
atoms 5, 25
Azores 21

basalt 17, 18, 19, 21, 22
beryl 20
building materials 2, 20

calcium chloride 5
cinders 12, 20, 21
concrete 20
crystals 5, 10, 16, 17, 18, 20

dolerite 16, 21

Earth's crust 6, 7, 8, 9, 10, 14, 24, 27
Earth's mantle 6, 7, 8, 14, 24, 27
erosion 22, 23
eruptions 11, 13, 14, 15
Etna 10
extrusive rocks 11, 16, 17, 18, 22

feldspar 5, 16
fossils 9, 17

gabbro 16, 17, 21
garnet 20
gems 5, 20
geological timeline 25
geologists 10, 22, 25
Giant's Causeway 17
glaciers 23
gneiss 24
granite 5, 16, 17, 18, 20, 21, 24

Half Dome 13
Hawaiian Islands 4, 15
hot spots 9, 10, 15
Hutton, James 22

intrusive rocks 13, 16, 18, 22

Kilauea 4

lava 4, 11, 12, 13, 14, 17, 18, 19, 22, 27, 29
Luzon 26

magma 10, 11, 13, 14, 18, 22, 24
marine geology 10
metamorphic rock 4, 7, 22, 24
meteorites 19
mica 16
mid-ocean ridges 8
minerals 4–5, 10, 16, 20
molten rock 4, 6, 8, 9, 10, 24, 27

obsidian 18, 21

Pantheon 20
pegmatite 16, 17, 20
pillow lava 14
planets and moons 19
plate boundaries 8–9, 15, 24
porphyry 16
pumice 19, 20, 21

quarries 26
quartz 16

radioactive decay 25
radiometric dating 25
rhyolite 17
rock cycle 5, 7, 13, 22, 26, 27

Saddle Tor 16
salt 5
seamounts 15
sedimentary rock 4, 7, 22
Stonehenge 21

Stromboli 11
Surtsey 15

tectonic plates 8–9, 10, 14, 22, 24
tuff 19

Vesuvius 12
volcanic ash 11, 12, 15, 19, 27
volcanic bombs 12, 19
volcanic glass 18
volcanic islands 15, 21
volcanoes 4, 9, 10, 11, 12, 14–15, 26, 27
volcanologists 15

weathering 22, 23
Wegener, Alfred 9

THE CORPORATE PLANNER'S YEARBOOK 1974-75
Edited by D.E. Hussey for the Society for Long Range Planning, London, England

An international guide for all executives concerned with the future of their organizations.
A reference book for researchers, for those in need of economic forecasting services,
computer planning models, special consulting services, and organizers of conferences on
planning.

PARTIAL CONTENTS: The Future Development of Corporate Strategy. Technological
Forecasting in Orbit. Seeking New Sources of Earnings. The Role of the Corporate
Planner. Director. Professional Societies – Corporate Planning and Related Fields. Economic Forecasting Services. The Selection of a Computerized Planning Model. Membership of the Society for Long Range Planning.
1974 ISBN 0-08-017817-0

THE SOCIOLOGY OF ORGANIZATIONAL CHANGE
By E.A. Johns, Slough College of Technology

Considers fully the question of organizational change and offers guidance on the range of methods available for handling change by the application of sociology to business. Sources quoted range from learned journals to popular management literature. The author's knowledge of the subject leads to a demonstration of the practical relevance of research conclusions and sociological theories.

CONTENTS: The Need for Constant Change. Change, Equilibrium, and Homeostasis. Sources of Resistance to Change. Organizational and Psychological Factors. Techniques for Implementing Change. T-Groups and Sensitivity Training in Organizational Change. Managerial Succession and the Organizational Climate. Conclusions.

1973   ISBN 0-08-017601-1 (hardbound)
                                        ISBN 0-08-017602-X (softcover)

CHANGING SUPERVISOR BEHAVIOR
By Arnold P. Goldstein , Syracuse University and
Melvin Sorcher, General Electric Company

The authors' major focus is upon training supervisors to manage *effectively,* with
emphasis on *both* improved employee performance and improved employee satisfaction.
The material in the book is derived from basic research on human learning. It is developed
to include modeling (what to do), role playing (how to do it), social reinforcement (why
to do it), and transfer training (where and when to do it). The book will be of direct use
in courses in organizational and industrial psychology as well as courses or seminars for
industrial supervisors and managers.

1974   ISBN 0-08-017742-5 (hardbound)
                                                             ISBN 0-08-017769-7   (softcover)

FUNDAMENTALS OF PUBLIC RELATIONS
Professional Guidelines, Concepts and Integrations
Pergamon Management and Business Series, Volume 4
By Lawrence W. Nolte

An introductory work which explores all aspects of public relations including the history of the subject. The author explains the function of public relations in our social and economic systems, the basic principles which are involved in the practice of public relations, and the practical information needed to implement successful public relations activities. Of special interest are the dialogues with non-commercial public relations practitioners which balance the basic business orientation of the book and the reproduction of twenty-nine minicase histories selected by the Public Relations Society of America as outstanding examples of public relations accomplishments. These miniature case histories tell what the problem was and how it was solved.

1974   **ISBN 0-08-017107-9 (hardbound)**

PRINCIPLES OF APPLIED STATISTICS
Pergamon Management and Business Series, Volume 3
By Myron Melnyk

A blend of theory and application, this book is designed for a first course in statistics for students of business and economics. Chapters one through four and a number of other sections are self-contained thus allowing more time to concentrate on harder subjects in the classroom. The task of the instructor is greatly facilitated by multiple examples and graphic illustrations. The difficult topic of sampling distributions is made more familiar through extensive experimentations. There are numerous approaches to such topics as comparison of frequencies and areas under the curve, comparison of frequency distributions, fitting of normal distribution, Bayesian formula, Poisson distribution, Bayesian statistics, chisquare test, coefficient of correlations, fitting of moving average to bisect cycles, and others. Almost every chapter introduces one or more interesting teaching innovations that will be found most helpful by the instructor in his presentations.

1974   **ISBN 0-08-017108-7 (hardbound)**

ENCOUNTERS IN ORGANIZATIONAL BEHAVIOR: Problem Situations
Pergamon Management and Business Series, Volume 2
By Robert D. Joyce

An organized series of problem situations about people at work and essentially people who work in large organizational settings. The book stresses how they feel about their jobs, co-workers, and organizations for which they work.

PARTIAL CONTENTS: Communication and Productivity. Leadership Styles and Techniques. Problem Analysis and Decision Making. Acquiring and Keeping Talent. Achievement, Growth, and Recognition. Problems in Motivation. Personal Problems and Job Effectiveness. Individual Identity, Values and Ethics. Group Conflict and Team Development. Technology and the Future.
1972

ISBN 0-08-017013-7 (hardbound)
ISBN 0-08-017116-8 (softcover)

THE PRACTICE OF MANAGERIAL PSYCHOLOGY
Concepts and Methods for Manager and Organization Development
Pergamon Management and Business Series, Volume 1
By Andrew J. DuBrin, College of Business, Rochester Institute of Technology, New York

Based upon the aurhor's research and practical experience as a consultant, this volume presents a variety of innovative, conceptual schema to enable the practitioner, student, and manager to understand the underlying factors that will determine if and to what degree psychological intervention will be beneficial, meaningless, or harmful to an organization.

Requiring only a basic background in business or psychology, the book offers such new conceptualizations as a list of behavioral changes needed by managers, the Conflict Matrix, the developmental Goal X Level Integrator, managerial motivational schema, and helpful interventions for managerial obsolescence. A unique Managerial Psychology Matrix specifies the proper conditions for applying such techniques as sensitivity training, performance appraisal, psychological assessment, team development meetings, organizational analysis, and super-subordinate counseling.

1972   ISBN 0-08-016764-0 (hardbound)
                                                 ISBN 0-08-018126-0   (softcover)